A LATIN GRAMMAR

FOR

SCHOOLS AND COLLEGES

BY

GEORGE M. LANE, Ph.D., **LL.D.**

PROFESSOR EMERITUS OF LATIN **IN**
HARVARD UNIVERSITY

REVISED EDITION

GREENWOOD PRESS, PUBLISHERS

NEW YORK

PRINTED IN THE UNITED STATES OF AMERICA

PREFACE TO THE FIRST EDITION.

GEORGE MARTIN LANE died on the thirtieth of June, 1897. His *Latin Grammar*, in the preparation of which he had been engaged, during the intervals of teaching in Harvard University, for nearly thirty years, was at that time approaching completion. The first two hundred and ninety-one pages had been stereotyped; the pages immediately following, on the *Relative Sentence* and the *Conjunctive Particle Sentence* through *quod* and *quia* (pages 292–302), together with the chapter on the *Infinitive* (pages 374–386), were ready for stereotyping; of the remainder of the book, pages 303–373 and 387–436 were in the form of a first draught; finally, he had received a few weeks before his death, but had never examined, the manuscript of the chapter on *Versification* (pages 442–485), written at his invitation by his former pupil, Dr. Herman W. Hayley, now of Wesleyan University.

It was found that my dear and honoured master had left a written request that his work should be completed by me, in consultation with his colleagues, Professors Frederic De Forest Allen and Clement Lawrence Smith. A month had scarcely passed when scholars everywhere had another heavy loss to mourn in the sudden death of Professor Allen. Almost immediately afterwards, Professor Smith left this country, to take charge for a year of the American School of Classical Studies in Rome, but not before we had agreed that circumstances required the early publication of the book, notwithstanding his absence. I was thus deprived of two eminent counsellors, whose knowledge and experience would have been of inestimable assistance.

About one hundred and twenty pages (303–373 and 387–436), exclusive of *Versification*, were yet to receive their final form. Professor Lane had determined the order in which the topics contained in these pages should be treated, and no change has been made in that order. Most of the main principles of syntax,

Preface.

too, have been left exactly as they were expressed in his draught. This draught was written some years ago, and, although he had corrected and annotated it from time to time, there is no doubt that in writing it out afresh he would have made many alterations and improvements which are not indicated in his notes. Consequently, he is not to be held responsible for errors and omissions in the pages which had not received his final approval. Yet I conceived it my duty to preserve, so far as possible, the very language of his corrected draught; and this, in the statement of almost all the main principles, I have been able to do. Some modifications and some radical alterations were inevitable ; in particular, the treatment of *quamvis*, *quando*, *quin*, the *Supine*, and *Numerals* seemed to call for much amplification and rearrangement. I have also deemed it necessary to add some seventy sections [1] under various heads, and Dr. Hayley has been good enough to write sections 2458–2510, which precede his chapter on *Versification*. But, in general, my principal function has been : first, to provide additional Latin examples of the principles which Professor Lane had formulated ; secondly, to enter, under the various principles, historical statements regarding the usage in the Latin writers, drawn from the best authorities at my disposal.

Professor Lane's own method was far from that of a compiler. He took nothing for granted without thorough investigation, however well established it might seem, and he followed the dictum of no man, however widely accepted as an authority. For example, his many pupils and correspondents will remember how untiring he was in his efforts to arrive at accuracy in even the minutest points of inflection. Thus, for the *List of Verbs* (§§ 922–1022), he made entirely new collections, and admitted no form among the 'principal parts' unless actually found represented in the authors. In the details of syntax, he was equally indefatigable ; the sections on the *Locative Proper* (1331–1341), for instance, contain the result of an immense amount of painful

---

[1] The sections which I have added are as follows : 1866, 1873, 1878, 1879, 1880, 1887, 1890, 1901, 1902, 1903, 1907, 1909, 1913, 1922, 1927, 1935, 1964, 1975, 1978, 1979, 1980, 1981, 1982, 1983, 1984, 1989, 1990, 2011, 2012, 2013, 2014, 2015, 2068, 2086, 2088, 2097, 2111, 2122, 2152, 2155, 2255, 2264, 2267, 2271, 2273, 2275, 2276, 2277, 2281, 2289, 2292, 2345, 2357, 2400, 2406, 2407, 2408, 2409, 2410, 2411, 2412, 2413, 2414, 2740–2745.

research. He devoted much anxious thought to the definitions and the titles of the various constructions: thus, the distinction between the *Present of Vivid Narration* (1590) and the *Annalistic Present* (1591) seems obvious now that it is stated; but to reach it many pages of examples were collected and compared. He held that examples printed in the grammar to illustrate syntactical principles should never be manufactured; they should be accurately quoted from the authors, without other alteration than the omission of words by which the construction under illustration was not affected. He was careful, also, not to use an example in which there was any serious doubt as to the text in that part which covered the principle illustrated by the example. To 'Hidden Quantity' he had given much attention, and many of the results of his studies in this subject were published, in 1889, in the *School Dictionary* by his friend Dr. Lewis. Since that time he had found reason to change his views with regard to some words, and these changes are embodied in the present book, in which he marked every vowel which he believed to be long in quantity.

The order in which the divisions and subdivisions of grammar are here presented will not seem strange to those who are acquainted with the recent grammars published by Germans. It is the scientific order of presentation, whatever order a teacher may think fit to follow in his actual practice. The table of contents has been made so full as to serve as a systematic exposition of the scheme, and to make needless any further words upon it here. In the *Appendix* Professor Lane would have inserted, out of deference to custom, a chapter on the *Arrangement of Words;* but the draught of it which he left was too fragmentary for publication. Since the proper preparation of the chapter would have greatly delayed the publication of the book, it was thought best to omit it altogether, at least for the present. This topic, in fact, like some others in the *Appendix*, belongs rather to a treatise on Latin Composition than to a Latin Grammar.

For the indexes, and for much valuable help in proof reading, I heartily thank Dr. J. W. Walden, another of Professor Lane's pupils.

In the course of his work, Professor Lane frequently consulted his colleagues and other distinguished scholars both in this country and in Europe. He gratefully welcomed their advice, and care

Preface.

fully considered and often adopted their suggestions. Had he lived to write a preface, he would doubtless have thanked by name those to whom he considered himself as under particular obliga tion, whether from direct correspondence or through the use of their published works; but it is obvious that the information in my possession will not allow me to attempt this pleasant duty. Of Professor Lane's pupils, also, not a few, while in residence as advanced students at the University, were from time to time engaged in the collection of material which he used in the grammar. They, like his other helpers, must now be content with the thought of the courteous acknowledgment which they would have received from him.

MORRIS H. MORGAN.

HARVARD UNIVERSITY,
CAMBRIDGE, *May*, 1898.

PREFATORY NOTE TO THE REVISED EDITION.

In this Revised Edition many changes and corrections in details have been introduced throughout the book, but no alterations have been made in the treatment of broad general principles, except in the chapter on Sound (§§ 16–179). This has been very largely rewritten and extended from nineteen to thirty-one pages by my friend, Professor Hanns Oertel, of Yale University, who has also been kind enough to make the changes in the chapters on Formation and Inflection rendered necessary by his rewriting of the sections on Sound. In this rewriting Mr. Oertel has proceeded upon the ideas that in a school grammar, even an advanced one, phonology should play a subordinate part; that nothing should be introduced that cannot be illustrated from such Latin and Greek as are available to the student; and that those points should be emphasized which assist in the analyzing of compounds and in the understanding of word-formation and inflection. With these ideas, which necessarily prevent the introduction of some important topics treated in works on phonetics, I am in entire sympathy.

My thanks are due to not a few scholars and reviewers who have pointed out passages in the first edition which in their opinion called for changes. Some of their suggestions I have adopted; with others I have found myself unable to agree.

M. H. M.

HARVARD UNIVERSITY,
CAMBRIDGE, May, 1903.

TABLE OF CONTENTS.

THE REFERENCES ARE TO SECTIONS.

Table of Contents.

Table of Contents.

PART SECOND: SENTENCES, 1023–2299.

THE SIMPLE SENTENCE, 1099–1635.

(A.) USE OF THE NOUN, 1099–1468.

Table of Contents.

Table of Contents.

Table of Contents.

Table of Contents.

LATIN GRAMMAR

1. Latin Grammar has two parts. I. The first part treats of words: (A.) their sound; (B.) their formation; (C.) their inflection. II. The second part shows how words are joined together in sentences.

PART FIRST ◦ WORDS

PARTS OF SPEECH.

2. The principal kinds of words or PARTS OF SPEECH are *Nouns Verbs*, and *Conjunctions*.

3. I. NOUNS are *Substantive* or *Adjective*.

4. (A.) NOUNS SUBSTANTIVE, otherwise called Substantives, are divided, as to meaning, into *Concrete* and *Abstract*.

5. (1.) CONCRETE SUBSTANTIVES denote persons or things. Concrete Substantives are subdivided into *Proper Names*, which denote individual persons or things: as, **Cicerō**, *Cicero;* **Rōma**, *Rome;* and *Common Names*, otherwise called *Appellatives*, which denote one or more of a class: as, **homo**, *man;* **taurus**, *bull.*

6. Appellatives which denote a collection of single things are called *Collectives:* as, **turba**, *crowd;* **exercitus**, *army.* Appellatives which denote stuff, quantity, material, things not counted, but having measure or weight, are called *Material Substantives:* as, **vīnum**, *wine;* **ferrum**, *iron;* **faba**, *horsebeans.*

7. (2.) ABSTRACT SUBSTANTIVES denote qualities, states, conditions: as, **rubor**, *redness;* **aequitās**, *fairness;* **sōlitūdō**, *loneliness.*

8. (B.) NOUNS ADJECTIVE, otherwise called Adjectives, attached to substantives, describe persons or things: as, **ruber**, *red;* **aequus**, *fair;* **sōlus**, *alone.*

9. PRONOUNS are words of universal application which serve ...s substitutes for nouns.

Thus, **taurus**, *bull*, names, and **ruber**, *red*, describes, particular things; but **ego**, *I*, is universally applicable to any speaker, and **meus**, *mine*, to anything belonging to any speaker.

1

10. ADVERBS are mostly cases of nouns used to denote manner, place, time or degree: as, subitō, *suddenly ;* forās, *out of doors ;* diū, *long ;* valdē, *mightily, very.*

11. PREPOSITIONS are adverbs which are used to modify as prefixes the meaning of verbs, or to define more nicely the meaning of cases : as, vocō, *I call,* ēvocō, *I call out ;* ex urbe, *from town.*

12. II. VERBS are words which denote action, including existence or condition : as, regit, *he guides ;* est, *he is ;* latet, *he is hid.*

13. III. CONJUNCTIONS connect sentences, nouns, or verbs : as, et, *and ;* sed, *but.*

14. INTERJECTIONS are cries which express feeling, and are not usually a part of the sentence: as, ā, *ah ;* heu, *alas.*

15. There is no ARTICLE in Latin : thus, mēnsa may denote *table, a table,* or *the table.*

———◆———

A. SOUND.

ALPHABET.

16. In Cicero's time, the sounds of the Latin language were denoted by twenty-one letters (*DN.* 2, 93).

Character	Name	pronounced	Character	Name	pronounced
A	a	*ah*	M	em	*em*
B	be	*bay*	N	en	*en*
C	ce	*kay*	O	o	*o*
D	de	*day*	P	pe	*pay*
E	e	*eh*	Q	qu	*koo*
F	ef	*ef*	R	er	*air*
G	ge	*gay*	S	es	*ess*
H	ha	*hah*	T	te	*tay*
I	i	*ee*	V	u	*oo*
K	ka	*kah*	X	ix	*eex*
L	el	*el*			

The names given above are those employed by Roman grammarians. The sound indicated by *-ay* is only approximate ; the true sound is that of the French *ê* in *fête ;* see 39. The names of the letters are indeclinable ; for their gender, see 412.

17. Two other letters were also in use to represent Greek sounds in Greek words ; these were always called by their Greek names, and were placed at the end of the alphabet ; they are Y, named *ü* (42), and Z, named zēta (71).

2

18. ORIGIN OF THE ALPHABET. The Latin alphabet, which originally consisted of capitals only, was adapted from the alphabet of Chalcidian colonies in Italy.

19. SPELLING. The signs for the Greek sounds denoted by φ and χ, and perhaps also that for θ, these three sounds being unknown in Latin, were used as numerals (2407). In words borrowed from the Greek the Romans at first represented θ by t, φ by p, and χ by c : as, tūs, *incense,* for θύος; Poenī, *Punians,* for Φοίνικες; calx, *chalk,* for χάλιξ. Occasionally also the Latin mute was doubled : as, struppus, *strap,* for στρόφος. Later, about the middle of the second century B.C., th, ph, and ch begin to be used : as, cothurnus, *boot,* for κόθορνος; amphora, *jar,* for ἀμφόρα; Achaea for Ἀχαιά. In some instances these aspirates were next introduced even into words purely Latin : as, chommodus, *affable,* for commodus, an affectation ridiculed by Catullus (Cat. 84) and disapproved by Quintilian (1, 5, 20). But pulcher, *pretty,* is the usual spelling for pulcer (formed by the suffix -cro- from the stem of the verb poliō, *I polish*). Even Cicero (*O.* 160) aspirated the c in this word as a concession to popular usage, as he did the t in Cethēgus, Karthāgō, and the p in triumphus, while he retained the unaspirated explosive in the proper names Orcīvius, *name of a* '*gens,*' Matō, Otō, Caepiō, and in sepulcrum, *tomb;* corōna, *crown;* and lacrima, *tear.* In a similar manner Greek ῥ was at first transcribed by r : as, rumpia, *a kind of weapon,* for ῥομφαία ; but later by rh : as, rhētor, *rhetorician,* for ῥήτωρ.

20. The letters C (first written ⟨) and K were at an early period used promiscuously, and C stood for both unvoiced k and voiced g : as, VIRCO, VIRGŌ, *virgin.* Afterwards K dropped out of general use except in the abbreviations K. or Kal. for kalendae, *first of the month,* and K. for the proper name Kaesō (Quint. 1, 7, 10). About 300 B.C. the sign ⟨ or C was used for the unvoiced k alone, while a separate sign, which became G, was set apart for the voiced g. But C continued to be used for g in the abbreviations C for Gāius, Ↄ for Gāia, and Cn. for Gnaeus. Occasionally q is written for c, almost always before the vowels o and u : as, qum for cum, *with;* qolunt for colunt, *they cultivate;* peqūnia, *money.* But ordinarily q is found before unsyllabic (consonantal) u (v) only (22).

21. Before the introduction of Y and Z (17), u was used for the Greek Υ: as, Burrus, later Pyrrhus (Cic. *O.* 160); and s, or, as a medial, ss, for Z : as, sōna, *belt,* later zōna; massa, *lump,* for μᾶζα; malacissō, *I soften,* for μαλακίζω. By a blunder, y was occasionally introduced in words of Latin origin : as, lacryma, *tear,* for lacrima, which was wrongly supposed to be derived from Greek δάκρυ.

22. The characters I and V represent not only the two vowels i and u, but also their cognate semivowels (52) i̯ and u̯ (83), called commonly *consonant* i and u, but with less ambiguity *unsyllabic* i and u (82; 83). They are equivalent to the English *y* and *w* respectively.

23. In words like maior, simple i was commonly written for the sound of i̯i̯ (153, 2; 82; 83). But Cicero in such cases wrote ii: as, aiiō, *I say,* Maiia, Troiia (Quint. 1, 4, 11). In the same way Lucretius spelled Graiiugenārum, *of Greek-born men,* and EIIVS, *of him,* CVIIVS, *whose,* occur in inscriptions. Sometimes the same sound is represented by a taller letter, '*i longa,*' especially in the imperial age : as, MAIOR, *greater.* There are also cases in which the two designations were confounded, a double i being written, and one or the other letter made taller : as, EIIVS or EIIVS, *of him.*

24. The tall i, I longa, was used not only to represent unsyllabic i (22), but, beginning with Sulla's time, also for long vowel i (29, 2, *b*): as, SIGNA, *signs;* QVINQVE, *five.* It also represents sometimes double i: as, vIs for viīs, *in the roads.* At the beginning of words it occurs without reference to quantity for both short and long i, and, by mistake, I is elsewhere found for short i.

3

25. The emperor Claudius (A.D. 41-54) introduced a separate sign for unsyllabic u (22), restricting the sign v to the vowel u (Quint. 1, 7, 26 ; Ta. 11, 14) ; but it did not become current.

26. In schoolbooks and most texts of the authors, the vowel u is printed U, u, and the consonant V, v. A character, J, j, was introduced in the 17th century, to indicate the consonant i. But this character is no longer usual in editions of the authors or in schoolbooks.

27. The distinction between u and v is not always made very consistently : q has regularly, and g and s have sometimes, an aftersound of w, best represented by v ; but the usual practice is to write u, as in the following disyllables : quōrum, *of whom;* anguis, *snake;* suāvis, *sweet.* qu is always counted as a single sound (177). See also 2504.

28. For the intermediate sound (103) between i and u, as in the first syllable of lubet, libet, *it pleases,* and in the second syllable of optimus, optumus, *best* (Quint. 1, 4, 8 ; 7, 21), the emperor Claudius invented a separate character. It failed of acceptance, as did also the sign which he attempted to introduce for ps.

29. The same characters were ordinarily used to denote both long and short vowels. But at different periods long vowels were sometimes indicated in inscriptions thus :

(1.) Long a, e, or u was sometimes doubled : as, AARA, *altar ;* PAASTORES, *shepherds;* LEEGE, *by law;* IVVS, *right.* This doubling, which was never frequent, seems to have been introduced into Latin from the Oscan by the poet Accius. It occurs most frequently in inscriptions about the year 150 B.C., but sporadically much later : as, CONVENTVVS, *of the assembly;* ARBITRATVV, *by the decree;* and in other stems in -u- (593).

(2.) Long i was often denoted (*a.*) By the spelling ei (after the pronunciation of this diphthong had been changed to *ī*, 98) : as, DAREI, *be given ;* REDIEIT, *hath come back;* INTERIEISTI, *hast died.* Some Roman grammarians prescribed this spelling for every long i ; others tried to regulate the use of ei for ī by special rules. At the end of the republic, the spelling EI had given way to uniform I. (*b.*) Since the time of Sulla, by a taller letter ('*i longa* ') : as, FIXA, *fastened* (23, 24).

(3.) A mark called an *apex* (ꓶꓶꓶ) was often put over a long vowel : as, FECIT, *made;* HORTENSIVS ; DVVMVIRATVS, *duumvirate.* The apex was written ′ in the imperial age ; the form ‾, which occurs in an inscription, was adopted by the grammarians, and is still in use to mark the long vowels. It may be mentioned that inscriptions which employ the apex are by no means consistent in its use, and that late inscriptions have it over short and long vowels, apparently for decorative purposes. Quintilian 1, 7, 2 prescribes it only for cases which otherwise might be ambiguous : as, MÁLVS (mālus), *mast,* to distinguish it from MALVS (malus), *bad.*

30. In schoolbooks, a long vowel is indicated by a horizontal line over it : as, āra, *altar ;* mēnsis, *month ;* ōrdō, *series.* A short vowel is sometimes indicated by a curved mark : as, pĕr, *through ;* dŭx, *leader ;* but this mark is unnecessary if long vowels are systematically marked. Usually the quantity of the vowels in each word is definitely fixed ; but in a few cases the same vowel may be now short, now long, as in English the *ee* of *been* is pronounced long by some (*bean*), short by others (*bin*). Thus (2446) mihi, ibi were sometimes pyrrhics (‿ ‿, 2522), sometimes iambi (‿—, 2521). See for other cases 134, 2443, 2452, 2453. Such vowels of variable quantity are termed *common* and marked ⌣ or ⌣ : as mihī, *to me* (2514).

4

PRONUNCIATION.

31. The pronunciation of Latin sounds may be approximately determined : (*a*) from the description of the native grammarians and incidental allusions in other Latin authors ; (*b*) from variations in spelling ; (*c*) from the Greek transliteration of Latin words ; (*d*) from the Latin transliteration of foreign words ; (*e*) from the development of the sounds in languages derived from the Latin.

VOWELS.

32. Vowels are sounds which are produced by the vibrations of the vocal chords (this may be easily felt by placing a finger on the throat at the Adam's apple) and without any audible friction or any obstruction anywhere in the passage above the vocal chords. The difference in the sound of the vowels is due to the different shape which the position of the tongue and the lips gives in each case to the cavity of the mouth. During the pronunciation of pure vowels no air escapes through the nose.

33. The simple vowels, **a, e, i, o, u (y)**, are either *long* or *short.* The sound of a long vowel is considered to be twice the length of that of a short.

34. That a long vowel is equal to two shorts is a rule of metrical theory (see 2515). In actual pronunciation, there were undoubtedly various degrees of length, as in English : e. g., *sea, seize* (long), *cease* (half-long).

QUANTITY OF VOWELS.

The quantity of vowels must in general be learned by observation ; but some convenient helps for the memory may be found in 2429 ; and the quantity of many vowels may be ascertained by the general principles given in 35 and 36. Except in the case of *Hidden Quantity* (2459), the quantity of vowels is in general ascertained from verse. But some information may also be gleaned from such rhetorical prose as exhibits well defined habits in the rhythmical endings selected for sentences (**clausulae,** Cic. *O.* 191–226).

(A.) SHORT VOWELS.

35. A vowel is short :

(1.) Before another vowel or h (124) : as, **eōs, ēvehō** ; compare **taceō** with **tacēre.** For exceptions in classical Latin, see 127 ; for exceptions in early Latin see 126.

(2.) Before nt and nd (128) if not the result of contraction : as, **calendae, centum** ; compare **amant, amandus,** with **amāre.**

(3.) Before final **t** and m, and, in words of more than one syllable, before final r and l (132) : compare **amat, amem,** with **amās** and **amēs.**

5

36. All vowels are long which are:

(1) Weakened from a diphthong (96–101 ; 108), or which are the result of contraction (118) : as, concīdō from caedō ; cōgō from co-agō.

(2) Lengthened by compensation (121) : as, quīnī for * quincnī.

(3) Before **nf, ns,** often before **nc** followed by a consonant, and, in some cases, before **gn** (122).

PRONUNCIATION OF VOWELS.

37. The following English sounds come nearest to the Latin pronunciation of the vowels:

38. LONG VOWELS. ā had the sound of *a* in *father ;* ē that of *a* in *fate* (but see 39); ī that of *i* in *machine ;* ō that of *o* in *tone ;* ū that of *u* in *rule*.

39. It must be noted, however, that all English long vowels, save *a* as in *father*, are more or less diphthongal, that is, they become gradually closer (46) ; *a* in *fate* ends in a vanishing sound of *ee* (not heard in the *ê* of French *fête*), and *o* in *no* ends in the sound of *oo*. Similarly the long *e* sound in *he* becomes closer and ends in a sound similar to the *y* in *year*. In Latin all long vowels had one sustained sound.

40. SHORT VOWELS. **a** sounded approximately like the English *a* in the first syllable of *aha ;* **e, i, o,** and **u** sounded like *e* in *step, i* in *pit, o* in *obey*, and *u* in *pull* respectively.

41. Latin short **a** did not differ, except in quantity, from long **ā** ; it never had the 'flat' sound of English *a* in *pat*. In the case of the other vowels, **i, e, o,** and **u,** the long vowels were closer (46) than the short ones. This is the same difference which the English shows in *keen* (long and close) and *kin* (short and open) ; *pool* (long and close) and *pull* (short and open). For this reason, open **i** is sometimes represented by **e** in inscriptions : as, ANEMA for **anima,** *soul ;* and **vea** was the rustic pronunciation for **via,** *road* (Varro, *R. R.* 1, 2, 14).

42. **Y,** which was a sound borrowed from the Greek (17), sounded like German *ü*. The sound, which is missing in English, is formed with the tongue in position for *i* (in *kin*) and the lips rounded as for *oo* (in *moon*).

CLASSIFICATION OF VOWELS.

43. Vowels are divided according to the position of the tongue. Latin **i** and **e** are called *front vowels,* because the front part of the tongue is elevated. This elevation is greater for **i** than for **e.** Latin **o** and **u** are called *back vowels,* because they require an elevation of the rear part of the tongue. This elevation is greater for **u** than for **o.** Latin **a** holds an intermediate position, no part of the tongue being raised, while the front part is depressed.

44. In the formation of **i** and **e,** the tongue approaches the hard palate ; hence these two vowels are also called *palatal vowels*. Similarly, **o** and **u** are called *velar* or *guttural vowels* because in their formation the tongue approaches the soft palate (**vēlum palatī**).

45. o and u require a rounding of the lips (**labia**); hence they are called *labial vowels.* The same is true for **y.**

46. Comparing the vowels in English *keen* and *kin*, it will be noted that the passage between the tongue and the hard palate is narrower in the former than in the latter case. The *ee* in *keen* is therefore said to be a *narrow* or *close* vowel, while the *i* in *kin* is *wide* or *open.* See 41.

DIPHTHONGS.

47. Two unlike (43–46) vowels pronounced under one stress and as one syllable form a *Diphthong.* All diphthongs are long.

In all diphthongs the transition from one vowel to the other is gradual. A diphthong is, therefore, not formed simply by pronouncing two vowels in succession, but the vocal organs pass through all the intermediate positions and consequently the sound is constantly changing.

48. In their origin diphthongs are of two kinds : (*a.*) primitive diphthongs : as in **foedus,** *treaty;* **aurum,** *gold;* or (*b.*) secondary diphthongs, the result of vowels meeting in formation, composition, or inflection : see 120.

49. The diphthongs which occur in classical Latin are **au, ae, oe,** and the rare **ui** and **eu.**

au sounded like *ou* in *house.* **ae** had the sound of short Latin **a** rapidly combined with the sound of *e* in English *men.* But it is the common practice now to give to **ae** the sound of *ay* or *ai* in *ay, aisle,* although the difference between Latin **ae** and the earlier **ai** from which it descended is thus obliterated. **oe** had the sound of short Latin **o** rapidly followed by the sound of *e* in English *men.* But it is now customary not to distinguish between Latin **oe** and **oi,** and to give to both the sound of *oi* in *boil.* **ui** is pronounced by combining Latin short **u** and **i** (40, 41) with the stress on the **i** like French *oui ;* **eu** by combining Latin short **e** and **u** with stress on the **u.**

50. Besides these, the following diphthongs occur in the older inscriptions : **ai** pronounced as *ai* in *aisle ;* **ei** as *ei* in *eight ;* **oi** as *oi* in *boil;* and **ou** which sounded very much like the final *o* in *no, go,* which is really a diphthong (see 39).

CONSONANTS.

51. Consonants are formed by stopping the breath somewhere in the cavity of the mouth or by squeezing it through a narrow channel or aperture.

52. SEMIVOWELS. There is no sharp line of demarcation between consonants and vowels. Some vowels in unsyllabic function (82, 83) notably **i** (*i̯*) and **u** (*u̯*) (corresponding to English *y* and *w*), though usually classed as consonants, are so closely related to the vowels that they are termed semivowels (2504). To these may be added also the liquids **l** and **r.** Contact of the semivowels **i** and **u** with their corresponding vowels **i** and **u** is avoided in classical times. See for **-vu-** 107 *c ;* for **-quu-** 157 ; and for **-ii-** 104, *c* (on **objicio**) ; 458 (**Bōī** for ***Bōi̯ī**). See 153, 3.

7

53. Most of the consonants are pronounced as in English. The following points must be noticed:

54. b before a surd, as s or t, has the sound of p. The spelling b is here simply etymological : as, **abs**, pronounced *aps* (the b retained in spelling because of **ab**); **urbs**, pronounced *urps* (the b retained because of the oblique cases **urbis**, **urbī**, etc.); **obterō**, pronounced *opterō* (Quint. 1, 7, 7), where the spelling of the preposition **ob** was kept (164).

55. c has always the sound of English *k.*

56. d before the surd s is pronounced t ; the spelling d is preserved for etymological reasons only : as, **adsum**, pronounced *atsum.*

57. g always has the sound of English *g* in *go*, never that of *g* in *gentle.* **gu**, when it makes one syllable with the following vowel, is pronounced like English *gw :* as, **sanguine** like *sanguine.*

58. h has a weak sound as *h* in British English (Southern), and by some was not counted as a consonant. Consequently the same uncertainty existed as to initial **h.** The omission of initial h is recognized in classical Latin for **ānser** (originally **hānser*). Elsewhere the omission of initial h in spelling, as **ostia** for **hostia**, is rare until the third century A.D.

Very rarely h is written between two vowels to denote that each should be pronounced separately (like our diaeresis in *coëxtensive*): as, **ahēneus**, *bronze*, with **aē** separate (116 *a*); but **aes**, *bronze*, with diphthongal **ae.**

59. Unsyllabic (22) or consonant i has the sound of English *y* in *year.*

60. There were two varieties of l. One was like the English *l*, guttural in character, because in its pronunciation not only the blade (front part) of the tongue touched the gums, but in addition to this the rear part of the tongue was elevated toward the soft palate. The other l was purely dental, and formed without such back elevation. This second variety appeared in the combination ll, or whenever l was followed by the front vowels (43) **e** or **i**, or when it was final. Elsewhere l was guttural.

61. From the earliest times final m in unaccented syllables had a faint sound or was even inaudible (Quint. 9, 4, 39). Consequently it is often omitted in writing in the older inscriptions both before an initial vowel or consonant: as, POCOLO for **pōcolom** ; OINO for **oinom** (**ūnum**), and the grammarian Verrius Flaccus proposed to write only half an **M** for final m before a vowel. In prosody, therefore, final m did not prevent elision (2493). The same is seen in prose in cases like **animadvertō**, *I pay heed to*, from **animum advertō**, *I turn my mind toward* (395) ; **vēnīre**, *to be sold* for **vēnum īre**, *to go to sale* (1165). But in monosyllables where m closes the accented syllable, it did not vanish (2494, 2495), and this difference in the treatment of final m is reflected in the Romance languages.

62. n stands for two sounds. It represents the dental nasal, as *n* in English *now*. But before the gutturals k, c, g, q, and the compound **x** (= cs), it represents the guttural nasal which is written *ng* in English *sing, wrong.* This second n is sometimes called n adulterīnum or ' spurious n,' thus: nc (in avunculus) as in *uncle ;* ng (in angulus) as in *angle ; ngu* (in sanguine) as in *sanguine ;* nqu (in inquit) as *inkw* in *inkwiper ;* nx (in pinxit) as in *lynx.*

8

63. Dental n before s had a reduced sound, and is therefore sometimes omitted in writing : as, CESOR for cēnsor ; COSOL for cōnsul, in older inscriptions ; and fōrmōsus by the side of fōrmōnsus ; vīcēsimus by the side of vicēnsimus, Cicero omitted the n in the adjective suffix -ēnsis : as, forēsia, *of the forum;* hortēsia, *garden plants.*

64. q, in classical Latin, appears only in the combination qu, sounded like English *qu* or *kw* (27). r was trilled.

65. s, in classical Latin was always unvoiced (surd, 75) like English *s* in *so, sin,* never voiced (sonant, 75) as English *s* in *ease.* su, when it makes one syllable with the following vowel, is like *sw* in *sweet* (27).

66. In old Latin, final s after a short vowel and before a consonant seems to have been reduced in sound or to have disappeared altogether. In the older inscriptions it is often omitted in the ending of the nominative singular -us, and in the pre-Ciceronian poets final s often does not make position (2468). But such omission was considered vulgar in Cicero's time (Cic. O. 161 ; Quint. 9, 4, 38).

67. In the archaic period Latin s stood also for the voiced sibilant (English *s* in *ease, z* in *zeal*), as in ASA, *altar* (154).

68. t is always sounded as in *time,* never as in *nation.* The pronunciation of ci and ti with the c and t as sibilants (as in English *cinder, nation*) is very late.

69. v is like the English *w.*

70. x is a compound consonant, standing for cs, and so sounded, never as English *gs* or *gz.*

71. z, being a Greek sound, should have retained its Greek pronunciation. This differed in the different dialects ; in the Attic of the fourth century B.C. it was approximately that of English *z* in *zeal,* while its earlier value was *zd.* The Romans had great difficulty in pronouncing this sound (Quint. 12, 10, 27 f.), but the grammarian Velius Longus expressly states that it should not be pronounced as a compound sound (*zd*).

72. About 100 B.C. the combinations ch, ph, and th were introduced in Greek words to represent χ, φ, and θ ; as Philippus, for the older PILIPVS. Somewhat later these combinations were in general use in some Latin words (19). ch is thought to have been pronounced like *kh* in *blockhead,* ph as in *uphill,* and th as in *hothouse.* But in practice ch is usually sounded as in the German *machen* or *ich,* ph as in *graphic,* and th as in *pathos.*

CLASSIFICATION OF CONSONANTS.

73. EXPLOSIVES. Consonants which are formed by stopping the breath in the oral cavity and then suddenly removing the obstruction are called *explosives.* They cannot be prolonged in sound. They are : c, k, q, g ; t, d ; p, b. These are often called *mutes.*

74. CONTINUANTS. Consonants which may be prolonged in sound are called *continuants.* They are : unsyllabic (83) i (59) and u (66) ; 1 (60), r ; 1, s, f ; n (62), m.

9

75. VOICED and UNVOICED. If during the emission of breath the vocal chords vibrate (32), the consonant is said to be *voiced* or *sonant:* g; d; b; n (62), m; l (60), r; unsyllabic (83) i (59) and u (69); otherwise it is said to be *unvoiced* or *surd:* c, k, q; t; p; h, s, f.

76. NASALS. In the majority of consonants, the breath escapes through the cavity of the mouth, and the cavity of the nose is closed in the rear by means of the raised soft palate. Those consonants in which the breath escapes through the nose, while the oral cavity is closed, are called *nasals:* as, n, m, n adulterīnum (see 62).

77. CLASSIFICATION ACCORDING TO PLACE OF FORMATION. Consonants are further divided according to the place where the breath is stopped or squeezed. (1.) If the breath is stopped by the lips, as in p, b, m, or squeezed through the lips, as in v (English *w*), we speak of *labials*. (2.) If the breath is forced through an opening between the upper teeth and the lower lip, as in f, we speak of a *labiodental*. (3.) Sounds which are produced by the point of the tongue touching the upper gums and teeth, as t, d, n, r, or by the formation of a narrow median channel in the same place, like s, or of a lateral channel, like l (60), are called *dentals*. (4.) *Palatals* are formed by an elevation of the front part of the tongue against the forward section of the palate, like i consonant (English *y*). (5) If the back of the tongue touches or approaches the rear part of the palate as in k, q, c, g, n adulterīnum (English *ng* in *sing*), and l (60), we speak of *gutturals* (*velars*); see 44.

78. SPIRANTS. Sounds which are produced by friction of the breath are called *spirants:* as, s, f, and h.

79. SIBILANTS. On account of its hissing sound, s is called a sibilant. English *s, z, th* are sibilants.

80. DOUBLING OF CONSONANTS. In English, double consonants as the *tt, nn, pp, mm* in *motto, Anna, tapping, grammar*, are sounded exactly like the corresponding single consonants in *cot, pan, tap, ram*. In Latin, on the other hand, double consonants (geminātae) were pronounced as they are in modern Italian. In the case of explosives (73), as in mitto, after the tongue had come in contact with the roof of the mouth (= first t) a short pause ensued before the explosion took place (= second t). In the case of continuants (74), as in summus, Apollo, the mm or ll was sounded appreciably longer than a single m or l, and at the beginning of the second half of the long continuant there was a slight increase of force.

81. Consonants were not doubled in writing till after 200 B.C.: as, FVISE for fuisse, *to have been*, and for more than a century afterward the usage is variable : as, in the same inscription, ESSENT, *they might be*, by the side of SVPERASES, *thou mayest have conquered ;* but it must not be inferred that they were pronounced as single consonants.

SYLLABIC AND UNSYLLABIC FUNCTION.

82. Whenever two or more sounds are combined in a syllable, one of them excels in acoustic prominence : as, *a* in English *pat ; n* in the group *pnd* in *opnd* (*opened*); *l* in the group *tld* in *bottld* (*bottled*); and *s* in the group *pst*. This sound is said to have *syllabic function* or to be *syllabic ;* in the examples given, *a, n, l*, and *s* are respectively syllabic. All the other members of each group are termed *unsyllabic*.

83. Vowels are almost always used in syllabic function. When, in rare cases, they are unsyllabic, this fact is usually indicated in phonetic works by an inverted half-circle, ͜, placed under the vowel; so in the case of diphthongs to indicate the subordinate member: as ai̯, o̯e, u̯i (49). Latin omnia and English *glorious*, when pronounced as words of two syllables, would be written omni̯a (2503), *glori̯ous.* When sounds other than vowels have, in rare cases, syllabic function, this fact is noted in phonetic works by a point, ., or circle, ₒ, under the letter: as, Latin *agr̥s, *agr̥s (111, *b*), English *opn̥d, opn̥d.*

ACCENT.

84. The relative force with which the different syllables of a word are uttered varies. Such variation in emphasis is called *stress accentuation.*

The degrees of stress are really infinite, but for practical purposes it is sufficient to distinguish between (1.) the strongest stress (chief accent); (2.) a weaker stress (secondary accent); and (3.) absence of stress (atonic syllable). In the English *contradict*, the last syllable has the chief accent, a secondary accent falls on the first, and the second syllable is unstressed.

85. It is not customary to indicate the place of accents in Latin by special signs. When, for special reasons, signs are used, ´ denotes the chief accent, the secondary accent, while the unstressed syllables are left unmarked.

THE CLASSICAL ACCENT.

86. In classical Latin the place of the chief accent may be determined by the following rules.

(1.) Words of two syllables have the accent on the penult (175): as,

hómo ; ácer.

(2.) Words of more than two syllables have the accent on the penult when that syllable is long (177); otherwise on the antepenult: as,

palúster, onústus (177) ; mulíebris, génetrīx (178) ; árborēs, árbutus, gladíolus.

87. A short penult retains the accent in the genitive and vocative with a single ī from stems in -io- (456, 459): as, genitive, cōnsílī ; impérī ; genitive or vocative, Vergílī ; Valérī ; Mercúri. For calefácis, &c., see 394.

88. In a few words which have lost a syllable the accent is retained on the last syllable; such are (1.) compounds of the imperatives dīc and dūc (113): as, ēdū́c ; (2.) nominatives of proper names in -ās and -īs for -ātis and -ītis : as, Arpīnā́s, for Arpīnātis ; Laenā́s ; Maecēnā́s ; Quirī́s ; Samnī́s ; also nostrā́s, vostrā́s ; (3.) words compounded with the abbreviated (113) enclitics -c for -ce and -n for -ne : as, illī́c ; tantṓn ; audistī́n (for the shortening of the final syllable: as, vidén, *dost see?*, see 129) ; (4.) audī́t, contracted from audīvit (154, 893). The Latin grammarians prescribe the circumflex (90) for all these long syllables.

EARLIER RECESSIVE ACCENT.

89. In the preliterary period of the Latin language, the accent tended to go as far from the end of the word as possible (*recessive accent*). Thus, while the classical accentuation is inimícus, the older period accented ínimicus. In literary Latin this early recessive accent has survived, only in Plautus's accentuation of words of the form ◡ ◡ ◡ ◡̱ (proceleusmatic or fourth paeon, see 2521), in which he stresses the first syllable: as, fácilius (classical facílius); vóluerat (classical volúerat). But in many instances the early recessive accent may be traced in literary Latin by the phonetic changes which it produced (102 ff.).

90. Musical element. The native Latin grammarians slight the stress accentuation and pay much attention instead to the variations in pitch. But they are so greatly dependent on their Greek models that they are unsafe guides in this matter. It is, however, probable that a stressed vowel was uttered on a higher key (acute) than an unstressed vowel (grave), and that in certain syllables the long, accented vowel showed a rise and fall (circumflex): as, illîc (88).

91. The force of the Latin stress accent must have varied at different periods and in different localities, as it now varies in the Romance countries. The early recessive accent seems to have been fairly emphatic; but the stress in classical Latin was probably weak and the difference between accented and unaccented syllables was much less marked than it is in English.

PROCLITICS AND ENCLITICS.

92. Proclitics are unaccented words which are pronounced as a part of the following word; they are: (1.) The relative and indefinite pronouns and their derivatives; (2.) Prepositions.

(*a.*) Thus, quō diē, pronounced quōdíē; qui vīxit, quivíxit; genus unde Latīnum, génus undeLatínum. Similarly quamdiū, *as long as;* iamdiū, *this long time.* A distinction is thus made between the interrogative quālis (1526), which is accented, and the relative quālis (1831) which is proclitic (Quint. 1, 5, 26); cf. the English *who*, which is accented when interrogative, and proclitic when relative (*b.*) circum lītora, pronounced circumlítora; ab ōrīs, pronounced abōrīs (Quint. 1, 5, 27); in inscriptions and manuscripts prepositions are often united in writing with the following word. Phrases like extemplō, *suddenly*, invicem (94), *in turn*, are commonly written and accented as one word. But the preposition is accented when it is followed by a monosyllabic unemphatic (and therefore enclitic) personal pronoun: as, ín mē; ábs tē (but abs tē, if tē is emphatic). All prepositions used as adverbs (1402) have an independent accent.

93. Enclitics are words which have no accent of their own, but are pronounced as a part of the word preceding. This increase of the number of syllables produced certain accentual changes, all the details of which are not clear. When the enclitic was monosyllabic the place of the accent seems to have been determined as in 86; thus vídēs, but vidēsne; Látiō, but Latióque. Again, when by the addition of a monosyllabic enclitic the accent falls on the fourth syllable from the end, a secondary (84, 85) accent was probably placed on the penult: as, perícula, but perículàque. The Roman grammarians agree, however, in demanding that everywhere the syllable preceding the enclitics -que, -ne, -ve, and -ce should be accented. In deinde and subinde there is authority for placing the accent on the first syllable.

Enclitics are : (1.) Unemphatic personal and indefinite pronouns : as, in mē, pronounced ˌínmē ; dā mihi, dắmihi ; sīc tibi, síctibi ; sī quis, síquis ; nē quid, nḗquid. ˌ (2.) Verbs when used as auxiliaries : as, possum for pót(e) sum (752) ; quí libet (2401) ; vidḗlicet, īlicet, scīlicet (712) ; quámvīs (1903) ; the forms of esse in compound tenses (719), so that est is frequently combined, even in writing, with the preceding past participle (747). (3.) The particles -ne (-n), -ve, and -ce (-c) : as, satísne or shortened satín ; Hyrcānísve Arabisve ; istíce or shortened istíc (90), adhûc (90). (4.) The copulative conjunction -que : as, Latiṓque, limináque . (5.) The preposition cum when it follows (1435) its case. (6.) The particle quidem : as, sī quidem, síquidem (131). (7.) Other enclitics are : -met (650) : as, egómet ; -dem : as, ibídem ; -nam : as, ubínam ; -dum (1573) : as, agédum ; -inde : as, déinde, próinde (which are disyllabic in verse), and súbinde ; -tum ; as, etiámtum ; -per : as, parúmper ; ˌthe vocative when it was closely joined to the preceding word, e.g. an imperative : as, díc puer (106).

94. Two words expressing what is really one single idea are often bound together by *one* accent, one of them acting the part of either a proclitic or enclitic.

Thus, with the earlier recessive accent (89), Iúpiter (133; 389; originally a vocative which came to be used as nominative ; for the change of pater to piter see 104) ; ínvicem, *in turn ;* dḗnuō for dē nóvō (106) ; with the later, classical accent, lēgislátor, paterfamíliās, orbisterrárum, extémplō, imprímīs. When unemphatic ille and iste preceded their noun and had practically the value of our definite article they formed a unit with the following noun and thus the accent might fall on their last syllable : as, illé pater, isté canis. This use is particularly common in vulgar and laʾe Latin (see 112).

CHANGE OF SOUND.

(A.) VOWEL CHANGE.

CHANGE OF DIPHTHONGS IN ACCENTED SYLLABLES.

95. Of the six original diphthongs au, ou, eu, and ai, oi, ei, the only one which preserved its original sound in the classical period is au. Of the rest only ae (for older ai) and, in a few words, oe (for older oi) remained diphthongs ; all the others had become monophthongs.

96. CHANGE OF ai. ai is common in inscriptions : as, AIDILIS, PRAITOR. Toward the end of the republic the two elements of the diphthong had been partially assimilated to ae (49) : as, aedīlis (Quint. 1, 7, 18). This is its pronunciation in the classical period. Between 130 and 100 B.C. ai is displaced by ae in public documents ; but the old-fashioned ai was often retained in private inscriptions. Still later the two elements completely converged to ē. In provincial Latin ē is found as early as 200 B.C. : as, CESVLA for CAESVLLA ; in Rome itself the pronunciation ' Cēcilius ' for Caecilius, and ' prētor ' for praetor was derided as boorish ; but by 71 A.D. ae was verging toward ē even in the court language : the coins of Vespasian have IVDEA as well as IVDAEA. In the 3d and 4th century A.D. ē became the prevalent sound.

97. CHANGE OF **au.** The diphthong **au,** which was preserved in educated speech. was changed to **ō** in rustic and colloquial pronunciation (see the anecdote related by Suetonius, *Vesp.* 22) : as, **cōpō,** *innkeeper,* for **caupō; plōstrum** for **plaustrum** (*barge*), *cart;* **Clōdius** for **Claudius.** Some of these gained literary currency : as, **cōdex,** *book,* **caudex,** *block;* **fōcāle,** *neckcloth,* **faucēs,** *throat.* The form **sōdēs** (1572) for **sī audēs = sī audēs** (Cic. *O.* 154) is a colloquialism.

98. CHANGE OF **ei.** **ei** as a genuine diphthong is common in old inscriptions : as,. SEI ; SEIVE ; ADEITVR ; DEIXERVNT ; FEIDA. In classical Latin it has passed into **ī** : thus, **sī,** *if;* **sīve,** *either;* **adītur,** *is approached;* **dīxērunt,** *they said;* **fīda,** *faithful.* An intermediate stage between the old diphthong **ei** and the classical **ī** was a very close (46) **ē**: as, PLOIRVME (465) for **plūrimī** ; IOVRE (501, 507) for **iūrī.** For the orthographical use of **ei** as a spelling for the long ī-sound, see 29.

99. CHANGE OF **oi.** The development of **oi** was parallel to that of **ai.** It first passed into **oe** : as, COIRAVERVNT and COERAVERVNT, *they cared;* OITILE, *useful,* and OETI, *to use;* LOIDOS and LOEDOS, *play,* — all in old Latin. In classical Latin it has further been changed in accented syllables to **ū** : as, **cūrāvērunt, ūtile, ūtī, lūdus.** But **oe** was retained in classical Latin (1.) when a secondary diphthong (48), the result of contraction (120), and (2.) in a few words like **foedus,** *treaty,* perhaps as an archaizing, legal term ; **foedus,** *ugly;* **poena,** *penalty,* perhaps through the influence of Greek ποινή (in the verb **pūnīre,** *to punish,* the regular **ū** appears) ; **proelium,** *skirmish;* **foetor,** *stench;* and **moenia,** *walls,* perhaps because there was a word **mūnia,** *services.* The connection of **nōn,** *not,* with **noenum** (455 ; 1444 ; 699) is difficult because of the unusual development of **oe** to **o,** for which the Praenestine form CORAVERONT is the only parallel.

100. CHANGE of **ou.** **ou,** found in inscriptions down to about 90 B.C., passed, in classical Latin, into **ū** : as, POVBLICOM, NOVNTIATA, IOVDEX ; later **pūblicum,** *public,* **nūntiāta,** *notified,* **iūdex,** *judge.*

101. CHANGE OF **eu.** Primitive (48) **eu** appears in classical Latin only in the interjections **eu, heu, ēheu, heus.** Every other original **eu** had, even in old Latin, passed into **ou** and developed like the latter : as, **neumen (Greek νεῦμα)* became first **noumen,* then (100) **nūmen.** With the exceptions noted above, the diphthong **eu,** as it appears in Latin, is always of secondary origin (48), the result of the two vowels **e** and **u** meeting in composition : as, **neu,** *neither,* from **nē-ve** ; **neutiquam,** from **nē** and **utiquam** (124).

WEAKENING IN UNACCENTED SYLLABLES.

102. The vowel of an unstressed (atonic) syllable is often weakened, changing its quantity or quality or both. This is especially the case in syllables immediately preceded by the chief accent (*posttonic syllables*). The following changes took place at an early period when Latin still possessed the old, recessive accent (89).

WEAKENING OF SIMPLE VOWELS IN MEDIAL SYLLABLES.

103. (*a.*) ATONIC MEDIAL **e** before a single consonant was weakened (with the exceptions given under *b.*) to **i** : as, **cólligō,** *collect,* from **legō** ; **óbsideō,** *besiege.* from **sedeō** ; **cértāminis,** *of the contest,* from **certāmen** (224) ; **flāminis,** from **flāmen**(470). And so probably **hic**(664) arose from **hec* or **hoc* (105, *g*) when used as proclitic (92). Before the labials **p, b, f,** and **m** this weakened sound was intermediate between **i** and **u** (28), and both spellings occur : as, **quadripēs** and **quadrupēs,** *four-footed;* **alimentum,** *nourishment;* **monumentum,** *monument.* The choice of **i** or **u** was probably governed by the quality of the stressed vowel in the preceding syllable : viz., **u** after **o** and **u,** and **i** after **a, e,** and **i.** But such distinction is only imperfectly maintained in classical Latin.

(*b*.) But before two consonants, before r, before vowels, and after i, atonic e does not change: as, lévāmentum (224), but lévāminis, *of consolation ;* óbsessus (but óbsideō), *possessed ;* sócietās, *society,* from the stem socie- (but nóvitās from the stem nove-) ; géneris, *of the kind ;* ádeunt, *they approach.*

104. (*c*.) Atonic medial a, except in the cases mentioned below under (*d*.), (*e*.), and (*f*.), was first weakened to e and then underwent the same changes as atonic medial e (103) : as (before single consonants), cōnficiō, *accomplish,* from faciō ; insiliō, *jump in,* from saliō (1019) ; rédditus, *restored,* from datus ; trícipitem, *three-headed,* from *trícapitem (caput), Cic. *O.* 159 ; occiput, *back of the head,* and sinciput, *jole* (478). In compounds of iaciō (940), -iaciō is weakened in early Latin to -ieciō (as, coneciō, 940), but later to -iciō (as, subiciō). This last form may be due to syncope (111, *a*) of the radical a. The spelling -iiciō (as, subiiciō) is late and faulty (52). It does not occur in republican inscriptions and owes its origin to a confusion of the two forms coneciō and coniciō. (On the quantity of the vowel of the prepositions in these compounds of iaciō, see 122 *e*) ; (before p, b, f, m) áccipiō, *accept,* and óccupō, *occupy,* from capiō ; cóntubernālis, *room-mate,* from taberna ; ábripiō, *to snatch away,* from rapiō ; (before two consonants) péperci, *I have spared,* from parcō ; áccentus, *accent,* from cantus ; (before r) péperi, *I brought forth,* from pariō.

(*d*.) But an a in the preceding syllable may protect the atonic a : as, ádagiō, ádagium, *proverb,* but prōdigium, *miracle* (144).

(*e*) Atonic medial a before the guttural nasal (62) n followed by g changed to i (138) : as, áttingō, *touch,* from tangō.

(*f*.) Atonic medial a before l followed by any consonant save l changed to u (both l and u being guttural, 60, 44) : as, éxsultāre, *to leap up,* from saltāre ; but féfelli, *I deceived,* from fallō.

105. (*g*.) ATONIC MEDIAL O, when followed by a single consonant, first changed to e and then underwent all further changes of medial atonic e : as, hóminis, from *homon-is (485) ; imáginis, for *imāgonis, 226 (nominative imāgō, 485) ; cúpīdinis, for * cupīdonis, 225 (nominative cupīdō, 485) ; vírginis, for *virgonis (nominātive virgō, 470) ; ilicō, from *in-slocō, *on the spot* (169, 6).

(*h*.) Before two consonants or before guttural l (60) atonic medial o changed to u : as, éuntis, from *éontis (Greek ἰόντος) ; sédulō, from sē dolō (1417). But a preceding v or u protects o (107, *c*).

(*i*.) Before r, atonic medial o was retained : as, témporis, *of time ;* except when u in the preceding syllable induced a change to u : as, fúlguris, *of lightning* (for the -r in the nominative singular fulgur instead of -s, see 154).

106. (*k*.) Medial -av-, -ov-, and -iv- in posttonic syllables were weakened to u : as, dēnuō from dēnovō (94) ; ábluō from ablavō. The form puer, *boy,* arose from the older POVER in enclitic vocatives (93, 7) and was thence transferred to the nominative like piter in Iūpiter (94).

WEAKENING OF SIMPLE VOWELS IN FINAL SYLLABLES.

107. (*a*.) In final syllables unaccented original e before s and t was weakened to i : as, salūtis, *of safety,* from older salūtes (507).

(*b*) Final i became e : as. ante for *anti (Greek ἀντί and anti-cipāre) ; nominative singular mare, from the stem mari- (526).

(*c*.) In final syllables o before consonants changed to u except when preceded by u or v : as, fīlius, *son,* for old Latin filios (452) ; ferunt, *they carry,* for older feront ; femur, *thigh,* nomin. sg. from the stem femor- (489) ; genus, *kind,* for *genos, Greek γένος ; but vīvont, *they live :* salvom, *safe.* Not long before the beginning of our era o here also changed to u and appears to have coalesced with the preceding v (Quint. 1, 7, 26): as, in inscriptions : INGENVS (nomin. sg) for ingenuos ; SERVM, *slave* (acc. sg.), for servom ; NOVM for novom, *something new ;*

so also **boum**, *oxen* (gen. pl.), for **bovom** (494). But inasmuch as the majority of forms in the paradigms of these words retained their **v**, it was restored in most cases, by analogy, to the forms which had lost it: as, **servum** for **serum**, because of **servī**, **servō**, etc. ; **vivunt** for **viunt**, because of **vīvō**, **vīvis**, **vīvit**, etc.

(*d.*) When the stems **fac-** (**facere**, *do*), **cap-** (**capere**, *take*) appear as second members of compounds, their **a** changes in final syllables to **e** : as, **artifex**, *artisan* ; **auceps**, *bird-catcher*. After the analogy of these words, compounds with **dīcere** and **īre** have **e** in the nom. sg.: as, **iūdex**, **iūdicis**, *judge* (from **iūs** and **dīcere**); **comes**, *companion* (from **com**, *with*, and **īre**) ; see 136, 2.

WEAKENING OF DIPHTHONGS IN UNACCENTED SYLLABLES.

108. Diphthongs, whether medial or final, are treated alike in atonic syllables.

(*a.*) Atonic **ei**, **oi**, and **ai** (**ae**) became **ī** : as, **lupī**, *wolves* (nom. pl.), for **lupoi (Gr. λύκοι); **bellī**, *in war* (loc. sg., 460, 1338), for **bellei (Greek οἴκει) or **belloi (Greek οἴκοι); **éxīstimō**, *I consider*, from **aestimō**; **cóncīdō**, *I strike down*, from **caedō**; Cicero, *O.* 159, mentions **inīcum**, *unfair*, for **inaecum, and **concīsum** for **cóncaesum; so also, probably, **hīc**, *this*, arose from **hoic** (662) when used as a proclitic (92).

(*b.*) Atonic **ou** and **au** became **ū** : as, **inclūdō**, *I include*, from **claudō** ; **áccūsāre**, *to accuse*, from **causa**.

109. There are not a few cases in which the atonic vowel does not conform to the rules given above (102-108). These are usually compounds which show the vowel of the simple verb. Some of these were formed at a time when the early recessive accent was no longer in force and consequently there was no cause for weakening: in others the vowel of the simple verb was by analogy substituted for the weakened vowel of the compound: as, **appetō**, *I strive after*, from **petō**, which ought to have **i** like **colligō**, *collect*, from **legō** ; **intermedius**, *intermediate*, but **dimidius**, *half;* **dēfraudāre**, *to cheat*, by the side of **dēfrūdāre** from **fraudāre**; instead of the common **redarguō**, *I refute*, Scipio Africanus minor Pauli filius (185-129 B.C.) said **rederguō**, and **pertīsum** for **pertaesum**, but both Cicero (*O.* 159) and Lucilius discountenance **pertīsum** as the sign of a pedantic prig. In a few cases the reverse process took place, and the weakened vowel which arose in the compound was transferred to the simple verb : as, **clūdō**, *I close* (958), for **claudō**, which owes its **ū** to compounds like **occlūdō**. For a case where the vowel of the preceding syllable acted as a stay to the expected change, see 104, *d.*

LOSS IN UNACCENTED SYLLABLES.

110. Only vowels which are short and atonic may be lost. The loss of a medial vowel is called *Syncope ;* of an initial vowel, *Aphaeresis ;* of a final vowel *Apocope.*

111. SYNCOPE. (*a.*) Loss of a posttonic vowel, entailing the loss of a syllable, occurs in **ardus** (Lucil. ; for **ă** see 128) for the common **āridus**, *dry ;* **caldus** by the side of **calidus**, *warm* (Quint. 1, 6, 19); **reppulī**, *I pushed back*, and **rettulī**, *I carried back*, stand for **répepulī and **rétetulī (861); **pergō**, *I proceed*, stands for **perregō from **regō** (cf. **cor-rigō**, **ē-rigō**, where the **e** is weakened, 103, and **porrigō**, **porgō**, where it is either weakened or lost), hence it forms its perfect **perrēxī** (953): **pōnō**, *I place*, is for **posnō (170, 2) from **po-sinō (112), hence it forms its past participle **positus** (972); for **iūrgō**, *I blame*, Plautus has **iūrigō** ; **ūsūripō (from **ūsus** and **rapere**) yields **ūsurpō**, *I utilize ;* **gāvideō, hence **gāvīsus** (801), gives **gaudeo**, *I rejoice*, converting **ău** to **au** before the following **d** (128); in a similar way **auceps**, *bird-catcher*, is formed from **aviceps (**avis**, *bird* and **capere**, *catch*); **claudere**, *lock*, from * **clāvidere (clāvis**, *key*); **aetās**, *age*, for **áevitās** (262); **praecō**, *herald*, for * **práevicō** (105, *g*) **prae-vocō** (211); also with change of **ou** to **ū** (100), **prūdēns**, *prudent*, for * **proudēns** from **provi-dēns**, *foreseeing;* **nūper**, *lately*, from * **noviper**; **nūntius**, *messenger*, from * **noventius** (333); **iūcundus**, *joyful*, from **iuvicundus** (Cic. *Fin.* 2, 14). But forms like **pōclum**, *cup*, **saeclum**, *age*, do not belong here, as they are original and not derived by syncope from **pōculum, saeculum**; cf. 172.

(*b.*) Where, through the loss of a vowel, **l** or **r** would come to stand between two consonants, or where they would be final and preceded by a consonant, **l** and **r** become syllabic (83) and the syllable is thus maintained. Syllabic **l** is represented by **ul**, syllabic **r** by **er** (172, 3) The development of such intercalary vowels as **u** before **l** and **e** before **r** is called *Anaptyxis* (172). Thus, * **sacri-dōts** (cf. **sacri-legium**) became first * **sacr̥dōts** by syncope, then **sacerdōs**, *priest*, by anaptyxis; * **ācribus** (cf. **ācri-mōnia**, *pungency*) first became * **ācr̥bus** then **ācerbus**, *pungent ;* * **agri-los** (267, cf. **agri-cola**, *farmer*) became first * **agr̥los**, then * **agerlos**, and finally, by assimilation of the **r** to **l** (166, 7), **agellus**, *small field;* from * **dis-ficilter** (adverb from **dis-** and **facilis**) arose * **difficl̥ter** and **difficulter**, *with difficulty*. The nominative sg. of the following words is to be explained thus. **ager** (451) was originally * **agros** (cf. Greek ἄγρος), which changed successively to * **agr̥s**, * **agers**, and **ager** (for the loss of **-s** see 171, 1 and 3). Similarly * **ācris**, passing through the stages of * **ācr̥s**, * **ācers**, became **ācer** (627), and * **famlos** by way of * **faml̥s**, * **famuls**, became **famul** (455), to which later the common ending of nouns of the **o**-declension was added, giving **famulus**.

112. APHAERESIS. Aphaeresis hardly occurs in literary Latin. In the pronoun **iste** the initial **i** is sometimes dropped (667); this loss implies an accented ultima (94). A trace of prehistoric aphaeresis is found in the prefix **po-** for * **apo** (Greek ἀπό) in **pōnō**, *I place*, for **po-s(i)nō** (111, *a*).

113. APOCOPE. Under the same conditions under which a medial vowel was syncopated, the final vowel of a word which stood in close union with the following word, as a preposition with its noun, was lost. In this way * **peri** (Greek περί) became **per** ; * **apo** (Greek ἀπό) became **ap, ab** (164, 2) ; * **eti** (Greek ἔτι) became **et**. Similarly the final **-e** of the enclitics **-ce, -ne**, *not*, and **-ne** interrogative was lost : * **sī-ce** became **sīc**, *so;* * **quī-ne**, **quīn**, *why not;* **habēsne, haben**, *hast thou ;* the imperatives **dīc**, *say*, **dūc**, *lead*, and **fac**, *do*, stand for earlier **dīce, dūce, face** (846); the shortened form **em** for **eme** (imperative of **emere**, *take*) has been turned into an interjection (1149). In the same way **nec** arose by the side of **ne-que;** **ac** by the side of **atque** (158). Final **-e** has also been dropped in the nominative sg. of a number of polysyllabic neuter stems in **-āli** and **-āri** (546): as, **animal**, *animal,* for * **animāle**, **exemplar**, *pattern*, for * **exemplāre**. See 536, 537. It must, however, be remembered that in most of the cases given the loss of a final vowel would also result from elision (119) before the initial vowel of the following word.

COMBINATION OF ADJACENT VOWELS.

114. HIATUS. A succession of two vowel sounds not making a diphthong is called *Hiatus*.

When in the formation of words by means of suffixes or prefixes or through the loss of an intervening consonant, two vowels come into contact within a word we speak of *internal hiatus;* the term *external hiatus* comprises those cases where, in connected discourse, the final vowel of one word comes into contact with the initial vowel of the following word. For the latter kind, see 2474.

115. The treatment of vowels in internal hiatus is four-fold: (1.) The hiatus may remain; (2.) the two vowels may be fused into one (*Contraction*); (3.) one of the two vowels may be dropped (*Elision*); and (4.) the two vowels may be combined into a diphthong.

116. HIATUS is maintained (*a.*) between two adjacent vowels the second of which is long and accented (according to the classical accentuation): as, coḗgī, *I forced*, and coāctus, *forced* (937); but cōgō (118, 3). For coepī, instead of coḗpī, *I began*, see 120.

(*b.*) In many prepositional compounds when the members were still felt to be independent: as, praeesse (the contracted form praesse is found in inscriptions); dēerunt, *they will be wanting*, by the side of dērunt; coalēscō, *grow together* (the contracted form cōlēscō appears in Varro); cooptāre, *coöpt*, cooperiō, *I cover up* (by the side of rare cōptāre, cō-perīre); coïtus, *meeting*, by the side of coetus (120).

(*c.*) A comparatively large number of vowel combinations remain unchanged: as ea and eā in eam, *her*, and meā, *by my* (fem. sing.); ia and iā in māria, *seas*, viātōris, *of the traveller;* ua and uā in bēlua, *monster*, suā, *through her* (fem. sg.); iē in quiēs, *quiet;* uē in luēs, *pestilence;* eī in meī, *of me;* uī in tuī, *of thee;* eō in meō, *by my* (masc. sing.).

117. SYNIZESIS. In these combinations the first vowel is sometimes made unsyllabic (83). This is called *synizesis* (2499) and is not rare in poets, being often the only means of adapting a word to the requirements of certain metres. Thus, fortuitus (_ ⌣ _ ⌣) must appear in a hexameter as fortvītus (fortu̯ītus). See 2499, 2503.

118. CONTRACTION. (1.) Two like vowels may unite in one long vowel; rapidity of utterance was favourable to such fusion. In compounds, the desire to keep the members distinct often prevented it. So always nēmō, *nobody*, for *neemō from *ne-hemō, *no man* (for the loss of h, see 58, 150; for e in *hemō, see 144); and by the side of the open forms, nīl from nihil, *nothing;* vēmēns from vehemēns, *rapid* (connected with the verb vehō); rarely dērunt, *they will be wanting*, and dēsse, *to be wanting*, for dēerunt, dēesse; dēlēram, *I had destroyed*, from *dēlēeram for dēlēveram (for the loss of v, see 153), see 890; passūm, *of paces*, for passuum (591).

(2.) A diphthong absorbs the following vowel: as, praetor, older praitor, *praetor*, from *prai-itor, *who goes before;* inscriptions show praerunt for praeerunt, *they will be before;* for praebēre, *to furnish*, the open form praehibēre occurs in Plautus (1004).

(3.) If two unlike vowels are contracted at all, they usually unite in the long sound of the first vowel. Thus, o and a yield ō: as, cōgō, *I force*, from co-agō; cōgitō, *I think*, from co-agitō. Similarly Varro has cōlēscat, *it may combine*, for co-alēscat. o and e yield ō: as, prōmō, *bring out*, cōmō, *put up*, for pro-emō, co-emō (953). ē and a yield ē: as, dēgō, *I pass away*, from dē-agō (937). i and a in the termination of the vocative of -io- stems probably contracted to -ī; as fīlī from *filie, 459. But in denominative (365) and other verbs of the first conjugation ā and ō contract into ō: as, amō, *I love*, from *amā-ō (cf. Greek τῑμά-ω); and ā and ē into ē: as, amēs, *thou mayest love*, for *amā-ēs.

119. ELISION. Only rarely the first of two successive vowels is dropped: as, **nūllus**, *no*, for * **ne-ūllus**; likewise the final vowel of the first member of nominal compounds: as, **multangulus**, *with many corners*, for * **multi-angulus** (cf. **multi-cavus**, *with many holes*) ; **flexanimus**, *heart-rending*, for * **flexi-animus** (cf. **flexi-pēs**, *with bent feet*).

120. COMBINATION INTO DIPHTHONGS. The union of two successive vowels into a diphthong is equally rare: **o** and **i** are combined to **oi**, **oe**, in **coetus**, *meeting*, by the side of the open form **coïtus** (116, *b*) ; the perfect **coepī** (812), *I began*, owes its diphthong **oe** to forms in which the **e** was short and unaccented, such as the rare present forms **coepiō** for **có-ĕpiō** (813) ; for **coēpī** (813, 863) would have remained unchanged (116, *a*). **neuter**, with the accent on the **e**, was pronounced as three syllables, later **eu** became diphthongal ; **neutiquam** with synizesis (117) of **e**. **e** and **ī** sometimes contract to **ēi** in **rēi** (601, 602) and in **dēinde**, **dēin** in the classic poets.

LENGTHENING.

121. COMPENSATIVE LENGTHENING. When certain groups of consonants are simplified by the dropping of a consonant, its time is absorbed by a preceding short vowel, which thereby becomes long. This is called *Compensation.* In many cases compensative lengthening is due to the loss of a preliterary sonant **s** (170, 2): as,

cānus, *gray*, from *casnus (cf. **cas-cus**, *very old*). See for other cases of this lengthening, 170, 5, **quīnī**, for *quincnī ; 170, 6, **īgnōscō**, for *in-gnōscō.

122. INDUCED LENGTHENING. Before certain groups of consonants short vowels have a tendency to become long: as,

(*a*.) The prefixes **in-** and **con-** before **s** or **f** lengthened their vowels in classical Latin (Cic. *O.* 159): as, **īnsānus**, *mad* ; **īnfēlix**, *unhappy* ; **cōnsuēvit**, *he grew used to* ; **cōnfēcit**, *he accomplished.* Elsewhere also the vowel before **ns** and **nf** appears to have been lengthened: as, **fōns**, *fountain* ; **pēnsus**, *weighty* (Gell. 9, 6) ; **forēnsis**, *forensic* ; **cēnsor**, *censor* ; **mēnsa**, *table* ; **mēnsis**, *mouth* ; **Valēns** ; **Clēmēns** ; the **o** of **īnsons**, *guiltless*, however, is marked as short by the grammarian Probus.

(*b*.) A similar lengthening of the vowel before **nc** followed by **t** or **s** appears: as, **ūnctus**, *anointed*, from **unguō** (Gell. 9, 6) ; **iūnctus**, *joined*, from **iungō** (954), **coniūnx**, *spouse*, genit. **coniugis** (472) ; **quīnctus**, *fifth*, whence **quīntus** (170, 4) and **quīnque**, *five*, derive their **ī** ; **sānctus**, *hallowed.*

(*c*.) Spellings like sIGNVM, *sign* (well supported in inscriptions), and DIGNE, *worthily* (less well supported) show that **i** was at times lengthened before **gn**. The grammarian Priscian demands this lengthening for all vowels preceding the ending -gnus, -gna, -gnum.

(*d*.) A lengthened vowel before **r** followed by a consonant is also certain for some words like **ōrdō**, *order* ; **fōrma**, *shape.*

(*e*.) Some speakers appear to have lengthened the vowel of prepositions like **con-**, **sub-**, **ob-**, in the compounds of **iaciō** (104, *c*) ; as **ōbicit**. This practice, which is disapproved by Gellius (4, 17), probably arose from the transfer by analogy of the quantity of the first syllable in forms like **con-ieciant** (940) to that of the shortened form. In the same way the occasional spelling CÓNIVNX, *spouse*, for **coniūnx**, may owe its long **ō** to the analogy of **cōiunx**, CÓIVGI (170, 6).

(*f.*) Many verb stems ending in -g have a long vowel in the past participle before the suffix -to- : as, tēctus, *covered*, from tego (916); tāctus, *touched*, from tangō (925); pāctus, *fixed*, from pangō (925); fīctus, *moulded*, from fingō (954); pīctus, *painted*, from pingō. The evidence for ā in maximus is very scanty: one case of A with the apex (29, 3) in a faulty inscription.

(*g.*) Of the induced lengthenings enumerated above, only those given in (*a.*) (*b.*) (*f.*) seem to have been universal in classical Latin. The rest appear to have been local peculiarities, which, while making inroads upon the literary language, never gained full recognition.

123. (1.) ANALOGICAL LENGTHENING. In noun stems in -o the stem vowel is lengthened in the genitive plural -ōrum (449, 462), by analogy to the stems in -ā (435): as, servōrum, *of slaves*, like mēnsārum, *of tables*. For other cases see 122, *e.*

(2.) METRICAL LENGTHENING. On the lengthening of a vowel (or a syllable) under the influence of verse-ictus, see 2505.

SHORTENING.

124. A vowel originally long is regularly shortened in classical Latin before another vowel, even though an h intervene : as,

taceō, *I am silent*, from the stem tacē- (365) ; seorsum, *apart*, deorsum, *downward*, from sē(v)orsum, dē(v)orsum (153).

125. In simple words a diphthong occurs before a vowel only in one or two proper names : as, Gnaeus, Annaeus, in which it remains long, and in Greek words. But the diphthong ae of the prefix prae is sometimes shortened before a vowel : as, praĕacūtus ; praĕeunt ; praĕhibeō ; hence prehendō for *prae-hendō. Sometimes it coalesces with a following vowel : as, praĕŏptāvistī.

126. An increased tendency to shorten a long vowel before another vowel can be traced in the history of the language : thus, classical fuī, *I was*, for Plautus's fūī (750) ; clueō, *I am called*, for Plautus's clūeō ; perfect pluit, *it rained*, for Varro's plūit (cf. plūvit, 823, 947) ; pius, *pious*, for Ennius's pīus ; see also 765.

127. But even in classical Latin there are cases where a vowel before another vowel remains long : thus,

(1.) Regularly, the ī of fīō, *I am made*, except before -er-, as in fierem (788, 789).

(2.) In dīus, *godly*, for dīvus (153), and the old ablatives dīū, dīō, *open sky* (used only in the expression sub dīū, sub dīō, i. e. sub dīvō).

(3.) In the ending ēī of the genitive and dative sg. of stems in -ē- (601) when an i precedes : as, diēī, *of a day*, aciēī, *of the battle line*, but reī, *of the thing*, for older rēī.

(4). It may be mentioned here that rēī is said to occur in verse 6 times (Plaut. G. 2, Lucr. G. 2, D. 2) ; reī 9 times (Plaut. G. 2, Ter. G. 4, D. 1, Juv. G. 1, Sulp. Apoll. G. 1) ; rĕī 27 times (Plaut. G. 2, D. 3, Enn. D. 1, Ter. G. 9, D. 8, Lucil. G. 1, D. 1, Lucr. G. 2). fidēī G. 3 times (Plaut., Enn., Lucr.) ; fideī 11 times (Enn. D. 1, Man. G. 2, D. 1, Sil. G. 4, D. 1, Juv. G. 2); fidĕī 5 times (Ter. G. 1, D. 3, Hor. 1). ēī 35 times (Plaut. 18, Ter. 8, Lucr. 9); eī some 17 times (Plaut. 12, Ter. 2, German. 1, Ter. Maur. 2); ĕī 23 times (Plaut. 11, Ter. 8, Lucil. 3, Cat. 1).

(5.) **Gāius** retains its **ā** before the vowel **i** : thus, **Gāius** (trisyllabic).

(6.) In the pronominal genitives in **-īus** (618), the quantity of **i** varied. The older dramatists use **ī**; later, **ī** was shortened, but variations in its quantity seem to have continued until long after the end of the republic; Cicero, *DO.* 3, 183, measures **illius**; Quintilian 1, 5, 18 **ūnīus**; the grammarian Priscian prescribes **-ius** for all except **alterius**, which should always have **i**, and **utrius**, in which the **i** is common (30). In verse the **i** is often short, except in **neutrīus**; **utriusque** has always short **i**.

(7.) The penult is long in the endings **-āī, -āīs, -ōī, -ōīs,** and **-ēī, -ēīs,** from stems in **-āio-, -ōio-,** and **-ēio-** (458) or **-iā-** (437) : as, **Gāī, Bōī, Pōmpēī, plēbēī** : **Gāīs, Bōīs, Pompēīs, plēbēīs, Bāīs ; aulāī, pictāī.**

(8.) **Dīāna** has **ī** as often as **ī**. **ohē** has **ŏ** ; **ĕheu** has **ĕ** in comedy, otherwise **ē.**

(9.) In many Greek words a long vowel comes before another vowel ; as, **āēr, Aenēās, Mēdēa.** But early importations from Greek followed the general rule and shortened the vowel : as, **platĕa** (πλατεῖα), **balinĕum, balnĕum** (βαλανεῖον).

128. A long vowel preceding unsyllabic **i** or **ụ** followed by a consonant is shortened : as, **gaudeō** for ***gāudeō** (cf. **gāvīsus,** 111) ; **claudo** for **clāudō** (cf. **clāụis,** 111).

Similarly a long vowel (unless long by contraction : as, **nūntius,** 111, *a,* **cōntiō**) preceding a liquid or nasal followed by a consonant is shortened : as, syncopated **ardus** from **āridus** (111), **habentem,** from the stem **habē-.** For cases of induced lengthening of the vowel before **n** followed by certain consonants, see 122.

129. IAMBIC SHORTENING. The law of iambic shortening (2470) produced a number of important changes : thus,

(1.) In old dramatic verse iambic words (◡ —) often shorten the long vowel. The poets after Plautus and Terence preserve the long vowel.

(*a.*) Nouns ; G. **eri, boni, preti.** D. **cani, ero, malo.** L. **domi, heri.** Ab. **levi, manu, domo, bona, fide.** Plural : N. **fores, viri.** D., Ab. **bonis.** Ac. **foris, viros, bonas.** (*b.*) Verbs : **eo, volo, ago ; ero. dabo ; vides ; loces ; voles ; dedi, dedin ; roga, veni ;** later poets sometimes retain **cave, vale,** and **vide.** The vowel may also be shortened when **-n** (1503) is added and **s** is dropped before **-n** (170, 2) : **rogan, abin ; viden** is also retained by later poets.

(2.) In a few pyrrhic words (◡ ◡) in **-i,** which were originally iambic (◡ —), the poets in all periods retained final **-ī** at pleasure : these are,

mihĭ, tibĭ, sibĭ ; ibĭ, ubĭ ; also **alicubĭ.** The **i** of **bi** is always short in **nēcubi** and **sīcubi,** and usually in **ubinam, ubivīs,** and **ubicumque ; ibidem** is used by the dramatists, **ibīdem** in hexameter. **ubīque** has always **ī.**

130. The following instances show that this law operated in prose speech also :

(1.) In iambic words of the **ā-** declension (432) the final **-ā** of the nominative singular was shortened ; hence ***equā** became **equa,** *mare.* From these iambic words short final **-a** spread so that all stems in **-ā-** shorten the final **ā** of the nom. sg. (434).

(2.) The final **-a** in the nominative plural of neuter nouns of the **o-** declension (446), which appears in **trīgintā,** *thirty,* was likewise shortened, first in iambic words like **iuga,** *yokes,* **bona,** *goods,* then everywhere (461).

(3.) This law explains the short final vowel in **homo** (2442) by the side of **sermō** (2437, *c*) and similar cases, like the adverbs **modo, cito** (2442), **bene, male** (2440). In the same way arose the short final **o** of the first person in conjugation (2443) : as, **volo, dabo, dīxero** by the side of **scrībō ;** so also **viden** for **vidēn** (129, 1 ; 170, 2).

(4.) Of imperatives only puta, used adverbially (2438, *c*), ave, have (805 ; Quint. 1, 6, 21 ; but Martial scans havē) as a salutation and cave, used as an auxiliary (1711), show the short final vowel in classical Latin. Elsewhere the long vowel has been restored, as amā, monē (845).

(5.) According to this rule calēfaciō, malēdīcō changed to calefaciō, maledīcō.

131. A long final vowel is shortened when an enclitic is added to the word : as siquidem from sī ; quoque from quō.

132. A long vowel is regularly shortened, in the classical period, before final -t and -m and, in words of more than one syllable, also before final r and l.

Thus, soror, *sister*, for Plautus's sorōr, from the stem sorōr- (487) ; ūtar, *I may use*, for Plautus's ūtār (cf. ūtāris) ; bacchanal for Plautus's bacchanāl ; animal, exemplar from the stems animāl- (530) and exemplār- (537) ; but the long vowel is retained in the monosyllables fūr, *thief*, sōl, *sun ;* pōnēbat, *he placed,* for Plautus's pōnēbāt (cf. pōnēbās) ; iūbet, *he commanded,* for Plautus's iūbēt ; eram, *I was*, but erās ; rēxerim, *I may have ruled*, but rēxerīs (877) ; -um in the genitive plural of -o- stems is for -ūm (462) ; mēnsam, *table*, for *mēnsām from the stem mensā- ; rem, from rē- (rēs), spem from spē- (spēs).

TRANSFER OF QUANTITY.

133. (1.) In a few cases the length of the vowel has been transferred to the following consonant, the length of which is then indicated by doubling it (81) : as, littera for lītera, LEITERAS : Iuppiter for Iūpiter ; parricīda for pāri-cīda, *murder of a member of the same clan* (*pāro-, *member of a clan*, Doric παός, *a relative*) ; cuppa for cūpa, *barrel*. The legal formula sī pāret, *if it appear*, was vulgarly pronounced sī parret (Festus).

(2.) Since the doubled unsyllabic i (i̯) between vowels (23 ; 166, 9 ; 153, 2) is commonly written single, the *vowel* preceding it is often erroneously marked long : as, āiō wrongly for aiō, *i. e.* ai̯i̯ō, *I say ;* māior wrongly for maior, *i.e.* mai̯i̯or, *greater ;* pēior wrongly for peior, *i.e.* pei̯i̯or, *worse ;* ēius, *of him,* cūius, *of whom,* hūius, *of him,* all wrongly for eius, cuius, huius *i. e.* ei̯i̯us, cui̯i̯us, hui̯i̯us (153, 2). In all these words the first *syllable* was long but not the vowel.

VARIATIONS OF QUANTITY.

134. (1.) In some foreign proper names and in a very few Latin words the quantity of a vowel varied. Vergil has Sӯchaeus and Sychaeus within six verses ; also Āsia and Asia, Lavīnium and Lāvinius ; so also glōmus (Lucr.), glomus (Hor.) ; cōturnīx (Plaut., Lucr.), coturnīx (Ov.).

(2.) Sometimes such variations in vowel quantity are only apparent : thus, the occasional long final -ē of the active infinitive (darē, prōmerē) has probably a different origin from the usual -ĕ. For metrical lengthening, see 2505.

QUANTITATIVE VOWEL GRADATION.

135. The same stem often shows a long vowel in some of its forms and a short vowel in others. In most cases these variations of quantity were not developed on Latin soil but inherited from a much earlier period. Such old inherited differences in vowel quantity are called *quantitative vowel gradation.*

(1.) Instances of this are **prō** for * **prōd** (149; cf. **prōdesse**) and **pro-** (Greek πρό); **nē** and **ne-** in **nescius**; the couples **regō**, *I rule*, **rēxī**; **vehō**, *I draw*, **vēxī**; **veniō**, *I come*, **vēnī**, where the long vowel is characteristic of the perfect stem (862); **vocō**, *I call*, and **vōx** *voice*: **regō**, *I rule*, and **rēx**, *ruler*; **legō**, *I read*, and **lēx**, *bill*; **sedeō**, *I sit*, and **sēdēs**, *seat*; **fīdēs**, *confidence*, and **fīdō**, *I trust*; **dux** (cf. **ducis**). *leader*, and **dūcō**, *I lead*, where verb and noun are differentiated by the quantity of the root vowel; and many others.

(2.) Sometimes the reduction of the vowel in certain forms amounts to complete loss, as in the adverbial ending **-is-** in **magis** (346, 363) compared with the comparative suffix **-ios, -iōs** (Nom. **-ior**, Genit. **-iōris**); in the oblique cases of the stem **carōn-** (nomin. sg. **carō**, 497), where the suffix becomes **-n-** (545), genitive **car-n-is**; in the suffix **-ter**, which becomes **-tr-** in all cases but the nom. sg. (**pater, patris**, etc., 470, 487); in the feminine **-tr-i-c-** to the suffix **-tor-**; but the nom. sing. **Caecīlis** (465) for **Caecīlios** is probably due to syncope.

QUALITATIVE VOWEL CHANGES.

136. (1.) **i** before an **r** which goes back to an earlier voiced **s** (154) was changed to **e**: as, **cineris**, *of ashes*, for *cinisis, from the stem **cinis** (491); **Falerii**, for ***Falisii**, cf. **Falis-cus**; (formed like **Etrūria**, for *Etrūsia, cf. **Etrūs-cī**).

(2.) In the nominative singular of compounds like **iūdex**, *judge* (from **iūs** and **dīcere**), **comes**, *companion* (from **com**, *with*, and **īre**, *go*), the **i** of the second member of the compounds is changed to **e** (470) after the analogy of words like **artifex**, *artisan*, etc. (107, *d*).

137. **e** before **-gn-** became **i**: as, **īlignus**, from the stem **īlec-** (cf. **īlex**).

138. **e** before the guttural nasal (62) followed by a guttural mute was changed to **i**: as, **septingentī**, from **septem**; **singulī**, from the stem **sem-** in **semel** (for the assimilation of **m** see 164, 3); **obtingō** (925), *I attain*, for *óbtengō (104, *c*) from *ob-tangō (104, *e*).

139. A similar change took place in the group **-enl-** which became first **-inl-** and then **-ill-**: as, ***signilum**, diminutive of **signum** (for **ī**, see 122, *c*), first changed by syncope (111) from *signilum to *signlum, then to *sigenlum (172, 3), then to *siginlum, and finally to **sigillum.**

140. **o** before **nc** became **u**: as, **homunculus**, *manikin* for *homonculus, from the stem **homon-** (485); **nūncupāre**, *name*, for *nōn-cupāre (**nōn-** for **nōm-** (164, 3) = syncopated **nōmen**); **hunc**, *him*, for *honc, from **hom-ce** (662).

141. **o** before **l** followed by any consonant save **l** was changed to **u**: as, **cultus**, *tilled*, for *coltus, from **colere**; **multa**, *fine*, for old Latin **molta**. But **o** before **ll** is retained: as, **collis**, *hill*.

142. **e** before guttural **l** (60) was changed to **o**: as, **solvō**, *I undo*, from *seluō (**se-**, as in **se-cordia**, **luō** = Greek λύω); **culmen**, *top*, for *celmen, from *cellō in **ex-cellō**; **volō**, *I wish*, for *velō; but **e** is preserved before dental **l** (60): as in **velle**, **velim** (773). Before **l** followed by any consonant save **l** this **o** changes to **u** (141): as, **vult.**

143. In a number of words, notably in **voster**, *your*, **vorsus**, *turned*, **vortex**, *eddy*, and **votāre**, *forbid*, the forms with **o** were replaced, about the second century B.C. by forms with **e**: as, **vester**, **versus**, **vertex**, **vetāre** (Quint. 1, 7, 25).

ASSIMILATION.

144. In a few cases a vowel is influenced by the vowel of a neighbouring syllable : as,

nisi, *unless,* for ***nesi** ; iīs, for **eīs,** *to them* (671, 674) ; diī, diīs, *gods,* for deī, deīs (450) ; nihil, *nothing,* for ***nehil** ; homō, *man,* for ***hemō** (cf. nēmō, from ne-hemō, 118) ; see also 104, *d ;* 105, *i.*

QUALITATIVE VOWEL GRADATION.

145. The same stem often shows different vowels in different forms. In most of these cases this difference was inherited from a very early period and continued in the Latin. Such old inherited variation of the quality of the stem-vowel is called *qualitative vowel gradation.* The qualitative variations may be accompanied by quantitative changes (135).

Often the verb and the noun are thus distinguished by different vowels : as, **tegō,** *I cover,* and **toga,** *a garment, toga ;* **precor,** *I beg,* and **procus,** *suitor,* cf. English *to sing* and *a song, to bind,* and *a bond.* The different tenses of some verbs show a like gradation : as, **capiō,** *I take,* **cēpī** ; **faciō,** *I make,* **fēcī,** cf. English *I sing, I sang ; I bring, I brought.* The same occurs in derivation : as **doceō,** *I teach,* by the side of **decet** ; **noceō,** *I harm,* by the side of **nex (nec-s).** The two vowels which occur most frequently in such gradation are **e** and **o** : as in stems in **-o-,** **domine, dominus** (for **dominos**) ; as variable vowel (824) ; **genos** (genus, 107, *c*) in the nom. sg. by the side of ***genes-** in the oblique cases (gen. **generis** for ***genesis,** 154) ; **honōs** by the side of **hones-** in **hones-tus** ; **modus,** *measure,* for ***modos** (originally a neuter **-s-** stem like **genus** (487, 491), but transferred later to the **-o-** declension), by the side of **modes-** in **modes-tus,** *seemly.* See 187.

(B.) CONSONANT CHANGE.

146. In a number of words which belong more or less clearly to the stem of the pronoun quo- (681), cu- (157), the initial **c** has disappeared before **u** : as,

uter, *which of the two,* **ubī,** *where,* **unde,** *whence* (711). For the conjunction **ut, utī,** *that,* connection with this pronominal stem is much more doubtful. The **c-** appears in the compounds with **sī** and **nē** : as, **sī-cubī** (cf. **sī-quidem, sī-quandō), sī-cunde, nē-cubi, ne-cunde, ne-cuter.**

147. **d** varies in a few words with **l** : as old Latin **dacruma,** *tear,* for later **lacrima** ; **dingua,** *tongue,* for later **lingua** ; **odor,** *smell,* by the side of **oleō,** *I smell.*

148. Very rarely, before labials, final **d** of the preposition **ad** varies with **r** : as, old Latin **arfuērunt,** *they were present,* for later **adfuērunt** (2257) ; **arvorsum,** *against,* for **advorsum.** The only instances of this in classical Latin are **arbiter,** *umpire,* and **arcēssō** (970), *I summon,* which shows **r** before a guttural.

149. (1.) Final **d** after a long vowel disappeared in classical Latin : thus, in the ablative singular of **-ā-** and **-o-** stems (426), and in the ablative-accusative forms **mēd, tēd, sēd** (648). The prepositions **prō** and **sē** (1417) originally ended in **-d** which is still seen in **prōdesse,** *be of advantage,* **prōd-īre,** *go forth ;* **sēd-itiō,** *a going-apart, sedition.* According to the grammarians, the negative **haud** preserved its **d** before vowels, but lost it before consonants (1450).

(2.) Late inscriptions confuse final **-d** and **-t**: as FECID (729), ALIVT for **aliud**. But in very old Latin **-d** in the third person singular seems to be the remnant of a secondary ending (cf. the Greek distinction of primary -ται and secondary -το).

150. In a number of words **f** varies dialectically with **h**. In some of these **f** appears to have been original, in others **h**: as, old Latin **fordeum**, *barley*, for classical **hordeum**; old Latin **haba**, *bean*, for classical **faba**. The word **filum**, *thread*, appears as ***hilum** in nihil, *nothing*, for ***ne-hilum**.

151. **h** being a weak sound (58) was often lost between two like vowels, especially in rapid utterance: as, **nīl**, *nothing*, **prēndere**, *take*, **vēmēns**, *rapid*, by the side of **nihil, prehendere, vehemēns**; and always **nēmō**, *nobody*, for ***ne-hemō**, *no man*.

152. In some words **h** between two vowels is not original, but goes back to a guttural aspirate *gh*. Before consonants this guttural appears: as, **vehō**, *I draw*, **vectus** (953) from a stem **vegh-**, **trahō**, *I drag*, **tractus** (953) from a stem **tragh-**.

153. (1.) **v** not infrequently disappeared between two like vowels: as, **dītior**, *richer*, for **dīvitior**; **sīs** (Cic. *O.* 154), for **sī vīs** (774); **lātrīna**, for **lavatrīna**; **fīnīsse**, for **fīnīvisse**; **dēlēram**, for **dēlēveram**; and later also in perfect forms in which the preceding and following vowel differed: as, **amāsse**, for **amāvisse**. The abbreviated forms of the perfects in -**vī** (890) were common in Cicero's (*O.* 157) and Quintilian's (1, 6, 17) time. **v** also disappeared before **o** in **deorsum, seorsum**.

(2.) Old and original unsyllabic **i** (82; 83) disappeared everywhere between vowels. Wherever unsyllabic **i** appears between two vowels it represents double **ii**, and is the result of the assimilation of **g** to **i** (166, 9), or **d** to **i** (166, 9), or of the combination of two **i**'s: as in **ei-ius, quoi-ius** (eius, quoius = cuius, 688). See 23; 166, 9. In all these cases the first **i** joined to the preceding vowel (83) formed with it a diphthong, and the syllable is thus long (133, 2).

(3.) The combinations of unsyllabic (83) **u** with the vowel **u** and of unsyllabic **i** with the vowel **i** were avoided in classical Latin; see 52.

(4.) In composition, unsyllabic (82) **i** after a consonant became syllabic in **quoniam**, *since*, for **quomiam** (164, 5), and **etiam**, *also*, for **etiam** (both compounds with **iam**).

154. In early Latin **s** between two vowels was voiced (75), and in the fourth century B. C. this voiced **s** changed into **r**. According to Cicero (*Fam.* 9, 21, 2) L. Papirius Crassus, consul in 336 B. C., changed his family name **Papīsius** to **Papīrius**. Old inscriptions show frequently **s** for **r**: as, ASA, *altar*, AVSELII. This change of intervocalic **s** to **r** plays an important part in declension, conjugation, and derivation: as,

Nominative **iūs**, *right*, genitive **iūris**; **spērō**, *I hope*, derived from **spēs**; **nefārius**, *wicked*, from **nefās**; **gerō**, *I carry*, from a stem **ges-** which appears in **ges-sī, ges-tus** (953); **erō**, *I shall be*, from the stem **es-** in **esse**; the subjunctive ending -**sem** in **es-sem** appears as -**rem** after vowels: as, **stārem**; the infinitive ending (894, 895) -**se** in **es-se** appears as -**re** after vowels: as, **legere**, for ***legese**, *to read*, **stāre**, for ***stāse**, *to stand*. Where all oblique cases show -**r**- and only the nominative singular -**s**, the latter is sometimes changed to -**r** by analogy: as, **arbor**, *tree*, **honor**, *honour*, for original **arbōs, honōs**, by analogy to the oblique cases **arboris, arborī, honōris, honōrī**, etc. (487, 488). The final -**s** of the prefix **dis-** follows this rule: as, **dir-imō**, *I take apart*, for ***dis-emō**; but an initial **s-** of the second member of a compound remains unchanged: as, **dē-sinō**, *I stop*.

155. Wherever intervocalic **s** is found in classical Latin it is not original, but the result (*a*.) of earlier -ns-: as, **formōsus**, *handsome*, for **formōnsus** (63); (*b*.) of earlier -ss- (170, 7): as, **ūsus** for **ūssus*, *use* (159); **causa**, *thing*, for **caussa** (Quint. 1, 7, 20); or (*c*.) it occurs in borrowed words like **asinus**, *ass*. (*d*.) There are a few words in which an **r** in a neighbouring syllable seems to have prevented the change: as **miser**, *miserable* (173).

156. Before the **o** described in 142 **qu** changed to **c**: as, **incola**, *inhabitant*, for **inquola*, from **inquela*; the stem **quel-** appears in **in-quil-īnus**, *lodger*.

157. As **v** before **u** (107, *c*), so **qu** was not tolerated before **u**, but changed to **c**.

Hence when, about the beginning of our era, the **o** of **quom**, *when*, **sequontur**, *they followed*, changed to **u** (107, *c*), they became **cum**, **secuntur**; thus **equos** but **ecus**, *horse* (452); **reliquom** but RELICVM, *the rest*; **loquor**, *I speak*, but **locūtus** (978). Much later, in the second century of our era, the grammarians restored the **qu** before **u** by analogy to those forms in the paradigm in which **qu** came before other vowels: as, **sequuntur** for **secuntur** by analogy to **sequor**, **sequeris**, **sequitur**, **sequimur**, **sequimini**, etc.; **equus**, **equum**, for **ecus**, **ecum**, by analogy to **equī**, **equō**, **eque**, **equōrum**, **equīs**, **equōs**.

158. **qu** before consonants or when final changed to **c**: as, **relictus** from the stem **liqu-**, *leave* (present, **linquō**, 938); **ac**, *and*, for **atc*, by apocope from **atque**; **nec**, *nor*, by apocope from **neque**. See also **torctus* (170, 3), **quīnctus** (170, 4).

159. When in the process of early word formation a **t** was followed by another **t**, the combination **tt**, unless followed by **r**, changed to **ss**: as, **obsessus**, *besieged*, *sat upon*, for **obsettus*, from **obsed-tus* (cf. **sedeō**). After long vowels, nasals, and liquids this double **ss** was simplified to **s** (170, 7): as, **ūsus** from **ūt-tus*, *used* (cf. **ūtor**); **scānsus**, *climbed*, from **scant-tus* for **scandtus* (cf. **scandō**).

In this way arose a suffix **-sus** (906, 912) for the past participle of verbs ending in a dental, and this spread to other verbs (912): as **mānsus**, *stayed*, from **maneō** (1000), **pulsus**, *pushed*, from **pellō** (932). The regular participles of these two verbs still appear in the derivative verbs **mantāre** and **pultāre**, which presuppose the past participles **mantus* and **pultus* (371). If the double **tt** was followed by **r** it changed to **st**: as, **assestrīx** from **assettrīx*, while **assettor* changed to **assessor**.

160. But wherever the combination **tt** arose in historical times it remained unchanged: as, **attineō**; **cette**, syncopated for **cé-d(i)te**, i. e. the particle **ce** (93, 3) which is here proclitic, and the imperative **date**, *give*.

161. Initial **dv** (**du̯**) changed to **b**, unless the **v** (**u̯**) was converted into the corresponding vowel: as, **bis**, *twice*, for **du̯is* (cf. **duo**); **bidēns** for **du̯idēns*, by the side of old Latin **du̯idēns** with vocalic **u**; **bonus**, *good*, for **du̯onus**, by the side of trisyllabic **duonus**; **bellum**, *war*, for **du̯ellum*, by the side of **duellum** with vocalic **u**; **bēs**, *two thirds*, for **du̯ēs** (2427). Cicero (*O.* 153) notes that the change of **duellum** to **bellum** affected even the proper name **Duellius** (name of the admiral who won the naval victory over the Carthaginians in 260 B. C.) which was changed to **Bellius**. Plautus always scans **du̯ellum** disyllabic with synizesis (2503).

CHANGES OF CONSONANT GROUPS.

162. Many groups of consonants undergo changes in order to facilitate their pronunciation in rapid speech. These changes involve (*a*.) Assimilation of consonants ; (*b*.) the development of consonantal glides; (*c*.) the loss of one member of the group ; and (*d*.) the development of a vowel between the consonants.

ASSIMILATION.

163. Of two successive consonants belonging to different syllables (175), the first is, as a rule, assimilated to the second (*regressive assimilation*), rarely the second to the first (*progressive assimilation*). A consonant may be assimilated, either entirely or partially, to another consonant.

Assimilation is very common in prepositions prefixed to a verb.

164. PARTIAL ASSIMILATION. (1.) A voiced mute before an unvoiced consonant became unvoiced : as, rēx, *king*, for *rēgs (cf. rēgis) ; rēxī, *I guided*, for *rēgsī (cf. regō) ; rēctus, *guided*, for *rēgtus ; scrīpsī, *I wrote*, for *scrībsī (cf. scrībō) ; scrīptus, *written*, for *scrībtus ; trāxī, *I dragged*, for *trāghsī, tractus, *dragged*, for *traghtus (152). The spelling did not always conform to this pronunciation : as, urbs, *city*, pronounced urps (54) but spelled with b by analogy to the oblique cases urbis, urbem, etc. ; obtineō, *I get*, pronounced optineō.

(2.) An unvoiced mute before a voiced consonant became voiced. The prepositions ob, ab, sub, for *op, *ap, *sup, owe their final b to their frequent position before voiced mutes : as, obdūcō, abdīcō, sub dīvō. The forms *op (still preserved in op-eriō, *I close*, 1019) *ap (preserved in ap-erio, *I open*, 1019 ; cf. Greek ἀπό) and *sup (preserved in the adjective supīnus, *supine*) were then crowded out by ob, ab, and sub.

(3.) Nasals changed their place of articulation to that of the following consonant. Thus, dental n before the labials p and b became labial m : as, imbibō, *I drink in*, impendeō, *I hang over*. Labial m before the gutturals c and g became guttural n (62): as, prīnceps, *leader*, singulī, *severally* (the original labials appear in prīmus, semel (138)) ; hunc for *homce (662). Labial m before the dentals t, d, s became dental n : as, cōnsecrō, *I consecrate*, from com (cum) and sacrō ; tantus, *so great*, from tam ; quondam, *once*, from quom ; tandem, *at length*, from tam. But sometimes the etymological spelling was retained : as, quamdiū, *as long as*. But m does not change to n before t or s in the inflection of verbs and nouns, where mt, ms develop into mpt, mps (167): as, sūmptus, sūmpsī, from sūmō.

(4.) p and b before n changed to m : as, somnus, *sleep*, for *sop-nus (cf. sopor) ; omnis, *all*, for *op-nis (cf. opēs) ; Samnium, for *Sabnium (cf. Sabīnī).

(5.) m before unsyllabic i (i̯) became n : as, quoniam (with vocalic i ; 153, 4), *since*, for *quoni̯am from quom iam (1882) ; coniungō, *I join together*, for *comiungō.

(6.) c between n and l, and before m, changed to g : as, angulus, *corner*, with anaptyctical (172) vowel u for *anglus, from *anclus (cf. ancus) ; segmentum, *section*, from the stem sec- in secāre.

165. It appears that at a very early period the neighbourhood of a nasal changed an unvoiced mute into a voiced one : as, ē-mungō, *I clean out*, by the side of mūcus ; pangō, *I fix*, by the side of pāc- in pāx, *peace* (gen. pāc-is).

27

166. ENTIRE ASSIMILATION. (1.) One mute is assimilated to another : thus **p** or **b** to **c**: as, **suc-currō**, *I assist;* **t** or **d** to **c**: as, **sic-cus**, *dry* (cf. **sit-is**, *thirst*), **accipiō**, *I accept;* **d** to **g**: as, **agglūtinō**, *I glue on ;* **t** or **d** to **qu**: as, **quicquam**, *anything ;* **t** or **d** to **p**: as, **appellō**, *I call;* **quippe**, *why?* (1690).

(2.) A mute is assimilated to a spirant: thus, **p** to **f** in **officīna**, *workshop*, for *opficīna, syncopated form of *opificīna ; **d** to **f**: as, **afferō**, *I bring hither ;* when **t** is thus assimilated to **s** the result is **ss** after a short vowel, and **s** after a long vowel (170, 7) or when final (171); as, in the -**s**- perfects, **concussī**, *I shook*, for *concutsī (concutiō, 961); **messuī**, *I mowed*, for *metsuī (metō, 835); **suāsī**, *I advised*, for *suātsī (suādeō, 1000); **clausī**, *I shut*, for *clautsī (claudō, 958); **haesī**, *I stuck*, for **haes-sī** (868) from **haerēre**, stem **haes-** (154); in the same way **possum**, *I can*, for *potsum (cf. **pot-est**, 752) ; **prōsum**, *I am of advantage*, for *prōtsum (cf. **prōd-esse**); **legēns**, *reading*, for *legents (from the stem **legent-**, cf. genitive **legent-is**). An **s** is never assimilated to a following **t**: as, **haustus**, *drained* (1014), from the stem **haus-**, present **hauriō** (154). Forms like the rare **hausūrus** (Verg.) are made after the analogy of dental stems.

(3.) One spirant, **s**, is assimilated to another, **f**: as, **difficilis**, *difficult*, **differō**, *I am unlike*, from **dis** and **facilis**, **ferō**.

(4.) A mute is assimilated to a nasal: thus **d** to **m** in **mamma**, *woman's breast*, from the stem **mad-** (cf. **madeō**, 1006); **rāmus**, *branch*, **rāmentum**, *splinter*, from the stem **rād-** (cf. **rādō**, 958) with simplification of the double **m** after the long vowel. **d** to **n** in **mercēnārius**, *hireling*, from the stem **mercēd-**, *reward*, (for **mercennarius**, see 133, 1); **p** to **m** in **summus**, *highest*, from the stem **sup-** (cf. **super**). A progressive assimilation of **nd** to **nn** belongs to the Oscan dialect, and occurs only very rarely in Latin : as, **tennitur** (Ter.), **distennite** (Plaut.) See 924; 950.

(5.) One nasal, **n**, is assimilated to another, **m**: as **immōtus**, *unmoved*. But an **m** before **n** is never assimilated: as, **amnis**, *river*.

(6). Mutes or nasals are assimilated to liquids; thus **n** to **l**: as, **homullus**, *manikin*, for *homon-lus (cf. **homun-culus**); **ūllus** (274); **d** to **l**: as, **sella**, *seat*, for *sed-la from the stem **sed-** (cf. **sedeō**); **caelum**, *chisel*, from the stem **caed-** (cf. **caedō**) with simplification of the double **l** after the diphthong (170, 7); **n** to **r**: as, **irruō**, *I rush in ;* and with progressive assimilation **n** to a preceding **l**: as, **tollō**, *I lift*, for *tolnō (833) ; **fallō**, *I cheat* (932); **pellō**, *I push* (932). But no assimilation is to be assumed for **parricīda**, which does not stand for **patricīda** (133, 1).

(7.) One liquid, **r**, is assimilated to another, **l**: as, **pelliciō**, *I lead astray* (956), for *per-liciō ; **agellus**, *small field*, for *agerlos ; **pūllus**, *clean*, from *pūr-los (cf. **pūrus**, *clean*).

(8.) A spirant, **s**, is assimilated to a preceding liquid in **velle**, *wish*, for *velse, **ferre**, *carry*, for *ferse (the infinitive ending -**se** appears in **es-se**, 895) ; **facillimus**, *easiest*, for *facilsimus (345); **sacerrimus**, *holiest*, for *sacersimus (344). But where **ls** and **rs** are not original but the result of lightening (170, 3 ; 10) they remain unchanged : as, **arsī**, *I burnt*, for *artsī from the stem **ard-** (cf. **ardeō**, 1000); **alsī**, *I felt cold*, for *alcsī from the stem **alg-** (cf. **algeō**, 1000).

(9.) **g** and **d** were assimilated to a following unsyllabic **i** (j) the result being (153, 2) **ii** (jj); thus **peiior**, *worse*, for *ped-jor, from the stem **ped-** (532), whence also the superlative **pessimus** for *petsimus (166, 2); **maiior**, *greater*, for *mag-jor (the stem **mag-** appears in **magis**); and so, for *ag-jō (the stem **ag-** appears in **ad-ag-ium**, **prōd-ig-ium**, 219). These forms were pronounced by Cicero with doubled **i** (23), and traces of the spelling with double **ii** are still found (23), though in common practice only one **i** is written (153, 2). On the confusion of syllabic quantity with vowel quantity in these words, see 133, 2.

CONSONANTAL GLIDES.

167. Pronunciation of two successive consonants is sometimes facilitated by the insertion of a consonant which serves as a glide. Such insertion is not frequent.

In inflection a **p** was thus developed between **m** and **s**, between **m** and **l**, and between **m** and **t** (elsewhere **mt** changed to **nt**, see 164, 3): as, sūmpsī, *I took*, sūmptus, *taken*, from sūmere for *sūmsī, *sūmtus ; and in the corresponding forms of cōmō, dēmō, prōmō (953); exemplum, *pattern*, for *exemlum from the stem em-, *take* (cf. eximere, 103, *a*).

DISAPPEARANCE.

168. A word may be lightened by the disappearance of an initial, a medial, or a final consonant.

Disappearance of an initial consonant is sometimes called *Aphaeresis*, of a medial, *Syncope*, of a final, *Apocope*.

169. INITIAL DISAPPEARANCE. (1.) Initial **tl** changed to **l**: as, lātus, *borne*, for *tlātus from tollō (187, 917).

(2.) Initial **gn** changed to **n**: as, nātus, *born*, for earlier GNATVS from the stem gen-, gnā (187); nōscō, *I find out*, for gnōscō, GNOSCIER (897); nārus, *knowing*, for the more frequent gnārus, nāvus, *active*, for gnāvus. Cf. the compounds cō-gnātus, cō-gnōscō, ī-gnārus, ī-gnāvus (170, 6) which preserve the **g**. But Gnaeus retained its **G**.

(3.) Initial **d** when followed by consonant **i** (j), disappeared: as, Iovis, Iūpiter, for *Djovis, *Djūpiter. Where the **i** was vocalic, **d** was retained: as, dīus.

(4.) Initial **stl-** first changed to **sl** and then to **l**: as, Old Latin stlocus, *place*, stlīs, *law-suit* (Quint. 1, 4, 16), STLOC, SLIS, classical locus, līs; also lātus, *wide*, for *stlātus. That a form *slocus existed is proved by īlicō (698, 703) from *in-slocō, *on the spot* (170, 2).

170. MEDIAL DISAPPEARANCE. (1.) **c**, **g**, **p**, and **b** disappear before **s** followed by an unvoiced consonant: as, sescentī, *six hundred*, for *sexcentī from sex; illūstris, *resplendent*, for *illūcstris from lūceō; discō, *I learn*, from *dicscō for *di-tc-scō (834), a reduplicated present from the root dec- (cf. decet) like gignō (from the root gen-), and sīdō (for *si-sd-ō, 170, 2, from the root sed-, 829). Sometimes prepositions follow this rule: as, asportō, *I carry off*, for *absportō, suscipiō, *I undertake*, for *subscipiō (subs formed from sub like abs from ab ; sub-cipiō gives succipiō); occasionally also ecferō, for exferō, *I carry out*. But more frequently prepositional compounds remain unchanged: as, obscūrus, *dark;* abscēdō, *I withdraw*. In some words the lost consonant has been restored by analogy: as, sextus, *sixth*, for *sestus (cf. Sēstius) after sex; textor, *weaver*, for *testor after texō.

(2.) **s** before voiced consonants was voiced (75) and is dropped. If a consonant precedes the **s** this is dropped also. In either case the preceding vowel is lengthened. Voiced **s** alone is dropped: as, prīmus, *first*, for *prīs-mus (cf. prīs-cus); cānus, *gray*, for *casnus (cf. cas-cus); adverb pōne, *behind*, for *posne (cf. pos, 1410); dīlābī, *glide apart*, for *dislābī; idem, *the same*, for ISDEM (678); iūdex, *judge*, for iūsdex, trēdecim, *thirteen*, for *trēsdecim. And with subsequent shortening of the final syllable (130, 3) abin, *goest thou?* for abisn(e), viden, *seest thou?* for vidēsn(e). Voiced **s** with the preceding consonant is dropped: as, trādūcō, *I lead across*, trānō, *I swim across*, for trānsdūcō, trānsnō; but in these prepositional compounds the -ns was often retained: as, trānsmittō, *I send across;* sēnī, *six each*, for *secsnī; sēmēnstris, *every six months*, for secsmēnstris; sēvirī, *the Board of Six*, for secsvirī; āla, *wing*, for *acsla (cf. ax-illa, Cic. *O.* 153); māvolō (779) for magsvolō from magisvolō, 396; tōles (plural), *goiter*, for *tōnsles (cf. tōnsillae, *tonsils*); pīlum, *pestle*, for *pinslum from pinsere, *crush;* two consonants and voiced **s** are dropped in scāla, *stair*, for *scand-sla (cf. scandō).

(3.) **c** falls away when it stands between a liquid and **t, s, m,** or **n** : as, **ultus,** *avenged,* for **ulctus* from ulc-iscor (980); **mulsī** for **mulcsī* from both **mulgeō,** *I milk,* and **mulceō,** *I stroke;* similarly other stems in -c and -g (1000, 1014); **quernus,** *oaken,* for **quercnus* from **quercus** ; **tortus,** *turned,* for **torctus* from **torqueō** (for the change of **qu** to **c,** see 158); for **fortis,** *brave,* **forctis** is found in old Latin.

(4.) **c** drops out when it stands between **n** and **t**: as, **quīntus,** *fifth,* for older **quīnctus** (2412), from **quīnque** (for the change of **qu** to **c,** see 158; for the long **ī** in **quīnque,** see 122, *b*). But verbs having stems in -nc or -ng retain the **c** in their past participles: as, **vīnctus,** *bound,* from **vincīre** (1014) ; **iūnctus,** *joined,* from **iungere** (954). In **pāstus** (965) **c** has dropped out between **s** and **t.**

(5.) The group **-ncn-** was simplified to simple **-n-,** and the preceding vowel was lengthened: as, **quīnī,** *five each,* for **quīnc-nī* (317); **cō-nīveō,** *wink and blink,* for con-cnīveō.

(6.) **n** before **gn** was dropped and the preceding vowel lengthened: as, **ī-gnōscō,** *I forgive,* for **in-gnōscō,* **cō-gnōscō,** *I know,* for **con-gnōscō.* In this manner (170, 5; 6) arises a form **cō-** by the side of **con-** (122, *e*): as, **cō-nectō, cō-nubium, cō-ligātus** (Gell. 2, 17, 8).

(7.) In the imperial age, **ss** after long vowels and diphthongs was regularly changed to **s**: as, **clausī,** *I closed;* **ūsus,** *used* (166, 2); but always **ēsse,** *to eat* (769) ; **ll** changed to **l** after diphthongs : as, **caelum,** *chisel* (166, 6) ; also when preceded by **ī** and followed by **i** : as, **vīlla,** *country-place,* but **vīlicus** (adject.) ; **mille,** *thousand,* but **mīlia** (642). Elsewhere **ll** was retained after long vowels: as, **pūllus** (166, 7), *clean* ; **rāllum,** *ploughshare,* from **rādō** with suffix **-lo-** (209). In Cicero's time (Quint. 1, 7, 20) the spelling was still **caussa** (155, *b*), *matter;* **cāssus** (930), *fallen;* **divīssiō** (cf. 912), *division.* Vergil also, according to Quintilian, retained the doubled consonants, and the best manuscripts of both Vergil and Plautus frequently show **ll** and **ss** for later **l** and **s,** as do inscriptions: as, PROMEISSERIT, *he might have promised* (49 B.C.) ; ACCVSSASSE, *to have accused.*

(8.) After a long vowel **d** was dropped before consonant **u (v)**: as, **svāvis,** *sweet,* for **svādvis* from **svād-** (cf. **svādeō**).

(9.) **r** before **st** was dropped: as, **tostus,** *roasted* (1004) for **torstus* from the stem **tors-** (cf. **torreō** with assimilated **-rs-,** 166, 8).

(10.) **-rts-** changed to **-rs-**: as, **arsī,** *I burnt,* for **artsī* (1000). **-rcsc-** changed to **-sc-**: as, **poscō,** *I demand,* for **porcscō* (834).

(11.) In **ipse,** *self,* for **is-pse,* an **s** has disappeared before **-ps-**

(12.) **d (t)** disappears between **r** and **c**: as, **cor-culum** for **cord(i)-culum** (275).

171. FINAL DISAPPEARANCE. (1.) A word never ends in a doubled consonant: as, **es** for **es-s,* *thou art,* which Plautus and Terence still scan as a long syllable ; and the following cases of assimilation : **ter** for **terr* from **ters* (cf. **terr-uncius,** *a quarter of an* **ās,** *a farthing,* 1272, for **ters-uncius,* 166, 8) ; **fār,** *spelt,* for **farr,* from **fars* (489) ; **fel,** *gall,* for **fell,* from **fels* (482) ; in **mīles,** *soldier,* for **mīless* from **mīlets* (cf. Gen. **mīlitis,** 477) the final syllable is still long in Plautus. **hoc,** *this,* for **hocc* from **hod-c(e)* (the neuter **hod* from the stem **ho-,** as **istud, illud** (107, *c*) from **isto-, illo-**) counts as a long syllable even in classical poetry.

(2.) No Latin word can end in two explosives : thus, final **t** is dropped in **lac,** *milk* (478) ; final **d** in **cor,** *heart* (476).

(3.) When final **s** was preceded by **r** or **l,** it was assimilated to these liquids, and final **rr** and **ll** were then simplified to **r** and **l.** See the examples under (1). Wherever final **-rs** and **-ls** appear they are not original but the result of the disappearance of an intervening consonant: as, **puls,** *pottage,* for **pults* (533) ; **pars,** *part,* for **parts* (533) ; all with syncope (111) of the vowel **i** in the nominative sg.

(4.) Original final **ns** was changed to **s** and the preceding vowel was lengthened: as, **sanguīs**, *blood* (2452), for *sanguins fiom the stem **sanguin-** (486). Wherever final **-ns** appears it is not original but the result of the disappearance of an intervening consonant: as, **ferēns**, *carrying*, for *ferents, from the stem **ferent-** ; **frōns**, *foliage*, for *fronds, from the stem **frond-**.

(5.) A dental mute before final **s** is dropped : as, **hērēs**, *heir*, for *hērēds (475); **virtūs**, *virtue*, for *virtūts (477); **nox**, *night*, for *nocts (533); a labial or guttural mute is retained : as, **fornāx** (**x** = **cs**), *furnace*, from the stem **fornāc-** (531); **lēx**, *law*, from the stem **lēg-** (472) ; **urbs**, *city*, from the stem **urb-** (480); **ops** from the stem **op-**, *help* (480).

DEVELOPMENT OF AN ANAPTYCTICAL VOWEL.

172. Certain consonant groups, notably those containing a liquid, are sometimes eased by the insertion of a vowel which develops between the consonants. This is called *Anaptyxis* (Greek ἀναπτύσσειν, *unfold*). It is the opposite of syncope of vowels (110, 111).

(1.) The suffix **-clo-** (242), changed to **-culo-**, being thus no longer distinguishable from the diminutive suffix **-culo-** (267) : as, **pōculum**, *cup*, for **pōclum** (Plaut.); **vehiculum**, *carriage*, for **vehiclum** (Plaut.). But **-clo-** is more common in Plautus than **-culo-**, especially after long vowels. The suffixes **-blo-** (245), and **-bli-** (294) always show the anaptyctical vowel. Its colour depends on the nature of the **l** (60) : as, **stabulum**, *resting-place;* **stabilis**, *steady.* The group **-ngl-** also changes to **-ngul-** : as, **angulus** (164, 6).

(2.) In words borrowed from the Greek an unfamiliar sequence of consonants was so lightened ; as, **mina**, *mina*, for *mna (μνᾶ); and in Old Latin **drachuma** (Plaut.) for later **drachma**, *drachma* (δραχμή); **techina**, *trick*, from Greek τέχνη ; **Tecumēssa** for **Tecmēssa** (Τέκμησσα).

(3.) Before syllabic (83) **l** and **r** a vowel is developed (111, *b*): as, **íncertus**, *uncertain*, for *íncr̥tus ; **fácultās**, *capability*, for **fácltās.** Likewise before syllabic **n** (139).

DISSIMILATION.

173. (1.) To avoid the repetition of the same liquid in successive syllables **l** is sometimes changed to **r**: as, **caeruleus**, *sky-blue*, for *caeluleus, from **caelum** ; **Parīlia**, by the side of **Palīlia**, from **Palēs** ; the suffix **-clo-** appears as **-cro-** after an **l**: as, **lavācrum**, *bath* . **simulācrum**, *image* (241) ; the suffix **-āli-** under like conditions changes to **-āri-'**; as, **molāre**, *of a mill* (313), but **augurāle**, *of an augur.*

(2.) In a few cases repetition is avoided by dropping the sound once: as, **praestīgiae**, *jugglery*, for **praestrīgiae.** This also applies to the spirant **s** followed by a consonant, a combination which is not tolerated in successive syllables : as in the reduplicated perfects **stetī**, for *stestī ; **spopondī**, for *spospondī (859), where the second syllable, and in **quisquiliae**, *sweepings*, for *squisquiliae, where the first syllable was lightened.

CHANGES WITHIN COMPOUNDS.

174. The final syllable of the first member of compounds (181) sometimes undergoes certain changes by analogy to other compounds :

(1.) The final **-ā** of **ā**-stems, by analogy to the more frequent **-o**-stems, usually changed to **-o**, which in atonic syllables became **-i** (105) : as, **āli-ger**, *winged*, for *ālo-ger from **ālā-**.

(2.) Stems in **-on-** substitute **-o-** for **-on-** by analogy to the **-o**-stems : as, **homi-cīda**, *murderer*, for *homo-cīda (105) from **homon-** (Nom. **homō**).

(3.) Some stems in **-s** substitute **-o-** by analogy to the **-o**-stems : as, **foedi-fragus**, *treaty-breaking*, for *foedo-fragus from the stem **foedos-** (Nom. **foedus**, Gen. **foederis**; 154).

31

SYLLABLES.

175. A word has as many syllables as it has separate vowels or diphthongs. The last syllable is called the *Ultima ;* the last syllable but one is called the *Penult ;* the last syllable but two is called the *Antepenult.*

176. The quantity of single sounds (e. g. the quantity of a vowel) must be carefully distinguished from the quantity of the group of sounds or the syllable of which the single sound forms a part.

LENGTH OF SYLLABLES.

177. A syllable is long if its vowel is long, or if·its vowel is followed by two consonants or by **x** or **z** : as,

dūcēbās ; volvunt. In dūcēbās both the vowels and the syllables are long ; in volvunt the vowels are short, but the syllables are long ; in cases like the last the syllables (not the vowels) are said to be *long by position.* h does not count as a consonant (58) and qu (or qv, 27) has the value of a single consonant only : thus, in adhūc and aqua the first syllable is short.

178. In prose or old dramatic verse a syllable with a short vowel before a mute or f followed by l or r is not long : as tenebrae. In other verse, however, such syllables are sometimes regarded as long. In compounds such syllables are long in any verse : as obruit.

LOSS OF SYLLABLES.

179. The first of two successive syllables which begin with the same sound is sometimes lost. This is called *Haplology.*

Thus, sēmodius for sēmimodius, *half a bushel ;* calamitōsus for *ca-lamitātōsus, from the stem calamitāt- (262) and suffix -oso- (336) ; voluntā-rius, for voluntātārius (262, 309) ; cōnsuētūdō, for cōnsuētitūdō (264). See also 255 ; 379.

B. FORMATION.

180. FORMATION is the process by which stems are formed from roots or from other stems.

181. A word containing a single stem is called a *Simple* word : as, magnus, *great,* stem magno- ; animus, *soul,* stem animo-. A word containing two or more stems is called a *Compound* word : as, magnanimus, *great-souled,* stem magnanimo-.

182. Most inflected words consist of two parts : a stem, which is usually a modified root (195), and an inflection ending : thus, in ductōrī, *for a leader,* the root is d u c-, *lead,* the stem is ductōr-, *leader,* and -ī is the inflection ending, meaning *for.*

ROOTS.

183. A ROOT is a monosyllable which gives the fundamental meaning to a word or group of words.

184. A root is not a real word; it is neither a noun, naming something, nor a verb, denoting action. Thus i u g-, *yoke*, does not mean *a yoke* nor *I yoke*; it merely *suggests* something about yoking. The root becomes a real word only when an inflection ending is added, or, more commonly, both a formative suffix and an inflection ending : as, iug-u-m, *a yoke*.

185. Roots are common to Latin and its cognate languages, such as the Sanskrit and the Greek. When a root is named in this book, the specific Latin form of the root is meant. This often differs somewhat from the form of the root which is assumed as applicable to all the cognate languages.

186. Almost all roots are noun and verb roots; that is, roots with a meaning which may be embodied either in a noun or in a verb, or in both. Besides these there is a small class, less than a dozen in number, of pronoun roots. There are many words which cannot be traced back to their roots.

187. A root sometimes has two or more forms : as, f ī d- (for f e i d-), f o e d-, f i d-, *trust ;* g e n-, g n-, *sire ;* t o l, t l, *bear ;* see 135, 145.

Thus, fīd- is found in fīd-us, *trusty,* fīd-ūcia, *confidence,* fīd-ūciō, *I pledge,* fīd-ūciārius, *in trust,* fid-ere, *put trust in,* fīd-ēns, *courageous,* fīd-entia, *courage ;* foed- in foed-us, *pledge of faith,* foed-erātus, *bound by a pledge of faith ;* fid- in fid-ēs, *faith,* fid-ēlis, *faithful,* fid-ēliter, *faithfully,* fid-ēlitās, *faithfulness,* per-fid-us, *faithless,* per-fid-ia, *faithlessness,* per-fid-iōsus, *full of faithlessness,* per-fid-iōsē, *faithlessly.* g e n- in gen-itor, *sire,* g n- in gi-gn-ere, *beget,* g n-ā-in gnā-tus, *son.*

188. A root ending in a vowel is called a *Vowel Root :* as, d a-, *give ;* a root ending in a consonant is called a *Consonant Root :* as, r u p-, *break.* Roots are conveniently indicated by the sign √ : as, √t e g-, to be read 'root t e g-.'

189. A root or a part of a root is sometimes doubled in forming a word; this is called *Reduplication :* as, mur-mur, *murmur ;* tur-tur, *turtle-dove ;* po-pul-us, *people ;* ul-ul-āre, *yell.*

PRESENT STEMS AS ROOTS.

190. Many nouns are formed from the present stems of verbs, which take the place of roots. Stems thus used are mostly those of verbs in -āre and -īre.

Thus, from ōrā-, stem of ōrāre, *speak,* are formed ōrā-tor, *speaker,* and ōrā-tiō, *speech ;* from audī-, stem of audīre, *hear,* are formed audī-tor, *hearer,* and audī-tiō, *hearing.*

191. Verbs in -ēre, and those in -āre and -īre in which the ā or ī is confined to the present system (868, 874) usually have parallel nouns formed directly from a root : as,

doc-tor, *teacher,* doc-umentum, *lesson,* doc-ilis, *teachable* (√ d o c-, docēre); sec-tor, *cutter* (√s e c-, secāre); dom-itor, *tamer,* dom-inus, *master,* dom-itus, *tamed* (√do m-, domāre); sarc-ina, *package* (√s a r c-, sarcīre).

192. But a noun is sometimes exceptionally formed from the present stem of a verb in -ēre : as, monē-ta, *mint* (monēre); acē-tum, *vinegar* (acēre); virē-tum, *a green* (virēre); suādē-la, *persuasion* (suādēre); habē-na, *rein* (habēre); egē-nus, *needy* (egēre); verē-cundus, *shamefast* (verērī); valē-tūdō, *health* (valēre).

193. Verbs in -ere, and particularly such as have a present in -nō, -scō, -tō or -iō (832), usually have their parallel nouns formed directly from a root: as,

vic-tor, *conqueror* (√vic-, vincere); incrē-mentum, *growth* (√crē-, crēscere); pul-sus, *a push* (√pol-, pellere).

194. Sometimes, however, nouns are formed from such verb stems, and not from roots: as, lecti-stern-ium, *a couch-spreading* (sternere, √ster-, strā-); vinc-ibilis, *conquerable* (vincere, √vīc-); pāsc-uum, *pasture* (pāscere, √pā-); pect-en, *comb* (pectere, √pec-); fall-āx, *deceitful* (fallere, √fal-).

STEMS.

195. A STEM is that part of a word which contains its meaning, and is either a root alone or more commonly a root with an addition called a *Formative Suffix*.

Thus, in the word ducis, *leader's*, the stem, which is identical with the root duc-, means *leader;* a root thus serving as a stem is called a *Root Stem ;* in ductōris, *leader's,* the stem is formed by the formative suffix -tōr-, denoting the agent, attached to the √duc-.

196. New stems are formed by adding a suffix to a stem. Thus, from ōrātōr-, *speaker*, is formed by the addition of the suffix -io-, a new stem ōrātōr-io-, N. ōrātōrius, *speaker's.*

197. The noun has usually only one form of the stem. The verb has different stems to indicate mood and tense ; these stems are all based on two principal tense stems, the present and the perfect active.

PRIMITIVES AND DENOMINATIVES.

198. I. A stem or word formed directly from a root or a verb stem is called a *Primitive.* II. A stem or word formed from a noun stem is called a *Denominative.*

(*a.*) Primitives: from √rēg-, reg-, *guide:* rēx, stem rēg-, *king;* rēg-num, stem rēg-no-, *kingdom;* rēctus, stem rēc-to-, *guided;* regere, stem reg-e-, *guide.* From ōrā-, stem of ōrāre, *speak:* ōrātor, stem ōrā-tōr-, *speaker;* ōrātiō, stem ōrā-tiōn-, *speech.*

(*b.*) Denominatives: from noun stem rēg-, *king:* rēgīna, stem rēg-īnā-, *queen:* rēgius, stem rēg-io-, rēgālis, stem rēg-āli-, *royal.* From ōrātiōn-, *speech:* ōrātiūncula, stem ōrātiūn-culā-, *little speech.* From rēg-no-, *kingdom:* rēgnāre, stem rēgnā-, *to rule.* From iūs, *law:* iūrāre, *swear,* stem iūrā (154).

(A.) FORMATION OF THE NOUN.

WITHOUT A FORMATIVE SUFFIX.

199. Some roots are used as noun stems : as, duc-, N. dux, *leader* (√duc-, *lead*); rēg-, N. rēx, *king* (√rēg-, *guide*); particularly at the end of a compound : as, con-iug-, N. coniūnx, *yoke-fellow, spouse* (com-, √jug-, *yoke*); tubi-cin-, N. tubicen, *trumpeter* (tubā-, √can-, *play*).

34

WITH A FORMATIVE SUFFIX.

200. SIMPLE formative suffixes are vowels: as, -ā-, -o-, -i-, -u-; also -io-, -uo-, (-vo-) ; or such little syllables as -mo-, -min-; -ro-, -lo-; -ōn-; -no-, -ni-, -nu-; -to-, -ti-, -tu-; -ter-, -tōr-; -unt- (-nt-); -es- (-er-), -ōr-; these syllables sometimes have slight modifications of form. COMPOUND suffixes consist of one or more simple suffixes attached to a simple suffix : as, -tōr-io-, -ti-mo-, &c., &c.

201. The following are examples of noun stems formed from roots or verb stems by simple suffixes added :

STEM.	NOMINATIVE.	FROM.	STEM.	NOMINATIVE.	FROM.
fug-ā-	fuga, *flight*	f u g-, *fly*	som-no-	somnus, *sleep*	s o p-, *sleep*
fīd-o-	fidus, *trusty*	f ī d-, *trust*	plē-no-	plēnus, *full*	p l ē-, *fill*
ac-u-	acus, *pin*	a c-, *point*	rēg-no-	rēgnum, *realm*	r ē g-, *guide*
od-io-	odium, *hate*	o d-, *hate*	da-to-	datus, *given*	d a-, *give*
pluv-iā-	pluvia, *rain*	p l o v-, *wet*	lec-to-	lectus, *bed*	l e g-, *lie*
ar-vo-	arvom, *tilth*	a r-, *till*	gen-ti-	gēns, *race*	g e n-, *beget*
al-vo-	alvos, *belly*	a l-, *nurture*	sta-tu-	status, *stand*	s t a-, *stand*
sal-vo-	salvos, *safe*	s a l-, *safe*	rēc-tōr-	rēctor, *ruler*	r ē g-, *guide*
fā-mā	fāma, *tale*	f ā-, *tell*	e-unt-,	iēns, *going*	i-, *go*
teg-min-	tegmen, *cover*	t e g-, *cover*	rege-nt-	regēns, *guiding*	rege-, *guide*
sel-lā-	sella, *seat*	s e d-, *sit*	gen-er-	genus, *race*	g e n-, *beget*
err-ōn-	errō, *stroller*	errā-, *stroll*	fur-ōr-	furor, *madness*	f u r-, *rave*

202. Formative suffixes are often preceded by a vowel, which in many instances is a stem vowel, real or presumed ; in others, the vowel has come to be regarded as a part of the suffix itself.

Thus, -lo- : fīlio-lo-, N. fīlio-lu-s, *little son* (fīlio-) ; hortu-lu-s, *little garden* (horto-, 105, *h*) ; but -ulo-: rēg-ulu-s, *petty king* (rēg-) ; ger-ulu-s, *porter* (√g e s-, *bear*). -ci-: pugnā-ci-, N. pugnā-x, *full of fight* (pugnā-re) ; but -āci-: fer-āx, *productive* (√f e r-, *bear*). -to-: laudā-to-, N. laudā-tu-s, *praised* (laudā-re) ; but -āto-: dent-ātus, *toothed* (denti-). -tu-: equitā-tu-, N. equitā-tu-s, *cavalry* (equitā-re) ; but -ātu-: sen-ātu-s, *senate* (sen-). -lā-: suādē-lā-, N. suādē-la, *persuasion* (suādē-re, 192) ; but -ēlā-: loqu-ēla, *talk* (√l o qu-, *speak*). -tāt-: cīvi-tāt-, N. cīvi-tā-s, *citizenship* (cīvi-) ; but -itāt-: auctōr-itā-s, *authority* (auctōr-). -cio-: aedīli-cio-, N. aedīli-ciu-s, *of an aedile* (aedīli-) ; but -icio-: patr-iciu-s, *patrician* (patr-). -timo-: fīni-timo-, N. fīni-timu-s, *bordering* (fīni-) ; but -itimo-: lēg-itimu-s, *of the law* (lēg-).

203. There are many formative suffixes of nouns. The commonest only can be named, and these may be conveniently grouped as below, by their meanings. Compound suffixes are arranged with reference to the last element of the suffix : thus, under the adjective suffix -io- (304) will be found -c-io-, -īc-io-, -tōr-io-, and -ār-io-. In many instances it is difficult to distinguish between simple and compound suffixes.

I. THE SUBSTANTIVE.

(A.) PRIMITIVES.

I. THE AGENT.

204. The suffixes **-tōr-, -o-, -ā-, -lo-,** and **-ōn-,** are used to denote the *Agent :* as,

STEM.	NOMINATIVE.	FROM.
lĕc-tōr-	lĕctor, *reader*	√lĕg-, *read*
scrīb-ā-	scrība, *writer*	√scrīb-, *write*
fig-ulo-	figulus, *potter*	√fig-, *mould*
err-ōn-	errō, *stroller*	errā-re, *stroll*

(1.) -tōr- (N. -tor).

205. -tōr-, N. -tor, or -sōr-, N. -sor (159, 202), is the commonest suffix of the agent; the feminine is **-trī-ci-,** N. **-trī-x,** -tōr- is sometimes used in a present sense, of action repeated or occurring at any time, and sometimes in a past sense.

206. (*a.*) -tōr- (-sōr-), in the present sense, often denotes one who makes a regular business of the action of the root or verb.

ōrā-tōr-, N. ōrā-tor, *spokesman, speaker* (ōrā-re) ; lĕc-tor, *reader* (√lĕg-, *read*). Workmen and tradesmen : arā-tor, *ploughman,* pās-tor, *shepherd,* pīc-tor, *painter,* sū-tor, *shoemaker.* Semi-professional : captā-tor, *legacy-hunter,* dēlā-tor, *professional informer.* Government officials : cēn-sor, *appraiser, censor,* imperā-tor, *commander,* prae-tor, (*leader*), *praetor,* dictā-tor, *lic-tor.* Of the law : āc-tor, *manager,* accūsā-tor, *accuser,* spōn-sor, *bondsman,* tū-tor, *guardian.* From presumed verb stems (202) : sen-ātor, *senator* (sen-) ; viā-tor, *wayfarer* (viā-) ; fundi-tor, *slinger* (fundā-). -tro-, N. -ter, has the meaning of -tōr-: as, aus-tro-, N. aus-ter (*scorcher*), *south-wester* (√aus-, *burn*).

207. In the present sense -tōr- (-sōr-) is also used to indicate permanent character, quality, capability, tendency, likelihood : as, bellā-tor, *a man of war, warlike;* dēlīberā-tor, *a man of caution;* cessā-tor, *a loiterer;* dēri-sor, *a mocker, ironical;* cōnsūmp-tor, *apt to destroy, destructive ;* aedificā-tor, *building-mad.*

208. (*b.*) -tōr- (-sōr-), in a perfect sense, is used particularly in old Latin, or to denote an agent who has acquired a permanent name by a single conspicuous action. In this sense it usually has a genitive of the object, or a possessive pronoun : thus,

castigā-tor meus, *my mentor,* or *the man who has upbraided me;* olīvae inven-tor, *the deviser of the olive* (Aristaeus); reper-tor vītis, *the author of the vine* (Bacchus); patriae līberā-tōrēs, *the emancipators of the nation.*

(2.) -o- (N. -u-s), -ā- (N. -a) ; -lo- (N. -lu-s); -ōn- (N. -ō).

209. -o- and -ā- stems may denote vocation or class ; many are compounds -o-, N. -u-s: coqu-o-, N. coqu-o-s or coc-u-s, *cook* (√coqu-, *cook*) ; causidic-u-s, *pleader* (causā-, √dic-, *speak*) -ā-, N. -a: scrīb-ā-, N. scrīb-a, *clerk* (√scrīb-, *write*); agricol-a, *husbandman* (agro-, √col-, *till*).

210. -u-lo-, N. -u-lu-s (202): ger-ulo-, N. ger-ulu-s, *bearer* (√g e s-, *bear*); fig-ulu-s, *potter* (√f i g-, *shape, mould*).

211. -ōn-, N. -ō-: err-ōn-, N. err-ō, *stroller* (errā-re); especially in compounds: praed-ō, *robber* (praedā-rī); praec-ō for *praevocō, *herald* (praevocā-re); combib-ō, *fellow-drinker* (com-, √b i b-, *drink*).

II. THE ACTION.

212. The suffixes -ā-, -io-, -iā- ; -min- ; -i-ōn-, -ti-ōn- ; -lā- ; -mā-, -nā- ; -tā-, -tu- ; -er-, -or-, -ōr-, are used to denote the *Action:* as,

STEM.	NOMINATIVE.	FROM.
od-io-	odium, *hate*	√o d-, *hate*
āc-tiōn-	āctiō, *action*	√ā g-, *do*
ques-tu-	questus, *complaint*	√qu e s-, *complain*
fur-ōr-	furor, *rage*	√f u r-, *rave*

213. Words denoting action (1470) in a substantive form have a wide range of meaning; they may denote, according to the connection, action intransitive, transitive, or passive, complete or incomplete; if the verb denotes condition or state, the word of action often comes very near to denominatives of quality; furthermore the idea of action is often lost, and passes over to result, concrete effect, means or instrument, or place.

(1.) -ā- (N. -a) ; -io- (N. -iu-m) ; -iā- (N. -ia), -iē- (N. -iē-s).

214. -ā-, N. -a, is rare in words of action: fug-ā-, N. fu̇g-a, *flight* (√f u g-, *fly*); most words are concrete: mol-a, *mill* (√m o l-, *grind*); tog-a, *covering* (√t e g-, *cover*).

215. -ūr-ā-, N. -ūr-a, is rare: fig-ūrā-, N. fig-ūra, *shape* (√f i g-, *shape*).

216. -tūr-ā-, N. -tūr-a, or -sūr-ā-, N. -sūr-a (159, 202), akin to the agent in -tōr- (-sōr-): armā-tūrā-, N. armā-tūra, *equipment* (armā-re); pīc-tūra, *painting*, i.e., *act of painting* or *picture* (√p i g-, *paint*). Words parallel with official personal names (206) denote office: cēn-sūra, *taxing, censor's office* (cf. cēnsōr-); prae-tūra, *praetorship* (cf. praetōr-).

217. -io-, N. -iu-m, sometimes denotes the effect or the object. The line cannot always be drawn very sharply between these stems in -io- (many of which may be formed through a presumed noun stem), and denominatives in -io- (249).

218. (*a.*) -io- is rarely suffixed to simple roots or verb stems: od-io-, N. od-iu-m, *hate, hateful thing, hateful conduct* (√o d-, *hate*); some words become concrete: lab-iu-m, *lip* (√l a b-, *lick*).

219. (*b.*) Most primitives in -io- are compounds: as, adag-iu-m, *proverb* (ad, √a g-, *speak*); ingen-iu-m, *disposition* (in, √g e n-, *beget*); dīscid-iu-m, *separation*, exscid-iu-m, *destruction* (dī-, ex, √s c i d-, *cleave*); incend-iu-m, *conflagration* (in, √c a n d-, *light*); obsequ-iu-m, *compliance* (ob-, √s e qu-, *follow*); conloqu-iu-m, *parley* (com-, √l o qu-, *talk*); obsid-iu-m, *sieg*⸱ (ob, √s e d-, *sit*).

220. -t-io-, N. -t-iu-m: spa-tio-, N. spa-tiu-m, *stretch* (√s p a-, *span, stretch*); sōlsti-tiu-m, *sun-stand, solstice* (sōl-, √s t a-, *stand*); ini-tiu-m, *a beginning* (in, √i-, *go*).

221. -iā-, N. -ia: fur-iā-, N. fur-iae, plural, *ravings, madness* (√f u r-, *rave*); pluvia, *rain* (√p l u v-, *rain*). Most stems in -iā- are compounds, used in the plural only, often with concrete or passive meaning: dēlic-iae, *allurements, pet* (dē, √l a c-, *allure*); excub-iae, *patrol* (ex, √c u b-, *lie*).

222. -iē-, N. -iē-s, a variation of -iā-, usually denotes result (604): ser-iē-, N. ser-iē-s, *row* (√s e r-, *string*); spec-iē-s, *sight, looks* (√s p e c-, *spy, see*); pernic-iē-s, *destruction* (per, √n e c-, *murder*).

223. -t-iē-, N. -t-iē-s: permi-tiē-, N. permi-tiē-s, *wasting away* (per, √m i-, *less*).

(2.) -min- (103) (N. -men); -din-, -gin- (105, g) (N. -dō,- gō).

224. -min-, N. -men (202), usually active, occasionally passive, is very common; it sometimes denotes the means, instrument, or effect.

certā-min-, N. certā-men, *contest* (certā-re); crī-men, *charge* (√c e r-, c r ī-, *sift*); spec-imen, *what is inspected, sample* (√s p e c-, *spy, see*); lū-men, *light* (√l ū c-, *light*); flū-men, *flood, stream* (√f l u g u̜-, *flow*); ag-men, *what is led, train* (√a g-, *lead*). Words in -min- often mean nearly the same as those in -mento- (239): as, levā-men, levā-mentu-m, *lightening;* teg-umen, teg-umentu-m, *covering.*

225. ē-din-, -ī-din- (202): -ē-din-, N. -ē-dō: grav-ēdin-, N. grav-ēdō, (*heaviness*), *catarrh* (√g r a v-, *heavy*). -ī-din-, N. -ī-dō: cup-īdin-, N. cup-īdō, *desire* (√c u p-, *desire*); lib-īdō, *whim* (√l i b-, *yearn*).

226. -ā-gin-, -ī-gin- (202): -ā-gin-, N. -ā-gō: vorā-gin-, N. vorā-gō, *gulf* (vorā-re); imā-gō, *representation* (*imā-, cf. imitārī). -ī-gin-, N. -ī-gō: orī-gin-, N. orī-gō, *source* (orī-rī); cāl-īgō, *darkness* (√c ā l-, *hide*). A few denominatives have -ū-gin-, N. -ū-gō: aer-ūgin-, N. aer-ūgō, *copper rust* (aer-).

(3.) -i-ōn- (N. -i-ō); -ti-ōn- or -si-ōn- (N. -ti-ō or -si-ō).

227. -i-ōn-, N. -i-ō: opīn-iōn-, N. opīn-iō, *notion* (opīnā-rī); condic-iō, *agreement* (com-, √d i c-, *say*); contāg-iō, *touch* (com-, √t a g-, *touch*). Some words are concrete: leg-iō, *pick, legion* (√l e g-, *pick*). A few are denominatives: commūn-iō, *mutual participation* (commūni-).

228. -ti-ōn-, N. -ti-ō, or -si-ōn-, N. -si-ō (159, 202), is very common, and may denote action either intransitive, transitive, or passive, or the manner or possibility of action.

cōgitā-tiōn-, N. cōgitā-tiō, *a thinking, a thought* (cōgitā-re); exīstimā-tiō, *judging, reputation* (exīstimā-re); coven-tiō, commonly cōn-tiō, *meeting, speech* (com-, √v e n-, *come*); dēpul-siō, *warding off* (dē-, √p o l-, *push*); oppugnā-tiō, *besieging, method of besieging* (oppugnā-re); occultā-tiō, *hiding, chance to hide, possibility of hiding* (occultā-re). Some words denote the place where: sta-tiō, *a stand* (√s t a-, *stand*); some become collectives or concretes: salūtā-tiō, *greeting, levee, guests at a levee* (salūtā-re); mūnī-tiō, *fortification,* i.e., *act of fortifying* or *works* (mūnī-re).

(4.) -ē-lā- (N. -ē-la), -tē-lā- (N. -tē-la).

229. -ē-lā-, N. -ē-la (202): suādē-lā-, N. suādē-la, *persuasion* (suādē-re): loqu-ēla, *talk* (√loqu-, *talk*); quer-ēla or quer-ēlla, *complaint* (√ques-, *complain*). Some words are concrete: candē-la, *candle* (candē-re).

230. -tē-lā-, N. -tē-la-: conrup-tēlā-, N. conrup-tēla, *a seduction* (com-, √rup-, *spoil, ruin*); tū-tēla, *protection* (√tū-, *watch, protect*).

(5.) -mā- (N. -ma), -nā- (N. -na) ; -trī-nā- (N. -trī-na).

231. -mā- and -nā- are rare, and denote result or something concrete. -mā-, N. -ma: fā-mā-, N. fā-ma, *tale* (√fā-, *tell*); -nā, N. -na: ur-na, *pitcher* (√urc- in urc-eus, *pitcher*, 170, 3); with original suffix -sna (170, 2): lū-na, *moon* (√lūc-, *light*); scāla, *stairs* (√scand-, *mount*).

232. -inā-, N. -ina: ang-inā-, N. ang-ina, *choking* (√ang-, *choke*); pāg-ina, *page* (√pāg-, *fasten*); sarc-ina, *package* (√sarc-, *patch*). -īnā-, N. -īna (202): ru-īnā-, N. ru-īna, *downfall* (√ru-, *tumble*); -īnā- is very common in denominatives: pisc-ina, *fish-pond* (pisci-).

233. -trī-nā-, N. -trī-na, akin to the agent in -tōr-: doc-trīnā-, N. doc-trīna, *teaching*, either *the act of teaching* or *what is taught* (√doc-, *teach*); sū-trīna, *shoemaking, shoemaker's trade, shoemaker's shop* (√sū-, *sew*).

(6.) -tā- or -sā- (N. -ta or -sa) ; -tu- or -su- (N. -tu-s or -su-s).

234. -tā-, N. -ta, or -sā-, N. -sa (159), is rare, and sometimes denotes result, or something concrete: as, no tā-, N. no-ta, *mark* (√gno-, *know*); por-ta (*passage*), *gate* (√por-, *fare*); fos-sa, *ditch* (√fod-, *dig*); repul-sa, *repulse* (re-, √pol-, *push*); offēn-sa, *offence* (ob, √fend-, *strike*).

235. -tu-, N. -tu-s, or -su-, N. -su-s (159, 202), denotes the action and its results: ques-tu-, N. ques-tu-s, *complaint* (√ques-, *complain*); gem-itus, *groan* (√gem-, *groan*). Stems in -ā-tu-, N. -ā-tu-s, sometimes denote office or officials: cōnsul-ātu-, N. cōnsul-ātu-s, *being consul, consulship* (cōnsul-); sen-ātu-s, *senate* (sen-). -tu- is seldom passive: vī-su-s, active, *sight*, passive, *looks* (√vīd-, *see*); apparā-tu-s, *preparation*, either *a getting ready*, or *what is got ready* (apparā-re). The supine (2269) is the accusative or ablative of substantives in -tu- (-su-). Most words in -tu- (-su-) are defective in case, and are chiefly used in the ablative (430).

(7.) -er- for -es- (N. -us) ; -ōr- (N. -or).

236. Neuter stems in -er- (for -es-), or in -or- (for -os-), N. -us, denote result, or have a concrete meaning: gen-er-, N. gen-us, *birth, race* (√gen-, *beget*); op-er-, N. op-us, *work* (√op-, *work*); frīg-or-, N. frīg-us, *cold* (√frīg-, *cold*). -ēs with lengthened ē is sometimes used in the nominative of gender words: as, nūb-ēs, *cloud* (√nūb-, *veil*); sēd-ēs, *seat* (√sēd-); vāt-ēs, *bard*. -n-er-, -n-or-, N. -n-us: vol-ner-, N. vol-nus, *wound* (√vol-, *tear*); fac-inor-, N. fac-inus, *deed* (√fac-, *do*, 202).

237. -ōr- (for an older form -ōs-, 154), N. -ōs, commonly -or, masculine, denotes a state. Many substantives in -ōr- have a parallel verb, usually in -ēre (368), and an adjective in -ido- (287).

od-ōr-, N. od-ōs or od-or *smell* (√o d-, *smell*, cf. olē-re) ; pall-or, *paleness* (cf. pallē-re) ; cal-or, *warmth* (cf. calē-re) ; ūm-or, *moisture* (cf. ūmē-re); am-or, *love* (cf. amā-re) ; ang-or, *choking, anguish* (√a n g-, *choke*).

III. THE INSTRUMENT OR MEANS.

238. The suffixes -men-to-, -tro-, -cro- or -culo-, -lo-, -bro- or -bulo-, are used to denote the *Instrument* or *Means :* as,

STEM.	NOMINATIVE.	FROM.
ōrnā-mento-	ōrnāmentum, *embellishment*	ōrnā-re, *embellish*
arā-tro-	arātrum, *plough*	arā-re, *plough*
pō-culo-	pōculum, *drinking-cup*	√p ō-, *drink*
pā-bulo-	pābulum, *fodder*	√p ā-, *feed*

239. -men-to-, N. -men-tu-m (202), is one of the commonest suffixes ; it sometimes denotes result of action, rarely action itself.

pig-mento-, N. pig-mentu-m, *paint* (√p ī g-, *paint*) ; experī-mentu-m, *test* (experī-rī) ; ōrnā-mentu-m, *ornament* (ōrnā-re) ; frag-mentu-m, *fragment* (√f r a g-, *break*); cae-mentu-m, *quarried stone* (√c a e d-, *cut*) ; incrē-mentu-m, *growth* (in, √c r ē-, *grow*) ; al-imentu-m, *nourishment* (√a l-, *nurture*) ; doc-umentu-m, *lesson* (√d o c-, *teach*). See also -min- (224). -men-tā-, N. -men-ta, F., is rare : ful-menta, *prop* (√f u l c-, *prop*) ; rā-menta, *scraping* (√r ā d-, *scrape*).

240. -tro-, N. -tru-m (202) : arā-tro-, N. arā-tru-m, *plough* (arā-re) ; fer-etru-m, *bier* (√f e r-, *bear*) ; rōs-tru-m, *beak* (√r ō d-, *peck*). Sometimes -stro-: mōn-stru-m, *warning* (√m o n-, *mind*) ; lu-stra, plural, *fen, jungle* (√l u-, *wash*); lū-stru-m, *purification* (√l o u-, *wash*). -trā-, N. -tra, F.: mulc-trā-, N. mulc-tra (also mulc-tru-m, Ne.), *milking-pail* (√m u l g-, *milk*). -es-trā-: fen-estra, *window*.

241. -cro-, N. -cru-m, used when an l precedes : ful-cro-, N. ful-cru-m, *couch-leg* (√f u l c-, *prop*). -cro- sometimes denotes the place where : ambulā-cru-m, *promenade* (ambulā-re); sometimes the effect : simulā-cru-m, *likeness* (simulā-re).

242. -culo-, N. -culu-m (202) : pō-culo-, N. pō-culu-m, *cup* (√p ō-, *drink*) ; fer-culu-m, *tray* (√f e r-, *bear*). -culo- sometimes denotes the place where : cub-iculu-m, *sleeping-room* (√c u b-, *lie*) ; cēnā-culu-m, originally *dining-room*, usually *garret* (cēnā-re).

243. -u-lo-, N. -u-lu-m (202) : chiefly after c or g : vinc-ulo-, N. vinc-ulu-m, *bond* (√v i n c-, *bind*); cing-ulu-m, *girdle* (√c i n g-, *gird*). -u-lā-, N. -u-la, F., rēg-ula, *rule* (√r ē g-, *guide*).

244. -bro-, N. -bru-m (202) : crī-bro-, N. crī-bru-m, *sieve* (√c e r-, c r ī-, *sift*); lā-bru-m, *wash-basin* (√l a v-, *wash*). -brā-, N. -bra, F.: dolā-bra, *chisel, mattock* (dolā-re) ; late-bra, *hiding-place* (√l a t-, *hide*).

245. -bulo-, N. -bulu-m (202) : pā-bulo-, N. pā-bulu-m, *fodder* (√p ā-, *keep*) ; vēnā-bulu-m, *hunting-spear* (vēnā-rī) ; pat-ibulu-m, *pillory* (√p a t-, *stretch*). -bulo- sometimes denotes the place where : sta-bulu-m, *standing-place, stall* (√s t a-, *stand*). -bulā-, N. -bula, F., rare : sū-bula, *awl* (√s u-, *sew*); ta-bula, *board* (√t a-, *stretch*); fā-bula, *talk* (√f ā-, *talk*).

(B.) DENOMINATIVES.

I. THE QUALITY.

246. The suffixes -io-, -iā-; -tā-, -tāt-, -tūt-, -tū-din-, are used to denote the *Quality :* as,

STEM.	NOMINATIVE.	FROM.
conlēg-io-	conlēgium, *colleagueship*	conlēgā-, N. conlēga, *colleague*
audāc-iā-	audācia, *boldness*	audāci-, N. audāx, *bold*
cīvi-tāt-	cīvitās, *citizenship*	cīvi-, N. cīvis, *citizen*
magni-tūdin-	magnitūdō, *greatness*	magno-, N. magnus, *great*

247. These abstracts are feminine, and come chiefly from adjectives or participles, except those in -io-, which are neuters, and come mostly from substantives. Sometimes the same stem takes two or more of these suffixes: as, clāri-tāt- or clāri-tūdin-, *brightness* (clāro-); iuven-tūt-, in poetry iuven-tāt- or iuven-tā-, *youth* (iuven-).

(1.) -io- (N. -iu-m), -iā- (N. -ia), -iē- (N. -iēs).

248. -iē- sometimes occurs as collateral form to -iā- (604) ; -io- or -iā- is sometimes attached to other suffixes : thus, -t-io-, -t-iā- (-t-iē-); -mōn-io-, -mōn-iā- ; -cin-io-.

249. -io-, N. -iu-m, chiefly used in compounds, denotes *belonging to*, with a very wide range of meaning ; many of these words are clearly neuter adjectives in -io- (305). Suffixed to personal names -io- often denotes the condition, action, or employment, which gives rise to the name ; this meaning sometimes passes over to that of result, relation of persons, collection of persons, or place.

250. (*a.*) From simple noun stems: sen-io-, N. sen-iu-m, *feeble old age* (sen-); somn-iu-m, *dream* (somno-); sāv-iu-m, *love-kiss* (suāvi-); silent-iu-m, *silence* (silenti-); crepund-ia, plural, *rattle* (*crepundo-); mendāc-iu-m, *lie* (mendāci-); sōlāc-iu-m, *comfort* (*sōlāci-, *comforting*).

251. (*b.*) Direct compounds (377) : aequinoct-iu-m, *equinox* (aequo-, nocti-); contubern-iu-m, *companionship* (com-, tabernā-); prīvilēg-iu-m, *special enactment* (prīvo-, lēg-).

252. (*c.*) Indirect compounds (377), chiefly from personal names : cōnsil-iu-m, *deliberating together, faculty of deliberation, conclusion, advice, deliberative body* (cōnsul-) ; auspic-iu-m, *taking auspices, auspices taken* (auspic-) ; rēmig-iu-m, *rowing, oars, oarsmen* (rēmig-); conlēg-iu-m, *colleagueship, corporation* (conlēgā-); aedific-iu-m, *building* (*aedific-, *builder*) ; perfug-iu-m, *asylum* (perfugā-).

253. -t-io- N. -t-iu-m, rare : servi-tio-, N. servi-tiu-m, *slavery, slaves* (servo-); calvi-tiu-m, *baldness* (calvo-).

254. -mōn-io-, N. -mōn-iu-m (202) : testi-mōnio-, N. testi-mōniu-m, *evidence* (testi-); mātr-imōniu-m, *marriage* (mātr-); patr-imōniu-m, *patrimony* (patr-).

41

255. -cin-io-, N. -cin-iu-m, rare: latrō-cinio-, N. latrō-ciniu-m, *robbery* (latrōn-); patrō-ciniu-m, *protection* (patrōno-).

256. -iā-, N. -ia, is very common indeed, forming abstracts from nouns, mostly adjectives or present participles.

audāc-iā-, N. audāc-ia, *boldness* (audāci-); miser-ia, *wretchedness* (misero-); abundant-ia, *plenty* (abundanti-); scient-ia, *knowledge* (scienti-); mīlit-ia, *warfare* (mīlit-); victōr-ia, *victory* (victōr-); māter-ia, *timber* (māter-); custōd-ia, *guard* (custōd-).

257. -iē-, N. -iē-s: pauper-iē-, N. pauper-iē-s, *moderate means* (pauper-). Most stems in -iē- are primitive (222).

258. -t-iā-, N. -t-ia, is suffixed to a few adjective stems, chiefly in -o-: iūsti-tiā-, N. iūsti-tia, *justice* (iūsto-); mali-tia, *wickedness* (malo-); pudīci-tia, *shamefastness* (pudīco-); trīsti-tia, *sadness* (trīsti-).

259. -t-iē-, N. -t-iē-s, particularly as a collateral form of -t-iā- in the N., Ac., and Ab. singular (604): molli-tiē-,· N. molli-tiē-s, *softness* (molli-).

260. -mōn-iā-, N. -mōn-ia (202): ācri-mōniā-, N. ācri-mōnia, *sharpness* (ācri-); parsi-mōnia, *economy* (parso-). Analogously from roots, quer-imōnia, *complaint* ($\sqrt{}$qu e s-, *complain*); al-imōnia, *nurture* ($\sqrt{}$a l-, *nurture*).

(2.) -tā- (N. -ta), -tāt- (N. -tā-s), -tūt- (N. -tū-s), -tū-din- (N. -tū-dō).

261. -tā-, N. -ta: chiefly poetic: iuven-tā-, N. iuven-ta, *youth* (iuven-); senec-ta, *age* (sen-ec-).

262. -tāt-, N. -tā-s (202), is one of the very commonest suffixes.

pie-tāt-, N. pie-tā-s, *dutifulness* (pio-, 105); fēlīci-tā-s, *happiness* (fēlīci-); cīvi-tā-s, *citizenship, the community* (cīvi-); facili-tā-s, *easiness*, facul-tā-s, *ability* (facili-); cāri-tā-s, *dearness* (cāro-); auctōr-itā-s, *authority* (auctōr·); līber-tā-s, *freedom* (lībro-, 111, *b*); maies-tā-s, *grandeur* (maiōs-); volun-tā-s, *wish* (*volunti-, 179); veṅus-tā-s, *grace* (venusto-, 179); ae-tā-s, *age* (aevo-, 111, *a*); tempes-tā-s, *kind of time, weather* (tempes-).

263. -tūt-, N. -tū-s, only in iuven-tūt-, N. iuven-tū-s, *youth* (iuven-), senec-tū-s, *age* (senec-), servi-tū-s, *slavery* (servo-), and vir-tū-s, *manhood* (viro-, 111).

264. -tū-din-, N. -tū-dō, suffixed to adjective stems: magni-tūdin-, N. magni-tūdō, *greatness* (magno-); forti-tūdō, *courage* (forti-); and to a few participles: cōnsuē-tūdō, *custom* (cōnsuēto-, 179); sollici-tūdō, *anxiety* (sollicito-); analogously valē-tūdō, *health* (*valēto-, valēre).

II. THE PERSON CONCERNED.

265. The suffixes -ārio-, -ōn-, -iōn-, -li-, -no-, and some others, are used to denote the *Person concerned* or *occupied* with a thing: as,

STEM.	NOMINATIVE.	FROM.
sīc-ārio-	sīcārius, *assassin*	sīcā-, N. sīca, *dagger*
āle-ōn-	āleō, *gambler*	āleā-, N. ālea, *die*
lūd-iōn-	lūdiō, *player*	lūdo-, N. lūdus, *play*
aedī-li-	aedīlis, *aedile*	aedi-, N. aedis, *house*
tribū-no-	tribūnus, *tribune*	tribu-, N. tribus, *tribe*

III. THE PLACE.

266. Neuters with the suffixes -tōrio-, -ārio-, -īli-, -to-, or -ēto- are often used to denote the *Place*: as,

STEM.	NOMINATIVE.	FROM.
audī-tōrio-	audī-tōrium, *lecture-room*	audītōr-, N. audītor, *hearer*
aer-ārio-	aerārium, *treasury*	aer-, N. aes, *money*
ov-īli-	ovīle, *sheepfold*	ovi-, N. ovis, *sheep*
murt-ēto-	murtēta, *myrtlegroves*	murto-, N. murtus, *myrtle*

IV. DIMINUTIVES.

267. The suffixes -lo-, -lā-, or -cu-lo-, -cu-lā-, are used to form substantives with a *Diminutive* meaning. Diminutives may denote:

268. (1.) Actual smallness: as, secūricula, *a little hatchet;* ventulus, *a bit of wind;* spēcula, *a ray of hope.*

269. (2.) Imputed smallness: implying, (*a.*) admiration, affection, or compassion; (*b.*) contempt or irony. This diminutive, which usually serves to add point to sentences themselves of a playful, patronizing, or slurring character, is very hard to translate; *little* and *small* are often inadequate; *old* or *poor* will sometimes do; but usually recourse must be had to free translations adapted to the particular context: as,

ōrātiuncula, *a gem of a speech, an attempt at a speech;* mātercula, *an anxious mother, poor mamma, dear mamma;* lectulus, *one's own little bed;* ānellus aureolus, *a gay gold ring;* Graeculī, *our Greek cousins, the good people in Greece;* Graeculus, *a regular Greek, your gentleman from Greece;* muliercula, *a pretty girl, a lady gay, one of the gentler sex, a mere woman, an unprotected female, a maiden all forlorn;* lacrimula, *a wee tear, a crocodile tear;* volpēcula, *Master Reynard, dan Russel;* tōnstrīcula, *a common barber girl;* popellus, *rabble;* nummulī, *filthy lucre;* mercēdula, *an apology for pay;* ratiuncula, *a first rate reason;* caupōnula, *a low tavern.*

270. Some diminutives have entirely lost the diminutive meaning: as, puella, *girl,* not necessarily *little girl;* others have changed their original meaning: as, avunculus, *uncle,* originally *grandpapa;* anguīlla, *eel,* originally *little snake.* Some words are only found in the diminutive form: as, stēlla, *star* (*ster-). Diminutives usually have the gender of their primitives; exceptions are rare: as, rāna, *frog,* F., rānunculus, *tadpole,* M.

(1.) -lo- (N., M. -lu-s, Ne. -lu-m), -lā- (N. -la).

271. Stems in -o-, -ā-, or a mute (-g-, -c-, -d-, or -t-), take -lo- or -lā-, which is usually preceded by -u- (202).

hortu-lo-, N. hortu-lu-s, *little garden* (horto-); oppidu-lu-m, *hamlet* (oppido-); serru-lā-, N. serru-la, *little saw* (serrā-); rēg-ulu-s, *chieftain* (rēg-); vōc-ula, *a bit of a voice* (vōc-); calc-ulu-s, *pebble* (calci-); nepōt-ulu-s, *a grandson dear* (nepōt-); aetāt-ula, *tender age* (aetāt-).

272. Stems in -eo-, -io-, or -vo-, retain -o- before -lo-; stems in -eā-, -iā-, or -vā-, also have -o- before -lā-.

alveo-lo-, N. alveo-lu-s, *little tray* (alveo-); gladio-lu-s, *little sword* (gladio-); servo-lu-s, *little slave* (servo-); nauseo-lā-, N. nauseo-la, *a slight squeamishness* (nauseā-); bēstio-la, *little animal* (bēstiā-); fīlio-la, *little daughter* (fīliā-).

273. Stems in -lo-, -ro-, -no-, and -lā-, -rā-, -nā-, commonly drop the stem vowel and assimilate -r- or -n- to -l-: thus: -el-lo-, -el-lā- (111; *b*; 166, 6, 7).

catel-lo-, for *catululo-, N. catel-lu-s, *puppy* (catulo-); agel-lu-s, *little field* (agro-); asel-lu-s, *donkey* (asino-); fābel-lā-, N. fābel-la, *short story* (fābulā-); umbel-la, *sunshade* (umbrā-); pāgel-la, *short page* (pāginā-). A few words are not thus changed: pueru-lo-, N. pueru-lu-s, *poor boy* (puero-), as well as puel-lu-s.

274. Another vowel than **e** (172, 3) appears in: Hispāl-lu-s (Hispāno-), Messāl-la (Messānā-), proper names; corōl-la, *chaplet* (corōnā-); ūl-lu-s, *the least one, any at all* (ūno-); Sūl-la (Sūrā-), proper name; lapil-lu-s, for *lapid-lu-s, *pebble* (lapid-). Also homul-lu-s, *son of the dust* (homon-).

(2.) -cu-lo- (N., M. -cu-lu-s, Ne. -cu-lu-m), -cu-lā- (N. -cu-la).

275. Stems in a continuous sound (-l-, -n-, -r-, or -s-), or in -i-, -u-, or -ē-, usually take -cu-lo- or -cu-lā-.

sermūn-culo-, N. sermūn-culu-s, *small-talk* (sermōn-); virgun-culā-, N. virgun-cula, *little maid* (virgon-); homun-culu-s, *son of earth* (homon-); arbus-cula, *tiny tree* (arbos-); cor-culu-m, *heart of hearts* (cord-, 170, 12); igni-culu-s, *spark* (igni-); ani-cula, *grandam* (anu-); diē-cula, *brief day* (diē-); analogously, volpē-cula (*vixen*), *little fox* (*volpē-). Rarely with ī: canī-cula, *little dog* (can-).

276. -un-culo-, N. -un-culu-s : av-unculo-, N. av-unculu-s, *uncle* (avo-); rān-unculu-s, *tadpole* (rānā-). -un-culā-, N. -un-cula : dom-unculā-, N. dom-uncula, *little house* (domo-).

277. Diminutives are sometimes formed from other diminutives: cistel-lu-la, *casket* (cistel-la, cistu-la, cistā-).

278. A few other suffixes have a diminutive meaning: as, -ciōn-, -leo-, -astro-, -ttā-: homun-ciō, *manikin, child of dust* (homon-); acu-leu-s, *sting* (acu-); Antōni-aster, *regular little Antony;* pīn-aster, *bastard pine;* Iūli-tta, *Juliet* (Iūliā-); Pōlli-tta, *little Polla* (Pōllā-).

V. PATRONYMICS.

279. Patronymics, or proper names which denote descent from a father or ancestor, have stems in -dā- (N. -dē-s), F. -d- (N. -s). These are chiefly Greek names used in poetry.

Prīami-dā-, N. Prīami-dē-s, *scion of Priam's house;* Tantali-d-, N. Tantali-s, *daughter of Tantalus.* Pēlī-dē-s (Pēleu-s); Aenea-dē-s (Aeneā-); Thestia-dē-s (Thestio-); Lāertia-dē-s (Lāertā-); Scīpia-dā-s (Scīpiōn-). F. sometimes -īnē or -ōnē: Neptūnīnē (Neptūno-); Acrisiōnē (Acrisio-).

44

II. THE ADJECTIVE.

(A.) PRIMITIVES.

280. Primitive adjectives may usually be divided into active and passive ; but the same suffix often has either an active or a passive meaning. Under primitive adjectives belong the participles ; but these will be mentioned in connection with the verb.

I. WITH AN ACTIVE MEANING.

281. The suffixes -o-, -uo-, -ci-, -lo-, and **-do-,** are used to form adjectives with an *Active* meaning : as,

STEM.	NOMINATIVE.	FROM.
vag-o-	vagus, *wandering*	√ v a g-, *wander*
contig-uo-	contiguus, *touching*	com-, √ t a g-, *touch*
minā-ci-	mināx, *threatening*	minā-rī, *threaten*
cali-do-	calidus, *warm*	√ c a l-, *warm*

(1.) -o- (N. -u-s); -uo- (N. -uu-s).

282. -o- (N. -u-s): such words express nature or capacity : **vag-o-,** N. vag-u-s, *roaming* (√ v a g-, *rŏam*); vīv-u-s, *living* (√ v ī v-, *live*); many are compounds : as, **male-dic-u-s,** *abusive* (male, √ d i c-, *say*); **pro-fug-u-s,** *flying on* (prō-, √ f u g-, *fly*). Passive : fīd-u-s, *trustworthy* (√ f ī d-, *trust*).

283. -uo-, N. -uu-s : adsid-uo-, N. adsid-uu-s, *unremitting* (ad, √ s e d-, *sit*); contig-uu-s, *touching* (com-, √ t a g-, *touch*); perpet-uu-s, *uninterrupted* (per, √ p e t-, *go*). Some words are passive: as, sal-vu-s, *safe* (√ s a l-, *save*); vac-uu-s, *empty* (√ v a c-, *empty*) ; relic-uo-s, *left behind* (re-, √ l i q u-, *leave*), later reliquos, relicus, reliquus (157).

(2.) -ci- (N. -x) ; -lo- (N. -lu-s) ; -do- (N. -du-s).

284. -ā-ci-, N. -ā-x (202), denotes capacity, habit, or inclination, often implying censure : pugnā-ci-, N. pugnā-x, *full of fight* (pugnā-re) ; minā-x, *threatening* (minā-rī) ; fer-āx, *productive* (√ f e r-, *bear*) ; dic-āx, *full of mother-wit, quick at a joke* (√ d i c-, *say*) ; rap-āx, *apt to snatch* (√ r a p-, *snatch*).

285. -u-lo-, N. -u-lu-s (202), denotes simple action: as, **pat-ulo-,** N. pat-ulu-s, *spreading* (√ p a t-, *spread*) ; or inclination: as, bib-ulu-s, *apt to drink* (√ b i b-, *drink*).

286. The suffixes -undo- (-endo-), -bundo-, and -cundo- form a group and are possibly related to the suffix in -do-.

287. -do-, N. -du-s (202), denotes a state, and usually has a parallel verb in -ēre (368) : cali-do-, N. cali-du-s *warm* (cf. calē-re) ; calli-du-s, *knowing* (cf. callē-re) ; niti-du-s, *shining* (cf. nitē-re) ; rarely in -ere : cupidu-s, *desirous* (cf. cupe-re) ; flui-du-s, *liquid* (cf. flue-re) ; rapi-du-s, *hurried* (cf. rape-re). -i-do- becomes -i-di- in viri-di-s, *green* (cf. virē-re). -do- sometimes occurs in denominatives : herbi-du-s, *grassy* (herbā-).

45

288. -undo- (-endo-), N. -undu-s, (-endu-s) is the suffix of the gerundive, which was originally neither active nor passive (2238). In a few words from reflexives, which have become adjectives, it has a reflexive or active meaning: lāb-undo-, N. lāb-undu-s, *gliding, slipping* (lābī); ori-undu-s, *arising* (orīrī); sec-undu-s, *following* (sequī); volv-endu-s, *rolling* (volvī). See 899.

289. -bundo-, N. -bundu-s (202), has the meaning of an exaggerated present participle: freme-bundo-, N. freme-bundu-s, *muttering away* (√frem-, *roar*); treme-bundu-s, *all in a flutter* (√trem-, *quiver*); fur-ibundu-s, *hot with rage* (√fur-, *rave*); cōntiōnā-bundu-s, *speaking a speech* (cōntiōnā-rī); minitā-bundu-s, *breathing out threatenings* (minitā-rī); vītā-bundu-s, *forever dodging* (vītā-re).

290. -cundo-, N. -cundu-s, denotes permanent quality: fā-cundo-, N. fā-cundu-s, *eloquent* (√fā-, *speak*); irā-cundu-s, *choleric* (irā-scī); iū-cundu-s, *pleasant, interesting* (√iuv-, *help*).

II. WITH A PASSIVE MEANING.

291. The suffixes -li-, -ti-li-, -bili-, -tīvo-, -no-, and -mino-, are used to form adjectives with a *Passive* meaning: as,

STEM.	NOMINATIVE.	FROM.
fac-ili-	facilis, *easy to do*	√fac-, *do*
duc-tili-	ductilis, *ductile*	√duc-, *draw*
amā-bili-	amābilis, *lovable*	amā-re, *love*
mag-no-	magnus, *great*	√mag-, *increase*

(1.) -li- (N. -li-s) ; -ti-li-, -bili- (N. -ti-li-s, -bili-s).

292. -i-li-, N. -i-li-s (202), denotes passive capability: fac-ili-, N. fac-ili-s, *easy to do* (√fac-, *do*); frag-ili-s, *breakable, frail* (√frag-, *break*); hab-ili-s, *manageable, handy* (√hab-, *hold*); nūb-ili-s, *marriageable* (√nūb-, *veil*).

293. -ti-li-, N. -ti-li-s, or -si-li-, N. -si-li-s (159), denotes capability or quality: as, duc-tili, N. duc-tili-s, *capable of being drawn out, ductile* (√duc-, *draw*); fis-sili-s, *cleavable* (√fid-, *split*); rā-sili-s, *scraped* (√rād-, *scrape*). Rarely active: as, fer-tili-s, *productive* (√fer-, *bear*).

294. -bili-, N. -bili-s (202), denotes passive capability like -i-li-, but is far more common: horr-ibili-s, *exciting a shudder* (cf. horrē-re); amā-bili-s, *lovable* (amā-re); flē-bili-s, *lamentable* (√flē-, *weep*). Rarely active: as, sta-bili-s, *that can stand* (√sta-, *stand*); penetrā-bili-s, *piercing* (penetrā-re). -ti-bili- (159), passive, rare: flexibili-s, *flexible* (√flec-, *bend*, 960).

295. -tīvo-, N. -tīvu-s, denotes the way a thing originated: as, cap-tīvu-s, *captive* (√cap-, *take*); sta-tīvu-s, *set* (√sta-, *set*).

(2.) -no- (N. -nu-s) ; -mino- (N. -minu-s).

296. -no-, N. -nu-s, an old passive participle suffix, denotes result: mag-nu-s (*enlarged*), *great* (√mag-, *great*); plē-nus, *full* (√plē-, *fill*). Neuter as substantive: dō-nu-m, *gift* (√dō-, *give*). Sometimes active: egē-nu-s, *needy* (egē-re, 192).

297. The suffix -mino- (for -meno-, 103, *a*) in its weakest form (135, 2) is found in a few substantives: as, **alu-mnu-s**, *nursling* (√**a l-**, *nurse*). The endings -minī (730) and -minō (731) are apparently case forms of the same suffix. -minō would seem to be an ablative ; -minī may be a nominative plural.

(B.) DENOMINATIVES.

298. Denominative adjectives may be divided into such as denote: I. *Material* or *Resemblance.* II. *Appurtenance:* implying sometimes *possession*, often *fitness, conformity, character*, or *origin.* III. *Supply.* IV. Diminutives. V. Comparatives and Superlatives ; a few of these are primitive.

I. MATERIAL OR RESEMBLANCE.

299. The suffixes -eo- and -n-eo- are used to form adjectives denoting *Material* or *Resemblance :* as,

STEM.	NOMINATIVE.	FROM.
aur-eo-	aureus, *golden*	auro-, N. aurum, *gold*
ahē–neo-	ahēneus, *bronze* (58)	aes-, N. aes, *bronze*

300. -eo-, N. -eu-s: aur-eo-, N. aur-eu-s, *golden, all gold, as good as gold* (auro-) ; ferr-eu-s, *iron* (ferro-) ; pulver-eu-s, *all dust* (pulver-) ; virgin-eu-s, *girlish* (virgin-).

301. -n-eo-, N. -n-eu-s: ahē-neu-s, *bronze* (ahē-, 58; aes-); quer-neu-s, *oaken* (quercu-). -no- is usually poetical : as, ebur-nu-s, *ivory* (ebur-); quer-nu-s, *oaken* (quercu-). -ā-neo-, N. -ā-neu-s : miscell-āneu-s, *mixed* (miscello-).

II. APPURTENANCE.

302. The suffixes -o-, -io-, -vo- ; -timo-, -li-, -no- ; -bri-, -cri-, -tri- ; -co-, -ti-, -si-, are used to form adjectives denoting *Belonging to :* as,

STEM.	NOMINATIVE.	FROM.
rēg-io-	rēgius, *kingly*	rēg-, N. rēx, *king*
mari-timo-	maritimus, *of the sea*	mari-, N. mare, *sea*
rēg-āli-	rēgālis, *of a king*	rēg-, N. rēx, *king*
can-īno-	canīnus, *of a dog*	can-, N. canis, *dog*
mulie-bri-	muliebris, *womanly*	mulier-, N. mulier, *woman*
cīvi-co-	cīvicus, *citizen's*	cīvi-, N. cīvis, *citizen*

(1.) -o- (N. -u-s), -io- (N. -iu-s), -vo- (N. -vu-s).

303. -o-, N. -u-s : decōr-o-, N. decōr-u-s, *becoming* (decōr-); canōr-u-s, *melodious* (canōr-) ; pervius, *passable* (via-).

304. -io- is one of the commonest suffixes, and is often added to other suffixes ; thus : -c-io-, -īc-io- ; -tōr-io- (-sōr-io-) ; -ār-io-.

47

305. -io-, N. -iu-s: rēg-io-, N. rēg-iu-s, *of* or *like a king* (rēg-) ; patr-iu-s, *of a father* (patr-). Here belong many gentile names : as, Sēst-iu-s (Sexto-). These are used with substantives as adjectives : as, lēx Cornēl-ia, lēx Iūl-ia. Furthermore patrial adjectives : as, Corinth-iu-s, *Corinthian* (Corintho-). In some, consonant -io- is used : plēbē-iu-s, *of the commons* (plēbē-). -io- is rare in primitives : exim-iu-s, *select* (ex, √e m-, *take*).

306. -c-io-, N. -c-iu-s (202): aedīli-cio, N. aedīli-ciu-s, *of an aedile* (aedīli-) ; patr-iciu-s, *of the fathers* (patr-) ; later-iciu-s, *of brick* (later-).

307. -īc-io-, N. -īc-iu-s: nov-īcio-, N. nov-īciu-s, *new, new-comer* (novo-) ; nātāl-īciu-s, *birthday's* (nātāli-) ; caement-īciu-s, *rubble* (caemento-). Usually suffixed to perfect participles to denote the quality derived from the past act : conduct-īciu-s, *hired* (conducto-) ; trālāt-īciu-s, *transferred* (trālāto-).

308. -tōr-io-, N. -tōr-iu-s, or -sōr-io-, N. -sōr-iu-s, from the agent (205) in -tōr- (-sōr-), is the commonest ending with -io- : imperā-tōrio-, N. imperā-tōriu-s, *of a commander* (imperātōr-). The neuter, as substantive, denotes the place where (266): audī-tōriu-m, *lecture-room* (audītōr-) ; dēvor-sōriu-m, *inn* (dēvorsōr-).

309. -ār-io-, N. -ār-iu-s, very common, is chiefly added to substantives : as, agr-ārio-, N. agr-āriu-s, *of land* (agro-). Often as substantive : not-āriu-s (265), *stenographer* (notā-) ; aer-āriu-m (266), *treasury* (aer-) ; sēmin-āriu-m, *nursery* (sēmin-) ; bell-āria, plural, *goodies, bonbons* (bello-).

310. -ī-vo-, N. -ī-vu-s (202): tempest-īvu-s, *seasonable* (tempestāt-, 126); aest-īvu-s, *summer's* (aestāt-). See 179.

(2.)   -timo- (N. -timu-s) ; -li- (N. -li-s) ; -no- (N. -nu-s).

311. -timo-, N. -timu-s (202), for an older -tumo- (28): mari-timo-, N. mari-timu-s, *of the sea* (mari-) ; fīni-timu-s, *of the border* (fīni-) ; lēg-itimu-s, *lawful* (lēg-).

312. -li- N. -li-s: humi-li-, N. humi-li-s, *lowly* (humo-) ; but almost always in denominatives -li- is preceded by a long vowel (202), usually -ā- or -ī-, thus : -ā-li- (-ā-ri-), -ī-li ; -ē-li-, -ū-li-.

313. -ā-li-, N. -ā-li-s: rēg-āli-, N. rēg-āli-s, *kingly* (rēg-) ; decemvir-āli-s, *of a decemvir* (decemviro-) ; fāt-āli-s, *fated* (fāto-) ; t-āli-s, *such* (stem to-, *that*) ; qu-āli-s, *as* (quo-). -ā-ri-, N. -ā-ri-s, is used for -āli- if an l precedes (173) : as, mol-āri-, N. mol-āri-s, *of a mill* (molā-) ; mīlit-āri-s, *of a soldier* (mīlit-). Neuters in -āli- and -āri- often become substantives (300): fōc-āle, *neckcloth* (fauci-) ; anim-al, *breathing thing* (animā-) ; calc-ar, *spur* (calci-).

314. -ī-li-, N. -ī-li-s: cīv-īli-, N. cīv-īli-s, *of a citizen* (cīvi-) ; puer-īli-s, *boyish* (puero-). The neuter, as substantive, sometimes denotes the place where (266) : ov-īle, *sheepfold* (ovi-).

315. -ē-li, N. -ē-li-s: fidē-li-, N. fidē-li-s, *faithful* (fidē-) ; crūd-ēli-s, *cruel* (crūdo-); patru-ēli-s, *cousin* (patruo-). -ū-li-, N. -ū-li-s: tribū-li-, N. tribū-li-s, *tribesman* (tribu-).

316. The old participle suffix -no- (296) is sometimes added at once to noun stems, sometimes to other suffixes : thus, -ā-no-, -ī-no- ; -ti-no-, -tī-no- ; -er-no-, -ur-no-.

317. -no-, N. -nu-s, is added to stems formed with the comparative suffix -ero- or -tero- (347), denoting place : super-no-, N. super-nu-s, *above;* inter-nu-s, *internal* (inter) ; exter-nu-s, *outside;* so, also, alter-nu-s, *every other* (altero-) ; and to a very few substantives : as, pater-nu-s, *fatherly* (patr-) ; frāter-nu-s, *brotherly* (frātr-) ; vēr-nu-s, *of spring* (vēr-). Also to cardinals, making distributives : as, bī-nī, *two by two* (for *du̯ī̆nī, duo-, 161).

318. -ā-no-, N. -ā-nu-s (202): arcā-no-, N. arc-ānu-s, *secret* (arcā-) ; Rōma-nu-s, *of Rome* (Rōmā-); mont-ānu-s, *of a mountain* (monti-) ; oppid-ānu-s, *of a town* (oppido-). -i-āno-: Cicerōn-iāno-, N. Cicerōn-iānu-s, *Cicero's.* Rarely -ā-neo- : mediterrā-neu-s, *midland* (medio-, terrā-).

319. -ī-no-, N. -ī-nu-s (202): mar-īno-, N. mar-īnu-s, *of the sea;* repent-īnu-s, *sudden* (repenti-) ; oftenest added to names of living beings : as, can-īnu-s, *of a dog* (can-) ; dīv-īnu-s, *of a god* (dīvo-) ; -ē-no- : lani-ēnu-s, ali-ēnu-s. Also to proper names : as, Plaut-īno-, N. Plaut-īnu-s, *of Plautus* (Plauto-) ; Alp-īnu-s, *Alpine* (Alpi-).

320. -ti-no-, N. -ti-nu-s, is used in some adjectives of time : crās-tinu-s, *to-morrow's* (crās-) ; diū-tinu-s, *lasting* (diū) ; prīs-tinu-s, *of aforetime* (prī-, prae).

321. -tī-no-, N. -tī-nu-s, is used in a few words of place and time : intes-tīno-, N. intes-tinu-s, *inward* (intus) ; vesper-tīnu-s, *at eventide* (vespero-).

322. From words like frāter-nus (from *fratr(i)-nus, 111, *b*), pater-nus, exter-nus, inter-nus, arose a new suffix -terno- : as, hes-ternus, from the stem hes- (cf. her-ī, 154), and -erno- in hodiernus. From the adverb *noctur (νύκτωρ) was derived noctur-nus, by analogy to which diurnus was formed. Elsewhere the -ur of -urnus and the -tur- of -turnus belong to the stem : as, ebur-nus ; tacitur-nus, from the agent *taci-tor (205).

(3.) -bri-, -cri-, -tri- (N. -ber or -bri-s, &c.).

323. -bri-, N. -ber or -bri-s : salū-bri-, N. salū-ber, *healthy* (salūt-) ; mulie-bri-s, *womanly* (mulier-).

324. -cri-, N. -cer or -cri-s (202): volu-cri-, N. volu-cer, *winged* (*volo-, *flying*); medio-cri-s, *middling* (medio-).

325. -tri-, N. -ter or -tri-s : eques-tri-, N. eques-ter, *of horsemen* (equit-, 152) ; sēmēs-tri-s, *of six months* (sex, mēns-). -es-tri- is used in a few words : camp-ester, *of fields* (campo-) ; silv-estri-s, *of woods* (silvā-).

(4.) -co- (N. -cu-s) ; -ti-, -si- (N. -s, -si-s).

326. -co- is often suffixed to -ti-, sometimes to -es-ti- ; thus : -ti-co-, -es-ti-co-.

327. -co-, N. -cu-s : cīvi-co-, N. cīvi-cu-s, *of a citizen* (cīvi-) ; belli-cu-s, *of war* (bello-); vīli-cu-s, *bailiff* (villā-). -ā-co-, -ī-co-, -ū-co- (202): merā-cu-s, amī-cu-s, antī-cu-s, aprī-cu-s, postī-cu-s, pudī-cu-s, cadū-cu-s. -ti-co-, N. -ti-cu-s: rūs-tico-, N. rūs-ticu-s, *of the country* (rūs-). -es-ti-co-, N. -es-ti-cu-s: dom-esticu-s, *of a house* (domo-, domu-).

328. -ti- or -si- denotes belonging to a place; usually -ā-ti-, -ī-ti-, -es-ti-, -en-ti-; -ēn-si-, or -i-ēn-si-.

329. -ti-, N. -s: Tībur-ti-, N. Tībur-s, *Tiburtine* (Tībur-). -ā-ti-: quoi-āti-, N. quoi-ā-s, *what countryman?* (quoio-); Anti-ā-s, *of Antium* (Antio-); optim-ātēs, *good men and true* (optimo-). -ī-ti-: Samn-īti-, N. Samn-ī-s, *Samnian* (Samnio-). -en-ti-: Vēi-enti-, N. Vēi-ēn-s, *of Vei* (Vēio-). -es-ti-, N. -es-ti-s: agr-esti-, N. agr-esti-s, *of the fields* (agro-); cael-esti-s, *heavenly* (caelo-).

330. -ēn-si-, N. -ēn-si-s (202), from appellatives of place or proper names of place: castr-ēnsi-, N. castr-ēnsi-s, *of a camp* (castro-); circ-ēnsi-s, *of the circus* (circo-); Hispāni-ēnsi-s (*temporarily*) *of Spain.* -i-ēnsi-: Karthāgin-iēnsi-s, *of Carthage* (Karthāgin-).

III. SUPPLY.

331. The suffixes -to- or -ōso- are used to form adjectives denoting *Supplied* or *Furnished with:* as,

STEM.	NOMINATIVE.	FROM.
barbā-to-	barbātus, *bearded*	barbā-, N. barba, *beard*
ann-ōso-	annōsus, *full of years*	anno-, N. annus, *year*

(1.) -to- (N. -tu-s); -len-to- (N. -len-tu-s).

332. -to-, the perfect participle suffix, is sometimes added at once to a noun stem, sometimes to other suffixes, thus: -āto-, -īto-, -ēto-, -ūto-, -ento-, -lento-.

333. -to-, N. -tu-s: onus-to-, N. onus-tu-s, *loaded* (onus-); vetus-tu-s, *full of years* (*vetus-, *year*); iūs-tu-s, *just* (iūs-); hones-tu-s, *honourable* (*hones-); fūnes-tu-s, *deadly* (fūnes-). -ā-to-: barbā-tu-s, *bearded* (barbā-); dent-ātu-s, *toothed* (denti-); -ī-to-: aurī-tu-s, *long-eared* (auri-); -ū-to-: cornū-tu-s, *horned* (cornu-). -en-to-, N. -en-tu-s: cru-ento-, N. cru-entu-s, *all gore* (*cruenti-, *cruēre*). As substantive, **arg-entu-m** (*white metal*), *silver;* flu-enta, plural, *streams* (fluenti-).

334. The neuter of stems in -to-, as a substantive, denotes the place where something, generally a plant, is found (266): arbus-tu-m, *vineyard* (arbos-); commonly preceded by -ē-, forming -ē-to- (202), usually plural: dūm-ēta, *thorn-thickets* (dūmo-); murt-ēta, *myrtle-groves* (murto-).

335. -len-to-, N. -len-tu-s (202): vīno-lento-, N. vīno-lentu-s, *drunken* (vīno-); sanguin-olentu-s, *all blood* (sanguin-); lūcu-lentu-s, *bright* (lūci-, 28); pulver-ulentu-s, *dusty* (pulver-). A shorter form -lenti- is rare: vi-olenti-, N. vi-olēn-s, *violent* (vi-); op-ulēn-s, *rich* (op-)

(2.) -ōso- (N. -ōsu-s).

336. -ōso- (sometimes -ōnso-, -ōsso-), N. -ōsu-s, *full of,* is very common indeed. -ōso- is sometimes attached to other suffixes, thus: -c-ōso-, -ul-ōso-, -ūc-ul-ōso-.

337. -ōso-, N. -ōsu-s : ann-ōso-, N. ann-ōsu-s, *full of years ;* fōrm-ōnsu-s, fōrm-ōssu-s or fōrm-ōsu-s, *shapely* (fōrmā-) ; perīcul-ōsu-s, *with danger fraught* (perīculo-) ; mōr-ōsu-s, *priggish, cross* (mōr-) ; calamit-ōsu-s, *full of damage* (calamitāt-, 179) ; superstiti-ōsu-s, *superstitious* (superstitiōn-, 179) ; frūctu-ōsu-s, *fruitful* (frūctu-, 116, *c*) ; mont-uōsu-s, *full of mountains* (monti-, 202) ; cūri-ōsu-s, *full of care* (cūrā-) ; labōr-iōsu-s, *toilsome* (labōr-, 202).

338. -c-ōso-, N. -c-ōsu-s : belli-cōso-, N. belli-cōsu-s, *warlike* (bello-, bellico-). -ul-ōso-, N. -ul-ōsu-s : formīd-ulōso-, N. formid-ulōsu-s, *terrible* (formīdin-, 179). -ūc-ul-ōso-, N. -ūc-ul-ōsu-s : met-ū-culoso-, N. met-ū-culōsu-s, *skittish* (metu-).

IV. DIMINUTIVES.

339. Diminutives are formed from adjectives, as from substantives (267).

-lo-, N. -lu-s : aureo-lo-, N. aureo-lu-s, *all gold, of precious gold, of red red gold, good as gold* (aureo-) ; ebrio-lu-s, *tipsy* (ebrio-) ; parvo-lu-s, or parvu-lu-s, *smallish* (parvo-) ; frīgidu-lu-s, *chilly* (frīgido-) ; vet-ulus, *little old* (vet-) ; tenellu-lu-s, *soft and sweet* (tenello-, tenero-) ; pulchel-lus, *sweet pretty* (pulchro-) ; bel-lu-s, *bonny* (bono-) ; novel-lu-s, *newborn* (*novolo-, novo-). -culo-, N. -culu-s : pauper-culo-, N. pauper-culu-s, *poorish* (pauper-) ; levi-culu-s, *somewhat vain* (levi-).

340. A peculiar class of diminutives is formed by adding -culo- to the comparative stem -ius- (346): as, nitidius-culo-, N. nitidius-culu-s, *a trifle sleeker* (nitidius-) ; longius-culu-s, *a bit longer* (longius-).

341. Adverbs sometimes have a diminutive form : as, bellē, *charmingly ;* paullulum, *a little bit ;* meliusculē, *a bit better* (340).

V. COMPARATIVES AND SUPERLATIVES.

342. Comparatives and superlatives are usually formed from the stem of the positive : as, dignior, *worthier,* dignissimus, *worthiest,* from digno-, stem of dignus. A few are formed directly from roots : thus, maior, *greater,* and maximus, *greatest,* are formed from the √m a g-, and not from magno-, stem of magnus.

(1.) COMPARATIVE -ior, SUPERLATIVE -issimus.

343. The nominative of comparative adjectives ends usually in -ior, and that of superlatives in -issimus : thus,

COMPARATIVE.			SUPERLATIVE.		
Masc.	Fem.	Neut.	Masc.	Fem.	Neut.
-ior	-ior	-ius	-issimus	-issima	-issimum

POSITIVE.	COMPARATIVE.	SUPERLATIVE.
altus, *high,*	altior, *higher,*	altissimus, *highest.*
trīstis, *sad,*	trīstior, *sadder,*	trīstissimus, *saddest.*

(2.) SUPERLATIVE -rimus.

344. Adjectives with the nominative in -**er** have the nominative of the superlative like the nominative of the positive with -**rimus** added (350): as,

POSITIVE.	COMPARATIVE.	SUPERLATIVE.
pauper, *poor,*	**pauperior,** *poorer,*	**pauperrimus,** *poorest.*
ācer, *sharp,*	**ācrior,** *sharper,*	**ācerrimus,** *sharpest.*

mātūrrimus occurs once (Tac.), for **mātūrissimus**, positive **mātūrus,** *ripe.*

(3.) SUPERLATIVE -limus.

345. humilis, difficilis, and facilis,
similis, dissimilis, and gracilis,

have the nominative of the superlative in -**limus**, following l of the stem (350): as,

POSITIVE.	COMPARATIVE.	SUPERLATIVE.
humilis, *lowly,*	**humilior,** *lowlier,*	**humillimus,** *lowliest.*

THE COMPARATIVE SUFFIX.

346. The comparative suffix is -**iōs**-, which becomes in the singular, nominative masculine and feminine, -**ior** (154; 132), neuter nominative and accusative, -**ius** (107, *c*); in all other cases -**iōr**- (154).

347. Other comparative suffixes are -**ro**- or -**ero**-, and -**tro**- or -**tero**-, used in a few words, principally designating place: as, **sup-erī,** *the upper ones,* **īnferī,** *the nether ones;* **ex-terī,** *outsiders,* **posterī,** *after-generations;* **alter,** *the other; whether; whether?* *which of the two?* (for **quo-ter,* 146) ; **dexter,** *right.*

348. Some words designating place have a doubled comparative suffix, -**er-iōr**-, or -**ter-iōr**- : as, **sup-er-ior,** *upper,* **inferior,** *lower.* **ci-ter-ior,** *hither,* **dēterior** (*lower*), *worse,* **exterior,** *outer,* **interior,** *inner,* **posterior,** *hinder, after,* **ulterior,** *further,* **dexterior,** *more to the right.* -**is-tro**- is used in two words which have become substantives: **min-is-ter** (*inferior*), *servant,* and **magister** (*superior*), *master.*

THE SUPERLATIVE SUFFIX.

349. The common superlative suffix is -**issimo**-, nominative -**issimus**, with older -**issumo**-, nominative -**issumus** (28).

350. Stems which end in -**ro**-, -**ri**-, or -**li**- (344, 345) take the suffix -**issimo**- (cf. -**simo**-, 351) with syncope of its initial i (111) and assimilation of the final l or r (166, 8).

351. The suffix -**timo**- is further used in a few root superlatives: **ci-timus, dextimus, extimus, intimus, optimus, postumus,** and **ultimus**; and -**simo**- in **maximus, pessimus,** and **proximus.**

352. The suffix -**mo**- or -**imo**- is used in **sum-mo-,** N. **summus,** *highest* (**sub**) ; **min-imo-,** N. **minimus,** *least;* **prīmus,** *first,* **septimus,** *seventh,* **decimus,** ·*tenth.* -**mo**- or -**imo**- is attached to -**is**- (135, 2) in **plūrimus** for ***plō-is-imo-s** (*fullest*), *most* (99); and to -**rē**- or -**trē**-, possibly an adverbial form (705), in **suprēmus, extrēmus,** and **postrēmus.**

PECULIARITIES OF COMPARISON.

353. Some positives have a comparative or superlative, or both, from a different form of the stem: such are,

frūgī, *thrifty,*	frūgālior,	frūgālissimus.
nēquam, *naughty,*	nēquior,	nēquissimus.
iuvenis, *young,*	iūnior,	(nātū minimus).
senex, *old,*	senior,	(nātū maximus).
magnus, *great,*	maior,	maximus (351).
beneficus, *kindly,*	beneficentior,	beneficentissimus.
honōrificus, *complimentary,*	honōrificentior,	honōrificentissimus.
magnificus, *grand,*	magnificentior,	magnificentissimus.

354. iuvenior, *younger,* is late (Sen., Plin., Tac.). benevolēns, *kindly,* benevolentior, benevolentissimus, and maledīcēns, *abusive,* maledīcentior (once each, Plaut.), maledīcentissimus, have usually as positive benevolus and maledicus respectively.

355. Some positives have a comparative or superlative, or both, from a wholly different stem: such are,

bonus, *good,*	melior,	optimus (351).
malus, *bad,*	peior,	pessimus (351).
multus, *much,*	plūs (sing. Ne. only),	plūrimus (352).
parvus, *little,*	minor,	minimus (352).

parvus has rarely parvissimus.

356. Four comparatives in -erior or -terior, denoting place (348), have two forms of the superlative; the nominative masculine singular of the positive is not in common use:

exterior,	extimus (351), or extrēmus (352), *outermost.*
īnferior,	īnfimus, or īmus, *lowest.*
posterior,	postumus (351), *lastborn,* or postrēmus (352), *last.*
superior,	summus (352), cr suprēmus (352), *highest.*

357. Six, denoting place, have the positive only as an adverb or preposition:

cis, *this side,*	citerior (348),	citimus (351), *hitherest.*
dē, *down,*	dēterior (348),	dēterrimus, *lowest, worst.*
in, *in,*	interior (348),	intimus, *inmost.*
prae, *before,*	prior,	prīmus (352), *first.*
prope, *near,*	propior,	proximus (351), *nearest.*
uls, *beyond,*	ulterior (348),	ultimus (351), *furthest.*

ōcior, *swifter,* ōcissimus, has no positive.

358. These have a superlative, but no comparative: bellus, *pretty,* falsus, *false,* inclutus, *famed,* invictus, *unconquered,* invītus, *unwilling,* meritus, *deserving,* novus, *new;* vetus, veterrimus, *old,* sacer, sacerrimus, *sacred,* vafer, vaferrimus, *sly;* malevolus, malevolentissimus (twice, Cic.), *spiteful;* maleficus, maleficentissimus (once, Suet.), *wicked,* mūnificus, mūnificentissimus (inscrr.; Cic. once), *generous.* mīrificus, mirificissimus (twice, Acc., Ter.), *strange.* Plautus has ipsissumus, *his very self.*

53

359. Most primitives in -ilis and -bilis (292, 294), have a comparative, but no superlative; but these have a superlative: **facilis** and **difficilis** (345), *easy* and *hard*, **ūtilis**, *useful;* also **fertilis**, *productive,* **amābilis**, *lovable,* **mōbilis**, *movable,* **nōbilis**, *well known.*

360. Many adjectives have no suffixes of comparison, and supply the place of these by **magis**, *more,* and **maximē**, *most:* as, **mīrus**, *strange,* **magis mīrus**, **maximē mīrus**. Many adjectives, from their meaning, do not admit of comparison.

COMPARATIVE AND SUPERLATIVE ADVERBS.

361. Adverbs derived from adjectives have as their comparative the accusative singular neuter of the comparative adjective; the superlative is formed like that of the adjective, but ends in -ē: as,

altē, *on high,*	altius,	altissimē.
ācriter, *sharply,*	ācrius,	ācerrimē.
facile, *easily,*	facilius,	facillimē.

362. An older superlative ending, -ēd for -ē, occurs in an inscription of 186 B.C.: FACILVMED, i.e. **facillimē**. A few adverbs have superlatives in -ō or -um : as, **meritissimō**, *most deservedly;* **prīmō**, *at first,* **prīmum**, *first;* **postrēmō**, *at last,* **postrēmum**, *for the last time.*

363. If the comparison of the adjective has peculiarities, they are retained in the adverb likewise : as, **bene**, *well,* **melius**, **optimē** ; **male**, *ill,* **peius**, **pessimē** ; **multum**, *much,* **plūs**, **plūrimum** ; **mātūrē**, *betimes,* **mātūrius**, **mātūrissimē** (Cic., Plin.), or **mātūrrimē** (Cic., Caes., Sall., Tac.). **ōcius**, *swifter,* no positive. **ōcissimē**. **minus**, *less,* is formed by the nominal suffix -es- (236), from √min- (minuō); for magis, *more,* see 135, 2. In poetry **magis** sometimes becomes **mage**, as if neuter of an adjective in -i-.

364. A few adverbs not derived from adjectives are compared : as, **diū**, *long,* **diūtius**, **diūtissimē** ; **saepe**, *often,* **saepius**, **saepissimē** ; **nūper**, *lately,* no comparative, **nūperrimē** ; **secus**, *otherwise,* **sētius**, *the less;* **temperī**, *betimes,* **temperius**, *earlier,* no superlative.

(B.) FORMATION OF DENOMINATIVE VERBS.

365. Denominative verb stems have present infinitives in -āre, -ēre, or -īre (-ārī, -ērī, or -īrī), and are formed from noun stems of all endings : as,

VERB.	FROM NOUN.	VERB.	FROM NOUN.
fugā-re, *rout*	fugā-, N. fuga	flōrē-re, *blossom*	flōr-, N. flōs
locā-re, *place*	loco-, N. locus	sordē-re, *be dirty*	sordi-, N. sordēs
nōminā-re, *name*	nōmin-, N. nōmen	pūnī-re, *punish*	poenā-, N. poena
levā-re, *lighten*	levi-, N. levis	condī-re, *season*	condo-, N. condus
sinuā-re, *bend*	sinu-, N. sinus	custōdī-re, *guard*	custōd-, N. custōs
albē-re, *be white*	albo-, N. albus	vestī-re, *dress*	vesti-, N. vestis
miserē-rī, *pity*	misero-, N. miser	gestī-re, *flutter*	gestu-, N. gestus

366. These present verb stems are formed by adding the suffix -i̯o-, -i̯e-
to the noun stem: as *fugā-i̯ō, *I flee;* the i̯ between two vowels was
dropped (153, 2) and the final vowel of noun stem was often contracted with
the ending (118, 3). The noun stem ending is often slightly modified.

367. In a half a dozen denominatives from stems in -u- the u of the noun stem
remains without modification, and is not contracted with the variable vowel (116, *c*) :
these are, **acuere,** *sharpen* (acu-), **metuere,** *fear,* **statuere,** *set,* **tribuere,**
assign; **arguere,** *make clear,* **bātuere,** *beat.*

368. Verbs in -āre are by far the most numerous class of denominatives ; they are usually transitive ; but deponents often express condition,
sometimes occupation : as, **domināri,** *lord it, play the lord ;* **aquāri,** *get oneself
water.* Most verbs in -īre also are transitive ; those in -ēre usually denote
a state : as, **calēre,** *be warm;* but some are causative : as, **monēre,** *remind.*

369. Many denominative verbs in -āre contain a noun suffix
which is not actually found in the noun itself ; such suffixes are :
-co-, -cin-, -lo-, -er-, -ro-, -to-, &c. : as,

-co- : albi-cāre, *be white* (*albi-co-) ; velli-cāre, *pluck* (*velli-co-,
plucker). -cin- : latrō-cinārī, *be a robber* (latrōn-) ; sermō-cinārī, *discourse* (sermōn-). -lo- : grātu-lārī, *give one joy* (*grātu-lo-) ; vi-olāre,
harm (*vi-olo-) ; heiu-lāri, *cry* 'heia' (*heiu-lo-). -er- : mod-erārī,
check (*mod-es-, 236). -ro- : tole-rāre, *endure* (*tole-ro-) ; flag-rāre,
blaze (*flag-ro-). -to- : dēbili-tāre, *lame* (*dēbili-to-) ; dubi-tāre, *doubt*
(*dubi-to-).

370. Many denominatives in -āre are indirect compounds (377),
often from compound noun stems which are not actually found. So,
particularly, when the first part is a preposition, or the second is from
the root f a c-, *make,* a g-, *drive, do,* or c a p-, *take :* as,

opi-tul-ārī, *bear help* (opitulo-) ; suf-fōc-āre, *suffocate* (*suf-fōc-o-,
fauci-) ; aedi-fic-āre (*housebuild*), *build* (*aedific- or *aedifico-, *house-
builder*) ; sīgni-fic-āre, *give token* (*sīgnifico-) ; fūm-ig-āre, *make smoke*
(*fūmigo-, *smoker,* fūmo-, √a g-) ; nāv-ig-āre, *sail,* and rēm-ig-āre, *row*
(nāvi-, *ship,* and rēmo-, *oar*) ; mīt-ig-āre, *make mild* (mīti-) ; iūr-ig-āre,
commonly iūr-g-āre, *quarrel* (iūr-) ; pūr-ig-āre, commonly pūr-g-āre,
clean (pūro-) ; gnār-ig-āre, *tell* (gnāro-, narrāre, 169, 2; 133, 1) ; anti-cipāre, *take beforehand* (*anticipo-, ante, √c a p-) ; oc-cup-āre, *seize* (*occupo-) ;
re-cup-er-āre, *get back* (*recupero-).

371. Many verbs in -tāre (-sāre), or -tārī (-sārī), express
frequent, intense, or sometimes attempted action. These are
called *Frequentatives* or *Intensives;* they are formed from perfect participle stems ; but stems in -ā-to- become -i-to- : as,

cant-āre, *sing* (canto-) ; cess-āre, *loiter* (cesso-) ; amplex-ārī, *em-
brace* (amplexo-) ; habit-āre, *live* (habito-) ; pollicit-ārī, *make overtures*
(pollicito-) ; dormīt-āre, *be sleepy* (dormīto-) ; neg-itāre, *keep denying* (for
*negā-tāre, with suffix -i-tāre, 910).

372. Some frequentatives in -tāre are formed from the present stem
of a verb in -ere ; the formative vowel before -tāre becomes i : as,

agi-tāre, *shake* (age-re) ; flui-tāre, *float* (flue-re) ; nōsci-tāre, *recognize* (nōsce-re) ; quaeri-tāre, *keep seeking* (quaere-re) ; scīsci-tārī, *enquire*
(scīsce-re) ; vēndi-tāre, *try to sell* (vēnde-re).

373. A few frequentatives add -tā- to the perfect participle stem: as, ācti-tāre, *act often* (ācto-); facti-tāre, *do repeatedly* (facto-); lēcti-tāre, *read again and again* (lēcto-); ūncti-tāre, *anoint often* (ūncto-). From a frequentative another frequentative is sometimes derived: as, dict-āre, *dictate*, dicti-tāre, *keep asserting* (dicto-).

374. Some verbs are found only as frequentatives: as, gust-āre, *taste* (*gusto-, √g u s-, *taste*); put-āre, *think* (puto-, √p u-, *clean*); aegrōt-āre, *be ill* (aegrōto-).

375. A few verbs in -uriō, -urīre, express desire; such are called *Desideratives:* as, ēss-urīre or ēs-urīre, *want to eat* (edere, ēsse). A few in -ssō, -ssere, express earnest action; such are called *Meditatives:* as, lacē-ssō, lacē-ssere, *provoke*.

COMPOSITION.

376. In compounds, the fundamental word is usually the second, which has its meaning qualified by the first.

377. A DIRECT COMPOUND is one formed directly from two parts: as, con-iug-, N. coniūnx, *yoke-fellow* (com-, *together*, √i u g-, *yoke*); con-iungere, *join together* (com-, iungere); an INDIRECT COMPOUND is one formed by the addition of a suffix to a direct compound: as, iūdic-io-, N. iūdicium, *trial* (iūdic-): iūdicā-re, *judge* (iūdic-).

378. A REAL COMPOUND is a word whose stem is formed from two stems, or an inseparable prefix and a stem, fused into one stem; an APPARENT COMPOUND is formed by the juxtaposition of an inflected word with another inflected word, a preposition, or an adverb.

I. COMPOSITION OF NOUNS.

(A.) REAL COMPOUNDS.

FORM OF COMPOUNDS.

379. If the first part is a noun, its stem is taken: as, Ahēno-barbus, *Redbeard, Barbarossa ;* usually with weakening of a stem vowel (103-105): as, aurifex, *jeweller* (auro-). On other changes of the final vowel in the first member of compounds, see 174. Sometimes with disappearance of a syllable (179); as, *venēni-ficus, venē-ficus, *poisoner* (venēno-); or of a vowel (111): as, man-ceps, *contractor* (manu-); particularly before a vowel (119): as, magn-animus, *great-souled* (magno-). Consonant stems are often extended by i before a consonant: as, mōri-gerus, *complaisant* (mōr-).

380. Stems in -s-, including those in -er-, -or- and -ōr- (236), are sometimes compounded as above (379): as, nemori-vagus, *woodranger;* honōri-ficus, *complimentary;* but usually they drop the suffix and take i : as, opi-fex, *workman* (oper-); foedi-fragus, *truce-breaker* (foeder-); volni-ficus, *wounding* (volner-); mūni-ficus, *generous* (mūner-); terri-ficus, *awe-inspiring* (terrōr-); horri-fer, *dreadful*, horri-sonus, *awful-sounding* (horrōr-).

381. The second part, which often has weakening of the vowel (102), is sometimes a bare root used as a stem (199), oftener a root with a formative suffix ; or a noun stem, sometimes with its stem ending modified : as, iū-dic-, N. iūdex, *juror* (√ d i c-, *declare*) ; causi-dic-o-, N. causidicus, *pleader* (209) ; in-gen-io-, N. ingenium, *disposition* (√ g e n-, *beget*, 219) ; con-tāg-iōn-, N. contāgiō, *touching together* (√ t a g-, *touch*, 227) ; im-berb-i-, N. imberbis, *beardless* (barbā-).

MEANING OF COMPOUNDS.

382. DETERMINATIVES are compounds in which the second part keeps its original meaning, though determined or modified by the first part. The meaning of a determinative may often be best expressed by two words.

383. (1.) The first part of a determinative may be an adjective, an adverb, a preposition, or an inseparable prefix ; the second part is a noun : as,

lāti-fundium, i.e. lātī fundī, *broad acres ;* prīvi-lēgium, i.e. prīva lēx, *special act ;* alti-sonāns, i.e. altē sonāns, *high-sounding;* con-discipulus, i.e. cum alterō discipulus, *fellow-pupil ;* per-magnus, i.e. valdē magnus, *very great ;* in-dignus, i.e. nōn dignus, *unworthy.*

384. (2.) The first part of a determinative may represent the oblique case of a noun, generally a substantive ; the second part is a noun or verb stem. These compounds are called *Objectives :* as,

Accusative of direct object (1132), armi-ger, i.e. quī arma gerit, *armour-bearer ;* dative of indirect object (1208), man-tēle, i.e. manibus tēla, *handkerchief, napkin ;* genitive (1227), sōl-stitium, i.e. sōlis statiō, *solstice ;* ablative instrumental (1300), tubi-cen, i.e. quī tubā canit, *trumpeter ;* locative (1331), Troiu-gena, i.e. Troiae nātus, *Troy-born ;* ablative locative (1350), nocti-vagus, *night-wandering ;* monti-vagus, *mountain-ranging.*

385. POSSESSIVES are adjective compounds in which the meaning of the second part is changed. The second part of a possessive is always formed from a substantive, qualified by the noun, adverb, or inseparable prefix of the first part, and the whole expresses an attribute which something *has :* as,

longi-manus, *longarms, long-armed ;* miseri-cors, *tender-hearted ;* bi-lin-guis, *two-tongued ;* magn-animus, *greatheart, great-hearted ;* im-berbis, *beardless.*

(B.) APPARENT COMPOUNDS.

386. Apparent Compounds are formed :

387. (1.) By two nouns combined, one with an unchanging case ending, the other with full inflections : as, aquae-ductus, *aqueduct ;* senātūs-cōn-sultum, *decree of the senate ;* pater-familiās, *father of a family ;* vērī-similis, *like the truth ;* in these words, aquae, senātūs, familiās, and vērī are genitives, and remain genitives, while the other part of the compound is declinable.

57

388. (2.) By a substantive with an adjective habitually agreeing with it, both parts being declined : as, rēs pūblica, *the common-weal ;* rēs gestae, *exploits ;* iūs iūrandum, *oath ;* pecūniae repetundae, *money claim.*

389. (3.) By nouns, chiefly substantives, in the same case placed loosely side by side and making one idea. The two words may be used : (*a.*) Copulatively : as, ūsus-frūctus, *use and enjoyment ;* pactum-conventum, *bargain and covenant ;* duo-decim, *two and ten, twelve ;* or (*b.*) Appositively : one word explaining the other (1045): as, Iuppiter, *Jove the Father* (94; 133); Mārspiter, *Mars the Father,* for Mārs pater.

390. (4.) From an original combination of an oblique case with a preposition : as, prōcōnsul, *proconsul,* from prō cōnsule, *for a consul ;* ēgregius, *select,* from ē grege, *out of the herd ;* dēlīrus, *astray, mad,* from dē līrā, *out of the furrow.*

II. COMPOSITION OF VERBS.

(A.) REAL COMPOUNDS.

391. Real Compounds are direct compounds of a verb with a preposition ; the root vowel or diphthong of the verb is often weakened (102) : as,

per-agere, *put through, accomplish ;* ab-igere, *drive away ;* ex-quīrere, *seek out.* The prefix, which was originally a separate adverb modifying the verb, is in poetry sometimes separated from the verb by another word; the disyllabic prepositions in particular often remain as juxtaposed adverbs (396).

392. Some prepositions are inseparable, that is, used only in composition : ambi-, *round,* an-, *up,* dis-, *in two, apart,* por-, *towards,* red-, re-, *back,* sēd-, sē-, *by oneself, away :* as, amb-īre, *go round to ;* an-hēlāre, *breathe up ;* dis-pellere, *drive apart ;* por-rigere, *stretch forth ;* red-dere, *give back ;* sē-iungere, *separate.*

(B.) APPARENT COMPOUNDS.

393. Apparent Compounds are formed by the juxtaposition of :

394. (1.) A verb with a verb : faciō and fīō are added to present stems, mostly of intransitive verbs in -ēre ; the -e- of the first verb is sometimes long, and sometimes short (130, 5) : as, calĕ-facere, *make warm* (calēre); excandĕ-facere, *make blaze* (candēre); madĕ-facere, *make wet* (madēre). In these apparent compounds, the accent of faciō remains the same as in the simple verb : as, calĕfácis.

395. (2.) A substantive with a verb : as, anim-advertere, *pay heed to,* animum advertere ; vēnum-dare, or vēndere, *sell,* vēnum dare ; vēn-īre, *be sold,* vēnum īre ; lucrī-facere, *make gain,* lucrī facere ; manū-mittere, *set free.*

396. (2) An adverb with a verb : as, circum-dare, *put round ;* satis-facere, satis-dare, *give satisfaction ;* intro-īre, *go inside ;* mālle, *prefer,* for magis velle (170, 2); nōlō, *be unwilling,* for ne volō ; ne-scīre, hau-scīre, *not know.*

C. INFLECTION.

397. INFLECTION is the change which nouns, pronouns, and verbs undergo, to indicate their relation in a sentence.

The inflection of a noun or pronoun is often called *Declension*, and that of a verb, *Conjugation*.

(A.) INFLECTION OF THE NOUN.

398. The noun or pronoun is inflected by attaching case endings to the stem.

The endings, which are called case endings for brevity, indicate number as well as case, and serve also to distinguish gender words from neuters in the nominative and accusative singular of some stems, and of all plurals. These endings are nearly the same for stems of all kinds.

THE STEM.

399. The stem contains the meaning of the noun. Noun stems are arranged in the following order: (1.) stems in -ā-, in -o-, in a consonant, or in -i-; these are substantive, including proper names, or adjective; (2.) stems in -u- or -ē-; these are substantive only, and include no proper names.

400. In some instances, a final stem vowel is retained before a case ending which begins with a vowel: as, **urbi-um, ācri-a, cornu-a, portu-ī, portu-um** (116, *c*); in others the stem vowel blends inseparably with the vowel of the case ending: as, **mēnsīs, dominīs** (108, *a*).

401. Some nouns have more than one form of the stem: as,

sēdēs (476); **femur, iecur** (489); **vās, mēnsis** (492); **vīrus, volgus** (493); **iter, nix, senex,** &c. (500); **vīs** (518); **caedēs** (523); **famēs, plēbēs** (524); **domus** (594); **angiportus,** &c. (595). Many nouns have a consonant stem in the singular, and an -i- stem in the plural: see 516; most substantives in -iē- or -tiē- have a collateral form in -iā- or -tiā- (604). Some adjectives have two different stems: as, **hilarus, hilara, hilarum,** and **hilaris, hilare; exanimus** and **exanimis.**

GENDER.

402. There are two genders, *Masculine* and *Feminine*. Masculine and feminine nouns are called *Gender nouns*. Nouns without gender are called *Neuter*.

403. Gender is, properly speaking, the distinction of sex. In Latin, a great many things without life have gender in grammar, and are masculine or feminine.

404. Some classes of substantives may be brought under general heads of signification, as below, like the names of rivers and winds (405), which are usually of the masculine gender, or of plants (407), which are usually of the feminine. When the gender cannot be determined thus, it must be learned from the special rules for the several stems and their nominatives.

GENDER OF SOME CLASSES OF SUBSTANTIVES.

MASCULINES.

405. Names of male beings, rivers, winds, and mountains, are masculine : as,

Caesar, Gāius, Sūlla, men's names ; pater, *father ;* erus, *master ;* scrība, *scrivener ;* Tiberis, *the Tiber ;* Aquilō, *a Norther ;* Lūcrētilis, *Mt. Lucretilis.*

406. The river names : Allia, Dūria, Sagra, Lēthē, and Styx are feminine. Also the mountain names Alpēs, plural, *the Alps,* and some Greek names of mountains in -a or -ē : as, Aetna, *Mt. Etna ;* Rhodopē, a Thracian range. A few are neuter, as Sōracte.

FEMININES.

407. Names of female beings, plants, flowers, shrubs, and trees, are feminine : as,

Gāia, Glycerium, women's names ; mālus, *apple-tree ;* quercus, *oak ;* īlex, *holm-oak ;* abiēs, *fir.*

408. Masculine are : bōlētus, *mushroom,* carduus, *thistle,* dūmī, plural, *brambles,* intibus, *endive,* iuncus, *rush,* oleaster, *bastard olive,* rubus, *bramble,* rumex, *sorrel,* scirpus, *bulrush,* and rarely fīcus, *fig.* Also some of Greek origin : as, acanthus, amāracus, asparagus, and crocus. Neuter are : apium, *parsley,* balsamum, *balsam-tree,* rōbur, *heart of oak,* and some names with stems in -er- (573).

MOBILE, COMMON, AND EPICENE NOUNS.

409. MOBILE NOUNS have different forms to distinguish sex : as, Iūlius, a man, *Julius,* Iūlia, a woman, *Julia ;* cervus, *stag,* cerva, *hind ;* socer, *father-in-law,* socrus, *mother-in-law ;* victor, *conqueror,* victrīx, *conqueress.* Adjectives 'of three endings' (611), belong to this class.

410. Some nouns have one ending, but are applicable to either sex. Such are said to be of *Common Gender :* as, adulēscēns, *young man* or *young woman ;* dux, *leader ;* infāns, *baby, child ;* and many other consonant stems or stems in -i-, denoting persons. Adjectives 'of two endings' or 'of one ending' (611), belong to this class.

411. EPICENES have one ending and one grammatical gender, though applicable to animals of either sex. Thus, aquila, *eagle,* is feminine, though it may denote a *he-eagle* as well as a *she-eagle :* anatēs, *ducks,* feminine, includes *drakes.*

NEUTERS.

412. Infinitives, words and expressions quoted or explained, and letters of the alphabet, are neuter: as,

vīvere ipsum, *mere living;* istūc 'taceō,' *your 'I won't mention;'* longum vale, *a long goodbye;* o Graecum, *Greek O.* But the letters have sometimes a feminine adjective, agreeing with **littera** understood.

VARIABLE GENDER.

413. Some substantives have different genders in the two numbers; the different gender is sometimes indicated by a difference of stem: as, **epulum**, neuter, **epulae**, feminine, *feast.* See **balneum, frēnum, jocus, locus, margarīta, ostrea, rāstrum,** in the dictionary.

NUMBER.

414. There are two numbers, the *Singular* used of one, the *Plural* of more than one.

415. ambō, *both,* and **duo,** *two,* nominative and accusative masculine and neuter, are the only remnants of an old *Dual* number, denoting two.

416. Some substantives, from their meaning, have no plural.

Such are: proper names: as, **Cicerō,** *Cicero;* **Rōma,** *Rome;* material and abstract substantives: as, **oleum,** *oil,* **vīnum,** *wine,* **iūstitia,** *justice;* and gerunds: as, **regendī,** *of guiding.* For the occasional use of the plural, 1105-1110.

417. Some substantives, from their meaning, have no singular.

Such are: names of persons of a class: as, **maiōrēs,** *ancestors;* **superī,** *the beings above;* **mānēs,** *ghosts;* of feasts, sacrifices, days: as, **Sāturnālia,** *festival of Saturn;* **kalendae,** *first of the month;* of things made of parts or consisting of a series of acts: as, **arma,** *arms;* **artūs,** *joints;* **quadrīgae,** *four-in-hand;* **exsequiae,** *funeral rites;* of some places: as, **Faleriī; Vēī; Pompēī; Athēnae,** *Athens;* **Alpēs,** *the Alps.*

418. Some substantives have different meanings in the two numbers: as,

aedis, *temple,* **aedēs,** *house;* **auxilium,** *aid,* **auxilia,** *auxiliaries;* **carcer,** *jail,* **carcerēs,** *race-barriers;* **Castrum,** *Castle,* **castra,** *camp;* **comitium,** *meeting-place,* **comitia,** *election;* **cōpia,** *abundance,* **cōpiae,** *troops;* **facultās,** *ability,* **facultātēs,** *wealth;* **fīnis,** *end,* **fīnēs,** *boundaries;* **grātia,** *favour,* **grātiae,** *thanks;* **impedīmentum,** *hindrance,* **impedīmenta,** *baggage;* **littera** *letter (of the alphabet),* **litterae,** *epistle;* **rōstrum,** *beak,* **rōstra,** *speaker's stand.* See also **aqua, bonum, fortūna, lūdus, opera, pars,** in the dictionary.

CASE.

419. Nouns have five cases, the *Nominative, Genitive, Dative, Accusative,* and *Ablative.*

The nominative represents a noun as subject, the accusative as object; the genitive denotes the relation of *of,* the dative of *to* or *for,* and the ablative of *from, with, in,* or *by.* But the meanings of the cases are best learnt from reading. All cases but the nominative and vocative (420) are called *Oblique Cases.*

420. Town names and a few appellatives have also a case denoting the place where, called the *Locative*. Masculine stems in -o- and some Greek stems with other endings have still another form used in addressing a person or thing, called the *Vocative*.

421. The stem of a noun is best seen in the genitive; in the genitive plural it is preserved without change, except that o of -o-stems is lengthened (123). In dictionaries the stem ending is indicated by the genitive singular, thus: -ae, -ī, -is, -ūs (-ĕī), indicate respectively stems in -ā-, -o-, a consonant or -i-, -u-, and -ē-, as follows:

GENITIVE SINGULAR.	GENITIVE PLURAL.	STEMS IN.
-ae, mēnsae, *table*	-ārum, mēnsā-rum	-ā-, mēnsā-, N. mēnsa
-ī, dominī, *master*	-ōrum, dominō-rum	-o-, domino-, N. dominus
-is, rēgis, *king*	-cons. um, rēg-um	-consonant, rēg-, N. rēx
-is, cīvis, *citizen*	-ium, cīvi-um	-i-, cīvi-, N. cīvis
-ūs, portūs, *port*	-uum, portu-um	-u-, portu-, N. portus
(-ĕī, rĕī), *thing*	(-ērum, rē-rum)	-ē-, rē-, N. rēs

422. Gender nominatives usually add -s to the stem: as, **servo-s** or servu-s, *slave*, rēx (164, 1), cīvi-s, portu-s, rē-s. But stems in -ā- or in a continuous consonant (-l-, -n-, -r-, or -s-) have no -s: as, mēnsa, cōnsul, *consul*, flāmen, *special priest*, patcr, *father*, flōs, *flower*.

423. Neuters have the nominative and accusative alike; in the singular the stem is used: as nōmen, *name;* or a shortened stem: as, exemplar, *pattern;* but stems in -o- take -m: as, aevo-m or aevu-m, *age*. In the plural -a is always used: as, rēgna, *kingdoms*, nōmina, cornua, *horns*. For -s in adjectives ' of one ending,' see 612.

424. Gender accusatives singular add -m to the stem: as, mēnsa-m, servo-m or servu-m, nāvi-m, *ship*, portu-m, die-m. The consonant stems have the ending -em: as, rēg-em; most substantive stems in -i-and all adjectives also drop -i- and take -em: as, nāv-em, trīst-em, *sad*. In the plural, gender stems add -s before which the vowel is long: as, mēnsā-s, servō-s, rēgē-s, nāvi-s or nāvē-s, portū-s, rē-s.

425. The ablative singular usually ends in the long vowel of the stem: as, mēnsā, dominō, nāvī, portū, rē. The ablative of consonant stems usually has -e (rarely -ī-, see 502): as, patre, *father;* and that of substantive -i- stems has -e more commonly than -ī: as, nāve.

426. The ablative singular of -ā- and -o- stems ended anciently in -ād and -ōd respectively: as, PRAIDAD, PREIVATOD; that of consonant stems in -īd: as, AIRID, COVENTIONID. But -d is almost entirely confined to inscriptions and disappeared early (149).

427. The genitive plural adds -rum to -ā-, -o-, and -ē- stems: as, mēnsā-rum, dominō-rum, rē-rum; and -um to consonant stems, -i-stems, and -u- stems: as, rēg-um, cīvi-um, portu-um.

428. The dative and ablative plural are always alike: stems in -ā- and -o- take -is, which blends with the stem vowel (400): as, mēnsīs, dominīs; other stems have -bus, before which consonant stems are extended by i: as, rēgi-bus, nāvi-bus, portu-bus or porti-bus, rē-bus.

429. Some pronouns and a few adjectives have some peculiar case endings; see 618-694.

430. Many nouns are defective in case.

Thus, many monosyllables have no genitive plural: as, **aes,** *copper,* **cor,** *heart,* **cōs,** *whetstone,* **dōs,** *dowry,* **ōs,** *face,* **pāx,** *peace,* **pix,** *pitch,* **rōs,** *dew,* **sāl,** *salt,* **lūx,** *light;* many words have no genitive, dative, or ablative plural: as, **hiemps,** *winter;* especially neuters: as, **fār,** *spelt,* **fel,** *gall,* **mel,** *honey,* **pūs,** *matter,* **rūs,** *country,* **tūs,** *frankincense.* Many words in -tu- (-su-) have only the ablative (235). For -ē- stems, see 600. Other words more or less defective are **exlēx, exspēs, fās** and **nefās, īnfitiās, inquiēs, īnstar, luēs, nēmō, opis** and **vicis** genitives, **pondō** and **sponte** ablatives, **secus, vīs.** Many adjectives 'of one ending' want the nominative and accusative neuter plural and genitive plural.

431. Some adjectives are altogether indeclinable: as, **frūgī,** *thrifty,* an old dative; **nēquam,** *naughty,* an old accusative; **quot,** *how many;* **tot,** *so many;* and most numerals (637). These adjectives are attached to any case of a substantive without varying their own forms.

———◆———

STEMS IN -ā-.

The First Declension.

Genitive singular -ae, genitive plural -ā-rum.

432. Stems in **-ā-** include substantives and adjectives; both substantives and adjectives are feminine.

433. Names of males are masculine (405): as, **scrība,** *writer;* also **Hadria,** *the Adriatic,* and rarely **damma,** *deer,* and **talpa,** *mole.*

434. The nominative of stems in **-ā-** ends in the shortened stem vowel **-a.**

435. Stems in **-ā-** are declined as follows:

Example Stem	mēnsa, *table,* mēnsā-, F.		Stem and case endings
Singular			
Nom.	mēnsa	*table, a* (or *the*) *table*	-a
Gen.	mēnsae	*a table's, of a table*	-ae
Dat.	mēnsae	*to* or *for a table*	-ae
Acc.	mēnsam	*a table*	-am
Abl.	mēnsā	*from, with,* or *by a table*	-ā
Plural			
Nom.	mēnsae	*tables* (or *the*) *tables*	-ae
Gen.	mēnsārum	*tables', of tables*	-ārum
Dat.	mēnsīs	*to* or *for tables*	-īs
Acc.	mēnsās	*tables*	-ās
Abl.	mēnsīs	*from, with,* or *by tables*	-īs

SINGULAR CASES.

436. -ā- of the stem was shortened in the nominative and accusative singular at an early period (130, 132). A few apparent examples of the nominative in -ā, found in the oldest writers, seem due to metrical causes : as, **aquilā** (Enn.). But -ā occurs in Greek proper names (445). A couple of old masculine nominatives in -ās are quoted (422) : **pāricīdās,** *murderer,* and **hosticapās,** *taker of enemies.* In the accusative singular -ām occurs once : **inimīcitiām** (Enn.).

437. The genitive sometimes ends (1.) in -āī in poetry : as, **aulāī,** *of the hall ;* **pīctāī,** *embroidered ;* (2.) in -ās : as, **molās,** *of a mill.* This genitive is rare, but was always kept up in the word **familiās** with **pater** or **māter,** sometimes with **fīlius** or **fīlia** : **pater familiās,** *the goodman,* **māter familiās,** *the housewife.* But **pater familiae,** or in the plural **patrēs familiārum,** is equally common.

438. Town names and a few appellatives have a locative case in -ae : as, **Rōmae,** *at Rome, in Rome ;* **mīlitiae,** *in war, in the field, in the army.*

PLURAL CASES.

439. Compounds ending with -cola, *inhabiting,* and -gena, *born,* and patronymics, sometimes have the genitive plural in -ŭm in poetry : as, **caelicolŭm,** *of occupants of heaven ;* **Graiugenŭm,** *of Greek-born men ;* **Aeneadŭm,** *of Aeneas's sons ;* also names of peoples : as, **Lapithŭm,** *of the Lapithae.* With these last -ŭm occurs even in prose : as, **Crotōniātŭm,** *of the Crotona people.* Others in -ŭm are **drachmŭm, amphorŭm.**

440. In the dative and ablative plural, -eis sometimes occurs (443) : as, **tueis ingrātieis,** *against your will* (Plaut.). Nouns in -ia have rarely a single ī : as, **pecūnīs,** *by moneys* (Cic.); **taenīs,** *with fillets* (Verg.); **nōnīs Iūnīs,** *on the fifth of June* (Cic.). See 24.

441. In the dative and ablative plural, words in -āia, or plural -āiae, have -āīs, and those in -ēia have -ēīs (127, 7) : as **KAL. MAIS,** *on the calends of May* (inscr.); **Bāīs,** *at Bajae* (Hor.); **plēbēīs,** *plebeian.*

442. The dative and ablative plural sometimes end in -ābus, particularly in **deābus,** *goddesses,* and **fīliābus,** *daughters,* to distinguish them from **deīs,** *gods,* and **filiīs,** *sons.* **ambae,** *both,* and **duae,** *two,* regularly have **ambābus** and **duābus.**

443. Other case forms are found in inscriptions, as follows :

G. -ai, which may be monosyllabic or disyllabic in pronunciation : **PVLCHRAI ; LAVERNAI ;** -āēs, after 80 B.C., chiefly in proper names, mostly Greek : **HERAES ;** rarely in appellatives : **DOMINAES ;** -ēs : **MINERVES ;** -ā, **VESTA ; COIRA,** i. e. **Cūrae.** D. -ai, in all periods (96) : **FILIAI ;** -ā : **FORTVNA :** -ē (96) : **FORTVNE.** Ac. -a (61) : **TAVRASIA ; MAGNA SAPIENTIA.** Ab. -ād (426) : **PRAIDAD.** Loc. -ai : **ROMAI.** Plural : N. -ai (96) : **TABELAI DATAI :** -ā, rare : **MATRONA ;** -ē, rare and provincial (96) : **MVSTE,** i.e. **mystae.** D. and Ab. -eis, very often (98) : **SCRIBEIS ;** D. -ās, once : **DEVAS CORNISCAS,** i.e. **dīvīs Cornīscīs.** Ab. -ēs once (98) : **NVGES,** i.e. **nūgīs.**

GREEK NOUNS.

444. Greek appellatives always take a Latin form in the dative singular and in the plural, and usually throughout : thus, **poēta,** M., *poet,* and **aula,** F., *court,* are declined like **mēnsa.** Masculines have sometimes a nominative -ēs and accusative -ēn : as, **anagnōstēs,** *reader,* **anagnōstēn ;** rarely an ablative -ē : as, **sophistē,** *sophist.* Greek feminines in -ē sometimes have Greek forms in late writers : as, N. **grammaticē,** *philology,* G. **grammaticēs,** Ac. **grammaticēn,** Ab. **grammaticē** (Quintil.).

445. Greek proper names sometimes have the following forms. Nominative masculine -ās, -ēs : as, **Prūsiās, Atrīdēs** ; feminine -ā : as, **Gelā, Phaedrā** ; -ē : as, **Circē.** Genitive feminine -ēs : as, **Circēs.** Accusative masculine -ān, -dēn : as, **Aenēān, Pēlĭdēn** ; feminine -ēn : as, **Circēn.** Ablative feminine -ē : as, **Tīsiphonē.** Vocative -ā or -a : as, **Atrīdā, Atrĭda, Thyesta** ; -tē : as, **Boōtē** ; -dē : as, **Aeacidē.**

STEMS IN -o-.

The Second Declension.

Genitive singular -ī, genitive plural -ō-**rum.**

446. Stems in -o- include substantives and **adjectives,** masculine or neuter.

447. Most names of plants in -us are feminine (407); also the following: **alvos** or **alvus,** *belly,* **colus,** *distaff,* **domus,** *house,* **humus,** *ground,* **vannus,** *fan.*

448. The nominative of masculines ends, including the stem vowel, in -o-s, or usually -u-s ; some end in -r ; neuters end in -o-m, or usually -u-m.

449. (1.) Stems in -o- with the nominative in -us or -um are declined as follows :

Examples Stems	dominus, *master,* domino-, M.	rēgnum, *kingdom,* rēgno-, Ne.	Stem and case endings	
			M.	Ne.
Singular				
Nom.	dominus, *a* (or *the*) *master*	rēgnum	-us	-um
Gen.	dominī, *a master's*	rēgnī	-ī	-ī
Dat.	dominō, *to* or *for a master*	rēgnō	-ō	-ō
Acc.	dominum, *a master* [*master*	rēgnum	-um	-um
Abl.	dominō, *from, with,* or *by a*	rēgnō	-ō	-ō
Voc.	domine, *master*		-e	
Plural				
Nom.	dominī, (*the*) *masters*	rēgna	-ī	-a
Gen.	dominōrum, *of masters* -	rēgnōrum	-ōrum	-ōrum
Dat.	dominīs, *to* or *for masters*	rēgnīs	-īs	-īs
Acc.	dominōs, *masters* [*masters*	rēgna	-ōs	-a
Abl.	dominīs, *from, with,* or *by*	rēgnīs	-īs	-īs

450. deus, *god,* is declined as follows : N. **deus,** G. **deī,** D. and Ab. **deō,** Ac. **deum.** Plural : N. **deī, diī,** commonly **dī,** G. **deōrum** or **deŭm,** D. and Ab. **deīs, diīs,** commonly **dīs,** Ac. **deōs.**

451. (2.) Stems in -o- with the nominative in -r or in -āius, -ēius, or -ōius are declined as follows:

Examples Stems	puer, *boy*, puero-, M.	ager, *field*, agro-, M.	Pompēius, *Pompey*, Pompēio-, M.
Singular			
Nom.	puer, *a* (or *the*) *boy*	ager	Pompēius
Gen.	puerī, *a boy's, of a boy*	agrī	Pompēī
Dat.	puerō, *to* or *for a boy*	agrō	Pompēiō
Acc.	puerum, *a boy*	agrum	Pompēium
Abl.	puerō, *from, with,* or *by a boy*	agrō	Pompēiō
Voc.			Pompēī, Pompeī͡
Plural			
Nom.	puerī, (*the*) *boys*	agrī	Pompēī
Gen.	puerōrum, *boys', of boys*	agrōrum	Pompēiōrum
Dat.	puerīs, *to* or *for boys*	agrīs	Pompēīs
Acc.	puerōs, *boys*	agrōs	Pompēiōs
Abl.	puerīs, *from, with,* or *by boys*	agrīs	Pompēīs

SINGULAR CASES.

452. -us and -um were originally -os and -om. But -us was used in the earliest times, -um somewhat later, and both became prevalent between 218 and 55 B.C. (107, *c*). After u or v, however, the -os and -om were retained till toward 50 A.D. (107, *c*); also after qu; but -cus and -cum often displaced -quos and -quom (157): as, equos, equom, or ecus, ecum, *horse;* antīquos, antīquom, or antīcus, antīcum, *ancient.* In the vocative -e was always used, and is retained by Plautus in puere, *thou boy.*

453. Words in -rus with a long penult, as, sevērus, *stern,* and the following substantives with a short penult are declined like dominus (449):

erus, *master*   umerus, *shoulder*
iūniperus, *juniper*   uterus, *womb*
numerus, *number*

For adjective stems in -ro- with nominative -rus, see 615.

454. Masculine stems in -ro- preceded by a short vowel or a mute, except those above (453), drop -os in the nominative, and have no vocative: as, stem puero-, N. puer, *boy* (111, *b*). Most masculines in -ro- have a vowel before r only in the nominative -er (111, *b*): as agro-, N. ager. But in compounds ending in -fer and -ger, *carrying, having,* and the following, the vowel before -r is a part of the stem, and is found in all the cases:

adulter, Līber, *paramour, Liber*   puer, vir, *boy, man*
gener, socer, *son-in-law, father-in-law* līberī, vesper, *children, evening*

For Mulciber, Hibēr, and Celtibēr, see the dictionary; for adjective stems in -ro- with nominative -r, see 616. Once socerus (Pl.).

66

455. nihilum, *nothing,* usually drops -um in the nominative and accusative, becoming nihil or nīl, and similarly nōn, *not,* may be for noenum, *naught* (99) famul is used for famulus, *slave,* by Ennius and Lucretius, once each (111, *b*).

456. Substantives ending in -ius or -ium (but never adjectives), have commonly a single -ī in the genitive singular: as,

Vergilius, G. Vergílī (87); fīlius, *son,* G. fīlī; cōnūbium, *marriage,* G. cōnūbī.

457. Vergil has once a genitive -iī, fluviī, *river's.* Propertius has -iī two or three times; with Ovid, Seneca, and later writers, -iī is common: as, gladiī, *of a sword;* even in proper names, which were the last to take -iī: as, Tarquiniī; but family names almost always retain a single -ī. Locatives have -iī: as, Iconiī (Cic.).

458. Proper names ending in -āius, -ēius, or -ōius have -āī, -ēī, or -ōī in the genitive and vocative singular and nominative plural, and -āīs, -ēīs, or -ōīs in the dative and ablative plural (127, 7): as,

Gāius, G., V., and N. Pl. Gāī, D. and Ab. Pl. Gāīs; Pompēī, Pompēīs; Bōī, Bōīs. In verse -ēī of the vocative is sometimes made one syllable (120): as, Pompeī; Volteī (Hor.).

459. Latin proper names in -ius have the vocative in -ī only: as,

Vergilius, V. Vergílī; Mercurius, V. Mercúrī (87). So, also, fīlius, fīlī, *son;* genius, genī, *good angel;* volturius, volturī, *vulture;* meus, mī, *my.*

460. Town names and a few appellatives have a locative case in -ī: as, Ephesī, *in Ephesus;* humī, *on the ground;* bellī, *in war.*

PLURAL CASES.

461. In the nominative plural masculine, -ei sometimes occurs (465): as, nātei geminei, *twins born* (Plaut.); -eis or -is is rare (465): as, Sardeis, *Sardians;* oculīs, *eyes;* not infrequently hīsce, *these here* (Plaut.); masculine stems in -io- have rarely a single -ī: as, fīlī, *sons.* For -āī, -ēī, or -ōī, see 458. The nominative and accusative plural of neuters ended anciently in -ā (130, 2). But -ā was shortened at an early period.

462. In the common genitive plural -ōrum, the -o- of the stem is lengthened (123). A genitive plural in -ŭm (or, after v, in -ŏm) is common from dīvos, dīvus, and deus, *god;* from dēnārius, *denar,* modius, *peck,* nummus, *money,* sēstertius, *sesterce,* and talentum, *talent,* with numerals; and from cardinals and distributives (641): as, dīvŏm, dīvŭm, deŭm; mīlle sēstertiŭm; ducentŭm; bīnŭm. The u was originally long (132); but it was shortened before 100 A.D.

463. Other masculine substantives have occasionally this genitive: as, līberŭm, *of children;* particularly in set phrases and in verse: as, centuria fabrŭm, *century of mechanics;* Graiŭm, *of Greeks.* With neuter substantives, as oppidŭm, for oppidōrum, *of towns,* and with adjectives it is rare.

464. In the dative and ablative plural, -eis is rare (98): as, Epidamnieis (Plaut.). Stems in -io- have rarely a single ī: as, fīlīs, *for sons.* For -āīs, -ēīs, or -ōīs, see 458. ambō, *both,* and duo, *two,* have ambōbus and duōbus (640).

67

465. Other case forms are found in inscriptions as follows :

N. **-os, -om,** with o retained (107, *c*): FILIOS, TRIBVNOS; POCOLOM; in proper names **-o** (66): CORNELIO; **-u,** rare: LECTV; **-is,** or **-i,** for **-ius** (135, 2): CAECILIS; CLAVDI; neuter **-o** (61): POCOLO. G. oldest form **-ī**: VRBANI; **-ei,** from 146 B.C. to Augustus: POPVLEI; CONLEGEI; **-ii** from stems in **-io-** not before Tiberius: COLLEGII. Ac. **-om** (107 *c*): VOLCANOM; **-o** (61): OPTVMO VIRO; **-u**: GREMIV. Ab. **-od,** not after 186 B.C. (426): POPLICOD, PREIVATOD. Plural: N. **-ei,** always common (98): VIREI; FILEI; **-ēs, -eis, -īs** (461): ATILIES; COQVES; LEIBEREIS, i.e. līberī; MAGISTREIS; MAGISTRIS; **-ē,** rare: PLOIRVME, i.e. **plūrumī.** G. **-ōm** or **-ō** (61) ROMANOM; ROMANO; **-ōro** (61): DVONORO. D. and Ab. **-eis,** the only form down to about 130 B.C. (98) : ANTIQVEIS; PROXSVMEIS; **-ēs,** twice: CAVATVRINES.

GREEK NOUNS.

466. Greek stems in **-o-** are generally declined like Latin nouns, but in the singular sometimes have **-os** in the nominative, **-on** in the nominative or accusative neuter, rarely **-ū** in the genitive, or **-ō** in the feminine ablative. Plural, nominative sometimes **-oe,** masculine or feminine, and genitive, chiefly in book-titles, **-ōn**: as,

Nominative **Īlios**; **Īlion** or **Īlium.** Genitive **Menandrū,** *of Menander.* Ablative feminine adjective **lectīcā octōphorō,** *in a sedan with eight bearers.* Plural: nominative **Adelphoe,** *the Brothers;* **canēphoroe,** *basket-bearers,* feminine. Genitive **Geōrgicōn** liber, *book of Husbandry.* For **Androgeōs, Athōs** and **Panthūs,** see the dictionary.

CONSONANT STEMS.

The Third Declension.

Genitive singular -is, genitive plural -um.

467. Consonant stems are mostly substantive, and include both gender words and neuters.

Comparatives and a few other words are adjective. For the gender of substantives, see 570.

468. The nominative of consonant stems ends in **-s** (or **-x**) ; or in **-n** (**-ō**), **-l, -r,** or **-s** of the stem, rarely in **-c** or **-t.**

469. Most consonant stems have one syllable less in the nominative than in the genitive.

Such words are called *Imparisyllabic* words or *Imparisyllables :* as, nominative **rēx,** *king,* one syllable; genitive **rēgis,** *of a king,* two syllables.

470. Many consonant stems have a double form : one form used in the nominative singular (neuters have this form in the accusative also), another form in the other cases : as,

iūdex, *juror*, stem of nominative iūdec- (136, 2), of other cases iūdic- ;
flāmen (103, *a*), *special priest*, flāmin- (103, *a*) ; **virgō**, *maid*, virgin- (105,*g*) ;
auceps (107, *d*), *fowler*, aucup- (104,*c*) ; **ebur** (107, *c*), *ivory*, ebor- ; **genus**,
race, **gener-** (145 ; 107, *c*) ; **trīstius** (346), *sadder*, trīstiōr- (346) ; **corpus** (107,*c*),
body, **corpor-** (105,*i*) ; **pater** (135, 2), *father*, **patr-**. In such instances the stem
of the oblique cases is taken for brevity to represent both forms of the stem.

I. MUTE STEMS.

471. (1.) Stems in a guttural mute, **-g-** or **-c-,** are declined
as follows :

Examples Stems	rēx, *king,* rēg-, M.	dux, *leader,* duc-, M.	iūdex, *juror,* iūdic-, M.,F.	Case endings
Singular				
Nom.	rēx, *a* (or *the*) *king*	dux	iūdex	-s (-x)
Gen.	rēgis, *a king's, of a king*	ducis	iūdicis	-is
Dat.	rēgī, *to* or *for a king*	ducī	iūdicī	-ī
Acc.	rēgem, *a king* [*king*	ducem	iūdicem	-em
Abl.	rēge, *from, with,* or *by a*	duce	iūdice	-e
Plural				
Nom.	rēgēs, (*the*) *kings*	ducēs	iūdicēs	-ēs
Gen.	rēgum, *kings', of kings*	ducum	iūdicum	-um
Dat.	rēgibus, *to* or *for kings*	ducibus	iūdicibus	-ibus
Acc.	rēgēs, *kings* [*kings*]	ducēs	iūdicēs	-ēs
Abl.	rēgibus, *from, with,* or *by*	ducibus	iūdicibus	-ibus

In the nominative and accusative, neuters have no case ending in the
singular, and **-a** in the plural. In the other cases they have the same case
endings as gender stems.

472. (*a.*) Examples of stems in **-g-**, with nominative **-x**, genitive
-gis, are :

-ex, -egis grex, M., (F.), *herd;* aquilex, M., *spring-hunter, hydraulic
engineer.*

-ēx, -ēgis rēx, M., *king;* interrēx, *regent;* lēx, F., *law;* and N. and Ac.
exlēx, exlēgem, *beyond the law,* adjective.

-ex, -igis rēmex, M., *oarsman.*

-īx, -īgis strīx, F., *screech-owl.*

-ūnx, -ugis coniūnx (122, *e*) or coniux, M., F., *spouse.*

-ux, -ūgis frūx, F., *fruit.*

69

473. (*b.*) Examples of stems in -c-, with nominative -x, genitive
-cis, are :

-ax, -acis   fax, F., *torch*, no G. Pl. in good writers (430).

-āx, -ācis   pāx, F., *peace*, Pl. only N. and Ac. pācēs ; līmāx, F., *snail.*

-ex, -ecis   faenisex, M., *haycutter ;* nex, F., *murder ;* precī, D., F., *prayer,*
         no N., usually plural.

-ēx, -ēcis   vervēx, M., *wether ;* allēx, F., *fish-pickle,* also allēc, Ne.

-ex, -icis   Masculines mostly : apex, *point ;* cārex, F., *rush ;* caudex or
         cōdex, *block, book ;* cimex, *bug ;* cortex, M., F., *bark ;* culex,
         gnat ; forfex, M., F., *shears ;* frutex, *shrub ;* ilex, F., *holm-oak ;*
         illex, M., F., *seducer ;* imbrex, *tile ;* latex, *fluid ;* mūrex, *purple-*
         shell ; obicc, Ab., M., F., *bar,* no N.; paelex, F., *concubine,*
         pollex, *thumb ;* pūlex, *flea ;* pūmex, *pumice-stone ;* rāmex, *blood-*
         vessel ; rumex, *sorrel ;* silex, M., F., *flint ;* sōrex, *shrew-mouse ;*
         vortex or vertex, *whirl ;* vitex, F., *a shrub.* Also some com-
         pounds : as, iūdex, *juror ;* artifex, *artisan ;* auspex, *bird-viewer.*

-ix, -icis   Feminines mostly : appendix, *addition ;* calix, M., *cup ;* filix,
         fern ; fulix, *gull ;* fornix, M., *arch ;* larix, *larch ;* pix, *pitch,*
         no G. Pl. (430); salix, *willow ;* vārix, *swollen vein ;* vicis, G.,
         change, no N., D., or G. Pl. (430).

-īx, -īcis   Feminines : cervīx, *neck ;* cicātrīx, *scar ;* cornīx, *crow ;* cŏturnīx
         (62), *quail ;* lōdīx, *blanket ;* rādīx, *root ;* struīx, *heap.* Also
         coxendīx, *hip,* later coxendix, coxendicis.

-ōx, -ōcis   vōx, F., *voice.*

-ux, -ucis   crux, F., *cross ;* dux, M., F., *leader ;* nux, F., *nut-tree, nut ;*
         trādux, M., *vinelayer.*

474. (2.) Stems in a dental mute, -d- or -t-, are declined as
follows :

Examples Stems	custōs, *keeper,* custōd-, M.	aetās, *age,* aetāt-, F.	virtūs, *virtue,* virtūt-, F.	mīles, *soldier,* mīlit-, M.
Singular				
Nom.	custōs	aetās	virtūs	mīles
Gen.	custōdis	aetātis	virtūtis	mīlitis
Dat.	custōdī	aetātī	virtūtī	mīlitī
Acc.	custōdem	aetātem	virtūtem	mīlitem
Abl.	custōde	aetāte	virtūte	mīlite
Plural				
Nom.	custōdēs	aetātēs	virtūtēs	mīlitēs
Gen.	custōdum	aetātum	virtūtum	mīlitum
Dat.	custōdibus	aetātibus	virtūtibus	mīlitibus
Acc.	custōdēs	aetātēs	virtūtēs	mīlitēs
Abl.	custōdibus	aetātibus	virtūtibus	mīlitibus

475. (*a.*) Examples of stems in -d-, with nominative **-s**, genitive **-dis**, are :

-as, -adis   vas, M., F., *personal surety*, no G. Pl. (430).

-aes, -aedis praes, M., *bondsman.*

-es, -idis   obses, M., F., *hostage;* praeses, M., F., *overseer.* *dēses, *slothful,* adjective.

-ēs, -edis   pēs, M., *foot.*

-ēs, -ēdis   hērēs, M., F., *heir;* exhērēs, *disinherited,* adjective; mercēs, F., *reward.*

-is, -idis   Feminines : capis, *cup;* cassis, *helmet;* cuspis, *spear-point;* prōmulsis, *appetizer;* lapis, M., *stone.*

-ōs, -ōdis   custōs, M., F., *guard.*

-aus, -audis laus, F., *praise.*

-us, -udis   pecus, F., *beast, head of cattle.*

-ūs, -ūdis   Feminines : incūs, *anvil;* palūs, *swamp,* nominative once in Horace palus, as from an -o- stem; subscūs, *dovetail.*

476. sēdēs, F., *seat,* has an -s- stem, namely -ēs (236), in the nominative, and sēd- in the other cases (401); G. Pl. sēdum, once sēdium (Vell. Pat.). The only example of a neuter stem in -d-, with nominative -r, genitive -dis, is cor (171, 2), *heart,* cordis, no G. Pl. (430).

477. (*b.*) Examples of stems in -t-, with nominative **-s**, genitive **-tis**, are :

-as, -atis   anas, F., *duck;* G. Pl. also anitum (Cic.), and Ac. Pl. anitēs (Plaut.).

-ās, -ātis   aetās, F., *age ;* also numerous other feminines in -tās (262).

-es, -etis   interpres, M., F., *go-between;* seges, F., *crop;* teges, F., *mat.*

-es, -itis   Masculines mostly : ames, *net-pole;* antistes, M., F., *overseer;* caespes, *sod;* comes, M., F., *companion;* eques, *horseman;* fōmes, *tinder;* gurges, *whirlpool;* hospes, M., F., *guest-friend;* līmes, *path;* merges, F., *sheaf;* mīles, M., F., *soldier;* palmes, *vine-sprout;* pedes, *man afoot. infantry;* poples, *hough;* stīpes, *trunk;* termes, *bough;* trāmes, *by-path.* dīves, *rich;* sōspes, *safe;* superstes, *surviving;* caelite, Ab., *occupant of heaven,* no N., adjectives.

-ēs, -etis   abiēs, F., *fir;* ariēs, M., *ram;* pariēs, M., *wall.*

-ēs, -ētis   Feminines : quiēs and requiēs, *rest,* no D., Ac. often requiem, Ab. usually requiē (603); inquiēs, *unrest,* N. only.

-os, -otis   compos, *master of,* adjective.

-ōs, -ōtis   nepōs, M., *grandson, profligate;* sacerdōs, M., *priest;* cōs, F., *whetstone,* no G. Pl. (130) ; dōs, F., *dowry,* no G. Pl. in good writers (43c) ; dōtum once (Val. Max.), and dōtium in the jurists.

-ūs, -ūtis   Feminines : iuventūs, *youth;* salūs, *existence;* senectūs, *old age;* servitūs, *slavery,* all singular only; and virtūs, *virtue,* with a plural.

478. vātēs, *bard,* has an -s- stem, namely -ēs (236), in the nominative, and **vāt-** in the other cases (401); G. Pl. **vātum,** but thrice **vātium** (Cic.). The only example of a neuter stem in -t-, with nominative -t, genitive -tis, is **caput,** *head,* **capitis,** and its compounds **occiput,** *back of the head* and **sinciput,** *jole.* **lac,** Ne., *milk,* **lactis,** has in old and late Latin nominative and accusative **lacte,** **lact** once in Varro (171, 2); acc. **lactem** occurs in Petronius once and later.

479. (3.) Stems in a labial mute, -b- or -p-, are declined as follows :

mūniceps, *burgess,* stem **mūnicip-,** M., F.

Singular: N. **mūniceps,** G. **mūnicipis,** D. **mūnicipī,** Ac. **mūnicipem,** Ab. **mūnicipe.** Plural : N. **mūnicipēs,** G. **mūnicipum,** D. **mūnicipibus,** Ac. **mūnicipēs,** Ab. **mūnicipibus.**

480. Examples of stems in -b- or -p-, with nominative -s, genitive -bis or -pis, are :

-ebs, -ibis caelebs, *unmarried,* adjective, the only stem in -b-.

——, **-apis dapis,** G., F., *feast,* N. and D. S., and G. Pl. not used (430).

-eps, -ipis adeps or **adips,** M., F., *fat,* no G. Pl. ; **forceps,** M., F., *pincers;* **mūniceps,** *burgher.* **particeps,** *sharing,* and **prīnceps,** *first,* adjectives.

-eps, -upis auceps, *fowler;* **manceps,** *contractor,* **mancupis** or **mancipis.**

——, **-ipis stipis,** G., F., *small change,* no N.

-ops, -opis Ops, F., old **Opis** (Plaut.), *goddess of power ;* **opis,** G., F., *help,* no N., D. once only, Pl. **opēs,** *means* (418).

II. STEMS IN A CONTINUOUS CONSONANT.

481. (1.) Stems in -l- and -n- are declined as follows :

Examples Stems	cōnsul, *consul,* cōnsul-, M.	leō, *lion,* leōn-, M.	imāgō, *likeness,* imāgin-, F.	nōmen, *name,* nōmin-, Ne.
Singular *Nom.*	cōnsul	leō	imāgō	nōmen
Gen.	cōnsulis	leōnis	imāginis	nōminis
Dat.	cōnsulī	leōnī	imāginī	nōminī
Acc.	cōnsulem	leōnem	imāginem	nōmen
Abl.	cōnsule	leōne	imāgine	nōmine
Plural *Nom.*	cōnsulēs	leōnēs	imāginēs	nōmina
Gen.	cōnsulum	leōnum	imāginum	nōminum
Dat.	cōnsulibus	leōnibus	imāginibus	nōminibus
Acc.	cōnsulēs	leōnēs	imāginēs	nōmina
Abl.	cōnsulibus	leōnibus	imāginibus	nōminibus

482. Examples of stems in -l-, with nominative -l, genitive **-lis, are :**

-āl, -alis   sāl, M., *salt*, sometimes Ne. in the singular; no G. Pl. (430).

-el, -ellis   fel (171, 1), Ne., *gall;* mel, Ne., *honey;* plural only **fella, mella.**

-il, -ilis   mūgil, M., *mullet;* pūgil, M., *boxer;* vigil, M., *watchman.*

-ōl, -ōlis   sōl, M., *sun*, no G. Pl. (430).

-ul, -ulis   cōnsul, *consul;* praesul, *head dancer;* exsul, *exile.*

483. (*a.*) Examples of stems in -n-, with nominative **-en,** genitive **-inis,** are :

flāmen, M.,*priest ;* pecten, M.,*comb ;* tībīcen, M.,*piper ;* tubicen, M., *trumpeter ;* sanguen, Ne., *blood.* Many neuters in **-men** (224) : as, certāmen, *contest.*

484. (*b.*) Examples of stems in -n-, with nominative -ō, genitive **-ōnis,** are :

Many masculine concretes : as, pugiō, *dagger ;* words of the agent (211) : as, praedō, *robber ;* and family names : as, Cicerō. Feminine abstracts in -iō (227), and many in -tiō or -siō (228) : as, opīniō, *notion ;* cōgitātiō, *thought.*

485. (*c.*) Examples of stems in -n-, with nominative -ō, genitive **-inis,** are :

Masculines : **Apollō** ; cardō, *hinge ;* ōrdō, *rank ;* turbō, *whirlwind.* homo, M., F., *human being ;* nēmō, *nobody ;* for G. and Ab., nūllīus and nūllō are generally used ; margō, M., F., *brink.* Feminines : grandō, *hail ;* harundō, *reed ;* hirundō, *swallow ;* hirūdō, *leech ;* testūdō, *tortoise ;* virgō, *maiden.* Many in -dō, -dinis (225), -gō, -ginis (226), and -tūdō, -tūdinis (264) : as, cupīdō, also M., *desire ;* imāgō, *likeness ;* sōlitūdō, *loneliness.*

486. sanguĭs, M., *blood,* stem sanguin-, takes -s in the nominative (171, 4). canis, M., F., *dog,* stem can-, and iuvenis, M., F., *young person,* stem iuven-, have the nominative formed like that ot -i- stems. For senex, *old man,* see 500.

487. (2.) Stems in -r- and -s- are declined as follows :

Examples Stems	pater, *father,* patr-, M.	dolor, *pain,* dolōr-, M.	flōs, *flower,* flōr-, M.	genus, *race,* gener-, Ne.
Singular				
Nom.	pater	dolor	flōs	genus
Gen.	patris	dolōris	flōris	generis
Dat.	patrī	dolōrī	flōrī	generī
Acc.	patrem	dolōrem	flōrem	genus
Abl.	patre	dolōre	flōre	genere
Plural				
Nom.	patrēs	dolōrēs	flōrēs	genera
Gen.	patrum	dolōrum	flōrum	generum
Dat.	patribus	dolōribus	flōribus	generibus
Acc.	patrēs	dolōrēs	flōrēs	genera
Abl.	patribus	dolōribus	flōribus	generibus

488. Many stems in -r- ended originally in -s-, which became -r- between two vowels, and in some words in the nominative also (154): as, flōs, M., *flower*, G. *flōsis, flōris; honōs, M., *honour*, G. honōris, N. honor.

489. (*a.*) Examples of stems in -r-, with nominative -r, genitive -ris, are :

-ar, -aris   baccar, Ne., *a plant;* iūbar, Ne., rarely M., *bright sky*, no Pl.

-ār, -aris   lār, M., *household god;* G. Pl. larum ; two or three times larium.

-ār, -arris fār (171, 1), Ne., *spelt;* Pl. only N. and Ac. farra.

-er, -eris   Masculines : acipēnser, *sturgeon;* agger, *mound;* ānser, rarely
             F., *goose;* asser, *pole;* carcer, *jail;* later, *brick;* mulier,
             F., *woman;* passer, *sparrow;* vōmer, *ploughshare.* Neuters :
             cadāver, *corpse;* tūber, *swelling;* ūber, *breast;* verberis, G.,
             lash, no N., generally Pl. ; acer, *maple*, and some other plant names :
             see 573. pauper, *poor*, adjective.

-ter, -tris accipiter, M., *hawk;* frāter, M., *brother;* māter, F., *mother;*
             pater, M., *father.*

-ēr, -ēris   vēr, Ne. ; no Pl.

-or, -oris   aequor, Ne., *sea;* marmor, Ne., *marble;* arbor, F., *tree.*

-or, -ōris   olor, M., *swan ;* soror, F., *sister;* uxor, F., *wife.* Many mascu-
             lines in -or for -ōs (237) : as, odor, *smell;* and in -tor, -tōris
             (205) : as, amātor, *lover.* Also gender comparatives of adjectives :
             as, trīstior (346), M., F., *sadder.*

-ur, -oris   Neuters : ebur, *ivory;* Pl. only ebora ; rōbur, *heart of oak;* Pl.
             rōbora common, rōborum and rōboribus twice each. Also femur
             thigh, femoris or feminis, and iecur, *liver*, iecoris, iecineris,
             or iocineris.

-ur, -uris   augur, M., F., *augur;* furfur, M., *bran ;* turtur, M., F., *turtle-
             dove ;* voltur or vultur, M., *vulture.* Neuters : fulgur, *lightning;*
             guttur, rarely M., *throat;* murmur, *murmur ;* sulpur, *sulphur.*
             cicur, *tame*, adjective.

-ūr, -ūris   fūr, M., *thief.*

490. volucris, F., *bird*, stem volucr-, has its nominative formed like that of -i- stems.

491. (*b.*) Examples of stems in -s-, or -r- for -s-, with nominative -s, genitive -ris, are :

-aes, -aeris aes, Ne., *copper, bronze ;* in the Pl. only aera and aerum are usual.

-ēs, -eris   Cerēs. pūbēs, *mangrown;* impūbēs, *immature*, adjectives ; for
             the last more commonly impūbis, like brevis (630).

-is, -eris   cinis, M., *ashes;* cucumis, M., *cucumber*, also with -i- stem ;
             pulvis, M., *dust;* vōmis, M., *ploughshare.*

-ōs, -oris   arbōs, F., *tree.*

-ōs, -ōris   Masculines : flōs, *flower;* mōs, *custom;* rōs, *dew*, no G. Pl. (430) ;
             lepōs, *grace;* honōs or honor, *honour*, and some old Latin words
             for later -or : as, odōs or odor, *smell* (489). ōs, Ne., *mouth, face*,
             no G. Pl. (430).

-us, -eris Neuters :_acus, *husk;* foedus, *treaty;* fūnus, *funeral;* genus, *race;* glŏmus (134), *clew;* holus, *green stuff;* latus, *side;* mūnus, *gift;* onus, *burden;* opus, *work;* pondus, *weight;* raudus or rūdus, *piece of copper;* scelus, *crime;* sīdus, *constellation;* ulcus, *sore;* vellus, *fleece;* vīscus, *bowel,* usually plural; volnus or vulnus, *wound.* Also Venus, F., and vetus, *old,* adjective.

-us, -oris Neuters: corpus, *body;* decus, *grace;* dēdecus, *disgrace;* facinus, *deed;* faenus, *interest;* frīgus, *cold;* lītus, *shore;* nemus, *grove;* pectus, *breast;* pecus, *flock;* penus, *store;* pignus, *pledge;* stercus, *dung;* tempus, *time;* tergus, *back.* Also lepus, M., *hare.*

-us, -ōris Neuter comparatives of adjectives : as, trīstius (346), *sadder.*

-ūs, -ūris Neuters : crūs, *leg;* iūs, *right,* Pl. iūra, G. Pl. twice only (Plaut.; Cato), no D. or Ab. Pl.; iūs, *broth,* pūs, *pus,* rūs, *country,* tūs, *frankincense,* Pl. only N. and Ac. iūra, &c. tellūs, F., *earth.*

492. vās, Ne., *vessel, utensil,* retains the s between two vowels : G. vāsis, D. vāsī, Ab. vāse, plural N. and Ac. vāsa; the G. vāsōrum, and D. and Ab. vāsis, are formed from an -o- stem, vāso- (401). mēnsis, M., *month,* mēnsis, has its nominative formed like that of -i- stems; G. Pl. mēnsum, sometimes mēnsuum or mēnsium. os (171, 1) Ne., *bone,* ossis, has no G. Pl. in good writers (430): ossium late.

493. The two neuters vīrus, *gall, poison,* and volgus or vulgus, *the crowd,* have -o- stems, except in the nominative and accusative (401), and no plural : thus, N. and Ac. volgus, G. volgī, D. and Ab. volgō. A masculine accusative volgum is sometimes found. The Greek neuter pelagus, *the deep,* has also G. pelagī, D. and Ab. pelagō, Pl. N. and Ac. pelagē (508).

III. STEMS IN -U- OR -V-.

494. Four substantives with stems in -ū- or -v-, grūs, F., *crane,* gruis ; sūs, M., F., *sow, swine,* suis ; bōs, M., F., *ox, cow,* bovis ; and nix, F., *snow,* nivis, follow the consonant declension; also the genitive Iovis, and the other oblique cases of Iuppiter (500). But sūs has in the plural dative and ablative suibus, sūbus, or subus ; bōs has in the plural genitive boum or bovum, rarely bovom (107, *c*), and in the dative and ablative bōbus, or oftener būbus ; nix has no genitive plural in good writers (430): nivium late, once nivum.

SINGULAR CASES.

495. (1.) The nominative singular of gender stems in a mute is formed by adding -s to the stem (422) : as,

rēg-, *king,* N. rēx (164, 1); duc-, *leader,* N. dux (135, 1); custōd-, *guard,* N. custōs (171, 5); aetāt-, *age,* N. aetās (171, 5); caelib-, *unmarried,* N. caelebs (54); mūnicip-, *burgher,* N. mūniceps. hiem-, *winter,* the only stem in -m-, N. hiemps (167) or hiems, also takes -s.

496. (2.) Stems in a continuous consonant, -l-, -n-, -r-, or -s-, and neuters have no nominative suffix (422, 423) : as,

cōnsul-, *consul,* N. cōnsul ; flāmin-, *special priest,* N. flāmen ; agger-, *mound,* N. agger ; iūr- for iūs-, *right,* N. iūs.

For cor, *heart,* see 476; lacte, lac, *milk,* 478; sanguis, *blood,* 486; -s in neuter adjectives, 612.

497. (*a.*) Stems in -ōn- drop -n- in the nominative; stems in -in- for -on- drop -n-, and end in -ō : as,

leōn-, *lion*, N. leō; imāgin- for imāgon-, *likeness*, N. imāgō.

498. (*b.*) Stems of one syllable in -r- for -s- usually retain -s in the nominative: as, flōr- for flōs-, M., *flower*, N. flōs; iūr- for iūs-, Ne., *right*, N. iūs. Some of more than one syllable also retain -s : see 491 ; but in others -s is changed to -r, and in masculines a preceding ō is shortened : as, odōs, *smell*, odor. lepōs, *grace*, retains -ōs.

499. (*c.*) Four stems in -er- for -is- have the nominative singular in -is : cinis, *ashes*, cineris ; cucumis, *cucumber*, cucumeris or cucumis ; pulvĭs, *dust*, pulveris ; and vōmis, oftener vōmer, *ploughshare*, vōmeris.

500. The following have the nominative singular formed from a different stem from that of the other cases (401):

iter, *journey*, itineris, stems iter-, itiner-; Iuppiter (389) Iovis ; supel-lēx, *furniture*, supellēctilis (545); senex, *old man, man of forty or more*, senis, stems senec-, sen-. For sēdēs, *seat*, see 476; vātēs, *bard*, 478. canis, *dog*, N. also canēs (Plaut. Enn., Lucil.), iuvenis, *young* or *middle-aged person* (486), volucris, *bird* (490), and mēnsis, *month* (492), have their nominatives formed like those of -i- stems.

501. An old dative in -ē is sometimes retained in set phrases (507): as, aerē, *money;* iūrē, *right.* See 98.

502. Substantives have rarely an ablative in -ī or -ei like -i- stems : as, capitī (Catull.), *head*, for capite ; dōtei (Plaut.), *dowry*, for dōte. Substantives used as adjectives have sometimes -ī : as artificī manū, *with artist hand ;* but often -e : as. ālite lāpsū, *with winged glide.* For -ē in old Latin there is no certain evidence.

503. Adjectives in the comparative degree have sometimes an ablative in -ī : as, meliōrī, *better*, for meliōre. Adjectives ' of one ending ' with consonant stems (624) have always -e, except vetus, *old*, which has sometimes veterī.

504. Town names and a few appellatives have a locative case in -ī: as, Karthāginī, *at Carthage;* rūrī, *a-field, in the country.*

PLURAL CASES.

505. The nominative and accusative plural masculine and feminine have rarely -īs, like stems in -i- : as sacerdōtīs, *priests;* meliōrīs, *better.* For -ā in neuters in old Latin, see 130, 2.

506. The genitive plural of stems in -tāt- (262) is sometimes -ium, like that of -ī- stems: as, cīvitātium, *communities;* voluptātium, *pleasures* (Cic.); but chiefly in or after the Augustan age. mēnsis, *month*, has mēnsum, but often mēnsuum, sometimes mēnsium. āles, *bird*, has sometimes ālituum in hexameter verse. For the dative and ablative -bŭs, see 2505.

507. Other case forms are found in inscriptions, as follows :

N. MVNICIPES: -ō for -ōs (66): MAIO, i.e. maiōs or maior. G. -es, as early as 218 B.C.: SALVTES ; -us, from 186 to 100 B.C.: NOMINVS ; -u (66): CAESARV. D. -ei: VIRTVTEI, soon after 290 B.C.; HEREDEI, 45 B.C. ; -ē, disappeared sooner than -ei except in set phrases (501), but is equally old: IVNONE ; IOVRE. Ac. -e (61): APICE. Ab. -īd (426): CONVENTIONID, i.e. cōntiōne ; -ei : VIRTVTEI; -ī: HEREDI. Plural: N. -īs: IOVDICIS. G. -om: POVMILIONOM; -ium: MVNICIPIVM. D. -ebus: TEMPESTATEBVS. Ac. -īs: MVNICIPIS.

GREEK NOUNS.

508. Greek appellatives of the consonant declension occasionally retain Greek case endings: as, **lampas**, *torch*, G. **lampados**, Ac. **lampada**. Plural: N. **lampades**, Ac. **lampadas**. **āēr**, *air*, has usually the accusative **āera**, and **aethēr**, *upper air*, always has **aethera**. In the plural nominative and accusative, **cētus**, *swimming monster*, **melos**, *strain of music*, and **pelagus** (493), *the deep*, have **-ē**: as, **cētē**. Genitive **-ōn**, rare: as, **epigrammatōn**, *epigrams*. Dative and ablative **-matīs** from words in **-ma, -matis**: as, **poēmatīs**, *poems* (401).

509. Greek proper names of the consonant declension are usually declined like Latin ones in old Latin and prose. From Vergil and Propertius on, Greek case endings grow more and more frequent, especially in poetry; they are best learned for every name from the dictionary; the commonest forms are:

Genitive **-os**: as, **Pān, Pānos**; **-ūs**, with nominative **-ō**: as, **Mantō, Mantūs**. Dative **-i**, rare: as, **Mīnōidi**. Accusative **-a**, common with names of persons in poetry, not in prose, more common with those of places, and even in prose: as, **Acheronta**; always **Pāna**; **-ō**, with feminines in **-ō, -ūs**: as, **Dīdō**. Vocative: **Pallās, Pallā**; in old Latin the nominative is commonly used instead of the vocative. Plural: Nominative **-es**: as, **Arcades**. Dative **-sin**, rare: as, **Lēmniasin**. Accusative **-as**, very common: as, **Lelegas**; in prose, **Macedonas**; also in words not Greek: as, **Allobrogas** (Caes.).

510. Names in **-eus**, like **Orpheus**, are usually declined like **-o-** stems (449). They have less frequently Greek forms: as, G. **Orpheos**, D. **Orphei** or **Orphī**, Ac. **Orphea**. Accusative rarely **-ēa**: as, **Īlionēa**.

511. Some names in **-ēs** have the genitive in **-is** or **-ī** and the accusative in **-em** or **-ēn** (401): as, **Sōcratēs**, G. **Sōcratis** or **Sōcratī**, Ac. usually **Sōcratem**, also **Sōcratēn**. **Achillēs** and **Ulixēs** have in the genitive **-eī, -ēī**, or **-ī**. Names in **-clēs** have rarely the accusative **-clea**: as, **Periclea**.

512. Some names in **-is** have forms either from a stem in **-id-**, or from one in **-i-**: as, **Paris**, G. **Paridis**, D. **Paridī**, Ac. **Paridem, Parim** or **Parin**, V. **Pari**.

STEMS IN -i- AND MIXED STEMS.

The Third Declension.

Genitive singular **-is**, genitive plural **-i-um.**

513. Stems in **-i-** include both substantives and adjectives, gender words and neuters.

For the gender of substantives, see 570.

514. The nominative of gender stems in **-i-** ends usually in **-s** (or **-x**), sometimes in **-l** or **-r**; that of neuter substantives has no suffix, and ends usually in **-e**, sometimes in **-l** or **-r**.

515. Most stems in **-i-** have as many syllables in the nominative as in the genitive.

Such words are called *Parisyllabic* words, or *Parisyllables :* as, nominative **cīvis,** *citizen,* two syllables ; genitive **cīvis,** *of a citizen,* also two syllables.

516. Stems in **-i-** are declined in the main like consonant stems, but have **-im** in the accusative of some substantives, and **-ī** in the ablative of adjectives, of some gender substantives, and of neuters; in the plural they have **-ium** in the genitive, **-īs** often in the accusative of gender words, and **-ia** in the nominative and accusative neuter.

I.   PARISYLLABLES.

517. (1.) Parisyllabic gender stems in **-i-** with the nominative in **-is** are declined as follows :

Examples Stems	tussis, *cough,* tussi-, F.	turris, *tower,* turri-, F.	amnis, *river,* amni-, M.	hostis, *enemy,* hosti-, M., F.	Stem and case endings
Singular					
Nom.	tussis	turris	amnis	hostis	-is
Gen.	tussis	turris	amnis	hostis	-is
Dat.	tussī	turrī	amnī	hostī	-ī
Acc.	tussim	turrim, -em	amnem	hostem	-im, -em
Abl.	tussī	turrī, -e	amne, -ī	hoste	-ī, -e
Plural					
Nom.	tussēs	turrēs	amnēs	hostēs	-ēs
Gen.		turrium	amnium	hostium	-ium
Dat.		turribus	amnibus	hostibus	-ibus
Acc.	tussīs, -ēs	turrīs, -ēs	amnīs, -ēs	hostīs, -ēs	-īs, -ēs
Abl.		turribus	amnibus	hostibus	-ibus

518. (*a.*) Like the singular of **tussis** are declined parisyllabic names of rivers and places, like Tiberis, Hispalis. Also cucumis, M., *cucumber* (but see 491), and the defectives sitis, F., *thirst,* Ac. sitim, Ab. sitī, no plural ; and vīs, F., *power,* Ac. vim, Ab. vī. Plural (401): N. vīrēs, G. vīrium, D. and Ab. vīribus, Ac. vīrīs or vīrēs. (The D. vī is only found twice ; a N. and Ac. Pl. vīs is very rare.)

519. (*b.*) The following feminines are declined like **turris,** with -im or -em in the accusative, and -ī or -e in the ablative :

| clāvis, *key* | nāvis, *vessel* | sēmentis, *planting* |
| febris, *fever* | puppis, *stern* | strigilis, *skin-scraper* |

So also in the oblique cases, **Liger,** *the Liger.* **Arar,** *the Arar,* has in the accusative -im, in the ablative -e or -ī.

520. secūris, *axe,* messis, *crop,* and restis, *rope,* also have **-im** or **-em** in the accusative, but only secūrī, messe, and reste in the ablative. **canālis,** *conduit,* has only -em in the accusative, and only -ī in the ablative.

521. (*c.*) The following are declined like **amnis**, with -em in the accusative, and -ī or -e in the ablative:

avis, *bird*	**cīvis,** *citizen*	**fūstis,** *club*
bīlis, *bile*	**classis,** *fleet*	**ignis,** *fire*

522. (*d.*) Most parisyllabic stems in -i-, with the nominative in -is, are declined like **hostis**: as,

ēnsis, M., *glaive;* piscis, M., *fish;* aedis, F., *temple,* Pl. *house* (418); **vītis,** F., *vine;* and a great many others. Also gender forms of adjectives in -i- 'of **two** endings' (630), except the ablative singular, which ends in -ī.

523. (2.) Parisyllables in -i- with the nominative in -ēs have their other cases like those of **hostis**: such are:

caedēs, *bloodshed;* **cautēs,** *rock;* **clādēs,** *disaster;* **indolēs,** *native disposition,* no Pl.; **lābēs,** *fall;* **mōlēs,** *pile;* **nūbēs,** *cloud;* **prōlēs,** *offspring,* no Pl.; **pūbēs,** *young population,* no Pl.; **rūpēs,** *crag;* **saepēs,** *hedge;* **strāgēs,** *slaughter;* **subolēs,** *offspring;* **tābēs,** *wasting,* no Pl., feminines; and some others. Masculine: **verrēs,** *boar;* **volpēs** or **vulpēs,** *fox.*

524. **famēs,** *hunger,* has G. twice famī (Cato, Lucil.), Ab. always famē (603), no Pl.; **plēbēs,** *commons,* N. also plēbs or plēps, has G. plēbeī (603), plēbī or plēbis, no Pl.

525. (3.) A few stems in -bri-, -cri-, or -tri-, are declined as follows:

imber, *shower,* stem imbri-, M.

Singular: N. imber, G. imbris, D. imbrī, Ac. imbrem, Ab. imbrī, oftener imbre. Plural: N imbrēs, G. imbrium, D. imbribus, Ac. imbrīs or imbrēs, Ab. imbribus. So also lunter or linter, F. (M.), *tub, boat,* ūter, M., *leather bag,* and venter, M., *belly,* but with only -e in the Ab.; and the masculine of adjectives in -bri-, -cri-, -tri-, N. -er (628); these last have in the Ab. always -ī.

526. (4.) Parisyllabic neuters in -i- with the nominative in -e are declined as follows:

Examples Stems	sedīle, *seat,* sedīli-, Ne.		mare, *sea,* mari-, Ne.		Stem and case endings	
	Singular	Plural	Singular	Plural	S.	Pl.
Nom.	sedīle	sedīlia	mare	maria	-e	-ia
Gen.	sedīlis	sedīlium	maris		-is	-ium
Dat.	sedīlī	sedīlibus	marī		-ī	-ibus
Acc.	sedīle	sedīlia	mare	maria	-e	-ia
Abl.	sedīlī	sedīlibus	marī		-ī	-ibus

527. mare has rarely the ablative mare in verse; in the plural only the nominative and accusative are usual; but a genitive marum is once quoted (Naev.), and the ablative maribus is once used by Caesar.

528. Examples of parisyllabic neuters in -i-, with the nominative in -e, genitive -is, are :

ancīle, *sacred shield ;* aplustre, *ancient ;* conclāve, *suite of rooms ;* īnsīgne, *ensign ;* praesaepe, *stall ;* rēte, *net,* Ab. rēte. Also the neuter of adjectives in -i- ' of two endings ' (630), and some words in -īle, -āle, -āre, originally adjectives (313, 314) : as, būbīle, *ox-stall ;* fōcāle, *neckcloth ;* cocleāre, *spoon.*

II. IMPARISYLLABLES.

529. Sometimes a plural stem in -i- is combined, in the singular, with a stem in a mute, in -l, or -r, or rarely in -s. These mixed stems thus become imparisyllables. Gender stems of this class are like consonant stems in the singular, except the ablative of adjectives, which has usually -ī.

530. Imparisyllabic stems in -i- are declined as follows :

Examples Stems	arx, *citadel,* arci-, F.	pars, *part,* parti-, F.	urbs, *city,* urbi-, F.	animal, *animal,* animāli-, Ne.
Singular *Nom.*	arx	pars	urbs	animal
Gen.	arcis	partis	urbis	animālis
Dat.	arcī	partī	urbī	animālī
Acc.	arcem	partem	urbem	animal
Abl.	arce	parte	urbe	animālī
Plural *Nom.*	arcēs	partēs	urbēs	animālia
Gen.	arcium	partium	urbium	animālium
Dat.	arcibus	partibus	urbibus	animālibus
Acc.	arcīs, -ēs	partīs, -ēs	urbīs, -ēs	animālia
Abl.	arcibus	partibus	urbibus	animālibus

531. Examples of stems in -ci-, with nominative -x, genitive -cis, are :

-āx, -ācis fornāx, F., *furnace.* Many adjectives (284) : as, audāx, *daring.*

-aex, -aecis faex, F., *dregs,* no G. Pl. (430).

-ex, -icis supplex, *suppliant,* Ab. -ī, sometimes -e, G. Pl. supplicum. Adjectives : duplex, *twofold ;* multiplex, *manifold ;* quadruplex, *fourfold ;* septemplex, *sevenfold ;* simplex, *simple ;* triplex, *threefold.* The foregoing have Ab. -ī : as, duplicī ; duplice once (Hor.), septemplice twice (Ov. ; Stat.) ; G. Pl. -ium, Ne. Pl. N. and Ac. -ia.

-ix. -īcis fēlīx, *happy ;* pernīx, *nimble,* adjectives. Also many feminines of the agent in -trīx (205) : as, victrīx, *victorious ;* these sometimes have a Ne. Pl. N. and Ac. : as, victrīcia ; in the G. Pl. they have -ium, or, as substantives, -um : as, nūtrīcum, *nurses.*

-lx, -lcis   calx, F. (M.), *heel;* calx, M., F., *limestone,* no G. Pl. (430); falx, F., *sickle.*

-nx, -ncis   lanx, F., *platter,* no G. Pl. (430); deŭnx, M., *eleven twelfths;* quĭncunx, M., *five twelfths.*

-ox, -ocis   praecox, *over-ripe,* older stem praecoqui- : as, G. praecoquis; rarely with -o- stem (401) : as, praecoquam.

-ōx, -ōcis   celōx, F., *clipper.* atrōx, *savage;* ferōx, *wild;* vēlōx, *swift,* adjectives.

-rx, -rcis   arx, F., *citadel,* G. Pl. rare and late; merx, F., *ware,* N. in old Latin sometimes mercēs or mers.

-ux, -ucis   Adjectives: trux, *savage,* Ab. -ī or -e, G. Pl. -ium; redux, *returning,* Ab. -ī or -e (558); no G. Pl. and no Ne. N. or Ac. (430).

-aux, ——   fauce, F., Ab., *throat,* N. faux once only and late, generally Pl.

-ūx, -ūcis   lūx, F. (581), *light,* Ab. sometimes -ī, no G. Pl. (430).

532. (*a.*) Examples of stems in -di-, with nominative -s, genitive -dis, are :

-ēs, -edis   Compounds of pēs, *foot:* compede, F., Ab., *fetter,* no N., G. Pl. compedium; adjectives: as, ālipēs, *wing-footed,* bipēs, *two-legged,* quadrupēs, *four-footed,* &c., Ab. -ī, Pl. G. -um only (563), Ne. N. and Ac. -ia, rare and late.

-ns, -ndis   Feminines: frōns, *foliage;* glāns, *acorn;* iūglāns, *walnut.*

-rs, -rdis   concors, *like-minded,* adjective, and other compounds of cor, Ab. -ī (559), Ne. Pl N. and Ac. -ia, G. Pl. not usual: discordium, *at variance,* and vēcordium, *frantic,* once each.

-aus,-audis fraus, F., *deceit,* G. Pl. fraudium, later fraudum.

533. (*b.*) Examples of stems in -ti-, with nominative -s (-x), genitive -tis, are:

-ās, -ātis   Arpīnās, *of Arpinum,* and adjectives from other town names; optimātēs, *good men and true,* G. Pl. -ium, less often -um; penātēs, *gods of the household store.*

-es, -etis   Adjectives: hebes, *dull;* teres, *cylindrical,* Ab. -ī (559), no G. Pl., Ne. Pl. hebetia, teretia, late and rare; perpes, *lasting through,* Ab. perpetī, late only; praepes, *swift-winged,* Ab -ī or -e, G. Pl. -um, no Ne. Pl. N. or Ac.

-ēs, -ētis   locuplēs, *rich,* adjective, Ab. usually -e of a person, -ī often of a thing, G. Pl. locuplētium, sometimes locuplētum, Ne. Pl. locuplētia once.

-īs, -ītis   līs, *contention;* dīs, *rich,* adjective, Ab. always -ī (559), Pl. G. -ium, once -um (Sen.), Ne. N. and Ac. -ia. Quirīs, Samnīs.

-ls, -ltis   puls, *pottage,* no G. Pl. (430).

-ns, -ntis   Masculines: **dēns**, *tooth;* **fōns**, *fountain;* **pōns**, *bridge;* **mōns**, *mountain*, N. once **montis** (Enn.); factors of twelve: **sextāns**, *one sixth;* **quadrāns**, **triēns**, **dōdrāns**, **dēxtāns**. Feminines: **frōns**, *forehead;* **gēns**, *clan;* **mēns**, *mind.* Present participles: as, re**gēns**, *guiding.* Many adjectives: as, **ingēns**, *gigantic*, Ab. -ī (559); **Vēiēns**, *of Vei;* compounds of **mēns**: as, **āmēns**, *out of one's head;* of **dēns**: as, **tridēns**, Ab. -ī, as substantive usually **-e**.

-eps, -ipitis Adjective compounds of **caput**, *head:* **anceps** (543), *two-headed*, once older **ancipēs** (Plaut.); **biceps**, *two-headed;* **triceps**, *three-headed;* **praeceps**, *head-first*, old **praecipēs** (Plaut.; Enn.), Ab. -ī (559), no G. Pl., Pl. N. and Ac. **-ia**.

-rs, -rtis   Feminines: **ars**, *art;* **cohors**, *cohort;* **fors**, *chance;* **mors**, *death;* **pars**, *part;* **sors**, *lot*, N. twice **sortis** (Plaut.; Ter.). Adjectives: **cōnsors**, *sharing*, **exsors**, *not sharing*, no G. Pl.; **expers**, *without part;* **iners**, *unskilled*, **sollers**, *all-skilled*, Ne. Pl. N. and Ac. **-ia**.

-x, -ctis   **nox**, F., *night;* Ab. also **noctū** (401); an old adverb form is **nox**, *nights.*

534. (*a.*) Stems in -bi-, with nominative -bs (149), genitive **-bis**, are :

trabs, F., *beam*, older N. **trabēs** (Enn.); **plēbs**, F., *commons*, N. sometimes **plēps**, for the older **plēbēs** (603), no Pl.; **urbs**, F., *city*.

535. (*b.*) Stems in -pi-, with nominative -ps, genitive **-pis**, are :

inops, *poor*, adjective, Ab. -ī (559), G. Pl. **-um**, no Ne. Pl. N. or Ac. (430); **stirps**, F. (M.), *trunk.*

536. Examples of stems in -li-, with nominative -l, genitive **-lis**, are :

-al, -ālis   Neuters, originally adjective (546): **animal**, *animal;* **bacchānal**, *shrine* or *feast of Bacchus;* **cervīcal**, *bolster;* **puteal**, *well-curb;* **toral**, *valance;* **tribūnal**, *tribunal;* **vectīgal**, *indirect tax.* Only N. or Ac.: **cubital**, *elbow-cushion;* **minūtal**, *minced-fish;* **capital**, **capitālia**, *death, capital crime.*

-il, -ilis   **vigil**, *wide-awake*, adjective, Ab. -ī, as substantive **-e** (561), G. Pl. **vigilum** (563), no Ne. Pl. N. or Ac. (430).

537. (*a.*) Examples of stems in -ri-, with nominative -r, genitive **-ris**, are :

-ar, -āris   Neuters, originally adjective (546): **calcar**, *spur;* **columbar**, *dovecote;* **exemplar**, *pattern;* **lacūnar**, *panel-ceiling;* **pulvīnar**, *couch;* **subligar**, *tights;* **torcular**, *wine-press.*

-ār, -aris   Adjectives: **pār**, *equal;* **dispār**, **impār**, *unequal*, for Ab., see 561 ; G. Pl. **-ium**, Ne. Pl. N. and Ac. **-ia**; **compār**, *co-mate*, as substantive has G. Pl. **-um**.

-er, -eris   Adjectives: **dēgener**, *degenerate*, Ab. -ī (559), no Ne. Pl. N. or Ac. (430); **über**, *fruitful*, Ab., -ī, late **-e**, Ne. Pl. **übera** once only (Acc.).

-or, -oris Adjectives: **memor,** *remembering;* **immemor,** *forgetful,* Ab. **-ī** (559), G. Pl. **memorum** (636) once only (Verg.), no Ne. Pl. N. or Ac. (430).

-or, -ōris Adjective compounds of **color**: as, **concolor,** *of like shade,* **discolor,** *of different shade,* both with Ab. **-ī** only; **versicolor,** *pied,* Ab. **-ī,** rarely **-e,** Ne. Pl. N. and Ac. **-ia;** the G. Pl. of these words is not usual, but **versicolōrum** once.

538. (*b.*) Stems in **-ri-,** with nominative **-s** of the stem, genitive **-ris,** are **glīs,** F., *dormouse,* **glīris; mās,** M., *male,* **maris; mūs,** F., *mouse,* **mūris.**

539. The only imparisyllabic stem in **-si-** is **ās** (171, 1), M., *unit, an as,* G. **assis,** with its compounds **bēs,** *two thirds,* G. **bessis,** and **sēmis,** *half an as,* *half,* G. **sēmissis.**

SINGULAR CASES.

540. (1.) The nominative singular of gender stems in -i- is usually formed by adding -s to the stem (422). But many gender substantives have the nominative in -ēs (236, 401): as,

amni-, *river,* N. **amnis; aedi-,** *temple,* N. **aedis; brevi-,** *short,* N. **brevis.** With N. **-ēs: nūbi-,** *cloud,* N. **nūbēs;** for other examples, see 523.

541. Some substantives form the nominative in both these ways: as, **vallēs** and **vallis,** *valley,* equally common; **aedis,** *temple,* later **aedēs;** for **caedēs,** *slaughter,* **clādēs,** *disaster,* and **mōlēs,** *pile,* **caedis,** &c., occur exceptionally.

542. A few stems in **-bri-, -cri-,** or **-tri-,** drop **-i-** in the nominative. The endings **brs, crs, trs,** then change to **-ber, -cer, -ter** (111, *b*): as, **imbrī-,** *shower,* N. **imber** (525).

543. Of gender imparisyllables, some have lost -i- of the stem before -s in the nominative; others have originally a consonant stem in the nominative (529–535).

Thus, **monti-,** *mountain,* and **sorti-,** *lot,* have N. **mōns** and **sors** for an older **montis** and **sortis;** but **dēns,** *tooth,* and **regēns,** *ruling,* have as original stems **dent-** and **regent-.** Adjectives in **-cipiti-** have N. **-ceps** (533).

544. A few adjective stems in **-li-** or **-ri-** drop **-i-** in the nominative without taking **-s** (536, 537): as, **vigili-,** *wide-awake,* N. **vigil; pari-,** *equal,* N. **pār;** so also **Arar** and **Liger.** Three substantives in **-ri-** for **-si-** likewise drop **-i-,** and end in the original **-s** (538): **glīri-** for **glīsi-,** *dormouse,* N. **glīs; mās,** *male;* **mūs,** *mouse.*

545. For **carō,** F., *flesh,* **carnis** (Ab. **-ī,** usually **-e,** no G. Pl) see 135, 2. **supellēx,** F., *furniture,* **supellēctilis** (Ab. **-ī** or **-e,** no Pl.), has the nominative formed from a different stem from that of the other cases (401).

546. (2) Neuter stems in -i- have no nominative suffix, and end in -e for -i- of the stem (107, *b*): as,

mari-, *sea,* N. **mare; brevi-,** *short,* N. **breve.** In some words, originally neuter adjectives in **-āle** and **-āre,** the **-e** is dropped and the **ā** shortened: as, **animāle,** *living thing,* **animal** (536); **exemplāre** (Lucr.), *pattern,* **exemplar** (537). Some neuter adjectives end in **-l** or **-r** (536, 537); and some 'of one ending' end in **-s** (612).

547. The accusative singular of gender substantives usually has -em, like consonant stems (424); but a few substantives with the nominative in -is have -im only, and some have either -im or -em.

548. (*a.*) Accusatives in -im
Are sitim, tussim, vim, *thirst, cough, strength*
And būrim, cucumim. *ploughtail, cucumber*

549. The accusative in -im is found in many adverbs (700): as, **partim,** *in part;* in some adverbial expressions: as, **adamussim, examussim,** *to a* T, **adfatim,** *to satiety,* **ad ravim,** *to hoarseness;* in some names of rivers and cities: as, **Tiberim, Hispalim**; and in some Greek words (565).

550. (*b.*) Six have the accusative commonly in -im, sometimes in -em :
febrim, -em, *fever* puppim, -em, *stern* secūrim, -em, *axe*
pelvim, -em, *basin* restim, -em, *rope* turrim, -em, *tower*

551. Six have the accusative commonly in -em, sometimes in -im :

bipennem, -im, *two-edged axe*	nāvem, -im, *ship*
clāvem, -im, *key*	sēmentem, -im, *planting*
messem, -im, *crop*	strigilem, -im, *skin-scraper*

552. In the ablative, gender substantives have usually -e, and neuters and adjectives have -ī : as,

hoste, *enemy ;* marī, *sea ;* ācrī, *sharp,* brevī, *short,* audācī, *daring.*

553. (1.) Of gender substantives with the nominative in -is, a few have only -ī in the ablative, and many have either -ī or -e.

554. (*a.*) These ablatives have only -ī :
secūrī, sitī, tussī, vī, *axe, thirst, cough, strength*
canālī, cucumī. *conduit, cucumber*

Some names of rivers and cities have only -ī : as, **Tiberī, Hispalī.** The locative also ends in -ī : as, **Neāpolī,** *at Neapolis.*

555. (*b.*) These ablatives of gender substantives with the nominative in -is have -ī or -e :

amne, -ī, *river*	clāvī, -e, *key*	orbī, -e, *circle*
ave, -ī, *bird*	febrī, -e, *fever*	puppī, -e, *stern*
bīle, -ī, *bile*	fūstī, -e, *club*	sēmentī, -e, *planting*
cīvī, -e, *citizen*	ignī, -e, *fire*	strigilī, -e, *skin-scraper*
classe, -ī, *fleet*	nāvī, -e, *ship*	turrī, -e, *tower*

556. A few other words in -is have occasionally an ablative in -ī : as, **anguis,** *snake,* **collis,** *hill,* **fīnis,** *end,* **postis,** *post,* **unguis,** *nail,* &c. **sors,** *lot,* **imber,** *shower,* and **lūx,** *light,* have also -e or -ī ; **supellēx,** *furniture,* has **supellēctilī** or -e ; **Arar** has -e or -ī ; **Liger,** -ī or -e.

557. Neuter names of towns with the nominative in -e have -e in the ablative : as, **Praeneste.** **rēte,** *net,* has only **rēte** ; **mare,** *sea,* has rarely **mare** (527).

558. (2.) Adjectives ' of two endings ' with stems in -i- (630) often have -e in the ablative when they are used as substantives, and sometimes in verse, when a short vowel is needed : as,

adfīnī, -e, *connection by marriage;* aedīle, -ī, *aedile;* familiārī, -e, *friend.*
But some, even as substantives, have -ī : as, aequālī, *of the same age,* cōnsulārī,
ex-consul, gentīlī, *tribesman.* Adjectives of place in -ēnsis (330) usually have
-ī, but sometimes -e : as, Tarquiniēnse. Proper names have usually - e : as,
Iuvenāle.

559. Adjectives 'of one ending' with stems in -i- (632), have commonly
-ī in the ablative. The following ablatives have only -ī :

āmentī, *frenzied,* ancipitī, *two-headed,* praecipitī, *head-first,* concolōrī,
of like hue, concordī, *harmonious,* discordī, *at variance,* sōcordī, *impercep-
tive,* dēgenerī, *degenerate,* dītī, *rich,* teretī, *rounded,* ingentī, *huge,* inopī,
without means, memorī, *remembering,* immemorī, *forgetful.*

560. Present participles, when used as adjectives, have -ī in the
ablative, otherwise -e : as,

ā sapientī virō, *by a wise man;* adulēscente, *youth,* substantive;
Rōmulō rēgnante, *in the reign of Romulus,* ablative absolute (1362).

561. Other adjectives 'of one ending' occasionally have -e in the
ablative when used as substantives or as epithets of persons, or in verse
when a short syllable is needed : as,

cōnsortī, *sharing,* parī, *equal,* vigilī, *wide-awake,* fēlīcī, *happy,* as adjectives ; but cōnsorte, &c., as substantives ; in prose, imparī, disparī, *unequal;*
in verse, impare, dispare. Proper names have -e : as, Fēlīce.

PLURAL CASES.

562. In the plural, gender nominatives have -ēs, rarely -īs or -eis,
and gender accusatives have -īs or -ēs indifferently, sometimes -eis ;
after about 50 A.D., -ēs was the prevalent ending for both cases.
Neuters add -a to the stem, making -ia ; for -iā in old Latin, cf. 2505.

563. In the genitive plural, present participles, some substantive stems
in -nt(i)-, and some adjectives 'of two endings' (631) have occasionally
-um : as,

amantum, *lovers;* rudentum, *rigging;* agrestum, *country folk;* caeles-
tum, *heaven's tenantry.* apis, *bee,* has commonly -um ; caedēs, *slaughter,*
and fraus, *deceit,* have rarely -um. For -um in some adjectives 'of one ending,'
see 636 ; for -būs in the dative and ablative in old Latin, see 2505.

564. Other case forms are found in inscriptions, as follows :

N. without -is : VECTIGAL, i.e. vectīgālis, adjective; -e for -is (66, 41):
MILITARE, i.e. mīlitāris, adjective; -ēs (540): AIDILES, i.e. aedīlis ; CIVES, i.e.
cīvis. G. -us, from 186 to 100 B.C. : PARTVS, i.e. partis. D. -ei : VRBEI.
Ac. -i (61) : PARTI, i.e. partem ; -e : AIDE, i.e. aedem. Ab. -ei : FONTEI;
-e : SERVILE, i.e. servīlī. Plural: N. -ēs : FINES; -eis : FINEIS; -īs : FINIS.

GREEK NOUNS.

565. Greek stems in -i- are usually declined like Latin ones, with the accusative in -im, and ablative in -ī. But the accusative sometimes has -n : as, poēsin,
poetry, Charybdin ; similarly Capyn ; and a vocative occurs : as, Charybdi.
The plural genitive Metamorphōseōn, and as ablative Metamorphōsesin,
occur as titles of books.

CHARACTERISTICS OF STEMS IN -i-.

566. Parisyllables with nominatives in **-is, -ēs**, or **-e**, and a few in **-er** ; and imparisyllables with nominatives in **-al**, and in **-ar** for **-āre**, have stems in **-i-**.

But **canis, iuvenis** (486), **volucris** (490), **mēnsis** (492), **sēdēs** (476), and **vātēs** (478), have consonant stems.

567. Under **-i-** stems may also conveniently be grouped the following classes, which have usually a consonant form in the singular, and an -i- form in the plural :

568. (*a.*) Imparisyllabic adjectives with the genitive in **-is**, except comparatives and the dozen with consonant stems (624), and imparisyllables with a nominative in **-s** or **-x** preceded by any consonant except **p**. But **cōniūnx** (472) and **caelebs** (480) have consonant stems.

569. (*b.*) The following monosyllables : **ās**, *unit, an as*, **faex**, *dregs*, **fraus**, *deceit*, **glīs**, *dormouse*, **līs**, *strife*, **lūx**, *light*, **mās**, *male*, **mūs**, *mouse*, **nox**, *night*, **stirps**, *trunk*, **vīs**, *strength.* Also **fauce**, *throat*, and **compede**, *fetter*, both Ab., no N., and **fornāx**, *furnace.*

GENDER OF CONSONANT STEMS AND -i- STEMS.

570. The gender of many of these substantives is determined by their meaning (404–412) ; that of participles used as substantives follows the gender of the substantive understood ; Greek substantives follow the Greek gender. The gender of other words may be conveniently arranged for the memory according to the nominative endings as follows.

MASCULINE.

571. Imparisyllables in **-es** or **-ēs** and substantives in **-er, -ō, -or**, and **-ōs** are masculine : as,

caespes, *sod ;* **pēs**, *foot ;* **agger**, *mound ;* **sermō**, *speech ;* **pallor**, *paleness ;* **flōs**, *flower.*

572. These imparisyllables in **-es** or **-ēs** are feminine : **merges**, *sheaf,* **seges**, *crop,* **teges**. *mat ;* **requiēs** and **quiēs**, *rest ;* **compedēs**, plural, *fetters ;* **mercēs**, *reward.* **aes**, *copper, bronze*, is neuter.

573. These substantives in **-er** are neuter : **cadāver**, *corpse,* **iter**, *way,* **tūber**, *swelling, truffle,* **ūber**, *udder,* **verberis**, *lash*, genitive, no nominative ; also names of plants in **-er** : as, **acer**, *maple,* **cicer**, *chickpea,* **papāver**, *poppy,* **piper**, *pepper,* **siler**, *osier,* **siser**, *skirret,* **sūber**, *corktree.* **linter**, *tub, boat*, is feminine, once masculine. **vēr**, *spring*, is neuter.

574. Substantives in **-ō**. with genitive **-inis** (485), are feminine ; as, **imāgō, imāginis**, *likeness ;* also **carō. carnis**, *flesh.* and words of action in **-iō** and **-tiō** (227, 228). But **cardō**, *hinge,* **ōrdō**, *rank*, and **turbō**, *whirlwind*, are masculine. **margō**, *brink*, and **cupīdō**, *desire*, are sometimes masculine.

575. These substantives in **-or** are neuter : **ador**, *spelt,* **aequor**, *sea,* **marmor**, *marble,* **cor**, *heart.* **arbor**, *tree*, is feminine.

576. These substantives in **-ōs** are feminine : **cōs**, *whetstone,* **arbōs**, *tree,* **dōs**, *dowry.* **ōs, ōris**, *mouth, face*, is neuter, also **os, ossis**, *bone.*

86

FEMININE.

577. Parisyllables in **-ēs,** and substantives in **-ās -aus, -is, -s** preceded by a consonant, and **-x,** are feminine: as,

nūbēs, *cloud;* aetās, *age;* laus, *praise;* nāvis, *ship;* urbs, *city;* pāx, *peace.*

578. ās, assis, *penny,* is masculine. vās, *vessel, utensil,* and the defectives fās, *right,* and nefās, *wrong,* are neuter.

579. Substantives in **-nis** are masculine; also twenty-nine others in **-is,** as follows:

axis, callis, caulis, anguis,	*axle, path, cabbage, snake*
fascis, fūstis, lapis, sanguĭs,	*bundle, club, stone, blood*
piscis, postis, pulvĭs, ēnsis,	*fish, post, dust, glaive*
torquis, torris, unguis, mēnsis,	*twisted collar, firebrand, nail,* **month**
vectis, vermis, vōmis, collis,	*lever, worm, ploughshare, hill*
glĭs, canālis, also follis,	*dormouse, conduit, ball*
cassēs, sentēs, veprēs, orbis,	*nets, brambles, thorns,* plurals, *circle*
cucumis, and sometimes corbis.	*cucumber, basket*

būrim, *ploughtail,* accusative only, is also masculine. A few of the above are sometimes feminine: as, amnis, anguis, callis, canālis, cinis, finis, fūnis, torquis, veprēs, &c.

580. Four in **-s** preceded by a consonant are masculine: dēns, *tooth,* fōns, *fountain,* pōns, *bridge,* mōns, *mountain;* also factors of twelve: sextāns, *one sixth,* quadrāns, triēns, dōdrāns, dēxtāns; rudēns, *rope,* once. adeps, *fat,* and forceps, *pincers,* are masculine or feminine. stirps, *stock,* is sometimes masculine.

581. calix, *cup,* fornix, *arch,* and trādux, *vinelayer,* are masculine; also substantives in **-ūnx** and **-ex;** except nex, *murder,* and precī, *prayer,* dative, no nominative, which are feminine; also rarely grex, *herd.* cortex, *bark,* forfex, *scissors,* silex, *flint,* and obice, *barrier,* ablative, no nominative, are either masculine or feminine. calx, *heel,* and calx, *lime,* are sometimes masculine, also lūx, *light,* in the ablative in old Latin.

NEUTER.

582. Substantives in **-c, -e, -l, -n, -t,** in **-ar, -ur, -us,** and **-ūs,** are neuter: as,

lac, *milk;* mare, *sea;* animal, *animal;* carmen, *song;* caput, *head;* calcar, *spur;* fulgur, *lightning;* corpus, *body;* iūs, *right.*

583. sōl, *sun,* pecten, *comb,* liēn, *spleen,* rēnēs, *kidneys,* plural, and furfur, *bran,* are masculine. So usually sāl, *salt,* but sometimes neuter in the singular. fār, *spelt,* is neuter.

584. pecus, *beast,* is feminine; also tellūs, *earth,* and the substantives in -ūs which have **-ūdis** (475) or **-ūtis** (477) in the genitive: as, palūs, *marsh;* iuventūs, *youth.*

STEMS IN -u-.

The Fourth Declension.

Genitive singular -ūs, genitive plural -u-um.

585. Stems in -u- are substantive only, and mostly masculine.

586. There are only three neuters in common use, **cornū**, *horn*, **genū**, *knee*, and **verū**, *a spit*. But some cases of other neuters are used: as, ablative **pecū**, *flock;* plural nominative and accusative **artua**, *limbs* (Plaut.); ossvA, *bones* (inscr.).

587. The nominative of stems in -u- ends, including the stem vowel, in -u-s in gender words, and in lengthened -ū of the stem in neuters.

588. Most substantives in -u- are masculines in -tu- or -su-, often defective in case (235). The following words are feminine: **acus**, *pin, needle*, **domus**, *house*, **manus**, *hand*, **porticus**, *colonnade ;* **tribus**, *tribe;* and the plurals **īdūs**, *ides*, and **quīnquātrūs**, *feast of Minerva ;* rarely **penus**, *store*, and **specus**, *cave*.

589. Stems in -u- are declined as follows:

Examples Stems	flūctus, *wave*, flūctu-, M.	cornū, *horn*, cornu-, Ne.	Stem and case endings	
Singular			M.	Ne.
Nom.	flūctus, *a* (or *the*) *wave*	cornū	-us	-ū
Gen.	flūctūs, *a wave's, of a wave*	cornūs	-ūs	-ūs
Dat.	flūctuī, -ū, *to* or *for a wave*	cornū	-uī, -ū	-ū
Acc.	flūctum, *a wave*	cornū	-um	-ū
Abl.	flūctū, *from, with,* or *by a wave*	cornū	-ū	-ū
Plural				
Nom.	flūctūs, (*the*) *waves*	cornua	-ūs	-ua
Gen.	flūctuum, *waves', of waves*	cornuum	-uum	-uum
Dat.	flūctibus, *to* or *for waves*	cornibus	-ibus	-ibus
Acc.	flūctūs, *waves* [*waves*]	cornua	-ūs	-ua
Abl.	flūctibus, *from, with,* or *by*	cornibus	-ibus	-ibus

SINGULAR CASES.

590. In the genitive, the uncontracted form -uis sometimes occurs: as, **anuis**, *old woman* (Ter.). A genitive in -tī is rather common: as, **adventī**, *arrival ;* **ōrnātī**, *embellishment* (Ter.); **senātī**, *senate*. In the dative, -ū is regularly found for -uī in neuters and often in gender words.

PLURAL CASES.

591. In the genitive plural, a shorter form in **-um** is occasionally found: as, **passum,** *steps* (Plaut., Mart.); **currum,** *chariots* (Verg.); EXERCITVM. The quantity of the u and the origin of this ending are uncertain.

592. In the dative and ablative plural, the following retain **-u-bus:** **acus,** *pin, needle,* **arcus,** *bow,* **partus,** *birth,* **tribus,** *tribe.* The following have **-u-bus** or **-i-bus** (28): **artūs,** plural, *joints,* **lacus,** *lake,* **portus,** *haven,* **specus,** *cave,* **genū,** *knee,* **verū,** *a spit.* All other words have **-i-bus** only.

593. Other case forms are found in inscriptions, as follows :·

G. **-uos**: SENATVOS; **-ū** (66) SENATV; **-uus,** in the imperial age (29, 1): EXERCITVVS. D. **-uei** (29, 2): SENATVEI. Ac. **-u** (61): MANV. Ab. **-uu** (29, 1): ARBITRATVV; **-uō,** once, by some thought to be for **-ūd** (426); MAGISTRATVO. Plural: N. **-uus** (29, 1): MAGISTRATVVS.

594. domus, *house,* F., has stems of two forms, **domu-** and **domo-** (401); it is declined as follows: N. **domus,** G. **domūs,** rarely **domī,** D. **domuī** or **domō,** Ac. **domum,** Ab. **domō** or **domū,** Locative **domī,** rarely **domuī.** Plural: N. **domūs,** G. **domuum,** later **domōrum,** D. and Ab. **domibus,** Ac. **domōs,** less commonly **domūs.**

595. Some other substantives have an **-u-** stem in some of their cases, and an **-o-** stem in others : see **angiportus, arcus, caestus, colus, cornū, cornus, cupressus, fīcus, fretus, gelus, laurus, murtus, penus, pīnus, quercus, rictus, tonitrus,** in the dictionary.

STEMS IN -ē-.

The Fifth Declension.

Genitive singular -ĕī, genitive plural -ē-rum.

596. Stems in **-ē-** are substantive only, and feminine.

597. diēs, *day,* is always masculine in the plural, and commonly in the singular; but the feminine is common when **diēs** denotes length of time or a set day. **merīdiēs,** *midday,* is masculine and singular only.

598. The nominative of stems in **-ē-** ends, including the stem vowel, in **-ē-s.**

599. Stems in **-ē-** are of two classes :

600. (1.) Stems of the first class have one or two syllables; there are four of them : **rēs,** *thing,* **spēs,** *hope,* **diēs,** *day,* and **fidēs,** *faith.*

Of this class, **rēs** and **diēs** have a plural throughout; **spēs** has only the nominative and accusative plural, and **fidēs** has no plural.

601. Stems in -ē- of the first class are declined as follows :

Examples Stems	rēs, *thing,* rē-, F.	diēs, *day,* diē-, M.	Stem and case endings
Singular			
Nom.	rēs, *a* (or *the*) *thing*	diēs	-ēs
Gen.	rēī, rēī, *a thing's, of a thing*	diēī, diēī	-ēī, -ēī, -ēī
Dat.	rēī, rēī, *to* or *for a thing*	diēī, diēī	-ēī, -ēī, -ēī
Acc.	rem, *a thing*	diem	-em
Abl.	rē, *from, with,* or *by a thing*	diē	-ē
Plural			
Nom.	rēs (*the*) *things*	diēs	-ēs
Gen.	rērum, *things', of things*	diērum	-ērum
Dat.	rēbus, *to* or *for things*	diēbus	-ēbus
Acc.	rēs, *things*	diēs	-ēs
Abl.	rēbus, *from, with,* or *by things*	diēbus	-ēbus

602. fidēs is declined like rēs ; it has once a genitive fidēs (Plaut.). For rēī, reī, or rēī, and fidēī, fideī, or fidēī, see 127, 4. dies has rarely a genitive diēs (Enn.) or diī (Verg.). spēs has only the genitive and dative spēī in verse. A genitive or dative in -ē is sometimes found : as, rē, diē, fidē.

603. A few cases of other words sometimes follow this class (401) : as, plēbēs (524), *commons*, G. plēbēī or plēbī ; famēs (524), *hunger*, Ab. always famē ; requiēs (477), *rest*, G. requiē (Sall.), Ac. requiem, Ab. requiē ; tābēs (523), *waste*, Ab. tābē, *cor.tāgēs, *contact*, Ab. contāgē (Lucr.), &c.

604. (2.) Stems of the second class are formed by the suffix -iē- or -tiē-, and have three or more syllables.

This class, which is parallel to stems in -iā-, has usually no genitive, dative, or plural. Many stems, especially those in -tiē-, have also a collateral form in -iā-, and the genitive and dative, when used at all, are commonly from a stem in -iā-.

605. Stems in -ē- of the second class are declined as follows :

lūxuriēs, *extravagance,* stem lūxuriē-, F.

Nom. lūxuriēs, *Acc.* lūxuriem, *Abl.* lūxuriē.

606. A few examples of the genitive of these stems are found : as, perniciī, perniciēs, or perniciē, *ruin* (Cic.) ; rabiēs, *fury* (Lucr.) ; aciē, *edge of battle* (Sall., Caes., auct. B. Afr.), faciē, *make* (Plaut., Lucil.), speciē, *looks* (Caes.) ; aciēī (auct. B. Afr.). And a very few of the dative : as, aciēī twice (Caes.) ; perniciēī, perniciī (Nep.) ; perniciē (Liv.).

607. ēluviēs, *offscouring, wash,* has the nominative of the plural, and glaciēs, *ice,* has the accusative of the plural. Five words only have the nominative and accusative plural :

seriēs, aciēs, *row, edge,* speciēs, faciēs, *look, make,* effigiēs, *likeness.*

THE ADJECTIVE.

608. Adjectives are declined like substantives, and it has been shown already how their cases are formed. But they differ from substantives in having different forms in some of their cases to denote different genders; it is convenient therefore to put their complete declension together.

609. Adjective stems end in -o- and -ā-, in a consonant, or in -i-.

610. An accusative plural of a stem in -u-, anguimanūs, *with a serpent for a hand,* is once used (Lucr.). There are no adjective stems in -ē-.

611. Adjectives are often conveniently said to be '*of three endings,*' '*of two endings,*' or '*of one ending.*'

By the 'ending' is meant the ending of the nominative singular: thus, **bonus, bona, bonum,** *good,* and **ācer, ācris, ācre,** *sharp,* are 'of three endings' (409); **brevis, breve,** *short,* is 'of two endings' (410); and **audāx,** *bold,* is 'of one ending' (410).

612. Adjectives 'of one ending' which form a gender nominative in -s, retain the -s irrationally in the nominative and accusative neuter singular: as, N. M. and F. **audāx,** N. and Ac. Ne. also **audāx.**

STEMS IN -o- AND -ā-.

613. Most adjectives with stems in -o- and -ā- are declined as follows:

Example Stems	M. bonus, F. bona, Ne. bonum, *good,* bono-, bonā-.					
	Singular.			Plural.		
	MASC.	FEM.	NEUT.	MASC.	FEM.	NEUT.
Nom.	bonus	bona	bonum	bonī	bonae	bona
Gen.	bonī	bonae	bonī	bonōrum	bonārum	bonōrum
Dat.	bonō	bonae	bonō	bonīs	bonīs	bonīs
Acc.	bonum	bonam	bonum	bonōs	bonās	bona
Abl.	bonō	bonā	bonō	bonīs	bonīs	bonīs
Voc.	bone					

614. Stems in -io- and -iā- have no consonant i in cases ending in -i or -īs (153, 3): as **plēbēius,** *plebeian,* G. S. M. and Ne., and N. Pl. M. **plēbēī,** D. and Ab. Pl. **plēbēīs.**

615. Stems in -ro- preceded by a long vowel retain -us in the nominative singular masculine and are declined like **bonus** (453): as, **sevērus,** *stern;* also

    ferus, merus, *wild, unmixed*   **properus,** *hasty*
    mōrigerus, *complaisant*   **prōsperus,** *lucky*
    praeposterus, *reversed*   **triquetrus,** *three-cornered*

91

616. (1.) Some stems in -ro- preceded by a short vowel end in -r in the nominative singular masculine and have no vocative (454); they are declined as follows:

Example Stems	M. līber, F. lībera, Ne. līberum, *free*, libero-, lībera-.					
	Singular.			Plural.		
	MASC.	FEM.	NEUT.	MASC.	FEM.	NEUT.
Nom.	līber	lībera	līberum	līberī	līberae	lībera
Gen.	līberī	līberae	līberī	līberōrum	līberārum	līberōrum
Dat.	līberō	līberae	līberō	līberīs	līberīs	līberīs
Acc.	līberum	līberam	līberum	līberōs	līberās	lībera
Abl.	līberō	līberā	līberō	līberīs	līberīs	līberīs

Such are: compounds, chiefly poetical, ending in -fer and -ger, *bearing, carrying, having:* as, caelifer, *heaven-upholding;* corniger, *horned;* also the following:

(alter, 618), asper, *other, rough*   satur, sēmifer, *full, half-beast*
lacer, līber, *torn, free*   tener, Trēver, *tender, Treveran*
gibber, miser, *hump-backed, forlorn*

dexter, *right,* has dextera, dexterum, or dextra, dextrum, G. dexterī, or dextrī, &c. sinister, *left,* has usually sinistra, &c., rarely sinisteram (Plaut., Ter.). asper has a plural accusative asprōs (Stat.), and ablative asprīs (Verg.).

617. (2.) Other stems in -ro- have a vowel before r only in the nominative singular masculine -er (454); they are declined as follows:

Example Stems	M. aeger, F. aegra, Ne. aegrum, *ill*, aegro-, aegrā-.					
	Singular.			Plural.		
	MASC.	FEM.	NEUT.	MASC.	FEM.	NEUT.
Nom.	aeger	aegra	aegrum	aegrī	aegrae	aegra
Gen.	aegrī	aegrae	aegrī	aegrōrum	aegrārum	aegrōrum
Dat.	aegrō	aegrae	aegrō	aegrīs	aegrīs	aegrīs
Acc.	aegrum	aegram	aegrum	aegrōs	aegrās	aegra
Abl.	aegrō	aegrā	aegrō	aegrīs	aegrīs	aegrīs

618. Nine adjectives or adjective pronouns have the pronoun form -īus in the genitive singular and -ī in the dative singular, for masculine, feminine, and neuter alike; they are the following:

alius, *another*   ūnus, *one*   alter, *the other*
sōlus, *alone*   ūllus, *any at all*   uter, *which of the two*
tōtus, *whole*   nūllus, *no*   neuter, *neither*

619. Of the above words, those with the nominative in -us are declined like ūnus (638). But **alius** has N. and Ac. Ne. aliud (659); for the G., **alterīus** is mostly used, except in the combination **alīus modī**, *of another sort;* the N. M. is rarely **alis**, Ne. **alid**, D. rarely **alī**. **alter** is declined like **līber** (616), except in the genitive singular **alterīus** (127, 6) and dative **alterī**. For **uter** and its derivatives, see 693.

620. The ordinary genitive and dative of -o- and -ā- stems, from some of the above words, is sometimes found: G. and D. **aliae, sōlae, alterae,** D. **aliō, alterae,** &c.

CONSONANT STEMS.

OF TWO ENDINGS.

621. The only consonant stems of two endings are comparatives (346); they are declined as follows :

Example Stems	M. and F. trīstior, Ne. trīstius, *sadder,* trīstiōr-, trīstius-.			
	Singular.		Plural.	
	MASC. AND FEM.	NEUT.	MASC. AND FEM.	NEUT.
Nom.	trīstior	trīstius	trīstiōrēs	trīstiōra
Gen.	trīstiōris	trīstiōris	trīstiōrum	trīstiōrum
Dat.	trīstiōrī	trīstiōrī	trīstiōribus	trīstiōribus
Acc.	trīstiōrem	trīstius	trīstiōres	trīstiōra
Abl.	trīstiōre	trīstiōre	trīstiōribus	trīstiōribus

622. The ablative rarely has -ī for -e : as, meliōrī (503); the accusative plural masculine and feminine rarely have -īs : as, meliōrīs (505).

623. plūs, *more*, has in the singular only Ne. N. and Ac. plūs, G. plūris, and Ab. plūre. Plural: N. M. and F. plūrēs, Ne. plūra, G. plūrium, D. and Ab. plūribus, Ac. M. and F. plūrēs or plūris, Ne. plūra. complūrēs, *a good many*, plural only, has N. M. and F. complūrēs, Ne. N. and Ac. complūria or complūra, G. complūrium, D. and Ab. complūribus, Ac. M. and F. complūrēs or complūris.

OF ONE ENDING.

624. A dozen adjectives 'of one ending,' mostly words applying to persons, with consonant stems throughout, have no nominative or accusative neuter plural; they are :

caelebs, compos, *unmarried, master of*
*dēses, dīves, *lazy, rich*
particeps, princeps, *sharing, first*

pūbēs, impūbēs, *mangrown, immature*
sōspes, superstes, *safe, surviving*
pauper, cicur, *poor, tame*

625. When these adjectives have a neuter, it is the same as the gender forms, except in the accusative singular ; they are declined as follows :

M. F. and Ne. dīves, *rich*, stem dīvit-.

Singular : N. dīves, G. dīvitis, D. dīvitī, Ac. M. and F. dīvitem, Ne. dīves, Ab. divite. Plural : N. and Ac. M. and F. dīvitēs, G. dīvitum, D. and Ab. dīvitibus.

626. The plural caelitēs, *heavenly, occupants of heaven*, is also declined like the plural of dīves ; the singular Ab. caelite occurs a couple of times. vetus, *old*, G. veteris, is also declined like dīves, but has a Ne. Pl. N. and Ac. vetera ; the Ab. S. is regularly vetere, but veterī is sometimes used.

STEMS IN -i-.

OF THREE ENDINGS.

627. A dozen adjectives with stems in -bri-, -cri-, or -tri-, have a distinctive form in -er for the masculine nominative singular ; they are :

celeber, *thronged*	volucer, *winged*	pedester, *foot-*
salūber, *healthy*	campester, *of a plain*	puter, *rotten*
ācer, *keen*	equester, *cavalry-*	silvester, *woody*
alacer, *lively*	palūster, *of a swamp*	terrester, *land-*

So also celer, *swift*. The names of months, September, Octōber, November, December, are also adjectives with stems in -bri-, but are not used in the neuter. Other adjectives with stems in -bri-, -cri-, or -tri-, have no distinctive form for the masculine nominative singular : as, muliebris, mediocris, inlūstris.

628. These adjectives are declined as follows :

Example Stem	M. ācer, F. ācris, Ne. ācre, *sharp*, ācri-.					
	Singular.			Plural.		
	MASC.	FEM.	NEUT.	MASC.	FEM.	NEUT.
Nom.	ācer	ācris	ācre	ācrēs	ācrēs	ācria
Gen.	ācris	ācris	ācris	ācrium	ācrium	ācrium
Dat.	ācrī	ācrī	ācrī	ācribus	ācribus	ācribus
Acc.	ācrem	ācrem	ācre	ācrīs, -ēs	ācrīs, -ēs	ācria
Abl.	ācrī	ācrī	ācrī	ācribus	ācribus	ācribus

629. In all cases but the masculine nominative singular these adjectives are just like those in -i- ' of two endings ' (630). But the ablative always has -ī, never -e, and the genitive plural always has -ium, never -um. In celer the second e belongs to the stem : M. celer, F. celeris, Ne. celere ; the genitive plural, which is celerum, is found only as a substantive. Most of these adjectives have now and then a masculine in -is, like adjectives 'of two endings' (630), and in old Latin the nominative -er is rarely feminine.

OF TWO ENDINGS.

630. Adjectives 'of two endings' with stems in **-i-** are declined as follows :

Example Stem	M. and F. brevis, Ne. breve, *short*, brevi-.			
	Singular.		Plural.	
	MASC. AND FEM.	NEUT.	MASC. AND FEM.	NEUT.
Nom.	brevis	breve	brevēs	brevia
Gen.	brevis	brevis	brevium	brevium
Dat.	brevī	brevī	brevibus	brevibus
Acc.	brevem	breve	brevīs, -ēs	brevia
Abl.	brevī	brevī	brevibus	brevibus

631. The ablative is sometimes **-e** when these adjectives are used substantively or in verse (558). The genitive plural is rarely **-um** for **-ium** (563).

OF ONE ENDING.

632. Most adjectives ' of one ending' have a consonant form of the stem in the singular, except usually in the ablative (633), and an **-i-** stem in the plural ; they are declined as follows :

Examples Stems	M. F. and Ne. audāx, *bold*, audāc(i)-.		M. F. and Ne. regēns, *ruling*, regent(i)-.	
Singular	MASC. & FEM.	NEUT.	MASC. & FEM.	NEUT.
Nom.	audāx	audāx	regēns	regēns
Gen.	audācis	audācis	regentis	regentis
Dat.	audācī	audācī	regentī	regentī
Acc.	audācem	audāx	regentem	regēns
Abl.	audācī	audācī	regente, -ī	regente, -ī
Plural	MASC. & FEM.	NEUT.	MASC. & FEM.	NEUT.
Nom.	audācēs	audācia	regentēs	regentia
Gen.	audācium	audācium	regentium	regentium
Dat.	audācibus	audācibus	regentibus	regentibus
Acc.	audācīs, -ēs	audācia	regentīs, -ēs	regentia
Abl.	audācibus	audācibus	regentibus	regentibus

633. Present participles have **-ī** in the ablative, when they are used as adjectives, otherwise **-e** (560). For **-ī** or **-e** in other words, see 559. 561. For **-ium** or **-um** in the genitive plural, 563.

634. Most adjectives 'of one ending' in -i- are declined as above (632); some of them have peculiarities in some of their cases, as follows:

635. (1.) **trux** (531), *savage*, has Ab. -ī or -e, G. Pl. -ium, no Ne. Pl. N. or Ac. **redux** (531), *returning*, has Ab. -ī or -e, no G. Pl. or Ne. Pl. N. or Ac. **hebes**, *dull*, **teres**, *cylindrical* (533), and compounds of **caput**, *head*, as **anceps**, (533), *two-headed*, have Ab. -ī, no G. Pl.; a Ne. Pl. N. or Ac. -ia is rare. For **locuplēs**, *rich*, see 533.

636. (2.) The following have -ī in the ablative, but -um of consonant stems in the genitive plural, and no nominative or accusative neuter plural: **inops** (535), *without means*, **vigil** (536), *wide-awake*, **memor** (537), *remembering*, **dēgener**, *degenerate*. **ūber** (537), *prolific*, has Ab. -ī, twice -e, Ne. Pl. once -a (Acc.). Compounds of **pēs**, as, **bipēs** (532), *two-legged*, have a late and rare Ne. Pl. N. and Ac. -ia.

THE NUMERAL ADJECTIVE.

637. Of the cardinals, **ūnus**, **duo**, **trēs**, and the hundreds except **centum** are declined. The other cardinals are not declined.

638. **ūnus**, *one*, is declined as follows:

	Singular.			Plural.		
	MASC.	FEM.	NEUT.	MASC.	FEM.	NEUT.
Nom.	ūnus	ūna	ūnum	ūnī	ūnae	ūna
Gen.	ūnīus	ūnīus	ūnīus	ūnōrum	ūnārum	ūnōrum
Dat.	ūnī	ūnī	ūnī	ūnīs	ūnīs	ūnīs
Acc.	ūnum	ūnam	ūnum	ūnōs	ūnās	ūna
Abl.	ūnō	ūnā	ūnō	ūnīs	ūnīs	ūnīs
Voc.	ūne					

In verse, the genitive singular is often **ūnius**.

639. **duo**, *two*, and **trēs**, *three*, are declined as follows:

	MASC.	FEM.	NEUT.	MASC. & FEM.	NEUT.
Nom.	duo	duae	duo	trēs	tria
Gen.	duōrum	duārum	duōrum	trium	trium
Dat.	duōbus	duābus	duōbus	tribus	tribus
Acc.	duo or duōs	duās	duo	trēs or trīs	tria
Abl.	duōbus	duābus	duōbus	tribus	tribus

640. In dramatic verse, **duō**, &c., is common. In the genitive plural, **duo** sometimes has **duŭm** (462). **ambō**, *both*, is declined like **duo**, but has -ō in the nominative and accusative, and only **ambōrum** and **ambārum** in the genitive plural. For the forms **duo**, **ambō**, see 415; **duōbus**, **duābus**, 464, 442.

641. Hundreds are declined like the plural of **bonus** (613): as, **ducentī, ducentae, ducenta**, *two hundred*, G. **ducentōrum** or **ducentŭm** (462), &c.

642. The adjective **mīlle**, *thousand*, is not declined. The substantive has in the singular only N. Ac. Ab. **mīlle**, or Ab. **mīllī**; plural: N. and Ac. **mīllia (mīlia)**, G. **mīllium (mīlium)**, D. and Ab. **mīllibus (mīlibus)**.

643. Ordinals, as **prīmus**, *first*, and distributives, as **bīnī**, *two each*, are declined like **bonus** (613). But distributives seldom have a singular, and often have the genitive plural -**ŭm** (462): as, **bīnŭm.**

———◆———

THE PRONOUN.

(A.) THE PERSONAL AND REFLEXIVE PRONOUN.

644. The pronoun of the first person, **ego**, *I*, of the second person, **tū**, *thou*, and the reflexive pronoun, **suī, sē**, *himself, herself, itself, themselves*, are declined as follows:

	ego, *I*		tū, *thou*		suī, *self*
	Sing.	Plur.	Sing.	Plur.	Sing. & Plur.
Nom.	ego	nōs	tū	vōs	
Gen.	meī	nostrŭm, -trī	tuī	vestrŭm, -trī	suī
Dat.	mihĭ, mī	nōbīs	tibĭ	vōbīs	sibĭ
Acc.	mē	nōs	tē	vōs	sē
Abl.	mē	nōbīs	tē	vōbīs	sē

645. The nominatives **ego** and **tū**, and the accusatives **mē, tē** and **sē**, have no case ending. The last vowel of **ego** is rarely long in Plautus, long or short in Lucilius. The nominative **ego** has a different stem from that of its other cases, and the plurals of **ego** and **tū** have a different stem from that of the singular.

646. meī, tuī, and **suī**, which are often monosyllables in old verse, were originally the genitive of the neuter possessives, used substantively. An old genitive **mīs** is quoted, and **tīs** occurs rarely in Plautus.

647. The relation of the ending -**bīs** in **vōbīs** to -**bĭ** in **tibĭ** may be due to analogy with **illīs, illī. nōbīs** is formed after **vōbīs**.

648. In old Latin, the ablative was **mēd, tēd, sēd** (426), which forms are also used irrationally for the accusative. But by Terence's time the -**d** was no longer used (143).

649. Older forms for **vestrŭm** and **vestrī** are **vostrŭm** and **vostrī.** The genitive plural was originally a genitive of the possessive: that in -**ī** being the neuter singular, that in -**ŭm** the masculine or feminine plural. In old Latin, **nostrōrum, nostrārum, vostrōrum, vostrārum** also occur.

650. Emphasis is given (1.) by reduplication (189): Ac. and Ab. **mēmē, tētē**, rare; **sēsē**, very common. (2.) by -**te** added to the N. of **tū : tūte.** (3.) by -**met** added to any case but the genitive plural: as, **egomet**; but **tū** has only **tūtemet** or **tūtimet.**

97

651. In inscriptions, the datives MIHEI, TIBEI, and SIBEI occur, so written in verse sometimes even when the last syllable is short; and MIHE, TIBE. Plural: D. and Ab. VOBEIS. Ac. ENOS in an old hymn; SEESE (29,1).

THE PERSONAL AND REFLEXIVE POSSESSIVE.

652. The possessives of **ego, tū,** and **suī,** are **meus,** *mine,* **tuus,** *thine,* and **suus,** *his, her, its, their* (*own*), declined like **bonus** (613), except that **meus** has **mī** in the vocative singular masculine (459); those of **nōs** and **vōs** are **noster,** *our,* and **voster,** later **vester,** *your,* declined like **aeger** (617).

653. Old forms are tuos, tuom, and suos, suom (452). In old verse meūs, mēī, &c., tūōs, tūī, &c., sūōs, sūī, &c., often occur. sōs for suōs, sās for suās, and sīs for suis, are old and rare.

654. Other case forms are found in inscriptions, as follows:

MEEIS, MIEIS, monosyllable; TOVAM; SVEI, SOVOM, SOVO, SVVO, SOVEIS, SVEIS, SVIEIS.

655. Emphasis is given (1.) by -met added to **suō, suā, suōs,** and to **mea** and **sua,** neuter plural: as, **suōmet;** (2.) by -pte, which is oftenest found with the ablative: as, **suōpte.**

(B.) OTHER PRONOUNS.

656. Some pronouns have a peculiar genitive singular in -ĭus and dative singular in -ī, for masculine, feminine, and neuter alike.

These are : **iste, ille, ipse, uter,** and their derivatives. Some other words of a pronoun character also have this form of the genitive and dative: see 618.

657. In verse, the -ĭ- of the genitive is often shortened, and always in utriusque ; but neutrīus is not found with short i. In dramatic verse, the genitive singular of iste, ille, or ipse, is often two syllables.

658. **hĭc, is, quī** or **quis,** and their derivatives have the genitive singular in -ius, thus: huius, eius, and quoius or cuius ; in dramatic verse, these genitives are often one syllable. Their datives are huic for hoice, ēī or ēī, and quoi or cui.

659. Six words have a peculiar neuter nominative and accusative singular in -d : id, illud, istud, quid, quod, aliud, and derivatives. In manuscripts, -t is sometimes found for -d: as, it, illut, istut, &c.; sometimes also in inscriptions of the empire. In hoc for *hod-ce and in istuc and illuc for *istud-ce, *illud-ce, the d has vanished (166, 1 ; 171, 1).

THE DEMONSTRATIVE PRONOUN.

660. The demonstrative pronouns are **hĭc,** *this, this near me;* **iste, istic,** *that, that near you;* and **ille, illic,** *yonder, that.*

661. The demonstrative pronoun **hīc**, *this, this near me*, is declined as follows:

	Singular.			Plural.		
	Masc.	Fem.	Neut.	Masc.	Fem.	Neut.
Nom.	hīc	haec	hoc	hī	hae	haec
Gen.	huius	huius	huius	hōrum	hārum	hōrum
Dat.	huic	huic	huic	hīs	hīs	hīs
Acc.	hunc	hanc	hoc	hōs	hās	haec
Abl.	hōc	hāc	hōc	hīs	hīs	hīs

662. The stem of **hīc** is **ho-, hā-**; to most of its cases a demonstrative **-c** for **-ce** is attached. The masculine and feminine nominative singular and nominative and accusative neuter plural take an **-i-**: **hīc** for *ho-i-ce (108, *a*); **haec** for ha-i-ce (96). **hunc, hanc,** are for *hom-ce, *ham-ce. For the quantity of the first syllable of **huius**, see 153, 2; of **hoc**, 171, 1.

663. Old forms with the full ending **-ce** are rare except after **-s**: Plural Ne. Acc. **haece** (Enn.); G. F. **hārumce** (Cato); also G. **hōrunc, hārunc** (Pl., T.); **hōsce**, D. and Ab. **hīsce** (Pl., T.). After 100 B.C., the full form **-ce** is not found, except occasionally after **-s**: **huiusce, hōsce, hāsce, hīsce.** Before **-ne** interrogative it is retained in the weakened form **-ci-**: as, **hīcine.** But **hīcne, hocne, huicne,** &c., are found, though rarely.

664. The nominative **hic** or **hicine** found in the dramatists and rarely later is probably for *ho-c, *he-c (103, *a*). A nominative plural feminine **haec** is found in writers of all ages. Other and rare forms are: Pl. N. M. **hīsce** (461), D. or Ab. **hibus.**

665. Other case forms of **hīc** are found in inscriptions, as follows:

N. M. HEC, HIC. G. HOIVS, HVIIVS (23), HVIVS, HOIVSCE, HOIVSQVE, HVIVSQVE. D. HOICE, HOIC, HOI, HVIC, HVI. Ac. M. HONC, HOC; F. HANCE; Ne. HOCE, HVC. Ab. M. and Ne. HOCE; F. HACE, oftener than HAC in republican inscriptions; HAACE (29, 1). Loc. HEICE, HEIC. Plural: N. M. HEISCE, HEIS, or HEI, HISCE or HIS; HI, not before Augustus; Ne. N. and Ac. HAICE, HAECE. G. HORVNC. D. and Ab. HEISCE, HIBVS. Ac. F. HASCE.

666. The demonstrative pronouns **iste**, *that, that near you*, and **ille**, *yonder*, are declined alike, as follows:

	Singular.			Plural.		
	Masc.	Fem.	Neut.	Masc.	Fem.	Neut.
Nom.	ille	illa	illud	illī	illae	illa
Gen.	illïus	illïus	illïus	illōrum	illārum	illōrum
Dat.	illī	illī	illī	illīs	illīs	illīs
Acc.	illum	illam	illud	illōs	illās	illa
Abl.	illō	illā	illō	illīs	illīs	illīs

667. The first syllable of iste and ille is often short in the dramatists. Old forms of **iste** are: N. **istus**, G. **istī**, in **istīmodī**, D. F. **istae.** The initial i of **iste** and of **istic** (669), is sometimes not written: as, **sta rēs** (Cic.), **stūc perīculum** (Ter.). Old forms of **ille** are: N. **olus** (81); **ollus** or **olle**, &c.: as, D. S. or N. Pl. **ollī**, D. Pl. **ollīs.** G. **illī**, in **illīmodī**, D. F. **illae.** The dramatists have **eccistam, eccilla, eccillud, eccillum, eccillam,** for ecce istam, &c., and **ellum, ellam,** for em illum, &c.

668. Other case forms of ille are found in inscriptions, as follows:

D. F. ILLAE. Plural: N. M. ILLEI. G. OLORVM (81). D. and Ab. OLLEIS, ILLEIS.

669. istic and illic, compounded of iste, ille, and -ce or -c, are declined alike, as follows:

	Singular.			Plural.		
	MASC.	FEM.	NEUT.	MASC.	FEM.	NEUT.
Nom.	illic	illaec	illuc	illīc	illaec	illaec
Acc.	illunc	illanc	illuc	illōsce	illāsce	illaec
Abl.	illōc	illāc	illōc	illīsce	illīsce	illīsce

670. Rare forms are: N. and Ac. Ne. **istoc, illoc,** G. **illīusce,** D. **illīc,** Ab. F. **istāce, illāce.** Plural: N. M. **illīsce** (461), **illīc,** Ac. **illōsce, illāsce.** Before **-ne** interrogative, **-ce** becomes **-ci-:** N. **illicine, istucine,** Ac. **illancine,** Ab. **istōcine, istācinē.** Pl. Ac. **istōscine.**

THE DETERMINATIVE PRONOUN.

671. The determinative pronoun is, *that, the aforesaid, the one,* is declined as follows:

	Singular.			Plural.		
	MASC.	FEM.	NEUT.	MASC.	FEM.	NEUT.
Nom.	is	ea	id	eī, iī, or ī	eae	ea
Gen.	eius	eius	eius	eōrum	eārum	eōrum
Dat.	ĕī	ĕī	ĕī	eīs, iīs, or īs	eīs, iīs, or īs	eīs, iīs, or īs
Acc.	eum	eam	id	eōs	eās	ea
Abl.	eō	eā	eō	eīs, iīs, or īs	eīs, iīs, or īs	eīs, iīs, or īs

672. is and id (659) are formed from a stem i-, and the other parts from a stem eo-, eā-. The genitive is sometimes written in Cicero and Plautus **eiius**; for the quantity of the first syllable of **eius**, see 153, 2; for **ĕi**, see 127, 3, and 127, 4.

673. In old verse, the genitive singular rarely has the first syllable short. Old and rare forms are: D. F. eae, Ac. M. im or em. Pl. D. and Ab. ĭbus, F. eābus (442). In dramatic verse, eum, eam, eī, eŏ, ea, and eī, eŏrum, eārum, eos, eas, eīs, are often found; also eccum, eccam, eccōs, eccās, ecca, for ecce eum, &c.

674. Other case forms of is are found in inscriptions, as follows:

N. EIS, 124 B.C. G. EIVS, EIIVS, EIIVS or EIIVS (23). D. EIEI, 123 B.C.; EEI, IEI; EI, 123 B.C., and common in all periods. Plural: N. EEIS, EIS, IEIS, till about 50 B.C.; EEI, EI, IEI. D. and Ab. EEIS, EIEIS, IEIS, IS; after the republic, IIS, IIS.

675. A rare and old pronoun equivalent to is is sum, sam, accusative singular, sōs, accusative plural, and sīs, dative plural.

THE PRONOUN OF IDENTITY.

676. The pronoun of identity, īdem, *the same*, is declined as follows:

	Singular.			Plural.		
	MASC.	FEM.	NEUT.	MASC.	FEM.	NEUT.
Nom.	īdem	eadem	idem	eīdem or īdem	eaedem	eadem
Gen.	eiusdem	eiusdem	eiusdem	eōrundem	eārundem	eōrundem
Dat.	eīdem	eīdem	eīdem	eīsdem or īsdem	eīsdem or īsdem	eīsdem or īsdem
Acc.	eundem	eandem	idem	eōsdem	eāsdem	eadem
Abl.	eōdem	eādem	eōdem	eīsdem or īsdem	eīsdem or īsdem	eīsdem or īsdem

677. In manuscripts and editions, the plural nominative masculine is often written iīdem, and the dative and ablative iīsdem. The singular nominative masculine is rarely eisdem or isdem (Plaut., Enn.), eidem (Cic., Varr.), neuter īdem (Plaut.). In verse, eundem, eandem, eīdem, eōdem, eadem, and eīdem, eaedem, eōrundem, eōsdem, eāsdem, are often found.

678. Other case forms of īdem are found in inscriptions, as follows:

N. M. EISDEM, 123 B.C., ISDEM, 59 B.C., both common till Caesar's time; EIDEM; Ne. EIDEM, 71 B.C. D. IDEM. Plural: N. M. EISDEM, ISDEM, EIDEM, till Caesar's time; IIDEM, once only. D. and Ab. ISDEM, very rarely IISDEM.

THE INTENSIVE PRONOUN.

679. The intensive pronoun ipse, *himself*, stems ipso-, ipsā-, is declined like ille (666), but has the nominative and accusative neuter singular ipsum.

680. In dramatic verse, ipse has rarely the first syllable short, and often has the older form ipsus. Plautus has these forms: N. F. eapse, Ac. eumpse, eampse, Ab. eōpse, eāpse, equivalent to ipsa, &c. So reāpse for rē ipsā.

THE RELATIVE, INTERROGATIVE, AND INDEFINITE PRONOUN.

(1.) quī AND quis.

681. The stem qui-, or quo-, quā-, is used in three ways : as a relative, *who, which;* as an interrogative, *who? which? what?* as an indefinite, *any.*

682. (*a.*) The relative **quī,** *who, which,* is declined as follows :

	Singular.			Plural.		
	MASC.	FEM.	NEUT.	MASC.	FEM.	NEUT.
Nom.	quī	quae	quod	quī	quae	quae
Gen.	cuius	cuius	cuius	quōrum	quārum	quōrum
Dat.	cui	cui	cui	quibus	quibus	quibus
Acc.	quem	quam	quod	quōs	quās	quae
Abl.	quō	quā	quō	quibus	quibus	quibus

683. (*b.*) The interrogative adjective **quī, quae, quod,** *which? what?* is declined like the relative **quī** (682).

684. The interrogative substantive has in the nominative singular **quis, quid,** *who? what?* the rest is like **quī** (682).

In old Latin, **quis** is both masculine and feminine, but a separate feminine form **quae** is used three or four times.

685. quis interrogative is sometimes used adjectively with appellatives : as, quis senātor? *what senator?* And quī is sometimes used substantively : as, quī prīmus Ameriam nūntiat? *who is the first to bring the tidings to Ameria?*

686. (*c.*) The indefinite **quis** or **quī,** *one, any,* has the following forms :

quis and **quid** masculine and neuter substantives, **quī** and **quod** adjectives ; feminine singular nominative and neuter plural nominative and accusative commonly **qua,** also **quae.** The rest is like **quī** (682).

687. quis, quem, quid, and quibus come from the stem qui- ; the other parts come from quo-, quā-. quae stands for an older quai (690). For quid and quod, see 659.

688. Old forms of the genitive singular are **quoius,** and of the dative **quoiei, quoiī,** or **quoi,** also in derivatives of quī or quis. A genitive plural **quōiūm** is old and rare. The dative and ablative plural is sometimes **quīs** from quo-, quā-. A nominative plural interrogative and indefinite **quēs** is rare (Pacuv.).

689. The ablative or locative is sometimes **quī,** from the stem qui- : as an interrogative, *how?* as a relative, *wherewith, whereby,* masculine, feminine, or neuter, in old Latin sometimes with a plural antecedent; especially referring to an indefinite person, and with cum attached, **quīcum ;** and as an indefinite, *somehow.*

690. Other case forms of **quī** or **quis** and their derivatives are found in inscriptions, as follows :

N. QVEI, prevalent in republican inscriptions; also QVI ; once QVE.   G. QVOIVS, regularly in republican inscriptions; CVIIVS, CVIIVS, CVIIVS (23), once QVIVS (20). D. QVOIEI, QVOI ; once F. QVAI.   Ab. QVEI.   Plural: N. M. QVEI, but after 120 B. C., occasionally QVI ; QVES, indefinite ; F. and Ne. QVAI.   G. QVOIVM.

DERIVATIVES OF quī AND quis.

691. The derivatives of **quī** and **quis** have commonly **quis** and **quid** as substantives, and **quī** and **quod** as adjectives.   Forms requiring special mention are named below :

692. quisquis, *whoever, whatever, everybody who, everything which,* an indefinite relative, has only these forms in common use: N. M. quisquis, sometimes F. in old Latin, Ne. N. and Ac. quicquid or quidquid, Ab. M. and Ne. as adjective quōquō.

Rare forms are: N. M. quīquī, Ac. quemquem, once Ab. F. quāquā, as adverb quīquī, once D. quibusquibus.   A short form of the genitive occurs in quoiquoimodī or cuicuimodī, *of whatsoever sort.*

aliquis or aliquī, aliqua, once aliquae (Lucr.), aliquid or aliquod, *some one, some* ; Ab. M. sometimes, Ne. often aliquī (689).   Pl. Ne. N. and Ac. only aliqua ; D. and Ab. sometimes aliquīs (6ε8).

ecquis or ecquī, ecqua or ecquae, ecquid or ecquod, *any ?*   Besides the nominative only these forms are found: D. eccui, Ac. ecquem, ecquam, ecquid, Ab. M. and Ne. ecquō.   Pl. N. ecquī, Ac. M. ecquōs, F. ecquās.

quīcumque, quaecumque, quodcumque, *whoever, whichever, everybody who, everything which.*   The cumque is sometimes separated from quī by an intervening word.   An older form is quīquomque, &c.

quīdam, quaedam, quiddam or quoddam, *a, a certain, some one, so and so ;* Ac. quendam, quandam.   Pl. G. quōrundam, quārundam.

quīlibet, quaelibet, quidlibet or quodlibet, *any you please.*

quisnam, rarely quīnam, quaenam, quidnam or quodnam, *who ever ? who in the world ?*   Sometimes nam quis, &c.

quispiam, quaepiam, quippiam, quidpiam or quodpiam, *any, any one ;* Ab. also quīpiam (689), sometimes as adverb, *in any way.*

quisquam, quicquam or quidquam, *anybody at all, anything at all,* generally a substantive, less frequently an adjective, *any at all.*   There is no distinctive feminine form, and quisquam and quemquam are rarely, and in old Latin, used as a feminine adjective.   Ab. also quīquam (689), sometimes as adverb, *in any way at all.*   No plural.

quisque, quaeque, quicque, quidque or quodque, *each.*   Sometimes ūnus is prefixed: ūnusquisque ; both parts are declined.   quisque and quemque are sometimes feminine.   Ab. S. quīque (689) rare, Ab. Pl. quīsque (688) once (Lucr.).

quīvīs, quaevīs, quidvīs or quodvīs, *which you will* ; Ab. also quīvīs (689).

(2.)   uter.

693. uter, utra, utrum, *whether? which of the two?* has the genitive singular **utrīus,** and the dative singular **utrī.**

The rest is like **aeger** (617). **uter** is sometimes relative, *whichsoever,* or indefinite, *either of the two.*

DERIVATIVES OF uter.

694. The derivatives of **uter** are declined like **uter**; they are:

neuter, *neither of the two,* genitive **neutrīus,** always with ī (657). When used as a grammatical term, *neuter,* the genitive is always **neutrī**: as, **generis neutrī,** *of neuter gender.*

utercumque, utracumque, utrumcumque, *whichever of the two, either of the two.*

uterlibet, *whichever you please.*

uterque, *whichsoever, both.*   G. always **utriusque** (657).

utervīs, *whichever you wish.*

alteruter, F. **altera utra,** Ne. **alterutrum** or **alterum utrum,** *one or the other,* G **alterīus utrīus,** once late **alterutrīus,** D. **alterutrī,** Ac. M. **alterutrum** or **alterum utrum,** F. **alterutram** once (Plin.) or **alteram utram,** Ab. **alterutrō** or **alterō utrō,** F. **alterā utrā.** No Pl., except D. **alterutrīs** once (Plin.).

CORRELATIVE PRONOUNS.

695. Pronouns often correspond with each other in meaning and form; some of the commonest correlatives are the following:

Kind.	Interrogative.	Indefinite.	Demonstrative, Determinative, &c.	Relative.
Simple	quis, quī, *who?*	quis, quī, aliquis	hīc, iste, ille is, quisque	quī
Alternative	uter, *which of the two?*	uter, alteruter	uterque	uter, quī
Number	quot, *how many?* (431)	aliquot	tot	quot
Quantity	quantus, *how large?* (613)	aliquantus, quantusvīs	tantus	quantus
Quality	quālis, *of what sort?* (630)	quālislibet	tālis	quālis

THE ADVERB,
THE CONJUNCTION, AND THE PREPOSITION.

I. NOUNS AS ADVERBS.

696. Adverbs, conjunctions, and prepositions are chiefly noun or pronoun cases which have become fixed in a specific form and with a specific meaning. Many of these words were still felt to be live cases, even in the developed period of the language; with others the consciousness of their noun character was lost.

697. Three cases are used adverbially : the accusative, the ablative, and the locative.

698. The rather indeterminate meaning of the accusative and the ablative is sometimes more exactly defined by a preposition. The preposition may either accompany its usual case : as, **adamussim, admodum, īlicō** ; or it may be loosely prefixed, with more of the nature of an adverb than of a preposition, to a case with which it is not ordinarily used : as, **examussim, intereā.** Sometimes it stands after the noun : as, **parumper,** *a little while.* Besides the three cases named above, other forms occur, some of which are undoubtedly old case endings, though they can no longer be recognized as such : see 710.

(1.) ACCUSATIVE.

(*a.*) ACCUSATIVE OF SUBSTANTIVES.

699. domum, *homeward, home ;* **rūs,** *afield ;* **forās,** *out of doors* (***forā-**) ; **vicem,** *instead ;* **partim,** *in part ;* old **noenum** or **noenu,** common **nōn,** for **ne-oenum,** i. e. **ūnum,** *not one, naught, not ;* **admodum,** *to a degree, very ;* **adamussim, examussim,** *to a* T ; **adfatim,** *to satiety ;* **invicem,** *in turn, each other.*

700. Many adverbs in **-tim** and **-sim** denote manner (549) : as, **cautim,** *warily,* **statim,** *at once,* **sēnsim,** *perceptibly, gradually ;* **ōstiātim,** *door by door,* **virītim,** *man by man,* **fūrtim,** *stealthily.*

(*b.*) ACCUSATIVE OF ADJECTIVES AND PRONOUNS.

701. Neuters : all comparative adverbs in **-ius** (361) : as, **doctius,** *more learnedly ;* so **minus,** *less,* **magis,** *more* (363). **prīmum,** *first,* **secundum,** *secondly,* &c.; **tum,** *then* (to-, *that*) : **commodum,** *just in time ;* **minimum,** *at least,* **potissimum,** *in preference,* **postrēmum,** *at last,* **summum,** *at most ;* **versum,** *toward,* **rursum, russum, rūsum,** *back ;* **facile,** *easily,* **impūne,** *scotfree,* **recēns,** *lately,* **semel,** *once* (simili-), **simul,** *together* (simili-). Plural : **cētera,** *for the rest ;* **quia,** *because* (qui-) ; in old Latin **frūstra,** *in vain* (fraud-).

702. Feminines : **bifāriam,** *twofold ;* **cōram,** *face to face* (**com-** or **co-,** ***ōrā-**) ; **tam,** *so* (tā-, *that*) ; **quam,** *as, how.* Plural : **aliās,** *on other occasions.*

(2.) ABLATIVE.

(*a.*) ABLATIVE OF SUBSTANTIVES.

703. domō, *from home,* rūre, *from the country ;* hodiē, *to-day* (ho-, diē-), volgō, *publicly,* vespere, *by twilight,* noctū, *by nights, nights,* lūce, *by light,* tempore, *in times, betimes ;* sponte, *voluntarily,* forte, *by chance ;* quotannīs, *yearly ;* grātiīs or grātis, *for nothing,* ingrātiīs or ingrātis, *against one's will ;* īlicō, *on the spot* (169, 4 ; 170, 2), foris, *out of doors* (*forā-).

(*b.*) ABLATIVE OF ADJECTIVES AND PRONOUNS.

704. Many adverbs in -ō are formed from adjectives of time : as, perpetuō, *to the end,* crēbrō, *frequently,* rārō, *seldom,* repentīnō, *suddenly,* sērō, *late,* prīmō, *at first.* Many denote manner : as, arcānō, *privily,* sēriō, *in earnest.* Some are formed from participles : as, auspicātō, *with auspices taken ;* compositō, *by agreement.* A plural is rare : alternīs, *alternately.*

705. Instead of -ō, neuter ablatives commonly have -ē : as, longē, *far,* doctē, *wisely.* So also superlatives : facillimē, *most easily,* anciently FACILVMED (362). Consonant stems have -e : as, repente, *suddenly.*

706. From pronouns some end in -ī (689) : as, quī, *how ?* indefinite, quī, *somehow ;* atquī, *but somehow ;* quī-quam, *in any way at all.*

707. Feminines : many in -ā : ūnā, *together ;* circā, *around :* contrā, *against* (com-, 347) ; extrā, *outside* (ex, 347) ; in classical Latin, frūstrā, *in vain* (fraud-). So, especially, adverbs denoting the 'route by which :' hāc, *this way ;* rēctā, *straightway.*

(3.) LOCATIVE.

708. In -ī, from names of towns and a few other words : Karthāginī, *at Carthage ;* Rōmae, for Rōmāi, *at Rome :* domī, *at home* illī, commonly illī-c, *there* (illo-), istī, commonly istī-c, *where you are,* hī-c, *here* (ho-) ; old sei, common sī, *at that, in that case, so, if* ; sīc, *so* (sī, -ce).

709. In -bī, from some pronouns : ibī, *there* (i-) ; ubī (for *quobī, 146), *where ;* alicubī, *somewhere ;* sī-cubi, *if anywhere,* nē-cubi, *lest anywhere.*

OTHER ENDINGS.

710. Besides the above, other endings are also found in words of this class : as,

-s in abs, *from,* ex, *out of ;* similarly us-que, *in every case, ever,* us-quam, *anywhere at all.* -tus has the meaning of an ablative : as, intus, *from within, within ;* antīquitus, *from old times, anciently ;* funditus, *from the bottom, entirely.* -ō denotes the 'place to which' in adverbs from pronoun stems : as, eō, *thither ;* quō, *whither ;* illō, or illūc, for illoi-ce, *thither,* after hūc ; hōc, commonly hūc, perhaps for hoi-ce (99) *hither.* -im denotes the 'place from which :' as, istim, commonly istinc, *from where you are ;* illim, commonly illinc, *from yonder ;* hinc, *hence ;* exim, *thereupon ;* also -de : as, unde, *whence* (quo-, 146), sī-cunde, *if from any place,* nē-cunde, *lest from anywhere.* -ter : as comparative (347) : praeter, *further, beyond,* inter, *between ;* denoting manner : ācriter, *sharply ;* amanter, *affectionately ;* rarely from -o- stems : as, firmiter, *steadfastly.*

CORRELATIVE ADVERBS.

711. Adverbs derived from pronoun stems often correspond with each other in meaning and form ; some of the commonest correlatives are the following :

	Interrogative.	Indefinite.	Demonstrative, Determinative, &c.	Relative.
Place	ubĭ, *where ?*	alicubĭ usquam uspiam ubivīs	hīc, istic, illīc ibĭ, ibĭdem	ubĭ
	quō, *whither ?*	aliquō quōlibet quōvīs	hūc, istūc, illūc eō, eōdem	quō
	quorsum, *whitherward ?*	aliquōvor-sum	horsum, istorsum	quorsum
	unde, *whence ?*	alicunde undelibet	hinc, istinc, illinc inde, indidem	unde
Time	quandō, *when?*	aliquandō umquam	nunc, tum, tunc	quom or cum
	quotiēns, *how often ?*	aliquotiēns	totiēns	quotiēns
Way	quā, *by what way ?*	aliquā quāvīs	hāc, istāc, illāc eā, eādem	quā
Manner	utī or ut, *how ?*	aliquā	ita, sīc	utī or ut (146)
Degree	quam, *how ?*	aliquam	tam	quam

II. SENTENCES AS ADVERBS.

712. Some adverbs are condensed sentences : as,

īlicet, *you may go, straightway* (īre licet) ; scīlicet, *you may know, obviously, of course* (scīre licet) ; vidēlicet, *you can see, plainly* (vidēre licet) ; nūdiustertius, *now is the third day, day before yesterday* (num dius, i.e. diēs, tertius) ; forsitan, *maybe* (fors sit an) ; mīrum quantum, *strange how much, astonishingly ;* nesciō quō pactō, nesciō quōmodo, *somehow or other, unfortunately.*

(B.) INFLECTION OF THE VERB.

713. The verb is inflected by attaching person endings to the several stems.

THE STEM.

714. The stem contains the meaning of the verb, and also denotes the mode (mood) and the time (tense) of the action as viewed by the speaker.

715. There are three MOODS, *Indicative, Subjunctive*, and *Imperative.*

716. There are six TENSES in the indicative, three of the present system, *Present, Imperfect*, and *Future;* and three of the perfect system, *Perfect, Pluperfect*, and *Future Perfect.* The subjunctive lacks the futures ; the imperative has only the present.

717. The meanings of the moods and tenses are best learnt from reading. No satisfactory translation can be given in the paradigms, especially of the subjunctive, which requires a variety of translations for its various uses.

718. The verb has two principal stems : I. The Present stem, which is the base of the present system ; II. The Perfect stem, which is the base of the perfect active system.

719. The perfect system has no passive ; its place is supplied by the perfect participle with a form of **sum**, *am*, or less frequently of **fuī**, *am become.*

720. Many verbs have only the present system : as, **maereō**, *mourn;* some have only the perfect system : as, **meminī**, *remember.* Some verbs have a present and perfect system made up of two separate roots or stems : as, present indicative **ferō**, *carry*, perfect indicative **tulī**, and perfect participle **lātus** ; present **possum**, *can*, perfect **potuī**.

THE PERSON ENDING.

721. The person ending limits the meaning of the stem by pointing out the person of the subject. There are three PERSONS, the *First*, used of the speaker, the *Second*, of what is spoken to, and the *Third*, of what is spoken of. The person ending furthermore indicates number and voice.

722. There are two NUMBERS : the *Singular*, used of one, and the *Plural*, used of more than one.

723. There are two VOICES : the *Active*, indicating that the subject acts, and the *Passive*, indicating that the subject acts on himself, or more commonly is acted on by another.

724. Only transitive verbs have all persons of the passive. Intransitive verbs have in the passive only the third person singular, used impersonally ; the participle in this construction is neuter.

725. Some verbs have only the passive person endings, but with a reflexive or an active meaning ; such are called *Deponents:* see 798.

726. The person endings are as follows :

Voice.	Active.				Passive.			
Mood.	IND. & SUB.		IMPERATIVE.		IND. & SUB.		IMPERATIVE.	
Number.	SING.	PLUR.	SING.	PLUR.	SING.	PLUR.	SING.	PLUR.
First person.	-m	-mus	*not used*	*not used*	-r	-mur	*not used*	*not used*
Second person.	-s	-tis	*none,* -tō	-te, -tōte	-ris, -re	[-minī]	-re, -tor	[-minī]
Third person.	-t	-nt	-tō	-ntō	-tur	-ntur	-tor	-ntor

727. In the perfect indicative active, the second person singular ends in -tī, and the third person plural in -runt for an older -ront, or in -re. -re is most used in poetry and history, and by Cato and Sallust; -runt by Cicero, and almost always by Caesar.

728. In the indicative -m is not used in the present (except in sum, *am,* and inquam, *quoth I*), in the perfect or future perfect, or in the future in -bō. -s is not used in es for ess, *thou art,* and in ēs, *eatest* (171, 1).

729. In inscriptions, -d sometimes stands for -t (149, 2) in the third person singular, and sometimes -t is not used: as, FECID, *made,* for fēcit ; DEDE, *gave,* for dedēt or dedit. And other forms of the third person plural of the indicative active are sometimes used: as, Pisaurian DEDROT, DEDRO (with syncope, 111) for dederunt, *gave;* EMERV, *bought,* for ēmērunt; once DEDERI, probably for dedēre (856).

730. In the passive second person singular, Terence has always, Plautus commonly -re ; later it is unusual in the present indicative, except in deponents; but in other tenses -re is preferred, especially in the future -bere, by Cicero, -ris by Livy and Tacitus. The second person plural passive is wanting; its place is supplied by a single participial form in -minī, which is used without reference to gender, for gender words and neuters alike (297).

731. Deponents have rarely **-mino**, in the imperative singular: as, second person, prōgredimino, *step forward thou* (Plaut.) ; in laws, as third person : FRVIMINO, *let him enjoy;* or -tō and -ntō for -tor and -ntor : as, ūtitō, *let him use ;* ūtuntō, *let them use.* In a real passive, -ntō is rare : as, CENSENTO, *let them be rated.*

NOUNS OF THE VERB.

732. The verb is accompanied by some nouns, which are conveniently, though not quite accurately, reckoned parts of the verb; they are:

Three Infinitives, *Present Active* and *Passive*, and *Perfect Active*, sometimes called the *Infinitive Mood*. For the future active and passive and the perfect passive, compound forms are used.

The *Gerund* and the *Gerundive*.

Two *Supines*.

Three Participles, *Present* and *Future Active*, and *Perfect Passive*.

PRINCIPAL PARTS.

733. The several verb stems can readily be found, when once the principal parts are known; these are given in the dictionary.

734. The PRINCIPAL PARTS of a verb are the *Present Indicative Active, Present Infinitive Active, Perfect Indicative Active,* and *Perfect Participle:* as,

PRES. INDIC.	PRES. INFIN.	PERF. INDIC.	PERF. PART.
regō, *rule*	regere	rēxī	rēctus
laudō, *praise*	laudāre	laudāvī	laudātus
moneō, *advise*	monēre	monuī	monitus
audiō, *hear*	audīre	audīvī	audītus

735. The Principal Parts of deponents are the *Present Indicative, Present Infinitive,* and *Perfect Participle:* as,

PRES. INDIC.	PRES. INFIN.	PERF. PART.
queror, *complain*	querī	questus
mīror, *wonder*	mīrārī	mīrātus
vereor, *fear*	verērī	veritus
partior, *share*	partīrī	partītus

DESIGNATION OF THE VERB.

736. A verb is usually named by the present indicative active first person singular: as, regō; laudō, moneō, audiō; or by the present infinitive active: as, regere; laudāre, monēre, audīre. Deponents are named by the corresponding passive forms: as, queror; mīror, vereor, partior; or querī; mīrārī, verērī, partīrī.

737. For convenience, verbs with -ere in the present infinitive active are called *Verbs in* -ere; those with -āre, -ēre, or -īre, *Verbs in* -āre, -ēre, or -īre, respectively. In like manner deponents are designated as *Verbs in* -ī; or *Verbs in* -ārī, -ērī, or -īrī, respectively.

THEME OF THE VERB.

738. The several stems of the verb come from a form called the *Theme.* In primitives, the theme is a root ; in denominatives, the theme is a noun stem.

Thus, **r e g-** in **reg-ō** is a root ; while **vesti-** in **vesti-ō**, *dress*, is a noun stem. The noun stem is sometimes modified in form. Oftentimes the noun stem is only presumed: as, **audi-** in **audi-ō**.

739. Some verbs have a denominative theme in the present system, and a primitive theme in the perfect system, others have the reverse.

740. Most verbs with an infinitive of more than two syllables in **-āre, -ēre**, or **-īre**, or, if deponent, in **-ārī, -ērī**, or **-īrī**, are denominative ; most other verbs are primitive.

Thus, **laudāre, monēre, audīre ; mīrārī, verērī, partīrī**, are denominative ; while **esse, dare, (dē)lēre, regere, querī**, are primitive. A few verbs, however, which have the appearance of denominatives, are thought to be primitive in their origin.

———◆———

ARRANGEMENT OF THE VERB.

741. Verbs are divided into two classes, according to the form of the present system : I. Root verbs, and verbs in **-ere**, mostly primitive ; II. Verbs in **-āre, -ēre**, or **-īre**, mostly denominative.

742. Verbs are sometimes arranged without regard to difference of kind, in the alphabetical order of the vowel before **-s** of the second person singular of the present indicative active, **ā, ē, i, ī**: thus, **laudās, monēs, regis, audīs**, sometimes called the *first, second, third*, and *fourth conjugation* respectively.

———

I. PRIMITIVE VERBS.

743. A few of the oldest and commonest verbs of everyday life have a bare root as stem in the present indicative or in parts of it ; and some of them have other peculiarities ; such are called *Root Verbs*, or by some, *irregular* (744–781). Most primitives are verbs in **-ere**, like **regō** (782).

(A.) ROOT VERBS.

Irregular Verbs.

(*a.*) WITH A PREVALENT BARE ROOT.

744. Primitives with the bare root as present indicative stem in almost all their forms are **sum**, *am*, **dō**, *give, put*, and compounds ; and with the root doubled, **bibō**, *drink*, **serō**, *sow*, and **sistō**, *set*.

III

(1.) sum, *am* (es-, s-).

745. sum, *am,* is used only in the present system **(720).**   The perfect system is supplied by forms of **fuī (fu-).**

PRINCIPAL PARTS.

PRES. INDIC.	PRES. INFIN.	PERF. INDIC.	PERF. PART.
sum	**esse**	**(fuī)**	————

INDICATIVE MOOD.

PRESENT TENSE.

Singular.	Plural.
sum, *I am*	sumus, *we are*
es, *thou art*	estis, *you are*
est, *he is*	sunt, *they are*

IMPERFECT TENSE.

eram, *I was*	erāmus, *we were*
erās, *thou wert*	erātis, *you were*
erat, *he was*	erant, *they were*

FUTURE TENSE.

erō, *I shall be*	erimus, *we shall be*
eris, *thou wilt be*	eritis, *you will be*
erit, *he will be*	erunt, *they will be*

PERFECT TENSE.

fuī, *I have been,* or *was*	fuimus, *we have been,* or *were*
fuistī, *thou hast been,* or *wert*	fuistis, *you have been,* or *were*
fuit, *he has been,* or *was*	fuērunt or -re, *they have been,* or *were*

PLUPERFECT TENSE.

fueram, *I had been*	fuerāmus, *we had been*
fuerās, *thou hadst been*	fuerātis, *you had been*
fuerat, *he had been*	fuerant, *they had been*

FUTURE PERFECT TENSE.

fuerō, *I shall have been*	fuerimus, *we shall have been*
fueris, *thou wilt have been*	fueritis, *you will have been*
fuerit, *he will have been*	fuerint, *they will have been*

SUBJUNCTIVE MOOD.

PRESENT TENSE.

Singular.	Plural.
sim, *may I be*	sīmus, *let us be*
sīs, *mayst thou be*	sītis, *be you, may you be*
sit, *let him be, may he be*	sint, *let them be, may they be*

IMPERFECT TENSE.

essem, *I should be*	essēmus, *we should be*
essēs, *thou wouldst be*	essētis, *you would be*
esset, *he would be*	essent, *they would be*

PERFECT TENSE.

fuerim, *I may have been*	fuerīmus, *we may have been*
fuerīs, *thou mayst have been*	fuerītis, *you may have been*
fuerit, *he may have been*	fuerint, *they may have been*

PLUPERFECT TENSE.

fuissem, *I should have been*	fuissēmus, *we should have been*
fuissēs, *thou wouldst have been*	fuissētis, *you would have been*
fuisset, *he would have been*	fuissent, *they would have been*

IMPERATIVE MOOD.

es or estō, *be thou, thou shalt be*	este or estōte, *be you, you shall be*
estō, *he shall be*	suntō, *they shall be*

NOUNS OF THE VERB.

INFINITIVE.	PARTICIPLE.
Pres. esse, *to be*	*Pres.* See 749
Perf. fuisse, *to have been*	*Perf.* ————
Fut. futūrus esse, *to be going to be*	*Fut.* futūrus, *going to be*

---

746. For the first person **sum,** Varro mentions **esum** as an archaic form. This **e** was probably prefixed by analogy with the other forms ; for the **-m,** and for **es,** see 728. For **sim,** &c., and **siem,** &c., see 841. In the imperfect **eram,** &c., and the future **erō,** &c., s has become **r** (154).

747. The indicative and imperative **es** is for older **ess** (171, 1), and is regularly used long by Plautus and Terence. The **e** of **es** and **est** is not pronounced after a vowel or **-m**, and is often omitted in writing: as **experrēcta es**, pronounced **experrēctas**; **epistula est**, pronounced **epistulaṣt**; **cōnsilium est**, pronounced **cōnsiliumst**. In the dramatists, **-s** preceded by a vowel, which is usually short, unites with a following **es** or **est**: thus, **tū servos es** becomes **tū servos**; **similis est**, **similist**; **virtūṣ est**, **virtūst**; **rēs est**, **rēst**.

748. Old forms are: SONT (inscr. about 120 B.C.); with suffix **-scō** (834), **escit** (for *esscit), *gets to be, will be*, **escunt**; present subjunctive, **siem, siēs, siet**, and **sient** (841), common in inscriptions down to 100 B.C., and in old verse; also in compounds; imperative **estōd** rare.

749. The present participle is used only as an adjective. It has two forms: **sontem** (accusative, no nominative), which has entirely lost its original meaning of *being, actual, the real man*, and has only the secondary meaning of *guilty*, and **īnsōns**, *innocent;* and **-sēns** in **absēns**, *away*, **praesēns**, *at hand*, **dī cōnsentēs**, *gods collective;* also once INSENTIBVS. **sum** has no gerund or gerundive.

750. A subjunctive present **fuam, fuās, fuat**, and **fuant** occurs in old Latin; and an imperfect **forem, forēs, foret**, and **forent**, in all periods. The present infinitive **fore**, *to get to be, become*, has a future meaning. Old forms in the perfect system are FVVEIT (29, 1), FVET; **fūit, fūimus, fūerim, fūerit, fūerint, fūisset** (Plaut., Enn.). **fui** has no perfect participle or supine.

751.   **possum,** *can.*

Principal parts: **possum, posse**; (**potuī**, see 875.)		
INDICATIVE MOOD.		
	Singular.	Plural.
Pres.	possum, potes, potest	possumus, potestis, possunt
Imp.	poteram, poterās, poterat	poterāmus, poterātis, poterant
Fut.	poterō, poteris, poterit	poterimus, poteritis, poterunt
SUBJUNCTIVE MOOD.		
Pres.	possim, possīs, possit	possīmus, possītis, possint
Imp.	possem, possēs, posset	possēmus, possētis, possent
	INFINITIVE.	PARTICIPLE.
Pres.	posse	—

752. **possum** is formed from **pote**, *able*, and **sum**, juxtaposed (166, 2; 396). The separate forms **potis sum**, &c., or **pote sum**, &c., are also used, and sometimes even **potis** or **pote** alone takes the place of a verb; in either case **potis** and **pote** are indeclinable, and are applied to gender words and neuters both.

753. **t** is retained before a vowel, except in **possem**, &c., for **potessem**, &c., and in **posse**; **t** before **s** changes to **s** (166, 2). Old forms are: **possiem**, &c., (748), **potessem, potisset, potesse**. Rare forms are POTESTO (inscr. 58 B.C.), and passives, as **potestur**, &c., with a passive infinitive (1484). **possum** has no participles; the perfect system, **potuī**, &c., is like **fui**, &c. (745).

(2.) dō, *give, put* (d ā-, d a-).

754. There are two verbs **dō,** one meaning *give,* and one meaning *put.* The **dō** meaning *put* is oftenest used in compounds ; the simple verb has been crowded out by **pōnō.** The present system of **dō** is as follows:

Principal parts : **dō, dare, dedī, datus.**

ACTIVE VOICE.
INDICATIVE MOOD.

	Singular.	Plural.
Pres.	dō, dās, dat	damus, datis, dant
Imp.	dabam, dabās, dabat	dabāmus, dabātis, dabant
Fut.	dabō, dabis, dabit	dabimus, dabitis, dabunt

SUBJUNCTIVE MOOD.

Pres.	dem, dēs, det	dēmus, dētis, dent
Imp.	darem, darēs, daret	darēmus, darētis, darent

IMPERATIVE MOOD.

	dā or datō, datō	date or datōte, dantō

	INFINITIVE.	PARTICIPLE.
Pres.	dare	**dāns**
	GERUND.	
Gen.	dandī, &c.	

PASSIVE VOICE.
INDICATIVE MOOD.

	Singular.	Plural.
Pres.	———, daris or -re, datur	damur, daminī, dantur
Imp.	dabar, dabāre or -ris, da-bātur	dabāmur, dabāminī, dabantur
Fut.	dabor, dabere or -ris, da-bitur	dabimur, dabiminī, dabuntur

SUBJUNCTIVE MOOD.

Pres.	———, dēre or -ris, dētur	———, dēminī, dentur
Imp.	darer, darēre or -ris, darē-tur	darēmur, darēminī, darentur

IMPERATIVE MOOD.

	dare or dator, dator	daminī, dantor

	INFINITIVE.	GERUNDIVE.
Pres.	darī	dandus

755. In the present system **a** is short throughout in the first syllable, except in **dās** and **dā.** For **dedī, datus,** and supines **datum, datū,** see 859 and 900.

756. Old forms: **danunt** of uncertain origin (833) for **dant.** From another form of the root come **duis, duit; interduō, concrēduō,** perfect **concrēduī;** subjunctive **duim, duīs** (**duās**), **duit** and **duint** (841), and compounds, used especially in law language, and in praying and cursing; **crēduam, crēduās** or **crēduīs, crēduat** or **crēduit.**

757. Real compounds of **dō** have a present system like **regō** (782); in the perfect and the perfect participle, **e** and **a** become **i**: as, **abdō,** *put away,* **abdere, abdidī, abditus; crēdō,** *put trust in.* **perdō,** *fordo, destroy,* and **vēndō,** *put for sale,* have gerundives **perdendus, vēndundus,** and perfect participles **perditus, vēnditus;** the rest of the passive is supplied by forms of **pereō** and **vēneō. reddō,** *give back,* has future **reddibō** 3 times (Plaut.). In the apparent compounds with **circum, pessum, satis,** and **vēnum, dō** remains without change, as in 754.

(3.) bibō, serō, and sistō.

758. **bibō,** *drink,* **serō,** *sow* (for *si-sō, 154), and **sistō,** *set,* form their present stem by reduplication of the root (189). The vowel before the person endings is the root vowel, which becomes variable, like a formative vowel (824). These verbs have the present system like **regō** (782).

(*b.*) With the Bare Root in parts.

inquam, eō, and queō.

759. **inquam, eō,** and **queō** have the bare root as present stem, in almost all their parts; in a few parts only the root is extended by a formative vowel (829).

(1.) inquam, *say I, quoth I.*

760. **inquam,** *say I,* is chiefly used in quoting a person's direct words; and, from its meaning, is naturally very defective. The only parts in common use are the following:

	INDICATIVE MOOD.			
	Singular.		Plural.	
Pres.	inquam, inquis, inquit	——,	——,	inquiunt
Fut.	——, inquiēs, inquiet	——,	——,	——

761. Rare forms are: subjunctive **inquiat** (Cornif.), indicative imperfect **inquiēbat** (Cic.), used twice each; indicative present **inquimus** (Hor.), perfect **inquiī** (Catull.). **inquīstī** (Cic.), once each; imperative **inque,** 4 times (Plaut. 2, Ter. 2), **inquitō,** 3 times (Plaut.). For **inquam,** see 728.

762. (2.) eō, *go* (ī- for e i-, i-).

	Principal parts: **eō, īre, iī, itum.**	

INDICATIVE MOOD.

	Singular.	Plural.
Pres.	eō, īs, it	īmus, ītis, eunt
Imp.	ībam, ībās, ībat	ībāmus, ībātis, ībant
Fut.	ībō, ībis, ībit	ībimus, ībitis, ībunt
Perf..	iī, īstī, iīt or īt	iimus, īstis, iērunt or -re
Plup.	ieram, ierās, ierat	ierāmus, ierātis, ierant
F. P.	ierō, ieris, ierit	ierimus, ieritis, ierint

SUBJUNCTIVE MOOD.

Pres.	eam, eās, eat	eāmus, eātis, eant
Imp.	īrem, īrēs, īret	īrēmus, īrētis, īrent
Perf.	ierim, ieris, ierit	ierīmus, ierītis, ierint
Plup.	īssem, īssēs, īsset	īssēmus, īssētis, īssent

IMPERATIVE MOOD.

	ī or ītō, ītō	īte or ītōte, euntō

INFINITIVE.		PARTICIPLE.
Pres.	īre	iēns, *Gen.* euntis
Perf.	īsse	itum
Fut.	itūrus esse	itūrus

GERUND.		SUPINE.
Gen.	eundī	
Dat.	eundō	
Acc.	eundum	——
Abl.	eundō	——

763. The passive is only used impersonally, and has a neuter gerundive **eundum** and participle **itum**; but transitive compounds, as **adeō**, *go up to,* have a complete passive: as, **adeor, adīris,** &c. **ambiō**, *go round, canvass,* follows denominatives in -īre (796), but has once or twice the imperfect **ambībat, ambībant, ambībātur** (Liv., Tac., Plin. *Ep.*), and once the future **ambībunt** (Plin.); future perfect **ambīssit, ambīssint**, once each (prol. Plaut.).

764. The ī is weakened from **ei** (98): as, **eis, eit, eite, abeis, abei** (Plaut.); EITVR, ABEI, ADEITVR (inscr. 130 B.C.), VENEIRE (49 B.C.), PRAETEREIS. Before **o, u,** or **a,** the root becomes **e.** For **u** in **euntis,** see 902.

765. Old forms are: **īerō** (Plaut.), **iī, īerant** (Ter.), once each (126); in an inscription of 186 B.C., ADIESET, ADIESENT, ADIESE, and of 146 B.C., REDIEIT (29, 2; 132); INTERIEISTI. A future in -iet, as **trānsiet** (Sen.), is late and rare.

117

766. A double i is found in iissēs and iisset once each (*Ciris*, Nepos), also sometimes in compounds of these forms: as rediissēs, interiisset. Compounds sometimes have it also in the perfect infinitive and in the second person singular of the perfect indicative: as, abiisse, abiistī; also in rediistis once (Stat.). In the first person of the perfect indicative a single long ī is found rarely in late writers in the singular: as, adī (Val. Fl.).

767. A few examples are found of a perfect system with v, as īvī, &c. This form is confined almost exclusively to poetry and late prose.

(*a*) Examples of simple forms with v are: īvisse (Plaut.), īvit (Cato), īvī (Varro), īverat (Catull.). (*b*) Compound forms: exīvī (Plaut.), obīvit (Verg.), subīvit (Stat.); trānsīvisse (Claud. ap. Tac.), inīvimus, trānsīvī, trānsīvimus (Curt.), trānsīvit, trānsīverant (Sen.), exīvit (Gell.). Apparent compounds (396): intrō īvit (C. Gracch., Piso, Gell.).

(3.) queō, *can.*

768. queō, *can,* and nequeō, *can't,* have the perfect quīvī, the rest like eō (762); but they have no imperative, gerundive, or future participle, and the present participle is rare. queō is commonly used with a negative, and some parts only so. Passive forms are rare, and only used with a passive infinitive (1484).

-----

edō; volō (nōlō, mālō) and ferō.

(1.) edō, *eat* (e d-, ē d-).

769. edō, *eat,* has a present system with a formative vowel like regō throughout (782); but in some parts of the present, and of the imperfect subjunctive, parallel root forms are usually found, with d of the root changed to s, and the vowel lengthened (135), as may be seen in the following:

Principal parts: edō, ēsse, ēdī, ēsus.	
INDICATIVE MOOD.	
Singular.	Plural.
Pres. edō, ēs or edis, ēst or edit	edimus, ēstis or editis, edunt
SUBJUNCTIVE MOOD.	
Pres. edim, edīs, edit	edīmus, edītis, edint
or edam, edās, edat	or edāmus, edātis, edant
Imp. ēssem, ēssēs, ēsset	ēssēmus, ———, ēssent
or ederem, ederēs, ederet	or ederēmus, ederētis, ederent
IMPERATIVE MOOD.	
ēs or ede, ēstō or editō	ēste or edite
INFINITIVE.	**PARTICIPLE.**
Pres. ēsse	edēns

770. For **ēs**, see 728; for **edim**, &c., 841. In the passive, the indicative present **ēstur** is used, and imperfect subjunctive **ēssētur**. The perfect participle **ēsus** is for an older **ēssus** (170, 7). Supines **ēssum, ēssū** (Plaut.).

771. comedō, *eat up*, has also the following root forms: **comēs, comēst, comēstis; comēstō; comēsse; comēssēs, comēsset, comēssēmus.** The present subjunctive has also **comedim, comedis, comedint.** The participle perfect is **comēssus, comēsus,** or **comēstus,** future **comēssūrus. exedō,** *eat out,* has **exēst** and **exēsse**; subjunctive **exedint. adedō,** *eat at,* has **adēst.**

772. volō (**nōlō, mālō**) and **ferō** have the bare root in some parts only of the present system; in other parts the root extended by a formative vowel, like **regō** (782). **volō** (**nōlō, mālō**) lack some forms, as will be seen below.

773. (2.) **volō,** *will, wish, want, am willing* (**v o l-, v e l-**).

	Principal parts : **volō, velle, voluī,** ⸺.	
	INDICATIVE MOOD.	
	Singular.	Plural.
Pres.	**volō, vīs, volt** or **vult**	**volumus, voltis** or **vultis, volunt**
Imp.	**volēbam, volēbās, volēbat**	**volēbāmus, volēbātis, volēbant**
Fut.	**volam, volēs, volet**	**volēmus, volētis, volent**
Perf.	**voluī, voluistī, voluit**	**voluimus, voluistis, voluērunt** or -re
Plup.	**volueram, voluerās, voluerat**	**voluerāmus, voluerātis, voluerant**
F.P.	**voluerō, volueris, voluerit**	**voluerimus, volueritis, voluerint**
	SUBJUNCTIVE MOOD.	
Pres.	**velim, velīs, velit**	**velīmus, velītis, velint**
Imp.	**vellem, vellēs, vellet**	**vellēmus, vellētis, vellent**
Perf.	**voluerim, volueris, voluerit**	**voluerīmus, voluerītis, voluerint**
Plup.	**voluissem, voluissēs, voluisset**	**voluissēmus, voluissētis, voluissent**
	INFINITIVE.	PARTICIPLE.
Pres.	**velle**	**volēns**
Perf.	**voluisse**	

774. volo for **volō** is rare (2443). **volt** and **voltis** became **vult** and **vultis** about the time of Augustus (141). For **volumus,** see 142; **velim,** &c., 841; **vellem,** &c., **velle,** 166, 8. **sīs,** *an thou wilt,* is common for **sī vīs** (Plaut. Ter., Cic., Liv.). **sultis,** *an 't please you,* is used by Plautus for **sī voltis.**

775. nōlō, *won't*, is formed from ne-, *not*, and volō, juxtaposed, and mālō, *like better*, abbreviated from mávolō for *magsvolo (779, 170, 2).

776.   nōlō, *won't, don't want, object, am not willing*.

Principal parts : nōlō, nōlle, nōluī, ——.

		INDICATIVE MOOD.	
		Singular.	Plural.
Pres.		nōlō, nōn vīs, nōn volt or vult	nōlumus, nōn voltis or vultis, nōlunt
Imp.		nōlēbam, nōlēbās, nōlēbat	nōlēbāmus, nōlēbātis, nōlēbant
Fut.		——, nōlēs, nōlet	nōlēmus, nōlētis, nōlent
		SUBJUNCTIVE MOOD.	
Pres.		nōlim, nōlīs, nōlit	nōlīmus, nōlītis, nōlint
Imp.		nōllem, nōllēs, nōllet	nōllēmus, nōllētis, nōllent
		IMPERATIVE MOOD.	
		nōlī or nōlītō, nōlītō	nōlīte or nōlītōte, nōluntō

	INFINITIVE.	PARTICIPLE.
Pres.	nōlle	——

777. nevīs and nevolt, from ne-, *not*, are found in Plautus. nōlō has usually no participles, but oblique cases of nōlēns are used a few times by post-Augustan writers (Cels., Luc., Quintil., Ta., Juv., Mart., Plin.). The perfect system, nōluī, &c., is like that of volō (772).

778.   mālō, *like better, choose rather*.

Principal parts : mālō, mālle, māluī, ——.

	INDICATIVE MOOD.	
	Singular.	Plural.
Pres.	mālō, māvīs, māvolt or māvult	mālumus, māvoltis or māvultis, mālunt
Imp.	mālēbam, mālēbās, mālēbat	mālēbāmus, mālēbātis, mālēbant
Fut.	——, mālēs, mālet	mālēmus, mālētis, mālent
	SUBJUNCTIVE MOOD.	
Pres.	mālim, mālīs, mālit	mālīmus, mālītis, mālint
Imp.	māllem, māllēs, māllet	māllēmus, māllētis, māllent

	INFINITIVE.	PARTICIPLE.
Pres.	mālle	——

779. Old forms are māvolō, māvolunt; māvolet; māvelim, māvelīs, māvelit; māvellem. The perfect system, māluī, &c., is like that of volō (772).

(3.) ferō, *carry* (fer-).

780. ferō, *carry,* is used only in the present system (720). The other parts are supplied by forms of **tollō,** *lift* (tol-, tlā-). The present system of **ferō** is as follows:

Principal parts : **ferō, ferre** ; (**tulī, lātus**).

ACTIVE VOICE.

INDICATIVE MOOD.

	Singular.	Plural.
Pres.	ferō, fers, fert	ferimus, fertis, ferunt
Imp.	ferēbam, ferēbās, ferēbat	ferēbāmus, ferēbātis, ferēbant
Fut.	feram, ferēs, feret	ferēmus, ferētis, ferent

SUBJUNCTIVE MOOD.

Pres.	feram, ferās, ferat	ferāmus, ferātis, ferant
Imp.	ferrem, ferrēs, ferret	ferrēmus, ferrētis, ferrent

IMPERATIVE MOOD.

	fer or fertō, fertō	ferte or fertōte, feruntō

	INFINITIVE.	PARTICIPLE.
Pres.	ferre	ferēns
	GERUND.	
Gen.	ferendī, &c.	

PASSIVE VOICE.

INDICATIVE MOOD.

	Singular.	Plural.
Pres.	feror, ferris or -re, fertur	ferimur, feriminī, feruntur
Imp.	ferēbar, ferēbāre or -ris, ferēbātur	ferēbāmur, ferēbāminī, ferēbantur
Fut.	ferar, ferēre or -ris, ferētur	ferēmur, ferēminī, ferentur

SUBJUNCTIVE MOOD.

Pres.	ferar, ferāre or -ris, ferātur	ferāmur, ferāminī, ferantur
Imp.	ferrer, ferrēre or -ris, ferrētur	ferrēmur, ferrēminī, ferrentur

IMPERATIVE MOOD.

	ferre or fertor, fertor	feriminī, feruntor

	INFINITIVE.	GERUNDIVE.
Pres.	ferrī	ferendus

781. For **tulī,** see 860; the full form **tetulī,** &c., is found in old Latin, and TOLI, &c., in inscriptions; the compound with **re-** is **rettulī** for *retetulī (861). For the participle **lātus,** see 169, 1.

(B.) VERBS IN -ere.
The Third Conjugation.

782.   rēgō, *rule.*

PRINCIPAL PARTS.

PRES. INDIC.	PRES. INFIN.	PERF. INDIC.	PERF. PART.
regō	regere	rēxī	rēctus

ACTIVE VOICE.
INDICATIVE MOOD.
PRESENT TENSE.

Singular.	Plural.
regō, *I rule,* or *am ruling*	regimus, *we rule,* or *are ruling*
regis, *thou rulest,* or *art ruling*	regitis, *you rule,* or *are ruling*
regit, *he rules,* or *is ruling*	regunt, *they rule,* or *are ruling*

IMPERFECT TENSE.

regēbam, *I was ruling,* or *I ruled*	regēbāmus, *we were ruling,* or *we ruled*
regēbās, *thou wert ruling,* or *thou ruledst*	regēbātis, *you were ruling,* or *you ruled*
regēbat, *he was ruling,* or *he ruled*	regēbant, *they were ruling,* or *they ruled*

FUTURE TENSE.

regam, *I shall rule*	regēmus, *we shall rule*
regēs, *thou wilt rule*	regētis, *you will rule*
reget, *he will rule*	regent, *they will rule*

PERFECT TENSE.

rēxī, *I have ruled,* or *I ruled*	rēximus, *we have ruled,* or *we ruled*
rēxistī, *thou hast ruled,* or *thou ruledst*	rēxistis, *you have ruled,* or *you ruled*
rēxit, *he has ruled,* or *he ruled*	rēxērunt or -re, *they have ruled,* or *they ruled*

PLUPERFECT TENSE.

rēxeram, *I had ruled*	rēxerāmus, *we had ruled*
rēxerās, *thou hadst ruled*	rēxerātis, *you had ruled*
rēxerat, *he had ruled*	rēxerant, *they had ruled*

FUTURE PERFECT TENSE.

rēxerō, *I shall have ruled*	rēxerimus, *we shall have ruled*
rēxeris, *thou wilt have ruled*	rēxeritis, *you will have ruled*
rēxerit, *he will have ruled*	rēxerint, *they will have ruled*

SUBJUNCTIVE MOOD.

PRESENT TENSE.

Singular.	Plural.
regam, *may I rule*	regāmus, *let us rule*
regās, *mayst thou rule*	regātis, *may you rule*
regat, *let him rule*	regant, *let them rule*

IMPERFECT TENSE.

regerem, *I should rule*	regerēmus, *we should rule*
regerēs, *thou wouldst rule*	regerētis, *you would rule*
regeret, *he would rule*	regerent, *they would rule*

PERFECT TENSE.

rēxerim, *I may have ruled*	rēxerīmus, *we may have ruled*
rēxerīs, *thou mayst have ruled*	rēxerītis, *you may have ruled*
rēxerit, *he may have ruled*	rēxerint, *they may have ruled*

PLUPERFECT TENSE.

rēxissem, *I should have ruled*	rēxissēmus, *we should have ruled*
rēxissēs, *thou wouldst have ruled*	rēxissētis, *you would have ruled*
rēxisset, *he would have ruled*	rēxissent, *they would have ruled*

IMPERATIVE MOOD.

rege or regitō, *rule, thou shalt rule*	regite or regitōte, *rule, you shall rule*
regitō, *he shall rule*	reguntō, *they shall rule*

NOUNS OF THE VERB.

INFINITIVE.		PARTICIPLE.	
Pres.	regere, *to rule*	*Pres.*	regēns, *ruling*
Perf.	rēxisse, *to have ruled*		
Fut.	rēctūrus esse, *to be going to rule*	*Fut.*	rēctūrus, *going to rule*

GERUND.		SUPINE.	
Gen.	regendī, *of ruling*		
Dat.	regendō, *for ruling*		
Acc.	regendum, *ruling*	*Acc.*	*rēctum, *to rule*, not used
Abl.	regendē, *by ruling*	*Abl.*	*rēctū, *in ruling*, not used

VERBS IN -ere.

The Third Conjugation.

783.   **regor,** *am ruled.*

PASSIVE VOICE.

INDICATIVE MOOD.

PRESENT TENSE.

Singular.	Plural.
regor, *I am ruled*	**regimur,** *we are ruled*
regeris or **-re,** *thou art ruled*	**regiminī,** *you are ruled*
regitur, *he is ruled*	**reguntur,** *they are ruled*

IMPERFECT TENSE.

regēbar, *I was ruled*	**regēbāmur,** *we were ruled*
regēbāre or **-ris,** *thou wert ruled*	**regēbāminī,** *you were ruled*
regēbātur, *he was ruled*	**regēbantur,** *they were ruled*

FUTURE TENSE.

regar, *I shall be ruled*	**regēmur,** *we shall be ruled*
regēre or **-ris,** *thou wilt be ruled*	**regēminī,** *you will be ruled*
regētur, *he will be ruled*	**regentur,** *they will be ruled*

PERFECT TENSE.

rēctus sum, *I have been,* or *was ruled*	**rēctī sumus,** *we have been,* or *were ruled*
rēctus es, *thou hast been,* or *wert ruled*	**rēctī estis,** *you have been,* or *were ruled*
rēctus est, *he has been,* or *was ruled*	**rēctī sunt,** *they have been,* or *were ruled*

PLUPERFECT TENSE.

rēctus eram, *I had been ruled*	**rēctī erāmus,** *we had been ruled*
rēctus erās, *thou hadst been ruled*	**rēctī erātis,** *you had been ruled*
rēctus erat, *he had been ruled*	**rēctī erant,** *they had been ruled*

FUTURE PERFECT TENSE.

rēctus erō, *I shall have been ruled*	**rēctī erimus,** *we shall have been ruled*
rēctus eris, *thou wilt have been ruled*	**rēctī eritis,** *you will have been ruled*
rēctus erit, *he will have been ruled*	**rēctī erunt,** *they will have been ruled*

SUBJUNCTIVE MOOD.

PRESENT TENSE.

Singular.	Plural.
regar, *may I be ruled*	regāmur, *may we be ruled*
regāre or -ris, *mayst thou be ruled*	regāminī, *may you be ruled*
regātur, *let him be ruled*	regantur, *let them be ruled*

IMPERFECT TENSE.

regerer, *I should be ruled*	regerēmur, *we should be ruled*
regerēre or -ris, *thou wouldst be ruled*	regerēminī, *you would be ruled*
regerētur, *he would be ruled*	regerentur, *they would be ruled*

PERFECT TENSE.

rēctus sim, *I may have been ruled*	rēctī sīmus, *we may have been ruled*
rēctus sīs, *thou mayst have been ruled*	rēctī sītis, *you may have been ruled*
rēctus sit, *he may have been ruled*	rēctī sint, *they may have been ruled*

PLUPERFECT TENSE.

rēctus essem, *I should have been ruled*	rēctī essēmus, *we should have been ruled*
rēctus essēs, *thou wouldst have been ruled*	rēctī essētis, *you would have been ruled*
rēctus esset, *he would have been ruled*	rēctī essent, *they would have been ruled*

IMPERATIVE MOOD.

regere or regitor, *be ruled, thou shalt be ruled*	regiminī, *be ruled*
regitor, *he shall be ruled*	reguntor, *they shall be ruled*

NOUNS OF THE VERB.

INFINITIVE.	GERUNDIVE.
Pres. regī, *to be ruled*	regendus, *to be ruled*
Perf. rēctus esse, *to have been ruled*	
Fut. *rēctum īrī, *to be going to be ruled*, not used (2273)	PERFECT PARTICIPLE.
	rēctus, *ruled*

VERBS IN -iō, -ere.

784. Verbs in -iō, -ere, as capiō, capere, *take* (c a p-), drop an l in some forms of the present and imperfect. The present system is as follows :

<table>
<tr><td colspan="3" align="center">ACTIVE VOICE.</td></tr>
<tr><td colspan="3" align="center">INDICATIVE MOOD.</td></tr>
<tr><td></td><td align="center">Singular.</td><td align="center">Plural.</td></tr>
<tr><td>*Pres.*</td><td>capiō, capis, capit</td><td>capimus, capitis, capiunt</td></tr>
<tr><td>*Imp.*</td><td>capiēbam, capiēbās, ca-
piēbat</td><td>capiēbāmus, capiēbātis, capiē-
bant</td></tr>
<tr><td>*Fut.*</td><td>capiam, capiēs, capiet</td><td>capiēmus, capiētis, capient</td></tr>
<tr><td colspan="3" align="center">SUBJUNCTIVE MOOD.</td></tr>
<tr><td>*Pres.*</td><td>capiam, capiās, capiat</td><td>capiāmus, capiātis, capiant</td></tr>
<tr><td>*Imp.*</td><td>caperem, caperēs, caperet</td><td>caperēmus, caperētis, caperent</td></tr>
<tr><td colspan="3" align="center">IMPERATIVE MOOD.</td></tr>
<tr><td colspan="3" align="center">cape or capitō, capitō | capite or capitōte, capiuntō</td></tr>
<tr><td></td><td align="center">INFINITIVE.</td><td align="center">PARTICIPLE.</td></tr>
<tr><td>*Pres.*</td><td>capere</td><td>capiēns</td></tr>
<tr><td></td><td align="center">GERUND.</td><td></td></tr>
<tr><td>*Gen.*</td><td>capiendī, &c.</td><td></td></tr>
<tr><td colspan="3" align="center">PASSIVE VOICE.</td></tr>
<tr><td colspan="3" align="center">INDICATIVE MOOD.</td></tr>
<tr><td></td><td align="center">Singular.</td><td align="center">Plural.</td></tr>
<tr><td>*Pres.*</td><td>capior, caperis or -re, ca-
pitur</td><td>capimur, capiminī, capiuntur</td></tr>
<tr><td>*Imp.*</td><td>capiēbar, capiēbāre or
-ris, capiēbātur</td><td>capiēbāmur, capiēbāminī, capi-
ēbantur</td></tr>
<tr><td>*Fut.*</td><td>capiar, capiēre or -ris, ca-
piētur</td><td>capiēmur, capiēminī, capientur</td></tr>
<tr><td colspan="3" align="center">SUBJUNCTIVE MOOD.</td></tr>
<tr><td>*Pres.*</td><td>capiar, capiāre or -ris, ca-
piātur</td><td>capiāmur, capiāminī, capiantur</td></tr>
<tr><td>*Imp.*</td><td>caperer, caperēre or -ris,
caperētur</td><td>caperēmur, caperēminī, cape-
rentur</td></tr>
<tr><td colspan="3" align="center">IMPERATIVE MOOD.</td></tr>
<tr><td colspan="3" align="center">capere or capitor, capitor | capiminī, capiuntor</td></tr>
<tr><td></td><td align="center">INFINITIVE.</td><td align="center">GERUNDIVE.</td></tr>
<tr><td>*Pres.*</td><td>capî</td><td>capiendus</td></tr>
</table>

785. There are a dozen verbs in -iō, -ere, like capiō, and three deponents in -ior, -ī, all formed from consonant roots with a short vowel : see 836. aiō, *say*, and fīō, *grow, become*, have certain peculiarities arising from the blending of the root with the suffix.

(1.) aiō, *say, say ay, avouch* (a g-).

786. aiō, *say*, is defective, and has only these parts in common use :

	Singular.	Plural.
Ind. Pres.	aiō, ais, ait	——, ——, aiunt
Ind. Imp.	aiēbam, aiēbās, aiēbat	aiēbāmus, aiēbātis, aiēbant
Subj. Pres.	——, aiās, aiāt	——, ——, ——

787. For aiō, sometimes written aiiō (23), see 153, 2. Old forms are : present ais, ais, āis, or with -n interrogative āin, āīn ; ait, ait, or āīt ; imperfect āibam, āibās, āibat, and āibant ; imperative once only, ai (Naev.). A participle aientibus, *affirmative*, occurs once (Cic.).

(2.) fīō, *become, am made.*

788. fīō, *become*, and factus sum supplement each other : in the present system, the passive of faciō, *make*, except the gerundive, faciendus, is not used, fīō, &c., taking its place ; in the perfect system, only factus sum, &c., is used.

	Singular.	Plural.
Ind. Pres.	fīō, fīs, fit	——, ——, fiunt
Ind. Imp.	fīēbam, fīēbās, fīēbat	fīēbāmus, fīēbātis, fīēbant
Ind. Fut.	fīam, fīēs, fīet	fīēmus, fīētis, fīent
Subj. Pres.	fīam, fīās, fīat	fīāmus, fīātis, fīant
Subj. Imp.	fierem, fierēs, fieret	fierēmus, fierētis, fierent
Imper.	fī	fīte
Infin. Pres.	fierī	*Part. Pres.* ——

789. In fīō, &c., ī represents an older ei, seen in FEIENT (inscr. 45 B.C.). The infinitive fierī for fierei owes its passive ending to analogy ; the active form fiere occurs twice (Enn., Laev.). The vowel before -er- in fierem, &c., and fierī, is sometimes long in the dramatists, where a cretic (_ ᵕ _) is required, but otherwise always short.

790. -fīō is used in apparent compounds (394) : as, patēfit. In real compounds commonly -ficior : as, cōnficior ; but sometimes -fīō : as, cōnfit, cōnfiunt, cōnfīat, cōnfieret, cōnfierent, cōnfīerī ; dēfit, dēfīet, dēfīat, dēfierī ; effit, effīant, ecfierī ; īnfit ; interfīat, interfierī ; superfit, superfīat.

791. Some verbs in -iō, -ere (or -ior, -ī), have occasionally the form of verbs in -īre (or -īrī), in some parts of the present system, oftenest before an r, and particularly in the passive infinitive : as,

fodīrī, 3 times (Cato, Col. 2), circumfodīrī (Col.), ecfodīrī (Plaut.) ; adgredīrī (adgredīrier), 4 times (Plaut.), prōgredīrī (Plaut.) ; morīrī 6 times (Plaut. 4. Pomp., Ov.), ēmorīrī twice (Plaut., Ter.) ; orīrī, always ; parīre, twice (Plaut., Enn.) ; usually potīrī (potīrier). Also cupīret (Lucr.) ; adgredīre, adgredībor, adgredīmur (Plaut.) ; morīmur (Enn.) : orīris (Varr., Sen.). adcrītur (Lucil., Lucr.). orīrētur (Cic., Nep., Sall., Liv.). adorīrētur (Liv., Suet.) ; paribis (Pomp.), PARIRET (inscr.) ; potīris (Manil.), potītur (Lucil., Ov.), &c., &c.

II. Denominative Verbs.
(1.) VERBS IN -āre.
The First Conjugation.

792. laudō, *praise.*

PRINCIPAL PARTS.			
PRES. INDIC.	PRES. INFIN.	PERF. INDIC.	PERF. PART.
laudō	**laudāre**	**laudāvī**	**laudātus**

ACTIVE VOICE.
INDICATIVE MOOD.
PRESENT TENSE.

Singular.	Plural.
laudō, *I praise,* or *am praising*	laudāmus, *we praise,* or *are praising*
laudās, *thou praisest,* or *art praising*	laudātis, *you praise,* or *are praising*
laudat, *he praises,* or *is praising*	laudant, *they praise,* or *are praising*

IMPERFECT TENSE.

laudābam, *I was praising,* or *I praised*	laudābāmus, *we were praising,* or *we praised*
laudābās, *thou wert praising,* or *thou praisedst*	laudābātis, *you were praising,* or *you praised*
laudābat, *he was praising,* or *he praised*	laudābant, *they were praising,* or *they praised*

FUTURE TENSE.

laudābō, *I shall praise*	laudābimus, *we shall praise*
laudābis, *thou wilt praise*	laudābitis, *you will praise*
laudābit, *he will praise*	laudābunt, *they will praise*

PERFECT TENSE.

laudāvī, *I have praised,* or *I praised*	laudāvimus, *we have praised,* or *we praised*
laudāvistī, *thou hast praised,* or *thou praisedst*	laudāvistis, *you have praised,* or *you praised*
laudāvit, *he has praised,* or *he praised*	laudāvērunt or -re, *they have praised,* or *they praised*

PLUPERFECT TENSE.

laudāveram, *I had praised*	laudāverāmus, *we had praised*
laudāverās, *thou hadst praised*	laudāverātis, *you had praised*
laudāverat, *he had praised*	laudāverant, *they had praised*

FUTURE PERFECT TENSE.

laudāverō, *I shall have praised*	laudāverimus, *we shall have praised*
laudāveris, *thou wilt have praised*	laudāveritis, *you will have praised*
laudāverit, *he will have praised*	laudāverint, *they will have praised*

SUBJUNCTIVE MOOD.

PRESENT TENSE.

Singular.	Plural.
laudem, *may I praise*	laudēmus, *let us praise*
laudēs, *mayst thou praise*	laudētis, *may you praise*
laudet, *let him praise*	laudent, *let them praise*

IMPERFECT TENSE.

laudārem, *I should praise*	laudārēmus, *we should praise*
laudārēs, *thou wouldst praise*	laudārētis, *you would praise*
laudāret, *he would praise*	laudārent, *they would praise*

PERFECT TENSE.

laudāverim, *I may have praised*	laudāverīmus, *we may have praised*
laudāverīs, *thou mayst have praised*	laudāverītis, *you may have praised*
laudāverit, *he may have praised*	laudāverint, *they may have praised*

PLUPERFECT TENSE.

laudāvissem, *I should have praised*	laudāvissēmus, *we should have praised*
laudāvissēs, *thou wouldst have praised*	laudāvissētis, *you would have praised*
laudāvisset, *he would have praised*	laudāvissent, *they would have praised*

IMPERATIVE MOOD.

laudā or laudātō, *praise, thou shalt praise*	laudāte or laudātōte, *praise, you shall praise*
laudātō, *he shall praise*	laudantō, *they shall praise*

NOUNS OF THE VERB.

INFINITIVE.

Pres.	laudāre, *to praise*
Perf.	laudāvisse, *to have praised*
Fut.	laudātūrus esse, *to be going to praise*

PARTICIPLE.

Pres.	laudāns, *praising*
Fut.	laudātūrus, *going to praise*

GERUND.

Gen.	laudandī, *of praising*
Dat.	laudandō, *for praising*
Acc.	laudandum, *praising*
Abl.	laudandō, *by praising*

SUPINE.

Acc.	laudātum, *to praise*
Abl.	*laudātū, *in praising*, not used

VERBS IN -āre.

The First Conjugation.

793. laudor, *am praised.*

PASSIVE VOICE.

INDICATIVE MOOD.

PRESENT TENSE.

Singular.	Plural.
laudor, *I am praised*	laudāmur, *we are praised*
laudāris or -re, *thou art praised*	laudāminī, *you are praised*
laudātur, *he is praised*	laudantur, *they are praised*

IMPERFECT TENSE.

laudābar, *I was praised*	laudābāmur, *we were praised*
laudābāre or -ris, *thou wert praised*	laudābāminī, *you were praised*
laudābātur, *he was praised*	laudābantur, *they were praised*

FUTURE TENSE.

laudābor, *I shall be praised*	laudābimur, *we shall be praised*
laudābere or -ris, *thou wilt be praised*	laudābiminī, *you will be praised*
laudābitur, *he will be praised*	laudābuntur, *they will be praised*

PERFECT TENSE.

laudātus sum, *I have been,* or *was praised*	laudātī sumus, *we have been,* or *were praised*
laudātus es, *thou hast been,* or *wert praised*	laudātī estis, *you have been,* or *were praised*
laudātus est, *he has been,* or *was praised*	laudātī sunt, *they have been,* or *were praised*

PLUPERFECT TENSE.

laudātus eram, *I had been praised*	laudātī erāmus, *we had been praised*
laudātus erās, *thou hadst been praised*	laudātī erātis, *you had been praised*
laudātus erat, *he had been praised*	laudātī erant, *they had been praised*

FUTURE PERFECT TENSE.

laudātus erō, *I shall have been praised*	laudātī erimus, *we shall have been praised*
laudātus eris, *thou wilt have been praised*	laudātī eritis, *you will have been praised*
laudātus erit, *he will have been praised*	laudātī erunt, *they will have been praised*

SUBJUNCTIVE MOOD.

PRESENT TENSE.

Singular.	Plural.
lauder, *may I be praised*	laudēmur, *may we be praised*
laudēre or -ris, *mayst thou be praised*	laudēminī, *may you be praised*
laudētur, *let him be praised*	laudentur, *let them be praised*

IMPERFECT TENSE.

laudārer, *I should be praised*	laudārēmur, *we should be praised*
laudārēre or -ris, *thou wouldst be praised*	laudārēminī, *you would be praised*
laudārētur, *he would be praised*	laudārentur, *they would be praised*

PERFECT TENSE.

laudātus sim, *I may have been praised*	laudātī sīmus, *we may have been praised*
laudātus sīs, *thou mayst have been praised*	laudātī sītis, *you may have been praised*
laudātus sit, *he may have been praised*	laudātī sint, *they may have been praised*

PLUPERFECT TENSE.

laudātus essem, *I should have been praised*	laudātī essēmus, *we should have been praised*
laudātus essēs, *thou wouldst have been praised*	laudātī essētis, *you would have been praised*
laudātus esset, *he would have been praised*	laudātī essent, *they would have been praised*

IMPERATIVE MOOD.

laudāre or laudātor, *be praised, thou shalt be praised*	laudāminī, *be praised*
laudātor, *he shall be praised*	laudantor, *they shall be praised*

NOUNS OF THE VERB.

INFINITIVE.	GERUNDIVE.
Pres. laudārī, *to be praised*	laudandus, *to be praised*
Perf. laudātus esse, *to have been praised*	**PERFECT PARTICIPLE.**
Fut. *laudātum īrī, *to be going to be praised*, not used (2273)	laudātus, *praised*

131

(2.) VERBS IN -ēre.
The Second Conjugation.
794.   **moneō,** *advise.*

PRINCIPAL PARTS.

PRES. INDIC.	PRES. INFIN.	PERF. INDIC.	PERF. PART.
moneō	**monēre**	**monuī**	**monitus**

ACTIVE VOICE.
INDICATIVE MOOD.
PRESENT TENSE.

Singular.	Plural.
moneō, *I advise,* or *am advising*	**monēmus,** *we advise,* or *are advising*
monēs, *thou advisest,* or *art advising*	**monētis,** *you advise,* or *are advising*
monet, *he advises,* or *is advising*	**monent,** *they advise,* or *are advising*

IMPERFECT TENSE.

monēbam, *I was advising,* or *I advised*	**monēbāmus,** *we were advising,* or *we advised*
monēbās, *thou wert advising,* or *thou advisedst*	**monēbātis,** *you were advising,* or *you advised*
monēbat, *he was advising,* or *he advised*	**monēbant,** *they were advising,* or *they advised*

FUTURE TENSE.

monēbō, *I shall advise*	**monēbimus,** *we shall advise*
monēbis, *thou wilt advise*	**monēbitis,** *you will advise*
monēbit, *he will advise*	**monēbunt,** *they will advise*

PERFECT TENSE.

monuī, *I have advised,* or *I advised*	**monuimus,** *we have advised,* or *we advised*
monuistī, *thou hast advised,* or *thou advisedst*	**monuistis,** *you have advised,* or *you advised*
monuit, *he has advised,* or *he advised*	**monuērunt** or **-re,** *they have advised,* or *they advised*

PLUPERFECT TENSE.

monueram, *I had advised*	**monuerāmus,** *we had advised*
monuerās, *thou hadst advised*	**monuerātis,** *you had advised*
monuerat, *he had advised*	**monuerant,** *they had advised*

FUTURE PERFECT TENSE.

monuerō, *I shall have advised*	**monuerimus,** *we shall have advised*
monueris, *thou wilt have advised*	**monueritis,** *you will have advised*
monuerit, *he will have advised*	**monuerint,** *they will have advised*

SUBJUNCTIVE MOOD.

PRESENT TENSE.

Singular.	Plural.
moneam, *may I advise*	moneāmus, *let us advise*
moneās, *mayst thou advise*	moneātis, *may you advise*
moneat, *let him advise*	moneant, *let them advise*

IMPERFECT TENSE.

monērem, *I should advise*	monērēmus, *we should advise*
monērēs, *thou wouldst advise*	monērētis, *you would advise*
monēret, *he would advise*	monērent, *they would advise*

PERFECT TENSE

monuerim, *I may have advised*	monuerīmus, *we may have advised*
monuerīs, *thou mayst have advised*	monuerītis, *you may have advised*
monuerit, *he may have advised*	monuerint, *they may have advised*

PLUPERFECT TENSE.

monuissem, *I should have advised*	monuissēmus, *we should have advised*
monuissēs, *thou wouldst have advised*	monuissētis, *you would have advised*
monuisset, *he would have advised*	monuissent, *they would have advised*

IMPERATIVE MOOD.

monē or monētō, *advise, thou shalt advise*	monēte or monētōte, *advise, you shall advise*
monētō, *he shall advise*	monentō, *they shall advise*

NOUNS OF THE VERB.

INFINITIVE.

Pres. monēre, *to advise*
Perf. monuisse, *to have advised*
Fut. monitūrus esse, *to be going to advise*

PARTICIPLE.

Pres. monēns, *advising*

Fut. monitūrus, *going to advise*

GERUND.

Gen. monendī, *of advising*
Dat. monendō, *for advising*
Acc monendum, *advising*
Abl. monendō, *by advising*

SUPINE.

Acc. *monitum, *to advise*, not used
Abl. monitū, *in advising*

133

VERBS IN -ēre.

The Second Conjugation.

795.   **moneor,** *am advised.*

PASSIVE VOICE.

INDICATIVE MOOD.

PRESENT TENSE.

Singular.	Plural.
moneor, *I am advised*	**monēmur,** *we are advised*
monēris or **-re,** *thou art advised*	**monēminī,** *you are advised*
monētur, *he is advised*	**monentur,** *they are advised*

IMPERFECT TENSE.

monēbar, *I was advised*	**monēbāmur,** *we were advised*
monēbāre or **-ris,** *thou wert advised*	**monēbāminī,** *you were advised*
monēbātur, *he was advised*	**monēbantur,** *they were advised*

FUTURE TENSE.

monēbor, *I shall be advised*	**monēbimur,** *we shall be advised*
monēbere or **-ris,** *thou wilt be advised*	**monēbiminī,** *you will be advised*
monēbitur, *he will be advised*	**monēbuntur,** *they will be advised*

PERFECT TENSE.

monitus sum, *I have been,* or *was advised*	**monitī sumus,** *we have been,* or *were advised*
monitus es, *thou hast been,* or *wert advised*	**monitī estis,** *you have been,* or *were advised*
monitus est, *he has been,* or *was advised*	**monitī sunt,** *they have been,* or *were advised*

PLUPERFECT TENSE.

monitus eram, *I had been advised*	**monitī erāmus,** *we had been advised*
monitus erās, *thou hadst been advised*	**monitī erātis,** *you had been advised*
monitus erat, *he had been advised*	**monitī erant,** *they had been advised*

FUTURE PERFECT TENSE.

monitus erō, *I shall have been advised*	**monitī erimus,** *we shall have been advised*
monitus eris, *thou wilt have been advised*	**monitī eritis,** *you will have been advised*
monitus erit, *he will have been advised*	**monitī erunt,** *they will have been advised*

SUBJUNCTIVE MOOD.

PRESENT TENSE.

Singular.	Plural.
monear, *may I be advised*	**moneāmur,** *may we be advised*
moneāre or **-ris,** *mayst thou be advised*	**moneāminī,** *may you be advised*
moneātur, *let him be advised*	**moneantur,** *let them be advised*

IMPERFECT TENSE.

monērer, *I should be advised*	**monērēmur,** *we should be advised*
monērēre or **-ris,** *thou wouldst be advised*	**monērēminī,** *you would be advised*
monērētur, *he would be advised*	**monērentur,** *they would be advised*

PERFECT TENSE.

monitus sim, *I may have been advised*	**monitī sīmus,** *we may have been advised*
monitus sīs, *thou mayst have been advised*	**monitī sītis,** *you may have been advised*
monitus sit, *he may have been advised*	**monitī sint,** *they may have been advised*

PLUPERFECT TENSE.

monitus essem, *I should have been advised*	**monitī essēmus,** *we should have been advised*
monitus essēs, *thou wouldst have been advised*	**monitī essētis,** *you would have been advised*
monitus esset, *he would have been advised*	**monitī essent,** *they would have been advised*

IMPERATIVE MOOD.

monēre or **monētor,** *be advised, thou shalt be advised*	**monēminī,** *be advised*
monētor, *he shall be advised*	**monentor,** *they shall be advised*

NOUNS OF THE VERB.

INFINITIVE.	GERUNDIVE.
Pres. **monērī,** *to be advised*	**monendus,** *to be advised*
Perf. **monitus esse,** *to have been advised*	PERFECT PARTICIPLE.
Fut. ***monitum īrī,** *to be going to be advised,* not used (2273)	**monitus,** *advised*

135

(3.) VERBS IN -īre.
The Fourth Conjugation.
796.   **audiō,** *hear.*

PRINCIPAL PARTS.			
PRES. INDIC.	PRES. INFIN.	PERF. INDIC.	PERF. PART.
audiō	**audīre**	**audīvī**	**audītus**

ACTIVE VOICE.
INDICATIVE MOOD.
PRESENT TENSE.

Singular.	Plural.
audiō, *I hear,* or *am hearing*	**audīmus,** *we hear,* or *are hearing*
audīs, *thou hearest,* or *art hearing*	**audītis,** *you hear,* or *are hearing*
audit, *he hears,* or *is hearing*	**audiunt,** *they hear,* or *are hearing*

IMPERFECT TENSE.

audiēbam, *I was hearing,* or *I heard*	**audiēbāmus,** *we were hearing,* or *we heard*
audiēbās, *thou wert hearing,* or *thou heardst*	**audiēbātis,** *you were hearing,* or *you heard*
audiēbat, *he was hearing,* or *he heard*	**audiēbant,** *they were hearing,* or *they heard*

FUTURE TENSE.

audiam, *I shall hear*	**audiēmus,** *we shall hear*
audiēs, *thou wilt hear*	**audiētis,** *you will hear*
audiet, *he will hear*	**audient,** *they will hear*

PERFECT TENSE.

audīvī, *I have heard,* or *I heard*	**audīvimus,** *we have heard,* or *we heard*
audīvistī, *thou hast heard,* or *thou heardst*	**audīvistis,** *you have heard,* or *you heard*
audīvit, *he has heard,* or *he heard*	**audīvērunt** or **-re,** *they have heard,* or *they heard*

PLUPERFECT TENSE.

audīveram, *I had heard*	**audīverāmus,** *we had heard*
audīverās, *thou hadst heard*	**audīverātis,** *you had heard*
audīverat, *he had heard*	**audīverant,** *they had heard*

FUTURE PERFECT TENSE.

audīverō, *I shall have heard*	**audīverimus,** *we shall have heard*
audīveris, *thou wilt have heard*	**audīveritis,** *you will have heard*
audīverit, *he will have heard*	**audīverint,** *they will have heard*

SUBJUNCTIVE MOOD.

PRESENT TENSE.

Singular.	Plural.
audiam, *may I hear*	audiāmus, *let us hear*
audiās, *mayst thou hear*	audiātis, *may you hear*
audiat, *let him hear*	audiant, *let them hear*

IMPERFECT TENSE.

audīrem, *I should hear*	audīrēmus, *we should hear*
audīrēs, *thou wouldst hear*	audīrētis, *you would hear*
audīret, *he would hear*	audīrent, *they would hear*

PERFECT TENSE.

audīverim, *I may have heard*	audīverīmus, *we may have heard*
audīverīs, *thou mayst have heard*	audīverītis, *you may have heard*
audīverit, *he may have heard*	audīverint, *they may have heard*

PLUPERFECT TENSE.

audīvissem, *I should have heard*	audīvissēmus, *we should have heard*
audīvissēs, *thou wouldst have heard*	audīvissētis, *you would have heard*
audīvisset, *he would have heard*	audīvissent, *they would have heard*

IMPERATIVE MOOD.

audī or audītō, *hear, thou shalt hear*	audīte or audītōte, *hear, you shall hear*
audītō, *he shall hear*	audiuntō, *they shall hear*

NOUNS OF THE VERB.

INFINITIVE.

Pres. audīre, *to hear*
Perf. audīvisse, *to have heard*
Fut. audītūrus esse, *to be going to hear*

PARTICIPLE.

Pres. audiēns, *hearing*
Fut. audītūrus, *going to hear*

GERUND.

Gen. audiendī, *of hearing*
Dat. audiendō, *for hearing*
Acc. audiendum, *hearing*
Abl. audiendō, *by hearing*

SUPINE.

Acc. audītum, *to hear*
Abl. audītū, *in hearing*

VERBS IN -īre.

The Fourth Conjugation.

797.   **audior,** *am heard.*

PASSIVE VOICE.

INDICATIVE MOOD.

PRESENT TENSE.

Singular.	Plural.
audior, *I am heard*	audīmur, *we are heard*
audīris or -re, *thou art heard*	audīminī, *you are heard*
audītur, *he is heard*	audiuntur, *they are heard*

IMPERFECT TENSE.

audiēbar, *I was heard*	audiēbāmur, *we were heard*
audiēbāre or -ris, *thou wert heard*	audiēbāminī, *you were heard*
audiēbātur, *he was heard*	audiēbantur, *they were heard*

FUTURE TENSE.

audiar, *I shall be heard*	audiēmur, *we shall be heard*
audiēre or -ris, *thou wilt be heard*	audiēminī, *you will be heard*
audiētur, *he will be heard*	audientur, *they will be heard*

PERFECT TENSE.

audītus sum, *I have been, or was heard*	audītī sumus, *we have been, or were heard*
audītus es, *thou hast been, or wert heard*	audītī estis, *you have been, or were heard*
audītus est, *he has been, or was heard*	audītī sunt, *they have been, or were heard*

PLUPERFECT TENSE.

audītus eram, *I had been heard*	audītī erāmus, *we had been heard*
audītus erās, *thou hadst been heard*	audītī erātis, *you had been heard*
audītus erat, *he had been heard*	audītī erant, *they had been heard*

FUTURE PERFECT TENSE.

audītus erō, *I shall have been heard*	audītī erimus, *we shall have been heard*
audītus eris, *thou wilt have been heard*	audītī eritis, *you will have been heard*
audītus erit, *he will have been heard*	audītī erunt, *they will have been heard*

SUBJUNCTIVE MOOD.

PRESENT TENSE.

Singular.	Plural.
audiar, *may I be heard*	audiāmur, *may we be heard*
audiāre or -ris, *mayst thou be heard*	audiāminī, *may you be heard*
audiātur, *let him be heard*	audiantur, *let them be heard*

IMPERFECT TENSE.

audīrer, *I should be heard*	audīrēmur, *we should be heard*
audīrēre or -ris, *thou wouldst be heard*	audīrēminī, *you would be heard*
audīrētur, *he would be heard*	audīrentur, *they would be heard*

PERFECT TENSE.

audītus sim, *I may have been heard*	audītī sīmus, *we may have been heard*
audītus sīs, *thou mayst have been heard*	audītī sītis, *you may have been heard*
audītus sit, *he may have been heard*	audītī sint, *they may have been heard*

PLUPERFECT TENSE.

audītus essem, *I should have been heard*	audītī essēmus, *we should have been heard*
audītus essēs, *thou wouldst have been heard*	audītī essētis, *you would have been heard*
audītus esset, *he would have been heard*	audītī essent, *they would have been heard*

IMPERATIVE MOOD.

audīre or audītor, *be heard, thou shalt be heard*	audīminī, *be heard*
audītor, *he shall be heard*	audiuntor, *they shall be heard*

NOUNS OF THE VERB.

INFINITIVE.	GERUNDIVE.
Pres. audīrī, *to be heard*	audiendus, *to be heard*
Perf. audītus esse, *to have been heard*	PERFECT PARTICIPLE.
Fut. audītum īrī, *to be going to be heard* (2273)	audītus, *heard*

THE DEPONENT VERB.

798. Deponents, that is, verbs with passive person endings and a reflexive or an active meaning (725), have these active noun forms : participles, the future infinitive, the gerund, and the supines. The perfect participle is usually active, but sometimes passive ; the gerundive always passive. The following is a synopsis of deponents :

PRINCIPAL PARTS.

queror, *complain,* querī, questus	mīror, *wonder,* mīrārī, mīrātus		
	vereor, *fear,* verērī, veritus		
	partior, *share,* partīrī, partītus		

	I. -ī	II. (1.) -ārī	(2.) -ērī	(3.) -īrī
		INDICATIVE MOOD.		
Pres.	queror	mīror	vereor	partior
Imp.	querēbar	mīrābar	verēbar	partiēbar
Fut.	querar	mīrābor	verēbor	partiar
Perf.	questus sum	mīrātus sum	veritus sum	partītus sum
Plup.	questus eram	mīrātus eram	veritus eram	partītus eram
F. P.	questus erō	mīrātus erō	veritus erō	partītus erō
		SUBJUNCTIVE MOOD.		
Pres.	querar	mīrer	verear	partiar
Imp.	quererer	mīrārer	verērer	partīrer
Perf.	questus sim	mīrātus sim	veritus sim	partītus sim
Plup.	questus essem	mīrātus essem	veritus essem	partītus essem
		IMPERATIVE MOOD.		
	querere	mīrāre	verēre	partīre
		PARTICIPLES.		
Pres.	querēns	mīrāns	verēns	partiēns
Perf.	questus	mīrātus	veritus	partītus
Fut.	questūrus	mīrātūrus	veritūrus	partītūrus
		INFINITIVE.		
Pres.	querī	mīrārī	verērī	partīrī
Perf.	questus esse	mīrātus esse	veritus esse	partītus esse
Fut.	questūrus esse	mīrātūrus esse	veritūrus esse	partītūrus esse
		GERUND AND GERUNDIVE.		
Gen.	querendī, &c.	mīrandī, &c.	verendī, &c.	partiendī, &c.
	querendus	mīrandus	verendus	partiendus
		SUPINE.		
Acc.	questum	*mīrātum	*veritum	*partītum
Abl.	*questū	mīrātū	*veritū	*partītū

799. Three deponents in -ior, -ī, gradior, *walk,* morior, *die,* and patior, *suffer,* and their compounds, have a present system like the passive of capiō (784). But adgredior and prōgredior and morior and ēmorior have sometimes the forms of verbs in -īrī; for these, and for orior, *arise,* orīrī, ortus, and potior, *become master of,* potīrī, potītus, see 791. By far the largest number of deponents are verbs in -ārī, like mīror, mīrārī (368).

800. Some verbs waver between active and passive person endings: as, adsentiō, *agree,* adsentīre, and adsentior, adsentīrī; populō, *ravage,* populāre, and populor, populārī: see 1481.

801. A few verbs are deponent in the present system only: as, dēvortor, *turn in,* perfect dēvortī; revortor, *turn back,* perfect revortī, but with active perfect participle revorsus. Four are deponent in the perfect system only: fīdō, *trust,* fīdere, fīsus, and the compounds, cōnfīdō, diffīdō; and audeō, *dare,* audēre, ausus, gaudeō, *feel glad,* gaudēre, gāvīsus, and soleō, *am used,* solēre, solitus. Most impersonals in -ēre have both an active and a deponent form in the perfect system: see 815, 816.

PERIPHRASTIC FORMS.

802. (1.) The future active participle with a form of sum is used to denote an intended or future action: as,

rēctūrus sum, *I am going to rule, intend to rule.*

	INDICATIVE MOOD.	
	Singular.	Plural.
Pres.	rēctūrus sum, es, est	rēctūrī sumus, estis, sunt
Imp.	rēctūrus eram, erās, erat	rēctūrī erāmus, erātis, erant
Fut.	rēctūrus erō, eris, erit	rēctūrī erimus, eritis, erunt
Perf.	rēctūrus fuī, fuistī, fuit	rēctūrī fuimus, fuistis, fuērunt
Plup.	rēctūrus fueram, fuerās, fuerat	rēctūrī fuerāmus, fuerātis, fuerant
	SUBJUNCTIVE MOOD.	
Pres.	rēctūrus sim, sīs, sit	rēctūrī sīmus, sītis, sint
Imp.	rēctūrus essem, essēs, esset	rēctūrī essēmus, essētis, essent
Perf.	rēctūrus fuerim, fuerīs, fuerit	rēctūrī fuerīmus, fuerītis, fuerint
Plup.	rēctūrus fuissem, fuissēs, fuisset	rēctūrī fuissēmus, fuissētis, fuissent
	INFINITIVE.	
Pres.	rēctūrus esse	
Perf.	rēctūrus fuisse	

803. A future perfect is hardly ever used: as, fuerit victūrus (Sen.). In the imperfect subjunctive, forem, forēs, foret, and forent are sometimes used (Nep., Sall., Liv., Vell.).

804. (2.) The gerundive with a form of **sum** is used to de-note action which requires to be done : as,

regendus sum, *I am to be ruled, must be ruled.*

	INDICATIVE MOOD.	
	Singular.	Plural.
Pres.	regendus sum, es, est	regendī sumus, estis, sunt
Imp.	regendus eram, erās, erat	regendī erāmus, erātis, erant
Fut.	regendus erō, eris, erit	regendī erimus, eritis, erunt
Perf.	regendus fuī, fuistī, fuit	regendī fuimus, fuistis, fuērunt
Plup.	regendus fueram, fuerās, fuerat	regendī fuerāmus, fuerātis, fuerant
	SUBJUNCTIVE MOOD	
Pres.	regendus sim, sīs, sit	regendī sīmus, sītis, sint
Imp.	regendus essem, essēs, esset	regendī essēmus, essētis, essent
Perf.	regendus fuerim, fuerīs, fuerit	regendī fuerīmus, fuerītis, fuerint
Plup.	regendus fuissem, fuissēs, fuisset	regendī fuissēmus, fuissētis, fuissent
	INFINITIVE.	
Pres.	regendus esse	
Perf.	regendus fuisse	

DEFECTIVE VERBS.

805. (1.) Some verbs have only a few forms : as,

inquam, *quoth I* (760) ; **aiō**, *avouch* (786). See also **apage**, *avaunt, get thee behind me,* **cedo**, *give, tell,* **fārī**, *to lift up one's voice,* **havē** or **avē** and **salvē**, *all hail,* **ovat**, *triumphs,* and **quaesō**, *prithee,* in the dictionary.

806. (2.) Many verbs have only the present system ; such are :

807. (*a.*) sum, *am* (745) ; **ferō**, *carry* (780) ; **fīō**, *grow, become* (788).

808. (*b.*) Some verbs in -ere : **angō**, *throttle,* **bītō**, *go,* **clangō**, *sound,* claudō or claudeō, *hobble,* **fatīscō**, *gape,* **glīscō**, *wax,* **glūbō**, *peel,* **hīscō**, *gape,* **temnō**, *scorn,* **vādō**, *go,* **vergō**, *slope.* Also many inceptives (834) : as, **dītēscō**, *get rich,* **dulcēscō**, *get sweet,* &c., &c.

809. (*c.*) Some verbs in -ēre : **albeō**, *am white,* **aveō**, *long,* **calveō**, *am bald,* **cāneō**, *am gray,* **clueō**, *am called, hight,* **flāveō**, *am yellow,* **hebeō**, *am blunt,* **immineō**, *threaten,* **lacteō**, *suck,* **līveō**, *look dark,* **maereō**, *mourn,* **polleō**, *am strong,* **renīdeō**, *am radiant,* **squāleō**, *am scaly,* **ūmeō**, *am wet.*

810. (*d.*) Some verbs in -īre : **balbūtiō**, *sputter,* **feriō**, *strike,* **ganniō**, *yelp,* **ineptiō**, *am a fool,* **superbiō**, *am stuck up,* **tussiō**, *cough.* Also most desideratives (375).

811. Many verbs are not attended by a perfect participle, and lack in consequence the perfect passive system, or, if deponent, the perfect active system.

812. (3.) Some verbs have only the perfect system: so particularly **coepī**, *have begun, began* (120); and with a present meaning, **ōdī**, *have come to hate, hate;* and **meminī**, *have called to mind, remember.* The following is a synopsis of these three verbs:

	INDICATIVE MOOD.			
	Active.	Passive.	Active.	Active.
Perf.	coepī	coeptus sum	ōdi	meminī
Plup.	coeperam	coeptus eram	ōderam	memineram
F. P.	coeperō	coeptus erō	ōderō	meminerō
	SUBJUNCTIVE MOOD.			
Perf.	coeperim	coeptus sim	ōderim	meminerim
Plup.	coepissem	coeptus essem	ōdissem	meminissem
	IMPERATIVE MOOD.			
Perf.	——	——	——	mementō, me-mentōte
	INFINITIVE.			
Perf.	coepisse	coeptus esse	ōdisse	meminisse
	PARTICIPLES.			
Perf.		coeptus	——	——
Fut.	coeptūrus		ōsūrus	——

813. A few forms of the present system of **coepī** occur in old writers: as, coepiō (Plaut.), **coepiam** (Caec., Cato), **coepiat** (Plaut.), **coeperet** (Ter.), and coepere (Plaut.); perfect once **coēpit** (Lucr.). **ōsus sum** or **fuī** (Plaut., C. Gracch., Gell.), **exōsus sum** (Verg., Sen., Curt., Gell.), and **perōsus sum** (Suet., Col., Quint.), are sometimes used as deponents. **memini** is the only verb which has a perfect imperative active. **ōdī** and **meminī** have no passive.

814. **coeptūrus** is rather rare and late (Liv. 2, Plin., Suet.), once as future infinitive (Quint.); and **ōsūrus** is very rare (Cic., Gell.). **exōsus** and **perōsus**, as active participles, *hating bitterly*, are not uncommon in writers of the empire; the simple **ōsus** is not used as a participle.

815. (4.) Impersonal verbs have usually only the third person singular, and the infinitive present and perfect: as,

(*a.*) **pluit**, *it rains*, **tonat**, *it thunders*, and other verbs denoting the operations of nature. (*b.*) Also a few verbs in **-ēre** denoting feeling: as, **miseret** (or **miserētur**, **miserēscit**), *it distresses*, **miseritum est**; **paenitet**, *it repents*, **paenituit**; **piget**, *it grieves*, **piguit** or **pigitum est**; **pudet**, *it shames*, **puduit** or **puditum est**; **taedet**, *it is a bore*, **taesum est**.

816. Some other verbs, less correctly called impersonal, with an infinitive or a sentence as subject, are likewise defective: as,

lubet or libet, *it suits,* lubitum or libitum est, lubuit or libuit; licet, *it is allowed,* licuit or licitum est; oportet, *it is proper,* oportuit; rē fert or rēfert, *it concerns,* rē ferre or rēferre, rē tulit or rētulit. For the impersonal use of the third person singular passive, as pugnātur, *there is fighting,* pugnandum est, *there must be fighting,* see 724.

817. Of the impersonals in -ēre, some have other forms besides the third person singular and the infinitives: as,

paenitēns, *repenting,* paenitendus, *to be regretted,* late; pigendus, *irksome;* pudēns, *modest,* pudendus, *shameful,* puditūrum, *going to shame;* lubēns or libēns, *with willing mind, gladly,* very common indeed; imperative LICETO, *be it allowed* (inscrr. 133–111 B.C.), licēns, *unrestrained,* licitus, *allowable;* gerunds pudendum, pudendō, pigendum.

REDUNDANT VERBS.

818. (1.) Some verbs have more than one form of the present stem: thus,

819. (*a.*) Verbs in -ere have rarely forms of verbs in -ēre in the present system: as, abnueō, *nod no,* abnuēbunt (Enn.), for abnuō, abnuent; congruēre, *to agree* (Ter.), for congruere. For verbs in -iō, -ere (or -ior, -ī), with forms of verbs in -īre (or -īrī), see 791. Once pīnsībant (Enn.).

820. (*b.*) Some verbs in -āre have occasionally a present stem like verbs in -ere: as, lavis, *washest,* lavit, &c., for lavās, lavat, &c.; sonit, *sounds,* sonunt, for sonat, sonant. Others have occasionally a present stem like verbs in -ēre: as, dēnseō, *thicken,* dēnsērī, for dēnsō, dēnsārī.

821. (*c.*) Some verbs in -ēre have occasionally a present stem like verbs in -ere: as, fervit, *boils,* fervont, for fervet, fervent. See also fulgeō, oleō, scateō, strīdeō, tergeō, tueor in the dictionary. cieō, *set a going,* sometimes has a present stem in -īre, particularly in compounds: as, cīmus, ciunt, for ciēmus, cient.

822. (*d.*) Some verbs in -īre have occasionally a present stem like verbs in -ere: as, ēvenunt, *turn out,* for ēveniunt; ēvenat, ēvenant, for ēveniat, ēveniant, and advenat, pervenat, for adveniat, perveniat (Plaut.).

823. (2.) Some verbs have more than one form of the perfect stem: as,

eō, *go,* old iī (765), common iī, rarely īvī (767); pluit, *it rains,* pluit, sometimes plūvit. See also pangō, parcō, clepō, vollō or vellō, intellegō, pōnō, nectō, and adnectō, saliō and īnsiliō, applicō, explicō and implicō, dīmicō and necō in the dictionary. Some compound verbs have a form of the perfect which is different from that of the simple verb: as, canō, *make music,* cecinī, concinuī, occinuī; pungō, *punch,* pupugī, compunxī, expunxī; legō, *pick up,* lēgī, dīlēxī, intellēxī, neglēxī; emō, *take, buy,* ēmī (adēmī, exēmī), cōmpsī, dēmpsī, prōmpsī, sūmpsī.

FORMATION OF STEMS.

VARIABLE VOWEL.

824. The final vowel of a tense stem is said to be *variable* when it is -o- in some of the forms, and -u-, -e-, or -i- in others.

825. The sign for the variable vowel is -o|e-: thus, **rego|e-**, which may be read 'rego- or rege-,' represents **rego-** or **regu-**, **rege-** or **regi-**, as seen in **rego-r** or **regu-nt**, **rege-re** or **regi-t**.

826. The variable vowel occurs in the present of verbs in -ere, except in the subjunctive, in the future in -bō or -bor, and in the future perfect, as may be seen in the paradigms. It is usually short; but in the active, o is long: as, **regō, laudābō, laudāverō**; and poets rarely lengthen i in the second and third person singular of the present. For the future perfect, see 882.

827. In old Latin, the stem vowel of the third person plural of the present was o: as, COSENTIONT; o was long retained after v, u, or qu (107, *c*): as, **vīvont, ruont, sequontur**; or, if o was not retained, qu became c: as, **secuntur**.

I. THE PRESENT SYSTEM.

PRESENT INDICATIVE STEM.

I. PRIMITIVES.

(A.) ROOT VERBS.

828. A root without addition is used as the present stem, in the present tense or parts of the present tense, in root verbs (744–781) : as,

es-t, *is;* da-t, *gives;* inqui-t, *quoth he;* i-t, *goes;* nequi-t, *can't;* ēs-t, *eats;* vol-t, *will;* fer-t, *carries.* With reduplicated root (189): bibi-t, *drinks;* seri-t, *sows;* sisti-t, *sets.*

(B.) VERBS IN -ere.

829. (1.) The present stem of many verbs in -ere is formed by adding a variable vowel -o|e-, which appears in the first person singular active as -ō, to a root ending in a consonant or in two consonants : as,

PRESENT STEM.	VERB.	FROM THEME.
rego|e-	regō, *guide*	reg-
verto|e-	vertō, *turn*	vert-

Other examples are : **tegō**, *cover*, **petō**, *make for ;* **mergō**, *dip*, **serpō**, *creep ;* **pendō**, *weigh ;* **dīcō**, *say*, **fīdō**, *trust*, **scrībō**, *write*, with long ī for ei (98); **dūcō**, *lead*, with long ū for eu, ou (100) ; **lūdō**, *play*, with long ū for oi, oe (99); **laedō**, *hit*, **claudō**, *shut ;* **rādō**, *scrape*, **cēdō**, *move along*, **fīgō**, *fix*, **rōdō**, *gnaw*, **glūbō**, *peel*. *furō, *rave ;* **agō**, *drive*, **alō**, *nurture*. **gignō**, *beget*, (g e n-, g n-), has reduplication, and **sīdō**, *settle, light* (s e d-, s d-), is also the result of an ancient reduplication (189).

830. In some present stems an original consonant has been modified : as, **gerō**, *carry* (g e s-), **ūrō**, *burn* (154) ; **trahō**, *draw* (t r a gh-), **vehō**, *cart* (152) ; or has disappeared : as, **fluō**, *flow* (f l ū gu-).

831. Some roots in a mute have a nasal before the mute in the present stem : as, **frangō**, *break* (f r a g-). Other examples are : **iungō**, *join*, **linquō**, *leave*, **pangō**, *fix*, **pingō**, *paint ;* **findō**, *cleave*, **fundō**, *pour ;* **-cumbō**, *lie*, **lambō**, *lick*, **rumpō**, *break* (164, 3). The nasal sometimes runs over into the perfect or perfect participle, or both.

832. (2.) The present stem of many verbs in -ere is formed by adding a suffix ending in a variable vowel -ᵒ|e-, which appears in the first person singular active as -ō, to a root : thus, -nō, -scō, -tō, -iō : as,

PRESENT STEM	VERB.	FROM THEME.
linᵒ|e-	linō, *besmear*	l i-
crēscᵒ|e-	crēscō, *grow*	c r ē-
pectᵒ|e-	pectō, *comb*	p e c-
capiᵒ|e-	capiō, *take*	c a p-

833. (*a.*) -nō is added to roots in a vowel, or in a continuous sound, -m-, -r-, or -l-.

So regularly **linō**, *besmear*, **sinō**, *let ;* **temnō**, *scorn*, **cernō**, *sift*, **spernō**, *spurn*, only. The third persons plural **danunt** (Naev., Plaut.) for **dant**, **prōdīnunt, redīnunt** (Enn.) for **prōdeunt, redeunt** hardly belong here ; their formation is obscure. In a few verbs, -n is assimilated (166, 6) : as, **tollō**, *lift*. Sometimes the doubled l runs into the perfect (855) : as, **vellī, fefellī**. **minuō**, *lessen*, and **sternuō**, *sneeze*, have a longer suffix -nuᵒ|e-.

834. (*b.*) -scō, usually meaning '*begin to*,' forms presents called *Inceptives* or *Inchoatives*.

-scō is attached : first, to roots : as, **nāscor**, *am born*, **nōscō**, *learn*, **pāscō**, *feed*, **scīscō**, *resolve ;* consonant roots have ī, less commonly ē, before the suffix : as, **tremīscō** or **tremēscō**, *fall a-trembling*, **nancīscor**, *get* (831) ; but **discō**, *learn* (170, 1), and **poscō**, *demand* (170, 10), are shortened ; see 168. Secondly, to a form of the present stem of denominative verbs, especially of those in -ēre : as, **clārēscō**, *brighten ;* the stem is often assumed only, as in **inveterāscō**, *grow old*, **mātūrēscō**, *get ripe*. Many inceptives are used only in composition : as, **extimēscō**, *get scared*, **obdormīscō**, *drop asleep*.

835. (*c.*) -tō occurs in the following presents from guttural roots : **flectō**, *turn*, **nectō**, *string*, **pectō** *comb*, **plector**, *am struck*, **amplector**, *hug*, **complector**, *clasp*. From a lingual root v i d-, comes **vīsō**, *go to see, call on* (153). From vowel roots : **bētō** or **bītō**, *go*, and **metō**, *mow.*

836. (*d.*) -iō is usually added to consonant roots with a short vowel; the following have presents formed by this suffix:

capiō, *take,* cupiō, *want,* faciō, *make,* fodiō, *dig,* fugiō, *run away,* iaciō, *throw,* pariō, *bring forth,* quatiō, *shake,* rapiō, *seize,* sapiō, *have sense,* and their compounds; the compounds of *laciō, *lure,* and speciō or spiciō, *spy,* and the deponents gradior, *step,* morior, *die,* and patior, *suffer,* and their compounds. For occasional forms like those of verbs in -īre (or -īrī), see 791. For aiō, see 786; for fiō, 788.

837. A few present stems are formed by adding a variable vowel -ᵒ|ₑ-, for an older -iᵒ|ₑ-, to a vowel root: as,

ruō, *tumble down,* rui-s, rui-t, rui-mus, rui-tis, ruu-nt (114). Vowel roots in -ā-, -ē-, or -ī- have a present stem like that of denominatives: as, stō, *stand,* stā-s, sta-t, stā-mus, stā-tis, sta-nt; fleō, *weep,* flē-s, fle-t, flē-mus, flē-tis, fle-nt; neō, *spin,* has once neu-nt for ne-nt (Tib.); sciō, *know,* scī-s, sci-t, scī-mus, scī-tis, sciu-nt.

838. Most present stems formed by adding the suffix -iō to a root ending in -l-, -r-, or -n-, and all formed by adding -iō to a long syllable, have the form of denominatives in -īre in the present system: as, saliō, *leap,* salīre, aperiō, *open,* aperīre, veniō, *come,* venīre; farciō, *cram,* farcīre.

II. DENOMINATIVES.

839. The present stem of denominatives is formed by attaching a variable vowel -ᵒ|ₑ-, for an older -iᵒ|ₑ-, to a theme consisting of a noun stem: as,

UNCONTRACTED PRESENT STEM.	VERB.	FROM THEME.
cēnaᵒ|ₑ-	cēnō, *dine*	cēnā-
flōreᵒ|ₑ-	flōreō, *blossom*	flōre-
vestiᵒ|ₑ-˙	vestiō, *dress*	vesti-
acuᵒ|ₑ-	acuō, *point*	acu-

The noun stem ending is often slightly modified in forming the theme: thus, laud- becomes laudā- in laudō for *laudā-ō, and flōr- becomes flōre- in flōre-ō.

840. In many of the forms, the final vowel of the theme is contracted with the variable vowel: as,

plantō, plantās (118, 3) for *plantāiō, *plantāies (153, 2); monēs for *monēies (118, 1), audīs for *audīies (118, 3). The long ā, ē, or ī, is regularly shortened in some of the forms: as, scit, arat, habet, for Plautine scīt, arāt, habēt. In a few forms no contraction occurs: as, moneō, audiō, audiu-nt, audie-ntis, &c., audie-ndus, &c. (114). Denominatives from stems in -u-, as acuō, are not contracted, and so have the forms of verbs in -ere (367).

PRESENT SUBJUNCTIVE.

841. The suffix of the present subjunctive of sum, *am,* is -ī-, which becomes -i- before -m, -t, and -nt: si-m, sī-s, si-t, sī-mus, sī-tis, si-nt (35, 2, 3). So also in the singular and in the third person plural, dui-m, &c. (756), and edi-m, &c. (769), and in all the persons, veli-m, &c. (nōli-m, &c., māli-m, &c.). An old suffix is -iē- (-ie-), in sie-m, siē-s, sie-t, and sie-nt.

842. (1.) The present subjunctive stem of verbs in -ere,
-ēre, and -īre, ends in -ā-, which becomes -a- in some of the
persons; this suffix replaces the variable vowel of the indicative: as,

rega-m, regā-s, rega-t, regā-mus, regā-tis, rega-nt; capia-m,
capiā-s, &c.; monea-m, moneā-s, &c; audia-m, audiā-s, &c. ea-m,
quea-m, fera-m, and the old fua-m (750), also have the formative subjunctive vowel.

843. (2.) The present subjunctive stem of verbs in -āre ends
in -ē-, which becomes -e- in some of the persons: as,

laude-m, laudē-s, laude-t, laudē-mus, laudē-tis, laude-nt. dō, *give,*
also has de-m, dē-s, &c.

IMPERATIVE.

844. Root verbs have a root as imperative stem (745–780): as, es, &c.,
fer, &c. But the imperative of nōlō has a stem in -ī-, like verbs in -īre: thus,
nōlī, nōlī-tō, nōlī-te, nōlī-tōte.

845. The imperative stem of verbs in -ere, and of verbs in
-āre, -ēre, and -īre, is the same as that of the indicative: as,

rege, regi-tō, regu-ntō, rege-re; cape, capi-tō, capiu-ntō; fī; laudā,
&c.; monē, &c.; audī, &c.

846. The second person singular imperative active of dīcō, dūcō, and
faciō, is usually dīc, dūc, and fac, respectively, though the full forms, dīce,
&c., are also used, and are commoner in old Latin. Compounds of dūcō
may have the short form: as, ēdūc. ingerō has once inger (Catull.). sciō
has regularly the singular scī-tō, plural scī-tōte, rarely scī-te.

IMPERFECT INDICATIVE.

847. The imperfect indicative stem ends in -bā-, which becomes -ba- in some of the persons: as,

daba-m, dabā-s, daba-t, dabā-mus, dabā-tis, daba-nt; iba-m;
quiba-m.   In verbs in -ere and -ēre, the suffix is preceded by a form
ending in -ē-: as, regēba-m; monēba-m; so also volēba-m (nōlēba-m,
mālēba-m), and ferēba-m; in verbs in -iō, -ere, and in -iō, -īre, by a form
ending in -iē-: as, capiēba-m; audiēba-m; in verbs in -āre, by one ending in -ā-: as, laudāba-m. In verse, verbs in -īre sometimes have -ī- before
the suffix (Plaut., Ter., Catull., Lucr., Verg., &c.): as, audība-t. āiō, *say,*
has sometimes aība-m, &c. (787).

848. The suffix of the imperfect indicative of sum, *am,* is -ā-, which becomes -a-
before -m, -t, and -nt (35, 2, 3) the s becomes r between the vowels (154): era-m,
erā-s, era-t, erā-mus, erā-tis, era-nt.

IMPERFECT SUBJUNCTIVE.

849. The imperfect subjunctive stem ends in -rē-, which becomes -re- in some of the persons: as,

dare-m, darē-s, dare-t, darē-mus, darē-tis, dare-nt; īre-m, fore-m, ferre-m. In verbs in -ere, the -rē- is preceded by a form ending in -e-: as, regere-m, capere-m; in verbs in -āre, -ēre, and -īre, by one ending in -ā-, -ē-, or -ī-, respectively: as, laudāre-m, monēre-m, audīre-m.

850. The suffix of the imperfect subjunctive of sum, *am*, is -sē-, which becomes -se- in some of the persons; esse-m, essē-s, esse-t, essē-mus, essē-tis, esse-nt; so also ēssē-s, &c. (769). volō, *wish*, nōlō, *won't*, and mālō, *prefer*, have velle-m, nōlle-m, and mālle-m respectively (166, 8.)

FUTURE.

851. The future stem of sum, *am*, is erº|ₑ-.: erō, eri-s, eri-t, eri-mus, eri-tis, eru-nt. dō has dabō, eō has ībō, and queō has quībō.

852. (1.) The future stem of verbs in -ere and -īre ends in -a- in the first person singular, otherwise in -ē-, which becomes -e- in some of the persons: as,

rega-m, regē-s, rege-t, regē-mus, regē-tis, rege-nt; capia-m, capiē-s, &c.; audia-m, audiē-s, &c. The first person singular is not a future form, but the subjunctive present, used with a future meaning (842); forms in -em occur in manuscripts of Plautus: as, faciem, sinem. Verbs in -īre sometimes have -bº|ₑ-, chiefly in the dramatists: as, scībō, opperībo-r (Plaut., Ter.), lēnību-nt (Prop.); rarely verbs in -ere (819): as, exsūgēbō (Plaut.). For reddibō, instead of the usual reddam, see 757.

853. (2.) The future stem of verbs in -āre and -ēre ends in -bº|ₑ-, which is preceded by a form ending in long -ā- or -ē- respectively: as,

laudābō, laudābi-s, laudābi-t, laudābi-mus, laudābi-tis, laudābu-nt. monēbō, monēbi-s, &c.

II. THE PERFECT SYSTEM.

PERFECT INDICATIVE STEM.

854. There are two kinds of perfect stems: (A.) Some verbs have as perfect stem a root, generally with some modification, but without a suffix (858–866). (B.) Some perfects are formed with a suffix, -s-, or -v- or -u- (867–875).

855. Some perfects of primitives are formed not from a root, but from the present stem without the formative vowel, treated as a root: as, prehendī, *seized*, from prehend- (866); poposcī, *asked*, fefellī, *deceived* (858); iūnxī, *joined* (867).

856. The first person of the perfect ends in -ī, sometimes written ei (29, 2). -t, -stī, sometimes written -stei (29, 2), -stis, and -mus are preceded by short i; -re is always, and -runt is usually, preceded by long ē: as,

rēxī, rēxi-stī, rēxi-t, rēxi-mus, rēxi-stis, rēxē-runt (rēxe-runt), or rēxē-re.

149

857. Sometimes -t is preceded by long ī: as, iīt, petiīt, REDIEIT (29, 2). -runt is sometimes preceded by short e (Plaut., Ter., Lucr., Hor., Ov., Verg., Phaedr.). This is the original form; -ē- is by analogy to -ēre.

(A.) PERFECT STEM WITHOUT A SUFFIX.

858. (1.) Some verbs in -ere form their perfect stem by prefixing to the root its initial consonant with the following vowel, which, if a, is usually represented by e ; this is called the *Reduplicated Perfect*, and the first syllable is called the *Reduplication:* as,

PERFECT STEM.	VERB.	FROM THEME.
pū-pug-	pungō, *punch*	p u g-
pe-pig-	pangō, *fix*	p a g-

Other examples are : cadō, *fall*, cecidī (c a d-, 104, *c*) ; pariō, *bring forth*, peperī (p a r-, 104, *c*) ; pellō, *push*, pepulī (p o l-, 105, *h*) ; poscō, *demand*, poposcī (855) ; fallō, *deceive*, fefellī (855, 104, *c*) ; see also 923–932. caedō, *cut*, has cecidī (108, *a*) ; and a few old forms are quoted from verbs having an o or an u in the root with e in the reduplication : as, memordī, pepugī.

859. Four verbs with vowel roots also have a reduplicated perfect stem : dō, *give, put*, dare, dedī ; bibō, *drink*, bibere, bibī ; stō, *stand*, stāre, stetī, and sistō, *set*, sistere, -stitī, rarely stitī. Also four verbs in -ēre : mordeō, *bite*, momordī, pendeō, *hang*, pependī, spondeō, *promise*, spopondī, tondeō, *clip*, -totondī. In the root syllable of spopondī, *promised*, stetī, *stood*, stitī, *set*, and the old scicidī, *clove*, an s is dropped (173, 2).

860. In compounds the reduplication is commonly dropped: as,

cecidī, *fell*, compound concidī, *tumbled down*. Compounds of cucurrī, *ran*, sometimes retain the reduplication : as, prōcucurrī. Compounds of bibī, *drank*, didicī, *learned*, poposcī, *asked*, stitī, *set*, stetī, *stood*, and dedī, *gave, put*, retain it, the last two weakening e to i : as, restitī, *staid back*. abscondidī, *hid away*, usually becomes abscondī ; in apparent compounds, e is usually retained : as, circum stetī, *stood round*, vēnum dedī, *put for sale*. The reduplication is also lost in the simple verbs tulī, *carried*, old tetulī, and in scindō, *split*, scidī, which last is rare as a simple verb.

861. Some compounds with re- drop only the vowel of the reduplication (111, *a*): as, reccidī, *fell back*; rettulī, *brought back* (see also 781) ; repperī, *found*; rettudī, *beat back*. Some perfects occur only in composition: as, percellō, *knock down*, perculī ; cōntundō, *smash to pieces*, contudī ; diffindō, *split apart*, diffidī ; but fidī also occurs a couple of times as a simple verb.

862. (2.) Some verbs in -ere have a perfect stem consisting of a consonant root with a long vowel (135, 1) : as,

PERFECT STEM.	VERB.	FROM THEME.
ēd-	edō, *eat*	e d-
lēg-	legō, *pick up, read*	l e g-

Other examples are : fodiō, *dig*, fōdī ; fundō, *pour*, fūdī ; linquō, *leave*, līquī ; see 936–946. Three verbs in -ēre also have this form, sedeō, *sit*, sēdī, strīdeō, *grate*, strīdī, videō, *see*, vīdī ; and one in -īre, veniō, *come*, vēnī.

863. The following verbs in -ere with a in the present stem, have long ē in the perfect stem (145):

agō, *do*, ēgī, frangō, *break*, frēgī, pangō, *fix*, rarely pēgī, but always compēgī, impēgī, oppēgī; capiō, *take*, cēpī, faciō, *make*, fēcī, iaciō, *throw*, iēcī. So also the old co-ēpī, *began*, common coepī.

864. Two verbs in -āre and some in -ēre have a perfect stem consisting of a root which ends in -v- and has a long vowel: iuvō, *help*, iuvāre, iūvī, lavō, *wash*, lavāre or lavere, lāvī; caveō, *look out*, cavēre, cāvī; see 996.

865. Verbs in -uō, -uere, both primitives and denominatives, have usually a perfect stem in short u of the theme (124): as, luō, *pay*, luī; acuō, *sharpen*, acuī: see 947, 948. Forms with long ū are old and rare (126): as, fūī, adnūī, cōnstitūī, īnstitūī. fluō, *flow*, and struō, *pile*, have flūxī and strūxī (830).

866. (3.) Some verbs in -ere from roots ending in two consonants have a perfect stem consisting of the root: as,

PERFECT STEM.	VERB.	FROM THEME.
mand-	mandō, *chew*	m a n d-
pand-	pandō, *open*	p a n d-

Other examples are: vortō or vertō, *turn*, vortī or vertī; scandō, *climb*, -scendī; prehendō, *seize*, prehendī (855); vollō or vellō, *pluck*, vollī or vellī; see 949–951. Similarly ferveō, *boil*, fervere or fervēre, has fervī or ferbuī (823), and prandeō, *lunch*, prandēre, has prandī.

(B.) PERFECT STEM IN -S-, OR IN -V- OR -U-.

PERFECT STEM IN -S-.

867. Many verbs in -ere form their perfect stem by adding the suffix -s- to a root, which generally ends in a mute: as,

PERFECT STEM.	VERB.	FROM THEME.
carp-s-	carpō, *pluck*	c a r p-
scalp-s	scalpō, *dig*	s c a l p-
ges-s-	gerō, *bear*	g e s-
dīx-	dīcō, *say*	d ī c-

Other examples are: dūcō, *lead*, dūxī (100); fingō, *mould*, fīnxī (855); lūdō, *play*, lūsī (166, 2); scrībō *write*, scrīpsī (164, 1); struō, *pile*, strūxī (164, 1); vīvō, *live*, vīxī (98). Some verbs with a short vowel in the present, have a long vowel in the perfect: as, regō, *guide*, rēxī (135); intellegō, *understand*, intellēxī (823); tegō, *cover*, tēxī; iungō, *join*, iūnxī (855). And some verbs with a long vowel in the present, have a short vowel in the perfect: as, ūrō, *burn*, ussī (830). See 952–961.

868. Some verbs in -ēre also have a perfect in -s-: as algeō, *am cold*, alsī (170, 3); haereō, *stick*, haesī (166, 2): see 999, 1000. Also some in ·īre: as, sarciō, *patch*, sarsī (170, 3): see 1014, 1015.

PERFECT STEM IN -V- OR -U-.

869. (1.) Some verbs in **-ere,** with vowel roots, and almost all verbs in **-āre** or **-īre,** form their perfect stem by adding the suffix **-v-** to a theme ending in a long vowel: as,

PERFECT STEM.	VERB.	FROM THEME.
crē-v-	crēscō, *grow*	c r ē-
laudā-v-	laudō, *praise*	laudā-
audī-v-	audiō, *hear*	audī-

For other verbs in **-ere** with a perfect stem in **-v-**, and particularly **terō, cernō, spernō,** and **sternō,** see 962–970.

870. A few verbs in **-ere** have a perfect stem in **-v-** attached to a presumed theme in long **ī** : as, **cupiō,** *want,* **cupīvī; petō,** *aim at,* **petīvī; quaerō,** *inquire,* **quaesīvī; arcēssō,** *fetch,* **arcēssīvī;** see 966–970.

871. A few verbs in **-ēre** also have a perfect stem in **-v-** : as, **fleō,** *weep,* **flēre, flēvī;** see 1001–1003.   And three verbs in **-ēscere** have a perfect stem in **-v-** attached to a presumed theme in long **ē** : **-olēscō,** *grow,* **-olēvī; quiēscō,** *get quiet,* **quiēvī; suēscō,** *get used,* **suēvī.**

872. One verb in **-āscere** has a perfect stem in **-v-** attached to a presumed theme in long **ā:** **advesperāscit,** *it gets dusk,* **advesperāvit.**

873. (2.) Many verbs in **-ere** form their perfect stem by adding the suffix **-u-** to a consonant root: as,

PERFECT STEM.	VERB.	FROM THEME.
al-u-	alō, *nurture*	a l-
gen-u-	gignō, *beget*	g e n-

Other examples are : **colō,** *cultivate,* **coluī ; cōnsulō,** *consult,* **cōnsuluī; -cumbō,** *lie,* **-cubuī ; fremō,** *roar,* **fremuī ; ēliciō,** *draw out,* **ēlicuī ; molō,** *grind,* **moluī ; rapiō,** *snatch,* **rapuī ; serō,** *string,* **-seruī ; stertō,** *snore,* **-stertuī ; strepō,** *make a racket,* **strepuī ; texō,** *weave,* **texuī ; volō,** *will,* **voluī ; compescō,** *check,* **compescuī (855) ;** see 971–976.

874. Some verbs in **-āre** also have a perfect stem in **-u-:** as, **crepō,** *rattle,* **crepāre, crepuī (993) ;** and many in **-ēre:** as, **moneō,** *warn,* **monēre, monuī:** see 1004–1006; also four in **-īre :** as, **saliō,** *leap,* **salīre, saluī (1019).**

875. The perfect **potuī** to the present **possum (751)** is from a lost present ***poteō, *potēre (922).** **pōnere** (for ***po-sinere,** 112; 170, 2) forms an old perfect **posīvī (964),** later **posuī,** as if **pos-** were the stem.

PERFECT SUBJUNCTIVE.

876. The perfect subjunctive stem ends in **-erī-,** for which **-eri-** is sometimes used (35, 2, 3) : as,

rēxeri-m, rēxerī-s, rēxeri-t, rēxerī-mus, rēxerī-tis, rēxeri-nt.

877. In the perfect subjunctive, long ī is found before the person endings **-s, -mus,** and **-tis,** some 25 times, as follows: **-īs,** 18 times (Plaut. 3, Pac., Enn., Ter., Hor., Tib., Sen., inscr., once each, Ov. 8), **-īmus,** 4 times (Plaut. 3, Ter. 1), **-ītis,** 3 times (Plaut. 2, Enn. 1).

878. In the perfect subjunctive, short i is found, as in the future perfect, some 9 times, thus: **-is,** 8 times (Plaut. in anapests 3, Verg. 2, Hor. 3), **-imus** once (Verg.). But before **-tis,** short i is not found.

PERFECT IMPERATIVE.

879. One verb only, **meminī,** *remember,* has a perfect imperative; in this imperative, the person endings are not preceded by a vowel, thus: **memen-tō, memen-tōte.**

PLUPERFECT INDICATIVE.

880. The pluperfect indicative stem ends in **-erā-,** which becomes **-era-** in some of the persons : as,

rēxera-m, rēxerā-s, rēxera-t, rēxerā-mus, rēxerā-tis, rēxera-nt.

PLUPERFECT SUBJUNCTIVE.

881. The pluperfect subjunctive stem ends in **-issē-,** which becomes **-isse-** in some of the persons : as,

rēxisse-m, rēxissē-s, rēxisse-t, rēxissē-mus, rēxissē-tis, rēxisse-nt.

FUTURE PERFECT.

882. The future perfect stem ends in **-erō-** and **-eri-** : as,

rēxerō, rēxeri-s, rēxeri-t, rēxeri-mus, rēxeri-tis, rēxeri-nt.

883. In the future perfect, short i is found before the person endings **-s, -mus,** and **-tis,** some 40 times, as follows : **-is,** 29 times (Plaut. 2, Cic. 1, Catull. 1, Verg. 7, Hor. 12, Ov. 4, Germ. 1, Juv. 1); **-imus,** 3 times (Plaut., Ter., Lucr.) ; **-itis,** 8 times (Enn. 1, Plaut. 5, Ov. 2).

884. In the future perfect, long ī is found, as in the perfect subjunctive, some 33 times, thus : **-īs,** 28 times (Plaut. 3, Hor. 5, Ov. 15, Prop., Stat., Mart., Priap., inscr., once each), **-īmus,** once (Catull.), **-ītis,** 4 times (Ov. 3, Priap. 1).

SHORT OR OLD FORMS.

885. (1.) Some shorter forms in the perfect system are principally found in old Latin.

886. (*a.*) Shorter forms in the perfect indicative, the pluperfect subjunctive, and the infinitive, most of them from perfects in **-s-** (867), occur chiefly in verse : thus,

Perfect indicative, second person singular, common : as, **dīxtī** (Plaut., Ter., Cic.); plural, rare : as, **accestis** (Verg.). Pluperfect subjunctive singular, not very common : as, **exstīnxem** (Verg.), **intellēxēs** (Plaut.), **vīxet** (Verg.) ; plural, once only, **ērēpsēmus** (Hor.). Infinitive, **dīxe** (Plaut.), **cōnsūmpse** (Lucr.).

887. (*b.*) A perfect subjunctive stem in -sī- or in -ssī-, and a future perfect indicative stem in -so|e- or in -sso|e-, occur chiefly in old laws and prayers, and in dramatic verse: as,

Perfect subjunctive: **faxim, faxīs,** FAXSEIS (inscr. 145 B.C.), **faxit, faxīmus, faxītis, faxint; ausim, ausīs, ausit; locāssim, amāssis, servāssit, amāssint, prohibēssis, prohibēssit, cohibēssit, licēssit.**

Future perfect indicative: **faxō, faxis, faxit, faxitis, capsō, recepsō, iussō, occīsit, capsimus; levāssō, invitāssitis, mulcāssitis, exoculāssitis, prohibēssis, prohibēssint.** Denominatives in -āre have also, in old Latin, a future perfect infinitive: as, **impetrāssere.**

888. Passive inflections, as future perfect **faxitur, turbāssitur,** deponent MERCASSITVR (inscr. 111 B.C.), are very rare; and, indeed, with the exception of **faxō** and **ausim,** even the active forms had become antiquated by 150 B.C. Denominatives in -īre never have the above formations. But **ambiō,** *canvass,* is thought to have a future perfect **ambīssit** twice (Plaut. prol.).

889. (2.) Shortened forms from perfect stems formed by the suffix -v- (869) are very common in all periods.

890. (*a.*) In tenses formed from perfect stems in -āv-, -ēv-, and -ōv-, **v** is often dropped before -is-, -ēr-, or -er-, and the vowels thus brought together are contracted (153, 1): as,

laudāvistī, laudāstī; laudāvistis, laudāstis; laudāvērunt, laudārunt (but the form in -re, as **laudāvēre,** is never contracted); **laudāverim, laudārim,** &c.; **laudāveram, laudāram,** &c.; **laudāvissem, laudāssem,** &c.; **laudāverō, laudārō,** &c.; **laudāvisse, laudāsse.**

-plēvistī, -plēstī; -plēvistis, -plēstis; -plēvērunt, -plērunt; plēverim, -plērim, &c.; **-plēveram, -plēram,** &c.; **-plēvissem, -plēssem,** &c.; **-plēverō, -plērō,** &c.; **-plēvisse, -plēsse.**

nōvistī, nōstī; nōvistis, nōstis; nōvērunt, nōrunt; nōverim, nōrim, &c.; **nōveram, nōram,** &c.; **nōvissem, nōssem,** &c.; **nōverō** always retains the **v,** but **cōgnōrō,** &c.; **nōvisse, nōsse.**

891. The verbs in which **v** belongs to the root (864), are not thus shortened, except **moveō,** mostly in compounds. From **iuvō, iuerint** (Catull.), **adiuerō** (Enn.), once each, and twice **adiuerit** (Plaut., Ter.) are unnecessary emendations.

892. Contractions in the perfect before **-t** and **-mus** are rare: as, **inrītāt, disturbāt; suēmus** or **suēmus** (Lucr.), **nōmus** (Enn.), **cōnsuēmus** (Prop.).

893. (*b.*) In tenses formed from perfect stems in -īv-, **v** is often dropped before -is-, -ēr-, or -er-; but contraction is common only in the forms which have -is-: as,

audīvistī, audīstī; audīvistis, audīstis; audīvērunt, audiērunt; audīverim, audierim, &c.; **audīveram, audieram,** &c.; **audīvissem, audīssem,** &c.; **audīverō, audierō,** &c.; **audīvisse, audīsse.** Sometimes **audiī, audiit, audīt.** Intermediate between the long and the short forms are **audiērās** and **audierit,** once each (Ter.). In the perfect subjunctive, **sinō** has **sīverīs** (Plaut., Cato), **sīrīs** (Plaut., Cato, Liv.), **sīreis** (Pac.), or **seirīs** (Plaut.), **sīrit** (Plaut., Liv.), **sīrītis** (Plaut.), **sīverint** (Plaut., Curt.), **sierint** (Cic., Curt.), or **sīrint** (Plaut.). **dēsinō** is thought to have **dēsīmus** in the perfect indicative a couple of times (Sen., Plin. *Ep.*).

NOUNS OF THE VERB.

INFINITIVE.

894. The active infinitive has the ending **-re** in the present, and **-isse** in the perfect : as,

dare; regere, capere; laudāre, monēre, audīre. rēxisse; laudāvisse or laudāsse, monuisse, audīvisse or audīsse.

895. For **-rē** in old Latin, see 134, 2. The infinitive of fīō, *become*, ends in **-rī**, fīerī, with a passive ending (789); twice fīere (Enn. Laev.). An older form for **-re** is **-se**, found in esse, *to be*, ēsse, *to eat*, and their compounds. For **velle**, *to wish* (mālle, nōlle), see 166, 8. In the perfect, eō, *go*, sometimes has **-iisse** in compounds (766), and in poetry, petō, *go to*, has rarely petiisse.

896. The present infinitive passive of verbs in **-ere** has the ending **-ī** ; that of other verbs has **-rī** : as,

regī, capī; laudārī, monērī, audīrī. ferō, *carry*, has ferrī. The length of the ī is sometimes indicated by the spelling ei (29, 2) : as, DAREI.

897. A longer form in **-ier** for **-ī**, and **-rier** for **-rī**, is common in old laws and dramatic verse, and occurs sometimes in other poetry: as, FIGIER, *to be posted*, GNOSCIER, *to be read* (inscr. 186 B.C.) ; dīcier, *to be said*, cūrārier, *to be looked after* (Plaut.); dominārier, *to be lord paramount* (Verg.).

898. The place of the perfect passive, future active, and future passive infinitive is supplied by a circumlocution, as seen in the paradigms. For the future perfect **-āssere**, see 887.

GERUNDIVE AND GERUND.

899. The gerundive stem is formed by adding **-ndo-**, nominative **-ndus, -nda, -ndum**, to the present stem : as,

dandus, stem dando- ; regendus, capiendus; laudandus, monendus, audiendus. Verbs in **-ere** and **-īre** often have **-undus**, when not preceded by u or v, especially in formal style: as, capiundus; eō, *go*, always has eundum, and orior, *rise*, oriundus. For the adjective use, see 288. The gerund is like the oblique cases of the neuter singular. For **-bundus**, see 289; **-cundus**, 290.

SUPINE.

900. The supine stem is formed by the suffix **-tu-**, which is often changed to **-su-** (912).

This suffix is attached to a root or to a form of the present stem after the manner of the perfect participle (906): as, nūntiātum, *to report*, nūntiātū, *in reporting*, stem nūntiātu-. Many of the commonest verbs have no supine: as, sum, eō, ferō; regō, emō, tegō; amō, dēleō, doceō, &c., &c.

PRESENT PARTICIPLE.

901. The present participle stem is formed by adding **-nt-** or **-nti-**, nominative **-ns**, to the present stem : as,

dāns, *giving*, stems dant-, danti- ; regēns, capiēns ; laudāns, monēns, audiēns.

902. The adjective **sontem** (accusative, no nominative), which was originally the participle of **sum**, has **o** before the suffix, and **absēns** and **praesēns** have **e**; the participle of **eō** has **ē** in the nominative singular, otherwise **u, iēns, euntis,** &c. **n** rarely drops before **-s** (63): as, LIBES (inscr.), **exsultās** (Enn.), **animās** (Lucr.).

903. Some adjectives which were originally present participles have no verb: as, **clēmēns,** *merciful*, **ēlegāns,** *choice*, **ēvidēns,** *clear*, **frequēns,** *thick*, **petulāns,** *wanton*, **recēns,** *fresh*, **repēns,** *sudden*, &c., &c. For **potēns,** *powerful*, see 922.

FUTURE PARTICIPLE.

904. The future participle suffix is **-tūro-,** nominative **-tūrus, -tūra, -tūrum,** which is often changed to **-sūro-,** nominative **-sūrus, -sūra, -sūrum** (912).

This suffix is added to a theme after the manner of the perfect participle (906) : as, **rēctūrus,** *going to guide;* **laudātūrus,** *going to praise.*

905. Some future participles have a different formation from that of the perfect participle: as, **mortuus,** *dead*, **moritūrus;** see also in the dictionary **arguō, fruor, orior, ruō, secō.** And some verbs have two forms of the future participle : as, **āgnōscō, īgnōscō, hauriō, iuvō, pariō.** Some verbs which have no perfect participle have a future participle : as, **acquiēscō, appāreō, ardeō, caleō, careō, doleō, ēsuriō, fugiō, haereō, incidō, iaceō, -nuō, parcō, rauciō, recidō, sonō, stō, valeō.**

PERFECT PARTICIPLE.

906. The perfect participle suffix is **-to-,** nominative **-tus, -ta, -tum,** which is often changed to **-so-,** nominative **-sus, -sa, -sum** (912).

907. The perfect participle was originally active as well as passive, and some participles have retained the active meaning : as,

adultus, *grown up;* **ēmersus,** *rising out from;* **exōsus, perōsus,** *hating bitterly;* **placitus,** *engaging;* **iūrātus,** *sworn*, **coniūrātus,** *conspiring;* **prānsus,** *having lunched*, **cēnātus,** *having dined*, **pōtus,** *drunk*, &c. The perfect participles of deponents are usually active, but sometimes passive : as, **meditātus,** *having studied*, or *studied.* Many verbs are not accompanied by a perfect participle (811), particularly verbs in **-ēre**, with a parallel adjective in **-idus** (287). Intransitive verbs have usually only the neuter. A perfect active participle **meminēns** is said to have been used twice (Plaut., Laev.).

908. The perfect participle is formed in one of two separate ways :

909. (1.) From a theme consisting of a root ; in this way the participles of most verbs in **-ere** and **-ēre** are formed : as,

gestus, *carried*, **aptus,** *fit*, **solūtus,** *loosed* (142), **iūnctus,** *joined* (831), **sparsus,** *sprinkled* (170, 3); **doctus,** *taught.*

910. In some consonant root participles of verbs in **-ere, -āre,** or **-ēre,** which have the suffix **-u-** in the perfect stem (873), the **-to-** is preceded by a short **i**: as, **genitus,** *born* (971–976); **domitus,** *tamed* (993); **monitus,** *warned* (1003, 1004, 1009). In old Latin, e occurs : as, MERETA (41); e is retained in **vegetus,** *sprightly.* One participle has **-tuo-** : **mortuus,** *dead.*

911. Some verbs in -āre have participles from consonant roots: as, **frictus**, *rubbed*, fricō, fricāre; see 993. Also some in -īre: as, **fartus**, *stuffed* (170, 3), farciō, farcīre; **fultus**, *propped*, fulciō, fulcīre; see 1011–1015, and 1017, 1019, 1020.

912. Roots in -d- and -t- change -to- to -so-, before which the dentals change to **s** (159). After long vowels, nasals, and liquids the double **ss** is simplified to **s**: as, **fossus**, *dug*, but **dīvīsus**, *divided;* **vorsus** or **versus**, *turned*. The suffix -so- is also found with some roots in -l-, -m-, or -r- and a few others: as, **pulsus** (159).

913. (2.) From a theme in long **ā** or in long **ī**; in this way participles are regularly formed from denominatives in -āre or -īre respectively: as,

> **laudātus**, *praised;* **audītus**, *heard*.

914. A few perfect participles of verbs in -ere are formed from a presumed theme in long **ī**, or long **ē**, or from one in long **ū**: as, **petītus**, *aimed at;* **exolētus**, *grown out;* see 967-970; **tribūtus**, *assigned;* see 947, 948.

915. (1.) Many perfect participles formed from consonant roots have a short root vowel (135, 1): as,

> **adspectus**, *beheld;* **captus**, *taken;* **coctus**, *cooked;* **commentus**, *devising;* **cultus**, *tilled;* **dictus**, *said*, verb dīcō; **ductus**, *led*, dūcō; **factus**, *made;* **fossus**, *dug;* **gestus**, *carried;* **inlectus**, *allured;* **questus**, *complaining;* **raptus**, *seized;* **tersus**, *neat;* **textus**, *woven;* **vorsus**, *turned*.

916. (2.) Some perfect participles formed from consonant roots have a long root vowel, sometimes even when the vowel of the parallel present stem is short (135, 1; 122, *f*): as,

> **fīxus**, *fastened*, verb fīgō; -**flīctus**, *dashed*, -flīgō; **pāstus**, *fed*, pāscō; **pollūctus**, *offered up*, pollūceō; **scrīptus**, *written*, scrībō; -**cāsus**, *fallen*, cadō. Also **āctus**, *driven*, agō; **vīsus**, *seen*, videō; **frūctus**, *enjoying*, fruor; **lēctus**, *culled*, legō; **pictus**, *painted*, pingō; **rēctus**, *ruled*, regō; **ēsus**, *eaten*, edō; **strūctus**, *piled*, struō; **tēctus**, *covered*, tegō; **ūnctus**, *anointed*, inguō; **frāctus**, *broken*, frangō; **pāctus**, *fixed*, pangō. Furthermore, **iūnctus**, *joined*, iungō; **sānctus**, *hallowed*, sanciō (831); also, **fūnctus**, *having performed*, fungor.

917. (1.) Most perfect participles formed from vowel roots have a long root vowel: as,

> **lātus**, *borne* (169, 1); **nātus**, *born;* -**plētus**, *filled;* **trītus**, *worn;* **nōtus**, *known;* **sūtus**, *sewed*. So also an isolated **rūtus** in the law phrase **rūta caesa**, or **rūta et caesa**, *diggings and cuttings*, i.e. *minerals and timber*.

918. (2.) Ten perfect participles formed from vowel roots have a short root vowel; they are:

citus, datus, *hurried, given*	-**rutus, satus**, *fallen, planted*
itum, ratus, *gone, thinking*	**situs, status**, *lying, set*
litus, quitus, *besmeared, been able*	

919. As **citus**, so always **percitus** and **incitus** (once **incītus**, doubtful); usually **concitus**, rarely **concītus**; **excitus** and **excītus** equally common; always **accītus**. **ambitus** always has long **ī** (763). **āgnitus**, *recognized*, **cōgnitus**, *known*, and the adjectives **inclutus** or **inclitus**, *of high renown*, and **putus**, *clean*, have a short root vowel. For **dēfrūtum**, **dēfrutum**, see 134, 1.

LIST OF VERBS

ARRANGED ACCORDING TO THE PRINCIPAL PARTS.

920. I. The principal parts of root verbs and of verbs in -ere are formed in a variety of ways and are best learned separately for every verb (922–986).

921. II. The principal parts of verbs in -āre, -ēre, and -īre, are usually formed as follows :

laudō, *praise*	laudāre	laudāvī	laudātus
moneō, *advise*	monēre	monuī	monitus
audiō, *hear*	audīre	audīvī	audītus

For other formations, see 989–1022.

I. Primitive Verbs.

(A.) ROOT VERBS.

922. Root verbs have their principal parts as follows :

sum, *am*	esse	——	——
——, *become, get, am*	fore	fuī	——

For **fuam,** &c., **forem,** &c., **fore,** see 750. **fuī,** &c., serves as the perfect system of **sum.**

pos-sum, *can*	pos-se	——	——
——, *can*	——	potuī	——

potuī, &c., serves as the perfect system of **possum.** Of the present system of **potuī,** only **potēns,** *powerful,* is used, and only as an adjective.

dō, *give, put*	dare	dedī	datus

For compounds, see 757.

bibō, *drink*	bibere	bibī	pōtus

So the compounds, with the reduplication preserved in the perfect system (860).

serō, *sow*	serere	sēvī	satus

Compounds have **i** for **a** in the perfect participle : as, **cōn-situs.**

sistō, *set*	sistere	-stitī, rarely stitī	status
inquam, *quoth I*	——	inquiī once	——
eō, *go*	īre	iī, very rarely īvī	itum, -itus
queō, *can*	quīre	quīvī	quitus
ne-queō, *can't*	ne-quīre	ne-quīvī	ne-quitus
edō, *eat*	ēsse	ēdī	ēsus
volō, *will, wish, want*	velle	voluī	——
nōlō, *won't*	nōlle	nōluī	——
mālō, *like better*	mālle	māluī	——
ferō, *carry*	ferre	(tulī)	(lātus)

For **tulī,** old **tetulī,** and **lātus,** see 780 ; for the perfect of **re-ferō,** 861

(B.) VERBS IN -ere.

(A.) PERFECT STEM WITHOUT A SUFFIX.

923. (1*a*.) The following verbs in **-ere** have a reduplicated perfect stem (858), and the perfect participle, when used, in **-tus** :

924. (*a.*) With the present stem in **-o|e-** (829).

canō, *make music*   **canere**   **cecinī**   **(cantātus)**

For **con-cinō, oc-cinō,** and **prae-cinō,** see 971 and 823.

tendō, *stretch*   **tendere**   **tetendī**   **tentus**

For **tennitur** (Ter.), **dis-tennite** (Plaut.), see 166, 4 ; late participle **tēnsus.** Compounds have **-tendī** (860) and **-tentus.** But sometimes **ex-tēnsus,** and in late writers, **dē-tēnsus, dis-tēnsus, os-tēnsus,** and **re-tēnsus.**

925. (*b.*) With the present stem in a nasalized root followed by **-o|e-** (831).

pangō, *fix*   **pangere**   **pepigī,** *agreed*   **pāctus**

In meaning, the perfect **pepigī** corresponds to **pacīscor ; pānxit,** *made, set in verse* (Enn.), **pānxerit,** *set* (Col.), **pēgit** (Pac.), **pēgerit** (Cic.), *fixed,* once each. For **com-pingo** and **im-pingō,** see 938.

pungō, *punch*   **pungere**   **pupugī**   **pūnctus**

For **com-pungō** and **ex-pungō,** see 954 and 823.

tangō, *touch*   **tangere**   **tetigī**   **tāctus**

In old Latin : **tagō** (Turp.), **tagit, tagam** (Pac.). Compounds have **i** for **a** in the present system : as, **con-tingō, con-tingere, con-tigī** (860), **con-tāctus ;** in old Latin : **at-tigās** (Plaut., Ter., Acc., Pac.), **at-tigat** (Pac.), **at-tigātis** (Plaut., Pac.).

926. (*c.*) With the present stem in **-lo|e-** (833).

tollō, *take off*   **tollere**   **(sus-tulī)**   **(sub-lātus)**

As the perfect and perfect participle of **tollō** are appropriated by **ferō, tollō** takes those of **sus-tollō.** The original perfect is **tetulī** (860).

927. (*d.*) With the present stem in **-sco|e-** (834).

discō, *learn*   **discere**   **didicī**   ——
poscō, *demand*   **poscere**   **poposcī**   ——

For **poposcī,** see 855. For **-didicī** and **-poposcī,** see 860.

928. (*e.*) With the present stem in **-io|e-** (836).

pariō, *bring forth*   **parere**   **peperī**   **partus**

For forms in **-īre,** see 791. **com-periō,** 1012 ; **re-periō,** 1011.

929. (1 *b.*) The following verbs in **-ere** have a reduplicated perfect stem (858), and the perfect participle, when used, is **-sus** (912).

930. (*a.*) With the present stem in **o-|e-** (829.)

cadō, *fall*   **cadere**   **cecidī**   **-cāsus**

Compounds have **i** for **a** in the present system : as, **oc-cidō, oc-cidere, oc-cidī** (860), **oc-cāsus.** Rarely **e** in the present and perfect systems (Enn. Lucr., Varr.) : as, **ac-cedere, ac-cedisset** (109). For the perfect of **re-cidō,** see 861.

caedō, *fell, cut*   **caedere**   **cecidī**   **caesus**

Compounds have **ī** for **ae** : as, **ac-cīdō, ac-cīdere, ac-cīdī** (860), **ac-cīsus.**

parcō, *spare*   parcere   pepercī   ——

pepercī, &c. (regularly in Cic., Caes., Hor., Ov., Mart.; Nep. once; also Plaut. twice, Ter. once). Old parsī, &c. (Plaut. 8, Cato, Ter., Nov., Nep., once each); once parcuīt (Naev.). Compounds: com-perce (Plaut.), con-parsit (Ter.), in-perce, im-percitō, re-percis (Plaut.), re-parcent (Lucr.).

pendō, *weigh, pay*   pendere   pependī   pēnsus

931. (*b.*) With the present stem in a nasalized root followed by -o|e- (831).

tundō, *pound*   tundere   tutudī not used   tūnsus

For the perfect of re-tundō, see 861 ; other compounds have the perfect -tudī (861), but once con-tūdit (Enn.). Perfect participle, tūsus (Plin., Mart.); compounds: con-tūnsus (Plin.), con-tūsus (Cato, Varr., Caes., Lucr., Sal., Verg., &c.); ob-tūnsus (Plaut., Verg., Liv., Sen.), op-tūsus, ob-tūsus (Lucr., Sen., Quintil., Tac.); per-tūssus (Plaut.), per-tūsus (Cato, Lucr., Liv., Sen., &c.); re-tūnsus (Plaut., Verg.), re-tūsus (Cic., Lucr., Hor.); sub-tūsus (Tib.).

932. (*c.*) With the present stem in -ro|e-, or -lo|e- (833).

currō, *run*   currere   cucurrī   cursum

For perfect of compounds, see 860.

fallō, *cheat*   fallere   fefellī   falsus

Compound re-fellō, re-fellere, re-fellī (860), ——.

pellō, *push*   pellere   pepulī   pulsus

For the perfect of re-pellō, see 861. Other compounds have -pulī (860).

933. (1 *c.*) The following verbs in **-ere** are without the reduplication (861):

934. (*a.*) With the present stem in a nasalized root followed by -o|e- (831).

findō, *split apart*   findere   -fidī, rarely fidī   fissus
scindō, *rend*   scindere   -scidī, rarely scidī   scissus

935. (*b.*) With the present stem in -lo|e- (833).

per-cellō, *knock down* per-cellere   per-culī   per-culsus

936. (2 *a.*) The following verbs in **-ere** have a perfect stem consisting of a consonant root with a long vowel (862), and the perfect participle, when used, in **-tus** :

937. (*a.*) With the present stem in -o|e- (829).

agō, *drive*   agere   ēgī   āctus

Real compounds have i for a in the present system: as, ab-igō, ab-igere, ab-ēgī, ab-āctus; but per-agō retains a. cōgō and dēgō are contracted: cōgō, cōgere, co-ēgī, co-āctus; dēgō, dēgere, ——, ——.

emō, *take, buy*   emere   ēmī   emptus

co-emō retains e in the present system, and usually inter-emō and per-emō ; other compounds have -imō. For cōmō, dēmō, prōmō, and sūmō, see 952.

——, *strike*   ——   īcī   ictus

Forms of the present system are īcit (Plaut., Lucr.), īcitur (Plin.), īcimur (Lucr.).

legō, *pick up, read*   legere   lēgī   lēctus

Compounds with ad, inter, nec-, per, prae, and re-, have -legō in the present system, others -ligō. For dī-ligō, intel-legō, neg-legō, see 952.

938. (*b.*) With the present stem in a nasalized root followed by -o|e- (831).

com-pingo, *fix together* com-pingere com-pēgī com-pāctus·

A compound of **pangō** (925, 823).

frangō, *smash* frangere frēgī frāctus

Compounds have **i** for **a** in the present system : as, cōn-fringō, cōn-fringere, cōn-frēgī, cōn-frāctus.

im-pingō, *drive in* im-pingere im-pēgī im-pāctus

A compound of **pangō** (925, 823). So also op-pēgī.

linquō, *leave* linquere līquī -lictus
rumpō, *burst* rumpere rūpī ruptus

So the compounds. But Plautus has con-rumptus and dir-rumptus.

vincō, *conquer* vincere vīcī victus

939. (*c.*) With the present stem in -sco|e- (834).

pavēscō, *get afraid* pavēscere ex-pāvī ———

940. (*d.*) With the present stem in -io|e- (836).

capiō, *take* capere cēpī captus

Compounds have **i** for **a** in the present system and **e** in the perfect participle : as, in-cipiō, in-cipere, in-cēpī, in-ceptus. In the present system, **e** is rare: as, re-cepit (Lucr.); **u** is frequent in old Latin.

coepiō, *begin* rare coepere once coepī coeptus

See 812–814.

faciō, *make* facere fēcī factus

For **fac**, see 846; for passive, 788. Compounds have **i** for **a** in the present system and **e** in the perfect participle: as, ef-ficiō, ef-ficere, ef-fēcī, ef-fectus.

fugiō, *run away* fugere fūgī ———
iaciō, *throw* iacere iēcī iactus

Compounds have -iciō (104, *c*), -icere, -iēcī, -iectus : as, ē-iciō, ē-icere, ē-iēcī, ē-iectus. In old Latin the present system has rarely -ieciō; -iecere. dis-sīciō is sometimes used (Lucr., Verg.) for dis-iciō.

941. (2 *b.*) The following verbs in -ere have a perfect stem consisting of a consonant root with a long vowel (862), and the perfect participle, when used, in -sus (912).

942. (*a.*) With the present stem in -o|e- (829).

cūdō, *hammer* cūdere -cūdī -cūsus

943. (*b.*) With reduplication and -o|e- in the present stem (829).

sīdō, *settle* sīdere sīdī, -sīdī, -sēdī -sessus

944. (*c.*) With the present stem in a nasalized root followed by -o|e- (831).

fundō, *pour* fundere fūdī fūsus

945. (*d.*) With the present stem in -so|e- for -to|e- (835).

vīsō, *go to see* vīsere vīsī ———

946. (*e.*) With the present stem in -io|e- (836).

fodiō, *dig* fodere fōdī fossus

For forms in -īre, see 791.

947. (2 *c.*) The following verbs in **-ere** (367) with the present stem in **-º|e-** (837, 840), have the perfect stem in **-u-** or in **-v-** of the theme (865), and the perfect participle, when used, in **-tus**:

acuō, *sharpen*	acuere	acuī	acūtus adjective
arguō, *make clear*	arguere	arguī	argūtus rare
con-gruō, *agree*	con-gruere	con-gruī	
ex-uō, *doff*	ex-uere	ex-uī	ex-ūtus
im-buō, *give a smack of*	im-buere	im-buī	im-būtus
ind-uō, *don*	ind-uere	ind-uī	ind-ūtus
in-gruō, *impend*	in-gruere	in-gruī	———
luō, *pay, atone for*	luere	luī	-lūtus, *washed*
metuō, *fear*	metuere	metuī	metūtus once
-nuō, *nod*	-nuere	-nuī	———
pluit, *it rains*	pluere	pluit, plūvit	———
ruō, *tumble down*	ruere	ruī	-rutus
so-lvō, *loose*	so-lvere	so-lvī	so-lūtus
spuō, *spit*	spuere	-spuī	———
statuō, *set*	statuere	statuī	statūtus

Compounds have **i** for **a** throughout: as, cōn-stituō, cōn-stituere, &c.

volvō, *roll*	volvere	volvī	volūtus
suō, *sew*	suere	-suī	sūtus
tribuō, *assign*	tribuere	tribuī	tribūtus

948. Two verbs in **-ere** with the present stem in **-nuº|e-** (833), have the perfect stem in **-nu-** (865), and the perfect participle, when used, in **-tus**:

minuō, *lessen*	minuere	minuī	minūtus
sternuō, *sneeze*	sternuere	sternuī	———

949. (3.) The following verbs in **-ere** have a perfect stem consisting of a root ending in two consonants (866), and the perfect participle in **-sus** (912):

950. (*a.*) With the present stem in **-º|e-** (829); most have a nasal (831).

-cendō, *light*	-cendere	-cendī	-cēnsus
-fendō, *hit*	-fendere	-fendī	-fēnsus
mandō, *chew*	mandere	mandī once	mānsus
pandō, *open*	pandere	pandī	passus, pānsus

For dis-pennite (Plaut.), see 166,4. dis-pandō, dis-pendō, has perfect participle dis-pessus (Plaut., Lucr.), dis-pānsus (Lucr., Plin., Suet.).

pre-hendō, *seize*	pre-hendere	pre-hendī	pre-hēnsus

Rarely prae-hendō; but very often prēndō, prēndere, prēndī, prēnsus.

scandō, *climb*	scandere	-scendī	-scēnsus

Compounds have **e** for **a** throughout: as, dē-scendō, dē-scendere, &c.

vorrō, verrō, *sweep*	vorrere, verrere	-vorrī, -verrī	vorsus, versus
vortō, vertō, *turn*	vortere, vertere	vortī, vertī	vorsus, versus

951. (*b.*) With the present stem in **-lº|e-** (833).

vollō, vellō, *tear*	vollere, vellere	vollī, vellī	volsus, vulsus

Late perfect vulsī (Sen., Luc.); -vulsī (Laber., Col., Sen., Luc.).

(B.) PERFECT STEM IN -s-, OR IN -v- OR -u-.

PERFECT STEM IN -S-.

952. (1*a*.) The following verbs in -ere have the perfect stem in -s- (867), and the perfect participle, when used, in -tus:

953. (*a.*) With the present stem in -°|e- (829).

carpō, *nibble, pluck*   carpere   carpsī   carptus
   Compounds have **e** for **a** : as, dē-cerpō, dē-cerpere, dē-cerpsī, dē-cerptus.

com-būrō, *burn up*   com-būrere   com-bussī   com-būstus
cōmō, *put up*   cōmere   cōmpsī   cōmptus
   Compound of **com-** and emō (937, 823). See also dēmō, prōmō, sūmō.

coquō, *cook*   coquere   coxī   coctus
dēmō, *take away*   dēmere   dēmpsī   dēmptus
dīcō, *say*   dīcere   dīxī   dictus
   For dīc, see 846.

dī-ligō, *esteem*   dī-ligere   dī-lēxī   dī-lēctus
   Compound of **dis-** and legō (937, 823). See also intel-legō and neg-legō.

dūcō, *lead*   dūcere   dūxī   ductus
   For dūc, ē-dūc, see 846.

-flīgō, *smash*   -flīgere   -flīxī   -flīctus
   Of the simple verb, flīgit occurs (L. Andr.), flīgēbant (Lucr.), and flīgī (L. Andr., Acc.).

gerō, *carry*   gerere   gessī   gestus
intel-legō, *understand*   intel-legere   intel-lēxī   intel-lēctus
neg-legō, *disregard*   neg-legere   neg-lēxī   neg-lēctus
   In the perfect system very rarely intel-lēgī and neg-lēgī (862, 823).

nūbō, *veil, marry (a man)* nūbere   nūpsī   nūpta
prōmō, *take out*   prōmere   prōmpsī   prōmptus
regō, *guide, rule*   regere   rēxī   rēctus
   In the present system, con-rigō and ē-rigō ; commonly por-rigō, sometimes porgō ; rarely sur-rigō, commonly surgō ; always pergō.

rēpō, *creep*   rēpere   rēpsī
scalpō, *dig*   scalpere   scalpsī   scalptus
scrībō, *write*   scrībere   scrīpsī   scrīptus
sculpō, *carve*   sculpere   sculpsī   sculptus
struō, *build up*   struere   strūxī   strūctus
sūgō, *suck*   sūgere   sūxī   suctus
sūmō, *take up*   sūmere   sūmpsī   sūmptus
tegō, *cover*   tegere   tēxī   tēctus
trahō, *drag*   trahere   trāxī   tractus
ūrō, *burn*   ūrere   ussī   ustus
vehō, *cart*   vehere   vēxī   vectus
vīvō, *live*   vīvere   vīxī   ———

954. (*b.*) With the present stem in a nasalized root followed by -o|e- (831)

cingō, *gird*	cingere	cīnxī	cīnctus
com-pungō, *prick over*	com-pungere	com-pūnxī	com-pūnctus

A compound of **pungō** (925, 823).

ē-mungō, *clean out*	ē-mungere	ē-mūnxī	ē-mūnctus
ex-pungō, *prick out*	ex-pungere	ex-pūnxī	ex-pūnctus

A compound of **pungō** (925, 823).

fingō, *mould*	fingere	fīnxī	fīctus
iungō, *join*	iungere	iūnxī	iūnctus
pingō, *paint*	pingere	pīnxī	pīctus
plangō, *beat*	plangere	plānxī	plānctus
stinguo, *poke, poke out*	stinguere	-stīnxī	-stīnctus
stringō, *peel, graze*	stringere	strīnxī	strīctus
tingō, *wet*	tingere	tīnxī	tīnctus
unguo, *anoint*	unguere	ūnxī	ūnctus

Sometimes **ungō**, **ungere**, &c., in the present system.

955. (*c.*) With the present stem in -no|e- (833).

temnō, *scorn*	temnere	(con-tempsī)	(con-temptus)

956. (*d.*) With the present stem in -io|e- (836).

ad-liciō, *lure*	ad-licere	ad-lexī	————
in-liciō, *inveigle*	in-licere	in-lexī	in-lectus
pel-liciō, *lead astray*	pel-licere	pel-lexī	pel-lectus
-spiciō, *spy*	-spicere	-spēxī	-spectus

Forms of the simple verb are old and rare : as, **specitur, spicit, spece** (Plaut.), **specimus** (Varr.), **spiciunt** (Cato), **spēxit** (Naev., Enn.).

957. (1 *b.*) The following verbs in -ere have the perfect stem in -s- (867), and the perfect participle, when used, in -sus (912):

958. (*a.*) With the present stem in -o|e- (829).

cēdō, *move along*	cēdere	cessī	cessus
claudō, *shut*	claudere	clausī	clausus

Sometimes **clūdō, clūdere, clūsī, clūsus.** Compounds have **ū** for **au** throughout.

dī-vidō, *separate*	dī-videre	dī-vīsī	dī-vīsus
fīgō, *pin*	fīgere	fīxī	fīxus, twice fīctus
fluō, *flow*	fluere	flūxī	fluxus adjective
laedō, *hurt*	laedere	laesī	laesus

Compounds have **ī** for **ae** throughout : as, in-līdō, in-līdere, &c.

lūdō, *play*	lüdere	lūsī	lūsus
mittō, *send*	mittere	mīsī	missus
mergō, *dip, duck*	mergere	mersī	mersus
plaudō, *clap*	plaudere	plausī	plausus

Also **ap-plaudō, ap-plaudere**, &c. Other compounds have usually **ō** for **au** throughout : as, **ex-plōdō**, &c. ; but **ex-plaudō** (Lucr.).

premō, *squeeze*	premere	pressī	pressus

Compounds have **i** for **e** in the present system : as, **com-primō**, &c.

rādō, *scrape*	rādere	rāsī	rāsus
rōdō, *gnaw*	rōdere	rōsī	rōsus
spargō, *scatter*	spargere	sparsī	sparsus

Compounds usually have **e** for **a** throughout: as, cōn-spergō, &c.

| trūdō, *shove* | trūdere | trūsī | trūsus |
| vādō, *go* | vādere | -vāsī | -vāsus |

959. (*b.*) With the present stem in -sco|e- (834).

algēscō, *get cold*	algēscere	alsī	——
ardēscō, *flame out*	ardēscere	arsī (ex-arsī)	——
lūcēscō, *grow light*	lūcēscere	-lūxī	——

Sometimes in the present system lūcīscō, lūcīscere, &c.

| frīgēscō, *grow cold* | frīgēscere | -frīxī | —— |
| vīvēscō, *get alive* | vīvēscere | (re-vīxī) | —— |

In composition, also re-vīvīscō, re-vīvīscere.

960. (*c.*) With the present stem in -to|e- (835).

| flectō, *turn* | flectere | flexī | flexus |
| nectō, *bind together* | nectere | nexī, nexuī | nexus |

Perfect system rare: nexit (Lucil., Acc.); nexuit, ad-nexuerant (Sall.).

| pectō, *comb* | pectere | pexī *once* | pexus |

961. (*d.*) With the present stem in -io|e- (836).

| quatiō, *shake* | quatere | -cussī | quassus |

Compounds drop the **a** (111, *a*): as, in-cutiō, in-cutere, in-cussī, in-cussus.

PERFECT STEM IN -V-.

962. (2 *a.*) The following verbs in -ere have the perfect stem in -v-, preceded by a long vowel of the root (869), and the perfect participle, when used, in -tus:

963. (*a.*) With the present stem in -o|e- (829).

| terō, *rub* | terere | trīvī | trītus |

Perfect infinitive once in pentameter verse (823) at-teruisse (Tib.).

964. (*b.*) With the present stem in -no|e- (833).

| cernō, *sift, separate, see* | cernere | crēvī, *decided* | certus, -crētus |
| linō, *besmear* | linere | lēvī, rarely līvī | litus |

In the present system some forms in -īre are used by late writers.

| sinō, *leave, let* | sinere | sīvī | situs |

Perfect system forms of sinō and dē-sinō in -v- are: sīvī (Plaut., Ter., Cic.); dē-sīvit (Sen.), sīvistis (Cic.), once each; sīverīs (Plaut., Cato), dē-sīverit (Cato, Gell.), sīverint (Plaut., Curt.), sīvisset (Cic., Liv.). Much oftener without -v-: as, dē-siī (Sen.), sīstī (Plaut., Cic.); dē-sīstī often, siit once (Ter.), dē-siit (Varr., Sen., &c.), dē-sīt (Mart., &c.), dē-siimus (Lent.), dē-sīmus (893), sīstis; dē-siērunt (Cic., Liv.); dē-sierat, dē-sierit (Cic.); dē-sīssem, &c., sīsset, sīssent, dē-sīsse. For sīrīs, &c., see 893; for pōnō, 972.

| spernō, *spurn* | spernere | sprēvī | sprētus |
| sternō, *strew* | sternere | strāvī | strātus |

965. (*c.*) With the present stem in -sco|e- (834).

crēscō, *grow*	crēscere	crēvī	crētus
nōscō, *get to know*	nōscere	nōvī	nōtus adjective

Compounds: ī-gnōscō, ī-gnōvī, ī-gnōtum; ā-gnōscō, ā-gnōvī, ā-gnitus; cō-gnōscō, cō-gnōvī, cō-gnitus; dī-nōscō, dī-nōvī, rarely dignōscō, dī-gnōvī, ——; inter-nōscō, inter-nōvī, ——. Old passive infinitive GNOSCIER (inscr. 186 B. C.).

pāscō, *feed*	pāscere	pāvī	pāstus
scīscō, *enact*	scīscere	scīvī	scītus

966. (2*b.*) The following verbs in -ere have the perfect stem in -v-, preceded by the long vowel of a presumed denominative stem (870), and the perfect participle, when used, in -tus :

967. (*a.*) With the present stem in -o|e- (829).

petō, *aim at*	petere	petīvī	petītus

In the perfect, sometimes petiī (Cic., Ov., Liv., Val. Fl., Plin. *Ep*), PETIEI (inscr.), petī late (Sen., Stat.); petiit (Cic., Hor., Tac., Suet.), petit (Verg, Ov., Phaedr., Sen., Luc., Suet.), petiisse (Verg., Hor., Ov., Val. Fl., Stat.).

quaerō, *inquire*	quaerere	quaesīvī	quaesītus

Compounds sometimes retain ae in old Latin, but usually have ī for ae throughout : as, con-quīrō, con-quīrere, &c.

968. (*b.*) With the present stem in -sco|e- (834).

ab-olēscō, *vanish away*	ab-olēscere	ab-olēvī	——
ad-olēscō, *grow up*	ad-olēscere	ad-olēvī	ad-ultus
con-cupīscō, *hanker for*	con-cupīscere	con-cupīvī	con-cupītus
-dormīscō, *fall asleep*	-dormīscere	-dormīvī	
ex-olēscō, *grow out*	ex-olēscere	ex-olēvī	ex-olētus
in-veterāscō, *get set*	in-veterāscere	in-veterāvī	——
obs-olēscō, *get worn out*	obs-olēscere	obs-olēvī	obs-olētus adj.
quiēscō, *get still*	quiēscere	quiēvī	quiētus adjective
re-sipīscō, *come to*	re-sipīscere	re-sipīvī	
suēscō, *get used*	suēscere	suēvī	suētus
vesperāscit, *gets dusk*	vesperāscere	vesperāvit	——

969. (*c.*) With the present stem in -io|e- (836).

cupiō, *want*	cupere	cupīvī	cupītus

Once with a form in -īre (791), cupīret (Lucr.).

sapiō, *have a smack*	sapere	sapīvī	——

Compounds have i for a: as, re-sipiō, &c.

970. (*d.*) With the present stem in -sso|e- (375).

ar-cēssō, *send for*	ar-cēssere	ar-cēssīvī	ar-cēssītus

Sometimes ac-cersō, &c.; infinitive rarely ar-cēssīrī or ac-cersīrī.

capēssō, *undertake*	capēssere	capēssīvī	——
facēssō, *do, make off*	facēssere	facēssīvī	facēssītus

Perfect system rare: facēssierīs or facēsserīs (Cic.), facēssīsset (Tac.).

in-cēssō, *attack*	in-cēssere	in-cēssīvī	——
lacēssō, *provoke*	lacēssere	lacēssīvī	lacēssītus

PERFECT STEM IN -u-.

971. (3.) The following verbs in **-ere** have the perfect stem in -u- (873), and the perfect participle, when used, in **-tus**; in some participles **-tus** is preceded by a short **i**, thus, **-itus** (910):

972. (*a.*) With the present stem in -o|e- (829).

alō, *bring up*	alere	aluī	altus, rarely alitus
colō, *till, stay round, court*	colere	coluī	cultus
con-cinō, *chime with*	con-cinere	con-cinuī	———

A compound of **canō** (924, 823). See also **oc-cinō** and **prae-cinō**.

cōn-sulō, *consult*	cōn-sulere	cōn-suluī	cōn-sultus
depsō, *knead*	depsere	depsuī	depstus
fremō, *growl*	fremere	fremuī	———
gemō, *groan*	gemere	gemuī	———
molō, *grind*	molere	moluī	molitus
oc-cinō, *sing ominously*	oc-cinere	oc-cinuī	———

Once with reduplication, **oc-cecinerit** (Liv.).

oc-culō, *hide*	oc-culere	oc-culuī	oc-cultus
pīsō, pīnsō, *bray*	pīsere, pīnsere	pīnsuī, pīsīvī	pistus

Once (818, 847) **pīnsībart** (Enn.). Perfect once **pīnsuī** (Pomp.), once (823, 893) **pīsiērunt** (Varr.). Perfect participle often **pīnsitus** (Col.), once **pīnsus** (Vitr.).

pōnō, *place*	pōnere	po-suī	po-situs

A compound of **po-** and **sinō** (964). Perfect in old Latin **po-sīvī** (893); **po-suī** is first used by Ennius (875). Perfect participle in verse sometimes, **po-stus, -po-stus**; inf. **inposisse** (Plaut.).

prae-cinō, *play before*	prae-cinere	prae-cinuī	———
serō, *string*	serere	-seruī	sertus
stertō, *snore*	stertere	(dē-stertuī)	———
strepō, *make a racket*	strepere	strepuī	———
texō, *weave*	texere	texuī	textus
tremō, *quake*	tremere	tremuī	———
vomō, *throw up*	vomere	vomuī	———

973. (*b.*) With reduplication and -o|e- in the present stem (829).

gignō, *beget*	gignere	genuī	genitus

Present sometimes also without reduplication, **genit**, &c. (Varr., Lucr.).

974. (*c.*) With the present stem in a nasalized root followed by -o|e- (831).

ac-cumbō, *lie by*	ac-cumbere	ac-cubuī	ac-cubitus

So also **in-cumbō**; **dis-cumbō** has **dis-cubuī**, **dis-cubitum**. Compounds with **dē**, **ob**, **prō**, **re-**, and **sub**, have **-cubuī**, ———.

975. (*d.*) With the present stem in -io|e- (836).

ē-liciō, *coax out*	ē-licere	ē-licuī	ē-licitus
rapiō, *seize*	rapere	rapuī	raptus

Compounds have **i** for **a** in the present and perfect systems, and **e** in the perfect participle: as, **ē-ripiō**, **ē-ripere**, **ē-ripuī**, **ē-reptus**. Old Latin has **u** in **dē-rupier** and in **sub-rupiō**, **sub-rupere**, **sub-rupuī**, **sub-ruptus**; shortened forms are: **surpuit**, **surpuerit** (Plaut.), **surpit** (Plaut. prol.), **surpere** (Lucr.), **surpite**, **surpuerat** (Hor.). For **sub-repsit** (Plaut.), see 887.

976. (*e.*) With the present stem in -sco|e- (835); for com-pēscuī, see 855.

acēscō, *get sour*	acēscere	-acuī	——
alēscō, *grow up*	alēscere	(co-aluī)	(co-alitus)
ārēscō, *dry up*	ārēscere	-āruī	——
calēscō, *get warm*	calēscere	-caluī	——
candēscō, *get white*	candēscere	-canduī	——
cānēscō, *get grey*	cānēscere	cānuī	——
clārēscō, *get bright*	clārēscere	clāruī	——
com-pescō, *check*	com-pescere	com-pescuī	——
con-ticēscō, *get all still*	con-ticēscere	con-ticuī	——

Also in the present system, con-ticīscō, con-ticīscere, &c.

crēbrēscō, *get common*	crēbrēscere	-crēbruī	——
crūdēscō, *wax bad*	crūdēscere	(re-crūduī)	——
-dolēscō, *get pained*	-dolēscere	-doluī	——
dūrēscō, *get hard*	dūrēscere	dūruī	——
ē-vīlēscō, *get cheap*	ē-vīlēscere	ē-viluī	——
fervēscō, *boil up*	fervēscere	-ferbuī, -fervī	——
flōrēscō, *blossom out*	flōrēscere	-flōruī	——
horrēscō, *bristle up*	horrēscere	-horruī	——
languēscō, *get weak*	languēscere	languī	——
latēscō, *hide away*	latēscere	-lituī	——
liquēscō, *melt*	liquēscere	(dē-licuī)	——
madēscō, *get moist*	madēscere	maduī	——
marcēscō, *pine away*	marcēscere	(ē-marcuī)	——
mātūrēscō, *ripen*	mātūrēscere	mātūruī	——
nigrēscō, *get black*	nigrēscere	nigruī	——
nōtēscō, *get known*	nōtēscere	nōtuī	——
ob-mūtēscō, *get still*	ob-mūtēscere	ob-mūtuī	——
ob-surdēscō, *get deaf*	ob-surdēscere	ob-surduī	——
oc-callēscō, *get hard*	oc-callēscere	oc-calluī	——
pallēscō, *grow pale*	pallēscere	palluī	——
pūtēscō, *get soaked*	pūtēscere	pūtuī	——
rigēscō, *stiffen up*	rigēscere	riguī	——
rubēscō, *redden*	rubēscere	rubuī	——
sānēscō, *get well*	sānēscere	-sānuī	——
senēscō, *grow old*	senēscere	-senuī	——
stupēscō, *get dazed*	stupēscere	(ob-stupuī)	——

Also op-stipēscō or ob-stipēscō, op-stipuī or ob-stipuī.

tābēscō, *waste away*	tābēscere	tābuī	——
tepēscō, *get lukewarm*	tepēscere	tepuī	——
-timēscō, *get scared*	-timēscere	-timuī	——
torpēscō, *get numb*	torpēscere	torpuī	——
tremēscō, *quake*	tremēscere	(con-tremuī)	——

Also in the present system, con-tremīscō, con-tremīscere, &c

tumēscō, *swell up*	tumēscere	-tumuī	——
valēscō, *get strong*	valēscere	-valuī	——
vānēscō, *wane*	vānēscere	(ē-vānuī)	——

DEPONENTS IN -ĭ.

977. (1.) The following deponents in -ĭ have the perfect participle in -tus, except **morior**, which has -tuus:

978. (*a*). With the present stem in -ᵒ|ₑ- (829).

fruor, *enjoy*	fruī	frūctus
loquor, *speak*	loquī	locūtus
queror, *complain*	querī	questus
sequor, *follow*	sequī	secūtus

979. (*b*.) With the present stem in a nasalized root followed by -ᵒ|ₑ- (831).

fungor, *get quit*	fungī	fūnctus

980. (*c*.) With the present stem in -scᵒ|ₑ- (834).

apīscor, *lay hold of*	apīscī	aptus

Compounds have i and e for a: as, ad-ipīscor, ad-ipīscī, ad-eptus.

com-minīscor, *devise*	com-minīscī	com-mentus
ex-pergīscor, *stretch myself,wake*	ex-pergīscī	ex-per-rēctus

Perfect participle rarely **ex-pergitus** (Lucil., Lucr.).

nancīscor, *get*	nancīscī	nactus, nănctus
nāscor, *am born*	nāscī	nātus
ob-līvīscor, *forget*	ob-līvīscī	ob-lītus
pacīscor, *bargain*	pacīscī	pactus

Compounds: dē-pecīscor, dē-pecīscī, dē-pectus; com-pectus.

pro-ficīscor, *start on*	pro-ficīscī	pro-fectus
ulcīscor, *avenge*	ulcīscī	ultus

981. (*d*.) With the present stem in -iᵒ|ₑ- (836).

morior, *die*	morī	mortuus
orior, *rise*	orīrī	ortus
potior, *master*	potīrī	potītus

For forms in -īrī of these three verbs, see 791. For **potīrī**, twice **potī** (Enn., Pac.).

982. (2.) The following deponents in -ĭ have the perfect participle in -sus (912):

983. (*a*.) With the present stem in -ᵒ|ₑ- (829).

lābor, *tumble down*	lābī	lapsus
nītor, *rest on*	nītī	nīsus, nīxus
ūtor, *use*	ūtī	ūsus

984. (*b*.) With the present stem in -scᵒ|ₑ- (834).

dē-fetīscor, *get tired out*	dē-fetīscī	dē-fessus

985. (*c*.) With the present stem in -tᵒ|ₑ- (835).

am-plector, *hug round*	am-plectī	am-plexus
com-plector, *hug up*	com-plectī	com-plexus

986. (*d*.) With the present stem in -iᵒ|ₑ- (836).

gradior, *step*	gradī	gressus
patior, *suffer*	patī	passus

Compounds of these two verbs have e for a: as, ad-gredior, per-petior, per-pessus; for forms of -gredior in -īrī, see 791.

II. DENOMINATIVE VERBS.

987. Most verbs in -āre, -ēre, and -īre (or in -ārī, -ērī, and -īrī), are denominatives.

988. Some primitives from vowel roots have the form of denominatives in the present system, or throughout; and some verbs with a denominative present system have the perfect and perfect participle formed directly from a root.

(1.) VERBS IN -āre.

(A.) PERFECT STEM WITHOUT A SUFFIX.

989. (1.) The following verb in -āre has a reduplicated perfect stem (859):

| stō, *stand* | stāre | stetī | ——— |

For -stitī, see 860. The compound **prae-stō** has rarely the perfect participle **prae-stātus** (Brut., Plin.), and **prae-stitus** (Liv.).

990. (2.) The following verbs in -āre have a perfect stem consisting of a root which ends in -v- and has a long vowel (864), and the perfect participle in -tus:

| iuvō, *help* | iuvāre | iūvī | iūtus once |

In the perfect system, **iuverint, adiuverō,** and **adiuverit** occur once each in Catull., Enn., Plaut., and Ter; see 891. Perfect participle usual only in the compound **ad-iūtus**.

| lavō, *bathe* | lavāre | lāvī | lautus |

Forms in -ere are very common in the present tense (820): **lavis** (Plaut., Hor.), **lavit** (Plaut., Lucr., Catull., Verg., Hor.), **lavimus** (Hor.), **lavitur** (Val. Fl.), **lavitō** (Cato), **lavere** often, **lavī** (Pomp.). Perfect participle often **lōtus** in writers of the empire; supine, **lautum, lavātum**.

(B.) PERFECT STEM IN -V- OR -u-.

PERFECT STEM IN -V-.

991. (1*a*.) Two verbs in -āre have the perfect stem in -v- (869), and the perfect participle, when used, in -tus, both preceded by a long -ā- of the root ·

| flō, *blow* | flāre | flāvī | flātus |
| nō, *swim* | nāre | nāvī | ——— |

992. (1*b*.) Most verbs in -āre have the perfect stem in -v- (869), and the perfect participle in -tus, both preceded by a form of the present stem in long -ā-: as,

laudō, *praise*	laudāre	laudāvī	laudātus
līberō, *free*	līberāre	līberāvī	līberātus
nōminō, *name*	nōmināre	nōmināvī	nōminātus
spērō, *hope*	spērāre	spērāvī	spērātus

PERFECT STEM IN -u-.

993. (2.) The following verbs in -āre have the perfect stem in -u (874), and the perfect participle, when used, in -tus; in some participles, -tus is preceded by a short i, thus, -itus (910):

crepō, *rattle*   crepāre   crepuī   (in-crepitus)

Forms of the perfect system in -v- (823) are: **in-crepāvit** (Plaut.), **discrepāvit** (Varr.), **in-crepārit** (Suet.).

cubō, *lie*   cubāre   cubuī   ——

Forms of the perfect system in -v- (823) are: **ex-cubāverant** (Caes.), **cubāris** (Prop.), **in-cubāvēre** (Plin.), **cubāsse** (Quintil.). Compound perfect participle **in-cubitus** (Plin.).

domō, *tame*   domāre   **domuī**   **domitus**

ē-necō, *murder*   ē-necāre   **ē-necuī**   **ē-nectus**

The simple verb has **necāvī, necātus**; twice **necuit** (Enn., Phaedr.). **ē-necō** sometimes has i for e in the present and perfect system: once (823) **ē-nicāvit**, and once (887) **ē-nicāssō** (Plaut.); perfect participle also **ē-necātus** (Plin.).

fricō, *rub down*   fricāre   fricuī   frictus

Perfect participle also **fricātus** (Vitr.), **cōn-fricātus** (Varr., Plin.), **dē-fricātus** (Catull., Col., Plin.), **īn-fricātus** (Col., Plin.), **per-fricātus** (Vitr., Plin.).

micō, *quiver*   micāre   micuī

So the compounds; except **dī-micō, dī-micāvī, dī-micātum**; twice in pentameter verse (823) **dī-micuisse** (Ov.).

-plicō, *fold*   -plicāre   -plicuī   -plicitus

A few forms of the present system of the simple verb occur. In the perfect and perfect participle usually **-plicāvī, -plicātus**; but sometimes **ap-plicuī** (Cic. once, Tib., Ov., Liv., Sen., &c.); **com-plicuī** (Sen.), **ex-plicuī** (Verg., Hor., Liv., Sen., &c.), **im-plicuī** (Verg., Tib., Ov., Sen., &c.); **ap-plicitus** (Col., Quintil., Plin. *Ep.*), **ex-plicitus** (Caes., Sen., Plin. *Ep.*), **im-plicitus** (Plaut., Cic., Liv.); once **re-plictus** (Stat.).

secō, *cut*   secāre   secuī   sectus

The compound with **ex** sometimes has i for e; once (823) **exicāveris** (Cato).

sonō, *sound*   sonāre   sonuī   ——

Also (820) **sonit, sonunt** (Enn., Acc.), **sonere** (Acc., Lucr.); **re-sonunt** (Enn.). Perfect (823) **re-sonārint** (Hor.), **re-sonāvit** (Man.), **sonātūrus** (Hor.)

tonō, *thunder*   tonāre   tonuī   (at-tonitus)

Once (820) **tonimus** (Varr.). Perfect participle once **in-tonātus** (Hor.).

vetō, *forbid*   vetāre   vetuī   vetitus

In old Latin, **votō**, &c. (143). Perfect once (823) **vetāvit** (Pers.).

DEPONENTS IN -ārī.

994. There are many deponents in -ārī, with the perfect participle in -ātus: as,

hortor, *exhort*   hortārī   hortātus

For the primitive **fārī**, *speak*, and compounds, see the dictionary.

(2.) VERBS IN -ēre.

(A.) PERFECT STEM WITHOUT A SUFFIX.

995. (1.) The following verbs in -ēre have a reduplicated perfect stem (859), and the perfect participle, when used, in -sus (912):

mordeō, *bite*	mordēre	momordī	morsus

The compound **prae-mordeō** has once (823) **prae-morsisset** (Plaut.).

pendeō, *am hung*	pendēre	pependī	——

The compound **prō-pendeō** has the perfect participle prō-pēnsus.

spondeō, *covenant*	spondēre	spopondī	spōnsus

For **dē-spondī** and **re-spondī**, see 860 ; rarely dē-spopondī (Plaut.).

tondeō, *shear*	tondēre	-totondī, -tondī	tōnsus

For **dē-tondunt** (Varr.), see 821. Perfect only in the compounds **at-tondī** and dē-tondī (860); once dē-totonderat (Varr.), and perhaps dē-totondit (Enn.).

996. (2*a*.) The following verbs in -ēre have a perfect stem consisting of a root which ends in -v- and has a long vowel (864), and the perfect participle, when used, in -tus :

caveō, *look out*	cavēre	cāvī	cautus
faveō, *am friendly*	favēre	fāvī	——
foveō, *warm, cherish*	fovēre	fōvī	fōtus
moveō, *move*	movēre	mōvī	mōtus

For short forms in the perfect system, particularly in compounds, see 891.

voveō, *vow*	vovēre	vōvī	vōtus

997. (2*b*.) Three verbs in -ēre have a perfect stem consisting of a consonant root with a long vowel (864), and the perfect participle in -sus (912):

sedeō, *sit*	sedēre	sēdī	-sessus

Real compounds have **i** for **e** in the present system : as, **ob-sideō**, &c. Compounds with **dis-**, **prae**, and **re-** have no perfect participle.

strīdeō, *grate*	strīdēre	strīdī	——

Often with a present system in **-ere** (821).

videō, *see*	vidēre	vīdī	vīsus

998. (3.) The following verbs in -ēre have a perfect stem ending in two consonants (866), and the perfect participle, when used, in -sus (912) :

ferveō, *boil*	fervēre	fervī, ferbuī	——

Sometimes with forms in **-ere** (821) in verse. The perfect system is rare.

prandeō, *lunch*	prandēre	prandī	prānsus

(B.) PERFECT STEM IN -s-, OR IN -v- OR -u-.

PERFECT STEM IN -S-.

999. (1*a*.) The following verbs in -ēre have the perfect stem in -s- (868), and the perfect participle, when used, in -tus :

augeō, *increase*	augēre	auxī	auctus
in-dulgeō, *am kind*	in-dulgēre	in-dulsī	——
lūceō, *beam*	lūcēre	lūxī	——
lūgeo, *mourn*	lūgēre	lūxī	——
torqueō, *twist*	torquēre	torsī	tortus

1000. (1*b*.) The following verbs in -ēre have the perfect stem in -s- (868), and the perfect participle, when used, in -sus (912):

algeō, *feel cold*	algēre	alsī	——
ardeō, *blaze*	ardēre	arsī	——
cō-nīveō, *wink and blink*	cō-nīvēre	cō-nīxī, cō-nīvī	——

The perfects cō-nīxī (Turp.), cō-nīvī (Crass.), occur once each.

fulgeō, *flash*	fulgēre	fulsī	——

Forms of the present in -ere (821) occur in verse: fulgit (Pomp., Lucil., Lucr.), fulgere (Pac., Acc., Lucil., Lucr., Verg.); ef-fulgere (Verg., Claud.).

haereō, *stick*	haerēre	haesī	——
iubeō, *order*	iubēre	iussī	iussus

In old Latin, IOVBEO, after IOVSI (IVSI); later iussī, iussus, after iubeō.

maneō, *stay*	manēre	mānsī	mānsum
mulceō, *stroke*	mulcēre	mulsī	mulsus adjective

Perfect participle per-mulsus rare (Cornif., Varr.).

mulgeō, *milk*	mulgēre	mulsī	mulsus once
rīdeō, *laugh*	rīdēre	rīsī	-rīsus
suādeō, *advise*	suādēre	suāsī	suāsus
tergeō, *wipe*	tergēre	tersī	tersus

For forms in -ere in the present, as tergit, &c. (Varr., Prop., Stat., Col.), see 821.

turgeō, *am swelling*	turgēre	tursī once	——

Of the perfect system, turserat (Enn.).

urgeō, *push*	urgēre	ursī	——

PERFECT STEM IN -v- OR -u-.

PERFECT STEM IN -V-.

1001. (1*a*.) The following verbs in -ēre have the perfect stem in -v- (869), and the perfect participle in -tus, both preceded by a long -ē- of the root:

dē-leō, *wipe out*	dē-lēre	dē-lēvī	dē-lētus
fleō, *weep*	flēre	flēvī	flētus
neō, *spin*	nēre	nēvī	——

For neunt (Tib.), see 837.

-pleō, *fill*	-plēre	-plēvī	-plētus

1002. (1*b*.) The following verb in -ēre has the perfect stem in -v- (869), preceded by long -ī-, and the perfect participle in -tus, preceded by short -i- of the root :

cieō, *set a going*   ciēre   cīvī   citus

Somewhat defective; also with a form in -īre (821).   For the perfect participle of compounds, see 919.

1003. (1*c*.) The following verb in -ēre has the perfect stem in -v- (869), and the perfect participle in -itus (910) :

ab-oleō, *destroy*   ab-olēre   ab-olēvī   ab-olitus

PERFECT STEM IN -u-.

1004. (2*a*.) Most verbs in -ēre have the perfect stem in -u- (874), and the perfect participle, when used, in -tus, which is usually preceded by a short i (910) : as,

| doceō, *teach* | docēre | docuī | doctus |
| habeō, *have* | habēre | habuī | habitus |

So also **post-habeō**; other compounds have i for **a** : as, **pro-hibeō**, **pro-hibēre**, **pro-hibuī**, **pro-hibitus**; twice contracted, **prōbet**, **prōbeat** (Lucr.). Compounds with **dē** and **prae** are regularly contracted, **dēbeō**, **praebeō**, &c. : but in Plautus once **de-hibuistī**, and regularly **prae-hibeō**, &c., throughout.

mereō, *earn*   merēre   meruī   meritus

Often deponent (800) : **mereor, merērī, meritus**.

misceō, *mix*   miscēre   miscuī   mixtus, mistus

The present stem is an extension of the suffix -scᵒ|ₑ- (834); -sc- of the present runs over into the perfect.

| moneō, *advise* | monēre | monuī | monitus |
| placeō, *am pleasing* | placēre | placuī | placitus |

So the compounds **com-placeō** and **per-placeō**; **dis-pliceō** has i for **a** throughout.

taceō, *hold my tongue* tacēre   tacuī   tacitus adjective

The compound **re-ticeō** has i for **a** and no perfect participle.

teneō, *hold*   tenēre   tenuī   -tentus

Compounds have i for **e** in the present and perfect : as, **dē-tineō, dē-tinuī, dē-tentus.**

| terreō, *scare* | terrēre | terruī | territus |
| torreō, *roast* | torrēre | torruī | tostus |

1005. (2*b*.) The following verb in -ēre has the perfect stem in -u- (874), and the perfect participle in -sus (912) :

cēnseō, *count, rate*   cēnsēre   cēnsuī   cēnsus

174

1006. (3.) The following verbs in -ēre have the perfect stem in -u- (874), and no perfect participle (907):

arceō, *check*	arcēre	arcuī	——

The compounds co-erceō and ex-erceō have e for a, and perfect participles co-ercitus and ex-ercitus.

caleō, *am warm*	calēre	caluī	——
candeō, *glow white*	candēre	canduī	——
careō, *have not*	carēre	caruī	——
doleō, *ache*	dolēre	doluī	——
egeō, *need*	egēre	eguī	——

The compound ind-igeō, ind-igēre, ind-iguī, ——, has i for e.

ē-mineō, *stick out*	ē-minēre	ē-minuī	——
flōreō, *bloom*	flōrēre	flōruī	——
horreō, *bristle up*	horrēre	horruī	——
iaceō, *lie*	iacēre	iacuī	——
lateō, *lie hid*	latēre	latuī	——
liceō, *am rated*	licēre	licuī	——
liqueō, *am melted*	liquēre	licuī	——
madeō, *am soaked*	madēre	maduī	——
niteō, *shine*	nitēre	nituī	——
noceō, *am hurtful*	nocēre	nocuī	——
oleō, *smell*	olēre	oluī	——

For forms in -ere in the present system, see 821.

palleō, *look pale*	pallēre	palluī	——
pāreō, *wait on, am obedient*	pārēre	pāruī	——
pateō, *am open*	patēre	patuī	——
rigeō, *am stiff*	rigēre	riguī	——
sileō, *am silent*	silēre	siluī	——
sorbeō, *suck up*	sorbēre	sorbuī	——

The perfect system of the simple verb is rare: sorbuit, sorbuerint (Plin.); also (823) sorpsit (Val. Max.): ab-sorbeō and ex-sorbeō have -sorbuī; but ab-sorpsī (Plin., Luc., Macr.), ex-sorpsī (Sen.).

studeō, *am eager*	studēre	studuī	——
stupeō, *am dazed*	stupēre	stupuī	——
timeō, *fear*	timēre	timuī	——
valeō, *am strong*	valēre	valuī	——
vigeō, *feel strong*	vigēre	viguī	——

1007. For audeō, gaudeō, and soleō, see 801; for lubet or libet, licet, miseret, oportet, paenitet, piget, pudet, taedet, see 815 and 816.

DEPONENTS IN -ērī.

1008. (1a.) The following deponent in -ērī has the perfect participle in -tus:

reor, *reckon, think*	rērī	ratus

1009. (1*b*.) The following deponents in -ērī have the perfect participle in **-tus,** which is preceded by a short **i** (910):

liceor, *bid*	licērī	licitus
misereor, *pity*	miserērī	miseritus

Perfect participle also **misertus** (Val. Max., Sen., Curt.). Active forms are: **miserēte, miserērent** (Enn.), **misereās** (Ter.), **miseret** (Lucr.), **miserent** (Val. Fl.). Passive forms are sometimes used impersonally (724): as, **miserētur,** &c.

tueor, *look to, protect*	tuērī	tuitus late

Forms in -ī also occur in verse (821). As perfect participle, generally **tūtātus.**

vereor, *am awed at*	verērī	veritus

1010. (2.) One deponent in -ērī has the perfect participle in **-sus** (912):

fateor, *confess*	fatērī	fassus

Compounds have **i** and **e** for **a**: as, **cōn-fiteor, cōn-fessus.**

(3.) VERBS IN -īre.

(A.) PERFECT STEM WITHOUT A SUFFIX.

1011. (1*a*.) The following verb in -īre has a reduplicated perfect stem (861), and the perfect participle in **-tus:**

re-periō, *find*	re-perīre	re-pperī	re-pertus

1012. (1*b*.) The following verb in -īre has no reduplication in the perfect stem, and the perfect participle in **-tus:**

com-periō, *find out*	com-perīre	com-perī	com-pertus

As deponent: **com-periar** (Ter.), com-perior (Sall., Tac.).

1013. (2.) The following verb in -īre has a perfect stem consisting of a consonant root with a long vowel (862), and the perfect participle in -**tus:**

veniō, *come*	venīre	vēnī	ventum, -ventus

For **ē-venunt, ē-venat, ē-venant, ad-venat, per-venat,** see 822.

(B.) PERFECT STEM IN -s-, OR IN -v- OR -u-.

PERFECT STEM IN -S-.

1014. (1.) The following verbs in -īre have the perfect stem in **-s-** (868), and the perfect participle in -**tus:**

farciō, *stuff*	farcīre	farsī	fartus

Compounds have usually **e** for **a** throughout.

fulciō, *prop*	fulcīre	fulsī	fultus
hauriō, *drain*	haurīre	hausī	haustus

A perfect subjunctive **haurierint** is quoted from Varro (82?).

saepiō, *hedge in*	saepīre	saepsī	saeptus
sanciō, *hallow*	sancīre	sānxī	sānctus adjective

Perfect participle rarely **sancītus** (Lucr., Liv.). A pluperfect **sancierat** is quoted from Pomponius Secundus (823).

sarciō, *patch*	sarcīre	sarsī	sartus
vinciō, *bind*	vincīre	vīnxī	vīnctus

1015. (2.) The following verb in -īre has the perfect stem in -s- (868), and the perfect participle in -sus (912):

sentiō, *feel*	sentīre	sēnsī	sēnsus

The compound with **ad** is generally deponent (800).

PERFECT STEM IN -V-.

1016. (1*a.*) The following verb in -īre has the perfect stem in -v- (869), and the perfect participle in -tus, both preceded by a long ī of the root :

sciō, *know*	scīre	scīvī	scītus

1017. (1*b.*) The following verb in -īre has the perfect stem in -v- (869). and the perfect participle in -tus :

sepeliō, *bury*	sepelīre	sepelīvī	sepultus

1018. (1*c.*) Most verbs in -īre have the perfect stem in -v- (869), and the perfect participle in -tus, both preceded by a form of the present stem in long -ī- : as,

audiō, *hear*	audīre	audīvī	audītus

PERFECT STEM IN -U-.

1019. (2.) The following verbs in -īre have the perfect stem in -u- (874), and the perfect participle, when used, in -tus :

am-iciō, *don*	am-icīre	am-icuī	am-ictus

Perfect rare: once **am-icuī** (Brut.), once **am-ixī** (Varr.).

ap-eriō, *open*	ap-erīre	ap-eruī	ap-ertus
op-eriō, *cover over*	op-erīre	op-eruī	op-ertus
saliō, *leap*	salīre	saluī	————

Compounds have i for a throughout: as, **īn-siliō**. A perfect system in -v- (823, 893), as **ex-silīvī**, occurs in late writers (Col., Sen., Plin., &c.).

DEPONENTS IN -īrī.

1020. (1*a.*) The following deponents in -īrī have the perfect participle in -tus:

ex-perior, *try*	ex-perīrī	ex-pertus
op-perior, *wait for*	op-perīrī	op-pertus

Perfect participle once **op-perītus** (Plaut.).

1021. (1*b*.) The following deponents in -**īrī** have the perfect participle in -**ītus**:

blandior, *am agreeable*	blandīrī	blandītus
largior, *shower*	largīrī	largītus
mentior, *tell lies*	mentīrī	mentītus
mōlior, *work hard*	mōlīrī	mōlītus
partior, *share*	partīrī	partītus
sortior, *draw lots*	sortīrī	sortītus

1022. (2.) The following deponents in -**īrī** have the perfect participle in -**sus** (912):

mētior, *measure*	mētīrī	mēnsus
ōrdior, *begin*	ōrdīrī	ōrsus

PART SECOND ♭ SENTENCES

1023. A SENTENCE is a thought expressed by means of a verb. The SUBJECT is that which is spoken of. The PREDICATE is that which is said of the subject.

1024. A SIMPLE SENTENCE is one which has only one subject and one predicate.

Thus, Rhodanus fluit, *the Rhone flows*, is a simple sentence: the subject is Rhodanus and the predicate is fluit.

1025. The sentence may be *declarative*, stating a fact, *exclamatory*, crying out about something, *interrogative*, asking a question, or *imperative*, giving a command.

THE SUBJECT.

1026. The subject is a substantive, or any word or words having the value of a substantive.

1027. The subject of a verb is in the nominative case.

1028. The subject may be expressed, or may be merely indicated by the person ending.

1029. (1.) With the first or the second person, the subject is expressed by a personal pronoun (ego tū, nōs vōs) only when somewhat emphatic, or in an indignant question. Otherwise the verb of the first or second person is not attended by a personal pronoun: as, eram, *I was*, erās, *thou wert*.

1030. The subject is regularly omitted when it is general and indefinite, in the first person plural; as, intellegimus, *we understand;* and second person singular, as: putārēs, *you*, or *anybody would have thought.*

1031. The subject of the first or second person is sometimes a substantive, contrary to the English idiom: as, Hannibal petō pācem, *I Hannibal am suing for peace.* pars spectātōrum scīs, *a part of you spectators knows.* exoriāre aliquis nostrīs ex ossibus ultor, *from out our bones mayst some avenger spring.* trecentī coniūrāvimus, *three hundred of us have sworn an oath together.*

179

1032. (2.) With the third person the subject is regularly expressed, unless the general 'he she it,' or 'they' implied in the person ending is definite enough.

1033. The third person plural often refers to people in general, particularly of verbs meaning *say, name* or *call, think,* and, with **volgō** added, of other verbs also: as, **ferunt,** *they say,* **people say,** or *the world says.* The singular verb **inquit,** is rarely used in the sense of *says somebody, it will be said,* or *quotha.*

1034. Some verbs have no subject at all in the third person singular; these are called *Impersonal.* Such are : a few verbs expressing 'operations of nature,' five verbs of 'mental distress,' and any verb used to denote merely the occurrence of action, without reference to any doer: as,

(*a.*) **lūcet,** *it is light,* **lūcēscit,** *it is getting light :* **pluit,** *it rains,* **fulget,** *it lightens,* **tonat,** *it thunders.* (*b.*) **miseret,** *it moves to pity,* **paenitet,** *it repents,* **piget,** *it grieves,* **pudet,** *it puts to shame,* **taedet,** *it bores.* (*c.*) **bene erat,** *it went well ;* **pugnātur,** *there is fighting,* **pugnātum est,** *there was fighting.* See also 816.

THE PREDICATE.

1035. The predicate is either a verb alone, or a verb of indeterminate meaning with a predicate nominative added to complete the sense.

Verbs of indeterminate meaning are such as mean *am* (something), *become, remain, seem, am thought, am called* or *named, am chosen.*

1036. The verb is sometimes omitted, when it is easily understood. So particularly such everyday verbs as mean *am, do, say, come,* and *go,* in proverbs and maxims, in short questions, and in emphatic or lively assertion or description : as,

quot hominēs, tot sententiae, sc. **sunt,** *as many men, so many minds.* **omnia praeclāra rāra,** sc. **sunt,** *all that's very fair is rare.* **mortuus Cūmīs,** sc. **est,** *he died at Cumae.* **bene mihǐ,** sc. **sit,** *be it well with me,* i. e. *a health to me.* **haec hāctenus,** sc. **dīcam,** *thus much only,* or *no more of this.*

ENLARGEMENT OF THE SIMPLE SENTENCE.

1037. The parts of the simple sentence may be enlarged by additions. The commonest enlargements of the subject and of the predicate are the following.

1038. I. The subject may be enlarged by the addition of attributes, appositives, or objects.

1039. (1.) An ATTRIBUTE is an essential addition to a substantive, uniting with it as one idea. The attribute may be :

1040. (*a.*) Genitive of a substantive of different meaning, denoting the agent, possessor, or the like : as, **metus hostium,** *fear of the enemy,* i. e. which they feel. **hostium castra,** *camp of the enemy.*

1041. (*b.*) Genitive or ablative of a substantive with an adjective in agreement : as, **puer sēdecim annōrum,** *a boy of sixteen years ;* **bovēs mīrā speciē,** *kine of wondrous beauty.*

1042. (*c.*) A noun in the same case, either an adjective or participle, or else a substantive used adjectively: as, **pugna Cannēnsis,** *the battle of Cannae;* **cīvitātēs victae,** *the conquered communities;* **victor Rōmulus rēx,** *victorious king Romulus.*

1043. (*d.*) A substantive in the accusative or ablative with a preposition: as, **pugna ad Cannās,** *the battle near Cannae.* **vir sine metū,** *a man without fear* (**1427**).

1044. An attribute is rarely attached immediately to a proper name: as, **fortem Gyān,** *Gyas the brave.* **Q. Lūcānius, eiusdem ōrdinis,** *Lucanius, of the same rank.* It is much oftener attached to a general word in apposition with the proper name: as, **vir clārissimus, M. Crassus,** *the illustrious Crassus.*

1045. (2.) An APPOSITIVE is a separate substantive added as an explanation to another substantive, and in the same case, but not like the attribute uniting with it as one idea: as,

avītum malum, rēgnī cupīdō, *the ancestral curse, ambition for a crown.* **Hamilcar, Mārs alter,** *Hamilcar, a second Mars.* **Cornēlia, māter Gracchōrum,** *Cornelia, mother of the Gracchi.* **Teutomatus, Ollivicōnis fīlius, rēx Nitiobrogum,** *Teutomatus, the son of Ollivico, the king of the Nitiobroges.*

1046. (3.) The OBJECT of a substantive is another substantive of different meaning in the genitive, denoting that on which action is exerted: as,

metus hostium, *fear of the enemy,* i. e. which is felt towards them. **vēnditiō bonōrum,** *sale of the goods.*

1047. A substantive in any case may be modified like the subject.

1048. II. The predicate may be enlarged by the addition of accusatives, datives, predicate nouns, or adverbial adjuncts.

1049. (1.) The ACCUSATIVE denotes the object of the verb; also extent, duration, and aim of motion. See **1124.**

1050. (2.) The DATIVE denotes that for or to which something is or is done. See **1175.**

1051. (3.) A predicate noun, either substantive or adjective, denoting 'office, time, age, order, condition,' or the like, is often added to other verbs besides those of indeterminate meaning (**1035**): as,

Iūnius aedem dictātor dēdicāvit, *Junius dedicated a temple in his capacity as dictator,* not *Junius the dictator.* **litterās Graecās senex didicī,** *I learned Greek when I was an old man.* **prīnceps in proelium ībat, ultimus excēdēbat,** *he was always the first to go into battle, the last to come out.* For the predicative dative of the substantive, see **1219.**

1052. In like manner a noun may be added as a predicate in agreement with a substantive in any oblique case: as,

sē incolumēs recipiunt, *they come back safe.* **ante mē cōnsulem,** *before my consulship.* **Dolābellā hoste dēcrētō,** *Dolabella having been voted an enemy.* **nātūrā duce,** *with nature as a guide.*

1053. (4.) An ADVERBIAL ADJUNCT is either an oblique case of a noun, often with a preposition, or an adverb denoting 'place, time, extent, degree, manner, cause,' or 'circumstances' generally: as,

silentiō proficīscitur, *he marches in silence.* in eō flūmine pōns erat, *over that river there was a bridge.*

1054. A predicate substantive may be modified like the subject. An adjective, either of the subject or of the predicate, may be modified by an oblique case or by an adverb.

COMBINATION OF SENTENCES.

1055. Simple sentences may be combined in two different ways. The added sentence may be I. Coordinate; or II. Subordinate.

Thus, in *he died and we lived,* the two sentences are coordinate, that is, of equal rank. But in *he died that we might live,* the sentence beginning with *that* is subordinate. In either combination the separate sentences are often called *Clauses* or *Members,* in contradistinction to the more comprehensive sentence of which they are parts.

I. THE COMPOUND SENTENCE.

1056. A COMPOUND SENTENCE is one which consists of two or more coordinate simple sentences: as,

tū mē amās, ego tē amō, Pl. *Most.* 305, *thou art in love with me, I'm in love with thee.* nox erat et caelō fulgēbat lūna serēnō inter minōra sīdera, H. *Epod.* 15, 1, *'twas night, and in a cloudless sky, bright rode the moon amid the lesser lights.* ā tē petō, mē dēfendās, *Fam.* 15, 8, *I ask it of you, protect me.*

1057. A compound sentence is usually abridged when the members have parts in common: as,

valēbant precēs et lacrimae, *Mil.* 34, *prayers and tears had weight,* compound subject, for valēbant precēs et valēbant lacrimae. rogat ōratque tē, *RA.* 144, *he begs and entreats you,* compound predicate, for rogat tē ōratque tē. arma virumque canō, V. 1, 1, *arms and the man I sing,* compound object, for arma canō virumque canō. diū atque ācriter pugnātum est, 1, 26, 1, *there was long and sharp fighting,* for diū pugnātum est atque ācriter pugnātum est.

II. THE COMPLEX SENTENCE.

1058. A COMPLEX SENTENCE is one which consists of a main and a subordinate sentence: as,

182

centuriōnēs praemittit (main sentence), quī locum idōneum castrīs dēligant (subordinate sentence), 2, 17, 1, *he sends some officers ahead to select a suitable spot for the camp.* nunc scio (main sentence), quid sit Amor (subordinate sentence), V. *E.* 8, 43, *now, now I know what Eros is.* ā tē petō (main sentence), ut mē dēfendās (subordinate sentence), *Fam.* 15, 7, *I ask it of you that you protect me.*

1059. Several sentences are often subordinate to one and the same main sentence, and subordinate sentences may in their turn be main sentences to other subordinate sentences.

Thus, in the following sentence *b* is subordinate to *A*, and *c* to *Ab:* (*c.*) quālis esset nātūra montis, (*b.*) quī cōgnōscerent, (*A.*) mīsit, 1, 21, 1, *he sent some people to see what the character of the hill was.*

1060. Subordinate sentences may be coordinated with each other, as well as main sentences.

Thus, in the following sentence, *b* and *b* are both subordinate to *A*, but coordinate with each other: (*A.*) hīs rēbus fīēbat, (*b.*) ut et minus lātē vagārentur (*b.*) et minus facile fīnitimīs bellum īnferre possent, 1, 2, 4, *so it came to pass that, in the first place, they did not roam round much, and secondly, they could not so easily make aggressive war on their neighbours.*

1061. A subordinate sentence introductory in thought to the main sentence, though not necessarily first in the order of the words, is called a *Protasis;* the main sentence which completes the thought is called an *Apodosis:* as,

quom vidēbis (protasis), tum sciēs (apodosis), Pl. *B.* 145, *when thou see'st, then thou'lt know.* ut sēmentem fēceris (protasis), ita metēs (apodosis), *DO.* 2, 261, *as a man soweth, so shall he reap.* sī sunt dī (protasis), beneficī in hominēs sunt (apodosis), *Div.* 2, 104, *if there are gods, they are kind to men.*

———◆———

AGREEMENT.

(A.) OF THE VERB.

1062. A verb agrees with its subject in number and person: as,

praedia mea tū possidēs, ego aliēnā misericordiā vīvō, *RA.* 145, *you, sir, hold my estates, it is by the compassion of other people that I am supported.* Rhodanus fluit, 1, 6, 2, *the Rhone flows.* nōs, nōs, dīcō apertē, cōnsulēs dēsumus, *C.* 1, 3, *it is ourselves, yes, ourselves, I will speak without reserve, the consuls, who fail in our duty.* vōs vōbīs cōnsulite, 7, 50, 4, *do you look out for yourselves* diffūgēre nivēs, H. 4, 7, 1, *scattered and gone are snows.*

1063. With a compound subject, two constructions are admissible, as follows.

1064. (1.) With two or more singular subjects, the verb is often in the plural : as,

(*a.*) Without connectives: persons : iīsdem ferē temporibus fuērunt C. Cotta, P. Sulpicius, Q. Varius, Cn. Pompōnius, *Br.* 182, *in about the same times lived Cotta, Sulpicius, Varius, and Pomponius.* Things : fidēs Rōmāna, iūstitia imperātōris in forō et cūriā celebrantur, L. 5, 27, 11, *the chivalrous principle of Rome and the square dealing of her captain are trumpeted in market place and council hall.* (*b.*) With atque, et, or -que : persons : ex hīs Cotta et Sulpicius facile prīmās tulērunt, *Br.* 182, *of these Cotta and Sulpicius indisputably bore the palm.* Things : nox et amor vīnumque nihil moderābile suādent, O. *Am.* 1, 6, 59, *darkness and love and wine to nothing governable tempt.* cum senātus populusque Rōmānus pācem comprobāverint, L. 37, 45, 14, *when the senate and the people of Rome sanction peace.* (*c.*) With et . . . et: persons : et Q. Maximus et L. Paullus iīs temporibus fuērunt, *Fam.* 4, 6, 1, *both Maximus and Paullus lived in such times.* Things : utrōsque et laudis cupiditās et timor īgnōminiae excitābant, 7, 80, 5, *both of these eagerness for glory in the first place and secondly fear of disgrace spurred on.*

1065. The plural is sometimes demanded by the meaning of the verb: as, iūs et iniūria nātūrā diiūdicantur, *Leg.* 1, 44, *right and wrong are naturally distinguished from each other.*

1066. (2.) Often, however, with two or more singular subjects, the verb is put in the singular : as,

(*a.*) Without connectives: persons : tum Gorgiās, Thrasymachus, Prodicus, Hippiās in magnō honōre fuit, *Br.* 30, *at that time Gorgias, Thrasymachus, Prodicus, and Hippias were in high renown.* Things : persuāsit nox, amor, vīnum, adulēscentia, T. *Ad.* 470, *the witchery was night, flirtation, wine, and youth* (*b.*) With atque, et, or -que : persons : cūr Lȳsiās et Hyperīdēs amātur? *Br.* 68, *why is a Lysias and a Hyperides idolized?* Things : Gallōs ā Belgīs Matrona et Sēquana dīvidit, 1, 2, 1, *the Matrona and Sequana cut off the Gauls from the Belgians.* senātus populusque Rōmānus voluit, L. 21, 40, 3, *senate and people of Rome ordained.* (*c.*) With et . . . et: persons : illam ratiōnem et Pompēius et Flaccus secūtus est, *Flacc.* 32, *that rule both Pompey and Flaccus followed.* Things : tālis senātōrum et dignitās et multitūdō fuit, *Ph.* 13, 13, *both the position and number of the senators was such.*

1067. With two or more singular subjects denoting things, and making a compound idea, a singular verb is very common, agreeing either with th. subjects taken as a unit, or with the nearest : as,

(*a.*) cum tempus necessitāsque postulat, dēcertandum manū est, *Off.* 1, 81, *when the emergency requires, we must fight it out by hand.* tanta laetitia ac grātulātiō fuit, L. 10, 26, 4, *so great was the demonstration of joy.* (*b.*) Cingetorīgī prīncipātus atque imperium est trāditum, 6, 8, 9, *the headship and command was assigned to Cingetorix.*

1068. (3.) With mixed subjects, singular and plural, the verb may likewise be either plural or singular : as, (*a.*) **vīta mors, dīvitiae paupertās omnīs hominēs permovent,** *Off.* 2, 37, *life and death, riches and poverty, tell much on everybody.* (*b.*) **quantō in perīculō et castra et legiōnēs et imperātor versārētur,** 2, 26, 5, *in what imminent peril camp and legions and commander were involved.* **hōc mihī et Peripatēticī et Acadēmia concēdit,** *Ac.* 2, 113, *this point both Peripatetics and Academy grant me.*

1069. The plural is sometimes used with a singular subject limited by an ablative with **cum,** *with:* as, **Syrus cum illō vostrō cōnsusurrant,** T. *Hau.* 473, *Syrus and yon man of yours are whispering together.* **Bocchus cum peditibus postrēmam Rōmānōrum aciem invādunt,** S. *I.* 101, 5, *Bocchus with the infantry falls on the rereward line of the Romans.* Cicero commonly uses a singular verb in this combination, Caesar has the plural once only.

1070. (4.) When the subjects are connected by **nec . . . nec, aut,** or **aut . . . aut,** the verb is likewise either plural or singular: as,

(*a.*) **neque multitūdō hostium neque tēlōrum vīs arcēre impetum eius virī potuērunt,** L. 26, 5, 17, *neither the numbers of the enemy nor the shower of missiles could arrest the onslaught of that intrepid soul.* **sī quid Sōcratēs aut Aristippus fēcerint,** *Off.* 1, 148, *if a Socrates or an Aristippus had done anything.* (*b.*) **neque pēs neque mēns satis suom officium facit,** T. *Eu.* 729, *nor foot nor mind its duty doth aright.* **sī Sōcratēs aut Antisthenēs dīceret,** *TD.* 5, 26, *if a Socrates or an Antisthenes should say it.*

1071. Collectives have usually a singular verb. But the plural is sometimes used, especially when the subject is separated from its verb, or is to be supplied from a preceding clause: as,

cum tanta multitūdō lapidēs conicerent, 2, 6, 3, *when such a throng were throwing stones.* **is cīvitātī persuāsit, ut dē fīnibus suīs exīrent,** 1, 2, 1, *this person succeeded in inducing the community to leave their territory.*

1072. The verb sometimes agrees with an appositive explaining the subject, or with a substantive in the predicate: as,

(*a.*) **flammae lātē fūsae, certiōris clādis indicium, prōgredī longius prohibuit,** L. 10, 43, 11, *wide-spread flames, sign of a surer disaster, prevented a further advance.* When **urbs, oppidum, cīvitās,** or the like, is added to plural names of places, the predicate usually agrees with the appellative: as, **Coriolī oppidum captum,** L. 2, 33, 9, *Corioli town was taken.* (*b.*) **amantium īrae amōris integrātiōst,** T. *Andr.* 555, *lovers' tiffs are love's renewal.* **summa omnium fuērunt ad mīlia** CCCLXVIII, 1, 29, 3, *the grand total was about three hundred and sixty eight thousand.* The verb regularly agrees with the predicate substantive when the subject is an infinitive: as, **contentum suīs rēbus esse maximae sunt dīvitiae,** *Par.* 51, *for a man to be content with his own estate is the greatest possible riches.*

1073. The verb sometimes agrees with a substantive introduced by such words as **quam, quantum, nisi,** or **praeterquam:** as, **quis illum cōnsulem nisi latrōnēs putant?** *Ph.* 4, 9, *who but brigands think that man a consul?* So also a predicate adjective or participle: as, **mihī nōn tam cōpia quam modus quaerendus est,** *IP.* 3, *I must aim not so much at comprehensiveness as at moderation.*

1074. A speaker in referring to himself sometimes uses the first person plural, as a more modest form of expression: as, **Molōnī dedimus operam,** *Br.* 307, *we attended Molo's instruction,* i. e. I. Similarly **nōs** in all its cases for **ego,** &c., and **noster,** &c., for **meus,** &c.

1075. The singular imperative **age** is sometimes used in addressing more than one, particularly in old Latin : as, **age licēminī**, Pl. *St.* 221, *come, people, give a bid.* **age igitur intrō abīte**, Pl. *MG.* 928, *come then go in.* Similarly, **cave dīrumpātis**, Pl. *Poen.* 117, *mind you don't break it off.* Similarly **ain**.

1076. If the subjects are of different persons, the first person is preferred to the second or the third, and the second to the third : as,

sī tū et Tullia, lūx nostra, valētis, ego et suāvissimus Cicerō valēmus, *Fam.* 14, 5, 1, *if you and Tullia, our sunbeam, are well, darling Ciceio and I are well.* But sometimes in contrasts the verb agrees with the nearest person : as, **quid indicat aut ipse Cornēlius aut vōs ?** *Sull.* 54, *what information does Cornelius himself give, or you people ?*

(B.) OF THE NOUN.

(1.) THE SUBSTANTIVE.

1077. A substantive which explains another substantive referring to the same thing is put in the same case.

This applies to the substantive used as attribute, appositive, or predicate. The two substantives often differ in gender or number, or both. (*a.*) Attribute : **tīrōne exercitū**, *Fam.* 7, 3, 2, *with a raw army.* **ā mīmā uxōre**, *Ph.* 2, 20, *from an actress-wife.* **mendīcōs hominēs**, Pl. *St.* 135, *beggar-men.* **oculī hominis histriōnis**, *DO.* 2, 193, *the eyes of an actor man.* **nēminī hominī**, Pl. *As.* 466, *to no human being.* **servom hominem**, T. *Ph.* 292, *a servant man.* **hominēs sīcāriōs**, *RA.* 8, *professional bravoes.* (*b.*) Appositive : **quid dīcam dē thēsaurō rērum omnium, memoriā ?** *DO.* 1, 18, *what shall I say of that universil storehouse, the memory?* **duo fulmina nostrī imperī, Cn. et P. Scīpiōnēs**, *Balb.* 34, *the two thunderbolts of our realm. the Scipios, Gnaeus and Publius.* (*c.*) Predicate : **īra furor brevis est,** H *E.* 1, 2, 62, *wrath is a madness brief.* · **Dolābellā hoste dēcrētō**, *Ph.* 11, 16, *Dolabella having been voted a public enemy.* Some apparent exceptions will be noticed from time to time hereafter.

1078. Mobile substantives take also the gender and number of the masculines or feminines they explain : as,

stilus optimus dīcendī magister, *DO.* 1. 150, *pen is the best professor of rhetoric.* **vīta rūstica parsimōniae magistra est**, *RA.* 75, *country life is a teacher of thrift.* **fluviōrum rēx Ēridanus**, V. *G.* 1, 482. *Eridanus, of rivers king.* **et genus et fōrmam rēgīna pecūnia dōnat**, H. *E.* 1, 6, 37, *both birth and shape the almighty dollar gives.* **ut omittam illās omnium doctrīnārum inventrīcēs Athēnās**, *DO.* 1, 13, *to say nothing of the great originator of all intellectual pursuits, Athens.*

1079. A substantive explaining two or more substantives, is put in the plural : as,

foedus inter Rōmam Lāvīniumque urbēs renovātum est, L. 1, 14, 3, *the treaty between the cities of Rome and Lavinium was renewed.* **Cn. et P. Scīpiōnēs**, *Balb.* 34, *the Scipios, Gnaeus and Publius.*

1080. A plural subject, expressed or implied, is sometimes defined by a singular word, which is generally a collective or distributive: as,

ut ambō exercitūs suās quisque abīrent domōs, L. 2, 7, 1, *so that both armies went back to their respective homes.* uterque eōrum ex castrīs exercitum ēdūcunt, Caes. C. 3, 30, 3, *they bring their army out of camp, each of them.* heus forās exīte hūc aliquis, Pl. *E.* 398, *hallo, you boys, come out of doors here, somebody.* alius alium percontāmur, Pl. *St.* 370, *we ask of one another.* cum accidisset ut alter alterum vidērēmus, *Fin.* 3, 8, *when it came to pass that we each saw the other.* The verb sometimes agrees with the defining singular: as, quandō duo cōnsulēs, alter morbō, alter ferrō periisset, L. 41, 18, 16, *since the two consuls had died, one a natural death, the other by the sword.*

1081. A substantive in the accusative or nominative is sometimes in apposition to a thought or clause : as,

manūs intentantēs, causam discordiae, Ta. 1, 27, *shaking their fists, a provocation to quarrel.* pars ingentī subiēre feretrō, trīste ministerium, V. 6, 222, *a part put shoulder to the mighty bier, a service sad.* nec Homērum audiō, quī Ganymēdēn ab dīs raptum ait propter fōrmam; nōn iūsta causa cūr Lāomedontī tanta fieret iniūria, *TD.* 1, 65, *nor will I lend an ear to Homer, who asserts that Ganymede was carried off by the gods for his beauty ; no just reason for doing Laomedon such injustice.*

(2.) THE ADJECTIVE.

1082. An adjective, adjective pronoun, or participle, agrees with its substantive in number, gender, and case : as,

vir bonus, H. *Ep.* 1, 16, 40, *a good man,* bona uxor, Pl. *MG.* 684, *a good wife,* oleum bonum, Cato, *RR.* 3, *good oil.* Gallia est omnis dīvīsa in partēs trēs, 1, 1, 1, *Gaul, including everything under the name, is divided into three parts.* et variae volucrēs nemora āvia pervolitantēs āera per tenerum liquidīs loca vōcibus opplent, Lucr. 2, 145, *and motley birds, in pathless woods that flit through lither sky, fill space with carols clear.*

1083. An adjective or participle, either attributive or predicate, sometimes takes the number and gender of the persons or things implied in the substantive: as,

(*a.*) concursus populī mīrantium quid rēī esset, L. 1, 41, 1, *a gathering of the public, wondering what was the matter.* (*b.*) pars subeuntium obrutī, pars cōnfīxī, Ta. *H.* 2, 22, *a part of those who came up were crushed, a part were run through.* Samnītium caesī tria mīlia ducentī, L. 10, 34, 3, *of the Samnites were slain three thousand two hundred.*

1084. (1.) An attributive adjective referring to several substantives is commonly expressed with one only, generally with the first or the last: as, rēs erat multae operae et labōris, 5, 11, 5, *it was a job that required much work and trouble.* semper amāvī ingenium, studia, mōrēs tuōs, *O. 33, I have always admired your ability, your scholarly tastes, and your character.* In lively style, the adjective is often used with every substantive.

1085. Two or more attributive adjectives in the singular connected by a conjunction may belong to a plural substantive : as,

circā portās Collīnam Ēsquilīnamque, L. 26, 10, 2, *about the gates, the Colline and the Esquiline.* But the substantive may also be in the singular : as, inter Ēsquilīnam Collīnamque portam, L. 26, 10, 1, *between the Esquiline and the Colline gate.*

1086. The combined idea of a substantive with an attributive adjective may be qualified by one or more adjectives : as,

nāvīs longās trīgintā veterēs, L. 27, 22, 12, *thirty old men-of-war.* prīvāta nāvis onerāria māxima, *V. 5, 136, a very large private freighting vessel.* āter aliēnus canis, T. *Ph. 706, a strange black dog.*

1087. (2.) A predicate adjective or participle referring to two or more substantives is usually in the plural ; its gender is determined as follows :

1088. (*a.*) If the substantives denote persons of the same gender, that gender is used ; if they denote persons of different gender, the masculine is used : as,

venēnō absūmptī Hannibal et Philopoemēn, L. 39, 52, 8, *it was by poison that Hannibal and Philopoemen were taken off.* quam prīdem pater mihī et māter mortuī essent, T. *Eu. 517, how long my father and my mother had been dead.*

1089. (*b.*) If the substantives denote things, and are of different genders, the neuter plural is used; also commonly when they are feminines denoting things : as,

mūrus et porta dē caelō tācta erant, L. 32, 29, 1, *the wall and town-gate had been struck by lightning.* īra et avāritia imperiō potentiōra erant, L. 37, 32, 13, *hot blood and greed proved stronger than authority.*

1090. (*c.*) If the substantives denote both persons and things, either the gender of the substantives denoting persons is used, or the neuter. The gender of the substantives denoting things is very rarely used : as,

et rēx rēgiaque classis ūnā profectī, L. 21, 50, 11, *the king too and the king's fleet set sail in his company.* inimīca inter sē līberam cīvitātem et rēgem, L. 44, 24, 2, *that a free state and a monarch were irreconcilable things.* Dolopas et Athamāniam ēreptās sibī querēns, L. 38, 10, 3, *complaining that the Dolopians and Athamania were wrested from him.*

1091. When the verb is attached to the nearest only of two or more subjects, a predicate participle or adjective naturally takes the gender of that substantive : as, ibī Orgetorīgis fīlia atque ūnus ē fīliīs captus est, 1, 26, 5, *there the daughter of Orgetorix and one of the sons too was made prisoner.* ut brāchia atque umerī līberī esse possent, 7, 56, 4, *so that their arms and shoulders might be unhampered.*

1092. The ablative singular absente is used once each by Terence and Afranius with a plural substantive : absente nōbīs, T. *Eu. 649, while we were out.*

1093. A neuter adjective or pronoun is sometimes used as a substantive in the predicate (1101) : as,

trīste lupus stabulīs, V. *E.* 3, 80, *a baleful thing the wolf for folds.* quod ego fuī ad Trāsumennum, id tū hodiē, L. 30, 30, 12, *what I was myself at Trasumene, that you are today.*

1094. A demonstrative, determinative, or relative pronoun used substantively takes the number and gender of the substantive it represents ; the case depends on the construction of the clause in which it stands : as,

erant peditēs, quōs dēlēgerant ; cum hīs in proeliīs versābantur ; ad eōs sē recipiēbant ; hī concurrēbant, 1, 48, 5, *there were foot-soldiers whom they had picked out ; with these men they kept company in action ; upon them they would fall back ; these people would always rally.* Hippiās glōriātus est ānulum quem habēret, pallium quō amictus, soccōs quibus indūtus esset, sē suā manū cōnfēcisse, *DO.* 3, 127, *Hippias bragged he had made with his own hand the ring which he wore, the cloak in which he was wrapped, and the slippers which he had on.*

1095. Sometimes, however, the number and gender of these pronouns are determined by the sense, and not by the form of the substantive represented : as,

equitātum omnem praemittit, quī videant, 1, 15, 1, *he sends all the horse ahead, for them to see.* hīc sunt quīnque minae. hoc tibī erus mē iussit ferre, Pl. *Ps.* 1149, *here are five minae ; this my master bade me bring for thee.* Domitius Massiliam pervenit atque ab iīs receptus urbī praeficitur, Caes. *C.* 1, 36, 1, *Domitius arrived at Massilia, and was received by the people and put in charge of the town.* ad hirundinīnum nīdum vīsast sīmia adscēnsiōnem ut faceret admōlīrier ; neque eās ēripere quībat inde, Pl. *R.* 598, *up to a swallow-nest methought an ape did strive to climb ; nor could she snatch the nestlings thence ;* the eās refers to hirundinēs, implied in hirundinīnum.

1096. A pronoun representing two or more substantives sometimes takes the number and gender of the nearest. But usually it is plural, and its gender is determined like that of an adjective (1087).

1097. A demonstrative, determinative, or relative pronoun used substantively is generally attracted to the number and gender of a predicate substantive in its own clause : as,

haec est nōbilis ad Trāsumennum pūgna, L. 22, 7, 1, *such is the far-famed fight at Trasumene,* 217 B. C. ista quidem vīs est, Suet. *Iul.* 82, *now that I call an outrage,* Caesar's dying words, 44 B.C. But with a negative, sometimes the neuter : as, nec sopor illud erat, V. 3, 173, *nor was that sleep.*

1098. A demonstrative, determinative, or relative pronoun in agreement with a substantive is often equivalent to a genitive limiting the substantive : as,

hōc metū vagārī prohibēbat, 5, 19, 2, *by fear of this he stopped the prowling round.* is pavor perculit Rōmānōs, L. 21, 46, 7, *the panic occasioned by this demoralized the Romans.* quā spē adductī, 4, 6, 4, *impelled by the hope of this.*

189

THE SIMPLE SENTENCE.

(A.) USE OF THE NOUN.

NUMBER AND GENDER.

1099. The singular of a word denoting a person is sometimes used in a collective sense.

This singular is generally a military designation: as, **mīles, eques, pedes, hostis, Rōmānus, Poenus.** But other substantives and adjectives are occasionally thus used.

1100. A substantive or adjective denoting a person is often used in the singular as representative of a class, particularly when two persons are contrasted: as,

sī tabulam dē naufrāgiō stultus adripuerit, extorquēbitne eam sapiēns? *Off.* 3, 89, *if a fool has seized a plank from a wreck, will the sage twitch it away?*

1101. The neuter singular of certain adjectives is used as an abstract substantive.

These adjectives have commonly stems in -o-, and are often used in the partitive genitive (1250). The nominative is rare, also the accusative and ablative, except in prepositional constructions. Such are: **bonum, malum; rēctum, prāvum; decōrum, indecōrum; honestum; vērum, falsum; iūstum, iniūstum; aequum; ambiguum; rīdiculum. ūtile, ināne, commūne, īnsīgne, simile,** &c.

1102. Certain adjectives, which originally agreed with an appellative denoting a thing, have dropped the appellative and become substantives.

Such are: **Āfricus,** sc. ventus; **Āfrica,** sc. terra; **calda,** sc. **aqua; cānī,** sc. capillī; **circēnsēs,** sc. lūdī; **decuma,** sc. pars; **fera,** sc. bēstia; **hīberna,** sc. castra; **merum,** sc. vīnum; **nātālis,** sc. diēs; **patria,** sc. terra; **praetexta,** sc. toga; **summa,** sc. rēs; **trirēmis,** sc. nāvis, and many others.

1103. Certain adjectives denoting relationship, friendship, hostility, connection, or age, may be used in both numbers as substantives.

Such are: (*a.*) **adfīnis, cōgnātus, cōnsanguineus, gentīlis, necessārius, propīnquus;** (*b.*) **adversārius, amīcus, inimīcus, familiāris, hostis, intimus, invidus, socius, sodālis;** (*c.*) **contubernālis, manipulāris, vīcīnus;** (*d.*) **adulēscēns, aequālis, iuvenis, senex.**

1104. The masculine plural of many adjectives is used substantively to denote a class.

Such are: **bonī,** *the good, the well-disposed, conservatives, patriots, our party;* **improbī,** *the wicked, the dangerous classes, revolutionists, anarchists, the opposite party;* **doctī, indoctī; piī, impiī,** and the like.

1105. Proper names of men are used in the plural to denote different persons of the same name, or as appellatives to express character, oftenest good character : as,

duo Metellī, Celer et Nepōs, *Br.* 247, *the two Metelluses, Celer and Nepos.* **quid Crassōs, quid Pompēiōs ēvertit ?** J. 10, 108, *what overthrew a Crassus, Pompey what?* i. e. men like Crassus and Pompey.

1106. The neuter plural of adjectives of all degrees of comparison is very often used as a substantive.

Such adjectives are usually in the nominative or accusative, and may have a pronoun, a numeral, or an adjective, agreeing with them. In English the singular is often preferred. Such are : **bona, mala ; vēra, falsa ; haec,** *this ;* **omnia,** *everything ;* **haec omnia,** *all this,* &c., &c.

1107. Names of countries are sometimes used in the plural when the country consists of several parts which are called by the same name as the whole country : as, **Galliae,** *the Gauls ;* **Germāniae,** *the Germanies.*

1108. Material substantives are often used in the plural to denote different sorts of the substance designated, its constituent parts, or objects made of it : as,

aera, *lumps of bronze, bronzes, coppers.* **aquae,** *water in different places, medicinal springs.* **cērae,** *pieces of wax, tablets, wax masks, waxworks.* **marmora,** *kinds of marble, blocks of marble, works of marble.* **nivēs,** *snowflakes, snowdrifts, snowstorms, repeated snows.* **spūmae,** *masses of foam.* **sulpura,** *lumps of sulphur.* **vīna,** *wines, different kinds of wine.*

1109. Abstract substantives are often used in the plural to denote different kinds or instances of the abstract idea, or an abstract idea pertaining to several persons or things : as,

sunt domesticae fortitūdinēs nōn īnferiōrēs mīlitāribus, *Off.* 1, 78, *there are cases of heroism in civil life fully equal to those in war.* **tē cōnscientiae stimulant maleficiōrum tuōrum,** *Par.* 18, *you are tormented by pricks of conscience for your sins.* **propter siccitātēs palūdum,** 4, 38, 2, *because the swamps were dry everywhere.*

1110. The plural is sometimes used in generalizations, and in poetry to magnify a single thing, to give mystery to the statement, or often merely for metrical convenience : as, **advēnisse familiārēs dīcitō,** Pl. *Am.* 353, *say that the people of the house are come,* the plural **familiārēs** denoting one person. **Priamī dum rēgna manēbant,** V. 2, 22, *while Priam's realms still stood.* **externōs optāte ducēs,** V. 8, 503, *choose captains from a foreign strand,* i. e. Aeneas.

CASE.

1111. There are two groups of cases, the principal and the secondary.

1112. The principal cases are the nominative and the accusative. The principal cases, which have more complete inflections than the secondary, express the two chief relations of the noun in the sentence, those of the subject and of the object. The secondary cases are used to express subordinate or supplementary relations.

THE NOMINATIVE.

1113. The nominative is principally used as the subject or predicate noun of a verb or of an infinitive. Besides this use, the nominative occurs in titles, exclamations, and addresses (1114–1123).

THE NOMINATIVE OF TITLE.

1114. The nominative is used in inscriptions, notices, titles, or headings: as,

L·CORNELIVS·CN·F·CN·N·SCIPIO, CIL. I, 34, on a tomb, *Lucius Cornelius Scipio, son* (fīlius) *of Gnaeus, grandson* (nepōs) *of Gnaeus.* LABYRINTHVS HIC HABITAT MINOTAVRVS, CIL. IV, 2331, on a plan of the Labyrinth scratched by a Pompei schoolboy, *The Maze. Here lives Minotaur.* PRIVATVM PRECARIO ADEITVR, CIL. I, 1215, *Private Grounds. No Admittance without leave.* Themistoclēs, Neoclī fīlius, Athēniēnsis, N. 2, 1, *Themistocles, son of Neocles, of Athens.*

1115. The title proper of a book is often put in the genitive, dependent on liber or librī: as, Cornēlī Tacitī Historiārum Liber Prīmus, *Tacitus's Histories, Book First.* Or prepositional expressions are used: as, M. Tullī Cicerōnis dē Fātō Liber, *Cicero, Fate, in One Book.* Cornēlī Tacitī ab Excessū dīvī Augustī Liber Prīmus, *Tacitus's Roman History from the Demise of the sainted Augustus, Book First.*

1116. Sometimes the nominative of a title or exclamation is retained in a sentence for some other case: as, Gabīniō cōgnōmen 'Cauchius' ūsurpāre concessit, Suet. *Cl.* 24, *he allowed Gabinius to take the surname 'Cauchius;'* (compare Catō quasi cōgnōmen habēbat Sapientis, *L.* 6, *Cato had the virtual surname of the Wise*). 'Marsya' nōmen habet, O. 6, 400, *it has the name of 'Marsyas;'* (compare nōmen Dānuvium habet, S. *Fr.* 3, 55, *it has the name Danube*). resonent mihi 'Cynthia' silvae, Prop. 1, 18, 31, *let woods reecho 'Cynthia' for me;* (compare tū, Tītyre, fōrmōsam resonāre docēs Amaryllida silvas, V. *E.* 1, 4, *thou, Tityrus, dost teach the woods to echo Amaryllis Fair*).

THE NOMINATIVE OF EXCLAMATION.

1117. The nominative is sometimes used in exclamations: as,

fortūnae fīlius, omnēs, H. *S.* 2, 6, 49, *'the child of Fortune,' all* exclaim. This nominative is often accompanied by an interjection, such as ecce, ēn, heu, ō, prō, vāh: as, ēn Priamus, V. 1, 461, *lo, Priam here.* ō fēstus diēs, T. *Eu.* 560, *oh day of cheer.* For eccilla, see 667.

THE VOCATIVE NOMINATIVE AND VOCATIVE PROPER.

1118. The vocative nominative is used when a person or thing is addressed: as,

quō usque tandem abūtēre, Catilīna, patientiā nostrā? *C.* 1, 1, *in heaven's name, how long, Catiline, wilt trifle with our patience?* valēte, dēsīderia mea, valēte, *Fam.* 14, 2, 4, *good bye, my absent loves, good bye.* Instead of a proper name, an emphatic tū is often used: as, advorte animum sīs tū, Pl. *Cap.* 110, *just pay attention, sirrah, please.*

1119. Masculine stems in **-o-** commonly use the special form for the second person singular called the vocative : as,

urbem, urbem, mī Rūfe, cole, *Fam.* 2, 12, 2, *stick to town, dear Rufus, yes, to town.* But the vocative nominative is sometimes used even of **-o-** stems : as, audī tū, populus Albānus, L. 1, 24, 7, *hear thou, the people of Alba.*

1120. Poets use the vocative nominative or vocative proper very freely, sometimes for liveliness, but often simply in place of other cases not allowed by the metre : as,

ōra manūsque tuā lavimus, Fērōnia, lymphā H. *S.* 1, 5, 24, *our faces and our hands, Feronia, in thy stream we wash.* occiderat Tatius, populīsque aequāta duōbus, Rōmule, iūra dabās, O. 14, 805, *now dead was Tatius, and to peoples twain thou gavest, Romulus, impartial laws.* longum tibi, Daedale, crīmen, O. 8, 240, *a lasting stigma, Daedalus, to thee.* In these three examples, Fērōniae, Rōmulus, and Daedalō would be impossible. In poetry, the vocative is particularly common in questions.

1121. Nominative forms and vocative forms are often combined : as, dulcis amīce, H. *E.* 1, 7, 12, *sweet friend.* mī vir, Pl. *Am.* 716, *my husband.* Iāne pater, J. 6, 394, *thou father Janus.*

1122. In verse the vocative is occasionally used even in the predicate : as, quō moritūre ruis ? V. 10, 811, *whither, on death intent, fliest thou ?* quibus, Hector, ab ōrīs exspectāte venīs ? V. 2, 282, *out of what limboes, Hector, dost thou gladly welcomed come ?*

1123. The vocative nominative or vocative proper is sometimes accompanied by ō, but only in impassioned addresses : as, ō fortūnāte adulēscēns, *Arch.* 24, *oh thou thrice blest youth;* also by prō in addresses to gods, by eho and heus in calls on men. Rarely by au, ehem, hem, ĕheu, eia or heia, iō.

———◆———

THE ACCUSATIVE.

1124. The accusative is used primarily with verbs, or with expressions equivalent to verbs. The relations expressed by the accusative are all of one general kind ; but they vary somewhat, according to the nature of the verb.

1125. I. With most verbs, the accusative either (*a.*) denotes that which is affected or apprehended, or is produced by the action of the verb (1132) ; or, less frequently (*b.*) it repeats the meaning of the verb in the form of a substantive (1140).

Such accusatives, called accusatives of the *Object*, are never attended by a preposition, and become nominative in the passive construction.

1126. II. With some verbs, the accusative denotes (*a.*) extent or duration (1151) ; with others it denotes (*b.*) aim of motion (1157).

Both these accusatives sometimes have their places taken by a prepositional expression, or by an adverb; in the passive construction, they are not convertible into a nominative, but remain accusative.

1127. Two or even three accusatives are sometimes used with one and the same verb: see 1167–1174.

1128. The accusative is sometimes disengaged from the verb, with which it originally stood, and used with a noun or a preposition.

1129. (1.) With substantives, the accusative is rare; it is used (*a.*) in a few attributive expressions, chiefly old set forms, and rarely to denote (*b.*) aim of motion.

Thus (*a.*) the predicative id aetātis, in id aetātis iam sumus, *we are now of that age*, becomes attributive in hominēs id aetātis, *people of that age.* And (*b.*) as domum, *home*, is used with the verb redeō, *go back*, so also rarely with the substantive reditiō, *a return*.

1130. With adjectives, the accusative is commonly that of extent : so with altus, *high*, lātus, *wide*, and longus, *long*, sometimes with crassus, *thick*.

Thus, in eōs surculōs facitō sint longī pedēs bīnōs, *see that the scions be two feet long*, the accusative pedēs, which belongs with the predicate sint longī, may be used with the attributive adjective longus alone, thus : surculī longī pedēs bīnōs, *scions two feet long*.

1131. (2.) The accusative is used with many prepositions : see 1410.

I. THE ACCUSATIVE OF THE OBJECT.

1132. The object of a verb is put in the accusative : as,

(*a.*) oppida sua omnia incendunt, 1, 5, 3, *they set all their towns afire.* cōnspexit adrāsum quendam, H. *E.* 1, 7, 49, *he spied a man all shaven and shorn.* (*b.*) duās fossās perdūxit, 7, 72, 3, *he made two trenches.* This accusative, is, as may be seen above, either (*a.*) receptive, i. e. existing independently of the action of the verb, and only affected or apprehended by it; or (*b.*) of product, i. e. produced by the action of the verb.

1133. Verbs thus used with an object are said to be *used transitively.* Such verbs may also be used intransitively, that is without an object, when stress is put on the action merely : thus,

(*a.*) Transitively: tū mē amās, egō tē amō, Pl. *Most.* 305, *thou lovest me, and I love thee.* nova dīruunt, alia aedificant, S. *C.* 20, 12, *they pull down new structures, and build up others.* (*b.*) Intransitively: amō, Pl. *B.* 511, *I 'm in love.* dīruit, aedificat, H. *E.* 1, 1, 100, *it pulleth down, it buildeth up.*

1134. Some verbs, in addition to the accusative, often take an infinitive also: thus, eum vident sedēre, *V.* 5, 107, *they see him sit, they see that he is sitting.* Here the accusative eum, originally the object, *they see him*, becomes at the same time the subject of the new statement appended, sedēre, *sit*, thus giving rise to the construction known as the *accusative with the infinitive.*

1135. Instead of the proper accusative of the object, another accusative is sometimes substituted. denoting the ultimate result: as,

rūpēre viam, L. 2, 50, 10. *they broke a path*, i. e. *they broke through the obstacles.* and so made *a path.* foedusque ferī, E. 33, *and strike a covenant*, i. e *strike* a victim, and so make *a covenant.*

1136. In Plautus, **quid tibĭ** with a substantive of action in **-tiō** and **est**, has an accusative like a verb used transitively: as, **quid tibĭ hanc cūrātiōst rem?** Pl. *Am.* 519, *what business hast thou with this?*

1137. Many verbs ordinarily used intransitively, particularly verbs of motion, have a transitive use when compounded with a preposition.

Such prepositions are, **ad, circum, ex, in, ob, per, prae, praeter, trāns,** and some others: as, **plūrēs paucōs circumsistēbant,** 4, 26, 2, *a good many took their stand round a few.* **Caesar omnem agrum Pīcēnum percurrit,** Caes. *C.* 1, 15, 1, *Caesar runs over the whole Picene territory.* **praeterīre nēmō pristrīnum potest,** Pl. *Cap.* 808, *no man can pass the mill.* **flūmen trānsiērunt,** 4, 4, 7, *they crossed the river.*

1138. A few verbs with a transitive use, have, when compounded with **circum** and **trāns,** besides the accusative of the object, a second accusative of the thing to which the preposition refers: as, **istum circumdūce hāsce aedĭs,** Pl. *Most.* 843, *take that man round this house.* **Caesar funditōrēs pontem trādūcit,** 2, 10, 1, *Caesar takes the slingers over the bridge.* **trānsfer līmen aureolōs pedēs,** Cat. 61, 166, *over the threshold put thy little golden foot.* In the passive, the accusative connected with the preposition is sometimes retained: as, **Apollōniam praetervehuntur,** Caes. *C.* 3, 26, 1, *they sail by Apollonia.*

1139. Verbs of weeping and wailing, and some other verbs of feeling, which commonly have an intransitive use, sometimes have a transitive use with an accusative: as,

(*a.*) **lūget senātus, maeret equester ōrdō,** *Mil.* 20, *the senate is in mourning, the equestrian order betrays its sadness.* (*b.*) **mātrōnae eum lūxērunt,** L. 2, 7, 4, *the married women wore mourning for him.* **maereō cāsum eius modī,** *Fam.* 14, 2, 2, *I cannot help showing my grief over a misfortune of such a kind.* **quid mortem congemis ac flēs,** Lucr. 3, 934, *why dost thou death bewail and weep?* Such verbs are **fleō,** *weep,* **gemō,** *wail,* **lāmentor,** **queror,** *bewail,* **doleō,** *am distressed,* **lūgeō,** *mourn,* **maereō,** *betray sadness.* Similarly, **horreō,** *shudder,* **reformīdō,** *am in dread,* **fastīdiō,** *feel disdain,* **rīdeō,** *laugh,* &c., &c. The object is oftener a thing than a person, and passive constructions are rare, and mostly confined to poetry.

The Emphasizing or Defining Accusative.

1140. The meaning of a verb, even of one ordinarily intransitive, may be emphasized or more exactly defined by an accusative of kindred derivation added.

(*a.*) Seldom without an adjective: as, **dum vītam vīvās,** Pl. *Per.* 494, *as long as life thou liv'st,* i. e. as long as you ever live and breathe. **quōrum maiōrum nēmō servitūtem servīvit,** *T.* 29, *of whose ancestors not one has served servitude,* i. e. been a regular slave. **vidē nē facinus faciās,** *Fin.* 2, 95, *mind you don't do a deed,* i. e. a misdeed. (*b.*) Commonly with an adjective: as, **scelestam servitūtem serviunt,** Pl. *Cu.* 40, *a wicked servitude they serve.* **facinus memorābile fēcistis,** L. 24, 22, 16, *you have done a deed well worth mentioning.* **mīrum atque īnscītum somniāvī somnium,** Pl. *R.* 597, *a strange and silly dream dreamed I.*

1141. The verb sometimes has an accusative of kindred meaning, but of different derivation: as,

ut vīvās aetātem miser, Pl. *Am.* 1023, *that thou mayst live thy days in woe.* nōn pugnāvit ingēns Īdomeneus Sthenelusve sōlus dīcenda Mū-sīs proelia, H. 4, 9, 19, *not towering Idomeneus nor Sthenelus alone has battles fought for Muses to rehearse.*

1142. The neuter singular accusative of a descriptive adjective is used, particularly by the poets, to denote manner : as,

magnum clāmat, Pl. *MG.* 823, *he's bellowing big.* suāve locus vōcī resonat conclūsus, H. *S.* 1, 4, 76, *sweet to the voice the pent-up place rings back.* suāve rubēns hyacinthus, V. *E.* 3, 63, *sweet-blushing hyacinth.* cūr tam cernis acūtum? H. *S.* 1, 3, 26, *why dost thou see so sharp?* The plural is not so common : as, asper, acerba tuēns, Lucr. 5, 33, V. 9, 794, *rough, staring savageness.*

1143. Some verbs of smell and of taste have an accusative defining what the smell or the taste is : as, pāstillōs Rūfillus olet, Gargōnius hircum, H. *S.* 1, 2, 27, *of lozenges Rufillus smells, Gargonius of the goat.* doctrīnam redolet puerī-lem, *DO.* 2, 109, *it smacks of A B C studies.* nōn omnēs possunt olere un-guenta exōtica, Pl. *Most.* 42, *not every man can of imported ointments reek.* meliōra unguenta sunt quae terram quam quae crocum sapiunt, Cic. in Plin. *NH.* 17, 5, 3, 38, *essences that smell of earth are better than those that smell of saffron.*

1144. Any verb or verbal expression may be defined in a general way by the neuter accusative of a pronoun or of an enumerative word. as,

id gaudeō, T. *Andr.* 362, *I'm glad of that.* id maestast, Pl. *R.* 397, *she's mournful over this.* id prōdeō, T. *Eu.* 1005, *I'm coming out for this.* cētera adsentior Crassō, *DO.* 1, 35, *on all the other points I agree with Cras-sus.* So also quod, *for which, on account of which,* aliquid, quicquam, nihil, &c., &c., and particularly quid, *why, in what respect, wherein, what,* or *what . . . for:* as, quid vēnistī, Pl. *Am.* 377, *why art thou come?* quid tibī obstō, *RA.* 145, *wherein do I stand in your way?*

1145. The accusative of an appellative is rarely used adverbially : as, magnam partem ex iambīs nostra cōnstat ōrātiō, *O.* 189, *our own speech is made up a great deal of iambs.* maximam partem lacte vīvunt, 4, 1, 8, *they live on milk the most part,* i. e. *chiefly.* Prepositional expressions are commoner: as, magnā ex parte, 1, 16, 6, *principally.* For vicem, *instead of, for,* or *like,* see the dictionary.

1146. The accusative is sometimes disengaged from a verb, and qualifies a sub-stantive as an attribute, chiefly in a few set expressions (1129): as, ōrātiōnēs aut aliquid id genus, *Att.* 13, 12, 3, *speeches or something that kind.* aucupium omne genus, Cat. 114, 3, *fowling of every kind.* nūgās hoc genus, H. *S.* 2, 6, 43, *small talk — this kind.* hoc genus in rēbus, Lucr. 6, 917, *in matters of this kind.* cum id aetātis fīliō, *Clu.* 141, *with a son of that age.* Similarly diēs quīndecim supplicātiō, 2, 35, 4, *a fortnight thanksgiving.*

THE ACCUSATIVE OF THE PART CONCERNED.

1147. Poets use the accusative to express the part concerned, especially a part of the human body: as,

tremit artūs, Lucr. 3, 489, V. *G.* 3, 84, *he shivers in his limbs.* tremis
ossa pavōre, H. *S.* 2, 7, 57, *thou tremblest in thy bones with fear.* viridī
membra sub arbutō strātus, H. 1, 1, 21, *stretching — his limbs — beneath*
an arbute green. ōs umerōsque deō similis, V. 1, 589, *in face and shoulders*
like a god.

The Accusative of the Thing put on.

1148. The accusative is used with reflexive verbs in poetry to denote the
thing put on : as,

comantem Androgeī galeam induitur, V. 2, 391, *Androgeus' high-haired*
helm he dons. exuviās indūtus Achillī, V. 2, 275, *clad in Achilles' spoils.*
Rarely to denote the thing taken off : as, priōrēs exuitur vultūs, St. *Th.*
10, 640, *she doffs her former looks.*

The Accusative of Exclamation.

1149. The accusative is used in exclamations, sometimes
merely to call attention to something, but generally with a predicate to express a judgment with emphasis.

(*a.*) In calling attention, ecce or em is used in old Latin : as, ecce mē,
Pl. *MG.* 663, *behold, your humble servant.* em Dāvom tibī, T. *Andr.* 842,
there, Davos sir. For ellum, eccillum, &c., see 667 and 673. Also, from
Cicero on, ēn : as, ēn quattuor ārās, V. *E.* 5, 65, *see, altars four.* (*b.*) In
emphatic judgments sometimes the accusative alone : as, fortūnātum Nī-
cobūlum, Pl. *B.* 455, *lucky man that Nicobulus.* testīs ēgregiōs, Cael. 63,
mighty fine witnesses; sometimes with an interjection : as, ō imperātōrem
probum, Pl. *B.* 759, *oh what a good commander;* rarely so with ēcastor,
edepol, eugē, heu, īlicet, *all's up,* ēheu. Interrogatively : hancine
impudentiam ? *V.* 5, 62, *possible, shamelessness like this?*

1150. The accusative is used in excited orders, appeals, and questions, without
any verb expressed, or even distinctly felt : as, Tiberium in Tiberim, Suet. *Tib.*
75, *Tiberius to the Tiber.* dī vostram fidem, T. *Andr.* 716, *ye gods your help.*
prō fidem, Thēbānī cīvēs, Pl. *Am.* 376, *oh help, or murder, ye citizens of*
Thebes. So with unde, quō, and quandō, often followed by mihī or tibī : as,
quō mihi fortūnam, sī nōn concēditur ūtī? H. *E.* 1, 5, 12, *why wealth for*
me, if wealth I may not use?

II. THE ACCUSATIVE OF SPACE AND TIME, AND OF
AIM OF MOTION.

The Accusative of Space and Time.

1151. Extent of space or duration of time is denoted
by the accusative : as,

(*a*.) mīlia passuum xx prōcēdit, 5, 47, 1, *he pushes on twenty miles.*
trīduī viam prōgressī, 4. 4, 4, *having advanced three days journey.* agge-
rem lātum pedēs cccxxx, altum pedēs lxxx exstrūxērunt, 7, 24, 1, *they
built up a mound three hundred and thirty feet wide, and eighty feet high*
(1130). (*b*.) mātrōnae annum lūxērunt, L. 2, 7, 4, *the married women wore
mourning a year.* ūndēvīgintī annōs nātus erat, *Br.* 229, *he was nineteen
years old.* secūtae sunt continuōs complūrēs diēs tempestātēs, 4, 34, 4,
there followed a good many days a succession of storms. triennium vagātī,
4, 4, 2, *having led a nomad life three years.* ūnum diem supplicātiō habita
est, L. 10, 47, 7, *a thanksgiving was held one day.* diēs quīndecim supplicātiō, 2, 35, 4, *a fortnight thanksgiving* (1129). Sometimes per is added:
as, lūdī per decem diēs factī sunt, *C.* 3, 20, *games were celebrated ten days
long.*

1152. The idea of traversing is sometimes not expressed : as, mīlia passuum
tria ab eōrum castrīs castra pōnit, 1, 22, 5, *he pitches camp three miles away
from their camp.* quadringentōs inde passūs cōnstituit signa, L. 34, 20,
4, *four hundred paces from there he set up the standards.* See 1399.

1153. With absum and distō, the ablative of amount of difference is sometimes
used (1393) : as, certior factus est Ariovistī cōpiās ā nostrīs mīlibus passuum quattuor et xx abesse, 1, 41, 5, *he was informed that Ariovistus's troops
were four and twenty miles away from ours.* If the place is not mentioned from
which distance is reckoned, ab or ā is sometimes used before the expression of distance : as, positīs castrīs ā mīlibus passuum xv, 6, 7, 3, *pitching camp fifteen
miles away.*

1154. The accusative is used with abhinc, ago: as, quaestor fuistī abhinc
annōs quattuordecim, *V.* 1, 34, *you were a quaestor fourteen years ago.* Rarely
the ablative (1393) : as, quō tempore ? abhinc annīs xv, *RC*, 37, *when ? fifteen
years ago;* and once or twice with abhinc, meaning *before* (1393): as, comitiīs
abhinc diēbus trīgintā factīs, *V.* 2, 130, *the election having been held thirty
days before.*

1155. The accusative singular is used with ordinals, to show the number of days,
months, or years since a particular event, including the day, month, or year of the
event itself : as, quod annum iam tertium et vīcēsimum rēgnat, *IP.* 7,
the circumstance that he has now been on the throne two and twenty years.

1156. The accusative in some pronominal expressions and adverbs passes over
from 'time through which' to a loose 'time at which': as, id temporis, *RA.* 97, *at
that time.* hoc noctis, Pl. *Am.* 163ʰ, *at this time of night.* tum, *then*, num,
nunc, *now*, nunc ipsum, Pl. *B.* 940, Att. 10, 4, 10, *this very minute*, commodum, *just in time.* For the locative ablative exceptionally used to denote duration,
see 1355.

THE ACCUSATIVE OF THE AIM OF MOTION.

1157. (1.) Proper names of towns and of little islands or peninsulas are put in the accusative to denote
the aim with expressions of motion : as,

Labiēnus Lutetiam proficīscitur, 7, 57, 1, *Labienus starts for Lutetia.*
Leucadem vēnimus, *Fam.* 16, 9, 1, *we came to Leucas.* nocturnus introitus
Zmyrnam, *Ph.* 11, 5, *the entrance into Smyrna by night* (1129) Plautus uses
Accherūns a few times like a town name : as, vīvom mē accersunt Ac-
cheruntem mortuī, *Most.* 509, *the dead are taking me to Acheron alive.*

1158. With singular names of towns and little islands, Plautus has the accusative alone twenty times, and twenty times with **in** ; Terence has, including **Lēmnum,** *Ph.* 567, and **Cyprum,** *Ad.* 224, 230, the accusative alone six times, and twice with in, in **Lēmnum,** *Ph.* 66, and **in Cyprum,** *Ad.* 278. Plural town names never have **in.**

1159. An appellative **urbem** or **oppidum** accompanying the accusative of a town name is usually preceded by **in** or **ad** : as, **ad urbem Fĭdēnās tendunt,** L. 4, 33, 10, *they make for the city of Fidenae.* **Iugurtha Thalam pervēnit, in oppidum magnum,** S. *I.* 75, 1, *Jugurtha arrived at Thala, a large town.*

1160. When merely 'motion towards' or 'nearness' is meant, **ad** is used : as, **trēs viae sunt ad Mutinam,** *Ph.* 12, 22, *there are three roads to Mutina.* **mīles ad Capuam profectus sum,** *CM.* 10, *I went to the war as a private, to the region round about Capua.*

1161. Proper names of countries are also sometimes put in the accusative in poetry, to denote aim of motion : as, **abĭit Ālidem,** Pl. *Cap.* 573, *he went away to Elis.* So in prose also, **Aegyptus** in Cicero, Caesar, Nepos, Livy, and Tacitus : as, **Germānicus Aegyptum proficīscitur,** Ta. 2, 59, *Germanicus sets out for Egypt.* Rarely and in poetry names of peoples : as, **sitientīs ĭbimus Āfrōs,** V. *E.* 1, 64, *to thirst-parched Afrians we shall go.* In general the accusative of country names is preceded by **in** or **ad,** as are also appellatives regularly in prose ; but in poetry, even appellatives without a preposition are common.

1162. (2.) The accusatives **domum, rūs,** and **forās,** are used like proper names of towns : as,

(*a.*) **eō domum,** Pl. *Mer.* 659, *I'm going home.* **equitēs domum contendērunt,** 2, 24, 4, *the cavalry hurried home.* **domum reditiōnis spē sublātā,** 1, 5, 3, *the hope of a return home being out of the question* (1129). (*b.*) **rūs ībō,** T. *Eu.* 216, *I shall go out of town.* (*c.*) **effūgī forās,** T. *Eu.* 945, *I ran out of doors.*

1163. The singular **domum** is always retained by Caesar, even when two or more separate persons or parties are spoken of. Plautus, Sallust, and Nepos, have the plural **domōs** once each, and Cicero and Livy use it occasionally.

1164. The accusative **domum** or **domōs** sometimes has an attribute, usually a possessive pronoun : as, **domum suam quemque reverti,** 2, 10, 4, *for every man to go back to his home.* **alius alium domōs suās invītant,** S. *I.* 66, 3, *they invite each other to their homes.* **aurum domum rēgiam comportant,** S. *I.* 76, 6, *they bring all the gold to the house royal.* **cum domum rēgis dēvertissēs,** *D.* 17, *when you went to stay at the king's palace.* The preposition **in** is sometimes used when the attribute is a genitive or a possessive pronoun, and commonly when it is any adjective but a possessive pronoun.

1165. (3.) In old Latin, **exsequiās** and **īnfitiās** are also used with **eō,** and sometimes **malam crucem** and **malam rem,** though these last more commonly have **in** : as,

exsequiās Chremētī īre, T. *Ph.* 1026, *to go to Chremes's funeral.* **ut eās malam crucem,** Pl. *Men.* 328, *that thou mayst get thee to the accursed cross.* Later writers, as Nepos, Livy, and Quintilian, use **īnfitiās eō** again, and, from Sallust on, **vēnum eō** and **vēnum dō** sometimes occur for **vēneō** and **vēndō.**

1166. With the accusative in **-tum** (or **-sum**), called the supine, the idea of 'aim' passes over into that of 'purpose :' as **mīlitātum abiīt,** T. *Hau.* 117, *he's gone away a soldiering* (2270).

TWO ACCUSATIVES COMBINED.

OBJECT AND PREDICATE.

1167. Many verbs may take two accusatives, an object and a predicate.

Such are verbs signifying *make, keep, choose, name* or *call, have, think, recognize* or *find, show oneself,* &c., &c.: as, longiōrem mēnsem faciunt, *V.* 2, 129, *they make the month longer.* eum certiōrem faciunt, 5, 37, 7, *they let him know.* Ancum Mārcium rēgem populus creāvit, L. 1, 32, 1, *the people made Ancus Marcius king.* mē cēpēre arbitrum, T. *Hau.* 500, *they've chosen me as referee.* Duellium 'Bellium' nōmināvērunt, *O.* 153, *Duellius they named 'Bellius.'* vīcīnam Capreıs īnsulam 'Aprāgopolim' appellābat, Suet. *Aug.* 98, *the island next to Capreae he called 'the Castle of Indolence.'* conlēgās adiūtōrēs habēbat, *Sest.* 87, *he had his colleagues as assistants.* tē sapientem exīstimant, L. 6, *they consider you a sage.* quem virum P. Crassum vīdimus, *CM.* 61, *what a man we saw in Crassus.* sevērum mē praebeō, *C.* 4, 12, *I show myself stern.* In the passive both the object and the predicate become nominatives : as, Caesar certior factus est, 3, 19, 5, *Caesar was informed.*

1168. In the sense of *consider as equivalent to,* dūcō and habeō, less frequently putō, have the ablative with prō. Other constructions with these and the above verbs may be found in the dictionary.

PERSON AND THING.

1169. (1.) Some verbs of teaching and hiding, demanding and questioning, may take two accusatives, one of a person and one of a thing.

The commonest of these verbs are doceō and its compounds, and cēlō ; flāgitō, ōrō, poscō, and rogō, interrogō. The thing is usually the neuter of a pronoun or enumerative word (1144) : as, (a.) peior magister tē istaec docuit, nōn ego, Pl. *B.* 163, *a worse instructor taught thee that, not I.* quid tē litterās doceam? *Pis.* 73, *why should I teach you your A B C's?* (b.) nōn tē cēlāvī sermōnem T. Ampiī, *Fam.* 2, 16, 3, *I have not kept you in the dark about the talk with Ampius.* (c.) interim cōtīdiē Caesar Aeduōs frūmentum flāgitāre, 1, 16, 1, *meantime Caesar every day a dunning the Aeduans for the grain.* Mīlēsiōs nāvem poposcit, *V.* 1, 86, *he called on the Miletus people for a vessel.* quid me istud rogās? *Fin.* 5, 83, *why do you ask me that?* Racilius mē sententiam rogāvit, *QFr.* 2, 1, 3, *Racilius asked me my opinion.*

1170. With doceō, meaning *inform,* cēlō, rogō, and interrogō, the ablative of the thing with dē is also used. And with flāgitō and poscō, sometimes the ablative of the person with ab, with cēlō the ablative of the person with dē.

1171. In the passive the person becomes the subject, and the accusative of a neuter pronoun or adjective is retained : as, nōsne hoc cēlātōs tam diū, T. *Hec.* 645, *for us not to be told of this so long;* rarely with reversed construction: quōr haec cēlāta mē sunt? Pl. *Ps.* 490, *why was this hid from me?* Accusatives of appellatives are rare: as, omnīs mīlitiae artīs ēdoctus fuerat, L. 25, 37, 3, *he had been thoroughly taught all the arts of war.* interrogātus sententiam, L. 36, 7, 1, *being asked his opinion.* Other constructions of doctus, and of the passive of cēlō, flāgitō, poscō, rogō and interrogō, may be found in the dictionary.

1172. (2.) Verbs of wishing, reminding, inducing, and accusing, and some others, also sometimes take an accusative of the person and one of the thing.

Such are volō, moneō and its compounds, hortor and cōgō; accūsō, arguō, īnsimulō, obiūrgō. The thing is usually the neuter of a pronoun or enumerative word (1144): as, quid mē voltis? Pl. *Mer.* 868, *what do you want of me?* illud tē esse admonitum velim, *Cael.* 8, *on this point I want you to be reminded* (1171). In old Latin, accusatives of appellatives also are thus used, and sometimes also with dōnō and condōnō.

1173. (3.) The defining accusative is sometimes combined with an accusative of the person: as, tam tē bāsia multa bāsiāre, Cat. 7, 9, *thee to kiss so many kisses* (1140). But usually with an accusative of the person, the ablative takes the place of the defining accusative: as, ōdissem tē odiō Vatīniānō, Cat. 14, 3, *I should hate thee with a Vatinian hate.*

OBJECT AND EXTENT, DURATION, OR AIM.

1174. The accusative of extent or duration, or of aim of motion is often combined with that of the object: as,

(*a.*) mīlia passuum decem novem mūrum perdūcit, 1, 8, 1, *he makes a wall nineteen miles* (1151). mātrōnae annum eum lūxērunt, L. 2, 7, 4, *the married women wore mourning for him a year* (1151). (*b.*) Ancus multitūdinem omnem Rōmam trādūxit, L. 1, 33, 1, *Ancus moved the whole population over to Rome* (1157). eōs domum remittit, 4, 21, 6, *he sends them home again* (1162). For other combinations, see 1138, 1198, and 2270.

THE DATIVE.

1175. The dative denotes that for or to which a thing is or is done, and either accompanies single words, such as verbs, adjectives, sometimes adverbs, rarely substantives, or serves to modify the entire sentence. It has two principal uses.

1176. I. The dative is used as a complement. Complements may be roughly distinguished as essential or optional. But these two complements are not always separated by a sharp line, and the same dative may sometimes be referred indifferently to either head.

1177. (1.) The ESSENTIAL COMPLEMENT is a dative of the person or thing added to an idea which is felt as incomplete without the dative (1180).

Thus, **pāret**, *he is obedient*, is a statement which is felt as incomplete without a dative added to denote what it is he is obedient to, in the sentence **pāret senātuī**, *he is obedient to the senate*. But when stress is put on the action merely, without reference to its bearing, such a verb may be used without a dative: as, **pāret**, *he is obedient, he yields obedience.*

1178. (2.) The OPTIONAL COMPLEMENT, that is, the dative of interest, advantage, or disadvantage, adds something to an idea that is already complete in itself (1205).

Thus, **carmina cantō**, *I chant verses*, is a statement entirely complete in itself; it may be modified or not, at option, by a dative, thus : **carmina virginibus puerīsque cantō**, *verses for maids and boys I chant.*

1179. II. The dative of certain substantives is used predicatively (1219).

I. THE COMPLEMENTARY DATIVE.

(1.) THE ESSENTIAL COMPLEMENT.

THE DATIVE WITH VERBS.

1180. Many verbs require a dative to complete their meaning.

WITH VERBS OF INTRANSITIVE USE.

1181. (1.) Many verbs of intransitive use, particularly such as denote a state, disposition, feeling, or quality, take the dative : as,

quodne vōbīs placeat, displiceat mihī ? Pl. *MG.* 614, *shall that which pleases you, displeasing be to me ?* sī Asiciō causa plūs prōfuit quam invidia nocuit, *Cael.* 23, *if his case has been more helpful to Asicius than the hostility has been damaging.* imperat aut servit collēcta pecūnia cuique, H. *E.* 1, 10, 47, *for every man his garnered hoard or master is or slave.* nōnne huic lēgī resistētis ? *Agr.* 2, 85, *will you not stand out against this law ?* gymnasiīs indulgent Graeculī, Traj. in Plin. *Ep.* 40 [49], 2, *our Greek cousins are partial to gymnasiums.* ignōscās velim huic festinātiōnī meae, in a letter, *Fam.* 5, 12, 1, *please excuse haste.* huic legiōnī Caesar cōnfidēbat maximē, 1, 40, 15, *Caesar trusted this legion most of all.* an C. Trebōniō ego persuāsī ? cui nē suādēre quidem ausus essem, *Ph.* 2, 27, *was it I that brought conviction to Trebonius ? a man to whom I should not have presumed even to offer advice.* In the passive, such verbs are used impersonally, the dative remaining (1034) ; personal constructions are rare and poetical.

1182. This dative is used with such verbs or verbal expressions as mean *am pleasing* or *displeasing, helpful* or *injurious, command, yield,* or *am obedient, am friendly, partial,* or *opposed; spare, pardon, threaten, trust, advise, persuade, happen, meet.*   But the English translation is not a safe guide: many of the verbs used with a dative are represented transitively in English; and some verbs of the meanings above are used transitively in Latin: as, dēlectō, iuvō, laedō, &c., &c.

1183. The dative is rarely used with a form of sum and a predicate noun corresponding in meaning with the verbs above (1181): as, quid mihi scelestō tibī erat auscultātiō? Pl. *R.* 502, i. e. quid tibī auscultābam? *why did I, illstarred wretch, lend ear to thee?* quī studiōsus reī nūllī aliaest, Pl. *MG.* 802, i. e. quī studet, *who lends his soul to nothing else.*   Or immediately with a noun: as, servitūs opulentō hominī, Pl. *Am.* 166, *slavery to a millionaire.* optemperātiō lēgibus, *Leg.* 1, 42, *obedience to the laws.*   aemula labra rosīs, Mart. 4, 42, 10, *lips rivalling the rose.*

1184. Some verbs have a variable use without any difference of meaning: thus, cūrō, decet, and vītō, have sometimes the dative in old Latin, but usually the accusative.   In Cicero, adūlor has the accusative; from Nepos on, the dative as well. medeor, medicor, and praestōlor take either the accusative or the dative.

1185. Some verbs have an accusative with one meaning, a dative of the complement, essential or optional, with another: see aemulor, caveō, comitor, cōnsulō, conveniō, cupiō, dēspērō, maneō, metuō, moderor, prōspiciō, temperō, timeō, and the different uses of invideō, in the dictionary.

1186. In poetry, verbs of union, of contention, and of difference, often take a dative: as, (*a.*) haeret laterī lētālis harundō, V. 4, 73, *sticks to her side the deadly shaft.*   So with coēō, concurrō, haereō, and similarly with iungō, misceō. (*b.*) quid enim contendat hirundō cycnīs? Lucr. 3, 6, *for how can swallow cope with swans?*   So with bellō, certō, contendō, pugnō. (*c.*) īnfīdō scurrae distābit amīcus, H. *E.* 1, 18, 4, *a friend will differ from a faithless hanger-on.*   So with differō, discrepō, dissentiō, distō.

1187. A verb often takes the dative, when combined with adversum, obviam, or praestō, also with bene, male, or satis, and the like: as,

fit ob viam Clōdiō, *Mil.* 29, *he runs across Clodius.*   cui bene dīxit umquam bonō? *Sest.* 110, *for what patriot had he ever a good word?*   nōs, virī fortēs, satis facere reī pūblicae vidēmur, *C.* 1, 2, *we doughty champions flatter ourselves we are doing our whole duty by the state.*   Similarly with verbs of transitive use.

1188. (2.) Many verbs of intransitive use compounded with a preposition take a dative connected in sense with the preposition: as,

manus extrēma nōn accessit operibus eius, *Br.* 126, *the last touch was not put upon his works.*   omnibus adfuit hīs pugnīs Dolābella, *Ph* 2, 75, *Dolabella was on hand in all these battles.*   pontō nox incubat ātra, V. 1, 89, *over the deep, night broodeth black.*   cōgnitiōnibus dē Chrīstiānīs interfuī numquam, Plin. *Ep. ad Trai.* 96 [97], 1, *I have never been to any of the trials of the Christians.*

1189. The prepositions are chiefly ad, ante, com-, in, inter, ob, prae, sub, or super.   In many compounds of these prepositions, however, the dative is due to the general meaning of the verb, as in cōnfīdit mihī, *he puts all trust in me* (1181), as contrasted with cōnsentit mihī, *he feels with me,* nearly equivalent to sentit mēcum (1188).

1190. Instead of the dative, such verbs often have a prepositional con-struction, particularly when place, literal or figurative, is distinctly to be expressed: as,

accēdere in fūnus, *Leg.* 2, 66, *to go to a funeral.* in morbum incidit, *Clu.* 175, *he fell ill.*

1191. Some verbs of intransitive use take, when compounded, either the dative or the accusative. See adiaceō, antecēdō, anteeō, praecurrō, praestō, incēdō, inlūdō, īnsultō, invādō, in the dictionary. And some compounds acquire a transitive use altogether, as obeō, oppugnō : see 1137.

WITH VERBS OF TRANSITIVE USE.

1192. (1.) Many verbs of transitive use take the dative : as,

ēī fīliam suam in mātrimōnium dat, 1, 3, 5, *he gives this person his own daughter in marriage.* decima legiō ēī grātiās ēgit, 1, 41, 1, *the tenth le-gion gave him thanks.* huic fert subsidium Puliō, 5, 44, 13, *to him Pulio brings aid.* multīs idem minātur Antōnius, *Ph.* 11, 2, *to many Antony threatens the same.* reliquī sēsē fugae mandārunt, 1, 12, 3, *the rest betook themselves to flight.* commendō vōbīs meum parvum fīlium, *C.* 4, 23, *unto your keeping do I commit the little son of mine.* multī sē aliēnissimīs crēdi-dērunt, 6, 31, 4, *many people put themselves in the hands of utter strangers.* equitēs imperat cīvitātibus, 6, 4, 6, *he issues orders to the communities for horse.*

1193. This dative is used with such verbs as dō, trādō, tribuō, dīvidō, ferō, praebeō, praestō, polliceor, prōmittō, dēbeō, negō, mōnstrō, dīcō, nārrō, mandō, praecipiō, &c., &c. In the passive construction, the accusa-tive becomes nominative, the dative remaining.

1194. (2.) Many verbs of transitive use compounded with a preposition take a dative connected in sense with the preposi-tion : as,

nihil novī vōbīs adferam, *RP.* 1, 21, *I shall not lay any novelty before you.* lēgēs omnium salūtem singulōrum salūtī antepōnunt, *Fin.* 3, 64, *the law always puts the general safety before the safety of the individual.* timō-rem bonīs iniēcistis, *Agr.* 1, 23, *you have struck terror into the hearts of patriots.* nōluērunt ferīs corpus obicere, *RA.* 71, *they would not cast his person before ravenous beasts.* nēminem huic praeferō, *N.* 8, 1, 1, *there is nobody I put before him.* hībernīs Labiēnum praeposuit, 1, 54, 2, *he put Labienus over the winter-quarters.* anitum ūva gallīnīs saepe suppōnimus, *DN.* 2, 124, *we often put ducks' eggs under hens.*

1195. The prepositions are circum, dē, ex, post, or those named in 1189. In many compounds of transitive use, however, the dative is due to the general meaning of the verb, as with those spoken of in 1189.

1196. With these verbs, a prepositional construction is often used, as with the verbs of intransitive use (1190): as,

iam diū nihil novī ad nōs adferēbātur, *Fam.* 2, 14, *no news has got to us this long time.* For compounds of circum and trāns with two accusa-tives, see 1138.

1197. Verbs of transitive use compounded with **com-** have oftener the ablative with **cum**: as, **cōnferte hanc pācem cum illō bellō**, *V.* 4, 115, *just compare this peace with that war.* See also in the dictionary, **coniungō** and **compōnō**; also the indirect compounds **comparō**, *compare*, from **compār**, and **commūnicō**.

1198. With a few compounds of **ad** or **in**, a second accusative is exceptionally used: as, **arbitrum illum adēgit**, *Off.* 3, 66, *he had the other man up before a daysman.* So with **inmittō**, Pl. *Cap.* 548, **īnsinuō**, Lucr. 1, 116, &c., &c. Regularly with **animum advertō**: as, **animum advertī columellam**, *TD.* 5, 65, *I noticed a modest shaft.* **quā rē animum adversā**, Caes. *C.* 1, 80, 4, *this fact being paid heed to:* compare 1138.

1199. A few compound verbs admit either the dative of the person or thing and accusative of the thing, or the accusative of the person or thing and ablative of the thing; such are **adspergō** and **īnspergō**, **circumdō**, **circumfundō**, **exuō** and **induō**, **impertiō**, **interclūdō**; also the uncompounded **dōnō**: as, **praedam mīlitibus dōnat**, 7, 11, 9, *he presents the booty to the soldiers.* **scrībam tuum ānulō dōnāstī**, *V.* 3, 185, *you presented your clerk with a ring.* For the different constructions of **interdīcō**, see the dictionary.

THE DATIVE WITH ADJECTIVES.

1200. The dative with many adjectives and some adverbs denotes that to which the quality is directed.

Such have the meaning of *useful, necessary, fit, easy, agreeable, known, near, belonging, friendly, faithful, like,* and most of their opposites; the adjective is often predicative: as, **vēr ūtile silvīs** (1036), *V. G.* 2, 323, *the spring is good for woods.* **est senātōrī necessārium nōsse rem pūblicam**, *Leg.* 3, 41, *for a senator it is indispensable to be conversant with government.* **ōrātiōnis genus pompae quam pugnae aptius**, *O.* 42, *a style better suited to the parade than to the field.* **convenienter nātūrae vīvere**, *Off.* 3, 13, *to live in touch with nature.*

1201. Some adjectives of this class have the dative of a person, the accusative with **ad** of a thing: so **accommodātus, aptus, idōneus, necessārius,** and **ūtilis**; and some denoting feeling have also the accusative with a preposition: **aequus, inīquus, fidēlis** with **in, benevolus** with **ergā,** and **impius** with **adversus.** **propior** and **proximus** sometimes accompany an accusative, like **prope, propius,** and **proximē.**

1202. The adjectives **commūnis, proprius** or **aliēnus, sacer, tōtus,** often accompany the construction of the genitive of the owner: see 1238. For **aliēnus** with the ablative, see 1306. Sometimes **aliēnus** has the ablative with **ab.**

1203. Some adjectives denoting relationship, connection, friendship or hostility, become substantives, and as such, admit the genitive also (1103); such are (*a.*) **adfīnis, cōgnātus;** (*b.*) **aequālis, familiāris, fīnitimus, pār** and **dispār, propinquus, vīcīnus;** (*c.*) **adversārius, amīcus, inimīcus, necessārius.**

1204. In Plautus and Terence, **similis,** *the like, the counterpart,* and its compounds, regularly take the genitive. The dative, as well as the genitive, is also used from Ennius on, particularly of a limited or approximate likeness: see the dictionary.

(2.) THE OPTIONAL COMPLEMENT.

1205. The dative of a person or thing interested, benefited, harmed, may be added at option to almost any verb : as,

cōnservāte parentī fīlium, parentem fīliō, *Cael.* 80, *save the son for the father, the father for the son.* mea domus tibĭ patet, mihĭ clausa est, *RA.* 145, *the very house I own is open for you, is shut upon me.* cui flāvam religās comam, simplex munditiīs ? H. 1, 5, 4, *for whom bind'st thou in wreaths thy golden hair, plain in thy neatness ?* nōn audēret facere haec viduae mulierī, quae in mē fēcit, T. *Hau.* 953, *he durst not to an unprotected female do what he hath done towards me.*

1206. The place of a verb with the dative of interest is sometimes filled by an interjection, ecce, ei, em, or vae : as, ei mihi quālis erat, E. 1, 7, V. 2, 274, *ah me, how ghastly he did look.* vae vīctīs, Pl. *Ps.* 1317, said by Brennus, 390 B. C., L. 5, 48, 9, *woe worth the worsted.* vae capitī atque aetātī tuae, Pl. *R.* 375, *a murrain on thy head and life.*

1207. The dative is often added to the entire sentence, where either a genitive or a possessive pronoun limiting a substantive might be used.

In such cases the dative expresses interest, advantage, or disadvantage, while the genitive would simply indicate the owner or the object : as, trānsfīgitur scūtum Puliōnī, 5, 44, 7, *unfortunately for Pulio, his shield gets pierced through and through.* mīlitantī in Hispāniā pater ēī moritur, L. 29, 29, 6, *while serving in Spain he had the misfortune to lose his father.* huic ego mē bellō ducem profiteor, *C.* 2, 11, *I here proclaim myself captain for this war.* sēsē Caesarī ad pedēs prōiēcērunt, 1, 31, 2, *they cast themselves at Caesar's feet.* nostrīs mīlitibus spem minuit, 5, 33, 5, *it dashed the hopes of our soldiers.* extergē tibi manūs, Pl. *Most.* 267, *wipe off thy hands.* vellunt tibi barbam lascīvī puerī, H. *S.* 1, 3, 133, *the wanton gamins pull thy beard, poor soul.*

1208. This dative is sometimes detached from the verb, and used immediately with a substantive, instead of the genitive : as, Philocōmasiō custōs, Pl. *MG.* 271, *the keeper for Philocomasium.* rēctor iuvenī, Ta. 1, 24, *a mentor for the young man.* So particularly with a gerundive in official expressions : as, cūrātor mūris reficiendīs, *OG.* 19, *commissioner for rebuilding the walls.*

1209. Verbs of warding off sometimes take a dative, especially in poetry, also those of robbing and ridding : as, (*a.*) hunc quoque arcēbis gravidō pecorī, V. *G.* 3, 154, *him also wilt thou for the pregnant herd keep far.* sōlstitium pecorī dēfendite. V. *E.* 7, 47, *the summer's heat keep distant for the flock.* (*b.*) torquem dētrāxit hostī, *Fin.* 1, 35, *he pulled a torque away from his enemy.* ēripiēs mihĭ hunc errōrem, *Att.* 10, 4, 6, *you will rid me of this mistake.*

1210. With verbs of motion the dative of the person interested denotes in poetry the end of motion also : as, multōs Danaūm dēmittimus Orcō, V. 2, 398, *we send down many a Danaan for the nether king.* So also the dative of personified words of place : as, it clāmor caelō, V. 5, 451, *up goes a shout for heaven,* i. e. heaven hears a shout. sēdibus hunc refer ante suīs, V. 6, 152, *first bear him duly to his place of rest,* i. e. let his expectant grave receive him.

THE EMOTIONAL DATIVE.

1211. The dative of the personal pronoun is often used with expressions of emotion, interest, surprise, or derision: as,

quid mihi Celsus agit? H. *E.* 1, 3, 15, *how fares me Celsus?* **Tongi-lium mihī ēdūxit,** *C.* 2, 4, *he took out Tongilius, bless my soul.* at tibī repente, cum minimē exspectārem, vēnit ad mē Canīnius māne, *Fam.* 9, 2, 1, *but bless you, sir, when I least dreamt of it, who should drop in on me all at once but Caninius, bright and early.*

THE DATIVE OF THE POSSESSOR.

1212. The dative is used with forms of **sum** to denote the possessor: as,

est hominī cum deō similitūdō, *Leg.* 1, 25, *man has a resemblance to god.* an nescīs longās rēgibus esse manūs? O. *E.* 16, 166, *dost possibly not know kings have long arms?* suos quoique mōs. T. *Ph.* 454, *to every man his own pet way.* So also with the compounds **absum, dēsum, supersum:** as, hoc ūnum Caesarī dēfuit, 4, 26, 5, *this was all Caesar lacked.*

1213. (1.) With **mihī est nōmen,** the name is put either in the dative or in the nominative: as,

mihī nōmen est Iūliō, or mihī nōmen est Iūlius, Gell. 15, 29, 1, *my name is Julius.* In old Latin and in Sallust, the dative: as, **nōmen Mercu-riōst mihī,** Pl. *Am. prol.* 19, *my name is Mercury;* later the nominative: as, canibus pigrīs nōmen erit Pardus, Tigris, Leo, J. 8, 34, *the craven cur shall sport the name of 'Lion, Tiger, Pard.'* Cicero uses the nominative or rarely the dative, Livy oftener the dative than the nominative. Tacitus puts adjectives in the dative, substantives in the nominative, rarely in the genitive. Caesar does not use the construction.

1214. (2.) With the actives **nōmen dō, indō, pōnō, tribuō,** &c., the name may be in the dative or in the accusative; with the passive of these expressions, the name may be in the dative or in the nominative: as,

quī tibi nōmen īnsānō posuēre, H. *S.* 2, 3, 47, *who've put on thee the nickname Crank.* quī fīliīs Philippum atque Alexandrum nōmina inposuerat, L. 35, 47, 5, *who had given his sons the names Philip and Alexander.* A genitive dependent on **nōmen** is used once by Tacitus and in very late Latin.

1215. With a gerundive, the dative of the possessor denotes the person who has the action to do: see 2243. For the ablative with **ab,** or for **habeō,** see 2243, 2245.

1216. This dative is sometimes used with the perfect participle, and the tenses formed with it: as, **mihī est ēlabōrātum,** *Caecil.* 40, *I have it all worked out.* carmina nūlla mihī sunt scrīpta, O. *Tr.* 5, 12, 35, *no poetry have I ready made.* Rarely with passives of the present system: as, nūlla placēre diū nec vīvere carmina possunt, quae scrībuntur aquae pōtōribus, H. *E.* 1, 19, 2, *no verse can take or be longlived that by teetotallers is writ.*

The Dative of Relation.

1217. The dative may denote the person viewing or judging : as, eris mihi magnus Apollō, V. *E.* 3, 104, *thou shalt to me the great Apollo be.* Quintia fōrmōsa est multīs, mihi candida, longa, rēcta est, Cat. 86, 1, *in many eyes is Quintia fair, to me she's bonny, tall, and straight.* From Caesar on, participles are often used to denote the person viewing or judging : as, est urbe ēgressīs tumulus, V. 2, 713, *there is, as you get out of town, a mound.* in ūniversum aestimantī, Ta. *G.* 6, *looking at it generally.*

1218. In imitation of a Greek idiom, volēns, cupiēns, or invītus, is used by Sallust and Tacitus in agreement with a dative dependent on a form of sum, the combination being equivalent to a subject with a form of volō, cupiō, or invītus sum, respectively : as, cēterīs remanēre volentibus fuit, Ta. *H.* 3, 43, i.e. cēterī remanēre voluērunt, *the rest were minded to bide where they were.* Once in Livy.

II. THE PREDICATIVE DATIVE.

The Dative of Tendency or Result.

1219. (1.) Certain datives are used with a form of sum to denote what a thing tends to, proves, or is. This dative is generally accompanied by a dative of the person interested : as,

auxiliō īs fuit, Pl. *Am. prol.* 92, *he was a help to them.* odiō sum Rō-mānīs, L. 35, 19, 6, *I am an abomination in the eyes of Rome.* potestne bonum cuiquam malō esse ? *Par.* 7, *can good prove bad for any human being ?* L. Cassius identidem quaerere solēbat, cui bonō fuisset, *RA.* 84, *Cassius used to ask for ever and ever, who the person benefited was,* or *who the gainer was.* nēminī meus adventus labōrī aut sūmptuī fuit, *V.* 1, 16, *my visit did not prove a bother or an expense to a soul.* rēs et fortūnae tuae mihĭ maximae cūrae sunt, *Fam.* 6, 5, 1, *your money-matters are an all-absorbing interest to me.*

1220. There are many of these datives, mostly abstracts and all singular ; some of the commonest are cūrae, ūsuī, praesidiō, cordī, odiō, auxiliō, impedī-mentō, salūtī, voluptātī. The adjectives magnus, maior, maximus, or tantus and quantus, are sometimes used in agreement with them ; and the dative frūgī sometimes has bonae.

1221. Instead of the dative of tendency, a predicative nominative or accusative is rarely used : thus, possessiōnem līberam Dardaniae sōlāciō fore, L. 40, 57, 9, *that the unrestricted occupancy of Dardania would prove comforting,* but, domestica quiēs sōlācium fuit, L. 6, 30, 9, *the peace that prevailed at home was a solid comfort.* Prepositional expressions with prō and in also occur.

1222. (2.) The dative is also used with a few verbs of consider-ing or accounting to denote what a thing is accounted.

So with such verbs as dō, dūcō, habeō, tribuō, and vertō: as, vitiō mihī dant, quod mortem hominis necessāriī graviter ferō, Matius in *Fam.* 11, 28, 2, *the world scores it against me that I take the murder of a near and dear friend to heart.* postquam paupertās probrō habērī coepit, S. *C.* 12, 1, *after lack of wealth began to count as a stigma.*

THE DATIVE OF PURPOSE OR INTENTION.

1223. A few datives are used to denote what a thing is intended to be. This dative is generally accompanied by a dative of the person interested.

So (*a.*) dōnō and mūnerī: as, ēmit eam dōnō mihī, T. *Eu.* 135, *he bought her as a gift for me.* centum bovēs mīlitibus dōnō dedit, L. 7, 37, 3, *he gave the soldiers a hundred oxen as a present.* Also (*b.*) auxiliō, praesidiō, and subsidiō, used of military operations, chiefly with verbs of motion: as, iī, quī praesidiō contrā castra erant relictī, subsidiō suīs iērunt, 7, 62, 8, *the men that had been left as a protection against the camp, went as a reinforcement to their own side.*

1224. For the datives dōnō and mūnerī, a predicative nominative or accusative is sometimes used: as, corōnam Iovī dōnum in capitōlium mittunt, L. 2, 22, 6, *they send a crown to the capitol as a present for Jupiter.* Prepositional expressions are also used for auxiliō, &c.: as, ad praesidium, L. 3, 5, 3, in praesidium, L. 31, 16, 7, *for protection,* auxiliī causā, L. 2, 24, 4, *to help.*

1225. The dative receptuī is also used in military language to denote purpose: as, Caesar receptuī canī iussit, 7, 47, 1, *Caesar ordered the retreat sounded.* Quīnctius receptuī canere iussit, L. 34, 39, 13. This dative is sometimes attached immediately to a substantive: as, receptuī signum, *Ph.* 13, 15, *the trumpet for retreat.*

———◆———

THE GENITIVE.

1226. The genitive is principally used with nouns, less frequently with verbs. Sometimes even when it seems to be dependent on a verb, it really depends on a substantive understood, or on a noun virtually contained or implied in the verb. Some verbs require an accusative also, in addition to the genitive.

———

I. THE GENITIVE WITH SUBSTANTIVES.

1227. A substantive is often limited by another substantive in the genitive.

The things denoted by the two words are usually distinct: as, metus hostium, *the fear of the enemy,* i. e. either (*a.*) which they feel (1231), or (*b.*) which is felt towards them (1260); magnī ponderis saxa, *stones of great weight* (1239). Sometimes, however, they are more or less the same: as, mīlitum pars, *part of the soldiers* (1242); magna multitūdō perditōrum hominum, *a perfect swarm of desperadoes* (1255).

1228. Two or even three genitives expressing different relations, sometimes limit one substantive: as, **superiōrum diērum Sabīnī cunctātiō,** 3, 18, 6, *Sabinus's dilatoriness in days preceding.* **eōrum diērum cōnsuētūdine itineris nostrī exercitūs perspectā,** 2, 17, 2, *studying up the order of march followed by our army in those days.*

1229. The limited substantive is often omitted, when it is obvious from the context: as, **ventum erat ad Vestae,** sc. aedem, H. *S.* 1, 9, 35, *to Vesta's were we come,* i. e. to her temple. **aberam bīduī,** sc. iter, *Att.* 5, 17, 1, *I was two days distant.* Usually so, when it is expressed with another genitive, which generally precedes: as, **quis est, quī possit cōnferre vītam Trebōnī cum Dolābellae?** *Ph.* 11, 9, *who is there that can compare the life of Trebonius with Dolabella's?*

1230. Instead of the genitive depending on a substantive, an equivalent adjective or a prepositional expression is often used. Such substitutions will be mentioned below in their appropriate places.

1231. The relations expressed by the limiting genitive vary very much according to the context. These relations may be put in classes, as below (1232–1260). But it must be remembered that as the genitive connects substantives in a loose way, the same construction may sometimes be referred to more than one head.

The Genitive of the Subject, Cause, Origin, or Owner.

1232. (1.) The genitive is used to denote that which does the action, or which causes, originates, or possesses the object designated by the substantive it limits: as,

metus hostium, Gell. 9, 12, 13, *the fear of the enemy,* i. e. which they feel. **adventus Caesaris,** 6, 41, 4, *the arrival of Caesar.* **bellum Venetōrum,** 3, 16, 1, *the war with the Venetans.* **illud Solōnis,** *CM.* 50, *Solon's memorable words.* **Canachī sīgna,** *Br.* 70, *statues by Canachus.* **Cupīdinis sīgnum,** *V.* 4, 135, *the statue representing Cupid.* **huius sīgnīs,** *V.* 3, 9, *with statues belonging to this man.* **pācem Ariovistī,** 1, 37, 2, *a peaceful policy on Ariovistus's part.* **Cannārum pugna,** L. 23, 43, 4, *the battle of Cannae* (1427). **abacī vāsa omnia,** *V.* 4, 35, *all the vessels on the sideboard.* **prīdiē eius diēī,** 1, 47, 2, *the day before that day* (1413). **labrōrum tenus,** Lucr. 1, 940, *the length of the lips* (1420).

1233. Instead of the genitive, an adjective is often used to express such relations; less frequently a prepositional construction: as,

(*a.*) **odium paternum,** N. 23, 1, 3, *the hatred felt by his father.* **servīlī tumultū,** 1, 40, 5, *in the slave insurrection.* **bellō Cassiānō,** 1, 13, 2, *in the war with Cassius.* **illud Cassiānum, cui bonō fuerit,** *Ph.* 2, 35, *Cassius's test question, 'who the gainer was.'* **erīlis patria,** Pl. *B.* 170, *my master's birthplace.* **intrā domesticōs parietēs,** *C.* 2, 1, *within the walls of our houses.* So usually with names of countries and of towns: as, **anus Corinthia,** T. *Hau.* 600, *an old woman of Corinth.* **pugna Cannēnsis,** L. 22, 50, 1, *the battle of Cannae.* Often in a generalizing sense: as, **paternus māternusque sanguīs,** *RA.* 66, *the blood of a father and of a mother.* (*b.*) **ad Cannās pugnam,** L. 22, 58, 1, *the battle of Cannae.*

1234. The possessive pronoun is regularly used instead of the possessive genitive of a personal or reflexive pronoun (1230) : as,

mea domus, *RA.* 145, *my own house.* **in tuā quādam epistolā,** *Att.* 9, 10, 3, *in a letter of yours.* But sometimes, for emphasis, the genitive of the personal or reflexive is used : as, **magnō suī cum perīculō,** 4, 28, 2, *with great personal risk ;* commonly so with **omnium** or **utriusque :** as, **voluntātī vestrūm omnium pāruī,** *DO.* 3, 208, *I yielded to your joint wish ;* see however 1235.

1235. A word in apposition with the possessive pronoun is put in the genitive: as, **meā ūnīus operā,** *Pis.* 6, *by my sole instrumentality.* **ad vestram omnium caedem,** *C.* 4, 4, *for the murder of you all* (1230). So particularly **ipse, omnis, sōlus,** and **ūnus.**

1236. The genitive is often used predicatively with verbs meaning *am, belong, become, make, seem, am accounted,* &c., &c. : as,

litterāriī ista sunt lūdī, Quint. 1, 4, 27, *such questions belong to the infant school.* **hīc versus Plautī nōn est, hīc est,** *Fam.* 9, 16, 4, *this line is not Plautus's, this one is.* **omnia, quae mulieris fuērunt, virī fiunt,** *Top.* 23, *everything which was the woman's becomes the man's.* **neque sē iūdicāre Galliam potius esse Ariovistī quam populī Rōmānī,** 1, 45, 1, *and that he did not think Gaul was any more Ariovistus's than it was the Romans'.* **hostiumst potīta,** Pl. *E.* 562, *into the foemen's hands she fell.*

1237. The possessive genitive of a person or of an abstract is particularly common when the subject of the verb is an infinitive or sentence : as,

(*a.*) **scyphīs pugnāre Thrācum est,** *H.* 1, 27, 1, *to fight with bowls is Vandal work.* **erat āmentis, cum aciem vidērēs, pācem cōgitāre,** *Lig.* 28, *it was a madman's act, dreaming of peace when you saw the troops in battalia.* **temporī cēdere semper sapientis est habitum,** *Fam.* 4, 9, 2, *shaping your course to circumstance has always passed as the sign of a wise man.* **mentīrī nōn est meum,** *l'. Hau.* 549, *telling lies is not my style* (1234). (*b.*) **nōn est pudōris meī, mē prōpugnātōrem P. Scīpiōnis profitērī,** *V.* 4, 80, *it is not in keeping with my delicacy to set up as the champion of Scipio.* **hārum rērum esse dēfēnsōrem magnī animī est,** *Sest.* 99, *to be the defender of these interests takes heroism.* **hoc sentīre prūdentiae est, facere fortitūdinis,** *Sest.* 86, *to think thus shows wisdom, to act thus, courage.* **negāvit mōris esse Graecōrum, ut in convīviō virōrum accumberent mulierēs,** *V.* 1, 66, *he said it was not manners among the Greeks to have women at table at a men's dinner-party.*

1238. With the possessive genitive, the limited substantive is sometimes defined by **commūnis, proprius** or **aliēnus, sacer,** or **tōtus** added: as, **hoc proprium virtūtis existimant,** 6, 23, 2, *this they consider a special characteristic of bravery.* **omnia quae nostra erant propria,** *RA.* 150, *everything which was our peculiar property* (1234). **illa īnsula eōrum deōrum sacra putātur,** *V.* 1, 48, *that island is considered the hallowed property of those gods.* **iam mē Pompeī tōtum esse scīs,** *Fam.* 2, 13, 2, *you are aware that I am become Pompey's, out and out.*

THE GENITIVE OF QUALITY.

1239. (2.) The genitive with an adjective in agreement is used to denote quality, either attributively or predicatively : as, (*a.*) Attributively : magnī ponderis saxa, 2, 29, 3, *stones of great weight.* summae speī adulēscentēs, 7, 63, 9, *young men of high promise.* diērum vīgintī supplicātiō, 4, 38, 5, *a twenty day thanksgiving.* bēlua multōrum es capitum, H. *E.* I, I, 76, *a many-headed beast art thou.* eius modī cōnsilium, 5, 29, 5, *such a plan.* dēmittō auriculās ut inīquae mentis asellus, II. *S.* I, 9, 20, *I drop my ears like Neddy in the sulks* (269). vāllō pedum IX, 5, 42. I, *with a nine foot palisade.* (*b.*) Predicatively : magnae habitus auctōritātis, 7, 77, 3, *passing for a man of great influence.* flūminis erat altitūdō circiter pedum trium, 2, 18, 3, *the depth of the river was about three feet.* The genitive of quality resembles the ablative of quality (1375) ; the two are sometimes combined : as, hominem maximī corporis terribilīque faciē, N. 15, 4, I, *a man of gigantic frame and with an awe-inspiring presence.* But the genitive is common in designations of size and number.

1240. A substantive expressing quality with aequus, pār, similis, or dissimilis in agreement, is put not in the genitive, but in the ablative, by Cicero, Caesar, Nepos, and Livy.

THE PARTITIVE GENITIVE.

1241. (3.) The partitive genitive denotes a whole of which the limited substantive denotes a part. There are two kinds of partitive genitive, the numerical and the quantitative : as,

(*a.*) mīlitum pars, 6, 40, 8, *part of the soldiers,* numerical partitive (1242). (*b.*) multum aestātis, 5, 22, 4, *much of the summer,* quantitative partitive (1247).

1242. (*a.*) The numerical partitive is a plural or a collective, limiting a word expressing part of the number : as,

mīlitum pars, 6, 40, 8, *part of the soldiers.* pars equitātūs, 4, 16, 2, *part of the cavalry.* alter cōnsulum, L. 6, 35, 5, *one of the two consuls.* uter est īnsānior hōrum ? H. *S.* 2, 3, 102, *which of these two is crazier ?* eōrum neuter, *Pis.* 62, *neither of the two.* multae istārum arborum, *CM.* 59, *many of the trees you see there.* quis omnium mortālium ? *V.* 5, 179, *who among all the sons of men ?* nēmō nostrūm, *RA.* 55, *not one of us.* nihil hōrum, *RA.* 138, *none of these things.* Stertinius, sapientum octāvōs, H. *S.* 2. 3. 296, *Stertinius, of sages eighth.* ō maior iuvenum, H. *AP.* 366, *O elder of the youths.* hōrum omnium fortissimī sunt Belgae, I, I, 3, *of all these the stoutest fighters are the Belgians.* Also with superlative adverbs : as, deōrum maximē Mercurium colunt, Ta. *G.* 9, *of the gods, they revere Mercury most.* minumē gentium, Pl. *Poen.* 690, T. *Eu.* 625, *no, never in the world.*

1243. uterque, *each, both,* often takes the genitive plural of a pronoun : as, quōrum uterque, uterque eōrum, hōrum. nostrūm, &c. ; sometimes of a substantive and pronoun combined : as, utriusque hārum rērum, *TD.* I, 65, *of each of these things.* quārum cīvitātum utraque, *V.* 5. 56, *each of these communities.* With a substantive alone, it is oftener attributive : as, uterque dux, *Marc.* 24, *each commander ,* and sometimes with neuter pronouns : as, quod utrumque, Brut. in *Fam.* II, I, I, N. 25, 2, 4. The plural utrīque is used both ways : as, ab utrīsque vestrūm, *Fam.* II, 21, 5, and ab utrīsque nōbīs, Brut. in *Fam.* II. 20, 3.

1244. The plurals **tot, totidem,** and **quot,** are not used partitively, and **omnēs** and **cūnctī** only so by poets and late prose writers. **plērīque** is used either way, in agreement, or with the genitive.

1245. The numerical partitive is exceptionally used in poetry with the positive of a descriptive adjective: as, **sāncte deōrum,** V. 4, 576, *thou holy of the gods.* And in late prose, particularly with words denoting a class of persons: as, **cum dēlēctis peditum,** L. 26, 5, 3, *with the pick of the infantry.* **levīs cohortium,** Ta. 3, 39, *the light-armed of the cohorts.*

1246. Instead of the numerical partitive, a prepositional expression with **ante, inter,** or **in,** or with **ex** or **dē,** is sometimes used: as, **ante aliōs acceptissimus,** L. 1, 15, 8, *most welcome before others.* So particularly **quīdam** and **ūnus, duo, trēs,** with **ex** or **dē**: as, **quīdam ex hīs,** 2, 17, 2, *one of these.* **ūnus dē multīs,** *Fin.* 2, 66, *one of the common herd.* But **ūnus** sometimes has the genitive: as, **ūnus multōrum,** H. *S.* 1, 9, 71. And usually so in a series, when **ūnus** is followed by **alter, alius, tertius,** &c.

1247. (*b.*) The quantitative partitive is usually a singular, limiting a neuter singular word denoting amount. The limited word is either a nominative, or an accusative without a prepòsition. This genitive often borders very closely on the genitive of definition (1255): as,

multum aestātis, 5, 22, 4, *much of the summer.* **amplius obsidum,** 6. 9, 7, *something more extensive in the way of hostages.* **minus dubitātiōnis,** 1, 14, 1, *less of hesitation.* **quam minimum spatiī,** 3, 19, 1, *as little time as possible.* **id aetātis,** *DO.* 1, 207, *at that time of life.* **id temporis,** *Fin.* 5, 1, *at that time of day.* **quid causae est ?** *Ac.* 1, 10, *what earthly reason is there ?* **hoc litterulārum,** *Att.* 12, 1, 1, *this apology for a letter,* or *this hasty line.* **hoc sibī sōlācī prōpōnēbant,** 7, 15, 2, *they laid this flattering unction to their souls.*

1248. Such neuters are: **multum, plērumque, plūrimum, amplius, plūs, paulum, minus, minimum, tantum, quantum, tantúndem, nimium ;** in poetry and late prose, also many other adjectives singular and plural. Furthermore, **id, hoc, illud, quod, quid,** &c., and **nihil ;** also **abunde, adfatim, largiter, nimis, partim, parum,** and **satis.**

1249. A few adjectives of place and time indicating a particular part of an object, are commonly used in immediate agreement with their substantives: as,

summus mōns, 1, 22, 1, *the highest part of the mountain,* or *the mountain-top.* **extrēmā hieme, mediā aestāte,** *IP.* 35, *at the end of the winter, in midsummer.* Such are: **prīmus, intimus, medius, extrēmus, postrēmus, ūltimus, summus, īnfimus, īmus, reliquus.** But the neuter is sometimes used partitively: as, **aestātis extrēmum erat,** S. *I.* 90, 1, *it was the end of summer.* **summa pectoris,** *Fam.* 1, 9, 15, *the upper parts of the breast.*

1250. The limiting genitive is often the neuter singular of an adjective used substantively: as,

aliquid bonī, T. *Andr.* 398, *something good.* **aliquid malī,** T. *Eu.* 999, *something bad.* **numquid tandem novī ?** *Br.* 10, *nothing new, pray ?* This use is ordinarily confined to stems in **-o- ;** rarely otherwise: as, **plūs inānis,** Lucr. 1, 365, *more of the void ;* and usually only when joined with an **-o-**stem: as, nihil solidī, nihil ēminentis, *DN.* 1, 75, *no solidity, no projection.*

1251. The partitive construction sometimes extends to the predicate : as, id erit sīgnī mē invītum facere, *RA.* 83, *this will be something of an indication that I act with reluctance;* sīgnī is here in the predicate, and yet made dependent on id. quid ergō est tuī cōnsilī ? Brut. in *Fam.* 11, 1, 3, *what then is your advice?* quid suī cōnsilī sit ostendit, 1, 21, 2, *he explains what his plan is.* quid est enim huic reliquī ? *Sull.* 89, *for what is there left for my client?* hī mīlitēs nihil reliquī victīs fēcēre, S. *C.* 11, 7, *these soldiers left nothing over to the conquered.* nihil ad celeritātem sibī reliquī fēcērunt, 2, 26, 5, *as for speed, they left no effort unspared.*

1252. The accusative with a preposition also sometimes has the genitive. as, in id redāctus sum locī, T. *Ph.* 979, *I am reduced to such a strait.* ad id locī, S. *C.* 45, 3, *to that spot.* ad id locōrum, S. *I.* 63, 6, *up to that time.* in multum diēī, L. 9, 44, 11, *till late in the day.* In Cicero, also the ablatives eō, eōdem, and quō, with locī : as, eō locī, *Sest.* 68, *in that position.* And in later writers, other ablatives, with or without a preposition, also have a genitive.

1253. Some appellatives of place are put in the genitive with adverbs of place : as, ubinam gentium ? Pl. *Mer.* 434, *C.* 1, 9, *where in the world?* nusquam gentium, T. *Ad.* 540, *nowhere in the world.* Similarly, locī with adverbs of time or order, as with intereā in Plautus and Terence, postideā in Plautus, posteā in Sallust, and inde in Lucretius ; also locōrum with adhūc and postid in Plautus.

1254. In Sallust, Livy, and Tacitus, genitives of abstracts are used with the adverbs eō, quō, and hūc : as, eō miseriārum, S. *I.* 14, 3, *to that pitch of distress.* Once with ut : ut quisque audentiae habuisset, adcurrerent, Ta. 15, 53, *they should run up, with a speed commensurate in every case to their daring.*

THE GENITIVE OF DEFINITION.

1255. (4.) The genitive is used to define that of which a thing consists : as,

magna multitūdō perditōrum hominum, 3, 17, 4, *a perfect swarm of desperadoes.* innumerābile pondus aurī, *Sest.* 93, *a weight of gold too great to count.* mīlle numerō nāvium clāssem, *V.* 1, 48, *an armada a thousand sail strong.*

1256. The genitive of an explicit word containing the leading idea is sometimes used to define a more general word ; as,

praedae pecudum hominumque, L. 24, 20, 5, *booty consisting of cattle and human beings.* pignora coniugum ac līberōrum, L. 2, 1, 5, *pledges in the shape of wives and children.* cōnfisus mūnītiōne fossae, Caes. *C.* 1, 42, 3, *relying on the defensive works in the shape of a moat.* Rarely in poetry and late prose, the proper name of a place, with urbs, prōmunturium, &c. : as, urbem Patavī, V. 1, 247, *the city of Patavium* (1045). Particularly with the words vōx, nōmen, genus, and especially causa : as, haec vōx voluptātis, *Fin.* 2, 6, *this word 'pleasure.'* nōmen amīcitiae, *Fin.* 2, 78, *the name 'friendship.'* Compare nōmen frāternum, 1, 36, 5, *the name of brothers* (1233). haec īgnōminiae causa, *Clu.* 120, *this reason, namely the censor's stigma.* parvulae causae vel falsae suspīciōnis vel terrōris repentīnī, Caes. *C.* 3, 72, 4, *insignificant causes, as for instance ungrounded suspicion or a panic.* propter eam causam sceleris istīus, *V.* 4, 113, *for this reason, namely the crime of the defendant.*

1257. The genitive of definition is very common with **causā**, less common with **grātiā**, to define what the motive or cause is : as,

amīcitiae causā, 1, 39, 2, *from motives of friendship.* Compare **vestrā magis hoc causā volēbam, quam meā**, *DO.* 1, 164, *I wished this more for your sake than for my own* (1 4). **honestātis amplitūdinisque grātiā**, *RA.* 15, *in compliment to their respectability and high social standing* So also sometimes with **nōmine**, and in old or official Latin, with **ergō**.

1258. Conversely, the gen.tive of a generic word denoting a person is sometimes added to a leading word defining the kind of a person : as, **frūstum puerī**, Pl. *Per.* 849, *thou bit of a boy.* **mōnstrum hominis**, T. *Eu.* 696, *thou fiend in human shape.* **quaedam pestēs hominum**, *Fam.* 5, 8, 2, *some regular plagues in the shape of men.*

1259. quidquid est, quantum est, quod est, or **quodcumque est,** with a genitive, is equivalent to an emphatic **omnis** : as, **quidquid patrum est,** L. 3, 17, 5, *whatever there is in the shape of senators,* i. e. *every single senator.* **quod est pecūniae, trādit,** Caes. *C.* 2, 20. 8, *what there is in the way of money, he hands over.* Similarly **tantum** for **tot** : as, **tantum hominum,** Pl. *Poen.* 619, *such a mass of men.*

THE OBJECTIVE GENITIVE.

1260. (5.) The objective genitive denotes the object of the action expressed in the limited substantive : as,

metus hostium, Gell. 9, 12, 13, *the fear of the enemy,* i. e. which is felt towards them. **vēnditiō bonōrum**, *RA.* 110, *sale of the goods.* **lūctū filī**, *DO.* 2, 193, *from grief for his son.* This construction is freely used, even when the parallel verb has a dative, an ablative, or a prepositional expression : as, **fidūciā locī**, 7, 19, 2, *from confidence in the position.* **līberātiōnem culpae**, *Lig.* 1, *acquittal from guilt.* **mīlitiae vacātiōnem**, 6, 14, 1, *exemption from military service.* **opīniōne trium legiōnum dēiectus**, 5, 48, 1, *disappointed in his hope of three legions.* **deōrum opīniō**, *TD.* 1, 30, *a conception of the gods.* **miserrima est contentiō honōrum**, *Off.* 1, 87, *a scramble for office is a pitiful thing.*

1261. Instead of the objective genitive, a prepositional expression is sometimes used with greater precision : as,

metus ā vī atque īrā deōrum, *DN.* 1, 45, *fear of the might and wrath of the gods.* So especially the accusative, usually denoting a person, with **in, ergā,** or **adversus,** combined with substantives denoting feeling : as, **odium in hominum ūniversum genus,** *TD.* 4, 25, *hatred to all mankind.* **vestra ergā mē voluntās,** *C.* 4, 1, *your good-will towards me.*

1262. A possessive pronoun or adjective is sometimes used for the objective genitive : as,

(*a.*) **odiō tuō**, T. *Ph.* 1016, *from hate to thee.* **tuā fidūciā**, *V.* 5, 176, *from his reliance on you.* **aspectūque suō**, Lucr. 1, 91, *and at the sight of her.* (*b.*) **metus hostīlis**, S. *I.* 41, 2, *fear felt of the enemy.* **servīlis percontātiō,** *DO.* 2, 327, *crossquestioning of the servant-girls.* **firmus adversus mīlitārem largītiōnem,** Ta. *H.* 2, 82, *dead-set against any largess to the military.*

II. THE GENITIVE WITH ADJECTIVES.

1263. (1.) The genitive is used with many adjectives to denote the object.

Such are chiefly adjectives meaning (*a.*) *desirous*, (*b.*) *knowing*, or *remembering*, (*c.*) *participating, controlling*, or *guilty*, (*d.*) *full*, and most of their opposites: as, (*a.*) **aurī cupidus**, Pl. *Poen.* 179, *eager for gold.* **sapientiae studiōsōs, id est enim philosophōs**, *TD.* 5, 9, *devotees of wisdom, for that is what 'philosophers' means.* So also **aemulus, avidus, fastīdiōsus, invidus.** (*b.*) **gnārus rēī pūblicae**, *Br.* 228, *familiar with government.* **rēī mīlitāris perītissimus**, 1, 21, 4, *a master of the art military.* **hominēs adulēscentulōs, inperītōs rērum**, T. *Andr.* 910, *mere hobbledehoys, not up in the world's ways.* **imperītus mōrum**, *RA.* 143, *behind the times.* **immemor beneficiōrum, memor patriae**, *Ph.* 2, 27, *forgetful of kindnesses, never forgetting his country.* So also **cōnscius, cōnsultus, īnscius, īnsolēns, īnsolitus, īnsuētus, iēiūnus, prōvidus, prūdēns, rudis.** (*c.*) **praedae participēs**, Caes. *C.* 3, 82, 1, *sharing in the booty.* **manifestus tantī sceleris**, S. *I.* 35, 8, *caught in committing this atrocious crime.* **expers glōriae**, *IP.* 57, *without a share in the glory.* So also **adfīnis, compos, cōnsors, exhērēs, potēns, reus.** (*d.*) **negōtī plēnus**, Pl. *Ps.* 380, *full of business.* **fōns plēnissimus piscium**, *V.* 4, 118, *a fountain swarming with fish.* **refertō praedōnum marī**, *IP.* 31, *when the sea was crammed with corsairs.* So also **fertilis, inops, līberālis, nūdus, prōfūsus.**

1264. In poetry and late prose, a great many other adjectives of these meanings, besides those mentioned above, are also used with the genitive. Such are principally: (*a.*) **avārus, cūriōsus, incūriōsus, sēcūrus.** (*b.*) **nescius, praesāgus, praescius, scītus.** (*c.*) **exsors, immūnis, impos, impotēns, innocēns, innoxius, īnsōns, noxius, suspectus.** (*d.*) **abundāns, dīves, egēnus, inānis, indigus, largus, parcus, pauper, prōdigus, sterilis, vacuus.**

1265. With **cōnscius** and the genitive of a thing, the dative of a person is sometimes added: as, **tot flāgitiōrum exercituī meō cōnscius**, Ta. 1, 43, *a participant with my army in so many outrages.* Sometimes **cōnscius** has the dative of a thing: as, **mēns cōnscia factīs**, Lucr. 3, 1018, *the mind of guilt aware.*

1266. (2.) The genitive of the object is often used with present participles which express permanent condition.

These participles are chiefly from verbs which have a transitive use. Not common in old Latin: as, **amantem uxōris**, Pl. *As.* 857, *devoted to his wife.* **fugitāns lītium**, T. *Ph.* 623, *inclined to dodge a suit at law.* Very common in Cicero: as, **semper appetentēs glōriae praeter cēterās gentīs fuistis**, *IP.* 7, *you have always been more hungry for glory than any other nation.* Especially in set expressions: as, **homo amantissimus patriae**, *Sull.* 34, **vir amantissimus rēī pūblicae**, *C.* 4, 13, *ever a devoted patriot.* **negōtī gerentēs**, *Sest.* 97, *business men.* **aliēnī appetēns**, *DO.* 2, 135, S. *C.* 5, 4, *always hankering after other people's things.* In Caesar seldom: as, **fugiēns labōris**, *C.* 1, 69, 3, *apt to shirk exertion.*

1267. The genitive is hardly ever found with adjectives in **-āx** (284): as, **huius rēi mendācem**, Pl. *As. 855, untruthful in this point.* But in poetry, from Vergil and Horace on, and in late prose, a few genitives occur with adjectives whose parallel verbs have a transitive use, such as **capāx, edāx, tenāx**, &c.: as, **tempus edāx rērum**, O. 15, 234, *thou all-devourer — time.*

1268. Some of the adjectives which usually take the genitive have occasionally other constructions.

Thus, with **adfīnis** the dative also occurs (1200), rarely with **aemulus** (1183); the ablative with adjectives of fulness, as **dīves, plēnus**, and **refertus** (1387); **iūre** with **cōnsultus** and **perītus** (1385). For **vacuus**, &c., see 1306. Prepositional constructions also occur with these adjectives, such as the accusative with **ad** or **in**, or the ablative with **ab, dē**, or **in**: see the dictionary.

1269. For the genitive, with words denoting relationship, connection, friendship, or hostility, see 1203; with **similis**, 1204. With **dignus** and **indignus**, *worthy* and *unworthy*, the ablative is regularly used (1392); rarely the genitive: as, **nōn ego sum dignus salūtis?** Pl. *Tri.* 1153, *don't I deserve a greeting too?* **indignus avōrum**, V. 12, 649, *unworthy of my sires.*

1270. (3.) In poetry and late prose, the genitive is used very freely with many adjectives of various meanings, often merely to indicate what they apply to: as,

nēmō mīlitāris rēi callidior habēbātur, Ta. *H.* 2, 32, *at soldiering nobody was thought to have a greater knack.* **vetus operis ac labōris**, Ta. 1, 20, *an old hand at the toil and moil of army life.* **aevī mātūrus Acestēs**, V. 5, 73, *Acestes, ripe in years.* **sērī studiōrum**, H. *S.* 1, 10, 21, *what laggards at your books.* **integer vītae scelerisque pūrus**, H. 1, 22, 1, *the man unspotted in his life and clean of sin.* **fessī rērum**, V. 1, 178, *in travail spent.* **satin tū sānu's mentis aut animī tuī?** Pl. *Tri.* 454, *art thou quite right in thy five wits?* (1339).

III. THE GENITIVE WITH VERBS.

VERBS OF VALUING.

1271. A few neuter adjectives of quantity are put in the genitive with verbs of valuing to denote the amount of estimation; such genitives are:

magnī, plūris, plūrimī; parvī, minōris, minimī; tantī, quantī.

The verbs with which these genitives are used are **aestimō, dūcō, faciō, habeō, pendō, putō**, and **sum**; rarely **exīstimō**: as, **magnī opera eius aestimāta est**, N. 24, 1, 2, *his services were rated high.* **nōn magnī pendō**, Pl. *As.* 460, *I don't care much.* **sua parvī pendere**, S. *C.* 12, 2, *a setting small store by what they had of their own.* **Verrēsne tibi tantī fuit?** *V.* 1, 77, *was Verres so important in your eyes?* **est mihī tantī.** *C.* 2, 15, *it is well worth my while.* **quantī is ā cīvibus suīs fieret īgnōrābās?** *V.* 4, 19, *did not you know how the man was prized by his own townsmen?* Rarely **maximī**: as, **maximī aestimāre**, *Clu.* 159, *to think all the world of.*

1272. In expressions of worthlessness, other genitives are also used thus; such are **nihilī**, or, usually with a negative, **āssis, floccī, naucī, pilī, teruncī** : as, **nōn āssis facis?** Cat. 43, 13, *car'st not a doit?* So also **huius** : as, **huius nōn faciam,** T. *Ad.* 163, *I shall not care a snap.*

1273. With **aestimō**, the ablatives **magnō** and **permagnō** are sometimes used: as, **quid? tū ista permagnō aestimās?** *V.* 4, 13, *tell me, do you rate that sort of thing very high yourself?* Compare 1390.

1274. The genitives **tantī** and **quantī, plūris** and **minōris** are also used with verbs of buying and selling, hiring and letting, and costing. But other words are put in the ablative with these verbs: see 1391. For **magnī**, &c., with **rēfert** and **interest,** see 1279.

1275. A similar genitive occurs in one or two set forms, such as **aequī bonīque dīcō,** or **faciō, aequī faciō,** and **bonī cōnsulō** : as, **istūc, Chremēs, aequī bonīque faciō,** T. *Hau.* 787, *I count that, Chremes, fair and good.* **aequī istūc faciō,** Pl. *MG.* 784, *that's all the same to me.*

THE VERBS **rēfert** AND **interest.**

1276. rēfert and **interest,** *it concerns,* are much alike in meaning and in construction. But the use of **rēfert** is characteristic of old Latin and poetry; in prose from Cicero on it is almost supplanted by **interest,** especially where persons are concerned.

1277. (1.) With **rēfert** and **interest,** a first or second person concerned is denoted by the possessive pronoun forms **meā, tuā, nostrā, vestrā** ; and, from Cicero on, the third person reflexive by **suā** : as,

(*a.*) **quid id rēfert meā?** Pl. *Cur.* 395, *what's that to me?* **tuā istūc rēfert maxumē,** Pl. *Tri.* 319, *that is of most concern to thee.* **nōn suā rēferre,** *Quinct.* 19, *that it did not concern him.* **nōn nostrā magis quam vestrā rēfert vōs nōn rebellāre,** L. 34, 17, 7, *it is not more for our interest than for your own that you should not make war again.* Without the verb: as, **quid istūc nostrā,** or **quid id nostrā?** T. *Ph.* 800, 940, *what's that to us?* (*b.*) **tuā et meā maximē interest tē valēre,** *Fam.* 16, 4, 4, *your health is a matter of the highest importance to you and to me.* **vestrā hōc maximē interest,** *Sull.* 79, *this is of vital moment to you.*

1278. (2.) With **interest,** from Cicero on, a third person or thing concerned is denoted by the genitive. Also with **rēfert,** a few times from Sallust on : as,

(*a.*) **quid eius intererat?** *RA.* 96, *what concern was it of his?* **interesse rēī pūblicae sē cum Pompēiō colloquī,** Caes. *C.* 1, 24, 5, *that it was of importance to the common weal that he should have a parley with Pompey.* (*b.*) **faciundum aliquid, quod illōrum magis quam suā rētulisse vidērētur,** S. *I.* 111, 1, *that he must do something which should seem more for the other side's good than his own.* For the accusative with **ad** with these verbs, or for the dative with **rēfert,** see the dictionary.

1279. The matter of concern is expressed by a sentence or infinitive, or by a neuter pronoun ; rarely by an appellative : as, **nōn quō meā interesset locī nātūra,** *Att.* 3, 19, 1, *not that the character of the place concerned me.* The degree of concern is expressed by an adverb, as **magnopere,** by a neuter accusative, as **multum,** or by a genitive of estimation, **magnī, permagnī, plūris, parvī, tantī, quantī** (1271).

JUDICIAL VERBS.

1280. Verbs of accusing, convicting, condemning, and acquitting, take a genitive of the charge : as,

C. Verrem īnsimulat avāritiae, *V.* 1, 128, *he charges Verres with avarice.* **accūsātus est prōditiōnis,** N. 1, 7, 5, *he was charged with treason.* **capitis arcēssere,** *D.* 30, *accuse on a capital charge.* **prōditiōnis damnātus est,** N. 2, 8, 2, *he was convicted of treason.* **Pollis pecūniae pūblicae est condemnātus,** *Flacc.* 43, *Pollis was condemned for embezzlement of government money.* **maiestātis absolūtī sunt permultī,** *Clu.* 116, *a good many were acquitted of high treason.* With this genitive, an ablative, **crīmine, iūdiciō, nōmine,** or **lēge,** is sometimes expressed (1377) : as, **nē quem umquam innocentem iūdiciō capitis arcēssās,** *Off.* 2, 51, *that you are never to accuse any innocent man on a charge affecting his status as a citizen.*

1281. The charge is sometimes denoted by a prepositional construction : as, **sescentī sunt, quī inter sīcāriōs et dē venēficiīs accūsābant,** *RA.* 90, *there are hundreds and hundreds that brought charges of murder, by steel and by poison.* So also **dē āleā,** *of gambling,* in Cicero regularly **dē pecūniīs repetundīs,** *of extortion,* and necessarily **dē vī,** *of an act of violence,* as **vīs** has no genitive. For the neuter accusative, see 1172.

1282. The penalty also is sometimes denoted by the genitive : as, **cupiō octuplī damnārī Aprōnium,** *V.* 3, 28, *I want to have Apronius condemned to a payment of eightfold.* **damnātusque longī Sīsyphus Aeolidēs labōris,** H. 2, 14, 19, *and Sisyphus the Aeolid, amerced with penance long.* Sometimes by the ablative : as, **capite,** *V.* 5, 109. So usually from Livy on, when the penalty is a definite sum of money or fractional part of a thing.

IMPERSONAL VERBS OF MENTAL DISTRESS.

1283. A genitive of the thing, commonly with an accusative of the person, is used with five impersonals of mental distress :

miseret, paenitet, piget, pudet, taedet : as,

tuī mē miseret, meī piget, E. in *Div.* 1, 66, *I pity thee, I loathe myself.* **frātris mē pudet pigetque,** T. *Ad.* 391, *my brother stirs my shame and my disgust.* **mī pater, mē tuī pudet,** T. *Ad.* 681, *dear father, in thy presence I'm abashed.* **galeātum sērō duellī paenitet,** J. 1, 169, *too late, with casque on head, a combatant repenteth him of war.* So also **miserētur,** and in old Latin inceptively, **miserēscit, commiserēscit.**

1284. These verbs sometimes have a sentence or a neuter pronoun as subject : as, **nōn tē haec pudent?** T. *Ad.* 754, *does not this make thee blush for shame?* Rarely an appellative : as, **mē quidem haec condiciō nōn paenitet,** Pl. *St.* 51, *for my part, with my wedded state I'm well content.* Or a person : as, **pudeō,** Pl. *Cas.* 877, *I feel ashamed.* For participles and gerundives, see 817.

1285. The genitive is used with the personals **misereor** or **misereō**, and in poetry with **miserēscō** : as,

aliquandō miserēminī sociōrum, *V.* I, 72, *do take pity on your allies, it is high time.* **nēminis miserēre certumst, quia meī miseret nēminem,** Pl. *Cap.* 764, *I'm bound to care for nobody, as no one cares for me.* **Arcadiī miserēscite rēgis,** *V.* 8, 573, *take pity on the king of Arcady.*

1286. Personal verbs of desiring, loathing, admiring, and dreading, sometimes take the genitive : as, **pol, quamquam domī cupiō, opperiar,** Pl. *Tri.* 841, *although I yearn for home, I vow I'll wait* (1263). **fastīdit meī,** Pl. *Aul.* 245, *he views me with disdain* (1263). **iūstitiaene prius mīrer, bellīne labōrum?** *V.* 11, 126, *thy justice first shall I admire? thy toils in war?* **nē tuī quidem testimōnī veritus,** *Att.* 8, 4, 1, *not having any awe about your recommendation either.*

VERBS OF MEMORY.

1287. The genitive is used with verbs of remembering and forgetting when they denote an inherent state of memory or of forgetfulness : as,

faciam ut meī meminerīs dum vītam vīvās, Pl. *Per.* 494, *I'll make you remember me as long as you live.* **num potuī magis oblīvīscī temporum meōrum, meminisse āctiōnum?** *Fam.* I, 9, 8, *could I have been more forgetful of my present interests, more mindful of my past career?* **reminīscerētur incommodī populī Rōmānī,** I, 13, 4, *he had better bear in mind the rebuff dealt out to Rome.* **oblītusque meōrum oblīvīscendus et illīs,** H. *E.* I, 11, 10, *of friends forgetful and by friends forgot.* See 1263.

1288. The accusative is used with these verbs when they denote the mere intellectual exercise of memory or a failure to remember: as,

equid meministī tuōm parentum nōmina? Pl. *Poen.* 1062, *do you remember your parents' names?* **Cinnam meminī vidī Sūllam,** *Ph.* 5, 17, *I can remember Cinna, I have seen Sulla.* **utinam mēmet possim oblīscier!** Accius ap. Non. 500, 5, *oh that myself I could forget!* **subitō tōtam causam oblītus est,** *Br.* 217, *suddenly he forgot the whole case.*

1289. recordor has once the genitive (*Pis.* 12), but from its meaning *bring to heart* it is naturally found oftener with the accusative. With it and with **meminī,** the ablative with **dē** also occurs. The rare **reminīscor** has the genitive once each in Caesar and Nepos; twice later; oftener the accusative. Neuter pronouns are in the accusative with all these verbs.

1290. The impersonal **venit in mentem** also takes the genitive: as, **venit mihī Platōnis in mentem,** *Fin.* 5, 2, *Plato comes into my head;* very exceptionally the ablative with **dē.** But the verb in this combination is often used personally, with the thing occurring to the mind as the subject, and regularly in Cicero, when it is **rēs** or **genus,** or a neuter pronoun.

1291. Verbs of reminding take the accusative of a person and sometimes with the genitive of a thing: as,

admonēbat alium egestātis, alium cupiditātis suae, S. *C.* 21, 4, *he reminded one man of his beggary, another of his greed.* So also **commoneō, commonēfaciō,** and, in Tacitus only, **moneō.** Oftener however the thing is in the ablative with **dē,** or, if it is a neuter pronoun or adjective, in the accusative (1172). Rarely a substantive equivalent to a neuter pronoun: as, **eam rem nōs locus admonuit,** S. *I.* 79, 1, *the place has reminded me of that.*

VERBS OF PARTICIPATION AND MASTERY.

1292. Verbs of participation and mastery sometimes take the genitive in old Latin and in poetry : as, **servom suī participat cōnsilī,** Pl. *Cist.* 163, *she makes a slav· a sharer in her plot* (1263). **quā Daunus agrestium rēgnāvit populō-rum,** H. 3, 30, 11, *where Daunus was the lord of rural folk* (1260). So, even in prose, **potior,** which usually has the ablative (1379) : as, **totīus Galliae sēsē potīrī posse spērant,** 1, 3, 8, *they hope they can get the mastery over the whole of Gaul.* Especially with persons, or with the genitive plural **rērum: rērum potior,** *get to be,* or often, *am, master of the situation,* or *I am monarch of all I survey.* Similarly in Tacitus **apīscor, adipīscor** : as, **arma, quīs Servius Galba rērum adeptus est,** Ta. 3, 55, *the war by which Galba became master of the throne.* In Plautus **crēdō** sometimes has the genitive of a thing and dative of a person.

VERBS OF FULNESS AND WANT.

1293. The genitive is sometimes used with verbs of filling, abounding, and lacking, as it is with the corresponding adjectives (1263) : as,

convīvium vīcīnōrum cōtīdiē compleō, *CM.* 46, *I fill out a dinner-party every day with neighbours.* **haec rēs vītae mē, soror, saturant,** Pl. *St.* 18, *these things, my sister, sicken me of life.* **terra ferārum nunc etiam scatit,** Lucr. 5, 39, *still teems the earth with ravin beasts.* So with **egeō** sometimes : as, **egeō cōnsilī,** *Att.* 7, 22, 2, *I am in need of some advice.* And usually with **indigeō** : as. **hoc bellum indiget celeritātis,** *Ph.* 6, 7, *this war requires rapid action.* But, from Livy on, the ablative is commoner with **indigeō** : see 1305.

1294. With verbs of separating and abstaining, the ablative is regularly used (1302). But the genitive is sometimes found in poetry : as, **mē omnium labōrum levās,** Pl. *R.* 247, *thou riddest me of all my woes.* **abstinētō īrārum calidae-que rixae,** H. 3, 27, 69, *from bursts of rage keep thou and hot affray.*

IV. THE GENITIVE OF EXCLAMATION.

1295. In poetry, the genitive with an adjective in agreement occurs two or three times in exclamation : as, **foederis heu tacitī,** Prop. 5, 7, 21, *alas, that secret covenant.* Usually the nominative (1117), or the accusative (1149).

THE ABLATIVE.

1296. The ablative is used principally with verbs and their participles, or with adjectives, and consists of three cases that were originally distinct.

1297. I. The ABLATIVE proper denotes that from which something parts or proceeds (1302).

The ablative proper is often accompanied by the prepositions **ab, dē, ex, prae, prō, sine,** or **tenus.**

1298. With the ablative proper two other cases, originally distinct, a locative case and an instrumental case, were confounded, and merged under the common name of the ablative.

1299. II. The LOCATIVE case denotes the place in, at, or on which action occurs. A few forms of the locative proper are still preserved (1331). But the place where is ordinarily denoted by the locative ablative (1342).

The locative ablative is often accompanied by the prepositions **in** or **sub.**

1300. III. The INSTRUMENTAL case denotes that by which or with which a main person or thing is attended (1356).

The instrumental ablative is often accompanied by the prepositions **cum** or **cōram.**

1301. The ablative or locative is sometimes attached immediately to a substantive.

Thus, (*a.*) sometimes to a substantive which denotes or implies action: as, **interitus ferrō**, *destruction with the sword*, like **intereō ferrō**; see 1307, 1331, 1342, 1376, 1377. (*b.*) In constructions in which the ablative is due to an older combination with a verb: as, **vir singulārī virtūte,** *a man of unexampled bravery.* See 1309 and 1375.

I. THE ABLATIVE PROPER.

THE ABLATIVE OF SEPARATION AND WANT, AND OF DEPARTURE.

1302. Verbs of separation take an ablative of the thing from which separation takes place : as,

(*a*) caruit forō posteā Pompēius, caruit senātū, caruit pūblicō, *Mil.* 18, *after that Pompey had to keep away from the market place, from the senate, from highways and byways.* adhūc Q. Ligārius omnī culpā vacat, *Lig.* 4. *thus far Ligarius proves devoid of any guilt.* egeō cōnsiliō, *Att.* 15, 1, A, 5, *I need advice* (1305). (*b*) Italiā prohibētur: nōn tū eum patriā prīvāre, quā caret, sed vītā vīs, *Lig.* 11, *he is kept out of Italy ; you want to deprive him not of his country, from which he is debarred, but of life.* līberēmus cūrā populum Rōmānum, L. 39, 51, 9, Hannibal's words when he took poison, 183 B. C , *let me relieve Rome of anxiety.*

1303. This ablative is used (*a*.) with such verbs as mean *abstain*, abstineō, dēsistō, supersedeō; *am devoid of*, careō, vacō; *need*, egeō; and in addition to the accusative of the object, (*b*.) with verbs used transitively, such as mean *keep off*, arceō, exclūdō and interclūdō, prohibeō; *drive away*, *remove*, pellō, moveō, and their compounds; *free*, expediō, līberō, levō, solvō and exsolvō; *deprive*, orbō, privō, spoliō, nūdō, fraudō.

1304. A preposition, **ab** or **ex**, is often used with these verbs, and regularly when the ablative denotes a person. But careō and egeō, and exsolvō and levō, never have a preposition.

1305. With egeō, the genitive is sometimes used, and often with indigeō : see 1293. Also in poetry, with verbs of abstaining and separating : see 1294.

1306. The ablative of separation is sometimes used with such adjectives as aliēnus, expers, līber, nūdus, vacuus, &c. : as, negant id esse aliēnum maiestāte deōrum, *Div.* 2, 105, *they maintain that this is not at variance with the greatness of the gods.* vacuī cūrīs, *Fin.* 2, 46, *devoid of cares.* arce et urbe orba sum, E. *Tr.* 114, *of tower and town bereft am I.* But sometimes the genitive: see 1263 and 1264; sometimes also prepositional constructions: for these, and particularly for the different constructions of aliēnus, see the dictionary.

TOWN AND ISLAND NAMES.

1307. (1.) Proper names of towns and of little islands are put in the ablative with verbs of motion, to denote the place from which motion proceeds: as,

Dāmarātus fūgit Tarquiniōs Corinthō, *TD.* 5, 109, *Damaratus ran away from Corinth to Tarquinii.* sīgnum Carthāgine captum, *V.* 4, 82, *the statue carried off from Carthage.* Megaribus, Pl. *Per.* 137, *from Megara.* Lēmnō, Pl. *Tru.* 90, *from Lemnos.* Rōmā accēperam litterās, *Att.* 5, 8, 2, *I had got a letter from Rome.* Rarely with a substantive of motion (1301): as, dē illīus Alexandrēā discessū, *Att.* 11, 18, 1, *about his departure from Alexandrea.* Also in dating letters: as, v kal. Sextīl., Rēgiō, *Fam.* 7, 19, *Regium*, 28 *July*; less often the locative: as, Īdibus Iūniīs, Thessalonicae, *QFr.* 1, 3, 10, *Thessalonica*, 13 *June.* Like a town name: Ācherunte, poet. in *TD.* 1, 37, *from Acheron.* With an attribute : ipsā Samō, *V.* 1, 51, *from Samos itself.* Teānō Sidicīnō, *Att.* 8, 11, B, 2, *from Sidicinian Teanum.*

1308. Singular town or island names sometimes have **ex** in old Latin : thus, Carystō, Pl. *Ps.* 730, *from Carystus*, or, ex Carystō, *Ps.* 737, indifferently. ex Andrō, T. *Andr.* 70, *from Andros.* In classical Latin, town names rarely have ab: as, ab Athēnīs proficīscī, Serv. in *Fam.* 4, 12, 2, *to start from Athens;* chiefly of neighbourhood: as, ab Gergoviā, 7, 43, 5 : 7, 59, 1, *from camp at Gergovia;* or direction : as, ā Salōnīs ad Ōricum, Caes. *C.* 3, 8, 4, *from Salonae to Oricum;* regularly with longē : as, longē ā Syrācūsīs, *V.* 4, 107, *far from Syracuse.*

1309. The ablative of a town or country name is rarely attached immediately to a substantive, to denote origin : as, Periphanēs Rhodō mercātor dīves, Pl *As.* 499, *Periphanes from Rhodes a chapman rich.* videō ibī hospitem Zacynthō, Pl. *Mer.* 940, *I see the friend there from Zacynthus.* Rarely in Cicero: as, Teānō Āpulō laudātōrēs, *Clu.* 197, *eulogists from Apulian Teanum;* in Caesar twice. In Livy with ab only: as, Turnus ab Arīciā, L. 1, 50, 3. *Turnus from Aricia.* But the Roman tribe one belongs to, is regularly in the ablative: as, Q. Verrem Rōmilā, sc. tribū, *V. a. pr.* 1, 23, *Verres of the tribe Romilia.*

223

1310. With a verb, country names regularly have a preposition, and always in Cicero, Sallust, and Livy : as, **ē Ciliciā dēcēdēns**, *Br.* 1. *going away from Cilicia.* The ablative alone is rare : as, **Aegyptō adveniō domum**, Pl. *Most.* 440, *from Egypt I come home.* Chiefly in Tacitus : as, **Aegyptō remeāns**, 2, 69, *coming back from Egypt.* In Caesar, by attraction : **cōgēbantur Corcȳrā atque Acarnāniā pābulum supportāre**, *C.* 3, 58, 4, *they were forced to fetch fodder from Corcyra and even Acarnania.*

1311. (2.) The ablatives **domō** and **rūre**, and in poetry **humō**, are used like proper names of towns : as,

(*a.*) **domō excesserant**, 4, 14, 5, *they had gone away from home.* Also metaphorically : as, **domō doctus**, Pl. *Mer.* 355, *by home-experience taught.*
(*b.*) **rūre rediit uxor mea**, Pl. *Mer.* 705, *my wife's come back from out of town.*
(*c.*) **humō**, in Vergil first : as, **vix oculōs attollit humō**, O. 2, 448, *scarce from the ground her eyes she lifts.*

THE ABLATIVE OF SOURCE, STUFF, OR MATERIAL.

1312. The verb **nāscor** and participles of origin take an ablative to denote parentage or rank in life.

Such participles are : **nātus, prōgnātus**, and **ortus** ; in poetry and late prose, also **crētus, ēditus, generātus, genitus, satus**, and **oriundus** : as, (*a.*) **Rōmulus deō prōgnātus**, L. 1, 40, 3, *Romulus, sprung from a god.* **dīs genite**, V. 9, 642, *thou sired of gods.* Of a parent, **ex** is sometimes used : as **ex mē hic nātus nōn est**, T. *Ad.* 40, *he's not my son ;* and of remoter ancestors, **ab**. (*b.*) **locō nātus honestō**, 5, 45, 2, *respectably descended.* **summō locō nātus**, 5, 25, 1, *of high birth.* **familiā antīquissimā nātum**, 7, 32, 4, *a member of an old family.* Rarely with **dē** : as, **quō dē genere gnātust Philocratēs ?** Pl. *Cap.* 277, *what is the parentage of Philocrates ?*

1313. The ablative with an attribute, attached to a substantive, sometimes denotes stuff or material : as, **aere cavō clipeum**, V. 3, 286, *a targe of hollow bronze.* **perennī fronde corōnam**, Lucr. 1, 118, *a crown of amaranthine leaf.* **solidōque adamante columnae**, V. 6, 552, *and pillars of the solid adamant.* This construction borders closely on the ablative of quality (1375). Rarely without an attribute : as, **pictās abiete puppīs**, V. 5, 663, *painted sterns of fir.*

1314. A substantive denoting stuff or material is generally put in the ablative with **dē** or **ex** ; thus,

(*a.*) Directly with a substantive : **pōcula ex aurō**, *V.* 4, 62, *cups of gold.*
(*b.*) Oftener with an auxiliary verb or participle : **sīgnum erat hoc Cupīdinis ē marmore**, *V.* 4, 5, *this statue of Cupid was made of marble.* **scūtīs ex cortice factīs**, 2, 33, 2, *with long shields made out of bark.* **ex ūnā gemmā pergrandī trūlla excavāta**, *V.* 4, 62, *a ladle scooped out of a single enormous semi-precious stone.*

1315. The ablative with forms of **faciō** and **sum** denotes that with which or to which something is done : as, **quid hōc homine faciās ?** *Sest.* 29, *what can you do with such a fellow ?* **quid mē fīet ?** T. *Andr.* 709, *what will become of me ?* But often the dative (1205): as, **quid tibī faciam ?** *Att.* 7, 3, 2, *what shall I do to you ?* Or the ablative with **dē** : as, **dē frātre quid fīet ?** T. *Ad.* 996, *as to my brother, what will come to pass ?*

THE ABLATIVE OF CAUSE, INFLUENCE, OR MOTIVE.

1316. The ablative is used to denote cause, influence, or motive: as,

madeō metū, Pl. *Most.* 395, *I'm drenched with dread.* tū imprūdentiā lāberis, *Mur.* 78, *you, sir, slip from inadvertence.* maerōre et lacrimīs cōnsenēscēbat, *Clu.* 13, *she just pined away in sorrow and tears.* īrā incendor, Pl. *Ps.* 201, *I'm getting hot with wrath.* premor lūctū, *Att.* 3, 22, 3, *I am bowed down with grief.* quod ego nōn superbiā faciēbam, *DO.* 1, 99, *I did not act thus from superciliousness, not I.* nōn movētur pecūniā, *V.* 4, 18, *he is not moved by money.* boat caelum fremitū virūm, Pl. *Am.* 232, *the welkin rings with roar of men.* dēlictō dolēre, corrēctiōne gaudēre, *L.* 90, *be pained by the sin, take pleasure in the reproof.* aetāte nōn quīs optuērier, Pl. *Most.* 840, *owing to age thou canst not see.* Iovis iussū veniō, Pl. *Am. prol.* 19, *at Jove's behest I come.* Sēiānus nimiā fortūnā sōcors, Ta. 4, 39, *Sejanus giddy with over-prosperity.* ferōx praedā glōriāque exercitus, Ta. *H.* 1, 51, *the army flushed with booty and glory.* exercitūs nostrī interitus ferrō, *Pis.* 40, *the annihilation of our army by the sword* (1301).

1317. Instead of the ablative, other constructions often occur, especially with verbs used transitively; such are:

(*a.*) Prepositional phrases with **dē** or **ex**, in Varro and Livy with **ab**; also with **ob, per**, or **propter**: as, multī in oppidum propter timōrem sēsē recipiunt, Caes. *C.* 2, 35, 6, *a good many retreated to the town from fear.* Sometimes with **prae**: as, prae amōre exclūstī hunc forās, T. *Eu.* 98, *it was for love you turned him out of doors:* in classical Latin, usually of hindrance: as, sōlem prae iaculōrum multitūdine nōn vidēbitis, *TD.* 1, 101, *you won't see the sun for the cloud of javelins.* (*b.*) Circumlocutions with **causā**, less frequently with **grātiā** (1257). (*c.*) Ablatives absolute, or participles, particularly auxiliary participles with an ablative to express cause, oftener motive, such as **captus, ductus, excitātus** or **incitātus, impulsus, incēnsus, īnflammātus, mōtus, perterritus**: as, nōnnūllī pudōre adductī remanēbant, 1, 39, 3, *some stuck by from shame.*

1318. The person by whom the action of a passive verb is done, is denoted by the ablative with **ab** or **ā.** Also occasionally with verbs equivalent to a passive, such as cadō, intereō, pereō, vēneō, &c., &c. Things or animals are sometimes represented as persons by the use of **ab**: as, animus bene īnfōrmātus ā nātūrā, *Off.* 1, 13, *a soul meetly fashioned by dame nature.* See 1476–1478.

1319. In poetry, an ablative denoting a person, with an adjective in agreement, is sometimes equivalent to an expression with an abstract substantive: as, et adsiduō ruptae lēctōre columnae, J. 1, 13, *and pillars by persistent reader riven,* i. e. adsiduitāte lēctōris, or adsiduā lēctiōne. cūrātus inaequālī tōnsōre capillōs, H. *E.* 1, 1, 94, *my locks by unsymmetric barber trimmed.*

THE ABLATIVE OF COMPARISON.

1320. (1.) The ablative may be used with a comparative adjective, when the first of two things compared is in the nominative, or is a subject-accusative.

Such an ablative is translated by *than:* as, (*a.*) **lūce sunt clāriōra nōbīs tua cōnsilia,** *C.* 1, 6, *your schemes are plainer to us than day.* **ō mātre pulchrā fīlia pulchrior,** H. 1, 16, 1, *O daughter fairer than a mother fair.* Particularly in sentences of negative import: as, **quis Karthāginiēnsium plūris fuit Hannibale?** *Sest.* 142, *of all the sons of Carthage, who was rated higher than Hannibal?* **nec mihī est tē iūcundius quicquam nec cārius,** *Fam.* 2, 10, 1, *and there is nothing in the world nearer and dearer to me than you.* (*b.*) **illud cōgnōscēs profectō, mihī tē neque cāriōrem neque iū-cundiōrem esse quemquam,** *Fam.* 2, 3, 2, *one thing I am sure you will see, that there is nobody nearer and dearer to me than you.*

1321. (2.) The ablative of comparison is similarly used when the first member of comparison is an accusative of the object: as,

exēgī monumentum aere perennius, H. 3, 30, 1, *I have builded up a monument more durable than bronze.* Particularly so in sentences of negative import: as, **hōc mihī grātius facere nihil potes,** *Fam.* 13, 44, *you can do nothing for me more welcome than this.* Also with predicate adjectives dependent on a verb of thinking (1167): as, **Hērodotum cūr vērāciōrem dūcam Enniō?** *Div.* 2, 116, *why should I count Herodotus any more truthful than Ennius?* Regularly when the second member of comparison is a rela- tive: as, **quā pecude nihil genuit nātūra fēcundius,** *DN.* 2, 160, *nature has created nothing more prolific than this animal,* i. e. the sow.

1322. (3.) In poetry, the ablative of comparison may be used with the first mem- ber of comparison in any case: as, **Lūcilī ritū, nostrūm meliōris utrōque,** H. *S.* 2, 1, 29, *after Lucilius's way, a better man than thou or I.*

1323. (4.) In sentences of negative import, the ablative is sometimes used with **alter** and **alius,** as with a comparative: as, **neque mēst alter quisquam,** Pl. *As.* 492, *and there's no other man than I.* **nec quicquam aliud lībertāte commūnī quaesīsse,** Brut. and Cass. in *Fam.* 11, 2, 2, *and to have aimed at nothing else than freedom for all.* But in prose, **quam** is commonly used.

1324. (1.) The second member of comparison is often introduced by **quam,** *than,* or in poetry by **atque** or **ac.** This member, whatever the case of the first member, is sometimes made the subject of a form of **sum** in a new sentence: as,

meliōrem quam ego sum suppōnō tibī, Pl. *Cur.* 256, *I give you as a substitute a better than I am myself.* **verba M. Varrōnis, hominis quam fuit Claudius doctiōris,** Gell. 10, 1, 4, *the words of Varro, a better scholar than Claudius ever was.* **ut tibī maiōrī quam Āfricānus fuit, mē ad- iūnctum esse patiāre,** *Fam.* 5, 7, 3, *so that you will allow me to be associated with you, a bigger man than Africanus ever was.*

1325. (2.) When the first member is in the nominative or accusative, **quam** is commonly a mere coordinating word, with both members in the same case: as,

(*a.*) **plūris est oculātus testis ūnus quam aurītī decem,** Pl. *Tru.* 490, *a single witness with an eye rates higher than a dozen with the ear.* (*b.*) **tū velim exīstimēs nēminem cuiquam neque cāriōrem neque iūcundiōrem umquam fuisse quam tē mihī,** *Fam.* 1, 9, 24, *I hope you will be convinced that nobody was ever nearer and dearer to anybody than you to me.*

1326. An introductory ablative of a demonstrative or relative pronoun sometimes precedes the construction with **quam**: as, **quid hōc est clārius, quam omnīs Segestae mātrōnās et virginēs convēnisse?** *V.* 4, 77, *what fact is there better known than this, to wit, that all the women in Segesta, married and single, came streaming together?*

1327. The ablative is sometimes used with comparative adverbs also.

So particularly in sentences of negative import: as, **nihil lacrimā citius ārēscit,** Corn. 2, 50, *nothing dries up quicker than a tear.* Less frequently in positive sentences in prose: as, **fortūna, quae plūs cōnsilīs hūmānīs pollet, contrāxit certāmen,** L. 44, 40, 3, *fortune, who is mightier than the devices of man, precipitated the engagement.* Very commonly, however, **quam** is used with comparative adverbs.

1328. Designations of number or extent are often qualified by **amplius, longius,** or **plūs,** *over,* or by **minus,** *under.*

The word thus qualified is put in the case which the context would require without any such qualification: as, **plūs septingentī captī,** L. 41, 12, 8, *over seven hundred were taken prisoners.* **tēcum plūs annum vīxit,** *Q.* 41, *he lived with you over a year* (1151). **cum equīs plūs quīngentīs,** L. 40, 32, 6, *with over five hundred horses.* Less frequently with **quam.** When these words are felt as real substantives in the nominative or accusative, the ablative of comparison may be used (1320): as, **plūs trīduō,** *RA.* 74, *more than three days.*

1329. In expressions of age with **nātus,** the adjectives **maior** and **minor** are used as well as **amplius** and **minus,** and with the same construction (1328): as, **annōs nātus maior quadrāgintā,** *RA.* 39, *over forty years old.* For other constructions, see the dictionary. Similarly **conlēctus aquae digitum nōn altior ūnum,** Lucr. 4, 414, *a pool no deeper than a finger's breadth* (1130). But commonly with comparative adjectives of extent, **quam** is used, or the ablative (1320): as, **palūs nōn lātior pedibus quīnquāgintā,** 7, 19, 1, *a marsh not wider than fifty feet.*

1330. With a comparative adjective or adverb, the ablatives **opīniōne, exspectātiōne,** and **spē,** and some others, chiefly in poetry, take the place of a sentence with **quam**: as,

opīniōne melius, Pl. *Cas.* 338, *better than you thought.* **minōra opīniōne,** Caes. *C.* 2, 31, 5, *more insignificant than is thought.* **lātius opīniōne dissēminātum est hoc malum,** *C.* 4, 6, *this infection is more sweeping than anybody dreams.* **spē omnium sērius,** L. 2, 3, 1, *later than was generally expected.*

II. THE LOCATIVE ABLATIVE.

(A.) THE LOCATIVE PROPER.

1331. (1.) Singular proper names of towns and of little islands are put in the locative to denote the place in or at which action occurs: as, quid **Rōmae** faciam? **mentīrī** nescio, J. 3, 41, *what can I do in Rome? I don't know how to lie.* **Corinthī** et **Karthāginī,** *Agr.* 2, 90, *at Corinth and at Carthage.* **Lacedaemonī,** N. *praef.* 4, *in Lacedaemon.* **Tīburī,** *Att.* 16, 3, 1, *at Tibur.* **Rhodī,** *Fam.* 4, 7, 4, *at Rhodes.* **mānsiōnēs** diutinae **Lēmnī,** T. *Ph.* 1012, *protracted stays at Lemnos* (1301). Sometimes in dates: as, **data Thessalonīcae,** *Att.* 3, 20, 3, *given at Thessalonica* (1307). The locative rarely means *near*: as, **Antiī,** L. 22, 1, 10, *round about Antium.* In Plautus only two singular town names with consonant stems occur, and these regularly in the locative, **Carthāginī** and **Sicyōnī,** three times each; once in a doubtful example, **Sicyōne,** *Cist.* 128. Terence has no examples of these stems. From Cicero on, the locative ablative is commoner with them (1343).

1332. With an adjective attribute also, the locative is used: as, **Teānī Āpulī,** *Clu.* 27, *at the Apulian Teanum.* **Suessae Auruncae,** L. 32, 9, 3, *at the Auruncan Suessa.* The appellative **forum,** *market place,* used, with an attribute, as a proper name, is sometimes put in the accusative with **ad**: as, **Claternae, ad Forum Cornēlium,** *Fam.* 12, 5, 2, *at Claterna and at Forum Cornelium;* sometimes in the locative ablative: **Forō Iūlī,** Plin. *Ep.* 5, 19, 7.

1333. When the locative is further explained by an appellative following, the appellative is put in the locative ablative, either alone, or with **in**: as, **Antiochīae, celebrī quondam urbe,** *Arch.* 4, *at Antioch, once a bustling town.* **Neāpolī, in celeberrimō oppidō,** *RabP.* 26, *at Neapolis, a town swarming with people.* An appellative in the ablative with **in** may be further defined by a proper name in the locative: as, **duābus in īnsulis, Melitae et Samī,** *V.* 5, 184, *in two islands — at Melita and Samos.* **in oppidō, Antiochīae,** *Att.* 5, 18, 1, *within town walls — at Antioch.* **in sēcessū, Apollōniae,** Suet. *Aug.* 94, *out of town — at Apollonia.* Or in the ablative: as, **in oppidō Citiō,** N. 5, 3, 4, *in the town of Citium.* **in urbe Rōmā,** L. 39, 14, 7, *in the city of Rome.*

1334. In Plautus, singular town names with stems in -ā- or -o- are put in the locative ten or twelve times, in the ablative with **in** some fifteen times. Three such have only **in,** never the locative: **in Anactoriō,** *Poen.* 896, **in Seleuciā,** *Tri.* 901, **in Spartā,** *Poen.* 663; furthermore, **in Epidamnō,** *Men.* 267, 380 twice, **in Ephesō,** *B.* 309, *MG.* 441, 778, and **in Epidaurō,** *Cur.* 341, 429, *E.* 540, 541, 554, but also **Epidamnī,** *Men. prol.* 51, **Ephesī,** *B.* 336, 1047, *MG.* 648, and **Epidaurī,** *E.* 636. Terence, who has only -o- stems, uses the locative six times, the ablative with **in** four times: only with **in**: **in Andrō,** *Andr.* 931, **in Imbrō,** *Hec.* 171. Furthermore **in Lēmnō,** *Ph.* 873, 1004, but also **Lēmnī,** *Ph.* 680, 942, 1013. Also **Mīlētī,** *Ad.* 654, **Rhodī,** *Eu.* 107, **Sūniī,** *Eu.* 519.

1335. A town name is sometimes put in the ablative with **in** by assimilation with a parallel **in**: as, **in Illyricō, in ipsā Alexandrēā,** *Att.* 11, 16, 1, *in Illyricum, and at Alexandrea itself.* **Antiochum in Syriā, Ptolemaeum in Alexandriā esse,** L. 42, 26, 7, *that Antiochus was in Syria, Ptolemy at Alexandria.* **in mōnte Albānō Lāviniōque,** L. 5, 52, 8, *on the Alban mount and at Lavinium.* Also without assimilation: as, **nāvis et in Caiētā est parāta nōbīs et Brundusiī,** *Att.* 8, 3, 6, *we have a vessel all chartered, one in Cajeta and one at Brundusium.* **in Hispalī,** Caes. *C.* 2, 18, 1, *in Hispalis.*

1336. With country names, the locative is very exceptional: as, **Chersonēsī,** N. 1, 2, 4, *at the Peninsula.* **Aegyptī,** Val. M. 4, 1, 15, *in Egypt.* Similarly **Accheruntī,** Pl. *Cap.* 689. 998, **Mer.** 606, *Tru.* 749, *in Acheron;* **Accherunte** however once: **Accheruntest,** Pl. *Poen.* 431. In Sallust, **Rōmae Numidiaeque,** *I.* 33, 4, with assimilation of **Numidiae** to **Rōmae.**

1337. (2.) The locatives **domī, rūrī, humī,** and rarely **orbī,** are used like proper names of towns: as, (*a.*) **cēnābō domī**, Pl. *St.* 482, *I shall dine at home.* Metaphorically, **domī est, nāscitur**, or **habeō**, *I can get at home, I need not go abroad for,* or *I have in plenty:* as, id quidem **domī est,** *Att.* 10, 14, 2, *as for that, I have it myself.* With a possessive pronoun or **aliēnus** in agreement, either the locative is used, or the ablative with **in**; for **domuī**, as, *Off.* 3, 99, see 594; with other adjectives the ablative with **in.** (*b.*) **rūrī,** T. *Ph.* 363, *up in the country;* for **rūre,** see 1344 and 1345. (*c.*) **humī,** *on the ground,* or *to the ground,* in Terence first: as, hunc ante nostram iānuam appōne :: obsecrō, **humīne?** T. *Andr.* 724, *set down this baby at our door :: good gracious ; on the ground?* iacēre **humī,** *C.* 1, 26, *sleeping on bare ground.* (*d.*) **orbī** with **terrae** or **terrārum:** as, amplissimum orbī terrārum monumentum, *V.* 4, 82, *the grandest monument in the wide wide world.*

1338. The locatives **bellī,** older **duellī,** and **mīlitiae** are sometimes used in contrast with **domī :** as, domi duellīque, Pl. *Cap. prol.* 68, domī bellīque, L. 2, 50, 11, domī mīlitiaeque, *TD.* 5, 55, mīlitiae et domī, T. *Ad.* 495, *at home and in the field.* Rarely without **domī :** as, bellī, *RP.* 2, 56, mīlitiae. S. *I.* 84, 2.

1339. (3.) Other appellatives rarely have the locative : as, **proxumae vīcīniae,** Pl. *B.* 205, *MG.* 273, *in the next neighbourhood.* **terrae,** L. 5, 51, 9, *in the earth.* With verbs of suspense, doubt, and distress, and with many adjectives, **animī,** *in soul,* is not infrequent ; and **animī** being mistaken for a genitive, **mentis** is also used: as, dēsipiēbam mentis, Pl. *E.* 138, *I was beside myself.* Oftener **animō** (1344).

1340. Many original locatives have become set as adverbs : as, **peregrī,** *abroad.* Particularly of pronouns : as, **illī,** Pl. *Am.* 249, *off there,* oftener **illīc ; istī** or **istic, hīc ;** sometimes further defined by an added expression: as, **hīc vīcīniae,** T. *Ph.* 95, *here in the neighbourhood.* **hīc** proxumae vīcīniae, *MG.* 273, *here in the house next door.* **hīc** in **Veneris** fānō meae vīcīniae, Pl. *R.* 613, *here, in the shrine of Venus, in my neighbourhood.* **hīc Rōmae,** *Arch.* 5, *here in Rome.*

1341. The locative proper sometimes denotes time when : as, **lūcī,** *by light,* **temperī,** *betimes,* **herī** or **here,** *yesterday,* **vesperī,** *at evening,* **herī vesperī,** *DO.* 2, 13, *last evening.* In Plautus, **diē septimī,** *Men.* 1156, *Per.* 260, *on the seventh day,* **māne sānē septimī,** *Men.* 1157, *bright and early on the seventh,* **diē crāstinī,** *Most.* 881, *tomorrow.* Often with an adjective juxtaposed : as, **postrīdiē,** *the day after,* postrīdiē māne, *Fam.* 11, 6, 1, *early next day,* **cōtīdiē,** *each day, daily,* **prīdiē,** *the day before.*

(B.) THE ABLATIVE USED AS LOCATIVE.

PLACE IN, ON, OR AT WHICH.

1342. (1.) Plural proper names of towns and of little islands are put in the locative ablative to denote the place in or at which action occurs : as,

mortuus Cūmīs, L. 2, 21, 5, *he died at Cumae.* **Athēnīs tenue caelum, crassum Thēbīs,** *Fat.* 7, *in Athens the air is thin, at Thebes it is thick.* **locus ostenditur Capreīs,** Suet. *Tib.* 62, *the place is pointed out at Capreae.* Rarely with substantives of action (1301) : as, **mānsiō Formiīs,** *Att.* 9, 5, 1, *the stay at Formiae.* With an attribute : **Athēnīs tuīs,** *Att.* 16, 6, 2, *in your darling Athens.* **Curibus Sabīnīs,** L. 1, 18, 1, *at the Sabine Cures.*

1343. (2.) Singular proper names of towns with consonant stems are oftener put in the locative ablative than in the locative proper : as,

adulēscentium gregēs **Lacedaemone** vīdimus, *TD.* 5, 77, *we have seen the companies of young men in Lacedaemon.* **Karthāgine,** *Att.* 16, 4, 2, *at Carthage.* **Tibure,** H. *E.* 1, 8, 12, *at Tibur.* **Nārbōne,** *Ph.* 2, 76, *at Narbo.* See 1331. So also **Acherunte,** Lucr. 3, 984, *in Acheron.* **Calydōne et Naupāctō,** Caes. *C.* 3, 35, 1, *at Calydon and Naupactus,* with **Naupāctō** attracted by **Calydōne.** With an attribute : **Carthāgine Novā,** L. 28, 17, 11, *at New Carthage.* **Acherunte profundō,** Lucr. 3, 978, *in vasty Acheron.*

1344. (3.) A few general appellatives are used in the locative ablative without an attribute, especially in set expressions, to denote the place where : as,

terrā marīque, *IP.* 48, *by land and sea ;* less commonly marī atque terrā, S. *C.* 53, 2, *by sea and land.* dextrā Pīraeus, sinistrā Corinthus, Cael. in *Fam.* 4, 5, 4, *Piraeus on the right, Corinth on the left.* Rarely, rūre, Pl. *Cas.* 110, H. *E.* 1, 7, 1, *in the country,* for rūrī (1337). So animō, animīs, with verbs of feeling : as, angor animō, *Br.* 7, *I am distressed in soul,* or *I am heart-broken.* Metaphorically : locō, (*a.*) *in the right place,* also suō locō, or in locō. (*b.*) locō, *instead ;* numerō, *in the category,* both with a genitive. prīncipiō, initiō, *in the beginning.*

1345. Certain appellatives, with an attribute, often denote the place where by the locative ablative ; so especially locō, locīs, rūre, librō, librīs, parte, partibus : as, remōtō, salūbri, amoenō locō, *Fam.* 7, 20, 2, *in a sequestered, healthy, and picturesque nook.* idōneō locō, 3, 17, 5, *in an advantageous spot.* inīquō locō, 5, 51, 1, *on unsuitable ground.* campestribus ac dēmissīs locīs, 7, 72, 2, *in level and sunken places.* rūre meō, H. *E.* 1, 15, 17, *at my own country box.* rūre paternō, H. *E.* 1, 18, 60, J. 6, 55, *on the ancestral farm.* aliō librō, *Off.* 2, 31, *in another book.*

1346. Substantives are often used in the locative ablative with tōtus in agreement, less often with cūnctus, omnis, or medius, to denote the place where : as, tōta Galliā, 5, 55, 3, *all over Gaul.* tōtīs trepidātur castrīs, 6, 37, 6, *there is a panic all over the camp.* omnibus oppidīs, *V.* 2, 136, *in all the towns.* omnibus oppidīs maritimīs, Caes. *C.* 3, 5, 1, *in all the seaports.* mediā urbe, L. 1, 33, 8, *in the heart of Rome.* But sometimes in is used, or the accusative with per.

1347. (4.) With country names and most appellatives, the place where is generally expressed by the ablative with in. But even without an attribute, the ablative alone is sometimes used, especially in poetry : as,

Ītaliā, *V.* 1, 263, *in Italy,* lītore, *V.* 1, 184, *upon the beach,* corde, *V.* 1, 209, *in heart,* pectore, *V.* 1, 657, *in breast,* thalamō, H. 1, 15, 16, *in bower,* umerō, *V.* 1, 501, *on shoulder,* Ēsquiliīs, *DN.* 3, 63, *on the Esquiline.* Once in Plautus Ālide, *Cap.* 330, *in Elis,* but eight times in Ālide.

1348. The locative ablative is sometimes used with such verbs as teneō and recipiō : as, (*a.*) Ariovistus exercitum castrīs continuit, 1, 48, 4, *Ariovistus kept his infantry in camp.* oppidō sēsē continēbant, 2, 30, 2, *they kept inside the town.* (*b.*) oppidīs recipere, 2, 3, 3, *to receive inside their towns.* rēx ecquis est, qui senātōrem tēctō ac domō nōn invitet ? *V.* 4, 25, *is there a monarch in the wide world that would not welcome a senator to house and home ?*

1349. The locative ablative is used with **fīdō** and **cōnfīdō**, **glōrior**, **laetor**, **nītor**, **stō**, and with **frētus**: as, barbarī cōnfisī locī nātūrā in aciē permānsērunt, 8, 15, 1, *the natives, trusting in the nature of their position, kept their s and in battle array.* superiōribus victōriis frētī, 3, 21, 1, *relying on their former victories.* For other constructions with these words, see the dictionary.

Time at which or Time within which.

1350. (1.) The locative ablative is used to denote the point of time at which action occurs.

So particularly of substantives denoting periods or points of time, thus : hieme, 5, 1, 1, *in the winter.* Kalendīs, H. *Epod.* 2, 70, *upon the first,* i. e. of the month. Generally with an attribute: as, prīmō vēre, 6, 3, 4, *in the first month of spring.* Mārtiīs Kalendis, H. 3, 8, 1. *upon the first of March.* With a parallel locative (1341): vesperī eōdem diē, *Att.* 8, 5, 1, *the evening of the same day.*

1351. Words not in themselves denoting periods or points of time, are in the same way put in the ablative : as,

patrum nostrōrum memoriā, 1, 12, 5, *in the memory of our fathers.* nōn modo illīs Pūnicīs bellīs, sed etiam hāc praedōnum multitūdine, *V.* 4, 103, *not only in the Punic wars of yore, but also in the present swarm of pirates.* proxumīs comitiīs, 7, 67, 7, *at the last election.* spectāculīs, *Att.* 2, 19, 3, *at the shows.* Especially substantives of action in -tus or -sus (235): as, sōlis occāsū, 1, 50, 3, *at sunset.* adventū in Galliam Caesaris, 5, 54, 2, *at Caesar's arrival in Gaul.* eōrum adventū, 7, 65, 5, *after these people came.* discessū cēterōrum, *C.* 1, 7, *when the rest went away.*

1352. (2.) The locative ablative is used to denote the space of time within which action occurs : as,

paucīs diēbus opus efficitur, 6, 9, 4, *the job is finished up in a few days.* tribus hōris Aduātucam venīre potestis, 6, 35, 8, *in three hours you can get to Aduatuca.* quae hīc mōnstra fiunt, annō vix possum ēloquī, Pl. *Most.* 505, *what ghost-transactions take place here I scarce could tell you in a year.* cum ad oppidum Senonum Vellaunodūnum vēnisset, id bīduō circumvāllāvit, 7, 11, 1, *arriving at Vellaunodunum, a town of the Senons, in two days time he invested it.* quicquid est, bīduō sciēmus, *Att.* 9, 14, 2, *whatever it may be, we shall know in a couple of days.*

1353. The ablative of the time at or within which action occurs is sometimes accompanied by in : as, in bellō, 6, 1, 3, *in the war.* in tempore, T. *Hau.* 364, *in the nick of time.* in adulēscentiā, Pl. *B.* 410, *in my young days.* in tālī tempore, Lucr. 1, 93, L. 22, 35, 7, *in such a stress, at such an hour.* in hōc trīduō, Pl. *Ps.* 316, *within the next three days* Especially of repeated action, in the sense of *a* or *every,* with numerals: as, ter in annō, Pl. *B.* 1127, *RA.* 132, *three times a year.* in hōrā saepe ducentōs versūs dictābat, H. *S.* 1, 4, 9, *two hundred verses in an hour he'd often dictate off.* But occasionally without in : as, mē deciēns diē ūnō extrūdit aedibus, Pl. *Aul.* 70, *ten times a day he thrusts me from the house.* septiēns diē, L. 28, 6, 10, *seven times a day.*

1354. An ablative of the time within which action occurs is sometimes followed by a relative pronoun sentence, with the relative pronoun likewise in the ablative : as, **quadrīduō, quō haec gesta sunt, rēs ad Chrȳsogonum dēfertur,** *R A.* 20, *within the four days space in which this occurred, the incident is reported to Chrysogonus,* i. e. four days after this occurred. **diēbus decem, quibus māteria coepta erat conportārī, omnī opere effectō,** 4, 18, 1, *the job being all done ten days after the carting of the stuff had begun.*

1355. The ablative is exceptionally used to denote duration of time : as, **tōtā nocte continenter iērunt,** 1, 26, 5, *they went on and on all night without interruption.* Regularly, however, the accusative (1151); but the ablative is common in inscriptions.

III. THE INSTRUMENTAL ABLATIVE.

(A.) THE ABLATIVE OF ATTENDANCE.

THE ABLATIVE OF ACCOMPANIMENT.

1356. A few indefinite designations of military forces denote accompaniment by the ablative alone, or oftener with **cum**: as,

(*a.*) **ad castra Caesaris omnibus cōpiis contendērunt,** 2, 7, 3, *they marched upon Caesar's camp with all their forces.* **omnibus cōpiīs ad Ilerdam proficīscitur,** Caes. *C.* 1, 41, 2, *he marches before Ilerda, horse, foot, and dragoons.* (*b.*) **is cīvitātī persuāsit, ut cum omnibus cōpiīs exīrent,** 1, 2, 1, *well, this man induced the community to emigrate in a body, bag and baggage.*

1357. The participles **iūnctus** and **coniūnctus** take the ablative of the thing joined with: as, **dēfēnsiōne iūncta laudātiō,** *Br.* 162, *a eulogy combined with a defence.* But sometimes the ablative with **cum** is used, or the dative (1186).

THE ABLATIVE OF MANNER.

1358. (1.) Certain substantives without an attribute are put in the ablative alone to denote manner ; but usually substantives without an attribute have **cum.**

(*a.*) Such adverbial ablatives are **iūre** and **iniūriā, ratiōne et viā, silentiō, vitiō, ōrdine, sponte, cōnsuētūdine,** &c. : as, **Arātus iūre laudātur,** *Off.* 2, 81, *Aratus is justly admired.* **iniūriā suspectum,** *C.* 1, 17, *wrongfully suspected.* **in omnibus, quae ratiōne docentur et viā,** *O.* 116, *in everything that is taught with philosophic method.* **silentiō ēgressus,** 7, 58, 2, *going out in silence.* **cēnsōrēs vitiō creātī,** *L.* 6, 27, 5, *censors irregularly appointed.* **ōrdine cūncta ēxposuit,** *L.* 3, 50, 4, *he told the whole story from beginning to end,* i. e. with all the particulars. (*b.*) With **cum: face rem hanc cum cūrā gerās,** Pl. *Per.* 198, *see that this job with care thou dost.* **cum virtūte vīvere,** *Fin.* 3, 29, *to live virtuously.*

1359. (2.) The ablative of a substantive with an attribute is often used to denote manner, sometimes with **cum** : as, (*a*.) ī pede faustō, H. *E*. 2, 2, 37, *go with a blessing on thy foot,* dat sonitū magnō strāgem, Lucr. 1, 288, *it deals destruction with a mighty roar.* ferārum rītū sternuntur, L. 5, 44, 6, *they throw themselves down beast-fashion.* apis Matīnae mōre modōque operōsa carmina fingō, H. 4, 2, 27, *in way and wise of Matin bee laborious lays I mould.* 'indoctus' dīcimus brevī prīmā litterā, 'īnsānus' prōductā, 'inhūmānus' brevī, 'īnfēlīx' longā, *O.* 159, *we pronounce* indoctus *with the first letter short,* īnsānus *with it long,* inhūmānus *with it short,* īnfēlīx *with it long* (167). ternō cōnsurgunt ōrdine rēmī, V. 5, 120, *with triple bank each time in concert rise the oars.* (*b*.) Allobroges magnā cum cūrā suōs fīnēs tuentur, 7, 65, 3, *the Allobrogans guard their own territory with great care.*

1360. With a substantive meaning *way* or *manner,* as modō, rītū, &c., *feeling* or *intention,* as hāc mente, aequō animō, *condition,* as eā condiciōne, or a part of the body, as in nūdō capite, *bareheaded,* cum is not used.

1361. Other expressions denoting manner, particularly prepositional expressions with per, may be found in the dictionary : as, per dolum, 4, 13, 1, *by deceit,* per iocum, *Agr.* 2, 96, *in fun,* per litterās, *Att.* 5, 21, 13, *by letter, in writing,* per vim, *RA.* 32, *violently,* per praestigiās, *V.* 4, 53, *by some hocus pocus or other,* &c., &c. Sometimes the ablative with ex.

The Ablative Absolute.

1362. (1.) The ablative of a substantive, with a predicate participle in agreement, is used to denote an attendant circumstance of an action.

In this construction, which is called the *Ablative Absolute,* (*a*.) the present participle is sometimes used : as, nūllō hoste prohibente incolumem legiōnem in Nantuātīs perdūxit, 3, 6, 5, *with no enemy hindering, he conducted the legion in safety to the Nantuates.* Much oftener, however, (*b*.) the perfect participle : as, hōc respōnsō datō discessit, 1, 14, 7, *this answer given he went away.* (*c*.) The future participle is also used in the ablative absolute from Livy on : as, hospite ventūrō, cessābit nēmo tuōrum, J. 14, 59, *a visitor to come, your slaves will bustle each and all.*

1363. A predicate ablative with a participle meaning *made, kept, chosen,* or the like, occurs in Cicero, Caesar, Nepos, and Livy, but is rare (1167) : as, Dolābellā hoste dēcrētō, *Ph.* 11, 16, *Dolabella having been voted an enemy of the state.*

1364. The perfect participles of deponents used actively in the ablative absolute, are chiefly those of intransitive use, such as nātus, mortuus, ortus, profectus. From Sallust on, other perfect deponent participles also are used actively with an accusative. Cicero and Caesar use a few deponent participles, such as ēmeritus, pactus, partītus, dēpopulātus, as passives, and later authors use many other participles so.

1365. (2.) The ablative of a substantive, with a predicate noun in agreement, is often used to denote an attendant circumstance of an action : as,

brevitātem secūtus sum tē magistrō, *Fam.* 11, 25, 1, *I aimed at brevity with you as a teacher.* **nātus dīs inimicis**, Pl *Most.* 563, *born under wrath of gods.* **M. Messālā et M. Pīsōne cōnsulibus**, 1, 2, 1, *in the consulship of Messala and Piso.* **istō praetōre vēnit Syrācūsās**, *V.* 4, 61, *in the defendant's praetorship he came to Syracuse.*

1366. The nominative **quisque, plerīque**, or **ipse**, sometimes accompanies the ablative absolute: as, **causā ipse prō sē dictā, damnātur**, L. 4, 44, 10, *he is condemned after pleading his case in person.*

1367. The ablative absolute may denote in a loose way various relations which might be more distinctly expressed by subordinate sentences.

So particularly: (*a.*) Time: as, **tertiā initā vigiliā exercitum ēdūcit**, Caes. *C.* 3, 54, 2, *at the beginning of the third watch he leads the army out.* (*b.*) Cause or means: as, **C. Flāminium Caelius religiōne neglēctā cecidisse apud Trāsumēnum scrībit**, *DN.* 2, 8, *Caelius writes that Flaminius fell at Trasumene in consequence of his neglect of religious observances.* (*c.*) Concession: as, **id paucīs dēfendentibus expugnāre nōn potuit**, 2, 12, 2, *though the defenders were few, he could not take it by storm.* (*d.*) Hypothesis: as, **quae potest esse vitae iūcunditās sublātīs amīcitiīs?** *Pl.* 80, *what pleasure can there be in life, if you take friendships away?* (*e.*) Description: as, **domum vēnit capite obvolūtō**, *Ph.* 2, 77, *he came home with his head all muffled up.*

1368. It may be seen from the examples above that a change of construction is often desirable in translating the ablative absolute. Particularly so in many set idiomatic expressions: as, **nūllā interpositā morā**, Caes. *C.* 3, 75, 1, *without a moment's delay, instantly.* **equō admissō**, 1, 22, 2, **equō citātō**, Caes. *C.* 3, 96. 3, *full gallop.* **clāmōre sublātō**, 7, 12, 5, *with a round of cheers.* **bene rē gestā salvos redeō**, Pl. *Tri.* 1182, *crowned with success I come back safe and sound.*

1369. The substantive of the ablative absolute usually denotes a different person or thing from any in the main sentence. But exceptions to this usage sometimes occur: as,

quibus audītīs, eōs domum remittit, 4, 21, 6, *after listening to these men, he sends them home again.* **sī ego mē sciente paterer**, Pl. *MG.* 559, *if I should wittingly myself allow*, more emphatic than **sciēns**. **sē iūdice nēmo nocēns absolvitur**, J. 13, 2, *himself the judge, no criminal gets free.*

1370. Two ablatives absolute often occur together, of which the first indicates the time, circumstances, or cause of the second: as, **exaudītō clāmōre perturbātīs ōrdinibus**, 2, 11, 5, *the ranks being demoralized from hearing the shouts.* **cōnsūmptīs omnibus tēlīs gladiīs dēstrictīs**, Caes. *C.* 1, 46, 1, *drawing their swords after expending all their missiles.*

1371. The substantive is sometimes omitted in the ablative absolute, particularly when it is a general word for a person or a thing which is explained by a relative: as, **praemissīs, quī repūrgārent iter**, L. 44, 4, 11, *sending sappers and miners ahead to clear a way.* **relātīs ōrdine, quae vīdissent**, L. 42, 25, 2, *telling circumstantially all they had seen.*

1372. The ablative neuter of some perfect participles is used impersonally (1034). This use is rare in old Latin, in classical Latin commonest in Cicero, and afterwards in Livy: as, **auspicātō**, *DN.* 2, 11, *with auspices taken.* **sortītō**, *V.* 2, 126, *lots being drawn*, or *by lot.* Such ablatives readily become adverbs (704). Substantives are also sometimes used alone: as, **austrō**, *Div.* 2, 58, *when the wind is south.* **tranquillitāte**, Plin. *Ep.* 8, 20, 6, *when it is calm.* **serēnō**, L. 37, 3, 3, *the day being clear.*

1373. The ablative neuter of some perfect participles is occasionally used in agreement with a sentence or an infinitive: as, **cōgnitō vivere Ptolomaeum,** L. 33, 41, 5, *it being known that Ptolomy was alive.* This construction is not used in old Latin, and is rare in classical Latin, but common in Livy and Tacitus. So adjectives also: as, **incertō quid vitārent,** L. 28, 36, 12, *it not being obvious what they were to steer clear of.*

1374. The ablative absolute is sometimes attended, especially in Livy and Tacitus, by an explanatory word, such as **etsī, tamen, nisi, quasi, quamquam,** or **quamvīs :** as, **etsī aliquō acceptō dētrimentō, tamen summā exercitūs salvā,** Caes. C. 1, 67, 5, *though with some loss, yet with the safety of the army as a whole.*

THE ABLATIVE OF QUALITY.

1375. The ablative with an adjective in agreement or with a limiting genitive is used to denote quality, either predicatively or attributively : as,

(*a.*) Predicatively : **capillō sunt prōmissō,** 5, 14, 3, *they have long hair,* or *let their hair grow long.* **singulārī fuit industriā,** N. 24, 3, 1, *he had unparalleled activity.* **animō bonō 's,** Pl. *Aul.* 732, *be of good cheer.* **ad flūmen Genusum, quod ripīs erat impedītīs,** Caes. C. 3, 75, 4, *to the river Genusus, which had impracticable banks.* (*b.*) Attributively : **difficilī trānsitū flūmen ripīsque praeruptīs,** 6, 7, 5, *a river hard to cross and with steep banks.* **interfectus est C. Gracchus, clārissimō patre, avō, maiōribus,** C. 1, 4, *Gracchus was done to death, a man with an illustrious father, grandfather, and ancestors in general* (1044). **bōs cervī figūrā,** 6, 26, 1, *an ox with the shape of a stag.* Compare the genitive of quality (1239).

THE ABLATIVE OF THE ROUTE TAKEN.

1376. The instrumental ablative is used with verbs of motion to denote the route taken : as.

Aurēliā viā profectus est, C. 2, 6, *he has gone off by the Aurelia Road.* **omnibus viīs sēmitīsque essedāriōs ex silvīs ēmittēbat,** 5, 19, 2, *he kept sending his chariot men out by all possible highways and byways.* **hīs pontibus pābulātum mittēbat,** Caes. C. 1, 40, 1, *by these bridges he sent foraging.* **frūmentum Tiberī vēnit,** L. 2, 34, 5, *some grain came by the Tiber.* **lupus Ēsquilīnā portā ingressus per portam Capēnam prope intāctus ēvāserat,** L. 33, 26, 9, *a wolf that came in town by the Esquiline gate had got out through the Capene gate, almost unscathed.* This construction gives rise to some adverbs : see 707. The ablative of the route is sometimes used with a substantive of action (1301): as, **nāvigātiō īnferō,** *Att.* 9, 5, 1, *the cruise by the lower sea.* **eōdem flūmine invectiō,** *Fin.* 5, 70, *entrance by the same river.*

(B.) THE INSTRUMENTAL PROPER.

THE ABLATIVE OF INSTRUMENT OR MEANS.

1377. The ablative is used to denote the instrument or means : as, pugnābant armīs, H. *S.* 1, 3, 103, *they fought with arms.* **clārē oculīs videō, sum pernīx pedibus, manibus mōbilis,** Pl. *MG.* 630, *I can see distinctly with my eyes, I'm nimble with my legs, and active with my arms.* **iuvābō aut rē tē aut operā aut cōnsiliō bonō,** Pl. *Ps.* 19, *I'll help thee either with my purse or hand or good advice.* **lacte et carne vīvunt, pellibusque sunt vestītī,** 5, 14, 2, *they live on milk and meat, and they are clad in skins.* **contentus paucīs lēctōribus,** H. *S.* 1, 10, 74, *content with readers few.* **centēnāque arbore flūctum verberat,** V. 10, 207, *and with an hundred beams at every stroke the wave he smites.* Rarely with substantives denoting action (1301) : as, **gestōrēs linguīs, audītōrēs auribus,** Pl. *Ps.* 429, *reporters with their tongues and listeners with their ears.* **tenerīs labellīs mollēs morsiunculae,** Pl. *Ps.* 67ᵃ, *caressing bites with velvet lips.*

1378. When the instrument is a person, the accusative with **per** is used: as, **haec quoque per explōrātōrēs ad hostēs dēferuntur,** 6, 7, 9, *this too is reported to the enemy through the medium of scouts.* Or a circumlocution, such as **virtūte, beneficiō, benignitāte,** or especially **operā,** with a genitive or possessive; as, **deūm virtūte multa bona bene parta habēmus,** Pl. *Tri.* 346, *thanks to the gods, we've many a pretty penny prettily put by.* **meā operā Tarentum recēpistī,** *CM.* 11, *it was through me you got Tarentum back.* Rarely the ablative of a person, the person being then regarded as a thing: as, **iacent suīs testibus,** *Mil.* 47, *they are cast by their own witnesses.*

1379. The instrumental ablative is used with the five deponents **fruor, fungor, potior, ūtor, vēscor,** and several of their compounds, and with **ūsus est** and **opus est**: as,

pāce numquam fruēmur, *Ph.* 7, 19, *we never shall enjoy ourselves with peace,* i. e. *we never shall enjoy peace.* **fungar vice cōtis,** H. *AP.* 304, *I'll play the whetstone's part.* **castrīs nostrī potītī sunt,** 1, 26, 4, *our people made themselves masters of the camp.* **vestrā operā ūtar,** L. 3, 46, 8, *I will avail myself of your services.* **carne vēscor,** *TD.* 5, 90, *I live on meat.* **opust chlamyde,** Pl. *Ps.* 734, *there is a job with a cloak,* i. e. *we need a cloak.*

1380. Instead of the instrumental ablative, some of the above verbs take the accusative occasionally in old and post-Augustan Latin: thus, in Plautus, Terence, Latin, always **abūtor,** also **fungor,** except once in Terence; **fruor** in Cato and Terence, and **perfungor** in Lucretius, once each; **potior** twice in Plautus and three times in Terence, often also the genitive (1292). The gerundive of these verbs is commonly used personally in the passive, as if the verbs were regularly used transitively (2244).

1381. ūtor often has a second predicative ablative : as, **administrīs druidibus ūtuntur,** 6, 16, 2, *they use the druids as assistants.* **facilī mē ūtētur patre,** T. *Hau.* 217, *an easy-going father he will find in me.*

1382. ūsus est and **opus est** sometimes take a neuter participle, especially in old Latin : as, **vīsō opust cautōst opus,** Pl. *Cap.* 225, *there's need of sight, there's need of care.* Sometimes the ablative with a predicate participle : as, **celeriter mī eō homine conventōst opus,** Pl. *Cur.* 302, *I needs must see that man at once.*

1383. With **opus est**, the thing wanted is often made the subject nominative or subject accusative, with **opus** in the predicate: as, **dux nōbīs et auctor opus est,** *Fam.* 2, 6, 4, *we need a leader and adviser.* Usually so when the thing needed is a neuter adjective or neuter pronoun: as, **multa sibī opus esse,** *V.* 1, 126, *that he needed much.* A genitive dependent on **opus** is found once or twice in late Latin (1227).

1384. **ūsus est** is employed chiefly in comedy, but also once or twice in Cicero, Lucretius, Vergil, and Livy.   Once with the accusative: **ūsust hominem astūtum**, Pl. *Ps.* 385, *there's need of a sharp man.*

THE ABLATIVE OF SPECIFICATION.

1385. The instrumental ablative is used to denote that in respect of which an assertion or a term is to be taken: as,

temporibus errāstī, *Ph.* 2, 23, *you have slipped up in your chronology.* excellēbat āctiōne, *Br.* 215, *his forte lay in delivery.* Helvētiī reliquōs Gallōs virtūte praecēdunt, I, I, 4, *the Helvetians outdo the rest of the Kelts in bravery.* hī omnēs linguā, īnstitūtīs, lēgibus inter sē differunt, I, I, 2, *these people all differ from each other in language, usages, and laws.* sunt quīdam hominēs nōn rē sed nōmine, *Off.* I, 105, *some people are human beings not in reality but in name.* ūna Suēba nātiōne, altera Nōrica, I, 53, 4, *one woman a Suebe by birth, the other Noric.* vīcistis cochleam tarditūdine, Pl. *Poen.* 532, *you've beaten snail in slowness.* dēmēns iūdiciō volgī, *H. S.* I, 6, 97, *mad in the judgement of the world.* sapiunt meā sententiā, *T. Ph.* 335, *in my opinion they are wise.* meā quidem sententiā, *CM.* 56, *in my humble opinion.* quis iūre perītior commemorārī potest? *Clu.* 107, *who can be named that is better versed in the law?*

THE ABLATIVE OF FULNESS.

1386. The instrumental ablative is used with verbs of abounding, filling, and furnishing: as,

vīlla abundat porcō, haedō, āgnō, *CM.* 56, *the country place is running over with swine, kid, and lamb.* tōtum montem hominibus complērī iussit, I, 24, 3, *he gave orders for the whole mountain to be covered over with men.* Māgōnem poenā adfēcērunt, N. 23, 8, 2, *they visited Mago with punishment.* legiōnēs nimis pulcrīs armīs praeditās, Pl. *Am.* 218, *brigades in goodliest arms arrayed.* cōnsulārī imperiō praeditus, *Pis.* 55, *vested with the authority of consul.*   For the genitive with compleō and impleō, see 1293.

1387. The ablative is sometimes used with adjectives of fulness, instead of the regular genitive (1263). Thus, in later Latin, rarely with **plēnus**: as, **maxima quaeque domus servīs est plēna superbīs**, J. 5, 66, *a grand establishment is always full of stuck-up slaves.* **et ille quidem plēnus annīs abiit, plēnus honōribus**, Plin. *Ep.* 2, 1, 7, *well, as for him, he has passed away, full of years and full of honours.*   So in Cicero and Caesar, once each.   Also with **dīves** in poetry, and, from Livy on, in prose.   With **refertus**, the ablative of things is common, while persons are usually in the genitive (1263).   With **onustus**, the ablative is generally used, rarely the genitive.

THE ABLATIVE OF MEASURE, EXCHANGE, AND PRICE.

1388. The instrumental ablative is used with verbs of measuring and of exchanging, and in expressions of value and price: as, (*a.*) quod magnōs hominēs virtūte mētīmur, N. 18, 1, 1, *because we gauge great men by their merit.* (*b.*) nēmō nisi victor pāce bellum mūtāvit, S. *C.* 58, 15, *nobody except a conqueror has ever exchanged war for peace.* (*c.*) haec signa sēstertiūm sex mīllibus quingentīs esse vēndita, *V.* 4, 12, *that these statues were sold for sixty-five hundred sesterces.* aestimāvit dēnāriis III, *V.* 3, 214, *he valued it at three denars.* trīgintā mīllibus dīxistis eum habitāre, *Cael.* 17, *you have said he pays thirty thousand rent.* quod nōn opus est, āsse cārum est, Cato in Sen. *Ep.* 94, 28, *what you don't need, at a penny is dear.* hem, istūc verbum, mea voluptās, vīlest vīgintī minīs, Pl. *Most.* 297, *bless me, that compliment, my charmer, were at twenty minas cheap.*

1389. With mūtō and commūtō, the ablative usually denotes the thing received. But sometimes in Plautus, and especially in Horace, Livy, and late prose, it denotes the thing parted with : as, cūr valle permūtem Sabīnā dīvitiās operōsiōres? H. 3, 1, 47, *why change my Sabine dale for wealth that brings more care?* Similarly with cum in the prose of Cicero's age : as, mortem cum vītā commūtāre, Sulp. in *Fam.* 4, 5, 3, *to exchange life for death.*

1390. The ablative of price or value is thus used chiefly with verbs or verbal expressions of bargaining, buying or selling, hiring or letting, costing, being cheap or dear. Also with aestimō, of a definite price, and sometimes magnō, permagnō (1273).

1391. The ablatives thus used, are (*a.*) those of general substantives of value and price, such as pretium, (*b.*) numerical designations of money, or (*c.*) neuter adjectives of quantity, magnō, permagnō, quam plūrimō, parvō, minimō, nihilō, nōnnihilō : as, magnō decumās vēndidī, *V.* 3, 40, *I sold the tithes at a high figure.* For tantī and quantī, plūris and minōris, see 1274.

1392. The ablative is also used with dignus and indignus : as,

dignī maiōrum locō, *Agr.* 2, 1, *well worthy of the high standing of their ancestors.* nūlla vōx est audīta populī Rōmānī maiestāte indigna, 7, 17, 3, *not a word was heard out of keeping with the grandeur of Rome.* See also dignor in the dictionary. Similarly in Plautus with condignē, decōrus, decet, aequē, aequos. For the genitive with dignus, see 1269; for the accusative with dignus and a form of sum, 1144.

THE ABLATIVE OF THE AMOUNT OF DIFFERENCE.

1393. The instrumental ablative is used to denote the amount of difference.

This ablative is used with any words whatever of comparative or of superlative meaning : as, ūnō diē longiōrem mēnsem faciunt aut bīduō, *V.* 2, 129, *they make the month longer by a day, or even by two days.* ubī adbibit plūs paulō, T. *Hau.* 220, *when he has drunk a drop too much.* nummō dīvitior, Pl. *Ps.* 1323, *a penny richer.* bīduō post, 1, 47, 1, *two days after.* multīs ante diēbus. 7, 9, 4, *many days before.* paucīs ante diēbus, *C.* 3, 3, *a few days ago.* nimiō praestat, Pl. *B.* 396, *'t is ever so much better.* multō mālim, *Br.* 184, *I would much rather.* multō maxima pars, *C.* 4, 17, *the largest part by far.*

1394. In expressions of time, the accusative is sometimes us-d with post, less frequently with ante, as prepositions, instead of the ablative of difference : as, post paucōs diēs, L. 21, 51, 2, post diēs paucōs, L. 37, 13, 6, paucōs post diēs, L. 33, 39, 2, *after a few days.* paucōs ante diēs, L. 39, 28, 4, diēs ante paucōs, L. 31, 24, 5, *a few days before.* With this prepositional construction, ordinals are common : as, post diem tertium, 4, 9, 1, *after the third day*, according to the Roman way of reckoning, i. e. the next day but one.

1395. (1.) When the time before or after which anything occurs is denoted by a substantive, the substantive is put in the accusative with ante or post : as,

paulō ante tertiam vigiliam, 7, 24, 2, *a little before the third watch.* bīduō ante victōriam, *Fam.* 10, 14, 1, *the day but one before the victory.* paucīs diēbus post mortem Āfricānī, *L.* 3, *a few days after the death of Africanus.*

1396. Sometimes in late writers, as Tacitus, Pliny the younger, and Suetonius, a genitive is loosely used: as, sextum post clādis annum, Ta. 1, 62, i. e. sextō post clādem annō, *six years after the humiliating defeat.* post decimum mortis annum, Plin. *Ep.* 6, 10, 3, *ten years after his death.* Similarly intrā sextum adoptiōnis diem, Suet. *Galb.* 17, *not longer than six days after the adoption-day.*

1397. (2.) When the time before or after which anything occurs is denoted by a sentence, the sentence may be introduced :

(*a.*) By quam : as, post diem tertium gesta rēs est quam dīxerat, *Mil.* 44, *it took place two days after he said it.* With quam, post is sometimes omitted. Or (*b.*) less frequently by cum : as, quem trīduō, cum hās dabam litterās, exspectābam, Planc. in *Fam.* 10, 23, 3, *I am looking for him three days after this writing* (1601). For a relative pronoun sentence, see 1354.

1398. Verbs of surpassing sometimes have an accusative of extent (1151): as, mīrāmur hunc hominem tantum excellere cēterīs? *IP.* 39, *are we surprised that this man so far outshines everybody else?* With comparatives, the accusative is rare : as, aliquantum inīquior, T. *Hau.* 201, *somewhat too hard.* Similarly permultum ante, *Fam.* 3, 11, 1, *long long before.*

1399. In numerical designations of distance, the words intervāllum and spatium are regularly put in the ablative: as, rēx VI mīlium passuum intervāllō ā Saburrā cōnsēderat, Caes. *C.* 2, 38, 3, *the king had pitched six miles away from Saburra.* So sometimes mīlle : as, mīlibus passuum VI a Caesaris castrīs sub monte cōnsēdit, 1, 48, 1. See 1152.

TWO OR MORE ABLATIVES COMBINED.

1400. Two or more ablatives denoting different relations are often combined in the same sentence: as,

Menippus, meō iūdiciō (1385) tōtā Asiā (1346) illīs temporibus (1350) disertissimus, *Br.* 315, *Menippus, in my opinion the most gifted speaker of that day in all Asia.* hāc habitā ōrātiōne (1362) mīlitibus studiō (1316) pugnae ardentibus (1370) tubā (1377) sīgnum dedit, Caes. *C.* 3, 90, 4, *seeing that his soldiers were hot for battle after this speech, he gave the signal by trumpet.*

USE OF CASES WITH PREPOSITIONS.

1401. Two cases, the accusative and the ablative, are used with prepositions.

1402. Prepositions were originally adverbs which served to define more exactly the meaning of a verb.

Thus, endo, *in, on,* the older form of in, is an adverb, in an injunction occurring in a law of the Twelve Tables, 451 B.C., manum endo iacitō, *let him lay hand on.* Similarly, trāns, *over,* in trānsque datō, *and he must hand over,* i. e. trāditōque.

1403. In the course of time such adverbs became verbal prefixes; the verbs compounded with them may take the case, accusative or ablative, required by the meaning of the compound. Thus, amīcōs adeō, *I go to my friends* (1137); urbe exeō, *I go out of town* (1302).

1404. For distinctness or emphasis, the prefix of the verb may be repeated before the case: as, ad amīcōs adeō; ex urbe exeō. And when it is thus separately expressed before the case, it may be dropped from the verb: as, ad amīcōs eō; ex urbe eō.

1405. The preposition thus detached from the verb becomes an attendant on a substantive, and serves to show the relation of the substantive in a sentence more distinctly than the case alone could.

1406. A great many adverbs which are never used in composition with a verb likewise become prepositions: as, apud, circiter, īnfrā, iūxtā, pōne, propter, &c., &c. The inflected forms of substantives, prīdiē, postrīdiē (1413), tenus (1420), and fīnī (1419), are also sometimes used as prepositions. And vicem (1145), causā, grātiā, nōmine, ergō (1257), resemble prepositions closely in meaning.

1407. A trace of the original adverbial use of prepositions is sometimes retained, chiefly in poetry, when the prefix is separated from its word by what is called *Tmesis:* as, īre inque gredī, i. e. ingrediīque, Lucr. 4, 887, *to walk and to step off.* per mihī mīrum vīsum est, *DO.* 1, 214, *passing strange it seemed to me.*

1408. Even such words as are used almost exclusively as prepositions sometimes retain their original adverbial meaning also: as, adque adque, E. in Gell. 10, 29, 2, *and up and up, and on and on,* or *and nearer still and still more near.* occīsīs ad hominum mīlibus quattuor, 2, 33, 5, *about four thousand men being killed.* susque dēque, *Att.* 14, 6, 1, *up and down, topsy turvy, no matter how.*

1409. On the other hand, some verbal prefixes are never used as separate prepositions with a substantive. These are called *Inseparable Prepositions;* they are: amb-, *round,* an-, *up,* dis-, *in two,* por-, *towards,* rēd-, *back.* Usually also sēd-, *apart* (1417).

PREPOSITIONS USED WITH THE ACCUSATIVE.

1410. The accusative is accompanied by the following prepositions:

ad, *to*, adversus or adversum, *towards, against*, ante, in composition also antid-, *before*, apud, *near, at*, circā, circum, circiter, *round, about*, cis, citrā, *this side of*, contrā, *opposite to*, ergā, *towards*, extrā, *outside*, īnfrā, *below*, inter, *between*, intrā, *within*, iūxtā, *near*, ob, *against*, penes, *in the possession of*, per, *through*, pōne, post, in Plautus postid, poste, pos, *behind*, praeter, *past*, prope (propius, proximē), propter, *near*, secundum, *after*, subter, *under*, suprā, *above*, trāns, *across*, uls, ultrā, *beyond*. For the various shades of meaning and applications of these prepositions, see the dictionary.

1411. Prepositions which accompany the accusative may be easily remembered in this order:

> ante, apud, ad, adversum,
>
> circum, cis, ob, trāns, secundum,
>
> penes, pōne, prope, per,
>
> post, and all in -ā and -ter.

1412. Of the above named words some are not used as prepositions till a relatively late period.

Thus, īnfrā is first used as a preposition by Terence and once only; circā somewhat before and citrā about Cicero's time; ultrā first by Cato; iūxtā by Varro. In Cicero iūxtā is still used only as an adverb, in Caesar and Nepos as a preposition.

1413. The substantive forms prīdiē, *the day before*, and postrīdiē, *the day after*, are sometimes used with an accusative like prepositions, mostly in Cicero, to denote dates: as, prīdiē nōnās Māiās, *Att.* 2, 11, 2, *the day before the nones of May*, i. e. *6 May.* postrīdiē lūdōs Apollinārīs, *Att.* 16, 4. 1, *the day after the games of Apollo*, i. e. *6 July.* For the genitive with these words, see 1232.

1414. The adverb vorsus or versus, *wards*, occurs as a post positive (1434) preposition rarely: once in Sallust, Aegyptum vorsus, J. 19, 3, *Egyptwards*, in Cicero a few times, twice in Pliny the elder. usque, *even to*, occurs with names of towns in Terence (once), Cicero, and later; with appellatives in Cato (once) and late writers.

1415. clam, *secretly*, is ordinarily an adverb. But in old Latin it is used often as a preposition, *unknown to*, with an accusative of a person. Terence has once the diminutive form clanculum, *Ad.* 52. With the ablative only in the MSS. of Caesar, once, clam vōbīs, *C.* 2, 32, 8, *without your knowledge*, and in *Bell. Afr.* 11, 4.

1416. subter, *under*, is used in poetry, once by Catullus and once by Vergil, with the locative ablative: as, Rhoetēō subter lītore, Cat. 65, 7, *beneath Rhoeteum's strand*.

PREPOSITIONS USED WITH THE ABLATIVE.

1417. The ablative is accompanied by the following prepositions:

abs, ab, or ā, *from*, cōram, *face to face*, dē, *down from, from, of*, ex or ē, *out of*, prae, *at the fore, in front of*, prō, *before*, quom or cum, *with*, sine, *without*. In official or legal language, also sēd or sē, *without*. For the different classes of ablatives with these prepositions, see 1297–1300; for the various shades of meanings and applications, see the dictionary.

1418. Prepositions which accompany the ablative may be easily remembered in this order:

abs (ab, ā), **c**um, cōram, dē,
prae, prō, sine, ex (or ē).

1419. The ablative **fīnī**, *as far as*, is used in old Latin as a preposition with the ablative: as, **osse fīnī**, Pl. *Men.* 859, *down to the bone.* **operitō terrā rādīcibus fīnī**, Cato, *RR.* 28, 2, *cover with loam the length of the roots.* Also, as a real substantive, with a genitive (1255): as, **ānsārum īnfimārum fīnī**, Cato, *RR.* 113, 2, *up to the bottom of the handles.* Rarely **fīne**, and before the genitive: as, **fīne genūs**, O. 10, 537, *as far as the knee.*

1420. **tenus**, *the length*, was originally a substantive accusative (1151). From Cicero on, it is used as a preposition with the ablative, and standing after its case: as, **Taurō tenus**, *D.* 36, *not further than Taurus.* **pectoribus tenus**, L. 21, 54, 9, *quite up to the breast.* **hāctenus**, *thus far, only thus far.* Also, as a real substantive, with a genitive, usually a plural, mostly in verse (1232): as, **labrōrum tenus**, Lucr. 1, 940, *the length of the lips, up to the lips.* **Cūmārum tenus**, Cael. in *Fam.* 8, 1, 2, *as far as Cumae.*

1421. The adverbs **palam**, *in presence of*, **procul**, *apart from*, either *near* or *far*, **simul**, *with*, are rarely used in poetry and late prose as prepositions with the ablative. **coram** occurs but once as a preposition (inscriptional) before Cicero's time. **absque** with the ablative occurs once each in Cicero and Quintilian; in Plautus and Terence only in a coordinate protasis (1701; 2110).

PREPOSITIONS USED WITH THE ACCUSATIVE OR THE ABLATIVE.

1422. Two cases, the accusative and the ablative, are accompanied by the prepositions **in**, older **endo, indu**, *into, in*, **sub**, *under*, and **super**, *over, on.*

1423. (1.) **in** and **sub** accompany the accusative of the end of motion, the locative ablative of rest: as,

(a.) **in cūriam vēnimus**, *V.* 4, 138, *we went to the senate-house.* **in vincla coniectus est**, *V.* 5, 17, *he was put in irons.* **hīc pāgus eius exercitum sub iugum mīserat**, 1, 12, 5, *this canton had sent his army under the yoke.* (b.) **erimus in castrīs**, *Ph.* 12, 28, *we shall be in camp.* **viridī membra sub arbutō strātus**, H. 1, 1, 21, *stretched out — his limbs — all under an arbute green.*

1424. Verbs of rest sometimes have **in** with the accusative, because of an implied idea of motion. And, conversely, verbs of motion sometimes have **in** with the ablative, because of an implied idea of rest: as,

(a.) **mihi in mentem fuit**, Pl. *Am.* 180, *it popped into my head*, i. e. came in and is in (compare **venit hoc mī in mentem**, Pl. *Aul.* 226. **in eius potestātem venīre nōlēbant**, *V.* 1, 150. **in eōrum potestātem portum futūrum intellegēbant**, *V.* 5, 98, *they knew full well the haven would get under the control of these people*). (b.) **Caesar exercitum in hībernīs conlocāvit**, 3, 29, 3, *Caesar put the army away in winter quarters*, i. e. put them into and left them in. **eam in lectō conlocārunt**, T. *Eu.* 593, *they laid the lady on her couch.* So commonly with **locō**. **conlocō, statuō, cōnstituō, pōnō**, and its compounds. For **expōnō** and **impōnō**, see the dictionary.

1425. (2.) **super** accompanies the ablative when it has colloquially the sense of dē, *about, in reference to :* as, hāc super rē scrībam ad tē Rēgiō, *Att.* 16, 6, 1, *I'll write you about this from Regium.* In other senses, the accusative, but somet.mes in poetry the ablative, chiefly in the sense of *on :* as, lĭgna super focō large repōnēns, H. 1, 9, 5, *piling on hearth the faggots high.* nocte super mediā, V. 9, 61, *at dead of night.* paulum silvae super hīs, H. *S.* 2, 6, 3, *a bit of wood to crown the whole.*

COMBINATION OF SUBSTANTIVES BY A PREPOSITION.

1426. (1.) Two substantives are sometimes connected by a preposition, to indicate certain attributive relations (1043) ; such are particularly :

(*a.*) Place : as, illam pugnam nāvālem ad Tenedum, *Mur.* 33, *the sea-fight off Tenedus.* excessum ē vītā, *Fin.* 3, 60, *the departure from life.* (*b.*) Source, origin, material : as, ex Aethiopiā ancillulam, T. *Eu.* 165, *a lady's maid from Aethiopia.* pōcula cx aurō, *V.* 4, 62, *bowls of gold* (1314). (*c.*) Direction of action, connection, separation : as, amor in patriam, *Fl.* 103, *love of country.* vestra ergā mē voluntās, *C.* 4, 1, *your good will towards me.* proelium cum Tūscīs ad Iāniculum, 1. 2, 52, 7, *the battle with the Tuscans at Janiculum.* vir sine metū, *TD.* 5, 48, *a man devoid of fear* (1043).

1427. (2.) Very commonly, however, other constructions are used, even to indicate the relations above : as,

bellum Venetōrum, 3, 16, 1, *war with the Venetans* (1231). bellō Cassiānō, 1, 13, 2, *in the war with Cassius* (1233). in aureīs pōculīs, *V.* 4, 54, *in golden bowls* (1233). scūtīs ex cortice factīs, 2, 33, 2, *with long shields made out of bark* (1314). post victōriam eius bellī, quod cum Persīs fuit, *Off.* 3, 49, *after the victory in the war with the Persians.*

1428. Prepositional expressions are sometimes used predicatively : as, sunt omnēs sine maculā, *Pl.* 6, 14, *they are all without spot or blemish.* And sometimes they are equivalent to adjectives : as, contrā nātūram, *TD.* 4, 11, *unnatural,* suprā hominem, *DN.* 2, 34, *superhuman.* Or to substantives : as, sine pondere, *O.* 1, 20, *things without weight.* Or to adverbs : as, sine labōre, Pl. *R.* 461, *easily.*

REPETITION OR OMISSION OF A PREPOSITION WITH SEVERAL SUBSTANTIVES.

1429. (1) A preposition is often repeated with emphasis before two or more substantives : as,

in labōre atque in dolōre, Pl. *Ps.* 685, *in toil and in trouble.* Particularly so with et . . . et, aut . . . aut, nōn sōlum . . . sed etiam, nōn minus . . . quam, &c., &c : as, et ex urbe et ex agrīs, *C.* 2, 21, *from Rome ana from the country too.*

1430. (2.) A preposition is often used with the first only of two or more substantives : as, in labōre ac dolōre, *TD.* 5, 41, *in toil and trouble.* incidit in eandem invidiam quam pater suus, N. 5, 3, 1, *he fell under the selfsame ban as his father.* Particularly when the second is in apposition : as, cum duōbus ducibus, Pyrrhō et Hannibale, *L.* 28, *with two commanders, Pyrrhus and Hannibal.*

Two Prepositions with one Substantive.

1431. (1.) When two prepositions belong to one and the same substantive, the substantive is expressed with the first. With the second, the substantive is repeated, or its place is taken by a pronoun : as,

contrā lēgem prōque lēge, L. 34, 8, 1, *against the law and for the law.* partim contrā Avītum, partim prō hōc, *Clu.* 88, *partly against Avitus, partly for him.* If, however, the two prepositions accompany the same case, the substantive need not be repeated : as, intrā extrāque mūnītiōnēs, Caes. *C.* 3, 72, 2, *inside and outside the works.*

1432. (2.) The second preposition is often used adverbially, without any substantive: as, et in corpore et extrā, *Fin.* 2, 68, *both in the body and outside.*

Position of Prepositions.

1433. In general a preposition precedes its case : see 178.

1434. Disyllabic prepositions sometimes follow their substantives. Thus, in Cicero, contrā, ultrā, and sine, sometimes stand after a relative; so likewise inter in Cicero, Caesar, and Sallust ; occasionally also penes and propter. For versus, see 1414 ; for fīnī, 1419; for tenus, 1420.

1435. Of monosyllables, ad and dē often follow a relative. Also cum often in Cicero and Sallust, and regularly in Caesar. With a personal or a reflexive pronoun, cum regularly follows, as mēcum, nōbīscum, sēcum.

1436. In poetry and late prose, prepositions are freely put after their cases.

1437. In oaths and adjurations, per is often separated from its proper accusative by the accusative of the object : as, per tē deōs ōrō, T. *Andr.* 538, *I beg thee by the gods, in the gods' name.*

USE OF ADVERBS.

1438. Adverbs qualify verbs, adjectives, or adverbs.

(*a.*) With verbs, all sorts of adverbs are used : as, of Place : quis istīc habet? Pl. *B.* 114, *who lives in there?* Time : tum dentēs mihi cadēbant prīmulum, Pl. *Men.* 1116, *my teeth were just beginning then to go.* Number : bis cōnsul fuerat P. Āfricānus, *Mur.* 58, *Africanus had twice been consul.* Degree, Amount : Ubiī magnopere ōrābant, 4, 16, 5, *the Ubians earnestly entreated.* Dumnorīx plūrimum poterat, 1, 9, 3, *Dumnorix was all-powerful.* Manner : bene quiēvit, libenter cibum sūmpsit, Plin. *Ep.* 3, 16, 4, *he has slept beautifully, he has relished his food.* (*b.*) With adjectives and adverbs, oftenest adverbs of degree or amount only, or their equivalents, such as bene, ēgregiē, &c. : as, valdē dīligēns, *Ac.* 2, 98, *very particular.* ēgregiē fortis, *DO.* 2, 268, *exceptionally brave.* Adverbs of manner, however, are also used, especially in poetry : as, turpiter hīrtum, H. *E.* 1, 3, 22, *disreputably rough,* i. e. disreputable and rough.

1439. An adverb is sometimes used with the meaning of an adjective : as,

reliquīs deincēps diēbus, 3, 29, 1, *the remaining successive days.* dē suīs prīvātim rēbus, 5, 3, 5, *in relation to their personal interests.* undique silvae, Plin. *Ep.* 1, 6, 2, *the surrounding woods.* Particularly when the substantive expresses character, like an adjective : as, vērē Metellus, *Sest.* 130, *a trueblooded Metellus.* rūsticānus vir, sed plānē vir, *TD.* 2, 53, *a country man, but every inch a man.*

1440. Perfect participles used as substantives are commonly qualified by an adverb, and not by an adjective. Particularly so dictum, factum, inventum, respōnsum, with bene and male, and their synonymes : as, rēctē ac turpiter factum, 7, 80, 5, *heroism and cowardice.* bene facta male locāta male facta arbitror, E. in *Off.* 2, 62, *good deeds ill put, bad deeds I count.* In superlative qualifications, however, the adjective is preferred.

1441. Other substantives also may be qualified by an adverb, when a verb construction or a participle is implied : as, C. Flāminius cōnsul iterum, *Div.* 1, 77, *Flaminius in his second consulship.* ō totiēns servos, H. *S.* 2, 7, 70, *time and again a slave.* ictū comminus, *Caecin.* 43, *by a hand-to-hand blow.* pūblicē testem, *V.* 2, 156, *a government witness.* populum lātē rēgem, *V.* 1, 21, *a nation regnant wide.* lātē tyrannus, H. 3, 17, 9, *lord paramount far and near.*

1442. An adverb sometimes takes the place of a substantive : as, cum amīcī partim dēseruerint mē, partim etiam prōdiderint, *QFr.* 1, 3, 5, *since my friends have some of them abandoned me, and others again have actually betrayed me,* i. e. aliī . . . aliī. postquam satis tūta circā vidēbantur, L. 1, 58, 2, *finding every thing round about looked pretty safe,* i. e. quae circā erant. palam laudārēs, sēcrēta male audiēbant, Ta. *H.* 1, 10, *his outward walk you would have admired; his private life was in bad odour,* i. e. quae palam fīēbant.

NEGATIVE ADVERBS.

1443. (1.) The negative oftenest used in declaration or interrogation is nōn, *not :* as,

nōn metuō mihi, Pl. *B.* 225, *I fear not for myself.* nōn semper imbrēs nūbibus hīspidōs mānant in agrōs, H. 2, 9, 1, *not always from the clouds do showers on stubbly fields come dripping dropping down.* nōn dīcēs hodiē? H. *S.* 2, 7, 21, *will you not say without delay ?*

1444. nōn is a modification of noenum or noenu, compounded of ne, *no,* and the accusative oinom or oenum, the older form of ūnum, *one thing.* noenum occurs in Plautus twice, in Ennius, Lucilius, Afranius, and Varro, once each, and noenu occurs twice in Lucretius (99).

1445. Negation is often expressed by other compounds of ne. In such cases the Latin idiom frequently differs from the English, and a transfer of the negative is required in translation.

Such compounds are : (*a.*) Verbs, such as negō, nequeō, nesciō, nōlō : as, negat vērum esse, *Mur.* 74, *he maintains it is not true.* (*b.*) Nouns, such as nēmō, neuter, nūllus, nihil : as, nēminī meus adventus labōrī fuit, *V.* 1, 16, *my visit did not trouble anybody.* (*c.*) Adverbs, such as numquam, nusquam. (*d.*) Similarly, the conjunction neque is used for *and not, but not,* unless a single word is to be emphasized or contrasted : as, nec frūstrā, 8, 5, 3, *and not in vain.*

245

1446. A form **nec** is used rarely in old Latin in the sense of **nōn** : as, **tū dīs nec rēctē dīcis**, Pl. *B.* 119, *thou dost abuse the gods*, i. e. **nōn rēctē** or **male dīcis**. After Plautus's time, **nec** for **nōn** occurs in a few set combinations, such as **nec opīnāns**, *not expecting*, and, from Livy on, **necdum**, *not yet*, i. e. **nōndum**.

1447. The form **nē** usually introduces an imperative or a subjunctive, as will be explained further on. But **nē** is also used in the combination **nē . . . quidem**, *not even*, *not . . . either*, with the emphatic word between **nē** and **quidem** : as, **nē tum quidem**, 1, 50, 2, *not even then*. **nē Vorēnus quidem sēsē vāllō continet**, 5, 44, 6, *Vorenus did not keep inside the palisade either*.

1448. The adjective **nūllus** is sometimes used, chiefly in colloquial language, for **nōn** or **nē** (1051): as, **Philotimus nūllus vēnit**, *Att.* 11, 24, 4, *no Philotimus has shown himself*. **nūllus crēduās**, Pl. *Tri.* 606, *you needn't believe it at all*.

1449. (2.) The negative **haut** or **haud**, *not*, is used principally with adjectives and adverbs, less frequently with verbs : as,

(*a.*) **haud mediocris vir**, *RP.* 2, 55, *no ordinary man*. **rem haud sānē difficilem**, *CM.* 4, *a thing not particularly hard*. **haud procul**, *CM.* 15, *not far*. In all periods of the language often combined with **quisquam**, **ūllus**, **umquam**, **usquam**. (*b.*) In old Latin **haud** is freely used with all sorts of verbs, especially with **possum**. In Cicero, it occurs here and there with a few verbs, such as **adsentior, errō, īgnōrō, nītor, amō**, but is principally confined to **sciō**, in the combination **haud sciō an**, *I don't know but* (**1782**). Caesar uses **haud** once only, and then in this combination.

1450. A shorter form, **hau**, occurs often in old Latin, and a few times in the classical period : as, **heic est sepulcrum hau pulcrum pulcrai fēminae**, CIL. I, 1007, 2, on the burial site of a woman, *here is the site not sightly of a sightly dame*. In Plautus it is juxtaposed with **sciō**, making **hausciō**, i. e. **nesciō**.

1451. (3.) Negation may also be intimated by such words as **vix**, *hardly*, **parum**, *not . . . enough, not quite*, **minus**, *less, not*, **minimē**, *least of all*, **male**, &c.

1452. Two negatives in the same sentence are usually equivalent to an affirmative.

Thus, with **nōn** first, an indefinite affirmative : as, **nōn nēmō**, *somebody, a certain gentleman, one or another*. **nōn nūllus**, *some*. **nōn nihil**, *something, somewhat*. **nōn numquam**, *sometimes*. With **nōn** second, a universal affirmative : as, **nēmō nōn**, *everybody, every human being*. **nūllus nōn**, *every*. **nihil nōn**, *every thing*. **numquam nōn**, *always*. **nōn possum nōn cōnfitērī**, *Fam.* 9, 14, 1, *I must confess*. **nēmō īgnōrat**, *V.* 2, 111, *everybody knows*.

1453. Sometimes, however, in old Latin, a second negation is used merely to emphasize the negative idea : as, **lapideō sunt corde multī, quōs nōn miseret nēminis**, E. in Fest. p. 162, *there's many a man with heart of stone, that feels for nobody*. For doubled negatives in compound sentences, see 1660.

USE OF DEGREES OF COMPARISON.

THE POSITIVE.

1454. The positive sometimes expresses an idea of disproportion : as,

prō multitūdine hominum angustōs sē fīnīs habēre arbitrābantur, 1, 2, 5, *in view of their large numbers they thought they had a cramped place to live in*. Generally, however, disproportion is expressed as in 1460 or 1461.

THE COMPARATIVE.

1455. When two things only are compared, the comparative is used : as,

uter igitur melior ? *Div.* 2, 133, *which of the two then is the better?* uter est īnsānior hōrum ? H. *S.* 2, 3, 102, *which of these two is crazier?* uter erātis, tūn an ille, maior ? Pl. *Men.* 1119, *you were — which of the two the bigger, thou or he?*

1456. The superlative is sometimes loosely used when only two things are meant : as, Numitōrī, quī stirpis maximus erat, rēgnum lēgat, L. 1, 3, 10, *to Numitor, who was the eldest of the family, he bequeaths the crown,* of two brothers, Numitor and Amulius. id meā minumē rēfert, quī sum nātū maximus, T. *Ad.* 881, *that is of small concern to me, who am the eldest son,* says Demea, who has only one brother.

1457. From Cicero on, an adjective or adverb is sometimes compared with another adjective or adverb. In such comparisons **quam** is always used.

In this case : (*a.*) Both members may have the positive form, the first with **magis** : as, Celer disertus magis est quam sapiēns, *Att.* 10, 1, 4, *Celer is more eloquent than wise.* magis audācter quam parātē, *Br.* 241, *with more assurance than preparation.* Or (*b*) Both members may have the comparative suffix : as, lubentius quam vērius, *Mil.* 78, *with greater satisfaction than truth.* pestilentia minācior quam perniciōsior, L. 4, 52, 3, *a plague more alarming than destructive.*

1458. But sometimes the second member is put in the positive, even when the first has the comparative suffix : as, ācrius quam cōnsīderātē, Ta. *H.* 1, 83, *with more spirit than deliberation.* And sometimes both members : as, clārīs maiōribus quam vetustīs, Ta. 4, 61, *of a house famous rather than ancient.*

1459. The comparative may be modified by ablatives of difference, such as multō, *far,* aliquantō, *considerably,* paullō or paulō, *a little,* nimiō, *too much, ever so much* (1393). Also by etiam, *even, still,* and in Catullus, Sallust, Vergil, and later Latin by longē, *far,* adhūc, *still.*

1460. The comparative of an adjective or adverb often denotes that which is more than usual or more than is right : as,

solēre aiunt rēgēs Persārum plūrēs uxōrēs habēre, *V.* 3, 76, *they say the Persian kings generally have several wives.* senectūs est nātūrā loquācior, *CM.* 55, *age is naturally rather garrulous.* stomachābātur senex, sī quid asperius dīxeram, *DN.* 1, 93, *the old gentleman always got provoked if I said anything a bit rough.*

1461. The comparative of disproportion is often defined by some added expression : as,

prīvātīs maiōra focīs, J. 4. 66, *something too great for private hearths* (1321). flāgrantior aequō nōn dēbet dolor esse virī, J. 13, 11, *the indignation of a man must not be over hot* (1330). In Livy and Tacitus by quam prō with the ablative : see the dictionary. Sometimes a new sentence is added : as, sum avidior, quam satis est, glōriae, *Fam.* 9, 14, 2, *I am over greedy of glory.* For **quam ut** or **quam quī,** see 1896.

1462. The comparative with a sentence of negative import is often preferred to the superlative with a positive sentence: as,

elephantō bēluārum nūlla prūdentior, *DN.* 1, 97, *of the larger beasts not one is more sagacious than the elephant,* or *the elephant is the most sagacious of beasts.* **sequāmur Polybium, quō nēmō fuit dīligentior,** *RP.* 2, 27, *let us follow Polybius, the most scrupulous of men.* For **nēmō** or **quis,** the more emphatic **nihil** or **quid** is often used: as, **Phaedrō nihil ēlegantius, nihil hūmānius,** *DN.* 1, 93, *Phaedrus was the most refined and sympathetic of men.*

1463. In colloquial language, a comparative suffix is sometimes emphasized by the addition of **magis**: as, **mollior magis,** Pl. *Aul.* 422, *more tenderer.* And sometimes by a mixture of construction, the comparative is modified by **aequē,** like the positive: as, **homo mē miserior nūllus est aequē,** Pl. *Mer.* 335, *there's not a man so woebegone as I,* for **miserior** alone, or **aequē miser.**

1464. The comparative with the ablative is particularly common, when a thing is illustrated by some striking typical object, usually an object of nature. In such illustrations, the positive with *as* is commonly used in English: as, **lūce clārius,** *V.* 2, 186, *plain as day.* **ō fōns Bandusiae, splendidior vitrō,** H. 3, 13, 1, *ye waters of Bandusia, as glittering as glass.* **melle dulcior ōrātiō,** E. in *CM.* 31, *words sweet as honey.* **ventīs ōcior,** *V.* 5, 319, *quick as the winds.* **vacca candidior nivibus,** O. *Am.* 3, 5, 10, *a cow as white as driven snow.* **caelum pice nigrius,** O. *H.* 17, 7, *a sky as black as pitch.* **dūrior ferrō et saxō,** O. 14, 712, *as hard as steel and stone.*

THE SUPERLATIVE.

1465. When more than two things are compared, the superlative is used to represent a quality as belonging in the highest degree to an individual or to a number of a class: as,

proximī sunt Germānīs, 1, 1, 3, *they live the nearest to the Germans.* **hōrum omnium fortissimī,** 1, 1, 3, *the bravest of these all.*

1466. The superlative may be strengthened by the addition of such words as **ūnus,** *preeminently,* usually with a genitive, **maximē, quam,** with or without a form of **possum,** *as possible,* &c., &c. (1892). In old Latin by **multō;** from Cicero on, by **longē,** *far,* and **vel,** *perhaps, even:* as,

cōnfirmāverim rem ūnam esse omnium difficillimam, *Br.* 25, *I am not afraid to avouch it is the one hardest thing in the world.* **longē nōbilissimus,** 1, 2, 1, *the man of highest birth by far.* **quam maximīs potest itineribus in Galliam contendit,** 1, 7, 1, *he pushes into Gaul by the quickest marches he can.* **quam mātūrrimē,** 1, 33, 4, *as early as possible.*

1467. The superlative is also used to denote a very high degree of the quality.

This superlative, called the *Absolute Superlative,* or the *Superlative of Eminence,* may be translated by the positive with some such word as *most, very:* as, **homo turpissimus,** *V.* 4, 16, *an utterly unprincipled man.* Often best by the positive alone: as, **vir fortissimus, Pīsō Aquītānus,** 4, 12, 4, *the heroic Piso of Aquitain* (1044).

1468. In exaggerated style, the superlative of eminence may be capped by a comparative: as, **stultior stultissumō,** Pl. *Am.* 907, *a greater than the greatest fool.* **ego miserior sum quam tū, quae es miserrima,** *Fam.* 14, 3, 1, *I am myself more unhappy than you, who are a most unhappy woman.*

(B.) USE OF THE VERB.

VOICE.

THE ACTIVE VOICE.

1469. In the active voice, the subject is represented as performing the action of the verb.

1470. By action is meant the operation of any verb, whether active or passive, and whether used intransitively or transitively.

1471. The active of one verb sometimes serves as the passive of another: thus, **pereō,** *go to destruction, die,* serves as the passive of **perdō,** *destroy,* and **vēneō,** *go to sale, am sold,* as the passive of **vēndō,** *put for sale, sell.* Similarly **fīō,** *become, get to be, am made,* is used in the present system as the passive of **faciō,** *make* (788).

THE PASSIVE VOICE.

1472. In the passive voice, the subject is represented as acted upon.

1473. The object accusative of the active voice becomes the subject of the passive voice (1125); and the predicate accusative of the active voice becomes a predicate nominative with the passive voice (1167).

Thus (*a.*) in the active construction: **illum laudābunt bonī, hunc etiam ipsī culpābunt malī,** Pl. *B.* 397, *the one the good will praise, the other e'en the bad themselves will blame.* In the passive: **laudātur ab hīs, culpātur ab illīs,** H. *S.* 1, 2, 11, *he's praised by some, by others blamed.* Active: **cīvēs Rōmānōs interficiunt,** 7, 3, 1, *they slay some citizens of Rome.* Passive: **Indutiomarus interficitur,** 5, 58, 6, *Indutiomarus is slain.* (*b.*) Active: **mīlitēs certiōrēs facit,** 3, 5, 3, *he informs the soldiers.* Passive: **certior factus est,** 2, 34, *he was informed.*

1474. Verbs which have two accusatives, one of the person and one of the thing in the active voice, generally have the person as subject in the passive, less frequently the thing: see 1171.

1475. An emphasizing or defining accusative, or an accusative of extent or duration, is occasionally made the subject of a passive: as,

haec illīc est pugnāta pugna, Pl. *Am.* 253, *this fight was fought off there* (1140). **tōta mihī dormītur hiems,** Mart. 13, 59, 1, *all winter long by me is slept,* i. e. **tōtam dormiō hiemem** (1151).

1476. The person by whom the action is done is put in the ablative with **ab** or **ā** (1318) ; the thing by which it is done is put in the instrumental ablative (1377) ; as,

(*a.*) nōn numquam latrō ā viātōre occīditur, *Mil.* 55, *once in a while the robber gets killed by the wayfarer.* respondit, ā cīve sē spoliārī mālle quam ab hoste vēnīre, Quintil. 12, 1, 43, *he said in reply that he would rather be plundered by a Roman than sold by an enemy* (1471). (*b.*) ūnīus virī prūdentiā Graecia līberāta est, N. 2, 5, 3, *Greece was saved from slavery by the sagacity of a single man,* i. e. Themistocles. Very often, however, the person or thing is not expressed, particularly with impersonals.

1477. When the person is represented as a mere instrument, the ablative is used without **ab** (1378) ; and when collectives, animals, or things without life are personified, the ablative takes **ab** (1318) : as,

(*a.*) neque vērō minus Platō dēlectātus est Diōne, N. 10, 2, 3, *and Plato on his part was just as much bewitched with Dion.* (*b.*) eius ōrātiō ā multitūdine et ā forō dēvorābātur, *Br.* 283, *his oratory was swallowed whole by the untutored many and by the bar.*

1478. Sometimes the person by whom the action is done is indicated by the dative of the possessor : see 1216. And regularly with the gerund and gerundive construction (2243).

1479. Only verbs of transitive use have ordinarily a complete passive. Verbs of intransitive use have only the impersonal forms of the passive (1034) : as,

diū atque ācriter pugnātum est, 1, 26, 1, *there was long and sharp fighting.* tōtīs trepidātur castrīs, 6, 37, 6, *all through the camp there was tumult and affright.* mihī quidem persuādērī numquam potuit, animōs ēmorī, *CM.* 80, *for my part, I never could be convinced that the soul becomes extinct at death* (1181). Similarly verbs which have a transitive use may also be used impersonally : as, diēs noctīsque ēstur, bibitur, Pl. *Most.* 235, *there is eating and drinking all day and all night* (1133).

1480. The complementary dative of a verb in the active voice is in poetry very rarely made the subject of a passive verb : as, invideor, H. *AP.* 56, *I am envied.* imperor, H. *E.* 1, 5, 21, *I charge myself.*

1481. The passive had originally a reflexive meaning, which is still to be seen in the passive of many verbs : as,

exercēbātur plūrimum currendō et lūctandō, N. 15, 2, 4, *he took a great deal of exercise in running and wrestling.* dēnsōs fertur in hostīs, V. 2, 511, *he tries to charge upon the serried foes.* quod semper movētur, aeternum est, *TD.* 1, 53, *anything that is always moving, is eternal.*

1482. The present participle of reflexives is sometimes used in a reflexive sense : as, exercēns, *exercising oneself, exercising,* ferēns, *tearing along,* vehēns, *riding,* and invehēns, *mounted on,* pāscēns, *browsing,* versāns, *playing, being,* volvēns, *rolling.* Also the gerund : as, iūs vehendī, *the privilege of riding.*

1483. Passive forms of coepī and dēsinō are commonly used in the perfect system, when a dependent infinitive is passive : as, litterīs ōrātiō est coepta mandārī, *Br.* 26, *oratory began to be put in black and white.* veterēs ōrātiōnēs legī sunt dēsitae, *Br.* 123, *the old speeches ceased to be read.* But the active forms are sometimes used by Cornificius, Sallust, and Livy, and regularly by Tacitus. The active forms are used with fierī also, which is not passive (789) ; but even with fierī, Livy uses the passive forms.

1484. Similar attractions with a passive infinitive occur in potestur, &c., quītur and quitus sum, nequītur, &c., rarely, and mostly in old Latin : as, fōrma in tenebrīs nōscī nōn quitast, T. *Hec.* 572, *her shape could hardly be distinguished in the dark.*

1485. Some perfect participles have an active meaning: as, adultus, *grown up.* See 907, and also in the dictionary cautus, cōnsultus, concrētus, dēflāgrātus, incōnsīderātus, occāsus, nūpta.

DEPONENTS.

1486. Many verbs have only passive inflections, but with the meaning of active inflections. Such verbs are called *Deponents*.

1487. In many deponents, a reflexive, passive, or reciprocal action is still clearly to be seen : as,

nāscor, *am born;* moror, *delay myself, get delayed;* ūtor, *avail myself;* amplectimur, *hug each other;* fābulāmur, *talk together;* partīmur, *share with one another.*

1488. Some verbs have both active and deponent inflections: as, adsentiō, *agree,* more commonly adsentior. mereō, *earn,* and mereor, *deserve.* See also in the dictionary altercor, auguror, comitor, cōnflīctor, fabricor, faeneror, mūneror, ōscitor, palpor, populor, revertor. The following have active inflections in the present system and deponent inflections in the perfect system : audeō, cōnfīdō and diffīdō, gaudeō, soleō: see also 801.

1489. In old Latin especially, many verbs which afterwards became fixed as deponents occur with active inflections also : as, adūlō, arbitrō, aucupō, auspicō, lūctō, lūdificō, morō, partiō, venerō, &c., &c.

1490. Verbs which are usually deponent are rarely found with a passive meaning : as, Sūllānās rēs dēfendere crīminor, *LAgr.* 3, 13, *I am charged with defending Sulla's policy.*

1491. When it is desirable to express the passive of a deponent, a synonyme is sometimes used : thus, the passive of mīror, *admire,* may sometimes be represented by laudor, *am praised.* Or some circumlocution : as, habet venerātiōnem quidquid excellit, *DN.* 1, 45, *anything best in its kind is looked on with respect,* as passive of veneror. familia in suspīciōnem est vocāta, *V.* 5, 10, *the household was suspected,* as passive of suspicor.

1492. The perfect participle of deponents is sometimes used with a passive meaning. Some of the commonest of these participles are : adeptus, commentus, complexus, cōnfessus, ēmentītus, expertus, meditātus, opīnātus, pactus, partītus, testātus, &c., &c.

MOOD.

THE INDICATIVE MOOD.

DECLARATIONS.

1493. The indicative mood is used in simple, absolute declarations : as,

arma virumque canō, V. 1, 1, *arms and the man I sing.* leve fit quod bene fertur onus, O. *A.* 4, 2, 10, *light gets the load that's bravely borne.*

1494. The negative used with the indicative is commonly nōn, *not* (1443). For other negative expressions, see 1445–1451.

1495. Certain verbs and verbal expressions denoting ability, duty, propriety, necessity, and the like, mostly with an infinitive, are regularly put in the indicative, even when the action of the infinitive is not performed.

This applies to declarations, questions, or exclamations : as, (*a.*) possum dē ichneumonum ūtilitāte dīcere, sed nōlō esse longus, *DN.* 1, 101, *I might expatiate on the usefulness of the ichneumon, but I do not care to be long-winded.* inter ferās satius est aetātem dēgere quam in hāc tantā immānitāte versārī, *RA.* 150, *it would be better to pass your days in the midst of howling beasts than to live and move among such brutish men.* (*b.*) stultī erat spērāre, *Ph.* 2. 23, *it would have been folly to hope.* quid enim facere poterāmus? *Pis.* 13, *for what else could we have done?* (*c.*) licuit uxōrem genere summō dūcere, Pl. *MG.* 680, *I might have married a wife of high degree.* nōn potuit pīctor rēctius dēscrībere eius fōrmam, Pl. *As.* 402, *no painter could have hit his likeness more exactly.* (*d.*) quantō melius fuerat prōmissum patris nōn esse servātum, *Off.* 3, 94, *how much better it would have been, for the father's word not to have been kept.*

1496. The principal verbs and verbal expressions thus used are: (*a.*) possum, licet, dēbeō, oportet, convenit, decet. (*b.*) aequum, aequius, iūstum, fās, necesse est; cōnsentāneum, satis, satius, optābile, optābilius est; ūtilius, melius, optimum, pār, rēctum est; facile, difficile, grave, īnfīnītum, longum, magnum est; est with the predicative genitive, or a possessive pronoun (1237). (*c.*) Similarly, but without an infinitive, forms of sum with a gerund, a gerundive, or a future participle.

1497. The imperfect of most of the above verbs and verbal expressions often relates to action not performed at the present time: as,

hīs aliās poteram subnectere causās ; sed eundum est, J. 3, 315, *to these I might add other grounds ; but I must go.* The context must determine whether the imperfect relates (*a.*) to action not performed either in the present as here, or in the past as in 1495, or (*b.*) to action performed in the past: as, sollicitāre poterat, audēbat, *C.* 3, 16, *he had at once the assurance and the ability to play the tempter's part.*

1498. Forms of **possum** are sometimes put in the subjunctive (1554). Thus, **possim**, &c., often (1556), also **possem**, &c., usually of present time (1560), less frequently of past time (1559), **potuissem**, &c., particularly in sentences of negative import (1561), rarely **potuerim**, &c. (1558). Sometimes also **dēbērem**, &c., of present time (1560), **dēbuissem**, &c., chiefly in apodosis.

QUESTIONS.

1499. The indicative is the mood ordinarily used in enquiries and in exclamations: as,

(*a*.) huic ego 'studēs?' inquam. respondit 'etiam.' 'ubī?' 'Mediōlānī.' 'cūr nōn hīc?' 'quia nūllōs hīc praeceptōrēs habēmus,' Plin. *Ep.* 4, 13, 3, *said I to the boy,* '*do you go to school?*' '*yes, sir,' said he;* '*where?*' '*at Mediolanum;*' '*why not here?*' '*oh because we haven't any teachers here.*' (*b*.) ut ego tuum amōrem et dolōrem dēsīderō, *Att.* 3, 11, 12, *how I always feel the absence of your affectionate sympathy.*

1500. Questions and exclamations are used much more freely in Latin than in English. Particularly common are two questions, of which the first is short and general, leading up to the real question: as,

sed quid ais? ubi nunc adulēscens habet? Pl. *Tri.* 156, *but tell me, where is the youngster living now?* estne? vīcī? et tibī saepe litterās dō? Cael. in *Fam.* 8, 3, 1, *is it true? have I beaten? and do I write to you often?* The real question is often preceded by quid est, quid dīcis, or by quid, quid vērō, quid tum, quid posteā, quid igitur, quid ergō, &c., &c.: as, quid? canis nōnne similis lupō? *DN.* 1, 97, *why, is not the dog like the wolf?*

1501. There are two kinds of questions: (1.) Such questions as call for the answer *yes* or *no* in English: as, *is he gone?* These may conveniently be called *Yes or No Questions*. (2.) Questions introduced by an interrogative pronoun, or by a word derived from an interrogative pronoun: as, *who is gone? where is he?* These are called *Pronoun Questions*.

YES OR NO QUESTIONS.

1502. (1.) Yes or No questions are sometimes put without any interrogative particle: as,

Thraex est Gallīna Syrō pār? H. *S.* 2, 5, 44, *of two gladiators, is Thracian Bantam for the Syrian a match?* Often intimating censure: as, rogās? Pl. *Aul.* 634, *dost ask?* or *what an absurd question.* prōmpsistī tū illī vīnum? :: nōn prōmpsī, Pl. *MG.* 830, *thou hast been broaching wine for him? :: not I.* Especially with nōn: as, patēre tua cōnsilia nōn sentīs? *C.* 1, 1, *you don't see that your schemes are out?* It is often doubtful whether such sentences are questions, exclamations, or declarations.

1503. (2.) Yes or No questions are usually introduced by one of the interrogative particles -ne or -n, nōnne, num, an, anne.

1504. A question with -ne or -n may enquire simply, without any implication as to the character of the answer, or it may either expect an affirmative answer like nōnne, or less frequently a negative answer like num: as, (*a.*) valen **?** Pl. *Tri.* 50, *art well ?* habētin aurum? Pl. *B.* 269, *have you got the gold ?* (*b.*) iussīn in splendōrem darī bullās hās foribus? Pl. *As.* 426, *did n't I give orders to polish up the bosses of the door ?* facitne ut dixī? Pl. *Am.* 526, *is n't he acting as I said ?* (*c*) istō immēnsō spatiō quaerō, Balbe, cūr Pronoea vestra cessāverit. labōremne fugiēbat? *DN.* 1, 22, *I want to know, Balbus, why your people's Providence lay idle all that immeasurable time ; it was work she was shirking, was it ?* quid, mundum praeter hunc umquamne vīdistī? negābis, *DN.* 1, 96, *tell me, did you ever see any universe except this one ? you will say no.*

1505. Sometimes the **-ne** of an interrogative sentence is transferred to a following relative, chiefly in Plautus and Terence: as, rogās **?** quīne arrabōnem ā mē accēpistī ob mulierem? Pl. *R.* 860, *how can you ask, when you have got the hansel for the girl from me ?* Similarly, ō sērī studiōrum, quīne putētis difficile, H. *S.* 1, 10, 21, *what laggards at your books, to think it hard,* i. e. nōnne estis sērī studiōrum, quī putētis difficile? Compare 1569.

1506. To a question with **nōnne**, a positive answer is usually expected, seldom a negative: as,

(*a.*) nōnne meministī **?** : : meminī vērō, *TD.* 2, 10, *don't you remember ? : : oh yes.* Sometimes a second or third question also has **nōnne**, but oftener **nōn** : as, nōnne ad tē L. Lentulus, nōn Q. Sanga, nōn L. Torquātus vēnit? *Pis.* 77, *did not Lentulus and Sanga and Torquatus come to see you ?* (*b.*) nōnne cōgitās? *RA.* 80, *do you bear in mind ?* nōnne is rare in Plautus, comparatively so in Terence, but very common in classical Latin.

1507. To a question with **num** a negative answer is generally expected. Less frequently either a positive or a negative answer indifferently : as,

(*a.*) num negāre audēs? *C.* 1, 8, *do you undertake to deny it ?* num, tibi cum faucēs ūrit sitis, aurea quaeris pōcula? H *S.* 1, 2, 114, *when thirst thy throat consumes, dost call for cups of gold ?* Rarely numne : as, quid, deum ipsum numne vīdistī? *DN* 1, 88, *tell me, did you ever see god in person ?* (*b.*) sed quid ais? num obdormīvistī dūdum? Pl. *Am.* 620, *but harkee, wert asleep a while ago ?* numquid vīs? Pl. *Tri.* 192, *hast any further wish ?*

1508. A question with **an**, less often **anne**, or if negative, with **an nōn**, usually challenges or comments emphatically on something previously expressed or implied: as,

an habent quās gallīnae manūs ? Pl. *Ps.* 29, *what, what, do hens have hands ?* an is also particularly common in argumentative language, in anticipating, criticising, or refuting an opponent: as, quid dīcis ? an bellō Siciliam virtūte tuā līberātam ? *V.* 1, 5, *what do you say ? possibly that it was by your prowess that Sicily was rid of the war ?* at vērō Cn. Pompēī voluntātem ā mē aliēnābat ōrātiō mea. an ille quemquam plūs dīlēxit ? *Ph.* 2, 38, *but it may be urged that my way of speaking estranged Pompey from me. why, was there anybody the man loved more ?* In old Latin, an is oftener used in a single than in an alternative question, while in classical Latin it is rather the reverse.

1509. (3.) Yes or No questions are sometimes introduced by ecquis, ecquō, ecquandō, or ēn umquam : as,

heus, ecquis hīc est ? Pl. *Am.* 420, *hollo, is e'er a person here ?* ecquid animadvertis hōrum silentium ? *C.* 1, 20, *do you possibly observe the silence of this audience ?* (1144). ō pater, ēn umquam aspiciam tē ? Pl. *Tri.* 588, *O father, shall I ever set mine eyes on thee ?*

1510. (4.) In Plautus, **satin** or **satin ut,** *really, actually,* sometimes becomes a mere interrogative or exclamatory particle: as, **satin abiīt ille?** Pl. *MG.* 481, *has that man really gone his way?*

POSITIVE AND NEGATIVE ANSWERS.

1511. There are no two current Latin words corresponding exactly with *yes* and *no* in answers.

1512. (1.) A positive answer is expressed by some emphatic word of the question, repeated with such change as the context may require: as,

an nōn dīxī esse hoc futūrum? :: **dīxtī,** T. *Andr.* 621, *didn't I say that this would be? :: you did.* **hūc abiīt Clītiphō** :: **sōlus?** :: **sōlus,** T. *Hau.* 904, *here Clitipho repaired :: alone? :: alone.* The repeated word may be emphasized by **sānē, vērō:** as, **dāsne manēre animōs post mortem?** :: **dō vērō,** *TD.* 1, 25, *do you grant that the soul lives on after death? :: oh yes.* Often, however, adverbs are used, without the repetition, such as **certē, certō, etiam, factum, ita, ita enimvērō, ita vērō, sānē, sānē quidem, scīlicet,** *oh of course,* **vērō,** rarely **vērum.**

1513. (2.) A negative answer is expressed by a similar repetition, with **nōn** or some other negative added: as,

estne frāter intus? :: **nōn est,** T. *Ad.* 569, *is brother in? :: he's not.* Or, without repetition, by such words as **nōn, nōn ita, nōn quidem, nōn hercle vērō, minimē, minimē quidem, minimē vērō, nihil minus.**

1514. **immō** introduces a sentence rectifying a mistake, implied doubt, or understatement in a question: as, **nūllane habēs vitia?** :: **immō alia, et fortasse minōra,** H. *S.* 1, 3, 20, *have you no faults? :: I beg your pardon, other faults, and peradventure lesser ones.* **causa igitur nōn bona est? immō optima,** *Att.* 9, 7, 4, *is n't the cause a good one then? good? yes, more than good, very good.*

ALTERNATIVE QUESTIONS.

1515. The alternative question belongs properly under the head of the compound sentence. But as the interrogative particles employed in the single question are also used in the alternative question, the alternative question is most conveniently considered here.

1516. In old English, the first of two alternative questions is often introduced by the interrogative particle *whether,* and the second by *or:* as, *whether is it easier to say, Thy sins be forgiven thee, or to say Arise?* In modern English, *whether* is not used thus.

1517. The history of the Latin alternative question is just the reverse of the English. In old Latin, the first question is very often put without any interrogative particle. Later, in the classical period, the use of **-ne,** or oftener of **utrum,** etymologically the same as *whether,* is overwhelmingly predominant.

1518. In the simplest form of the alternative sentence, neither question is introduced by an interrogative particle: as,

quid agō? adeō, maneō? T. *Ph.* 736, *what shall I do? go up and speak, or wait?* (1531).

1519. Of two alternative questions, the first either has no interrogative particle at all, or is more commonly introduced by **utrum, -ne,** or **-n.** The second is introduced by **an,** rarely by **anne,** or if it is negative, by **an nōn:** as,

(*a.*) album an ātrum vīnum pōtās? Pl. *Men.* 915, *do you take light wine or dark?* Tacitus es an Plīnius? Plin. *Ep.* 9, 23, 3, *are you Tacitus or Pliny?* sortiētur an nōn? *PC.* 37, *will he draw lots or not?* (*b.*) iam id porrō utrum libentēs an invītī dabant? *V.* 3, 118, *then furthermore did they offer it voluntarily or did they consent to give it under stress?* utrum cētera nōmina in cōdicem acceptī et expēnsī dīgesta habēs an nōn? *RC.* 9, *have you all other items methodically posted in your ledger or not?* (*c.*) servosne es an līber? Pl. *Am.* 343, *art bond or free?* esne tū an nōn es ab illō mīlitī Macedoniō? Pl. *Ps.* 616, *art thou or art thou not the Macedonian captain's man?* videōn Clīniam an nōn? T. *Hau.* 405, *do I see Clinia or not?*

1520. necne for an nōn is rare: as, sēmina praetereā linquontur necne animāī corpore in exanimō? Lucr. 3, 713, *are seeds moreover left or not of soul within the lifeless frame?* Twice in Cicero: as, sunt haec tua verba necne? *TD.* 3, 41, *are these your words or not?* But necne is common in indirect questions.

1521. Instead of a single second question with **an,** several questions may be used if the thought requires it, each introduced by **an.**

1522. Sometimes an introductory **utrum** precedes two alternative questions with **-ne** and **an:** as, utrum tū māsne an fēmina's? Pl. *R.* 104, *which is it, art thou man or maid?* This construction has its origin in questions in which utrum is used as a live pronoun: as, utrum māvīs? statimne nōs vēla facere an paululum rēmigāre? *TD.* 4, 9, *which would you rather do, have us make sail at once, or row just a little bit?* In Horace and late prose, utrumne . . . an is found a few times.

1523. Sometimes a second alternative question is not put at all: as, utrum hōc bellum nōn est? *Ph.* 8, 7, in old English, *whether is not this war?*

1524. Two or more separate questions asked with **-ne** . . . **-ne,** or with num . . . num, must not be mistaken for alternative questions: as, num Homērum, num Hēsiodum coēgit obmūtēscere senectūs? *CM.* 23, *did length of days compel either Homer or Hesiod to hush his voice?* (1692).

1525. An alternative question is answered by repeating one member or some part of it, with such changes as the context may require.

PRONOUN QUESTIONS.

1526. Pronoun questions or exclamations are introduced by interrogative pronouns, or words of pronoun origin.

Such words are: (*a.*) quis quī, quoius, uter, quālis, quantus, quotus: as, quid rīdēs? H. *S.* 2, 5, 3, *why dost thou laugh?* (1144). uter est insānior hōrum? H. *S.* 2, 3, 102, *which of these is the greater crank?* hōra quota est? H. *S.* 2, 6, 44, *what's o'clock?* (*b.*) Or unde, ubī, quō, quōr or cūr, quī ablative, *how,* quīn, *why not,* quam, *how,* quandō, quotiēns: as, unde venīs et quō tendis? H. *S.* 1, 9, 62, *whence dost thou come, and whither art thou bound?* deus fallī quī potuit? *DN.* 3, 76, *how could a god have been taken in?* (1495). quam bellum erat cōnfitērī nescīre, *DN.* 1, 84, *how pretty it would have been, to own up that you did not know* (1495).

1527. Sometimes **quin** loses its interrogative force, and introduces an impatient imperative, particularly in Plautus and Terence, or an indicative of sudden declaration of something obvious or startling: as,

(*a.*) quīn mē aspice, Pl. *Most.* 172, *why look me over, won't you?* i. e. mē aspice, quin aspicis? So twice in Cicero's orations. (*b.*) quīn discupiō dīcere, Pl. *Tri.* 932, *why I am bursting with desire to tell.*

1528. In Plautus, Terence, Horace, and Livy, **ut,** *how,* also is used in questions: as, **ut valēs?** Pl. *R.* 1304, *how do you do?* **ut sēsē in Samniō rēs habent?** L. 10, 18, 11, *how is every thing in Samnium?* Very commonly, and in Cicero only so, in exclamations also: as, **ut fortūnātī sunt fabrī ferrāriī, quī apud carbōnēs adsident; semper calent,** Pl. *R.* 531, *what lucky dogs the blacksmiths be, that sit by redhot coals; they're always warm.*

1529. In poetry, **quis, uter,** and **quantus** are found a few times with **-ne** attached; as, **uterne ad cāsūs dubiōs fīdet sibi certius?** H. *S.* 2, 2, 107, *which of the two in doubtful straits will better in himself confide?*

1530. Two or more questions or exclamations are sometimes united with one and the same verb: as,

unde quō vēnī? H. 3, 27, 37, *whence whither am I come?* quot diēs quam frīgidīs rēbus absūmpsī, Plin. *Ep.* 1, 9, 3, *how many days have I frittered away in utter vapidities.* quantae quotiēns occāsiōnēs quam praeclārae fuērunt, *Mil.* 38, *what great chances there were, time and again, splendid ones too.*

Some Applications of Questions.

1531. A question in the indicative present or future may be used to intimate command or exhortation, deliberation, or appeal: as,

(*a.*) abin hinc? T. *Eu.* 861, *will you get out of this?* abin an nōn? :: abeō, Pl. *Aul.* 660, *will you begone or not?* :: *I'll go.* quīn abīs? Pl. *MG.* 1087, *why won't you begone?* or *get you gone, begone.* nōn tacēs? T. *Ph.* 987, *won't you just hold your tongue?* ecquis currit pollinctōrem arcēssere? Pl. *As.* 910, *won't some one run to fetch the undertaker man?* quīn cōnscendimus equōs? L. 1, 57, 7, *why not mount?* or *to horse, to horse.* (*b.*) quid est, Crasse, īmusne sessum? *DO.* 3, 17, *what say you, Crassus, shall we go and take a seat?* quoi dōnō lepidum novum libellum? Cat. 1, 1, *unto whom shall I give the neat new booklet?* quid agō? adeō, maneō? T. *Ph.* 736, *what shall I do? go up and speak, or wait?* (*c.*) eōn? vocō hūc hominem? :: ī, vocā, Pl. *Most.* 774, *shall I go, and shall I call him here?* :: *go call him.* See also 1623. Such indicative questions occur particularly in old Latin, in Catullus, in Cicero's early works and letters, and in Vergil.

1532. Some set forms occur repeatedly, especially in questions of curiosity, surprise, incredulity, wrath, or captiousness: as,

sed quid ais? T. *Andr.* 575, *but apropos,* or *but by the way* (1500). quid istīc? T. *Andr.* 572, *well, well, have it your way:* compare quid istīc verba facimus? Pl. *E.* 141. ain tū? *Br.* 152, *no, not seriously?* itane? T. *Eu.* 1058, *not really?* Frequently egone: as, quid nunc facere cōgitās? :: egone? T. *Hau.* 608, *what do you think of doing now?* :: *what, I?* In Plautus, threats are sometimes introduced by scīn quō modō? *do you know how?* i. e. at your peril.

257

1533. A question is sometimes united with a participle, or an ablative absolute, or thrown into a subordinate sentence: as,

quem frūctum petentēs scīre cupimus illa quō modō moveantur? *Fin.* 3, 37, *with what practical end in view do we seek to know how yon bodies in the sky keep in motion?* quā frequentiā prōsequente crēditis nōs illinc profectōs? L. 7, 30, 21, *by what multitudes do you think we were seen off when we left that town?* ' hominēs ' inquit ' ēmistī.' quid utī faceret? *Sest.* 84, *'you bought up men' says he; with what purpose?*

THE INFINITIVE OF INTIMATION.

1534. The infinitive is principally used in subordination, and will be spoken of under that head. One use, however, of the present infinitive in main sentences, as a kind of substitute for a past indicative, requires mention here.

1535. In animated narration, the present infinitive with a subject in the nominative sometimes takes the place of the imperfect or perfect indicative: as,

interim cōtīdiē Caesar Aeduōs frūmentum flāgitāre, 1, 16, 1, *there was Caesar meantime every day dunning and dunning the Aeduans for the grain.* Diodōrus sordidātus circum hospitēs cursāre, rem omnibus nārrāre, *V.* 4, 41, *Diodorus kept running round in sackcloth and ashes from friend to friend, telling his tale to everybody.* intereā Catilīna in prīmā aciē versārī, labōrantibus succurrere, S. *C.* 60, 4, *Catiline meantime bustling round in the forefront of battle, helping them that were sore bestead.* tum vērō ingentī sonō caelum strepere, et micāre ignēs, metū omnēs torpēre, L. 21, 58, 5, *at this crisis the welkin ringing with a dreadful roar, fires flashing, everybody paralyzed with fear.* This infinitive occurs in almost all writers, for instance, Plautus, Terence, Cicero, Horace, and particularly Sallust, Livy, and Tacitus. Less commonly in Caesar. Usually two or more infinitives are combined, and infinitives are freely mixed with indicatives. The subject is never in the second person.

1536. This infinitive is used to sketch or outline persistent, striking, or portentous action, where description fails; and as it merely *intimates* the action, without distinct declaration, and without notation of time, number, or person, it is called the *Infinitive of Intimation.* It cannot be adequately represented in English.

1537. The infinitive of intimation is sometimes used without a subject, when emphasis centres in the action alone; as,

ubī turrim procul cōnstituī vīdērunt, inrīdēre ex mūrō, 2, 30, 3, *when they saw the tower planted some way off, jeer after jeer from the wall.* tum spectāculum horribile in campīs patentibus: sequī fugere, occīdī capī, S. *I.* 101, 11, *then a heartrending spectacle in the open fields: chasing and racing, killing and catching.*

1538. Terence and Petronius have it in questions: as, rēx tē ergō in oculīs : : scīlicet : : gestāre? : : vērō, T. *Eu.* 401, *your king then always bearing you : : of course, of course : : in eye? : : oh yes.* quī morī timōre nisi ego? Petr. 62.

1539. It may be mentioned here, that the infinitive of intimation is sometimes used from Sallust on in relative clauses and with **cum**, *when.* Also by Tacitus in a temporal protasis with **ubī, ut, dōnec,** or **postquam,** coordinated with a present or imperfect indicative protasis : as,

(*a.*) cingēbātur interim mīlite domus, cum Libō vocāre percussō-rem, Ta. 2, 31, *the house meantime was encompassed with soldiers, when Libo called for somebody to kill him* (1869). (*b.*) ubī crūdēscere sēditiō et ā conviciīs ad tēla trānsībant, inicī catēnās Flāviānō iubet, Ta. *H.* 3, 10, *when the riot was waxing hot, and they were proceeding from invectives to open violence, he orders Flavian to be clapped in irons* (1933).

THE SUBJUNCTIVE MOOD.

DECLARATIONS.

I. THE SUBJUNCTIVE OF DESIRE.

(A.) WISH.

1540. The subjunctive may be used to express a wish.

Wishes are often introduced by **utinam**, in old and poetical Latin also by **utī, ut,** and curses in old Latin by **quī** ; these words were originally interrogative, *how.* Sometimes the wish is limited by **modo,** *only.* In negative wishes **nē** is used, either alone, or preceded by **utinam** or **modo** ; rarely **nōn,** or the old-fashioned **nec,** *not* (1446).

1541. (1.) The present and perfect represent a wish as practicable ; although a hopeless wish may, of course, if the speaker chooses, be represented as practicable : as,

(*a.*) tē spectem, suprēma mihī cum vēnerit hōra, Tib. 1, 1, 59, *on thee I'd gaze, when my last hour shall come.* utinam illum diem videam, Att. 3, 3, *I hope I may see the day.* (*b.*) utinam cōnēre, Ph. 2, 101, *I hope you may make the effort.* (*c.*) dī vortant bene quod agās, T. *Hec.* 196, *may gods speed well whate'er you undertake.* quī illum dī omnēs perduint, T. *Ph.* 123, *him may all gods fordo.* ō utinam hībernae duplicentur tempora brūmae, Prop. 1, 8, 9, *oh that the winter's time may doubled be.* utinam revīvīscat frāter, Gell. 10, 6, 2, *I hope my brother may rise from his grave.* nē istūc Iuppiter sīrit, L. 28, 28, 11, *now Jupiter forefend.* The perfect is found principally in old Latin.

1542. The present is very common in asseveration : as,

pereram, nisi sollicitus sum, *Fam.* 15, 19, 4, *may I die, if I am not worried.* sollicitat, ita vivam, me tua valētūdō, *Fam.* 16, 20, *your state of health worries me, as I hope to live.* ita vīvam, ut maximōs sūmptūs faciō, *Att.* 5, 15, 2, *as I hope to be saved, I am making great outlays.* See also 1622.

1543. The perfect subjunctive sometimes refers to past action now completed. as, **utinam abierit malam crucem,** Pl. *Poen.* 799, *I hope he's got him to the bitter cross* (1165). **utinam spem implēverim,** Plin. *Ep.* 1, 10, 3, *I hope I may have fulfilled the expectations.*

1544. (2.) The imperfect represents a wish as hopeless in the present or immediate future, the pluperfect represents it as unfulfilled in the past : as,

(*a.*) **tēcum lūdere sīcut ipsa possem,** Cat. 2, 9, *could I with thee but play, e'en as thy mistress' self,* to Lesbia's sparrow. **utinam ego tertius vō-bīs amīcus adscrīberer,** *TD.* 5, 63, *would that I could be enrolled with you myself, as the third friend,* says tyrant Dionysius to Damon and Phintias. (*b.*) **utinam mē mortuum prius vīdissēs,** *QFr.* 1, 3, 1, *I wish you had seen me dead first.* (*c.*) **utinam nē in nemore Pēliō secūribus caesa accē-disset abiēgna ad terram trabēs,** E. in Cornif. 2, 34, *had but, in Pelion's grove, by axes felled, ne'er fallen to the earth the beam of fir,* i. e. for the Argo. **utinam ille omnīs sēcum cōpiās ēdūxisset,** *C.* 2, 4, *I only wish the man had marched out all his train-bands with him.*

1545. In old or poetical Latin, the imperfect sometimes denotes unfulfilled past action, like the usual pluperfect ; as, **utinam in Siciliā perbīterēs,** Pl. *R.* 494, *would thou hadst died in Sicily.* **utinam tē dī prius perderent,** Pl. *Cap.* 537, *I wish the gods had cut thee off before.* See 2075.

1546. In poetry, a wish is sometimes thrown into the form of a conditional protasis with **sī** or **ō sī :** as, **ō sī urnam argentī fōrs quae mihi mōnstret,** H. *S.* 2, 6, 10, *oh if some chance a pot of money may to me reveal.*

(B.) Exhortation, Direction, Statement of Propriety.

1547. The subjunctive may be used to express an exhortation, a direction, or a statement of propriety.

The subjunctive of exhortation is sometimes preceded in old Latin by **utī** or **ut,** originally interrogative. In negative exhortations or directions, **nē, nēmō, nihil,** or **numquam,** &c., is used, rarely **nōn.**

1548. (1.) The present expresses what is to be done or is not to be done in the future : as,

(*a.*) **hoc quod coepī prīmum ēnārrem,** T. *Hau.* 273, *first let me tell the story I've begun.* **taceam nunc iam,** Pl. *B.* 1058, *let me now hold my tongue.* **cōnsīdāmus hīc in umbrā,** *Leg.* 2, 7, *let us sit down here in the shade.* **nē difficilia optēmus,** *V.* 4, 15, *let us not hanker after impossibilities.* (*b.*) HAICE · VTEI · IN · COVENTIONID · EXDEICATIS, CIL. I, 196, 23, *this you are to proclaim in public assembly.* (*c.*) **nōmina dēclīnāre et verba in prīmīs puerī sciant,** Quintil. 1, 4, 22, *first and foremost boys are to know how to inflect nouns and verbs.* **utī adserventur magnā dīligentiā,** Pl. *Cap.* 115, *let them be watched with all due care.* **nē quis tamquam parva fastīdiat grammaticēs ele-menta,** Quintil. 1, 4, 6, *let no man look down on the rudiments of grammar fancying them insignificant.*

1549. (2.) The perfect subjunctive is rare: as, **idem dictum sit,** Quintil. 1, 1, 8, *the same be said, once for all.* Mostly in prohibitions: as, **morātus sit nēmō quō minus abeant,** L. 9, 11, 13, *let no man hinder them from going away.*

1550. In positive commands, the second person singular often has a definite subject in old or epistolary Latin, and particularly **sīs,** for the imperative **es** or **estō.** Usually however an indefinite subject (1030): as,

(*a.*) **eās,** Pl. *R.* 519, *be off.* **hīc apud nōs hodiē cēnēs,** Pl. *Most.* 1129, *dine here with us today.* **cautus sīs, mī Tirō,** *Fam.* 16, 9, 4, *you must be careful, dear Tiro.* (*b.*) **istō bonō ūtāre, dum adsit,** *CM.* 33, *enjoy this blessing while you have it with you.*

1551. When a prohibition is expressed in the subjunctive, the second person of the present is often used in old Latin, sometimes the perfect. Later, however, the perfect is generally prevalent. In the classical period, the present is almost confined to poetry. For the imperative in prohibitions, see 1581–1586.

(*a.*) **nē illum verberēs,** Pl. *B.* 747, *you must n't thrash the man.* Once in Horace: **nē sīs patruos mihī,** *S.* 2, 3, 88, *don't play stern governor to me.* (*b.*) **nē trānsierīs Ibērum,** L. 21, 44, 6, *do not cross the Iberus.* **quod dubitās nē fēcerīs,** Plin. *Ep.* 1, 18, 5, *what you have doubt about, never do.*

1552. (3.) The imperfect or (but not in old Latin) pluperfect subjunctive is sometimes used to express past obligation or necessity: as,

(*a.*) Imperfect: **quae hīc erant cūrārēs,** T. *Hec.* 230, *thou shouldst have looked to matters here.* **paterētur,** T. *Hau.* 202, *he should have stood it.* **quod sī meīs incommodīs laetābantur, urbis tamen perīculō commovērentur,** *Sest.* 54, *well, if they did gloat over my mishaps, still they ought to have been touched by the danger to Rome.* **crās īrēs potius,** Pl. *Per.* 710, *you'd better have gone tomorrow,* i. e. have resolved to go tomorrow. **poenās penderēs,** Pl. *B.* 427, *thou hadst to pay a penalty.* (*b.*) Pluperfect: **restitissēs, rēpugnāssēs, mortem pugnāns oppetīssēs,** Poet. in *Sest.* 45, *thou shouldst have made a stand, fought back, and fighting met thy fate.* **quid facere dēbuistī? frūmentum nē ēmissēs,** *V.* 3, 195, *what ought you to have done? you should not have bought any wheat.* Usually, however, past obligation or necessity is expressed by the gerundive construction, or by some separate verb meaning *ought* (1496).

(C.) Willingness, Assumption, Concession.

1553. The subjunctive of desire may be used to denote willingness, assumption, or concession: as,

ōderint dum metuant, Poet. in Suet. *Cal.* 30, *they are welcome to hate, as long as they fear.* **nē sit sānē summum malum dolor, malum certē est.** *TD.* 2, 14, *grant for aught I care that pain is not the worst evil, an evil it certainly is.* **nīl fēcerit, estō,** J. 6, 222, *he may be guiltless, be it so.*

II. THE SUBJUNCTIVE OF ACTION CONCEIVABLE.

1554. The subjunctive is often used to represent action as conceivable, without asserting that it actually takes place.

In some of its applications, this subjunctive is often more exactly defined by an expression of doubt or of assurance: as, **fors fuat an** in Plautus, **forsitan** from Terence on (rarely **forsan, fors**), **fortasse**, *may be, perhaps;* **opīnor**, **haud sciō an**, *I fancy;* facile, *easily,* sine **ūllā dubitātiōne**, *unhesitatingly*, &c., &c. The negative used with this subjunctive is **nōn**.

1555. This subjunctive is particularly common in guarded or diffident statements: thus, **velim**, *I could wish*, **nōlim**, *I should not be willing*, **mālim**, *I would rather*, **dīxerim**, *I should say*, are often preferred to a blunter **volō**, *I insist*, **nōlō**, *I won't*, **mālō**, *I prefer*, or **dīcō**, *I say*.

1556. The present denotes action in an indefinite future : as,

(*a.*) ego forsitan in grege adnumerer, *RA.* 89, *as for me, I might perhaps be counted in the common herd.* mūtuom argentum rogem, Pl. *Tri.* 758, *money I might borrow.* haud sciō an rēctē dīcāmus, *Sest.* 58, *I rather think we may say with propriety.* (*b.*) The second person singular generally has an imaginary subject (1030): as, dīcās hīc forsitan, J. 1, 150, *here peradventure thou mayst say*, i. e. anybody may say. rogēs mē quid sit deus, **auctōre** ūtar Simōnidē, *DN.* 1, 60, *you may ask me what god is; I should follow the lead of Simonides.* migrantīs cernās, V. 4, 401, *thou canst descry them on the move* (1635). Often with some generalizing word, such as **saepe**, **numquam**, **plūrēs**: as, saepe videās, H. *S.* 1, 4, 86, *thou oft canst see.* **Fortūnam** citius reperiās quam retineās, Publil. Syr. 168, *dame Fortune thou mayst sooner find than bind.* (*c.*) nunc aliquis dīcat mihi, H. *S.* 1, 3, 19, *now somebody may say to me* (more commonly dīcet aliquis, dīcēs, 1620). forsitan aliquis dīcat, L. 5, 52, 5, *perhaps somebody may say.* hoc vōbīs incrēdibile videātur, V. 3, 109, *this may seem incredible to you.*

1557. (1.) The perfect seldom occurs in old Latin. Later, it is rarely used of past time. In this use it resembles the perfect of concession (1553): as,

(*a.*) forsitan temere fēcerim, *RA.* 31, *peradventure I may have acted rashly.* errāverim fortasse, Plin. *Ep.* 1, 23, 2, *I may have been mistaken perhaps.* (*b.*) concēdō; forsitan aliquis aliquandō eius modī quippiam fēcerit, V. 2, 78, *I grant it; perhaps somebody, at some time or other, may have done something of the sort.* haec ipsa forsitan fuerint nōn necessāria, *Br.* 52, *even this may perhaps have been superfluous.*

1558. (2.) The perfect is oftenest used with a future meaning, and particularly the first person singular active of verbs meaning *think* or *say:* as,

(*a.*) nōn facile dīxerim, *TD.* 5, 121, *I could not readily say.* hoc sine ūllā dubitātiōne cōnfirmāverim, *Br.* 25, *this I can assert without any hesitation.* pāce tuā dīxerim, *TD.* 5, 12, *by your leave I would say.* The first person plural occurs first in Cornificius, and is rare: as, hunc deum rīte beātum dīxerīmus, *DN.* 1, 52, *such a god we should be right in pronouncing happy.* (*b.*) plānē perfectum Dēmosthenem facile dīxerīs, *Br.* 35, *you would readily pronounce Demosthenes absolutely perfect* (1030). tū vērō eum nec nimis valdē umquam nec nimis saepe laudāverīs, *Leg.* 3, 1, *oh no, rest assured you never can praise him too emphatically nor too often.* conluviem istam nōn nisi metū coērcuerīs, Ta. 14, 44, *such a motley rabble you can only keep under by terrorism.* (*c.*) forsitan quispiam dīxerit, *Off.* 3, 29, *perhaps somebody may say.*

1559. (1.) The imperfect properly denotes action which might have taken place in the past : as,

(*a*.) nōn ego hoc ferrem calidus iuventā cōnsule Plancō, H. 3, 14, 27, *this I should not have brooked in my hot youth, in Plancus' consulate.* (*b*.) The second person singular, particularly of verbs meaning *see, make out, think, say,* generally has an imaginary subject (1030) : as, vidērēs, H. S. 2, 8, 77, *thou mightst have seen.* cernerēs, L. 22, 7, 12, *you might have descried.* nescīrēs, L. 3, 35, 3, *you could not have told.* tē columen rēi pūblicae dīcerēs intuērī, *Sest.* 19, *you would have sworn you were gazing on a pillar of the state.* (*c*.) quī vidēret, urbem captam dīceret, *V.* 4, 52, *anybody who saw it, would have said it was a captured city.* dīcī hoc in tē nōn potest, posset in Tarquiniō, cum rēgnō esset expulsus, *TD.* 1, 88, *this cannot be said in your case ; it might have been said in Tarquin's, when he was driven from the throne.* numquam faceret, T. *Ph.* 121, *he never would have done it.*

1560. (2.) The imperfect often denotes action not performed at the present time ; so especially vellem (nōllem, māllem) : as,

(*a*.) nimis vellem habēre perticam, Pl. *As.* 589, *I wish so much I had a stick.* vellem adesse posset Panaetius ; quaererem ex eō, *TD.* 1, 81, *I only wish Panaetius could be with us : I should ask him* (Panaetius was dead). cuperem voltum vidēre tuum, *Att.* 4, 16, 7, *I should like to see the expression of your face.* māllem Cerberum metuerēs, *TD.* 1, 12, *I would rather you stood in dread of Cerberus.* possem idem facere, *TD.* 1, 84, *I could do the same.* (*b*.) melius sequerēre cupīdine captam, O. 14, 28, *better for thee it were a loving bride to woo.* (*c*.) in hāc fortūnā perūtilis eius opera esset, *Att.* 9, 17, 2, *in the present pinch his services would be extremely valuable.*

1561. The pluperfect represents action which did not take place in the past : as,

(*a*.) vellem quidem licēret : hoc dīxissem, *RA.* 138, *I only wish it were allowed ; I should have said so and so.* (*b*.) dedissēs huic animō pār corpus, fēcisset quod optābat, Plin. *Ep.* 1, 12, 8, *you might have given this spirit a body to match ; he would have done what he craved to do.* (*c*.) urbēs et rēgna celeriter tanta nēquitia dēvorāre potuisset, *Ph.* 2, 67, *such colossal prodigality might have been capable of swallowing down cities and kingdoms speedily.* vīcissent inprobōs bonī ; quid deinde ? *Sest.* 43, *the good might have overpowered the bad ; what next ?*

1562. It may be mentioned here, that the subjunctive of action conceivable often extends to subordinate sentences : see 1731.

QUESTIONS.

1563. I. The subjunctive is often used to ask what action or whether any action is desired, commanded, proper, or necessary.

In many instances a negative answer or no answer at all is expected. The negative is nē, sometimes nōn.

(*a*.) **quō mē vertam?** *Scaur.* 19, *which way shall I turn?* **quid faciam, praescrībe :: quiēscās :: nē faciam, inquis, omnīnō versūs?** H. *S.* 2, 1, 5, *lay down the law, what I'm to do :: keep still :: wilt have me write, sayst thou, no verse at all?* **quid igitur faciam? nōn eam?** T. *Eu.* 46, *what then am I to do? not go?* **quid nī meminerim?** *DO.* 2, 273, *why should not I remember?* or *of course I remember.* **huic cēdāmus? huius condiciōnēs audiāmus?** *Ph.* 13, 16, *shall we bow the knee to him? shall we listen to his terms?* (*b*.) **quid tandem mē facere decuit? quiēscerem et paterer?** L. 42, 41, 12, *what in the world ought I to have done? keep inactive and stand it?*

1564. Such questions sometimes have the alternative form : as, **Corinthiīs bellum indīcāmus, an nōn?** *Inv.* 1, 17, *are we to declare war against Corinth, or not?* **utrum indicāre mē êı thēnsaurum aequom fuit, an ego alium dominum paterer fierī hīsce aedibus?** Pl. *Tri.* 175, *should I have pointed out the hoard to him, or should I have allowed another to become the owner of this house?* here **paterer** is equivalent to **aequom fuit patī** (1495).

1565. II. The subjunctive is often used to ask whether action is conceivable : as,

(*a*.) **quis putet celeritātem ingenī L. Brūtō dēfuisse?** *Br.* 53, *who can suppose that Brutus lacked ready wit?* i. e. **nēmō putet** (1556), **putābit** (1620), or **putāre potest. sī enim Zēnōnī licuit, cūr nōn liceat Catōnī?** *Fin* 3, 15, *for if it was allowed Zeno, why should not it be allowed Cato?* (*b*.) **hoc tantum bellum quis umquam arbitrārētur ab ūnō imperātōre cōnficī posse?** *IP.* 31, *who would ever have dreamed that this stupendous war could be brought to a close by a single commander?* The imperfect sometimes denotes action not performed at the present time (1560) : **quis enim cīvis rēgī nōn favēret?** *D.* 6, *for what Roman would not feel for the king?* (*c*.) **ego tē vidēre nōluerim?** *QFr.* 1, 3, 1, *I have objected to seeing you?*

1566. The subjunctive is often used in interrogative outbursts of surprise, disapprobation, indignation, or captious rejoinder. In such questions a pronoun, **ego, tū (ille),** is usually expressed. The negative is **nōn.**

This subjunctive occurs in Plautus and Terence, in Cicero, oftenest the letters, in Horace, Vergil, and Livy. Not in Caesar nor Sallust.

1567. (1.) The question may have no interrogative word, or may have -ne, especially in comedy : as,

(*a*.) **nōn tacēs? :: taceam?** T. *Ph.* 987, *you hold your tongue :: I hold my tongue?* **nē flē :: egone illum nōn fleam?** Pl. *Cap.* 139, *weep not :: what, I not weep for him?* **tū pulsēs omne quod obstat?** H. *S.* 2, 6, 30, *what, you, sir, punch whatever's in your way?* **faveās tū hostī? ille litterās ad tē mittat?** *Ph.* 7, 5, *you, sir, sympathize with the enemy? he correspond with you?* **sapiēnsne nōn timeat?** *Ac.* 2, 135, *a sage not be afraid?* (*b*.) **ego mihī umquam bonōrum praesidium dēfutūrum putārem?** *Mil.* 94, *could I have dreamed that I should ever lack the protection of the patriotic?* (*c*.) ' **apud exercitum mihī fuerīs'** inquit '**tot annōs?**' *Mur.* 21, ' *to think of your having been with the army, bless my soul,' says he, ' so many years.'* (*d*.) **mihī cuiusquam salūs tantī fuisset, ut meam neglegerem?** *Sull.* 45, *could anybody's safety have been so important in my eyes as to make me disregard my own?*

1568. (2.) The question may have utī or ut: as,

tē ut ūlla rēs frangat? tū ut umquam tē corrigās? *C.* 1, 22, *any thing break you down? you ever reform?* pater ut obesse fīliō dēbeat? *Planc.* 31, *a father morally bound to work against his son?*

1569. (3.) The question with utī or ut is sometimes attended by a remnant of another question with -ne or -n. In this combination, -ne either precedes, joined to an emphatic word, or it is attached directly to utī or ut: as,

(*a.*) egone ut tē interpellem? *TD.* 2, 42, *what I? interrupt you?* illīne ut impūne concitent finitima bella? *L.* 4, 2, 12, *what, they be allowed to stir up border warfare with impunity?* virgō haec līberast :: meane ancilla lībera ut sit, quam ego numquam ēmīsī manū? Pl. *Cur.* 615, *this girl is free :: my servant-girl? she to be free, when I have never set her free?* (*b.*) utne tegam spurcō Dāmae latus? H. *S.* 2, 5, 18, *what, I'm to shield a nasty Dama's side?* somnium. utine haec īgnōrāret suōm patrem? T. *Ph.* 874, *oh bosh, not to have known the father that begat her?* See 1505 and 1532.

1570. It may be mentioned here, that the interrogative subjunctive is often used in subordinate sentences : see **1731**.

THE IMPERATIVE MOOD.

COMMAND.

1571. The second person of the imperative mood is used in commands, either particular or general.

Commands are very often attended by a vocative or vocative nominative, or by tū, *sir, sirrah,* or vōs, *gentlemen, you people* (1118). They are of various kinds, as follows : (*a.*) Order, often to an inferior : thus, to an official : līctor, conligā manūs, *Rab.* 13, L. 1, 26, 7, Gell. 12, 3, 2, *lictor, tie up his wrists.* To soldiers : as, dēsilīte mīlitēs, 4, 25, 3, *overboard, my men* sīgnifer, statue sīgnum, L. 5, 55, 1, *standardbearer, plant your standard.* īnfer mīles sīgnum, L. 6, 8, 1, *advance your standard, man,* or *charge.* To sailors : as, hūc dīrigite nāvēs, L. 29, 27, 13, *head your galleys this way.* To slaves : as, convorrite aedēs scōpīs, agite strēnuē, Pl. *B.* 10, *sweep up the house with brooms, be brisk.* Also to an equal : as, aperīte aliquis, Pl *Mer.* 130, *open the door there somebody* (1080). Or to a superior : as, heus, exī, Phaedrome, Pl. *Cur.* 276, *ho Phaedromus, come out.* (*b.*) Exhortation, entreaty, summons, request, prayer, imprecation, wish, concession, &c. : as, vōs vōbīs cōnsulite, 7, 50, 5, *every man of you for himself.* ēs, bibe, animō obsequere, Pl. *MG.* 677. *eat, drink, and be merry.* sperne voluptātēs, H. *E.* 1, 2, 55, *scorn thou delights.* quīn tū ī intrō, Pl. *Most.* 815, *go in, go in, won't you go in?* (1527). patent portae, proficīscere, ēdūc tēcum etiam omnīs tuōs, *C.* 1, 10, *the gates are open, march forth ; take out all your myrmidons with you too.* audī, Iuppiter, L. 1, 32, 6, *bow down thine ear, Jupiter.* ī in crucem, Pl. *As.* 940, *get you gone to the cross.* vīve valēque, H. *S.* 2, 5, 109, *long live and thrive,* or *farewell.* tibī habē, Pl. *Men.* 690, *you keep it yourself.*

1572. The imperative is often softened by the addition of **amābō, obsecrō, quaesō,** *prithee, I beg,* or **sīs, sultis, sōdēs,** *please* (97). It is sharpened by **age, agedum** or **agidum, age sīs,** *mark me,* or **ī,** *go, come on,* or by **modo,** *only.* The concessive imperative sometimes has **sānē,** *for all me.*

1573. In Plautus and Terence, the enclitic **dum,** *a while, a minute, just,* is often attached to the imperative: as, **manedum,** Pl. *As.* 585, *wait a minute.* In classical Latin, **dum** is retained with **age** and **agite** : as, **agedum cōnferte cum illīus vītā P. Sullae,** *Sull. 72, come now, compare Sulla's life with that man's* (1075).

1574. It may be mentioned here, that the imperative is often used in the protasis of a conditional sentence : as,

> **tolle hanc opīniōnem, lūctum sustuleris,** *TD.* 1, 30, *do away with this notion, and you will do away with mourning for the dead.* Once only in old Latin, but often in late Latin, with a copulative : as, **perge, ac facile ecfēceris,** Pl. *B.* 695, *start on, and you will do it easily.*

1575. (1.) The third person, and the longer forms of the second person, are used particularly in laws, legal documents, and treaties, and also in impressive general rules and maxims : as,

> (*a.*) **rēgiō imperiō duō suntō,** *Leg.* 3, 8, *there shall be two men vested with the power of kings.* **amīcitia rēgī Antiochō cum populō Rōmānō hīs lēgibus estō,** L. 38, 38, 1, *there shall be amity between king Antiochus and Rome on the following terms.* (*b.*) **vīcīnīs bonus estō,** Cato, *RR.* 4, *always be good to your neighbours.* **mōribus vīvitō antīquīs,** Pl. *Tri.* 295, *live thou in old-time ways.* The longer forms are often called the *Future Imperative.*

1576. (2.) The longer forms of the second person are also sometimes used in the ordinary speech of everyday life : as, **cavētō,** *QFr.* 1, 3, 8, *beware.* In old Latin, often **ēs,** *be thou,* but in classical Latin, oftener **estō** (or **sīs**). Usually **habētō,** meaning *keep,* or *consider,* regularly **scītō, scītōte,** *you must know* (846). In verse, the long forms may sometimes be due to the metre : as, **hīc hodiē cēnātō,** Pl. *R.* 1417, *take dinner here today.* **pār prō parī refertō,** T. *Eu.* 445, *pay tit for tat.* But also without such necessity : as, **aufertō intrō,** Pl. *Tru.* 914, *take it within.* **quiētus estō, inquam,** T. *Ph.* 713, *be not concerned, I say.*

1577. (3.) It may be mentioned here, that the longer forms are very often used in the apodosis of a complex sentence, particularly with a future or a future perfect protasis : as,

> **sī iste ībit, itō,** Pl. *Ps.* 863, *if he shall go, go thou.* **medicō mercēdis quantum poscet, prōmittī iubētō,** *Fam.* 16, 14, 1, *you must order your medical man to be promised all he shall charge in the way of a fee.* **ubī nihil erit quod scrībās, id ipsum scrībitō,** *Att.* 4, 8 b, 4, *when you don't have anything to write, then write just that.* **cum ego P. Grānium testem prōdūxerō, refellitō, sī poteris,** *V.* 5, 154, *when I put Granius on the witness stand, refute him if you can.*

1578. In such combinations, however, the shorter forms are sometimes found : as, **ubi volēs, accerse,** T. *Andr.* 848, *fetch me when you will.* And conversely the longer forms are also found with a present protasis : as, **ūnum illud vidētō, sī mē amās,** *Fam.* 16, 1, 2, *attend to this one thing, an thou lovest me.*

1579. A command is sometimes expressed by the subjunctive, accompanying **fac, facitō, fac ut, facitō ut, cūrā ut, cūrātō ut, vidē, vidē ut, volō,** or particularly **velim** : as,

266

magnum fac animum habeās et spem bonam, *QFr.* 1, 2, 16, *see that you keep up an heroic soul and unabated hope* (1712). fac cōgitēs, *Fam.* 11, 3, 4, *see that you bear in mind.* cūrā ut valeās, *Fam.* 12, 29, 3, *take good care of yourself.* velim exīstimēs, *Fam.* 12, 29, 2, *I should like to have you consider.* For commands in the subjunctive alone, see 1547; in the future indicative, 1624; in the form of a question, 1531.

1580. A periphrastic perfect passive form is rare: as, iūre caesus estō, Twelve Tables in Macrob. *Sat.* 1, 4, 19, *he shall be regarded as killed with justifying circumstances.* probē factum estō, L. 22, 10, 6, *let it be considered justified.* at vōs admonitī nostrīs quoque cāsibus este, O. *Tr.* 4, 8, 51, *but be ye warned by our misfortunes too.*

PROHIBITION.

1581. (1.) In prohibitions with the second person, the imperative with nē is used in old Latin, and with nēve as a connective, rarely neque : as,

nē flē, Pl. *Cap.* 139, *weep not.* nē saevī tantō opere, T. *Andr.* 868, *be not thus wroth.* Sometimes in classical poetry also, in imitation of old style : as, nē saevī, magna sacerdōs, V. 6, 544, *rave not, thou priestess grand.* Once in Livy : nē timēte, 3, 2, 9, *be not afraid.*

1582. From Ovid on, nōn is used a few times for nē : as, nōn cāris aurēs onerāte lapillīs, O. *AA.* 3, 129, *load not with precious stones your ears.*

1583. (2.) Prohibitions in the second person are usually expressed by nōlī or nōlīte with the infinitive, particularly in classical prose : as,

obiūrgāre nōlī, *Att.* 3, 11, 2, *don't scold.* nōlīte id velle quod fierī nōn potest, *Ph.* 7, 25, *don't yearn after the unattainable.*

1584. In poetry, equivalents for nōlī are sometimes used with the infinitive, such as fuge, parce or comperce, conpesce, mitte or omitte, absiste : as, quid sit futūrum crās, fuge quaerere, H. 1, 9, 13, *what fate the morrow brings, forbear to ask.* Livy has once parce, 34, 32, 20.

1585. (3.) A prohibition in the second person is often expressed by the subjunctive accompanying cavĕ, fac nē, vidē nē, vidētō nē, cūrā nē, cūrātō nē, or nōlim, and in old Latin cavĕ nē : as,

cavē festīnēs, *Fam.* 16, 12, 6, *don't be in a hurry.* cavētō nē suscēnseās, Pl. *As.* 372, *see that thou beest not wroth.* hoc nōlim mē iocārī putēs, *Fam.* 9, 15, 4, *I should hate to have you think I am saying this in fun.* For prohibitions in the second person with nē and the present or perfect subjunctive, see 1551. For the subjunctive coordinated with cavĕ, see 1711.

1586. In law language, prohibitions are expressed by the third person of the imperative with nē, and with nēve as a connective : as,

hominem mortuom in urbe nē sepelītō nēve ūritō, Twelve Tables in *Leg.* 2, 58, *he shall not bury nor yet shall he burn a dead man in town.* mulierēs genās nē rāduntō nēve lessum fūneris ergō habentō, Twelve Tables in *Leg.* 2, 59, *women shall not tear their cheeks nor shall they keen in lamentation for the dead* (1257). Likewise with nēmō : as, nēminī pārentō, Twelve Tables in *Leg.* 3, 8, *they shall not be subject to anybody.* See also 1548.

267

TENSE.

THE TENSES OF THE INDICATIVE.

The Present Tense.

1587. The present indicative represents action as going on at the time of speaking or writing : as,

scrībō, *I write*, or *I am writing.* nunc prīmum audiō, T. *Andr.* 936, *for the first time I hear.* notat ad caedem ūnum quemque nostrūm, *C.* 1, 2, *he is marking us out for death, each and all.* domus aedificātur, *Att.* 4, 2, 7, *the house is building.*

1588. The present is used to denote action customary or repeated at any time, or a general truth : as,

agrī cultūrae nōn student, 6, 22, 1, *they do not apply themselves to farming.* virī in uxōrēs vītae necisque habent potestātem, 6, 19, 3, *the married men have power of life and death over their wives.* probitās laudātur et alget, J 1, 74, *uprightness gets extolled, and left out in the cold.* dum vītant stultī vitia, in contrāria currunt, H. *S.* 1, 2, 24, *while fools essay a vice to shun, into its opposite they run.* mors sōla fatētur quantula sint hominum corpuscula, J. 10, 172, *death is the only thing that tells what pygmy things men's bodies be.* stultōrum plēna sunt omnia, *Fam.* 9, 22, 4, *the world is full of fools.* rīsū ineptō rēs ineptior nūllast, Cat. 39, 16, *there's nothing sillier than a silly laugh.*

1589. The present, when accompanied by some expression of duration of time, is often used to denote action which has been going on some time and is still going on.

This present is translated by the English perfect : as, Lilybaeī multōs iam annōs habitat, *V.* 4, 38, *he has lived at Lilybaeum this many a year.* iam dūdum auscultō, H. *S.* 2, 7, 1, *I have been listening for an age.* satis diū hōc iam saxum vorsō, T. *Eu.* 1085, *I've trundled at this boulder long enough as 'tis.* nimium diū tē castra dēsīderant, *C.* 1, 10, *the camp has felt your absence altogether too long.* iam diū īgnōrō quid agās, *Fam.* 7, 9, 1, *I have not known this long time how you are getting on.* This use extends to the subjunctive and to nouns of the verb also. But if the action is conceived as completed, the perfect is used : as, sērō resistimus ēī, quem per annōs decem aluimus, *Att.* 7, 5, 5, *it is too late to oppose a man whom we have been supporting ten long years.*

1590. The present is often used to represent past action as going on now. This is called the *Present of Vivid Narration :* as,

trānsfīgitur scūtum Puliōni et verūtum in balteō dēfīgitur. āvertit hīc cāsus vāgīnam, inpedītumque hostēs circumsistunt, 5, 44, 7, *Pulio has his shield run through, and a javelin sticks fast in his sword belt. This mischance puts his scabbard out of reach, and the enemy encompass him in this hampered condition.* This present often stands side by side with a past tense. It is common in subordinate sentences also.

1591. The present is sometimes used in brief historical or personal memoranda, to note incidents day by day or year by year as they occur. This is called the *Annalistic Present:* as,

Proca deinde rēgnat. is Numitōrem prōcreat. **Numitōrī rēgnum vetustum Silviae gentis lēgat,** L. 1, 3, 9, *after this Proca is king ; this man begets Numitor ; to Numitor he bequeaths the ancient throne of the Silvian race.* duplicātur cīvium numerus. Caelius additur urbī mōns, L. 1, 30, 1, *number of citizens doubled ; Mt. Caelius added to city.* in **Māmurrārum lassī deinde urbe manēmus,** H. *S.* 1, 5, 37, *in the Mamurras' city then forspent we sleep.* Particularly common with dates: as, **A. Vergīnius inde et T. Vetusius cōnsulātum ineunt,** L. 2, 28, 1, *then Verginius and Vetusius enter on the consulship.* **M. Sīlānō L. Nōrbānō cōnsulibus Germānicus Aegyptum** proficīscitur, Ta. 2, 59, *in the consulship of Silanus and Norbanus, Germanicus leaves for Egypt.*

1592. Verbs of hearing, seeing, and saying are often put in the present, even when they refer to action really past : as,

audiō **Valerium Mārtiālem** dēcessisse, Plin. *Ep.* 3, 21, 1, *I hear that Martial is dead,* i. e. the epigrammatist, 102 A. D. Particularly of things mentioned in books, or in quoting what an author says: as, **Hercyniam silvam, quam Eratosthenī nōtam esse** videō, 6, 24, 2, *the Hercynian forest, which I see was known to Eratosthenes.* **Platō ' ēscam malōrum ' appellat voluptātem,** *CM.* 44, *Plato calls pleasure the ' bait of sin.'*

1593. The present is sometimes loosely used of future action : as,

crās est mihī iūdicium, T. *Eu.* 338, *tomorrow I've a case in court.* ego **sȳcophantam iam condūcō dē forō,** Pl. *Tri.* 815, *for me, a sharper from the market place I'll straight engage.* **quam mox inruimus?** T. *Eu.* 788, *how soon do we pitch in ?* This present is also used in subordinate sentences with antequam and priusquam (1912, 1915), with dum, *until* (2006), and sometimes with sī.

THE IMPERFECT TENSE.

1594. The imperfect indicative represents action as going on in past time : as,

scrībēbam, *I was writing,* or *I wrote.* ei mihi quālis erat, V. 2, 274, *woe's me, how ghastly he appeared.* multōsque per annōs errābant āctī fātīs, V. 1, 31, *and they for many a year were roaming round, by fates pursued.*

1595. The imperfect often denotes past action lasting while something else occurred : as,

an tum erās cōnsul, cum mea domus ardēbat? *Pis.* 26, *were you perhaps consul at the time my house was burning down?* neque vērō tum ignōrābat sē ad exquīsīta supplicia proficīscī, *Off.* 3, 100, *and all the time he knew perfectly well that he was starting off to suffer studied torments.*

1596. The imperfect is used to denote repeated or customary past action or condition : as,

commentābar dēclāmitāns cōtīdiē, *Br.* 310, *I always practised speaking my compositions every day.* noctū ambulābat in pūblicō Themistoclēs, *TD.* 4, 44, *Themistocles used to promenade the streets nights.*

1597. The imperfect, when accompanied by some expression of duration of time, is used to denote action which had been going on for some time, and was still going on.

This imperfect, which is translated by the English pluperfect, is analogous to the present in 1589: as, **pater grandis nātū iam diū lectō tenēbā-tur**, *V*. 5, 16, *his aged father had long been bedridden.* **hōram amplius iam permultī hominēs mōliēbantur,** *V*. 4, 95, *something over an hour a good many men had been prizing away.* But if the action is conceived as completed at a past time, the pluperfect is used: as, **diem iam quīntum cibō caruerat,** 6, 38, 1, *four whole days he had gone without eating.*

1598. In a few examples, the imperfect is used to denote action suddenly recognized, though going on before: as, **ehem, Parmenō, tūn hīc erās?** T. *Hec.* 340, *why bless me, Parmeno, were you here all this time?*

1599. In descriptions of place or in general truths, where the present might be expected, the imperfect is sometimes used, by assimilation to past action in the context: as, **ipsum erat oppidum Alesia in colle summō,** 7, 69, 1, *Alesia proper was situated on the top of a hill.* Often also in subordinate sentences.

1600. For the imperfect indicative of certain verbs relating to action not performed at the present time, see 1497; for the conative use, see 2302.

1601. In letters, the imperfect may denote action at the time of writing, the writer transferring himself to the time of the reader: as,

haec tibi dictābam post fānum putre Vacūnae, H. *E.* 1, 10, 49, *I dictate this for thee behind Vacuna's crumbling shrine.* **nihil habēbam quod scrīberem,** *Att.* 9, 10, 1, *I have nothing to write.* Similarly in the delivery of messages: as, **scrībae ōrābant,** H. *S.* 2, 6, 36, *the clerks request.* The present, however, is very often used where the imperfect would be applicable. Compare 1616.

THE PERFECT TENSE.

1602. The Latin perfect indicative represents two English tenses: thus, the preterite, *I wrote,* and the perfect, *I have written,* are both expressed by the perfect **scrīpsī.** In the first sense, this perfect is called the *Historical Perfect;* in the second sense, it is called the *Perfect Definite.*

THE HISTORICAL PERFECT.

1603. The historical perfect simply expresses action as having occurred at an indefinite past time, without implying anything as to the duration of the action: as,

scrīpsī, *I wrote.* **vēnī, vīdī, vīcī,** Caesar in Suet. *Iul.* 37, *came, saw, over-came.* **apud Helvētiōs longē nōbilissimus fuit Orgetorīx,** 1, 2, 1, *among the Helvetians, the man of highest birth by all odds was Orgetorix.* Diodōrus prope triennium domō caruit, *V*. 4, 41, *for nearly three years Diodorus had to keep away from home.* **in Graeciā mūsicī flōruērunt, discēbantque id omnēs,** *TD.* 1, 4, *in Greece musicians stood high, and everybody studied the art* (1596).

1604. It may be mentioned here, that in subordinate sentences the historical perfect is sometimes loosely used from the writer's po.nt of view, instead of the more exact pluperfect demanded by the context : as, **aliquantum spatiī ex eō locō, ubī pugnātum est, aufūgerat,** L. 1, 25, 8, *he had run off some distance from the spot where the fighting had occurred.* See 1925.

THE PERFECT DEFINITE.

1605. The perfect definite expresses action which is already completed at the present time, and the effects of which are regarded as continuing : as,

scrīpsī, *I have written.* **dīxērunt,** *Clu.* 73, **dīxēre,** Quintil. 1, 5, 43, *they have finished speaking.* **spectātōrēs, fābula haec est ācta,** Pl. *Most.* 1181, *ladies and gentlemen, this play is done.*

1606. In old Latin, **habeō** with the perfect participle is sometimes equivalent to a periphrastic perfect : as, **illa omnia missa habeō,** Pl. *Ps.* 602, *I've dropped all that,* i. e. **mīsī.** But in classical Latin, the participle and a tense of **habeō** are more or less distinct in their force : as, **Caesar aciem īnstrūctam habuit,** 1, 48,3, *Caesar kept his line drawn up,* not *had drawn up.* Compare 2297.

1607. With verbs of inceptive meaning the perfect definite is equivalent to the English present : as,

cōnsistō, *take my stand,* **cōnstitī,** *stand,* **cōnsuēscō,** *get used,* **cōnsuēvī,** *am used,* **nōscō,** *learn,* **nōvī,** *know.* Similarly **meminī,** *remember,* and **ōdī,** *hate.* The pluperfect of such verbs is represented by the English imperfect, and the future perfect by the English future.

1608. The perfect often denotes a present resulting state: as, **vīcīne, periī, interiī,** Pl. *Most.* 1031, *my neighbour, I am dead and gone.* Particularly in the passive voice : as, **Gallia est omnis dīvīsa in partēs trēs,** 1, 1, 1, *Gaul, including everything under the name, is divided into three parts.* Compare 1615.

1609. In the perfect passive, forms of **fuī,** &c., are sometimes used to represent a state no longer existing : as, **monumentō statua superimposita fuit, quam dēiectam nūper vīdimus ipsī,** L. 38, 56, 3, *on the monument there once stood a statue which I saw not long ago with my own eyes, lying flat on the ground.* Similarly, in the pluperfect, **fueram,** &c. : as, **arma quae fīxa in parietibus fuerant, ea sunt humī inventa;** *Div.* 1, 74, *the arms which had once been fastened on the walls were found on the floor.* Sometimes, however, forms of **fuī,** &c., **fueram,** &c., and **fuerō,** &c., are used by Plautus, Cicero, especially in his letters, Nepos, Sallust, and particularly Livy, in passives and deponents, quite in the sense of **sum,** &c.

1610. The perfect of some verbs may imply a negative idea emphatically by understatement, as :

fuit Īlium, V. 2, 325, *Ilium has been,* i. e. Ilium is no more. **vīximus, flōruimus,** *Fam.* 14, 4. 5, *we have lived our life, we have had our day.* **fīlium ūnicum adulēscentulum habeō. āh, quid dīxī? habēre mē? immō habuī,** T. *Hau.* 93, *I have one only son, a growing boy. Ah me, what did I say, I have? Oh no, have had.*

1611. The perfect may denote an action often done, or never done: as,

iam saepe hominēs patriam cārōsque parentēs prōdiderunt, Lucr. 3, 85, *time and again have men their land betrayed and parents dear.* nōn aeris acervus et auri dēdūxit corpore febrīs, H. *E.* 1, 2, 47, *no pile of brass and gold hath fevers from the body drawn.* multī, cum obesse vellent, prōfuērunt et, cum prōdesse, obfuērunt, *DN.* 3, 70, *many a man has done good, when he meant to do harm, and when he meant to do good, has done harm.* Common from Cicero, Sallust, and Catullus on, especially in poetry.

1612. The perfect is sometimes used as a lively future perfect to express completed future action: as,

quam mox coctumst prandium? Pl. *R.* 342, *how soon is lunch all cooked?* cui sī esse in urbe licēbit, vīcimus, *Att.* 14, 20, 3, *if he shall be allowed to stay in town, the day is ours.* periī, sī mē aspexerit, Pl. *Am.* 320, *I'm gone, if he lays eyes on me.*

1613. It may be mentioned here, that the perfect is regularly used in a subordinate sentence denoting time anterior to a present of repeated action (1588). In such sentences the present is preferred in English: as,

reliquī, quī domī mānsērunt, sē atque illōs alunt, 4, 1, 5, *the others, that stay at home, always support themselves and the above-mentioned also.* sī quī aut prīvātus aut populus eōrum dēcrētō nōn stetit, sacrificiīs interdīcunt, 6, 13, 6, *if any man or any community does not abide by their decree, they always debar them from sacrifices.* So also with quom or cum, quotiēns, simul atque, ubī. Compare 1618.

The Pluperfect Tense.

1614. The pluperfect indicative expresses past action, completed before another past action expressed or understood: as,

scrīpseram, *I had written.* Pyrrhī temporibus iam Apollō versūs facere dēsierat, *Div.* 2, 116, *in Pyrrhus's day Apollo had quite given up making poetry.* mortuus erat Agis rēx. fīlium relīquerat Leōtychidem, N. 17, 1, 4, *Agis the king had died; he had left a son Leotychides.*

1615. The pluperfect often expresses a past resulting state: as,

castra oportūnīs locīs erant posita, 7, 69, 7, *the camp was pitched on favourable ground.* ita ūnō tempore et longās nāvēs aestus complēverat, et onerāriās tempestās adflīctābat, 4, 29, 2, *thus at one and the same time the tide had filled the men-of-war, and the gale of wind kept knocking the transports about.* This use is analogous to that of the perfect in 1608.

1616. In letters, the pluperfect is sometimes used to denote action occurring previous to the time of writing, the writer transferring himself to the time of the reader: as,

ūnam adhūc ā tē epistolam accēperam, *Att.* 7, 12, 1, *I have only had one letter from you thus far.* This use is analogous to that of the imperfect in 1601, and very often, where this pluperfect would be applicable, the perfect is used.

1617. The pluperfect is sometimes used where the perfect would be expected. Particularly so when it anticipates a past tense to follow in a new sentence: as, **quod factum prīmō populāris coniūrātiōnis concusserat. neque tamen Catilīnae furor minuēbātur,** S. *C.* 24, 1, *this terrified the conspirators at first; and yet Catiline's frenzy was not getting abated.* Verbs of saying are also often put in the pluperfect in subordinate sentences referring to a preceding statement: as, **Epidamniēnsis ille, quem dūdum dīxeram, adoptat illum puerum surruptīcium,** Pl. *Men. prol.* 57, *said man of Epidamnus that I named erewhile adopts said kidnapped boy.*

1618. It may be mentioned here, that the pluperfect is used in a subordinate sentence denoting time anterior to a past tense of repeated action. In such sentences the preterite is preferred in English: as,

hostēs ubī aliquōs singulārēs cōnspexerant, incitātīs equīs adoriēbantur, 4, 26, 2, *every time the enemy caught sight of detached parties, they would always charge full gallop.* Compare the analogous perfect in 1613.

The Future Tense.

1619. The future indicative expresses future action, either momentary or continuous: as,

scrībam, *I shall write, I shall be writing,* or *I will write, I will be writing.* The future commonly expresses either prediction, or will, determination, promise, threat: as, (*a.*) **tuās litterās exspectābō,** *Att.* 5, 7, *I shall be on the lookout for letters from you.* (*b.*) **vīvum tē nōn relinquam; moriēre virgīs,** *V.* 4, 85, *I will not leave you alive; you shall die under the rod.* But separate forms to mark the sharp distinction which exists between *shall* and *will* in the English future and future perfect are utterly unknown in Latin: thus, in **occīdar equidem, sed victus nōn perībō,** Cornif. 4, 65, *I shall be murdered, to be sure, but I will not die a vanquished man,* the difference between the prediction contained in *I shall,* and the determination contained in *I will,* cannot be expressed in Latin by the future indicative.

1620. The future is often used in diffident assertion, to express an assumption, a belief, conviction, or concession, of the speaker himself, without implying its universal acceptance: as,

dīcēs, *TD.* 2, 60, *you will say.* **dīcet aliquis,** *TD.* 3, 46, *somebody will say* (1556). **dabit hoc Zēnōnī Polemō,** *Fin.* 4, 51, *Polemo will concede this point to Zeno.* **excūdent aliī spīrantia mollius aera, crēdō equidem,** V. 6, 847, *with greater grace, I well believe, shall others shape the bronze that breathes.* Particularly in conclusions: as, **sequētur igitur vel ad supplicium beāta vīta virtūtem,** *TD.* 5, 87, *happiness then will walk with goodness even to the scaffold.* Or in general truths: as, **cantābit vacuus cōram latrōne viātor,** J. 10, 22, *the pourë man whan he goth by the weye, bifore the thevës he may synge and pleye.*

1621. The future sometimes predicts that a thing not yet known to be true will prove to be true: as, **haec erit bonō genere nāta,** Pl. *Per.* 645, *this maid, you'll find, is come of honest stock,* i. e. **esse reperiētur.** Compare the imperfect in 1598.

1622. In Plautus and Terence, the future is sometimes used in protestations, wishes, or thanks: as, **ita mē dī amābunt,** T. *Hau.* 749, *so help me heaven.* **dī tē amābunt,** Pl. *Mèn.* 278, *the gods shall bless thee.* Usually, however, the subjunctive: see 1542 and 1541.

1623. The future is sometimes used in questions of deliberation or appeal : as, dēdēmus ergō Hannibalem ? L. 21, 10, 11, *are we then to surrender Hannibal :* hancine ego ad rem nātam memorābō ? Pl. *R.* 188, *am I to say that I was born for such a fate?* Oftener the present subjunctive (1563), or sometimes the present indicative (1531).

1624. The future is sometimes used, particularly in the second person, to express an exhortation, a direction, a request, a command, or with nōn a prohibition : as,

crās ferrāmenta Teānum tollētis, H. *E.* 1, 1, 86, *tomorrow to Teanum you will take your tools.* bonā veniā mē audiēs, *DN.* 1, 59, *you will listen to me with kind indulgence.* tū intereā nōn cessābis, *Fam.* 5, 12, 10, *meantime you will not be inactive.* haec igitur tibī erunt cūrae, *Fam.* 3, 9, 4, *you will attend to this then,* i. e. haec cūrābis.

1625. It may be mentioned here, that the future is used in sentences subordinate to a future, an imperative, or a subjunctive implying a future : as,

profectō nihil accipiam iniūriae, sī tū aderis, *Att.* 5, 18, 3, *I am sure I shall suffer no harm, if you are with me.* ut mēd esse volēs, ita erō, Pl. *Ps.* 239, *as you will have me be, so will I be.* ut is quī audiet, cōgitet plūra, quam videat, *DO.* 2, 242, *so that the hearer may imagine more than he sees.* But sometimes a present is used (1593).

THE FUTURE PERFECT TENSE.

1626. The future perfect indicative expresses completed future action : as,

scrīpserō, *I shall have written,* or *I will have written.* The future perfect is very common in Latin, particularly in protasis with a relative, with cum, ubī, &c., with antequam or priusquam, with ut (. . . ita), *as* (. . . *so*), or with sī, to express action anterior in time to a future ; in English, this future perfect is usually represented by a loose present or perfect : as, quicquid fēceris, adprobābō, *Fam.* 3, 3, 2, *whatever you do, I shall think right.* Examples will be given further on, in speaking of the complex sentence.

1627. It may be mentioned here that the future perfect in protasis and apodosis both denotes two actions occurring at one and the same time; these actions are usually identical : as,

quī Antōnium oppresserit, is hoc bellum taeterrimum cōnfēcerit, *Fam.* 10, 19, 2, *the man that puts down Antony will put an end to this cruel war,* i. e. putting down Antony will be ending the war. respīrārō, sī tē vīderō, *Att.* 2, 24, 5, *I shall take breath again, if I set eyes on you.*

1628. The future perfect sometimes denotes a future resulting state : as,

molestus certē eī fuerō, T. *Andr.* 641, *at all events I shall have proved a bane to him.* meum rēī pūblicae atque imperātōrī officium praestiterō, 4, 25, 3, *I will have my duty all done to country and commander too.*

1629. The future perfect is sometimes used to express rapidity of future action, often with the implication of assurance, promise, or threat: as,

abierō, Pl. *Mos.* 590, *I'll instantly be gone.* iam hūc revererō, Pl. *MG.* 863, *B.* 1066, *i 'll be back here again forthwit'..* prīmus impetus castra cēperit, L. 25, 38, 17, *the first rush will see the camp carried.*

1630. The future perfect often denotes action postponed to a more con-venient season, or thrown upon another person.

Often thus with **post, aliās,** and particularly **mox: as, vōbīs post nār-rāverō,** Pl. *Ps.* 721, *I'll tell you by and by,* i. e. I won't tell you now. **ad frātrem mox ierō,** Pl. *Cap.* 194, *I'll to my brother's by and by,* i. e. not yet. **fuerit ista eius dēlīberātiō,** L. 1, 23, 8, *that is a question for him to settle,* i. e. not me. Especially **vīderō: as, quae fuerit causa, mox vīderō,** *Fin.* 1, 35, *what the reason was, I won't consider now.* **rēctē secusne aliās vīde-rimus,** *Ac.* 2, 135, *whether right or not, we will consider some other time,* i. e. never. **vōs vīderitis,** L. 1, 58, 10, *that is a question for you,* i. e. not me.

1631. The future perfect sometimes denotes action which will have oc-curred while something else takes place : as,

nōn erō vōbīs morae: tībīcen vōs intereā hīc dēlectāverit, Pl. *Ps.* 573ᵃ, *I will not keep you long ; meantime the piper will have entertained you here.* **tū invītā mulierēs, ego accīverō puerōs,** *Att.* 5, 1, 3, *do you, sir, in-vite the ladies, and I will meantime have fetched the children.*

1632. The future perfect is often not perceptibly different from the future, especially in the first person singular in old Latin : as,

ego mihī prōvīderō, Pl. *Most.* 526, *I'll look out for myself.* **erōs in obsidiōne linquet, inimīcūm animōs auxerit,** Pl. *As.* 280, *he'll leave his owners in a state of siege, he'll swell the courage of the enemy* Similarly Cicero, in the protases **sī potuerō, sī voluerō, sī licuerit, sī placuerit.**

The Future Active Participle with sum.

1633. The future active participle combined with the tenses of **sum** expresses action impending, resolved on, or destined, at the time indicated by the tense of the verb : as,

cum hōc equite pugnātūrī estis, L. 21, 40, 10, *with this kind of cavalry are you going to fight.* **bellum scrīptūrus sum, quod populus Rōmānus cum Iugurthā gessit,** Sall. *I.* 5, 1, *I purpose to write the history of the war that the people of Rome carried on with Jugurtha.* **fīet illud, quod futūrum est,** *Div.* 2, 21, *whatever is destined to be, will be.* **Delphōs petiit, ubī co-lumnās, quibus impositūrī statuās rēgis Perseī fuerant, suīs statuīs dēstināvit,** L. 45, 27, 6, *he went to Delphi, where he appropriated for his own statues the pillars on which they had intended to put statues of king Perses.*

THE TENSES OF THE SUBJUNCTIVE.

1634. In simple sentences, the tenses of the subjunctive correspond in general to the same tenses of the indicative. But the present has a future meaning ; the imperfect sometimes expresses past, sometimes present action; and the perfect sometimes expresses past action, and sometimes future action.

1635. The present subjunctive is sometimes used in reference to past action, like the indicative present of vivid narration (1590) : as, **migrantīs cernās,** *V.* 4, 401, *you can descry them swarming out* (1556). **comprehendī iussit ; quis nōn pertimēscat?** *V.* 5, 14, *he ordered them to be arrested ; who would not be thor-oughly scared?* (1565). See also 2075.

THE COMPOUND SENTENCE, OR COORDINATION.

1636. Two or more independent simple sentences may be coordinated to form a compound sentence in one of two ways: either without a connective, or with a connective.

What applies to the coordination of sentences, also applies to the coordination of the parts of sentences in abridged sentences (1057).

(A.) WITHOUT A CONNECTIVE.

1637. When simple sentences or parts of sentences are co-ordinated without any connective, this mode of arrangement is called *Asyndetic Coordination* or *Asyndeton.*

Asyndeton, whether in unabridged or in abridged sentences, is more usual with three or more members than with two. It occurs particularly often in Plautus, Terence, Ennius, and Cato, also in Cicero, especially in his early works and letters.

1638. The sentences in which asyndeton occurs are commonly such as might be connected by words meaning *and* or *but;* less often by words meaning *as, for,* &c. Asyndeton is especially common:

1639. (*a.*) In animated narration of events happening at the same moment, in description, and in climaxes. Also in mention of colleagues in office, and in many set phrases and formulas: as,

vēnī, vīdī, vīcī, Caesar in Suet. *Iul.* 37, *came, saw, overcame.* nostrī celeriter ad arma concurrunt, vāllum cōnscendunt, 5, 39, 3, *our men rush speedily to arms, clamber up the palisade.* huic s. c. intercessit C. Caelius, C. Pānsa, tribūnī pl., *Fam.* 8, 8, 7, *this decree of the senate was objected to by Caelius and Pansa, tribunes of the commons.* hī ferre agere plēbem, L. 3, 37, 7, *there were these people worrying and harrying the commons* (1535).

1640. (*b.*) In contrasts or antitheses: as,

opīniōnis commenta dēlet diēs, nātūrae iūdicia cōnfirmat, *DN.* 2, 5, *the fictions of speculation are swept away by time, but the judgements of nature are confirmed.* Particularly when either member is positive, the other negative: vincere scīs, Hannibal, victōriā ūtī nescīs, L. 22, 51, 4, *you know how to conquer, Hannibal, but not how to use victory,* says Maharbal after Cannae, 216 B. C.

1641. Asyndeton is very common with two or more imperatives: as, ēgredere ex urbe, Catilīna, līberā rem pūblicam metū, in exsilium proficīscere, *C.* 1, 20, *go forth from Rome, Catiline, relieve the commonwealth from its fear, depart into exile.* Particularly when the first is age, *come on, mark me,* or ī, *go* (1572). But from Horace on, ī nunc, *go to now,* is followed by et with a second imperative in derisive orders. In old Latin, the imperatives may be joined by et or even atque.

1642. Asyndeton is also common with parentheses. These often take the place of a modern foot-note: as, **lēgātus capite vēlātō fīlō** (lānae vēlāmen est) '**audī, Iuppiter,**' inquit, L. 1, 32, 6, *the envoy with his head covered with a 'filum' (that is to say a wrap of wool) says 'bow down thine ear, Jupiter.'* Parentheses however are often introduced, from Terence on by **nam,** and from Sallust and Cicero on, by **et, neque, autem, enim,** &c.

(B.) With a Connective.

(1.) CONJUNCTIONS AS CONNECTIVES.

1643. Simple sentences or parts of sentences may be connected by copulative, disjunctive, or adversative conjunctions.

(*a.*) COPULATIVE CONJUNCTIONS.

1644. Copulative conjunctions denote union, and connect both the sentences and their meaning. They are **et, -que, atque** or **ac,** *and,* and **neque** or **nec,** *neither.*

1645. (1.) **et,** *and,* is the commonest copulative, and connects either likes or unlikes ; with two members only, it is either used between them, or is prefixed for emphasis to both : as,

Dumnorix apud Sēquanōs plūrimum poterat et Helvētiīs erat amīcus, 1, 9, 3, *Dumnorix was very influential among the Sequani and a friend to the Helvetians.* **Dēmocritus alba discernere et ātra nōn poterat,** *TD.* 5, 114, *Democritus could not tell white and black apart.* **et discipulus et magister perhibēbantur inprobī,** Pl. *B.* 425, *both pupil and master were rated as knaves.*

1646. With three or more members, **et** is either used between the members or, frequently, prefixed for emphasis to all. Often, however, it is omitted throughout (1637), or a third member is appended by **-que** (1651): as,

persuādent Rauricīs et Tulingīs et Latovicīs utī ūnā cum hīs proficīscantur, 1, 5, 4, *they induce the Rauricans, Tulingans, and Latovicans to join them in their march.* **is et in custōdiam cīvēs Rōmānōs dedit et supplicātiōnem mihī dēcrēvit et indicēs maximīs praemiīs adfēcit,** *C.* 4, 10, *this person voted in the first place to put Roman citizens in ward, then to decree a thanksgiving in my honour, and lastly to reward the informers with liberal gifts.*

1647. Two members belonging closely together as a pair, and connected by **et, atque,** or **-que,** are sometimes put asyndetically with another member or members : as,

Aeduī ferunt sē dēiectōs prīncipātū ; queruntur fortūnae commūtātiōnem et Caesaris indulgentiam in sē requīrunt, 7, 63, 8, *the Aeduans set forth that they were cast down from the chief place ; they complain of the change of fortune, and say they miss Caesar's former kindness to them.* **nūntiātum est equitēs Ariovistī propius tumulum accēdere et ad nostrōs adequitāre ; lapidēs in nostrōs conicere,** 1, 46, 1, *it was reported that Ariovistus's cavalry were moving nearer the hillock and galloping up to the Romans ; that they were throwing stones at our men.*

1648. et has sometimes the meaning of *also* or of *and also,* particularly when there is a change of speakers, or before a pronoun : as, et hoc sciō, Plin. *Ep.* 1, 12, 11, *I know that too.* Sometimes also after vērum, nam, and simul, especially when a pronoun follows. Not in Caesar.

1649. (2.) -que, *and,* combines members which belong together and make a whole, though they may be different or opposed to each other; the second member is often a mere appendage : as,

rogat ōratque tē, *RA.* 144, *he begs and entreats you,* or *he earnestly entreats you.* libertī servolīque nōbilium, *RA.* 141, *the freedmen and slaves of the great,* or *retainers, bond and free.* omnēs ea, quae bona videntur, sequuntur fugiuntque contrāria, *TD.* 4, 12, *everybody runs after what seems good and avoids the opposite.* -que is usually put after the first word of the new member. It is particularly common in old or legal style.

1650. The combination -que . . . -que, *both . . . and,* is very common in poetry : as, noctēsque diēsque, E. in *CM.* 1, *both night and day.* In prose, it is used by Sallust when the first word is a pronoun : as, mēque rēgnumque meum, *I.* 10, 2, *both myself and my throne :* and by Livy to connect two relative sentences : as, omnēs quīque Rōmae quīque in exercitū erant, 22, 26, 5, *everybody, both people in Rome and people in the army.*

1651. After two members without a connective, a third member is sometimes appended by -que : as,

satis habēbat hostem rapīnīs, pābulātiōnibus, populātiōnibusque prohibēre, 1, 15, 4, *he was satisfied with keeping the enemy from plundering, foraging, and ravaging.*

1652. (3.) atque, or before any consonant except h often ac, *and, and besides,* adds something belonging essentially to what goes before, but more important as a supplement or extension ; as,

sē ex nāvī prōiēcit atque in hostēs aquilam ferre coepit, 4, 25, 4, *he sprang overboard and furthermore proceeded to bear the eagle upon the enemy.* magna dīs immortālibus habenda est atque huic Iovī Statōrī grātia, *C.* 1, 11, *we owe a great debt of gratitude to the gods immortal in general, and to yon Jove the Stayer in particular.* atque . . . atque occurs for et . . . et once in Vergil, and once in Silius Italicus.

1653. atque is used in comparisons, after words of likeness and unlikeness : as,

parī spatiō trānsmissus, atque ex Galliā est in Britanniam, 5, 13, 2, *the journey across is just as long as it is from Gaul to Britain.* idemque iussērunt simulācrum Iovis facere maius et contrā, atque anteā fuerat, ad orientem convertere, *C.* 3, 20, *and they furthermore gave orders to make a statue of Jupiter, a bigger one, and to turn it round to the east, the opposite of the way it originally faced.* Sometimes et is thus used after alius, aliter, aequē, pariter, &c. : see the dictionary.

1654. With adjectives and adverbs in the comparative degree, atque sometimes takes the place of quam *than,* when the first member of comparison is negative (1895) : as, amīcior mihi nūllus vīvit atque is est, Pl. *Mer.* 897, *I have no greater friend alive than that man is.* So in Plautus, Terence, Lucretius, Catullus, Vergil, rarely in Cicero, and in Horace even when the first member is positive.

1655. A sentence is often introduced by **et, -que,** or **atque,** where *but* would be used in English, particularly so when a positive sentence follows a negative one : as,

Sōcratēs nec patrōnum quaesīvit nec iūdicibus supplex fuit adhibuitque līberam contumāciam, *TD.* 1, 71, *Socrates did not try to find an advocate nor bow the knee to his judges, but he was plain-spoken and defiant.* nostrōrum mīlitum impetum hostēs ferre nōn potuērunt ac terga vertērunt, 4, 35, 2, *the enemy could not stand the dash of our people, but turned their backs.* hominis nē Graecī quidem ac Mȳsī potius, *QFr.* 1, 1, 19, *a creature who is not even a Greek, but more of a Mysian.*

1656. Two sentences, one of which would ordinarily be introduced by a subordinating temporal conjunction, are sometimes, mostly in poetry, coordinated by **et** or **-que:** as, dīxit et in silvam pennīs ablāta refūgit, V. 3, 258. *she spake, and on her pinions sweeping, vanished to the wood,* i.e. simul atque dīxit, refūgit.

1657. (4.) **neque** or **nec,** *neither, nor, and … not, but … not,* is used as a negative copulative, sometimes as a negative adversative : as,

opīniōnibus volgī rapimur in errōrem nec vēra cernimus, *Leg.* 2, 43, *we are swept into error by the delusions of the world and cannot make out the truth.* nōn enim temere nec fortuītō creātī sumus, *TD.* 1, 118, *for we were not created at adventure nor by accident.* subsidiō suīs iērunt collemque cēpērunt, neque nostrōrum mīlitum impetum sustinēre potuērunt, 7, 62, 8, *they went to aid their people and carried the hill, but they could not stand the fiery onset of our soldiers.* **neque** or **nec** is often repeated : as, nec meliōrēs nec beātiōrēs esse possumus, *RP.* 1, 32, *we can neither be better nor wiser.*

1658. **nec** is rarely used in the sense of **nē … quidem,** *not even, not … either:* as, **nec nunc,** H. *S.* 2, 3, 262, *not even now,* a free quotation of **nē nunc quidem,** T. *Eu.* 46. **nec … quidem,** *and not even,* is used once or twice for the common **ac nē … quidem** or **et nē … quidem.**

1659. Instead of **neque** or **nec,** *and not,* the copulatives **et, atque,** rarely **-que,** followed by a negative, **nōn, nēmō, nihil,** &c., are sometimes used in Cicero and Livy, less often in old Latin, and rarely in Caesar and Sallust : as, quid tū fēcissēs, sī tē Tarentum et nōn Samarobrīvam mīsissem? *Fam.* 7, 12, 1, *what would you have done, if I had sent you to Tarentum, and not to Samarobriva?* Particularly thus **et nōn,** or oftener **ac nōn,** in corrections. But ordinarily **neque** or **nec** is preferred to **et nōn,** and **nec quisquam,** &c., to **et nēmō,** &c. (1445).

1660. When **neque** is followed by another negative, the assertion is positive (1452) : as,

nec hoc ille nōn vīdit, *Fin.* 4, 60, *and the man did not fail to see this.* This positive use begins with Varro. In old Latin two negatives, and particularly **neque … haud,** are often used, as in old English, to strengthen the negation (1453).

1661. After a general negative, a word may be emphasized by **nē … quidem** or **nōn modo,** or the parts of a compound sentence may be distributed by **neque … neque,** without destroying the negation: as, nihil in locīs commūnibus, nē in fānīs quidem, nihil istum neque prīvātī neque pūblicī tōtā in Siciliā relīquisse, *V.* 4, 2, *that the defendant has left nothing untouched in public places, no, not even in the temples, nothing either in the way of private or of public property, in all Sicily.* Similarly when a coordinate member is appended with neque: as, nequeō satis mīrārī neque conicere, T. *Eu.* 547, *I can't quite puzzle out or guess.*

COMBINATION OF DIFFERENT COPULATIVES.

1662. Different copulatives are sometimes combined, as follows.

1663. (1.) The affirmative copulatives et and -que are sometimes combined, particularly in abridged sentences: as,

et Epamīnōndās praeclārē cecinisse dīcitur, Themistoclēsque est habitus indoctior, *TD.* 1, 4, *Epaminondas in the first place is said to have played beautifully, and Themistocles was not considered exactly an educated man.* This combination is used by Cicero rarely, by Horace in the satires, and rarely by late writers.

1664. The sequence -que . . . et is rare in old Latin, and not used by Caesar, Vergil, or Horace. -que . . . atque is first used by Lucretius, then by Vergil, Ovid, Livy, and Tacitus.

1665. (2.) Affirmative and negative copulatives are sometimes combined. Thus neque or nec combined with et, in the sequences neque . . . et and et . . . neque, which is rare in old Latin, is common in Cicero: as,

nec mīror et gaudeō, *Fam.* 10, 1, 4, *in the first place I am not surprised, and in the second place I feel glad;* neque . . . et nōn, however, is rare. patēbat via et certa neque longa, *Ph.* 11, 4, *there lay a road open at once plain and not long.* neque . . . -que begins with Cicero, but is rare (1655), neque . . . ac begins with Tacitus.

1666. Of all the Latin writers, Tacitus aims most at variety by combination of asyndeton and by the use of different copulatives: as, rēgem Rhamsēn Libyā Aethiopiā Mēdīsque et Persīs et Bactriānō ac Scythā potītum, 2, 60, *that king Rhamses got control of Libya and Aethiopia and the Medes and Persians, and the Bactrian and Scythian.*

(*b.*) DISJUNCTIVE CONJUNCTIONS.

1667. Disjunctive conjunctions connect the sentences, but disconnect the meaning. They are aut, vel, sīve or seu, -ve, and an, *or.* Of thesè conjunctions, aut, vel, and sīve, are often placed before two or more members of a sentence in the sense of *either . . . or.* And in poetry, -ve . . . -ve sometimes occurs.

1668. (1.) aut, *or*, sometimes *or even, or at least,* is used between two members which are to be represented as essentially different in meaning, and of which one excludes the other: as, hīc vincendum aut moriendum, mīlitēs, est, L. 21, 43, 5, *here you must conquer, my men, or die.* hōrae mōmentō cita mors venit aut victōria laeta, H. *S.* 1, 1, 7, *within an hour's brief turn comes speedy death or victory glad.* aut vīvam aut moriar, T. *Ph.* 483, *I shall either live or die.* sīderibus dubiīs aut illō tempore quō sē frīgida circumagunt pigrī serrāca Boōtae, J. 5, 22, *when stars blink faint, or even at the time when round rolls slow Boōtes' frigid wain.* quā rē vī aut clam agendum est, *Att.* 10, 12, 5 [10, 12 b, 2], *so we must use force, or at any rate secrecy.* Sometimes aut connects kindred ideas : as, equī ictī aut vulnerātī cōnsternā\ bantur, L. 21, 33, 6, *the horses kept getting frantic from being hit or wounded.*

1669. aut, in the sense of *otherwise, or else,* sometimes introduces a statement of what necessarily follows, if something else is not done : as,

audendum est aliquid ūniversīs, aut omnia singulīs patienda, L. 6, 18, 7, *you must make some bold dash collectively, or else you must suffer every thing individually.* vel is also occasionally used in this sense.

1670. (2.) vel, *or,* introduces an alternative as a matter of choice or preference, and often relates merely to the selection of an expression : as,

eius modī coniūnctiōnem tēctōrum oppidum vel urbem appellāvērunt, *RP.* 1, 41, *such a collection of dwelling-houses they called, well, a town or a city, whichever you please.* vel imperātōre vel mīlite mē ūtiminī, S. *C.* 20, 16, *use me as your generalissimo or as a private, whichever you will.* Catilīnam ex urbe vel ēiēcimus vel ēmīsimus vel ipsum ēgredientem verbīs prōsecūtī sumus, *C.* 2, 1, *we have — what shall I say ? — driven Catiline out of town, or allowed him to go out, or, when he was going out of his own accord, wished him a pleasant journey.* vel is often followed by etiam, potius, or dīcam. From Tacitus on, vel is sometimes used in the sense of aut : as, vincendum vel cadendum esse, Ta. 14, 35, *they must do or die* (1668).

1671. vel is sometimes used in the sense of *if you will, even,* or *perhaps,* especially before superlatives, or in the sense of *for instance :* as,

huius domus est vel optima Messānae, nōtissima quidem certē, *V.* 4, 3, *this gentleman's house is perhaps the finest in all Messana, at any rate the best known.* amant tēd omnēs mulierēs, neque iniūriā : vel illae, quae here palliō mē reprehendērunt, Pl. *MG.* 58, *the girls all idolize you, well they may ; for instance those that buttonholed me yesterday.*

1672. (3.) sīve or seu, *or,* used as a disjunctive conjunction, denotes a distinction which is not essential, or the speaker's uncertainty as to some matter of detail ; when used once only, it is chiefly in corrections, often with potius, *rather,* added ; as,

is Ascanius urbem mātrī seu novercae relīquit, L. 1, 3, 3, *said Ascanius left the city to his mother, or his stepmother, if you prefer.* dīxit Pompēius, sīve voluit, *QFr.* 2, 3, 2, *Pompey made a speech, or rather attempted to make one.*

1673. sīve is often repeated in the sense of *either,* or *no matter whether . . . or :* as, ita sīve cāsū sīve cōnsiliō deōrum, quae pars calamitātem populō Rōmānō intulerat, ea prīnceps poenās persolvit, 1, 12, 6, *thus, no matter whether from chance or through special providence, the part which had done damage to Rome was the first to pay penalty in full.*

1674. (4.) -ve rarely connects main sentences, usually only the less important parts of the sentence, or, oftener still, subordinate sentences : as,

cūr timeam dubitemve locum dēfendere ? J. 1, 103, *why should I fear or hesitate to stand my ground?* Appius ad mē bis terve litterās mīserat, *Att.* 6, 1, 2, *Appius had written me two or three times.* With nē it forms nēve or neu, which is used as a continuation of nē or ut : see 1581 ; 1586; 1947.

1675. (5.) The interrogative particle an sometimes becomes a disjunctive conjunction, *or, or possibly, or perhaps:* as, Simōnidēs an quis alius, *Fin.* 2, 104, *Simonides or possibly somebody else.* Common in Cicero, though not so in his speeches, and in Livy, commonest in Tacitus.

(*c.*) ADVERSATIVE CONJUNCTIONS.

1676. Adversative conjunctions connect the sentences, but contrast the meaning. They are autem, *on the other hand,* sed, vērum, cēterum, *but,* vērō, *but, indeed,* at, *but,* tamen, nihilō minus, *nevertheless.*

Of these conjunctions, autem and vērō are put after one word, or sometimes after two closely connected words ; tamen is put either at the beginning, or after an emphatic word.

1677. (1.) autem, *again, on the other hand, however,* simply continues the discourse by a statement appended to the preceding, without setting it aside : as,

hōrum prīncipibus pecūniās, cīvitātī autem imperium tōtīus prōvinciae pollicētur, 7, 64, 8, *to the chieftains of this nation on the one hand he promises moneys, and to the community on the other hand the hegemony of the whole province.* The opposition in a sentence introduced by autem, *again,* is often so weak that a copulative, *and,* might be used : as, ille quī Dīogenem adulēscēns, post autem Panaetium audierat, *Fin.* 2, 24, *the man who in his early youth had sat at the feet of Diogenes, and afterwards of Panaetius.* autem is oftenest used in philosophical or didactic discourse, 'ess frequently in history, oratory, or poetry.

1678. autem is often used in questions: as, metuō crēdere : : crēdere autem ? Pl. *Ps.* 304, *I am afraid to trust : · trust, do you say?*

1679. (2.) sed or set, and vērum, *but,* are used either in restriction, or, after a negative, in direct opposition : as,

vēra dīcō, sed nēquīquam, quoniam nōn vīs crēdere, Pl. *Am.* 835, *I tell the truth, but all in vain, since you are bent not to believe.* nōn ego erus tibī, sed servos sum, Pl. *Cap.* 241, *I am not your master, but your slave.*

1680. nōn modo, or nōn sōlum, *not only, not alone,* is followed by sed etiam or vērum etiam, *but also,* by sed . . . quoque, *but . . . as well,* or sometimes by sed or vērum alone : as, quī nōn sōlum interfuit hīs rēbus, sed etiam praefuit, *Fam.* 1, 8, 1, *who has not had a hand only in these matters, but complete charge.* quī omnibus negōtiīs nōn interfuit sōlum, sed praefuit, *Fam.* 1, 6, 1. nōn tantum is sometimes used by Livy, and once or twice by Cicero, but not by Caesar or Sallust, for nōn modo. Livy and Tacitus sometimes omit sed or vērum.

1681. nōn modo has sometimes the meaning of nōn dīcam : as, nōn modo ad certam mortem, sed in magnum vītae discrīmen, *Sest.* 45, *I won't say to certain death, but to great risk of life.*

1682. nōn modo or nōn sōlum, when attended by another negative, may also be followed by sed nē . . . quidem, *but not even,* or sed vix, *but hardly :* as,

nōn modo tibī nōn īrāscor, sed nē reprehendō quidem factum tuum, *Sull.* 50, *so far from being angry with you I do not even criticise your action.* When both members have the same predicate, usually placed last, the negation in nē . . . quidem or vix usually applies to the first member also : as, tālis vir nōn modo facere, sed nē cōgitāre quidem quicquam audēbit, quod nōn audeat praedicāre, *Off.* 3, 77, *a man of this kind will not only not venture to do, but not even to conceive anything which he would not venture to trumpet to the world,* or *will not venture to conceive, much less do.*

1683. (3.) cēterum is sometimes used in the sense of sed, in Terence, Sallust, and Livy. Sometimes also in the sense of sed rē vērā, in Sallust and Tacitus, to contrast reality with pretence.

1684. (4.) vērō, *but, indeed,* introduces an emphatic contrast or a climax : as,

sed sunt haec leviōra, illa vērō gravia atque magna, *Pl.* 86, *however, all this is less important, but the following is weighty and great.* scīmus mūsicēn nostrīs mōribus abesse ā prīncipis persōnā, saltāre vērō etiam in vitiīs pōnī, N. 15, 1, 2, *we know that, according to our Roman code of ethics, music is not in keeping with the character of an eminent man, and as to dancing, why that is classed among vices.* In Plautus, vērō is only used as an adverb ; its use as an adversative conjunction begins with Terence. In the historians, vērō is often equivalent to autem.

1685. (5.) at, *but,* denotes emphatic lively opposition, an objection. or a contrast : as,

brevis ā nātūrā nōbīs vīta data est ; at memoria bene redditae vītae sempiterna, *Ph.* 14, 32, *a short life hath been given by nature unto man ; but the memory of a life laid down in a good cause endureth for ever.* at is often used before a word indicating a person or a place, to shift the scene, especially in history. In law language, ast sometimes occurs, and ast is also sometimes used, generally for the metre, in Vergil, Horace, and late poetry.

1686. (6.) tamen, nihilō minus, *nevertheless.*

accūsātus capitis absolvitur, multātur tamen pecūniā, N. 4, 2, 6, *he is accused on a capital charge and acquitted, but is nevertheless fined in a sum of money.* minus dolendum fuit rē nōn perfectā, sed poeniendum certē nihilō minus, *Mil.* 19, *there was less occasion for sorrow because the thing was not done, but certainly none the less for punishment.*

(2.) OTHER WORDS AS CONNECTIVES.

1687. Instead of a conjunction, other words are often used as connectives: as, **pars** . . . **pars, alii** . . . **alii**; adverbs of order or time: as, **primum,** *first,* or **primo,** *at first* . . . **deinde** . . . **tum,** &c.; and particularly adverbs in pairs: as, **modo** . . . **modo, tum** . . . **tum** less frequently **quā** . . . **quā, simul** . . . **simul**: as,

multitūdō pars prōcurrit in viās, pars in vestibulīs stat, pars ex tēctīs prōspectant, L. 24, 21, 8, *part of the throng runs out into the streets, others stand in the fore-courts, others gaze from the house-tops.* prōferēbant alii purpuram, tūs alii, gemmās alii, *V.* 5, 146, *they produced some of them purple, others frankincense, others precious stones.* prīmō pecūniae, deinde imperī cupīdō crēvit, S. *C.* 10, 3, *at first a love of money waxed strong, then of power.* tum hoc mihī probābilius, tum illud vidētur, *Ac.* 2, 134, *one minute this seems to me more likely, and another minute that.*

1688. Simple sentences may also be coordinated by words denoting inference or cause, such as **ergō, igitur, itaque,** *therefore;* **nam, namque, enim,** *for,* **etenim,** *for you see:* as,

adfectus animī in bonō virō laudābilis, et vīta igitur laudābilis bonī virī, et honesta ergō, quoniam laudābilis, *TD.* 5, 47. *the disposition in a good man is praiseworthy, and the life therefore of a good man is praiseworthy, and virtuous accordingly, seeing it is praiseworthy.* Of these words, **nam, namque,** and **itaque** are usually put first in the sentence; **enim** and **igitur,** usually after one word, rarely after two. But in Plautus regularly, and generally in Terence, **enim** has the meaning of *indeed, verily, truly, depend upon it,* and may stand at the beginning.

1689. In Plautus, the combination **ergō igitur** occurs, and in Terence and Livy, **itaque ergō**: as, **itaque ergō cōnsulibus diēs dicta est,** L. 3, 31, 5, *accordingly then a day was set for the trial of the consuls.*

1690. The interrogative **quippe,** *why?* losing its interrogative meaning, is also used as a coordinating word, **why,** or *for:* as, **hōc genus omne maestum ac sollicitum est cantōris morte Tigellī: quippe benignus erat,** H. *S.* 1, 2, 2, *such worthies all are sad, are woebegone over Tigellius the minstrel's death; why he was generosity itself.*

1691. Simple sentences may also be coordinated by pronominal words, such as **hinc, inde,** *hence,* **eō, ideō, idcircō, proptereā,** *so, on that account,* &c.: as,

nocte perveniēbant; eō custōdiās hostium fallēbant. L. 23, 19, 10, *they got there in the night; in that way they eluded the enemy's pickets.* But **eō** and **ideō** are not used thus by Cicero, Caesar, or Sallust, or **idcircō** and **proptereā** by Cicero or Caesar.

1692. In animated rhetorical discourse any word repeated with emphasis may serve as a copulative; this is called *Anaphora:* as,

mīles in forum, mīles in cūriam comitābātur, Ta. 1, 7, *soldiers went with him to the forum, soldiers to the senate chamber.* ēreptī estis ex interitū, ēreptī sine sanguine, sine exercitū, sine dīmicātiōne, *C.* 3, 23, *you are rescued from death, rescued without bloodshed, without an army, without a struggle.*

THE INTERMEDIATE COORDINATE SENTENCE.

1693. A sentence coordinate in form with another sentence is often equivalent in meaning to a subordinate sentence. Such sentences are called *Intermediate Coordinate Sentences.*

The most varied relations of a subordinate sentence may be thus expressed by a coordinate sentence, and the combination of the two coordinate sentences is in sense equivalent to a complex sentence.

1694. Such coordinated sentences are a survival of a more primitive state of the language. They occur oftenest in Plautus and Terence, in Cicero's philosophical works and letters, in Horace's satires and epistles, and in Juvenal. In general they have been superseded by complex sentences, even in the oldest specimens of the language.

1695. I. The relation of the two members may not be indicated by the mood, but left to be determined from the context.

Thus, in the combination **amat, sapit,** Pl. *Am.* 995, *he is in love, he shows his sense,* the two members **amat** and **sapit** are alike in form. But in sense, **sapit** is the main member and **amat** is the subordinate member. Just what the relation of the **amat** is, whether it is **sī amat,** *if he is in love,* **cum amat,** *when he is in love,* **quod amat,** *because he is in love,* or **etsī amat,** *though he is in love,* &c., &c., is left to the reader to make out. The following are some of the commonest combinations of this class :

1696. (1.) The coordinated member may stand instead of the commoner accusative and infinitive with a verb of perceiving, thinking, knowing, or saying (2175). Such are **crēdō, fateor, opīnor, putō, certum est,** &c.: as,

lūdōs mē facitis, intellegō, Pl. *Per.* 802, *you are making game of me, I am aware.* **nārrō tibī: plānē relēgātus mihī videor,** *Att.* 2, 11, 1, *I tell you what, I seem to myself regularly banished.* **spērō, servābit fidem,** Pl. *E.* 124, *I hope he 'll keep his word* (2235).

1697. (2.) The coordinated member may be a direct question or an exclamation.

Thus (*a.*) in enquiries calling for an answer : as, **sīgnī dīc quid est,** Pl. *Am.* 421, *tell me, what is there in the shape of seal?* (1251). Or (*b.*) in ejaculation : as, **viden ut astat furcifer?** Pl. *Most.* 1172, *seest how the knave is posing there?* **vidēte quaesō, quid potest pecūnia,** Pl. *St.* 410, *see pray how all-commanding money is.* This construction occurs oftenest in comedy, and with an imperative meaning *say, tell,* or *look.* The subordinate construction is the rule : see 1773.

1698. (3.) The coordinated member rarely represents a relative sentence (1816) : as,

urbs antīqua fuit, Tyriī tenuēre colōnī, V. 1, 12, *there was an ancient town, which Tyrian settlers held.* **est locus, Hesperiam Grāī cōgnōmine dīcunt,** V. 1, 530. *there is a place. the Greeks by name Hesperia call,* imitated from **est locus Hesperiam quam mortālēs perhibēbant,** E. in Macrob *Sat.* 6, 1, *there is a place which sons of men Hesperia called.*

1699. (4.) The coordinated member may represent a subordinate temporal member : as,

vēnit hiemps, teritur Sicuōnia bāca trapētis, V. *G.* 2, 519, *has winter come, in mills is Sicyon's olive ground* (1860). vix prōram attigerat, rumpit Sāturnia fūnem, V. 12, 650, *scarce had he touched the prow, Saturnia snaps the rope*, i. e. cum rumpit (1869). lūcēbat iam ferē, prōcēdit in medium, *V.* 5, 94, *it was just about light, when he presents himself before them.* fuit ōrnandus in Mānīliā lēge Pompēius ; temperātā ōrātiōne ōrnandī cōpiam persecūtī sumus, *O.* 102, *when I had to glorify Pompey in the matter of the Manilius law, I went through the ample material for glorification in moderate language.*

1700. (5.) The coordinated member may be equivalent to a member with **ut**, expressing result (1965) : as,

iam faxō sciēs, T. *Eu.* 663, *I'll let you know at once*, i. e. sciās (1712) or ut sciās (1965). iam faxō hīc erunt, Pl. *B.* 715, *I'll warrant they shall soon be here.* adeō rēs rediit, adulēscentulus victus est, T. *Hau.* 113, *things came to such a pass the youngster was put down.* cētera dē genere hōc, adeō sunt multa, loquācem dēlassāre valent Fabium, H. *S.* 1, 1, 11, *the other cases of the kind, so plentiful are they, might tire the gabbling Fabius out.* ita haec ūmōre tigna pūtent, nōn videor mihi sarcīre posse aedīs meās, Pl. *Most.* 146, *so sopping rotten are these joists, I don't think I can patch my house.* ita avidō ingeniō fuit, numquam indicāre id filiō voluit suō, Pl. *Aul. prol.* 9, *so niggardly was he, he'd never point it out to his own son.* tanta incepta rēs est, haud somnīculōsē hoc agundumst, Pl. *Cap.* 227, *so big a job have we begun, not drowsily must this be done.*

1701. (6.) The coordinated member may be equivalent to a conditional protasis : as,

(*a.*) fīliam quis habet, pecūniā opus est, *Par.* 44, *a man has a daughter, he needs money.* trīstis es, indignor, O. *Tr.* 4, 3, 33, *if you are sad, I feel provoked.* (*b.*) sī iste ībit, ītō ; stābit, astātō simul, Pl. *Ps.* 863, *if he shall move, move thou ; but shall he stand, stand by his side.* in caelum, iusseris, ībit, J. 3, 78, *say but the word, he'll mount the sky.* (*c.*) subdūc cibum ūnum diem āthlētae, Iovem Olympium inplōrābit, *TD.* 2, 40, *cut off an athlete from his food just a day, he will pray to Jupiter aloft in Olympus* (1574). (*d.*) Zēnōnem rogēs, respondeat totidem verbis, *Fin.* 4, 69, *you may ask Zeno, he would answer in just as many words* (1556). (*e.*) tū quoque magnam partem opere in tantō, sineret dolor, Īcare, habērēs, V. 6, 31, *thou too a goodly space in work so vast, had grief allowed, O Icarus, hadst filled* (1559). at darēs hanc vim M. Crassō, in forō saltāret, *Off.* 3, 75, *but had you given this chance to Crassus, he would have capered in the market place* (1559). nam absque tē esset, hodiē numquam ad sōlem occāsum vīverem, Pl. *Men.* 1022, *for were it not for you, I ne'er should live this blessed day till set of sun* (1560, 2110). (*f.*) ūnā fuissēmus, cōnsilium certē nōn dēfuisset, *Att.* 9, 6, 6, *had we been together, we certainly should not have lacked a programme* (1561).

1702. (7.) The coordinated member may be equivalent to a concession : as,

id fortasse nōn perfēcimus, cōnātī quidem sumus, O. 210 ; *though we have perhaps not attained unto this, yet we have attempted it.* ergō illī intellegunt quid Epicūrus dīcat, ego nōn intellegō ? *Fin.* 2, 13, *do those gentlemen then understand what Epicurus means, and I not ?*

1703. (8.) The coordinated member may denote efficient cause or rea·son : as,

peregrīnus ego sum, Sauream nōn nōvī, Pl. *As.* 464, *I am a stranger, and I don't know Saurea.* mulier es, audācter iūrās, Pl. *Am.* 836, *because you are a woman, you are bold to swear.* tacent, satis laudant, T. *Eu.* 476, *their silence is sufficient praise.*

1704. (9.) The coordinated member may represent the protasis of a comparative sentence with ut (1937): as,

ita mē dī ament, honestust, T. *Eu.* 474, *so help me heaven, he is a proper man.* sollicitat, ita vīvam, mē tua, mī Tirō, valētūdō, *Fam.* 16, 20, *your health, dear Tiro, keeps me fidgety, as I hope to live.*

1705. II. The subordinate idea is often indicated by the subjunctive of desire coordinated with another verb, usually with one which has a different subject.

Thus, the combination amēs: oportet, *you should love; it is right* (1547), in which the two verbs are used separately, blends into one whole, amēs oportet, *Fin.* 2, 35, *it is right you should love.* The verb with which the subjunctive is coordinated specifies more exactly the general idea of desire contained in the subjunctive itself. The tense of the coordinate subjunctive is regulated by that of the other verb.

1706. The negative employed with coordinated subjunctives is the adverb nē, *not.*

Thus, the combination vidē: nē mē lūdās, *see to it; don't you fool me* (1547), in which the two verbs are used separately, blends into one whole, vidē nē mē lūdās, Pl. *Cur.* 325, *see to it you don't fool me.* Similarly, metuō: nē peccet, *I am afraid; let her not slip up* (1548), becomes metuō nē peccet, Pl. *Per.* 624, *I am afraid she may slip up.* From its frequent use in sentences of subordinate meaning, nē came at an early period to be regarded as a subordinating conjunction also, *lest, that . . . not,* as well as an adverb, and took the place of the less usual ut nē. Hence members with nē are more conveniently treated under the head of subordination (1947).

1707. (1.) The subjunctive is often coordinated with verbs of wishing. Such are volō, nōlō, rarely mālō, optō, placet, &c.: as,

animum advortās volō, Pl. *Cap.* 388, *I wish you would pay heed* (1548). quid vīs faciam? T. *Hau.* 846, *what wilt thou I should do?* (1563). vin conmūtēmus? tuam ego dūcam et tū meam? Pl. *Tri.* 59, *would you like to swap? I take your wife, and you take mine?* (1563). mālō tē sapiēns hostis metuat, quam stultī cīvēs laudent, L. 22, 39, 20, *I would rather a wise enemy should fear you, than stupid fellow-citizens admire you* (1548). Coordination is the rule with velim, vellem, &c., used in the sense of utinam (1540) : as, dē Menedēmō vellem vērum fuisset, dē rēgīnā velim vērum sit, *Att.* 15, 4, 4, *about Menedemus I could wish it had been true, about the queen I hope it may be true.* tellūs optem prius īma dehīscat, V. 4, 24, *I would the earth to deepest depths might sooner yawn.* L. Domitius dīxit placēre sibī sententiās dē singulīs ferrent, Caes. *C.* 3, 83, 3, *Domitius said his view was they should vote on the men separately.*

287

1708. (2.) The subjunctive is often coordinated with verbs of request, entreaty, encouragement, exhortation, charge, direction, command. Such are **precor, rogō, ōrō, petō, hortor, postulō, moneō, cēnseō; mandō, imperō, praecipiō, dēcernō**; and chiefly in old Latin, **iubeō** : as,

(*a*.) **reddās incolumem precor,** H. I, 3, 7, *deliver him up safe I pray.* **rogat fīnem ōrandī faciat,** I, 20, 5, *he requests him to make an end of entreaty.* **ā tē id quod suēstī petō, mē absentem dēfendās,** *Fam.* 15, 8, *I ask you to do as you always do, stand up for me when I am away.* **nōn hortor sōlum sed etiam rogō atque ōrō, tē colligās virumque praebeās,** *Fam.* 5, 18, 1, *I not only exhort you, but more than that I beg and entreat you, pull yourself together and quit you like a man.* **postulō etiam atque etiam cōnsiderēs quō prōgrediāre,** L. 3, 45, 10, *I charge you think again and again what you are coming to.* **tē moneō videās, quid agās.** **magnō opere cēnseō, dēsistās,** *V.* 5, 174, *I advise you to consider what you are doing. I earnestly recommend you to stop.* **hunc admonet iter cautē faciat,** 5, 49, 3, *he warns him he must pursue his march with care.* (*b*.) **huic mandat Rēmōs adeat,** 3, 11, 2, *he directs him to go to the Remans.* **praecipit ūnum omnēs peterent Indutiomarum,** 5, 58, 5, *he says they must all concentrate their attack on Indutiomarus.* **huic imperat quās possit adeat cīvitātēs,** 4, 21, 8, *he orders him to visit such communities as he can.* **senātus dēcrēvit darent operam cōnsulēs nē quid rēs pūblica dētrīmentī caperet,** S. C. 29, 2, *the senate decreed the consuls must see to it that the commonwealth received no harm.* **iube maneat,** T. *Hau.* 737, *tell her she must stay.* **mīlitēs certiōrēs facit, paulisper intermitterent proelium,** 3, 5, 3, *he tells the soldiers they must stop fighting a little while.* **abī, nūntiā patribus urbem Rōmānam mūniant,** L. 22, 49, 10, *go tell the fathers they must fortify Rome town.* **dīxī equidem in carcerem īrēs,** Pl. *St.* 624, *I'm sure I told you you must go to jail.* **scrībit Labiēnō cum legiōne veniat,** 5, 46, 3, *he writes to Labienus he must come with a legion.* **lēgātiōnem mittunt sī velit suōs recipere, obsidēs sibī remittat,** 3, 8, 5, *they send an embassy, if he wishes to get his own men back, he must send back the hostages to them.*

1709. (3.) The subjunctive is often coordinated with expressions of propriety or necessity. Such are **oportet, optumum est, opus est, decet, necesse est.**

mē ipsum amēs oportet, nōn mea, *Fin.* 2, 85, *it is myself you should love, not my possessions.* **quoniam habēs istum equom, aut ēmerīs oportet, aut hērēditāte possideās, aut surripueris necesse est,** *Inv.* 1, 84, *since you are in possession of that horse, you must either have bought him or inherited him, or else you must necessarily have stolen him.* **sed taceam optumumst,** Pl. *E.* 60, *but I'd best hold my tongue.* **nihil opust rescīscat,** Pl. *Mer.* 1004, *she need n't find it out at all.* **condemnētur necesse est,** *RA.* 111, *be condemned he needs must.*

1710. (4.) The subjunctive is sometimes coordinated with verbs of permission or concession. Such are **permittō** in Sallust and Livy, **concēdō**, also **sinō**, mostly in the imperative, chiefly in old Latin and poetry, and the impersonal **licet** (used thus often in Cicero, rarely before or after) : as,

supplēmentum scrīberent cōnsulēs, permissum, L. 27, 22, 11, *leave was given that the consuls might fill up the army.* **sine sciam,** L. 2, 40, 5, *let me know.* **sine modo adveniat senex,** Pl. *Most.* 11, *let but the old man come.* **fremant omnēs licet, dīcam quod sentiō,** *DO.* 1, 195, *though everybody may growl, I will say what I think.* See 1904.

288

1711. (5.) The subjunctive is often coordinated with the imperative cavĕ, cavētō, cavēte, *beware,* used in the sense of nē (1585): as,

cavē faciās, *Att.* 13, 33, 4, *don't do it.* cave dīrumpātis, Pl. *Poen. prol.* 117, *don't break it off* (1075).

1712. (6.) The subjunctive is often coordinated with verbs of giving, persuading, accomplishing, taking care. In this case the subjunctive has the meaning of purpose or result. Such are the imperative cedo, and dō, persuādeō, impetrō, cūrō, also faciō, particularly fac and facitō: as,

cedo bibam, Pl. *Most.* 373, *give me to drink.* date bibat tībīcinī, Pl. *St.* 757, *give the piper to drink.* huic Sp. Albīnus persuādet rēgnum Numidiae ā senātū petat, S. *I.* 35, 2, *Albinus induces him to ask of the senate the throne of Numidia.* tandem inpetrāvī abiret, Pl. *Tri.* 591, *at last I've coaxed him to clear out.* fac sciam, *Fam.* 7, 16, 3, *let me know.* faxō sciās, Pl. *Men.* 644, *I'll let you know,* much oftener sciēs or scībis (1700). fac bellus revertāre, *Fam.* 16, 18, 1, *mind you come back a beauty* (1579).

1713. A subjunctive is now and then loosely coordinated with verbs in general, to indicate the purpose of the action : as,

ēvocāte hūc Sōsiam, Blepharōnem arcēssat, Pl. *Am.* 949, *call Sosia here, let him fetch Blepharo.* clārē advorsum fābulābor, hic auscultet quae loquar, Pl. *Am.* 300, *I'll speak distinctly face to face, that he may hear what I shall say.* operam hanc subrupuī tibī, ex mē scīrēs, Pl. *Am.* 523, *I did this secretly for you, that you might learn from me.* manibus date līlia plēnīs, purpureōs spargam flōrēs, V. 6, 883, *lilies in handfuls give, I fain would scatter purple flowers,* that is, *that I may scatter.*

THE COMPLEX SENTENCE, OR SUBORDINATION.

1714. In a complex sentence, that is one consisting of a main and a subordinate sentence, the subordinate member is introduced by some subordinating word: such are,

I. Interrogative words, in indirect questions; II. Relative pronouns; III. Relative conjunctive particles, or conjunctive particles not of relative origin.

1715. Subordinate sentences may have the value of a substantive, usually as subject or as object; of an attributive; or of an adverb or adverbial adjunct : as,

(*a.*) eādem nocte accidit ut esset lūna plēna, 4, 29, 1, *it came to pass the same night that there was a full moon.* videō quid agās, *Fam.* 16, 17, *I see what you are driving at.* (*b.*) fundus quī est in agrō, quī Sabīnus vocātur, eum meum esse aiō, *Mur.* 26, *the estate which is in the territory which is called Sabine, that I maintain is mine,* lawyers' wordiness for fundus Sabīnus. (*c.*) cum advesperāsceret, ad pontem Mulvium pervēnērunt, *C.* 3, 5, *when it was getting dark, they reached the Mulvius bridge,* i. e. vespere, or prīmō vespere.

1716. Subordinate sentences which express time or place, are called *Temporal* or *Local* sentences; comparison or manner, *Comparative* or *Modal* sentences; condition, cause, or concession, *Conditional, Causal,* or *Concessive* sentences; purpose, *Final* sentences; result, *Consecutive* sentences.

1717. In a main sentence, the indicative present, future, and future perfect, and the imperative, are called *Primary Tenses ;* the indicative imperfect, historical perfect, and pluperfect, and the infinitive of intimation, are called *Secondary Tenses.* The perfect definite and the present of vivid narration are sometimes regarded as primary tenses, oftener as secondary tenses.

1718. Verbs which have an implication of futurity, such as those meaning *can, ought, must,* &c., with an infinitive, also subjunctives of wish (1540) or of exhortation (1547), may be called *Virtual Futures.*

1719. Sometimes the subjunctive serves as a main sentence : see 1762 ; sometimes a noun of the verb : see 1766.

MOOD OF THE SUBORDINATE SENTENCE.

1720. The indicative and the subjunctive are both used in subordinate sentences, as will be shown in the treatment of the several words of subordination. Some general uses may be mentioned collectively here.

THE INDICATIVE MOOD.

1721. The indicative is ordinarily used in sentences introduced by a relative pronoun, or by a causal conjunctive word other than cum.

pontem, quī erat ad Genāvam, iubet rescindī. I, 7, 2, *he orders the bridge which was near Geneva torn up.* concēdō, quia necesse est, *RA.* 145, *I give up, because I have to.* In sentences of this class, however, the subjunctive is often required, particularly in indirect discourse (1722), or in cases of attraction (1728).

THE SUBJUNCTIVE MOOD.

THE SUBJUNCTIVE OF INDIRECT DISCOURSE AND OF ATTRACTION.

1722. The subjunctive is used in relative, causal, temporal. and conditional sentences in indirect discourse, and in cases of attraction.

1723. A direct quotation or question gives the words of the original speaker without alteration. When the original words of a quotation or question are changed to conform to the construction of the sentence in which they are quoted, it is called *Indirect Discourse.*

1724. In the complete form of indirect discourse, the subjunctive is subordinate to an infinitive or an accusative with the infinitive, dependent on a verb of saying or thinking (2175) : as,

negat Epicūrus iūcundē posse vīvī, nisi cum virtūte vīvātur, *TD.* 3, 49, *Epicurus avers there is no living happily, without living virtuously ;* directly, iūcundē vīvī nōn potest, nisi cum virtūte vīvitur. Sōcratēs dīcere solēbat, omnēs in eō quod scīrent, satis esse ēloquentēs, *DO.* 1, 63, *Socrates used to maintain that all men were eloquent enough in a matter they knew ;* directly, omnēs in eō quod sciunt satis sunt ēloquentēs.

1725. The idea of saying or thinking is often not formally expressed in the main sentence, and the indirect discourse is intimated by the subordinate subjunctive only : as,

noctū ambulābat in pūblicō Themistoclēs, quod somnum capere nōn posset, *TD.* 4, 44, *Themistocles used to walk the streets nights, ' because he could not sleep,'* given as Themistocles's reason ; the writer's would be poterat. Paetus omnēs librōs, quōs frāter suus reliquisset, mihī dōnāvit, *Att.* 2, 1, 12, *Paetus made me a present of all the books ' that his brother had left.'* dum reliquae nāvēs eō convenīrent, in ancorīs expectāvit, 4, 23, 4, *he waited at anchor till the rest of the vessels should gather there* (2005). pervēnit priusquam Pompēius sentīre posset, Caes. *C.* 3, 67, 4, *he got there before Pompey should be able to learn of his coming* (1919). Xerxēs praemium prōposuit, quī invēnisset novam voluptātem, *TD.* 5, 20, *Xerxes offered a reward to anybody who should devise a new form of entertainment* (2110).

1726. A speaker or writer may quote his own thoughts in the indirect form, like another person's : as, haec tibi dictābam post fānum putre Vacūnae, exceptō quod nōn simul essēs, cētera laetus, H. *E.* 1, 10, 49, *I write thee this behind Vacuna's mouldering pile, in all else well, except that thou 'rt not here the while* (1601).

1727. Instead of an intimation of indirect discourse by a mere subjunctive, a verb of thinking or saying is sometimes introduced by quī, or especially quod, sometimes by cum, and put illogically itself in the subjunctive : as, litterās, quās mē sibī mīsisse dīceret, recitāvit, *Ph.* 2, 7, *he read off a letter, which he said I sent him*, i. e. quās mīsissem. impetrāre nōn potuī, quod religiōne sē impedīrī dīcerent, Sulpicius in *Fam.* 4, 12, 3, *I could not get leave, because they said they were hampered by religious scruple*, i. e. quod impedīrentur. cum dīceret, *DN.* 3, 83, *saying as he did.* This construction is common in Cicero, somewhat so in Caesar, rare in Sallust.

1728. The subjunctive is used in sentences expressing an essential part of the thought, which are subordinate to another subjunctive, or to an infinitive. This is called the *Subjunctive of Attraction,* or *of Assimilation :* as, vereor nē, dum minuere velim labōrem, augeam, *Leg.* 1, 12, *I am afraid I may make the work harder, while I am aiming to make it less.* sī sōlōs eōs dīcerēs miserōs, quibus moriendum esset, nēminem eōrum, quī vīverent exciperēs, *TD.* 1, 9, *if you should pronounce only such people unhappy as had to die, you would not except one of those who were living.* mōs est Syrācūsīs, ut sī quā dē rē ad senātum referātur, dīcat sententiam quī velit, *V.* 4, 142, *it is the custom at Syracuse, that if any question is discussed in the senate, anybody who pleases may express his opinion.* sapiēns nōn dubitat, sī ita melius sit, migrāre dē vītā, *Fin.* 1, 62, *the sage does not hesitate, if this be the better course, to withdraw from life.* mōs est Athēnīs laudārī in cōntiōne eōs, quī sint in proeliīs interfectī, *O.* 151, *it is the custom in Athens to eulogize in public assembly such as have fallen in action.*

1729. The indicative is kept in subordinate statements added or vouched for by the person reporting, and also in circumlocutions equivalent to a substantive : as,

nūntiātum est Ariovistum ad occupandum Vesontiōnem, quod est oppidum maximum Sēquanōrum, contendere, 1, 38, 1, *it was reported that Ariovistus was pressing on to seize Vesontio, which is the most considerable town of the Sequans.* prūdentissima cīvitās Athēniēnsium, dum ea rērum potīta est, fuisse trāditur, *RA.* 70, *Athens is said to have been passing wise, as long as she held the hegemony.* vīs, quae restant, mē loquī? T. *Andr.* 195, *wilt have me tell the rest?* i. e. relicua. fierī potest, ut id quod sentit polītē ēloquī nōn possit, *TD.* 1, 6, *it may be that he cannot express his thought in polished style,* i. e. sententiam suam.

The Subjunctive of Repeated Action.

1730. The subjunctive is sometimes used in relative, temporal, or conditional sentences, to express action repeated or occurring at no particular time : as,

(*a.*) neque aliter sī faciat, ūllam inter suōs habet auctōritātem, 6, 11, 4, *and if he does not do this, he never has any ascendancy at all over his people.* With the present and perfect, however, this subjunctive is confined principally to the indefinite second person singular (1030): as, bonus sēgnior fit, ubī neglegās, S. *I.* 31, 28, *the good man always gets slacker, when you are neglectful.* sīquoi mūtuom quid dederīs, fit prō propriō perditum, Pl. *Tri.* 1050, *if you've lent anything to any man, 'tis not your own, but lost.* (*b.*) The imperfect and pluperfect subjunctive begin with Catullus and Caesar, and get to be common with Livy and Tacitus : as, sī quis prehenderētur, cōnsēnsū mīlitum ēripiēbātur, Caes. *C.* 3, 110, 4, *every time a man was taken up, he was rescued by the joint action of the rank and file.* quemcumque līctor prēndisset, tribūnus mittī iubēbat, L. 3, 11, 2, *every man the lictor arrested, a tribune would order released.*

The Subjunctive as in the Simple Sentence.

1731. The subjunctive of wish, of action conceivable, or of interrogation, is sometimes used in a subordinate sentence exactly as in main sentences : as,

haec diē nātālī meō scrīpsī, quō utinam susceptus nōn essem, *Att.*
11, 9, 3, *this I have written on my birthday, on which day I wish I had never
been lifted from the ground* (1544). ut videās, Lucr. 3, 348, *so that you can
see* (1556). neque id faciō, ut forsitan quibusdam videar, simulātiōne,
Fam. 1, 8, 2, *nor do I do it, as perhaps I may seem to some to do, from hypoc-
risy* (1556). etiamst paucīs vōs quod monitōs voluerim, Pl. *Cap.* 53,
there's one point more, on which I'd have you briefly warned (1558). erant
eiusmodī sitūs oppidōrum, ut neque pedibus aditum habērent neque
nāvibus, quod minuente aestū nāvēs in vadīs adflīctārentur, 3, 12, 1,
*the towns were so situated that there was no access to them by land, nor by boat
either, because at ebb tide vessels would pound on the shoals* (1559). vix erat
hoc imperātum, cum illum spoliātum vidērēs, *V.* 4, 86, *hardly was the
order from his lips, when you might have seen the man stript* (1559). quō mē
vertam nesciō, *Clu.* 4, *I don't know which way to turn* (1563).

TENSE OF THE SUBORDINATE SENTENCE.

THE TENSES OF THE INDICATIVE.

1732. I. The tense of a subordinate indicative often indicates
a close relation of time with the tense of the leading verb, particularly in cases of repeated contemporaneous or antecedent
action. The subordinate sentence in such combinations is said
to have *Relative* time.

1733. (1.) The subordinate indicative tense may express action concurrent with the main action. Two concurrent sentences
are usually put in the same tense.

Concurrent action is said to be (*a.*) *congruent*, when two actions merely
cover the same time : as, dum legō, adsentior, *TD.* 1, 24, *as long as I am
reading, I assent.* dum necesse erat, ūnus omnia poterat, *RA.* 139, *so
long as it had to be, one man controlled the world.* dum Latīnae loquentur
litterae, quercus huic locō nōn deerit, *Leg.* 1, 2, *as long as Latin literature
has the gift of speech, this spot will not lack its oak.* vīxit, dum vīxit, bene,
T. *Hec.* 461, *he lived well all the time he lived.* quoad potuit, fortissimē
restitit, 4, 12, 5, *as long as he could, he made a manful stand.* Or (*b.*) *coincident*, when one action is virtually the same as the other : as, cum tacent,
clāmant, *C.* 1, 21, *while they are dumb, they cry out*, i. e. their silence is as
telling as a shout. fēcistī mihī pergrātum, quod Serāpiōnis librum
mīsistī, *Att.* 2, 4, 1, *you have obliged me very much by sending Serapio's book.*

1734. (2.) The subordinate indicative tense may express
action contemporaneous, antecedent, or subsequent, in relation
to the main action.

1735. (*a.*) Action contemporaneous with a main present is expressed by a present, with a main future or virtual future, by a future,
with a main secondary tense by an imperfect : as,

quod est, eō decet ūtī, *CM.* 27, *what you have, that you should avail yourself of.* hōrologium mittam, sī erit sūdum, *Fam.* 16, 18, 3, *I will send the clock, if it is pleasant* (1625). paulātim dabis, sī sapiēs, T. *Hau.* 870, *you'll give in driblets, if you are wise.* cum relaxāre animōs volent, caveant intemperantiam, *Off.* 1, 122, *when they want to unbend, let them beware of excess* (1625; 1718). omnia deerant, quae ad reficiendās nāvēs erant ūsuī, 4, 29, 4, *they were out of everything that was serviceable for repairing their vessels.*

1736. (*b.*) Action antecedent to a main present is expressed by a perfect, to a main future or virtual future by a future perfect, to a main secondary tense by a pluperfect: as,

quōcumque aspexistī tuae tibī occurrunt iniūriae, *Par.* 18, *wherever you turn your gaze, you are confronted by your own abominable acts.* cum posuī librum, adsēnsiō omnis ēlābitur, *TD.* 1, 24, *when I drop the book, all assent melts away* (1860). quicquid fēceris, adprobābō, *Fam.* 3, 3, 2, *no matter what you do, I shall think it well* (1626). ut quisque istīus animum offenderat, in lautumiās statim coniciēbātur, *V.* 5, 143, *any man that wounded his sensibilities was always flung into the quarries without any ado.*

1737. (*c.*) Action subsequent to a main present is expressed by the future participle with a present form of **sum**, to a main future or virtual future by the future participle with a future form of **sum**, and to a main secondary tense by the future participle with an imperfect form of **sum**: as,

decem diēs sunt ante lūdōs, quōs Cn. Pompēius factūrus est, *V. a. pr.* 31, *there are ten days before the shows which Pompey is to manage.* attentōs faciēmus, sī dēmōnstrābimus ea, quae dictūrī erimus, magna esse, *Inv.* 1, 23, *we shall make people attentive if we show that what we are going to say is important.* rēx, quia nōn interfutūrus nāvālī certāminī erat, Magnēsiam concessit, L. 36, 43, 9, *as the king was not to have a hand in the action at sea, he moved off to Magnesia.*

1738. II. A subordinate indicative tense is said to be *Independent* when it simply expresses time of its own, without any close relation to the time of the main action.

Such independent tenses may denote general present action: as, ībam forte viā sacrā, sīcut meus est mōs, H. *S.* 1, 9, 1, *in Sacred Street, as is my wont, I happened to be promenading* (relatively, erat mōs, 1735). nōn mē appellābis, sī sapis, Pl. *Most.* 515, *you won't address me, if you have sense* (relatively, sī sapiēs, 1735). Or past action, either continuous, completed, or indefinite: as, ut mōs fuit Bīthȳniae rēgibus, lectīcā ferēbātur, *V.* 5, 27, *he regularly rode in a litter, as was the practice of the despots of Bithynia;* here fuit denotes action simply as past, without further definition of time (1603), whereas erat, relative to the time of ferēbātur, would imply *which was then the practice* (1595).

1739 With dum, *in the time while,* an independent present is used: see 1995. With postquam, &c., *after,* an independent perfect is used of a single action; see 1925.

THE TENSES OF THE SUBJUNCTIVE.

1740. Subordinate subjunctive sentences were originally independent coordinate sentences, in the tense required to express the thought. By degrees the subordinate sentence blended closely with the main sentence, and the combination of the two was regarded as one whole.

1741. I. The time of the subordinate subjunctive is usually *Relative*, that is either contemporaneous, antecedent, or subsequent, in relation to that of the main action.

1742. Action contemporaneous with the main action is expressed by a present or imperfect subjunctive. Action antecedent is expressed by a perfect or a pluperfect subjunctive. Action subsequent is expressed by the future participle with a form of **sim** or of **essem**.

1743. Subordinate sentences with verbs of will or aim, with verbs of fear, also final sentences and many consecutive sentences are expressed in Latin as contemporaneous with the main action, not as subsequent to it.

1744. II. The main and subordinate sentences may express wholly different spheres of time by tenses not commonly used together, when the thought requires it. In such cases the tense of the subordinate member is called *Independent*, like the analogous tenses of the indicative (1738).

1745. The use of subordinate subjunctive tenses relatively to the main tense, or what is commonly called the *Sequence of Tenses*, is as follows :

Tense subordinate to an Indicative.

1746. (1.) The present, or perfect subjunctive, or the future participle with a form of **sim**, is used in sentences subordinate to a primary tense (1717): as,

(*a.*) tē hortor, ut Rōmam pergās, *QFr.* 1, 3, 4, *I urge you to repair to Rome.* cūrā, ut quam prīmum veniās, *Fam.* 4, 10, 1, *mind that you come as soon as you can.* ego quid accēperim sciō, *RA.* 58, *I know what I have received.* quam sum sollicitus quidnam futūrum sit, *Att.* 8, 6, 3. *how anxious I am to know what in the world is to come.* (*b.*) in eum locum rēs dēducta est ut salvī esse nequeāmus, *Fam.* 16, 12, 1, *to such a pass has it come that we cannot be saved.* an oblītus es quid initiō dīxerim? *DN.* 2, 2, *have you possibly forgotten what I said at the start?* quoniam in eam ratiōnem vītae nōs fortūna dēdūxit, ut sempiternus sermō dē nōbīs futūrus sit, caveāmus, *QFr.* 1, 1, 38, *since fortune has set us in such a walk of life that we are to be eternally talked about, let us be on our guard.* (*c.*) efficiam, ut intellegātis, *Clu.* 7, *I will see that you understand.* dīcent quid statuerint, *V.* 2, 175, *they will tell what they decided on.* quae fuerit causa, mox vīderō, *Fin.* 1, 35, *what the reason was I won't consider till by and by* (1630). tē disertum putābō, sī ostenderis quō modō sīs eōs inter sīcāriōs dēfēnsūrus, *Ph.* 2, 8, *I shall think you a most effective speaker, if you show how you are going to defend them on the charge of murder.*

1747. (2.) The imperfect, or pluperfect subjunctive, or the future participle with a form of essem, is used in sentences subordinate to a secondary tense (1717) : as,

(*a.*) hīs rēbus fīēbat, ut minus lātē vagārentur, 1, 2, 4, *so it came to pass that they did not roam round much.* docēbat, ut tōtīus Galliae prīncipātum Aeduī tenuissent, 1, 43, 6, *he showed how the Aeduans had had the mastery over all Gaul.* Flaccus quid aliī posteā factūrī essent scīre nōn poterat, *Fl.* 33, *Flaccus could not tell what other people would do in the future.* (*b.*) is cīvitātī persuāsit, ut dē fīnibus suīs cum omnibus cōpiīs exīrent, 1, 2, 1, *this man prevailed on his community to emigrate from their place of abode, bag and baggage.* quās rēs in Hispāniā gessisset, disseruit, L. 28, 38, 2, *he discoursed on his military career in Spain.* an Lacedaemoniī quaesīvērunt num sē esset morī prohibitūrus? *TD.* 5, 42, *did the Spartans ask whether he was going to prevent them from dying ?* (*c.*) Ariovistus tantōs sibī spīritūs sūmpserat, ut ferendus nōn vidērētur, 1, 33, 5, *Ariovistus had put on such high and mighty airs that he seemed intolerable.* hīc pāgus, cum domō exīsset patrum nostrōrum memoriā, L. Cassium cōnsulem interfēcerat, 1, 12, 5, *this canton, sallying out from home in our fathers' recollection, had put Cassius, the consul, to death.* illud quod mihī extrēmum prōposueram, cum essem de bellī genere dictūrus, *IP.* 17, *the point I had reserved till the end, when I was going to discourse on the character of the war.*

1748. With any kind of a secondary main sentence, a subordinate general truth usually stands in the past, contrary to the English idiom: as,

hīc cōgnōscī licuit, quantum esset hominibus praesidī in animī firmitūdine, Caes. *C.* 3, 28, 4, *here there was a chance to learn what a bulwark man has in courage.* In the direct form est (1588).

1749. A subsequent relation is sometimes loosely suggested by a simple subjunctive; necessarily so with verbs which lack the future participle, or which are in the passive: as, sum sollicitus quidnam dē prōvinciīs dēcernātur, *Fam.* 2, 11, 1, *I am anxious to see what in the world may be decided on about the provinces.*

1750. In a single example, a future perfect of resulting state is represented in subordination as follows : nec dubitō quīn cōnfecta iam rēs futūra sit, *Fam.* 6, 12, 3, *and I have no doubt the job will soon be completely finished up*, directly, sine dubiō cōnfecta iam rēs erit.

1751. (1.) An imperfect subjunctive expressing a particular past result, cause, reason, &c., is sometimes connected with a main general present tense (1744) : as,

cuius praeceptī tanta vīs est, ut ea Delphicō deō tribuerētur, *Leg.* 1, 58, *the power of this rule is so mighty that it was ascribed to the Delphic god.* cuius rēī tanta est vīs, ut Ithacam illam sapientissimus vir immortālitātī antepōneret, *DO.* 1, 196, *so irresistible is the power of this sentiment that the shrewdest of men loved his little Ithaca better than life eternal ;* of Ulixes. laudantur ōrātōrēs veterēs quod crīmina dīluere dīlūcidē solērent, *V.* 2, 191, *the orators of old are admired ' because they were always clear in explaining accusations away.'* The secondary sequence is also sometimes exceptionally used with ordinary presents.

1752. (2.) The present of vivid narration is commonly regarded as a secondary tense, especially when the subordinate sentence precedes, and regularly with narrative **cum**. Sometimes however as a primary tense : as,

(*a.*) **servīs suīs Rubrius, ut iānuam clauderent, imperat,** *V.* 1, 66, *Rubrius orders his slaves to shut the front door.* **Aeduī, cum sē dēfendere nōn possent, lēgātōs ad Caesarem mittunt,** 1, 11, 2, *the Aeduans, finding they could not defend themselves, send some envoys to Caesar.* (*b.*) **hortātur, ut arma capiant,** 7, 4, 4, *he urges them to fly to arms.* Sometimes the two sequences stand side by side, or a subjunctive of primary sequence has itself a second subordinate subjunctive of secondary sequence. Either sequence is used with the present of quotation also (1592).

1753. (3.) Subordinate sentences of past action conceivable, of action non-occurrent, or dubitative questions of the past, retain their past unchanged with a main primary tense : as,

(*a.*) **vērī simile nōn est, ut ille monumentīs maiōrum pecūniam antepōneret,** *V.* 4, 11, *it is not conceivable that the man would have thought more of money than of his heirlooms,* i. e. **nōn antepōneret** (1559). (*b.*) **omnia sīc erunt inlūstria, ut ad ea probanda tōtam Siciliam testem adhibēre possem,** *V.* 5, 139, *everything will be so self-evident, that I could use all Sicily as a witness to prove it* (1560). **taceō, nē haec quidem conligō, quae fortasse valērent apud iūdicem,** *Lig.* 30, *I'll hold my tongue, I won't even gather together the following arguments, which might perhaps be telling with a juryman* (1560). (*c.*) **quaerō ā tē cūr C. Cornēlium nōn dēfenderem,** *Vat.* 5, *I put the question to you, why I was not to defend Cornelius* (1563).

1754. A final subjunctive subordinate to a perfect definite sometimes has the primary sequence, but more commonly the secondary : as,

(*a.*) **etiamne ad subsellia cum ferrō vēnistis, ut hīc iugulētis Sex. Rōscium?** *RA.* 32, *have you actually come to the court-room knife in hand, to cut Roscius's throat on the spot?* (*b.*) **nē īgnōrārētis esse aliquās pācis vōbīs condiciōnēs, ad vōs vēnī,** *L.* 21, 13, 2, *I have come to you to let you know that you have some chances of peace.* **addūxī hominem in quō satis facere exterīs nātiōnibus possētis,** *V. a. pr.* 2, *I have brought up a man in whose person you can give satisfaction to foreign nations.*

1755. An independent present or perfect subjunctive may be put with a main secondary tense (1744) :

1756. (1.) In relative, causal, or concessive sentences : as,

cum in cēterīs colōniīs duūmvirī appellentur, hī sē praetōrēs appellārī volēbant, *Agr.* 2, 93, *though they are styled in all other colonies The Two, these men wanted to be styled praetors.* **qui adulēscēns nihil umquam nisi sevērissimē et gravissimē fēcerit, is eā aetāte saltāvit?** *D.* 27, *did the man who in his growing years invariably behaved with austere propriety, dance and caper round in his old age?* **hōc tōtō proeliō cum ab hōrā septimā ad vesperum pugnātum sit, āversum hostem vidēre nēmō potuit,** 1, 26, 2, *during the whole of this engagement, though the fighting went on from an hour past noon till evening, nobody could catch a glimpse of an enemy's back.*

1757. (2.) Often in consecutive sentences : as,

(*a.*) in prōvinciā Siciliā, quam iste per triennium ita vexāvit, ut ea restituī in antīquum statum nūllō modō possit, *V. a. pr.* 12, *in the province of Sicily, which the defendant so effectually tormented three years running that it cannot be restored at all to its original estate.* priōrēs ita rēgnārunt, ut omnēs conditōrēs partium certē urbis numerentur, L. 2, 1, 2, *such was the administration of the monarchs preceding, that they are all accounted founders of parts at least of Rome.* (*b.*) The perfect subjunctive sometimes represents the time of the perfect definite : as, tantum in aerārium pecūniae invēxit; ut ūnīus imperātōris praeda fīnem attulerit tribūtōrum, *Off.* 2, 76, *he conveyed such quantities of money into the treasury, that the plunder turned in by a single commander has put an end to tribute for good and all.* eō usque sē praebēbat patientem atque impigrum, ut eum nēmō umquam in equō sedentem vīderit, *V.* 5, 27, *he showed himself so indefatigably active that no human being has ever seen him astride a horse.* Sometimes the time of the historical perfect : as, temporis tanta fuit exiguitās, ut ad galeās induendās tempus dēfuerit, 2, 21, 5, *so scant was the time that they had not time to put their helmets on.* hīc ita quiēvit, ut eō tempore omnī Neāpolī fuerit, 17, *this man held so quiet that he staid all that time at Neapolis.* In Cicero a negative subordinate perfect is not uncommon ; an affirmative one is very rare. This construction is more common in Nepos, Livy, and Tacitus, and is the prevalent one in Suetonius.

1758. The imperfect only is used in complementary sentences with past verbs of happening, such as accidit, contigit, &c. (1966).

1759. When two consecutive subjunctives are coordinated, they usually have the same tense. Sometimes however the first is perfect and the second imperfect, or the reverse.

1760. (3.) An indirect question in the present or perfect sometimes retains its original tense with a main secondary tense (1744) : as,

hīc quantum in bellō fortūna possit, cōgnōscī potuit, 6, 35, 2, *here there was a chance to see how potent dame Fortune is in war.* Here possit represents potest of a general truth (1588) ; but usually general truths have the regular sequence (1748). cūr abstinuerit spectāculō ipse, variē trahēbant, Ta. 1, 76, *why the emperor did not go to the show, they accounted for in this way and that,* representing cūr abstinuit ? quō cōnsiliō redierim initiō audīstis, post estis expertī, *Ph.* 10, 8, *what my idea was in coming back, you learned first by hearsay, afterwards by personal observation,* representing quō cōnsiliō rediī ?

1761. The subordinate subjunctive has sometimes the sequence of the nearest verb, instead of that of its proper verb : as, cūrāvit, quod semper in rē pūblicā tenendum est, nē plūrimum valeant plūrimī, *RP.* 2, 39, *he arranged it so, a point which is always to be held fast in government, that the greatest number may not have the greatest power.*

TENSE SUBORDINATE TO A SUBJUNCTIVE.

1762. When the leading verb is a subjunctive, the present is regarded as primary, and the imperfect and pluperfect as secondary : as, (*a.*) exspectō eius modī litterās ex quibus nōn quid fīat, sed quid futūrum sit sciam, *Att.* 5, 12, 2, *I am expecting a letter of a kind to let me know not what is going on, but what will be going on.* quid prōfēcerim faciās mē velim certiōrem, *Fam.* 7, 10, 3, *how far I have succeeded I wish you would let me know.* (*b.*) quālis esset nātūra montis quī cōgnōscerent mīsit, 1, 21, 1, *he sent some scouts to find out what the character of the mountain was.* quid mē prohibēret Epicūrēum esse, sī probārem quae dīceret, *Fin.* 1, 27, *what would prevent me from being an Epicurean, if I accepted what he said?* quae sī bis bīna quot essent didicisset Epicūrus, certē nōn dīceret, *DN.* 2, 49, *Epicurus would certainly not say this, if he had ever been taught how much twice two is* (1748).

1763. An imperfect subjunctive of action non-occurrent at the present time has occasionally the present sequence: as, mīrārēris, sī interessēs, quā patientiā valētūdinem toleret, Plin. *Ep.* 1, 22, 7, *you would be amazed to find, if you were with him, with what dogged endurance he bears up under his illness.* But the secondary sequence is far more common.

1764. (1.) The perfect subjunctive in independent main sentences of prohibition (1551) or of action conceivable (1558) is regarded as a primary tense: as,

nē dubitārīs quīn id mihī futūrum sit antīquius, *Att.* 7, 3, 2, *don't entertain any doubt that this course will be preferable in my eyes.* quid nōn sit citius quam quid sit dīxerim, *DN.* 1, 60, *I could sooner tell what is not, than what is.*

1765. (2.) In subordinate sentences, the perfect subjunctive has the main sequence when it represents the indicative perfect definite, and the secondary when it represents the indicative historical perfect or the imperfect: as,

(*a.*) nēmō ferē vestrūm est, quīn, quem ad modum captae sint Syrācūsae saepe audierit, *V.* 4, 115, *there is hardly a man of your number but has heard over and over again how Syracuse was taken.* (*b.*) quā rē acciderit ut id suspicārēre quod scrībis nesciō, *Fam.* 2, 16, 1, *how it came to pass that you suspected what you write, I can't imagine.*

TENSE SUBORDINATE TO A NOUN OF THE VERB.

1766. (1.) A subjunctive subordinate to one of the nouns of the verb, except the perfect infinitive or the perfect participle, follows the sequence of the verb: as,

dēsinō quaerere cūr ēmeris, *V.* 4, 10, *I cease to ask why you bought.* nēminem tam āmentem fore putāvērunt, ut emeret argentum, *V.* 4, 9, *they did not dream anybody would be crazy enough to buy plate.* secūrī percussī, adeō torpentibus metū quī aderant, ut nē gemitus quidem exaudīrētur, L. 28, 29, 11, *they were beheaded, everybody there being so completely paralyzed with fear that not even a groan could be heard.* Q. Fabius Pīctor Delphōs missus est scīscitātum, quibus precibus deōs possent plācāre, L. 22, 57, 5, *Fabius Pictor was sent to Delphi to find out by what sort of prayers they could get the ear of the gods.* cupīdō incessit animōs iuvenum scīscitandī ad quem eōrum rēgnum esset ventūrum, L. 1, 56, 10, *the youths were possessed with a desire to find out to which one of their number the throne was to fall.*

1767. (2.) With a perfect infinitive or perfect participle, the subordinate subjunctive may be in the imperfect or pluperfect, even with a primary leading verb: as,

satis mihǐ multa verba fēcisse videor, quā rē esset hoc bellum necessārium, *IP.* 27, *I fancy I have said enough to show why this war is unavoidable.* hunc istǐ aiunt, cum taurum immolāvisset, mortuum concidisse, *Br.* 43, *your gentlemen say that this man, after sacrificing a bull, tumbled down dead.* viātor bene vestītus causa grassātōrī fuisse dīcētur cūr ab eō spoliārētur, *Fat.* 34, *a well-dressed traveller will be said to have been a temptation for a footpad to rob him.* versābor in rē saepe quaesītā, suffrāgia clam an palam ferre melius esset, *Leg.* 3, 33, *I shall be working on a question that has often been put, whether it was better to vote secretly or openly.*

1768. The sequence with a perfect infinitive is, however, often primary: as, hīc sī fīnem faciam dīcendī, satis iūdicī fēcisse videar cūr secundum Rōscium iūdicārī dēbeat, *RC.* 14, *if I should stop speaking here, I should feel I had made it plain enough to the court why a judgement should be rendered for Roscius.*

1769. The secondary sequence is used with meminī, *remember,* even when it has the present infinitive (2220): as, L. Metellum meminī ita bonīs esse vīribus extrēmō tempore aetātis, ut adulēscentiam nōn requīreret, *CM.* 30, *I can remember Metellus's being so good and strong in the very last part of his life that he did not feel the want of youth.*

1770. Sentences with a subjunctive due to another subjunctive or to an infinitive are put as follows:

1771. (1.) Sentences of relative time express contemporaneous, antecedent, and subsequent action like corresponding indicative sentences, with the appropriate sequence: as,

vereor, nē, dum minuere velim labōrem, augeam, *Leg.* 1, 12, *I am afraid that while I wish to make the work less, I may make it more.* crocodīlōs dīcunt, cum in terrā partum ēdiderint, obruere ōva, *DN.* 2, 129, *they say that the crocodile, after laying on land, buries her eggs.* dīcēbam quoad metuerēs, omnia tē prōmissūrum: simul ac timēre desīssēs, similem tē futūrum tuī, *Ph.* 2, 89, *I said that as long as you were afraid, you would promise everything; the moment you ceased to fear, you would be just like yourself.* cōnstituērunt ea, quae ad proficīscendum pertinērent, comparāre, 1, 3, 1, *they resolved to get such things ready as were necessary for the march.* erat scrīptum: nisi domum reverterētur, sē capitis eum damnātūrōs, *N.* 4, 3, 4, *it stood written that, if he did not come back home, they would condemn him to death* (direct form nisi revertēris, damnābimus). lēgātī vēnērunt, quī sē ea, quae imperāsset, factūrōs pollicērentur, 4, 22, 1, *some envoys came, to engage to do what he ordered* (direct form quae imperāris, faciēmus). Venetī cōnfīdēbant Rōmānōs neque ūllam facultātem habēre nāvium, neque eōrum locōrum ubǐ bellum gestūrī essent portūs nōvisse, 3, 19, 6, *the Venetans felt assured that the Romans had not any proper supply of ships, and were not acquainted with the ports in the places where they were to fight.*

1772. (2.) Sentences with independent time retain the independent time in the subjunctive in primary sequence (1744); in secondary sequence the present becomes imperfect, and the perfect becomes pluperfect: as, (*a.*) quamquam opīniō est, eum quī multīs annīs ante hōs fuerit, Pīsistratum, multum valuisse dīcendō, *Br.* 27, *though there is an impression that the man who lived years and years before these people, Pisistratus, was a very telling orator* (direct form, quī fuit, 1738). dīcitur, posteā quam vēnerit, paucīs diēbus esse mortuus, *Clu.* 175, *he is said to have died a few days after he came* (1739). (*b.*) cōgnōvit Suēbōs, posteā quam pontem fierī comperissent, nūntiōs in omnēs partēs dīmīsisse, 4, 19, 2, *he ascertained that after the Suebans had learned of the building of the bridge, they had sent out messengers in every direction.*

THE INDIRECT QUESTION.

1773. The subjunctive is used in indirect questions or exclamations.

Thus, when the direct question, quī scīs, *how do you know?* is subordinated to a main sentence, such as quaerō, *I ask*, the scīs becomes sciās: quaerō quī sciās, *RA.* 59, *I ask how you know.* Questions or exclamations thus subordinated are called *Indirect* (1723). In English, indirect questions are usually characterized simply by the position of the words, the subject standing before the verb.

1774. The indirect question is one of the commonest of constructions. It depends on verbs or expressions meaning not only *ask*, but also *tell, inform, ascertain, see, hear, know, consider, deliberate, doubt, wonder, fear*, &c., &c.

Yes or No Questions.

1775. Indirect Yes or No questions are introduced by the same interrogative particles that are used in direct questions (1503). But in indirect questions, num and -ne are used without any essential difference, in the sense of *whether, if.* nōnne is used thus only by Cicero, and by him only with quaerō: as,

quaeris num disertus sit? *Planc.* 62, *do you ask whether he is a good speaker?* quaesīvī cōgnōsceretne sīgnum, *C.* 3, 10, *I asked if he recognized the seal.* quaerō nōnne tibī faciendum idem sit, *Fin.* 3, 13, *I ask whether you ought not to do the same.* vidēte num dubitandum vōbīs sit, *IP.* 1, *consider whether you ought to have any hesitation.*

1776. The combinations -ne . . . -ne, and an . . . an, introducing two separate questions, are rare; -ne . . . -ne is mostly confined to poetry. In a few instances such questions can hardly be distinguished from alternatives.

1777. A conditional protasis with sī, *if, to see if*, or sī forte, *if perchance*, sometimes takes the place of an indirect question in expressions or implications of trial, hope, or expectation: as, ībō, vīsam sī domīst, *T. Haut.* 170, *I'll go and see if he's at home.* Usually with the subjunctive: as, exspectābam, sī quid scrīberēs, *Att.* 16, 2, 4, *I was waiting to see whether you would write anything.* circumfunduntur hostēs, sī quem aditum reperīre possent, 6, 37, 4, *the enemy came streaming round, to see if they could find any way of getting in.*

ALTERNATIVE QUESTIONS.

1778. Indirect alternative questions are introduced like direct questions (1519). But when the second member is negative, it has oftener **necne** than an **nōn** : as,

hoc quaerāmus, vērum sit an falsum, *Clu.* 124, *let us ask this question, whether it is true or false.* quaesivī ā Catilīnā in conventū fuisset, necne, *C.* 2, 13, *I asked Catiline whether he had been at the meeting or not.* permultum interest utrum perturbātiōne animī, an cōnsultō fīat iniūria, *Off.* 1, 27, *it makes a vast difference whether wrong be done in heat of passion, or with deliberate intent.* quaerō, eum Brūtine similem mālīs an Antōnii, *Ph.* 10, 5, *I ask whether you would rather have him like Brutus or like Antony.*

1779. An introductory **utrum** preceding an alternative question with -ne and **an** occurs a few times in Plautus and Cicero; **utrumne . . . an** occurs once in Cicero, and twice in Horace and Tacitus each; compare 1522. After **utrum**, a second alternative is sometimes suppressed, as in the direct question (1523).

1780. -ne in the second member only of an alternative question is rare, and not used by Caesar or Sallust: as, sine sciam captīva māterne sim, L. 2, 40, 5, *let me know whether I am a captive or a mother.*

1781. (1.) A few times in Plautus and Terence, the second member only of an alternative question is expressed with **quī sciō an ?** or **quī scīs an ?** equivalent to *perhaps:* as, quī scīs an quae iubeam faciat? T. *Eu.* 790, *perhaps she 'll do as I direct.* Horace has once **quī scīs an,** *AP.* 462, in the sense of *perhaps,* and once **quis scit an,** 4, 7, 17, in the sense of *perhaps not.*

1782. (2.) The second member only of an alternative question is often expressed after **haud sciō an,** *I don't know but, possibly, perhaps,* with **nōn, nēmō, nūllus,** &c., if the sentence is negative: as,

haud sciō an fierī possit, *V.* 3, 162, *I don't know but it is possible.* Similarly, though not often, with **nesciō an, haud sciam an, dubitō an, dubitārim an, dubium an, incertum an,** &c.: as, **ēloquentiā nesciō an habuisset parem nēminem.** *Br.* 126, *in oratory I fancy he would have had no peer.* This use, in which **haud sciō an** becomes adverbial, and the subjunctive approaches closely that of modest assertion, is principally confined to Cicero. In later Latin, **haud sciō an,** &c., sometimes has a negative sense, *I don't know whether,* with **ūllus,** &c.

1783. From Curtius on, **an** is used quite like **num** or -ne, in a single indirect question, without implication of alternatives.

1784. Two alternatives are rarely used without any interrogative particles at all: as, velit nōlit scīre difficile est, *QFr.* 3, 8, 4, *will he nill he, it is hard to know,* i. e. whether he will or not. Compare 1518.

PRONOUN QUESTIONS.

1785. Indirect pronoun questions are introduced by the same pronominal words that are used in direct pronoun questions (1526): as,

cōgnōscit, quae gerantur, 5, 48, 2, *he ascertains what is going on.* vidētis ut omnēs dēspiciat, *RA.* 135, *you can see how he looks down on everybody.* quid agās et ut tē oblectēs scīre cupiō, *QFr.* 2, 3, 7, *I am eager to know how you do and how you are amusing yourself.*

ORIGINAL SUBJUNCTIVES.

1786. Questions already in the subjunctive may also become indirect.

Thus, **quō mē vertam?** *V.* 5, 2, *which way shall I turn?* (1563) becomes indirect in **quō mē vertam nesciō,** *Clu.* 4, *I don't know which way I am to turn.* **quid faciam?** H. *S.* 2, 1, 24, *what shall I do?* (1563) becomes indirect in **quid faciam, praescrībe,** H. *S.* 2, 1, 5, *lay down the law, what I'm to do.* **neque satis cōnstābat quid agerent,** 3, 14, 3, *and it was not at all clear what they had best do.* **dubitāvī hōsce hominēs emerem an nōn emerem,** Pl. *Cap.* 455, *I had my doubts, whether to buy these men or not to buy* (1564).

INDICATIVE QUESTIONS APPARENTLY INDIRECT.

1787. In old Latin, the indicative occurs often in connections where the subjunctive would be used in classical Latin : as,

dīc, quis est, Pl. *B.* 558, *say, who is it?* whereas **dīc quis sit** would mean *say who it is.* In such cases the question is not subordinate, but coordinate, usually with an imperative (1697), or with some such expression as **tē rogō, volō scīre, scīn,** or the like. Such coordination occurs exceptionally in the classical period : as, **et vidē, quam conversa rēs est,** *Att.* 8, 13, 2, *and observe, how everything is changed.* **adspice, ut ingreditur,** V. 6, 856, *see, how he marches off.*

1788. The indicative is used with **nesciō** followed by a pronominal interrogative, when this combination is equivalent to an indefinite pronoun or adverb : as,

prōdit nesciō quis, T. *Ad.* 635, *there's some one coming out.* This is a condensed form for **prōdit nesciō quis sit,** *there's coming out I don't know who it is,* the real question, sit, being suppressed, and **nesciō quis** acquiring the meaning of aliquis, *somebody.* Similarly **nesciō** with unde, ubī, quandō, quot, &c., in writers of all ages. Plautus uses sciō quid, sciō ut, &c., somewhat in this way once or twice with the indicative : as, **scio quid agō,** *B.* 78, *I'm doing I know what.*

1789. This combination often expresses admiration, contempt, or regret : as, **contendō tum illud nesciō quid praeclārum solēre existere,** *Arch.* 15, *I maintain that in such a combination the beau ideal of perfection always bursts into being.* **paulum nesciō quid,** *R.A.* 115, *an unconsidered trifle.* **dīvīsa est sententia, postulante nesciō quō,** *Mil.* 14, *the question was divided, on motion of what's his name.* **nesciō quō pactō,** *C.* 31, *unfortunately.*

1790. The indicative is used in like manner with many expressions, originally exclamatory, which have become adverbs : such are **immāne quantum,** *prodigiously,* **mīrum quantum,** *wonderfully,* **sānē quam,** *immensely,* &c., &c. See 712 and the dictionary.

1791. Relative constructions often have the appearance of indirect questions, and care must be taken not to confound the two. Thus, **ut** is a relative in **hanc rem, ut factast, ēloquar,** Pl. *Am.* 1129, *I'll tell this thing as it occurred,* i. e. not *how it occurred.* **nōstī quae sequontur,** *T.D.* 4, 77, *you know the things that follow,* i. e. not *what follows*

THE RELATIVE SENTENCE.

1792. Relative sentences are introduced by relative words, the most important of which is the pronoun **quī**, *who, which*, or *that*. The relative pronoun may be in any case required by the context, and may represent any of the three persons.

1793. The relative adverbs, **ubĭ, quō, unde**, often take the place of a relative pronoun with a preposition, chiefly in designations of place, and regularly with town and island names. Less frequently of persons, though **unde** is not uncommonly thus used.

1794. In a wider sense, sentences introduced by any relative conjunctive particle, such as **ubĭ**, *when*, are sometimes called relative sentences. Such sentences, however, are more conveniently treated separately, under the head of the several conjunctive particles.

1795. (1.) The relative pronoun, like the English relative *who, which*, was developed from the interrogative. Originally, the relative sentence precedes, and the main sentence follows, just as in question and answer.

Thus, **quae mūtat, ea corrumpit**, *Fin.* 1, 21, *what he changes, that he spoils*, is a modification of the older question and answer: **quae mūtat ? ea corrumpit**, *what does he change? that he spoils*. With adjective relatives, the substantive is expressed in both members, in old or formal Latin: as, **quae rēs apud nostrōs nōn erant, eārum rērum nōmina nōn poterant esse ūsitāta**, Cornif. 4, 10, *what things did not exist among our countrymen, of those things the names could not have been in common use.*

1796. (2.) The relative sentence may also come last. As early as Plautus, this had become the prevalent arrangement, and the substantive of the main sentence is called the *Antecedent:* as,

ultrā eum locum, quō in locō Germānī cōnsēderant, castrīs idōneum locum dēlēgit, 1, 49, 1, *beyond the place in which place the Germans had established themselves, he selected a suitable spot for his camp.* The three words **diēs, locus**, and **rēs**, are very commonly expressed thus both in the antecedent and the relative sentence. This repetition is rare in Livy, and disappears after his time.

1797. In old Latin, rarely in classical poetry, a sentence sometimes begins with an emphasized antecedent put before the relative, and in the case of the relative: as, **urbem quam statuō vostra est**, V. 1, 573, *the city which I found is yours;* for **quam urbem statuō, ea vostra est.** In the main sentence, **is, hĭc, iste**, or **ille**, is often used; less frequently, as in this example, an appellative.

1798. The main sentence often has the determinative or demonstrative, or the substantive, or both omitted: as,

(*a.*) **ubĭ intellēxit diem īnstāre, quō diē frūmentum mīlitibus mētīrī oportēret**, 1, 16, 5, *when he saw the day was drawing nigh, on which day the grain was to be measured out to his men.* (*b.*) **quōs āmīsimus cīvĭs, eōs Mārtis vīs perculit**, *Marc.* 17, *what fellow-citizens we have lost, those the fury of the War-god smote down.* (*c.*) **Sabīnus quōs tribūnōs mīlitum circum sē habēbat, sē sequī iubet**, 5, 37, 1, *Sabinus ordered what tribunes of the soldiers he had about him, to follow him.*

1799. The antecedent is often omitted when it is indefinite, or is obvious from the context : as,

sunt quī mīrentur, *V.* 1, 6, *there be who wonder.* dēlēgistī quōs Rōmae relinquerēs, *C.* 1, 9, *you picked out people to leave in Rome.* quod periīt, periīt, Pl. *Cist.* 703, *gone is gone.* Caesar cōgnōvit Cōnsidium, quod nōn vīdisset, prō vīsō sibī renūntiāvisse, 1, 22, 4, *Caesar ascertained that Considius had reported to him as seen what he had not seen.*

1800. An ablative or nominative abstract in the relative sentence sometimes represents an ablative of manner or quality omitted from the main sentence : as, quā prūdentiā es, nihil tē fugiet, *Fam.* 11, 13, 1, *with what sense you have, nothing will elude you,* i. e. eā quā es prūdentiā, nihil tē fugiet. spērō, quae tua prūdentia est, tē valēre, *Att.* 6, 9, 1, *I hope that, with your characteristic caution, you are well.* at Āiāx, quō animō trāditur, mīlliēs oppetere mortem quam illa perpetī māluissset, *Off.* 1, 113, *Ajax, on the contrary, with his traditional vehemence, would have chosen rather to die a thousand deaths than to submit to such indignities.* This ellipsis begins with Cicero, and is found a few times only in later writers.

Agreement of the Relative.

1801. The agreement of the relative has already been spoken of in a general way (1082–1098). For convenience, however, it may be set forth here more explicitly.

1802. A relative pronoun agrees with its antecedent in gender and number, but its case depends on the construction of the sentence in which it stands : as,

Hippiās glōriātus est ānulum quem habēret, pallium quō amictus, soccōs quibus indūtus esset, sē suā manū cōnfēcisse, *DO.* 3, 127, *Hippias prided himself that he had made with his own hand the ring that he wore, the cloak in which he was wrapped, and the slippers that he had on.* This holds of all relatives with inflected form, such as quīcumque, quālis, quantus, &c., &c.

1803. When the relative refers to two or more antecedents of different gender, its gender is determined like that of a predicate adjective (1087) : as,

mātrēs et līberī, quōrum aetās misericordiam vestram requīrēbat, *V.* 5, 129, *mothers and babies, whose years would appeal to your sympathy* (1088). ōtium atque dīvitiae, quae prīma mortālēs putant, S. *C.* 36, 4, *peace and prosperity, which the sons of men count chiefest of blessings* (1089). fortūna, quam nēmō ab incōnstantiā et temeritāte sēiunget, quae digna nōn sunt deō, *DN.* 3, 61, *fortune, which nobody will distinguish from caprice ana hazard, qualities which are not befitting god* (1089). Sometimes the relative agrees with the nearest substantive : as, eās frūgēs atque frūctūs, quōs terra gignit, *DN.* 2, 37, *the crops, and the fruits of the trees that earth produces.*

1804. The relative is sometimes regulated by the sense, and not by the form of the antecedent : as, equitātum praemittit quī videant, 1, 15, 1, *he sends the cavalry ahead, for them to see* (1095). ūnus ex eō numerō, quī ad caedem parātī erant, S. *I.* 35, 6, *one of the number that were ready to do murder* (1095). duo prōdigia, quōs improbitās tribūnō cōnstrictōs addīxerat, *Sest.* 38, *a pair of monstrosities, whom their depravity had delivered over in irons to the tribune.* scrība pontificis, quōs nunc minōrēs pontificēs appellant, L. 22, 57, 3, *a clerk of the pontiff, which clerks they call nowadays lesser pontiffs,* i. e. quōs scrībās. Vēiēns bellum exortum, quibus Sabīnī arma coniūnxerant, L. 2, 53, 1, *a Vejan war broke out, with whom the Sabines had allied themselves,* i. e. bellum cum Vēientibus.

1805. A relative referring to a proper name and explanatory appellative combined, may take the gender of either: as, flūmine Rhēnō, quī agrum Helvētium ā Germānīs dīvidit, 1, 2, 3, *by the river Rhine, which is the boundary between Helvetians and Germans.* ad flūmen Scaldem quod īnfluit in Mosam, 6, 33, 3, *to the river Scheldt, that empties itself into the Maas.*

1806. With verbs of indeterminate meaning (1035), the relative pronoun sometimes agrees with the predicate substantive: as, Thēbae ipsae, quod Boeōtiae caput est, L. 42, 44, 3, *Thebes itself, which is the capital of Boeotia.* Often, however, with the antecedent: as, flūmen quod appellātur Tamesis, 5, 11, 8, *the river which is called the Thames.*

1807. When the relative is subject, its verb agrees with the person of the antecedent: as,

haec omnia is fēcī, quī sodālis Dolābellae eram, *Fam.* 12, 14, 7, *all this I did, I that was Dolabella's bosom friend.* iniquos es, quī mē tacēre postulēs, T. *Hau.* 1011, *thou art unfair, expecting me to hold my tongue.* So also when the antecedent is implied in a possessive: as, cum tū nostrā, quī remānsissēmus, caede tē contentum esse dīcēbās, *C.* 1, 7, *when you said you were satisfied with murdering us, who had staid behind.*

1808. For an accusative of the relative with an ablative antecedent the ablative is rarely used: as, notante iūdice quō nōstī populō, H. *S.* 1, 6, 15, *the judge condemning — thou know'st who — the world.* This represents the older interrogative conception: notante iūdice — quō? — nōstī, populō (1795).

1809. A new substantive added in explanation of an antecedent is put after the relative, and in the same case: as, ad Amānum contendī, quī mōns erat hostium plēnus, *Att.* 5, 20, 3, *I pushed on to Amanus, a mountain that was packed with the enemy.* This use begins with Cicero; but from Livy on, the explanatory word is also put as an appositive, with the relative following: as, Decius Magius, vir cui nihil dēfuit, L. 23, 7, 4, *Magius, a man that lacked nothing.*

1810. An adjective, especially a comparative, superlative, or numeral, explanatory of a substantive in the main sentence, is often put in the relative sentence: as,

palūs quae perpetua intercēdēbat Rōmānōs ad īnsequendum tardābat, 7, 26, 2, *a morass, that lay unbroken between, hindered the Romans from pursuit.*

1811. When reference is made to the substance of a sentence, the neuter quod is used, or more commonly id quod, either usually in parenthesis: as, intellegitur, id quod iam ante dīxī, imprūdente **L. Sūllā scelera haec fierī,** *RA.* 25, *it is plain, as I have said once before, that these crimes are committed without the cognizance of Sulla.* In continuations, **quae rēs** : as, **nāvēs removērī iussit, quae rēs māgnō ūsuī nostrīs fuit,** 4, 25, 1, *he ordered the vessels to be withdrawn, a course which proved very advantageous for our people.*

MOODS IN THE RELATIVE SENTENCE.

1812. The relative is sometimes equivalent to a conditional protasis. When thus used, it may have either the indicative or the subjunctive, as the sense requires : as,

(*a.*) **quod beātum est, nec habet nec exhibet cuiquam negōtium,** *DN.* 1, 85, *whatsoever is blessed, has no trouble and makes none to anybody.* **quisquis hūc vēnerit, pugnōs edet,** Pl. *Am.* 309, *whoever comes this way, shall have a taste of fists* (1796). **omnia mala ingerēbat quemquem adspexerat,** Pl. *Men.* 717, *she showered all possible bad names on every man she saw* (1795). (*b.*) **haec quī videat, nōnne cōgātur cōnfitērī deōs esse,** *DN.* 2, 12, *whoso should see this would be forced, wouldn't he?* to admit the *existence of gods.* **quī vidēret, equom Trōiānum intrōductum dīceret,** *V.* 4, 52, *whoever saw it would have sworn it was the Trojan horse brought in* (1559).

THE INDICATIVE MOOD.

1813. The indicative is used in simple declarations or descriptions introduced by a relative : as,

quem dī dīligunt, adulēscēns moritur, Pl. *B.* 816, *whom the gods love, dies young.* **reliquī, quī domī mānsērunt, sē alunt,** 4, 1, 5, *the others, that stay at home, support themselves* (1736). **quōs labōrantēs cōnspexerat, hīs subsidia submittēbat,** 4, 26, 4, *to such as he saw in stress, he kept sending reinforcements* (1736). **tū quod volēs faciēs,** *QFr.* 3, 4, 5, *do what you like* (1735).

1814. The indicative is also used with indefinite relative pronouns and adverbs : as, **quidquid volt, valdē volt,** *Att.* 14, 1, 2, *whatever he wants, he wants mightily.* **quisquis est,** *TD.* 4. 37, *whoever he may be.* **quācumque iter fēcit,** *V.* 1, 44, *wherever he made his way.* In later writers the imperfect or pluperfect is often in the subjunctive : see 1730.

1815. An original indicative often becomes subjunctive, particularly in indirect discourse (1722) ; or by attraction (1728) ; or to indicate repeated action (1730). See also 1727 and 1731.

THE SUBJUNCTIVE MOOD.

1816. Relative pronoun sentences take the subjunctive to denote (1.) a purpose, (2.) a characteristic or result, (3.) a cause, reason, proof, or a concession.

SENTENCES OF PURPOSE.

1817. (1.) Relative sentences of purpose are equivalent to subjunctive sentences introduced by ut, *in order that, to* (1947): as,

ea quī cōnficeret, C. Trebōnium relinquit, 7, 11, 3, *he left Trebonius to manage this.* quālis esset nātūra montis, quī cōgnōscerent, mīsit, 1, 21, 1, *he sent some scouts to ascertain what the character of the mountain was.* haec habuī dē amīcitiā quae dīcerem, *L.* 104, *this was what I had to say of friendship.* Sentences of purpose are an extension of the subjunctive of desire (1540).

SENTENCES OF CHARACTERISTIC OR RESULT.

1818. (2.) Relative sentences of characteristic or result are equivalent to subjunctive sentences introduced by ut, *so as to, so that* (1947).

The main sentence sometimes has a word denoting character, such as is, eius modī, rarely ṭālis: as, neque is sum, quī mortis perīculō terrear, 5, 30, 2, *but I am not the man to be scared by danger of death, no not I.* Often, however, character is intimated by the mood alone: as, secūtae sunt tempestātēs quae nostrōs in castrīs continērent, 4, 34, 4, *there followed a succession of storms to keep our people in camp.* quod miserandum sit labōrātīs, *DN.* 3, 62, *you struggle away to a pitiable degree.* Sentences of result are an extension of the subjunctive of action conceivable (1554).

1819. The subjunctive with quī is often used with dignus, indignus, or idōneus, usually with a form of sum: as, Līviānae fābulae nōn satis dignae quae iterum legantur, *Br.* 71, *Livy's plays are not worth reading twice.* nōn erit idōneus quī ad bellum mittātur, *IP.* 66, *he will not be a fit person to be sent to the war.* Twice thus, aptus, once in Cicero, once in Ovid. In poetry and late prose these adjectives sometimes have the infinitive. dignus and indignus have also ut in Plautus, Livy, and Quintilian.

1820. Relative subjunctive sentences are sometimes coordinated by et or sed, with a substantive, adjective, or participle: as, audāx et coetūs possit quae ferre virōrum, *J.* 6, 399, *a brazen minx, and one quite capable of facing crowds of men.*

1821. Relative sentences after assertions or questions of existence or non-existence, usually take the subjunctive: as,

sunt quī putent, *TD.* 1, 18, *there be people to think, there be who think,* or *some people think.* nēmō est quī nesciat, *Fam.* 1, 4, 2, *there is nobody that does n't know.* sapientia est ūna quae maestitiam pellat ex animīs, *Fin.* 1, 43, *wisdom is the only thing to drive sadness from the soul.*

1822. Such expressions are: est (exsistit, exortus est), quī; sunt (reperiuntur, nōn dēsunt), quī; nēmō est, quī; quis est, quī; sōlus or ūnus est, quī; est, nihil est, quod; quid est, quod? habeō, nōn habeō, nihil habeō, quod, &c., &c. Indefinite subjects are sometimes used with these verbs: as, multī, quīdam, nōnnūllī, aliī, paucī; sometimes appellatives: as, hominēs, philosophī.

1823. The indicative, however, is not infrequently found in affirmative sentences, particularly in old Latin and in poetry: as, sunt quōs sciō esse amīcōs. Pl. *Tri.* 91, *some men there are I know to be my friends.* interdum volgus rēctum videt, est ubi peccat, *H. E.* 2, 1, 63, *sometimes the world sees right, there be times when it errs.* sunt item, quae appellantur alcēs, 6, 27, 1, *then again there are what they call elks.*

SENTENCES OF CAUSE OR CONCESSION.

1824. (3.) Relative sentences of cause, reason, proof, or of concession, are equivalent to subjunctive sentences introduced by cum,
since, though (1877): as,

(*a*.) hospes, quī nihil suspicārētur, hominem retinēre coepit, *V.* 1, 64,
the friend, suspecting nothing, undertook to hold on to the man. Often justifying the use of a single word : as, ō fortūnāte adulēscēns, quī tuae virtūtis
Homērum praecōnem invēnerīs, *Arch.* 24, *oh youth thrice-blest, with Homer
trumpeter of thy prowess.* ad mē vēnit Hēraclius, homo nōbilis, quī sacerdōs Iovis fuisset, *V.* 4, 137, *I had a call from Heraclius, a man of high standing, as is proved by his having been a priest of Jupiter.* (*b*.) Cicerō, quī mīlitēs in castrīs continuisset, quīnque cohortēs frūmentātum mittit, 6, 36, 1,
though Cicero had kept his men in camp, he sends five cohorts foraging.

1825. With quī tamen, however, the indicative is usual : as, alter, quī tamen
sē continuerat, nōn tenuit eum locum, *Sest.* 114, *the other, though he had
observed a quiet policy, did not hold the place.*

1826. Oftentimes, where a causal relation might be expected, a simple
declaratory indicative is used: as,

habeō senectūtī magnam grātiam, quae mihī sermōnis aviditātem
auxit, *CM.* 46, *I feel greatly indebted to age, which has increased my eagerness
for conversation.* Particularly thus in old Latin : as, sed sumne ego stultus,
quī rem cūrō pūblicam ? Pl. *Per.* 75, *but am I not a fool, who bother with the
common weal?* Compared with : sed ego sum īnsipientior, quī rēbus
cūrem pūplicīs, Pl. *Tri.* 1057, *but I 'm a very fool, to bother with the common
weal.* Often of coincident action (1733) : as, stultē fēcī, quī hunc āmīsī,
Pl. *MG.* 1376, *I 've acted like a fool, in letting this man off.*

1827. The causal relative is often introduced by quippe, less frequently
by ut, or ut pote, *naturally :* as,

' convīvia cum patre nōn inībat ; ' quippe quī nē in oppidum quidem
nisi perrārō venīret, *RA.* 52, ' *he never went to dinner-parties with his father ;* ' *why, of course not, since he never went to a simple country town even,
except very rarely.* dictātor tamen, ut quī magis animīs quam vīribus
frētus ad certāmen dēscenderet, omnia circumspicere coepit, L. 7, 14,
6, *but the dictator, naturally, since he went into the struggle trusting to mind
rather than muscle, now began to be all on the alert.* With quippe quī, the
indicative only is used by Sallust, and is preferred by Plautus and Terence.
Cicero has, with one exception, the subjunctive, Tacitus and Nepos have it
always. Livy has either mood. Not in Caesar. ut quī has the subjunctive.
It occurs a few times in Plautus, Cicero, once in Caesar, oftenest in Livy.
With the indicative once in Cicero, and once in Tacitus. ut pote quī has
the subjunctive. It is used by Plautus, by Cicero, once with the indicative,
by Sallust, and Catullus.

1828. The indefinite ablative quī, *somehow, surely,* sometimes follows quippe
or ut in old Latin, in which case it must not be confounded with the relative : as,
quippe quī ex tē audīvī, Pl. *Am.* 745, *why, sure I 've heard from you ;* it
cannot be the relative here, as the speaker is a woman.

1829. The subjunctive is used in parenthetical sentences of restriction : as,

---

quod sciam, Pl. *Men.* 500 ; T. *Ad.* 641 ; *RA.* 17, *to the best of my knowledge and belief.* **quod sine molestiā tuā fiat**, *Fam.* 13, 23, 2, *as far as may be without trouble to yourself.* **quī** is often followed by **quidem** : as, **omnium ōrātōrum, quōs quidem ego cōgnōverim, acūtissimum iūdicō Q**. Sertō-rium, *Br.* 180, *of all orators, at least of all that I have made the acquaintance of myself, I count Sertorius the sharpest.*

1830. The indicative, however, is used in **quod attinet ad**, *as to*, and usually with **quantum**, and with forms of **sum** and **possum**: as, **quod sine molestiā tuā facere poteris**, *Att.* 1, 5, 7, *as far as you can without troubling yourself.*

CORRELATIVE SENTENCES.

1831. Sentences are said to be *correlative*, when a relative pronoun or adverb has a corresponding determinative or demonstrative pronoun or adverb in the main sentence.

Thus, the ordinary correlative of **quī** is **is**, less frequently **hīc, ille, īdem**. Similarly **tot** . . . **quot** are used as correlatives; also **quō** . . . **eō, quantō** . . . **tantō ; quantum** . . . **tantum ; tam** . . . **quam; totiēns** . . . **quotiēns; tālis** . . . **quālis; ubī** . . . **ibī ; ut** . . . **ita, sīc**, or **item ; cum** . . . **tum.**

RELATIVE SENTENCES COMBINED.

(A.) COORDINATION OF A RELATIVE.

1832. (1.) When two coordinate relative sentences would have the second relative in the same case as the first, the second relative is usually omitted : as,

Dumnorīgī quī prīncipātum optinēbat, ac maximē plēbī acceptus erat, persuādet, 1, 3, 5, *he prevails with Dumnorix, who held the headship, and was popular with the commons.*

1833. (2.) When two coordinate relative sentences require two different cases of the relative, the relative is usually expressed with both, or else the second relative, which is usually nominative or accusative, is omitted, or is, **hīc, ille**, or **īdem**, is substituted for it : as,

(*a*.) **cūr loquimur dē eō hoste, quī iam fatētur sē esse hostem, et quem nōn timeō ?** *C.* 2, 17, *why am I talking about an enemy who admits himself he is an enemy, and whom I do not fear ?* (*b*.) **Bocchus cum pedi-tibus, quōs Volux addūxerat, neque in priōre pugnā adfuerant**, S. *I.* 101, 5, *Bocchus with the infantry whom Volux had brought up, and who had not been engaged in the first skirmish.* (*c*.) **Viriāthus, quem C. Laelius frēgit, ferōcitātemque eius repressit**, *Off.* 2, 40, *Viriathus, whom Laelius crushed, and curbed his fiery soul.* This last use is chiefly limited to old Latin, Cicero, and Lucretius.

(B.) SUBORDINATION OF A RELATIVE.

1834. A sentence consisting of a main and a relative member, **may be** further modified by a more specific relative sentence : as, proximī sunt Germānīs quī trāns Rhēnum incolunt (general), **quibuscum continenter bellum gerunt** (specific), 1, 1, 3, *they are nearest to the Germans that live beyond the Rhine, with whom they carry on uninterrupted hostilities.* īdem artifex Cupīdinem fēcit illum quī est Thespiīs (general), **propter quem Thespiae vīsuntur** (specific), *V.* 4, 4, *the selfsame artist made the world-renowned Cupid at Thespiae, which is the attraction for tourists in Thespiae.*

THE RELATIVE INTRODUCING A MAIN SENTENCE.

1835. Besides the ordinary use of the relative, to introduce a subordinate sentence, it is often used like **hīc,** or **is,** or like **et is, is autem, is enim,** or **is igitur,** to append a fresh main sentence or period to the foregoing: as,

cōnsiliō convocātō sententiās exquīrere coepit, quō in cōnsiliō nōnnūllae huius modī sententiae dīcēbantur, 3, 3, 1, *calling a council of war, he proceeded to ask their opinion, and in this council some opinions of the following import were set forth.* centuriōnēs hostēs vocāre coepērunt; quōrum prōgredī ausus est nēmō, 5, 43, 6, *the officers proceeded to call the enemy; but not a man of them ventured to step forward.* perūtilēs Xenophōntis librī sunt; quōs legite studiōsē, *CM.* 59, *Xenophon's works are extremely profitable reading; so do read them attentively.* In Plautus this use is rare; but it becomes more and more prevalent, and in the time of Cicero the relative is one of the commonest connectives.

1836. From this use of the relative come many introductory formulas, such as quō factō, quā rē cōgnitā, quae cum ita sint, &c., &c.

1837. A connective **quod** is often used before **sī, nisi,** or **etsī,** less frequently before **quia, quoniam, utinam, quī,** &c.

This **quod** may be translated *so, but, now, whereas, as to that,* &c., or it is often best omitted in translation. See 2132.

---•---

THE CONJUNCTIVE PARTICLE SENTENCE.

quod.

1838. The conjunctive particle **quod,** originally the neuter of the relative pronoun, has both a declarative sense, *that,* and a causal sense, *because.* In both senses it regularly introduces the indicative (1721). For special reasons, however, the subjunctive is often used, and particularly in indirect discourse (1722).

1839. In some of its applications, particularly in old Latin, the conjunctive particle **quod** can hardly be distinguished from the pronoun **quod,** as follows:

1840. (1) In old Latin, **quod**, *why, for what*, is sometimes used with **veniō** and **mittō.** Thus, as in id **vēnimus**, Pl. *MG.* 1158, *that's why we've come*, id is used to define the purpose of the motion (1144), so also **quod**, in **quod vēnī, ēloquar**, T. *Hau. prol.* 3, *what I've come for, I'll set forth.* Instead of **quod**, more explicitly **quam ob rem** : as, **quam ob rem hūc sum missa**, Pl. *R.* 430, *what I am sent here for.*

1841. (2.) **quod**, *why, for what*, is used in such expansions as **quid est quod** ? **quid habēs quod** ? or **nihil est quod** : as,

quid est quod mē excīvistī ? Pl. *E.* 570, *why is it that you've called me out ?* (1144). Usually with the subjunctive (1563) : as, **quid est quod plūra dīcāmus** ? *Clu.* 59, *what reason is there for saying more ?* For **quod**, sometimes **quā rē, quam ob rem, cūr**, &c. _ The question itself is also sometimes varied : as, **quid fuit causae, cūr in Africam Caesarem nōn sequerēre** ? *Ph.* 2, 71, *what earthly reason was there, why you should not have followed Caesar to Africa ?*

1842. (3.) **quod**, *as to what*, or *that*, is used, especially at the beginning of a sentence, to introduce a fact on which something is to be said, often by way of protest or refutation : as,

vērum quod tū dīcis, nōn tē mī īrāscī decet, Pl. *Am.* 522, *but as to what you say, it is n't right that you should get provoked with me.* **quod multitūdinem Germānōrum in Galliam trādūcat, id sē suī mūniendī causā facere**, 1, 44, 6, *as to his moving a great many Germans over to Gaul, that he did for self-protection* (1722). This construction is particularly common in Caesar, and in Cicero's letters.

1843. When **quod**, *in case, suppose, although*, introduces a mere conjecture or a concession, the subjunctive is used (1554) : as, **quod quispiam ignem quaerat, extinguī volō**, Pl. *Aul.* 91, *in case a man may come for fire, I want the fire put out.* This use is principally found in old Latin, but once or twice also in Cicero.

1844. quod, *that, the fact that,* is often used in subordinate sentences which serve to complete the sense of the main sentence.

1845. The sentence with **quod** may represent a subject, as with **accēdit** ; an object, as with **praetereō**, &c. ; or any case of a substantive ; frequently it is in apposition with a demonstrative or an appellative : as,

(*a.*) **accēdēbat, quod suōs ab sē līberōs abstrāctōs dolēbant**, 3, 2, 5, *there was added this fact, that they lamented that their own children were torn from them ;* or less clumsily, *then too they lamented.* **praetereō, quod eam sibī domum sēdemque dēlēgit, in quā cōtīdiē virī mortis indicia vidēret**, *Clu.* 188, *I pass over the fact that she picked out a house to live in, in which she would see, day in day out, things to remind her of her husband's death.* **illud minus cūrō, quod congessistī operāriōs omnēs**, *Br.* 297, *I am not particularly interested in the fact that you have lumped together all sorts of cobblers and tinkers.* (*b.*) **Caesar senātūs in eum beneficia commemorāvit, quod rēx appellātus esset ā senātū**, 1, 43, 4, *Caesar told off the kindnesses of the senate to the man, the fact that ' he had been styled king by the senate '* (1722). **quō factō duās rēs cōnsecūtus est, quod animōs centuriōnum** dēvinxit et mīlitum voluntātēs redēmit, Caes. *C.* 1, 39, 4, *thus he killed two birds with one stone: he won the hearts of the officers, and he bought golden opinions of the rank and file.* ¯hōc ūnō praestāmus vel maximē ferīs, quod conloquimur inter nōs, *DO.* 1, 32, *in this one circumstance do we perhaps most of all surpass brutes, that we can talk with each other.* labōre et industriā et quod adhibēbat grātiam, in prīncipibus patrōnīs fuit, *Br.* 233, *thanks to his untiring industry, and to his bringing his winning manners to bear, he figured among the leaders of the bar.*

1846. accēdit, as the passive of addō, often has the subjunctive with ut : see 1965. addō quod, especially in the imperative form adde quod, occurs in Accius, Terence, Lucretius, Horace, and Ovid. adiciō quod begins with Livy.

1847. The sentence with quod is often introduced by a prepositional expression, such as eō with dē, ex, in, prō, rarely with cum ; or id with ad in Livy, super in Tacitus.

1848. nisi quod, or in Plautus and Terence nisi quia, *but for the fact that, except, only that,* and praeter quam quod, *besides the fact that,* are used in limitations : as, nihil peccat, nisi quod nihil peccat, Plin.. *Ep.* 9, 26, 1, *he erreth naught, save that he naught doth err.* Livy has also super quam quod. tantum quod in the sense of nisi quod is rare; more commonly of time, *just, hardly.*

1849. quid quod? for quid dē eō dīcam quod? *what of the fact that,* or *nay more,* marks an important transition : as, quid quod salūs sociōrum in perīculum vocātur? *IP.* 12, *nay more, the very existence of our allies is endangered.*

1850. With verbs of doing or happening, accompanied by some word of manner, quod introduces a verb of coincident action (1733) : as,

bene facis quod mē adiuvās, *Fin.* 3, 16, *you are very kind in helping me.* videor mihī grātum fēcisse Siculīs, quod eōrum iniūriās sum persecūtus, *V.* 2, 16, *I flatter myself that I have won the gratitude of the Sicilians in acting as avenger of their wrongs.* In this sense quī (1826) or cum (1874) is often used, or in Plautus and once in Horace quia.

1851. quod, *that, because,* is used to denote cause with verbs of emotion.

Thus, as with id in id gaudeō, T. *Andr.* 362, *I'm glad of that* (1144), so with an object sentence, as gaudeō quod tē interpellāvī, *Leg.* 3, 1, *I'm glad that I interrupted you.* Such verbs are : gaudeō, laetor ; mīror ; doleō, maereō, angor, indignor, suscēnseō, īrāscor, &c. In old Latin, Cicero's letters, Livy, and rarely in Tacitus such verbs may have quia, sometimes quom (1875). For the accusative with the infinitive, see 2187.

1852. Verbs of praising, blaming, accusing, and condemning, often take quod : as,

quod bene cōgitāstī aliquandō, laudō, *Ph.* 2, 34, *that you have ever had good intentions, I commend.* laudat Āfricānum Panaetius, quod fuerit abstinēns, *Off.* 2, 76, *Panaetius eulogizes Africanus, 'for being so abstinent'* (1725). ut cum Sōcratēs accūsātus est quod corrumperet iuventūtem, Quintil. 4, 4, 5, *as when Socrates was charged with 'demoralizing the rising generation'* (1725). grātulor, *congratulate,* and grātiās agō, *thank.* have regularly quod or cum (1875). Verbs of accusing sometimes have cūr.

1853. Causal **quod,** *owing to the fact that, because,* introduces an efficient cause, or a reason or motive : as,

(*a.*) in hīs locīs, quod omnis Gallia ad septentriōnēs vergit, mātūrae sunt hiemēs, 4, 20, 1, *in these parts the winter sets in early, owing to the fact that Gaul in general lies to the north.* Helvētiī reliquōs Gallōs virtūte praecēdunt, quod ferē cōtīdiānīs proeliīs cum Germānīs contendunt, 1, 1, 4, *the Helvetians outshine the rest of the Gauls in bravery, because they do battle with the Germans almost every day.* hōrum fortissimī sunt Belgae, proptereā quod a cultū prōvinciae longissimē absunt, 1, 1, 3, *of these the stoutest fighting-men are the Belgians, for the reason that they live furthest away from the comforts of the province.* (*b.*) T. Mānlius Torquātus fīlium suum, quod is contrā imperium in hostem pugnāverat, necārī iussit, S. *C.* 52, 30, *Torquatus ordered his own son to be put to death, because the young man had fought with the enemy contrary to orders.* exōrāvit tyrannum ut abīre licēret, quod iam beātus nōllet esse, *TD.* 5, 62, *he induced the monarch to let him go, 'because he didn't care to be Fortune's pet any longer'* (1725). Bellovacī suum numerum nōn contulērunt, quod sē suō arbitriō bellum esse gestūrōs dīcerent, 7, 75, 5, *the Bellovacans would not put in their proper quota, saying they meant to make war on their own responsibility* (1727).

1854. quod often has a correlative in the main sentence, such as eō, ideō, idcircō, proptereā. In Sallust, eā grātiā. In Plautus, causal quod is very rare compared to causal quia.

1855. An untenable reason is introduced in Plautus by nōn eō quia, in Terence by nōn eō quō; in Cicero very rarely by neque or non eō quō, usually by nōn quod or nōn quō; by nōn quia rarely in classical Latin, but commonly from Livy on. The valid reason follows, with sed quod, sed quia, or with sed and a fresh main sentence.

The mood is usually subjunctive (1725) : as, pugilēs ingemīscunt, nōn quod doleant, sed quia prōfundendā vōce omne corpus intenditur, *TD.* 2, 56, *boxers grunt and groan, not because they feel pain, but because by explosion of voice the whole system gets braced up.* Sometimes, but very rarely in classical prose, the indicative. Correlatives, such as idcircō, ideō, &c., are not uncommon. Reversed constructions occur, with magis followed by quam, as : magis quod, quō, or quia, followed by quam quō, quod, or quia. The negative *not that . . . not,* is expressed by nōn quod nōn, nōn quō nōn, or nōn quin.

---

quia.

1856. quia, a neuter accusative plural of the relative stem (701) is used in both a declarative and a causal sense, like quod (1838). It is, however, more prevalent in Plautus, less so from Terence on.

1857. For the uses of declarative quia, see under 1848, 1850, 1851.

1858. Causal quia, with or without a correlative, such as ideō, eō, proptereā, &c., is common in old Latin (1854) and poetry, unusual in prose (once in Caesar) before Tacitus. For nōn quia, &c., see 1855.

quom or cum.

1859. **quom** or **cum** (157, 711), used as a **relative conjunctive** particle (1794), has a temporal meaning, *when*, which readily passes over to an explanatory or causal meaning, *in that, since* or *although*. In both meanings it introduces the indicative in old Latin. In classical Latin, temporal **cum** in certain connections, and causal **cum** regularly, introduces the subjunctive. The subjunctive is also used with **cum** for special reasons, as in the indefinite second person (1731), by attraction (1728), and commonly by late writers to express repeated past action (1730). **cum**, *when*, is often used as a synonym of **sī**, *if*, and may then introduce any form of a conditional protasis (2016, 2110).

(A.) TEMPORAL cum.

WITH THE INDICATIVE.

1860. **cum**, *when, whenever, if,* of indefinite time, may introduce any tense of the indicative required by the context: as,

facile omnēs, quom valēmus, rēcta cōnsilia aegrōtīs damus, T. *Andr.* 309, *we all, when well, give good advice to sick folk easily.* Rōmae videor esse, cum tuās litterās legō, *Att.* 2, 15, 1, *I always fancy myself in Rome, when I am reading a letter from you.* cum posuī librum, adsēnsiō omnis ēlābitur, *TD.* 1, 24, *when I drop the book, all assent melts away* (1613). incenderis cupiditāte lībertātis, cum potestātem gustandī fēceris, *RP.* 2, 50, *you will inspire them with a passion for freedom, when you give them a chance to taste it* (1627). hīs cum fūnēs comprehēnsī adductīque erant, 3, 14, 6, *every time the lines were caught by these and hauled taut, they would part* (1618). The subjunctive is used, chiefly by late writers, rarely by Cicero and Caesar, to express repeated past action (1730): as, cum in convīvium vēnisset, sī quicquam caelātī adspexerat, manūs abstinēre nōn poterat, *V.* 4, 48, *when he went to a dinner party, if he ever caught sight of a bit of chased work, he never could keep his hands off* (2050).

1861. **cum**, *when,* of definite time, regularly introduces the indicative in old Latin, even where the subjunctive is required in classical Latin (1872): as,

nam illa, quom tē ad sē vocābat, mēmet esse crēdidit, Pl. *Men.* 1145, *for when that lady asked you in, she thought 'twas I.* postīculum hoc recēpit, quom aedīs vēndidit, Pl. *Tri.* 194, *this back part he excepted, when he sold the house.*

1862. **cum**, *when,* of definite time, regularly introduces the indicative of any action, not of past time: as,

sed dē hīs etiam rēbus, ōtiōsī cum erimus, loquēmur, *Fam.* 9, 4, *but we will talk of this when we have time.* cum ego P. Grānium testem prōdūxerō, refellitō, sī poteris, *V.* 5, 154, *when I put Granius on the witness stand, refute him if you can.*

315

1863. With **cum**, *when*, the indicative is used of definite past time to date the action of the main clause, as follows:

1864. (1.) The indicative imperfect is regularly used with **cum**, *when*, to denote a continued action parallel and coincident in duration with another continued action, also in the imperfect: as,

quom pugnābant maxumē, ego tum fugiēbam maxumē, Pl. *Am.* 199, *while they were fighting hardest, then I was running hardest.* tum cum rem habēbās, quaesticulus tē faciēbat attentiōrem, *Fam.* 9, 16, 7, *as long as you were a man of substance, the fun of making money made you a little close.*

1865. (2.) The indicative imperfect is often used with **cum**, *when*, denoting a continued action, to date an apodosis in the perfect: as,

legiōnēs quom pugnābant maxumē, quid in tabernāclō fēcistī? Pl. *Am.* 427, *what did'st thou in the tent what time the legions fought their mightiest?* hīs librīs adnumerandī sunt sex dē rē pūblicā, quōs tum scrīpsimus cum gubernācula rēī pūblicae tenēbāmus, *Div.* 2, 3, *to these books are to be added the six On the State, which I wrote at the time I was holding the helm of state.* But when the object of the clause is not distinctly to date the apodosis, its verb is in the subjunctive (1872).

1866. (3.) The indicative perfect or present of vivid narration is used with **cum**, *when*, to date an apodosis in the perfect or present of vivid narration: as,

'per tuās statuās' vērō cum dīxit, vehementius rīsimus, *DO.* 2, 242, *but when he uttered the words 'by your statues,' we burst into a louder laugh.* cum occīditur Sex. Rōscius, ibīdem fuērunt, *RA.* 120, *when Roscius was murdered, they were on the spot.* cum diēs vēnit, causā ipse prō sē dictā, damnātur, L. 4, 44, 10, *when the day of the trial came, he spoke in his own defence and was condemned.* The present is particularly common in old colloquial Latin: as, vivom, quom abīmus, līquimus, Pl. *Cap.* 282, *we left him alive when we came away.* For cum prīmum in narration, see 1925; for cum extemplō, 1926.

1867. (4.) The indicative perfect or present of vivid narration is regularly used with **cum**, *when*, to denote a momentary action when the apodosis denotes continued action: as,

cum Caesar in Galliam vēnit, alterīus factiōnis prīncipēs erant Aeduī, alterīus Sēquanī, 6, 12, 1, *when Caesar came to Gaul, the leaders of one party were the Aeduans, of the other the Sequanians.* eō cum veniō, praetor quiēscēbat, *V.* 4, 32, *when I got there, the praetor was taking a nap.*

1868. An emphatic indicative clause with **cum**, *while*, often follows the main action.

The clause with **cum** is usually inconsistent with the main action, and cum is often attended by intereā, interim, *all the time*, etiam tum, *still*, nōndum, hauddum, *not yet, no longer*, quidem, *by the way*, or tamen, nihilōminus, *nevertheless*: as,

316

caedēbātur virgīs in mediō forō Messānae cīvis Rōmānus, cum
intereā nūllus gemitus audiēbātur, *V.* 5, 162, *there was flogged with rods in
open market place at Messana a citizen of Rome, while all the time not a groan
was to be heard.* ēvolārat iam ē cōnspectū quadrirēmis, cum etiam
tum cēterae nāvēs ūnō in locō mōliēbantur, *V.* 5, 88, *she had already sped
out of sight, the four-banker, while the rest of the vessels were still struggling
round in one and the same spot.* This use is very rare in old Latin. Not
in Caesar. With the infinitive of intimation, see 1539.

1869. An indicative clause with cum, usually expressing sudden
or unexpected action, sometimes contains the main idea, and is put
last.

In this case cum is often attended by subitō or repente, *suddenly,* and
the first clause contains iam, *already, by this time,* vix, aegrē, *hardly,* vix-
dum, *hardly yet,* or nōndum, *not yet.* The first verb is commonly in the
imperfect or pluperfect, and the second in the perfect or present of vivid
narration: as,

dīxerat hoc ille, cum puer nūntiāvit venīre Laelium, *RP.* 1, 18,
*scarcely had he said this, when a slave announced that Laelius was com-
ing.* vix ea fātus eram, gemitū cum tālia reddit, V. 2, 323, *scarce had
I spoke the words, when with a groan he answers thus.* Hannibal iam
subībat mūrōs, cum repente in eum patēfactā portā ērumpunt Rōmānī,
L. 29, 7, 8, *Hannibal was already moving up to the walls, when all of a sudden the gate flies open and the Romans come pouring out upon him.* iamque
hoc facere apparābant, cum mātrēs familiae repente prōcurrērunt, 7,
26, 3, *they were already preparing to do it, when suddenly the married women
rushed forward.* This use is very rare in old Latin. From Sallust on,
it is found occasionally with the infinitive of intimation (1539).

1870. A clause with cum is often used attributively with words denoting
time, or with est, fuit, or erit.

The mood is the same as with a relative pronoun, sometimes the indicative, and regularly in old Latin, but usually the subjunctive: as, fuit quoddam tempus cum in agrīs hominēs vagābantur, *Inv.* 1, 2, *there was an
age of the world when men roved round in the fields* (1813, 1823). fuit
tempus cum rūra colerent hominēs, Varro, *RR.* 3, 1, 1, *there was a time
when men dwelt in the fields* (1818, 1821). est cum exōrnātiō praetermit-
tenda est, Cornif. 2, 30, *sometimes ornamentation should be avoided.* fuit
anteā tempus, cum Germānōs Gallī virtūte superārent, 6, 24, 1, *there
was a time when the Gauls outdid the Germans in valour.* The subjunctive
is also used with audiō cum (1722), but with meminī cum the indicative:
as, saepe ex socerō meō audīvī, cum is dīceret, *DO.* 2, 22, *I have often
heard my father-in-law saying.* meminī cum mihī dēsipere vidēbāre,
Fam. 7, 28, 1, *I remember when I thought you showed bad taste.*

1871. The indicative present or perfect with cum is used in expressions equivalent to an emphasized accusative or ablative of time, the main verb being est or sunt:
as, annī prope quadringentī sunt, cum hoc probātur, *O.* 171, *it is nearly
four hundred years that this has been liked.* nōndum centum et decem annī
sunt, cum lāta lēx est, *Off.* 2, 75, *it is not a hundred and ten years yet since
the law was passed.* In old Latin, the clause with cum is made the subject of est,
and the substantive of time is put in the accusative: as, hanc domum iam multōs
annōs est quom possideō, Pl. *Aul.* 3, *'tis many years now I have occupied this
house.*

317

WITH THE SUBJUNCTIVE.

1872. With **cum**, *when*, the imperfect or pluperfect subjunctive is used to describe the circumstances under which the action of the main clause took place : as,

cum rēx Pyrrhus populō Rōmānō bellum intulisset cumque dē imperiō certāmen esset cum rēge potentī, perfuga ab eō vēnit in castra Fabricii, *Off.* 3, 86, *king Pyrrhus having made war on the Roman nation, and there being a struggle for sovereignty with a powerful king, a deserter from him came into Fabricius's camp.* eōdem tempore Attalus rēx moritur alterō et septuāgēsimō annō, cum quattuor et quadrāgintā annōs rēgnāsset, L. 33, 21, 1, *the same year Attalus the king dies, in his seventy-second year, having reigned forty-four years.* hīc pāgus, cum domō exīsset patrum nostrōrum memoriā, L. Cassium cōnsulem interfēcerat, 1, 12, 5, *this canton, sallying out from home in our fathers' recollection, had put Cassius, the consul, to death.* nam cum inambulārem in xystō, M. ad mē Brūtus vēnerat, *Br.* 10, *for as I was pacing up and down my portico, Brutus had come to see me.* Antigonus in proeliō, cum adversus Seleucum et Lȳsimachum dīmicāret, occīsus est, N. 21, 3, 2, *Antigonus was killed in battle fighting against Seleucus and Lysimachus.* haec cum Crassus dīxisset, silentium est cōnsecūtum, *DO.* 1, 160, *a deep silence ensued after Crassus had finished speaking.* cum annōs iam complūrīs societās esset, moritur in Galliā Quīnctius, cum adesset Naevius, *Quinct.* 14, *the partnership having lasted several years, Quinctius died in Gaul, Naevius being there at the time.*

In this use, as the examples show, **cum** with the subjunctive is often equivalent to a participle or an ablative absolute. The use is not found in Plautus (1861). Ennius and Terence have possibly each an instance (disputed) of it, but it was certainly rare until the classical period, when it became one of the commonest of constructions. It must not be confounded with the special uses of the subjunctive mentioned in 1859.

1873. The difference in meaning between **cum** with the indicative and **cum** with the subjunctive may be illustrated by the following examples :

Gallō nārrāvī, cum proximē Rōmae fuī, quid audīssem, *Att.* 13, 49, 2, *I told Gallus, when I was last in Rome, what I had heard* (1866). a. d. III kal. Maiās cum essem in Cūmānō, accēpī tuās litterās, *Fam.* 4, 2, 1, *I received your letter on the twenty-eighth of April, being in my villa at Cumae* (1872). cum vāricēs secābantur C. Mariō, dolēbat, *TD.* 2, 35, *while Marius was having his varicose veins lanced, he was in pain* (1864). C. Marius, cum secārētur, ut suprā dīxī, vetuit sē adligārī, *TD.* 2, 53, *Marius being under the surgeon's knife, as above mentioned, refused to be bound* (1872). num P. Decius, cum sē dēvovēret et in mediam aciem inruēbat, aliquid dē voluptātibus suīs cōgitābat ? *Fin.* 2, 61, *did Decius, offering himself up, and while he was dashing straight into the host, have any thought of pleasures of his own ?* (1872, 1864).

(B.) EXPLANATORY AND CAUSAL cum.

1874. The indicative is often used with explanatory **cum** when the action of the protasis is coincident with that of the apodosis (1733).

In this use **cum** passes from the meaning of *when* to *that, in that,* or *in* or *by* with a verbal in *-ing :* as, hoc verbum quom illī quoidam dīcō, praemōstrō tibī, Pl. *Tri.* 342, *in laying down this lesson for your unknown friend I'm warning you.* cum quiēscunt, probant, *C.* 1, 21, *their inaction is approval.* Denoting the means: as, tūte tibi prōdes plūrumum, quom servitūtem ita fers ut ferrī decet, Pl. *Cap.* 371, *you do yourself most good by bearing slavery as it should be borne.* For similar uses of quod, quia, and quī, see 1850.

1875. Explanatory cum is also used with verbs of emotion; likewise with grātulor and grātiās agō: as, quom tu 's liber, gaudeō, Pl. *Men.* 1148, *that you are free, I'm glad.* grātulor tibī, cum tantum valēs apud Dolābellam, *Fam.* 9, 14, 3, *I give you joy that you stand so well with Dolabella.* tibī maximās grātiās agō, cum tantum litterae meae potuērunt, *Fam.* 13, 24, 2, *I thank you most heartily in that my letter had such influence.* For similar uses of quod and quia, see 1851, 1852.

1876. Explanatory **cum** is also used in the sense of *since, although,* or *even though.* In these meanings it introduces the indicative in old Latin (1878): as,

Denoting cause: istō tū pauper es, quom nimis sānctē piu 's, Pl. *R.* 1234, *that's why are poor yourself, since you are over-scrupulously good.* quom hoc nōn possum, illud minus possem, T. *Ph.* 208, *since this I can't, that even less could I.* Adversative cause: īnsānīre mē aiunt, quom ipsī īnsāniunt, Pl. *Men.* 831, *they say I'm mad, whereas they are mad themselves.* Concession: sat sīc suspectus sum, quom careō noxiā, Pl. *B.* 1005, *I am enough distrusted as it is, even though I'm void of wrong.*

1877. cum, *since, although, even though,* usually introduces the subjunctive: as,

Denoting cause: cum in commūnibus suggestīs cōnsistere nōn audēret, contiōnārī ex turrī altā solēbat, *TD.* 5, 59, *since he did not dare to stand up on an ordinary platform, he always did his speaking from a lofty tower,* of Dionysius, tyrant of Syracuse. Aeduī cum sē dēfendere nōn possent, lēgātōs ad Caesarem mittunt, 1, 11, 2, *since the Aeduans could not defend themselves, they sent ambassadors to Caesar.* Adversative cause: fuit perpetuō pauper, cum dīvitissimus esse posset, N. 19, 1, 2, *he was always poor, whereas he might have been very rich,* of Phocion. Pyladēs cum sīs, dīcēs tē esse Orestēn? *Fin.* 2, 79, *whereas you are Pylades, will you declare yourself Orestes?* Concession: ipse Cicerō, cum tenuissimā valētūdine esset, nē nocturnum quidem sibī tempus ad quiētem relinquēbat, 5, 40, 7, *Cicero himself, though he was in extremely delicate health, did not allow himself even the night-time for rest.* ille Catō, cum esset Tusculī nātus, in populī Rōmānī cīvitātem susceptus est, *Leg.* 2, 5, *the great Cato, though born at Tusculum, was received into the citizenship of the Roman nation.*

1878. This use of the subjunctive is not found in Plautus. It is thought to have begun in the time of Terence, who may have a couple of instances (disputed). Thereafter, it grew common and was the regular mood used with explanatory and causal **cum** in the classical period.

1879. Explanatory **cum** is sometimes introduced by **quippe**, rarely by **ut pote**, *naturally:* as,

tum vērō gravior cūra patribus incessit, quippe cum prōdī causam ab suis cernerent, L. 4, 57, 10, *then the senators were still more seriously concerned, and naturally enough, since they beheld their cause betrayed by their own people.* valētūdō, ē quā iam ēmerseram, ut pote cum sine febrī labōrāssem, *Att.* 5, 8, 1, *an illness from which I had already recovered, naturally, since it was unaccompanied by fever.* quippe cum occurs in Cicero, Nepos, and Livy; ut pote cum is used once in Cicero's letters, once by Pollio to Cicero, and in late writers. For quippe and ut pote with a causal relative, see 1827.

1880. The adversative idea is often emphasized by the use of **tamen** in the main clause: as, cum prīmī ōrdinēs hostium concidissent, tamen ācerrimē reliquī resistēbant, 7, 62, 4, *though the front ranks of the enemy had fallen, yet the rest made a most spirited resistance.*

(C.) cum . . . tum.

1881. A protasis with **cum** is often followed by an emphatic apodosis introduced by **tum.**

The protasis denotes what is general or common or old; the apodosis what is special or strange or new. In classical Latin **tum** is often emphasized by **maximē, in prīmīs, vērō,** &c.

In this use the mood is more commonly the indicative and the time of the two verbs is apt to be identical: as, quom mihi paveō, tum Antiphō mē excruciat animī, T. *Ph.* 187, *whilst for myself I tremble, Antipho puts me in a perfect agony of soul.* But cum anteā distinēbar maximīs occupātiōnibus, tum hōc tempore multō distineor vehementius, *Fam.* 12, 30, 2, *I was distracted by most important engagements before, but now I am very much more distracted.* Less frequently the subjunctive, to denote cause or concession (1877): as, cum tē ā pueritiā tuā dīlēxerim, tum hōc multō ācrius dīligō, *Fam.* 15, 9, 1, *whereas I have always loved you from your boyhood, for this I love you with a far intenser love.* By abridgement of the sentence (1057), cum . . . tum come to be copulative conjunctions (1687): as, mōvit patrēs cōnscrīptōs cum causa tum auctor, L. 9, 10, 1, *both the cause and its supporter touched the conscript fathers.*

———◆———

quoniam.

1882. quoniam, compounded of **quom** and **iam,** *when now,* refers primarily to time, but is seldom so used and only by early writers. The temporal meaning passed early into an exclusively causal meaning, *since.* In both meanings it regularly introduces the indicative (1721). For special reasons, however, the subjunctive is used, as in indirect discourse (1725), or by attraction (1728).

1883. (1.) quoniam, *when now,* used of time in early Latin, has some-times as a correlative continuō, subitō, or extemplō; it usually introduces the present indicative (1590): as,

is quoniam moritur, numquam indicāre id fīliō voluit suō, Pl. *Aul.* 9, *when he was on his dying bed, he ne'er would point it out to his own son,* of a hidden treasure. quoniam sentiō quae rēs gererētur, nāvem extemplō statuimus, Pl. *B.* 290, *when now I saw what was doing, we stopped the ship at once.*

1884. (2.) quoniam, *since, seeing that, now that,* with the indica-tive, introduces a reason, usually one known to the person addressed, or one generally known: as,

vēra dīcō, sed nēquīquam, quoniam nōn vīs crēdere, Pl. *Am.* 835, *the truth I speak, but all in vain, since thou wilt not believe.* vōs, Quirītēs, quoniam iam nox est, in vestra tecta discēdite, *C.* 3, 29, *do you, citizens, since it is now grown dark, depart and go to your own several homes.* quoniam in eam ratiōnem vītae nōs fortūna dēdūxit, ut sempiternus sermō dē nōbīs futūrus sit, caveāmus, *QFr.* 1, 1, 38, *since fortune has set us in such a walk of life that we are to be eternally talked about, let us be on our guard.* Often in transition: as, quoniam dē genere bellī dīxī, nunc dē magnitū-dine pauca dīcam, *IP.* 20, *since I have finished speaking about the character of the war, I will now speak briefly about its extent.* With the subjunctive in indirect discourse (1725): as, crēbrīs Pompēī litterīs castīgābantur, quo-niam prīmō venientem Caesarem nōn prohibuissent, Caes. *C.* 3, 25, 3, *they were rebuked in numerous letters of Pompey, 'because they had not kept Caesar off as soon as he came.'*

———◆———

quotiēns, quotiēnscumque.

1885. ·The relative particle quotiēns (711), or quotiēnscumque, *every time that, whenever,* introduces the indicative: as,

quotiēns quaeque cohors prōcurrerat, magnus numerus hostium cadēbat, 5, 34, 2, *as the cohorts successively charged, a great number of the enemy fell every time.* quoius quotiēns sepulcrum vidēs, sacruficās, Pl. *E.* 175, *every time you see her tomb, you offer sacrifice.* nec quotiēns-cumque mē vīderit, ingemīscet, *Sest.* 146, *neither shall he fall a-groaning whenever he sees me* (1736). quotiēnsque is late and rare.

1886. quotiēns has sometimes as a correlative totiēns, or a combination with tot which is equivalent to totiēns: as, quotiēns dīcimus, totiēns dē nōbīs iūdicātur, *DO.* 1, 125, *every time we make a speech, the world sits in judgement on us.* sī tot cōnsulibus meruisset, quotiēns ipse cōnsul fuit, *Balb.* 47, *if he had been in the army as many years as he was consul.*

1887. The subjunctive imperfect and pluperfect are common in the later writers to indicate repeated action (1730): as, quotiēns super tālī negōtiō cōnsul-tāret, ēditā domūs parte ac lībertī ūnīus cōnscientiā ūtēbātur, *Ta.* 6, 27, *whenever he had recourse to astrologers, it was in the upper part of his house and with the cognizance of only a single freedman.*

321

quam.

1888. quam, *as* or *than*, introduces an indicative protasis in periods of comparison. For special reasons, however, the subjunctive is used, as by attraction (1728), or of action conceivable (1731); see also 1896, 1897.

But usually periods of comparison are abridged (1057) by the omission of the verb or of other parts in the protasis (1325).

WITH THE INDICATIVE.

1889. (1.) quam, *as*, is used in the protasis of a comparative period of equality, generally with **tam** as correlative in the apodosis : as,

tam facile vincēs quam pirum volpēs comēst, Pl. *Most.* 559, *you'll beat as easily as Reynard eats a pear.* tam excoctam reddam atque ātram quam carbōst, T. *Ad.* 849, *I'll have her stewed all out and black as is a coal.* From Cicero on, the apodosis is in general negative or interrogative : as, quōrum neutrum tam facile quam tū arbitrāris concēditur, *Div.* 1, 10, *neither of these points is as readily granted as you suppose.* quid est ōrātōrī tam necessārium quam vōx? *DO.* 1, 251, *what is so indispensable to the speaker as voice?* Otherwise nōn minus . . . quam, *no less than, just as much*, or nōn magis . . . quam, *just as little* or *just as much*, is often preferred to tam . . . quam : as, accēpī nōn minus interdum ōrātōrium esse tacēre quam dīcere, Plin. *Ep.* 7, 6, 7, *I have observed that silence is sometimes quite as eloquent as speech.* nōn magis mihī deerit inimīcus quam Verrī dēfuit, *V.* 3, 162, *I shall lack an enemy as little as Verres did.* domus erat nōn dominō magis ōrnāmentō quam cīvitātī, *V.* 4, 5, *the house was as much a pride to the state as to its owner.*

1890. Instead of **tam**, another correlative is sometimes used in the apodosis. Thus, **aequē** . . . **quam** occurs in Plautus and in Livy and later writers, generally after a negative expression ; **perinde** . . . **quam** in Tacitus and Suetonius ; **iūxtā** . . . **quam** once in Livy. Sometimes the apodosis contains no correlative.

1891. tam . . . **quam** become by abridgement coordinating words : as,

tam vēra quam falsa cernimus, *Ac.* 2, 111, *we make out things both true and false.*

1892. The highest possible degree is expressed by **tam** . . . **quam quī** and a superlative without a verb; or by **quam** and a superlative with or without a form of **possum** (1466) ; sometimes by **quantus** or **ut** : as,

(*a.*) tam sum misericors quam vōs; tam mītis quam quī lēnissimus, *Sull.* 87, *I am as tender-hearted as you ; as mild as the gentlest man living.* tam sum amīcus rēī pūblicae quam quī maximē, *Fam.* 5, 2, 6, *I am as devoted a patriot as anybody can be.* (*b.*) quam maximīs potest itineribus in Galliam contendit, 1, 7, 1, *he pushes into Gaul by as rapid marches as he can.* cōnstituērunt iūmentōrum quam maximum numerum coëmere, 1, 3, 1, *they determined to buy up the greatest possible number of beasts of burden.* (*c.*) tanta est inter eōs, quanta maxima potest esse, mōrum distantia, *L.* 74, *there is the greatest possible difference of character between them.* Or without any superlative : fuge domum quantum potest, Pl. *Men.* 850, *run home as quick as e'er you can.* ut potuī accūrātissimē tē tūtātus sum, *Fam.* 5, 17, 2, *I defended you as carefully as I could.*

1893. quam . . . tam, with two comparatives or superlatives, is equivalent to the more common quo . . . eo with two comparatives (1973) : as,

(*a*.) magis quam id reputō, tam magis ūror, Pl. *B.* 1091, *the more I think it over, the sorer do I feel.* This use is found in Plautus, Lucretius, and Vergil. (*b*.) quam quisque pessumē fēcit, tam maxumē tūtus est, S. *I.* 31, 14, *the worse a man has acted, the safer he always is.* This use is found in Plautus, Terence, Cato, Varro, and Sallust.

1894. (2.) quam, *than,* is used in the protasis of a comparative period of inequality, with a comparative in the apodosis : as,

meliōrem quam ego sum suppōnō tibī, Pl. *Cu.* 256, *I give you in my place a better man than I am.* plūra dīxī quam voluī, *V.* 5, 79, *I have said more than I intended.* Antōniō quam est, volō peius esse, *Att.* 15, 3, 2, *I hope Antony may be worse off than he is.* doctrīna paulō dūrior quam nātūra patitur, *Mur.* 60, *principles somewhat sterner than nature doth support.* potius sērō quam numquam, L. 4, 2, 11, *better late than never.* corpus patiēns algōris suprā quam cuiquam crēdibile est, S. *C.* 5, 3, *a constitution capable of enduring cold beyond what anybody could believe.* suprā quam is found in Cicero, Sallust, and often in late writers; īnfrā and ultrā quam in Cicero, Livy, and late writers (īnfrā quam also in Varro) ; extrā quam in Ennius, Cato, and in legal and official language in Cicero and Livy.

1895. quam is also used with some virtual comparatives: thus, nihil aliud, nōn aliud quam, *no other than,* often as adverb, *only ;* secus quam with a negative, *not otherwise than ;* bis tantō quam, *twice as much as ;* and prae quam in old Latin, *in comparison with how ;* and similar phrases : as,

(*a*.) per bīduum nihil aliud quam stetērunt parātī ad pugnandum, L. 34, 46, 7, *for two days they merely stood in battle array.* This use occurs first in Sallust, then in Nepos, Livy, and later writers. (*b*.) mihī erit cūrae nē quid fīat secus quam volumus, *Att.* 6, 2, 2, *I will see to it that nothing be done save as we wish.* This use occurs in Plautus, Terence, Sallust, Cicero, Livy, and later writers. With both aliud and secus the clause is rarely positive, with aliud not before Livy. For atque (ac) instead of quam when the first clause is negative, see 1654. (*c*.) bis tantō valeō quam valuī prius, Pl. *Merc.* 297, *I am twice as capable as I was before.* (*d*.) nīl hōc quidem est trīgintā minae, prae quam aliōs sūmptūs facit, Pl. *Most.* 981, *oh, this is nothing, thirty minae, when you think what other sums he spends* prae quam is found only in Plautus rarely. Similar phrases are : contrā quam, in Cicero, Livy, and later writers ; praeter quam, in Plautus, Naevius, and frequently in other writers when followed by quod (1848) ; super quam quod (1848) and īnsuper quam in Livy ; prō quam in Lucretius ; advorsum quam, once in Plautus. prae quam is sometimes followed by a relative clause : as, prae quam quod molestumst, Pl. *Am.* 634, *compared with what is painful.* For ante (or prius) and post quam, see 1911, 1923.

WITH THE SUBJUNCTIVE.

1896. The subjunctive is used with quam or quam ut after comparatives denoting disproportion (1461) : as, quicquid erat oneris Segestānīs impōnēbat, aliquantō amplius quam ferre possent, *V.* 4, 76, *he would impose every possible burden on the Segestans, far too much for them to bear.* quis nōn intellegit Canachī sīgna rigidiōra esse, quam ut imitentur vēritātem ? *Br.* 70, *who does not feel that the statues of Canachus are too stiff to be true to nature ?* clārior rēs erat quam ut dissimulārī posset, L. 26, 51, 11, *the thing was too notorious to be hushed up.* Instead of ut, quī is also used by Livy and later writers : as, maior sum quam cui possit Fortūna nocēre, O. 6, 195, *too strong am I for Fortune to break down,* says infatuated Niobe. All these sentences are extensions of the subjunctive of action conceivable (1554, 1818).

1897. The subjunctive is used in clauses introduced by potius quam, *rather than,* to denote action merely assumed. citius, ante, or prius, *sooner,* is sometimes used in the sense of potius : as,

potius quam tē inimīcum habeam, faciam ut iusseris, T. *Eu.* 174, *rather than make you my enemy, I will do as you tell me.* dēpugnā potius quam serviās, *Att.* 7, 7, 7, *fight it out rather than be a slave.* potius vituperātiōnem incōnstantiae suscipiam, quam in tē sim crūdēlis, *V.* 5, 105, *I will submit to the charge of inconsistency rather than be cruel towards you.* animam omittunt prius quam locō dēmigrent, Pl. *Am.* 240, *they lose their lives sooner than yield their ground.* Livy has also potius quam ut. All these sentences are extensions of the subjunctive of desire (1540, 1817).

With the Infinitive.

1898. When the main clause is an infinitive, quam is often followed by an infinitive : as,

mālim morīrī meōs quam mendīcārier, Pl. *Vid.* 96, *better my bairns be dead than begging bread.* vōcēs audiēbantur sē cortice ex arboribus victūrōs, quam Pompēium ē manibus dīmissūrōs, Caes. *C.* 3, 49, 1, *shouts were heard that they would live on the bark of trees sooner than let Pompey slip through their fingers.*

---

quamquam.

1899. (1) quamquam is used in old Latin as an indefinite adverb, *ever so much, however much :* as,

quamquam negōtiumst, sī quid veis, Dēmiphō, nōn sum occupātus umquam amīcō operam dare, Pl. *Mer.* 287, *however busy I may be* (1814), *if anything you wish, dear Demipho, I'm not too busy ever to a friend mine aid to lend.* id quoque possum ferre, quamquam iniūriumst, T. *Ad.* 205, *that also I can bear, however so unfair.* From an adverb, quamquam became a conjunction, *although.*

1900. (2.) quamquam, *although,* introduces the indicative in the concession of a definite fact. In the later writers it is also sometimes used with the subjunctive, sometimes with a participle or an adjective.

(*a.*) **quamquam premuntur aere aliēnō, dominātiōnem tamen exspectant,** *C.* 2, 19, *though they are staggering under debt, they yet look forward to being lords and masters.* **quamquam nōn vēnit ad fīnem tam audāx inceptum, tamen haud omnīnō vānum fuit,** L. 10, 32, 5, *though the bold attempt did not attain its purpose, yet it was not altogether fruitless.* This is the classical use ; but see 1901. (*b.*) **nam et tribūnīs plēbis senātūs habendī iūs erat, quamquam senātōrēs nōn essent,** Varro in Gell. 14, 8, 2, *for even the tribunes of the people, though they were not senators, had the right to hold a meeting of the senate.* **haud cunctātus est Germānicus, quamquam fingī ea intellegeret,** Ta. 2, 26, *Germanicus did not delay, though he was aware this was all made up.* This use is found first in Varro, often in the Augustan poets, sometimes in Livy, always in Juvenal. It does not become common before Tacitus and the younger Pliny. (*c.*) **sequente, quamquam nōn probante, Amynandrō,** L. 31, 41, 7, *Amynander accompanying though not approving* (1374). **nē Aquītānia quidem, quamquam in verba Othōnis obstricta, diū mānsit,** Ta. *H.* 1, 76, *Aquitania, though bound by the oath of allegiance to Otho, did not hold out long either.* This use is found once each in Cicero and Sallust, half a dozen times in Livy, oftener in Tacitus.

1901. The subjunctive is also used often with **quamquam** for special reasons, as by attraction (1728), in indirect discourse (1725), and of action conceivable (1731).

1902. For **quamquam** appending a fresh main sentence, see 2153; for its use with the infinitive, 2317.

------

quam vīs or quamvīs.

1903. **quam vīs** or **quamvīs** is used as an indefinite adverb (712), *as much as you please,* and is often joined with an adjective or other adverb to take the place of a superlative : as,

quam vīs rīdiculus est, ubī uxor nōn adest, Pl. *Men.* 318, *he's as droll as you please when his wife is n't by.* **quamveis īnsipiēns poterat persentīscere,** Pl. *Merc.* 687, *the veriest dullard could detect.* **quamvīs paucī adīre audent,** 4, 2, 5, *the merest handful dares attack.* **quamvīs callidē,** *V.* 2, 134, *ever so craftily.* **quamvīs** is also sometimes used to strengthen a superlative (1466), though not in classical prose.

1904. (I.) The indefinite adverb **quam vīs,** *as much as you please,* is often used in subjunctive clauses of concession or permission ; such subjunctives are sometimes coordinated with **licet** : as,

quod turpe est, id quam vīs occultētur, tamen honestum fierī nūllō modō potest, *Off.* 3, 78, *if a thing is base, let it be hidden as much as you will, yet it cannot be made respectable* (1553). **locus hīc apud nōs, quam vīs subitō veniās, semper līber est,** Pl. *B.* 82, *our house is always open, come as sudden as you may* (1553). **praeter eōs quam vīs ēnumerēs multōs licet, nōnnūllōs reperiēs perniciōsōs tribūnōs,** *Leg.* 3, 24, *besides these you may tell off as many as you please, you will still find some dangerous tribunes* (1710). The combination with **licet** occurs first in Lucretius, then in Cicero.

Instead of **vīs,** other forms are sometimes used: as, **volumus, volent, velit,** &c.: thus, **quam volent facētī sint,** *Cael.* 67, *they may be as witty as they please* (1735). **quam volet Epicūrus iocētur et dīcat sē nōn posse intellegere, numquam mē movēbit,** *DN.* 2, 46, *Epicurus may joke and say he can't understand it as much as he likes, he will never shake me.* From an adverb, **quam vīs** became a conjunction, *however much, even if.*

1905. (2.) The subjunctive with the conjunction **quamvīs,** *however much, even if, though,* denotes action merely assumed; when the action is to be denoted as real, **ut** or **sīcut** or the like, with the indicative, usually follows in the best prose (1943): as,

(*a.*) **quamvīs sint hominēs quī Cn. Carbōnem ōderint, tamen hī dēbent quid metuendum sit cōgitāre,** *V.* 1, 39, *though there may be men who hate Carbo, still these men ought to consider what they have to fear.* **nōn enim possīs, quamvīs excellās,** *L.* 73, *you may not have the power, however eminent you may be.* This use begins with Cicero and Varro, and gets common in late writers. Not in Livy. (*b.*) **illa quamvīs rīdicula essent, sīcut erant, mihī tamen rīsum nōn mōvērunt,** *Fam.* 7, 32, 3, *droll as this really was, it nevertheless did not make me laugh.* **quamvīs enim multīs locīs dīcat Epicūrus, sīcutī dīcit, satis fortiter dē dolōre, tamen nōn id spectandum est quid dīcat,** *Off.* 3, 117, *even though Epicurus really does speak in many places pretty heroically about pain, still we must not have an eye to what he says.* In the Augustan poets rarely, and often in Tacitus, the younger Pliny, and late writers, the subjunctive, without a parenthetical phrase introduced by **ut** or the like, is used of an action denoted as real: as, **expalluit notābiliter, quamvīs palleat semper,** Plin. *Ep.* 1, 5, 13, *he grew pale perceptibly, though he is always a pale man.* **maestus erat, quamvīs laetitiam simulāret,** Ta. 15, 54, *sad he was, though he pretended to be gay.*

1906. **quamvīs,** *even if, though,* is also sometimes used with the indicative (1900): as,

erat dignitāte rēgiā, quamvīs carēbat nōmine, N. 1, 2, 3, *he had the authority of a king, though not the title.* **quamvīs tacet Hermogenēs, cantor est,** H. *S.* 1, 3, 129, *though he open not his mouth, Hermogenes remains a singer still.* This use occurs twice in Lucretius, once in Cicero, Nepos, and Livy each, in Varro, in the Augustan poets, and sometimes in late writers. Not in Tacitus, Pliny the younger, Juvenal, Martial, or Suetonius.

1907. It may be mentioned here that the indefinite adverb **quamlibet,** *however you please,* is used in subjunctive clauses of concession or permission (1904) once or twice by Lucretius, Ovid, and Quintilian. Velleius has it with the participle, a construction sometimes found with **quamvīs** in late writers.

---

tamquam.

1908. **tamquam,** *just as,* introduces an indicative protasis in periods of comparison.

The **tam** properly belongs to the apodosis and is attracted to the protasis. **tamquam** has sometimes as correlative **sīc** or **ita.**

tē hortor ut tamquam poētae bonī solent, sīc tū in extrēmā parte mūneris tuī dīligentissimus sīs, *QFr.* I, I, 46, *I urge you to be very particular at the end of your task, just as good poets always are.* tamquam philosophōrum habent disciplīnae ex ipsīs vocābula, parasītī ita ut Gnathōnicī vocentur, T. *Eu.* 263, *that so parasites may be called Gnathonites even as schools of philosophy are named from the masters.* Usually, however, ut (1944) or quemadmodum is used in this sense; and tamquam occurs oftenest in abridged sentences (1057), particularly to show that an illustration is untrue or figurative: as, Odyssīa Latina est sīc tamquam opus aliquod Daedalī, *Br.* 71, *the Odyssey in Latin is, you may say, a regular work of Daedalus.* oculī tamquam speculātōrēs altissimum locum obtinent, *DN.* 2, 140, *the eyes occupy the highest part, as a sort of watchmen.*

1909. In late writers, especially in Tacitus, tamquam is often used to introduce a reason or motive, or a thought indirectly expressed: as, invīsus tamquam plūs quam cīvīlia agitāret, Ta. I, 12, *hated on the ground that his designs were too lofty for a private citizen* (1725). lēgātōs increpuit, tamquam nōn omnēs reōs perēgissent, Plin. *Ep.* 3, 9, 36, *he reproved the embassy 'for not having completed the prosecution of all the defendants'* (1852, 1725). suspectus tamquam ipse suās incenderit aedīs, J. 3, 222, *suspected of having set his own house afire.*

1910. For tamquam instead of tamquam sī, see 2118; with a participle, 2121.

---

antequam, priusquam.

1911. antequam and priusquam accompany both the indicative and the subjunctive.

ante and prius properly belong to the apodosis, and regularly stand with it if it is negative; but otherwise they are usually attracted to the protasis.

antequam is very seldom found in old Latin, and it is in general much rarer than priusquam, except in Tacitus.

IN GENERAL STATEMENTS.

1912. In general present statements, **antequam** and **priusquam** regularly introduce the perfect indicative or the present subjunctive: as,

membrīs ūtimur priusquam didicimus cuius ea causā ūtilitātis habeāmus, *Fin.* 3, 66, *we always use our limbs before we learn for what purposes of utility we have them* (1613). priusquam lūcet, adsunt, Pl. *MG.* 709, *before 'tis light they're always here;* here lūcet is equivalent to inlūxit. ante vidēmus fulgōrem quam sonum audiāmus, Sen. *QN.* 2, 12, 6, *we always see the flash before we hear the sound.* priusquam sēmen mātūrum siet, secātō, Cato, *RR.* 53, *always cut before the seed is ripe* (1575). With the perfect subjunctive in the indefinite second person (1030): as, hoc malum opprimit antequam prōspicere potueris, *V.* I, 39, *this calamity always overwhelms you before you can anticipate it* (1731, 1558). For prius quam, *sooner than,* see 1897.

1913. The future indicative is used a few times in general statements by old and late writers, and the perfect subjunctive after a negative clause rarely by Tacitus: as, bovēs priusquam in viam agēs, pice cornua īnfima unguitō, Cato, *RR. 72, always smear the hoofs of your oxen with pitch before you drive them on the road* (1625, 1577). deŭm honor prīncipī nōn ante habētur quam agere inter hominēs dēsierit, Ta. 15, 74, *divine honours are not paid to an emperor before he has ceased to live among men.* Cicero has the perfect subjunctive in a definition: thus, prōvidentia, per quam futūrum aliquid vidētur antequam factum sit, *Inv.* 2, 160, *foresight is the faculty through which a future event is seen before it has taken place.* He also has the present indicative once: *Div.* 1, 120.

1914. In general past statements antequam and priusquam introduce the subjunctive imperfect or pluperfect; but this use is very rare: as, dormīre priusquam somnī cupīdō esset, S. *C.* 13, 3, *a-sleeping always before they felt sleepy.* ita saepe magna indolēs virtūtis, priusquam rēī pūblicae prōdesse potuisset, extīncta est, *Ph.* 5, 47, *thus character of unusual promise was oftentimes cut off, before it could do the government any good.*

IN PARTICULAR STATEMENTS.

1915. In particular present or future statements, antequam and priusquam introduce a present, either indicative or subjunctive; in future statements the future perfect is also used, and regularly when the main verb is future perfect: as,

antequam ad sententiam redeō, dē mē pauca dīcam, *C.* 4, 20, *before I come back to the motion, I will say a little about myself* (1593). est etiam prius quam abīs quod volo loquī, Pl. *As.* 232, *there's something else I want to say before you go.* antequam veniat in Pontum, litterās ad Cn. Pompēium mittet, *Agr.* 2, 53, *before he reaches Pontus, he will send a letter to Pompey.* prius quam ad portam veniās, est pistrīlla, T. *Ad.* 583, *there's a little bakery just before you get to the gate.* nihil contrā disputābō priusquam dīxerit, *Fl.* 51, *I will not argue to the contrary before he has spoken* (1626). neque prius, quam dēbellāverō, absistam, L. 49, 39, 9, *and I will not leave off before I have brought the war to an end.* sī quid mihī acciderit priusquam hōc tantum malī vīderō, *Mil.* 99, *if anything shall befall me before I see this great calamity.* neque prōmittō quicquam neque respondeō prius quam gnātum vīderō, T. *Ph.* 1044, *I'm not promising anything nor making any answer before I see my son* (1593). Tacitus uses neither the present indicative nor the future perfect.

1916. In old Latin the future and the perfect subjunctive also occur: as, prius quam quoiquam convīvae dabis, gustātō tūte prius, Pl. *Ps.* 885, *before you help a single guest, taste first yourself;* but Terence does not use the future, and it is found only once or twice later. nūllō pactō potest prius haec in aedīs recipī, quam illam āmīserim, Pl. *MG.* 1095, *on no terms can I take my new love to the house, before I've let the old love drop;* but usually the perfect subjunctive is due to indirect discourse.

1917. In particular past statements antequam and priusquam introduce the perfect indicative, especially when the apodosis is negative. The imperfect subjunctive rarely occurs, chiefly in late writers.

(*a.*) omnia ista ante facta sunt quam iste Ĭtaliam attigit, *V.* 2, 161, *all these incidents occurred before the defendant set foot in Italy.* neque prius fugere dēstitērunt quam ad Rhēnum pervēnērunt, 1, 53, 1, *and they did not stay their flight before they fairly arrived at the Rhine.* prius quam hinc abiit quīndecim mīles minās dederat, Pl. *Ps.* 53, *the captain had paid down fifteen minae before he left here.* (*b.*) nec prius sunt vīsī quam castrīs adpropinquārent, 6, 37, 2, *they were not seen before they drew near to the camp.* This use of the imperfect subjunctive, not to be confounded with that mentioned in 1919, is not found in old Latin or in Cicero. It is found in Nepos and Livy.

1918. The present indicative also occurs in particular past statements in old Latin: as, is priusquam moritur mihi dedit, Pl. *Cu.* 637, *before he died he gave it me.* The indicative imperfect occurs four times in Livy and once in late Latin, the pluperfect once in old Latin and once in Cicero.

1919. When the action of the protasis was forestalled, or when action conceivable or purpose is expressed, **antequam** and **priusquam** regularly introduce the imperfect subjunctive in particular past statements : as,

plērīque interfectī sunt, priusquam occultum hostem vidērent, L. 35, 29, 3, *most of them were slain before they could see the hidden enemy.* antequam verbum facerem, dē sellā surrēxit, *V.* 4, 147, *before I could utter a word he arose from his seat.* pervēnit priusquam Pompēius sentīre posset, Caes. *C.* 3, 67, 4, *he arrived before Pompey should be able to learn of his coming* (1725). The present and perfect subjunctive occur rarely, generally when the main clause contains a present of vivid narration (1590). The imperfect is not found in old Latin.

1920. The perfect indicative or imperfect subjunctive with **antequam** is often used attributively with nouns denoting time : as,

fābulam docuit, annō ipsō ante quam nātus est Ennius, *Br.* 72, *he exhibited a play just a year before Ennius was born.* ducentīs annīs ante quam Rōmam caperent, in Italiam Gallī trānscendērunt, L. 5, 33, 5, *two hundred years before they took Rome, the Gauls crossed over to Italy.* The pluperfect also occurs, when the main verb is pluperfect : as, Stāiēnus bienniō antequam causam recēpisset, sescentīs mīllibus nummūm sē iūdicium conruptūrum dīxerat, *Clu.* 68, *Stajenus had said two years before he undertook the case, that he would bribe the court for six hundred thousand sesterces.*

1921. The pluperfect subjunctive is rarely introduced by **antequam** or **priusquam** except in indirect discourse : as,

antequam dē meō adventū audīre potuissent, in Macedoniam perrēxī, *Pl.* 98, *before they should be able to hear of my arrival, I proceeded to Macedonia* (1725). āvertit equōs in castra priusquam pābula gustāssent Trōiae Xanthumque bibissent, V. 1, 472, *he drave the horses off to camp, or ever they should taste of Troja's grass and Xanthus drink* (1725).

1922. It may be mentioned here that postrīdiē quam and prīdiē quam occur a few times in Plautus and Cicero with the indicative ; postrīdiē quam with the indicative in Suetonius ; and prīdiē quam with the subjunctive in Livy, Valerius Maximus, and Suetonius.

posteā quam or postquam.

ubī, ut, cum prīmum, simul atque.

1923. With posteā quam, postquam (posquam), *after,* the following words may conveniently be treated : ubī, ut, *when ;* ubī prīmum, ut prīmum, cum prīmum, *when first,* and in Plautus quom extemplō ; simul atque (or ac, less frequently et or ut, or simul alone), *at the same time with, as soon as.*

postquam, ubī, ut, cum prīmum, simul atque, accompany the indicative.

For examples of the use of tenses, see 1924-1934.

1924. In clauses introduced by posteā quam or postquam, the imperfect or pluperfect subjunctive, found a dozen times in the manuscripts of Cicero's works and elsewhere, is generally corrected in modern editions or usually the conjunctive particle is emended to posteā quom (cum). But the subjunctive may of course be used with this and the other particles mentioned in 1923 for special reasons, as with the indefinite second person (1731), by attraction (1728), and in indirect discourse (1725). For the subjunctive of repeated past action with ubī and ut, see 1932. The infinitive of intimation occurs in Tacitus (1539): as, postquam exuī aequālitās, prōvēnēre dominātiōnēs, Ta. 3, 26, *after equality between man and man was dropped, there came a crop of tyrants.*

1925. In narration the perfect indicative is regularly used in clauses introduced by postquam, ubī, ut, cum prīmum, simul atque (1739) : as,

postquam tuās litterās lēgī, Postumia tua mē convēnit, *Fam.* 4, 2, 1, *after I read your letter, your Postumia called on me.* postquam aurum abstulimus, in nāvem cōnscendimus, Pl. *B.* 277, *after we got away the money, we took ship.* ubī ad ipsum vēnī dēvorticulum, cōnstitī, T. *Eu.* 635, *when I came exactly to the side street, I pulled up.* ubī sē diūtius dūcī intellēxit, graviter eōs accūsat, 1, 16, 5, *when he came to see that he was put off a good while, he takes them roundly to task.* quī ut perōrāvit, surrēxit Clōdius, *QFr.* 2, 3, 2, *when he had finished speaking, up jumped Clodius.* ut abiī abs tē, fit forte obviam mihi Phormiō, T. *Ph.* 617, *when I left you, Phormio happened to fall in my way.* crimen eius modī est, ut, cum prīmum ad mē dēlātum est, ūsūrum mē illō nōn putārem, *V.* 5, 158, *the charge is of such a sort that, when first it was reported to me, I thought I should not use it.* cum prīmum Crētae litus attigit, nūntiōs mīsit, L. 37, 60, 4. *as soon as he touched the shore of Crete, he sent messengers.* ut prīmum loquī posse coepī, inquam, *RP.* 6, 15, *as soon as I began to be able to speak, I said.* quem simul atque oppidānī cōnspexērunt, mūrum complēre coepērunt, 7, 12, 5, *as soon as the garrison espied him, they began to man the wall.* at hostēs, ubī prīmum nostrōs equitēs cōnspexērunt, impetū factō celeriter nostrōs perturbāvērunt, 4, 12, 1, *but as soon as the enemy caught sight of our cavalry, they attacked and threw our men into disorder.* The conjunction simul atque is very rarely found in old Latin.

1926. The present indicative of vivid narration (1590) sometimes occurs : as,

postquam iam **puerī septuennēs** sunt, pater onerāvit nāvim mag-
nam, Pl. *Men. prol.* 24, *after the boys were seven year olds, their father freighted
a big ship.* quid ait, ubı mē nōminās, T. *Hau.* 303, *what sayeth she when
you name me?* ubī neutrī trānseundī initium faciunt, Caesar suōs ın
castra redūxit, 2, 9, 2, *neither party taking the initiative ın crossing, Caesar
marched his men back to camp.* Verbs of perceiving, especially videō, occur
oftenest in this use, which is common in Plautus and Terence : as, postquam
videt nūptiās adparārī, missast ancilla īlicō, T. *Andr.* 513, *after she sees
a marriage on foot, her maid is sent forthwith.* abeō ab illīs, postquam
videō mē lūdificārier, Pl. *Cap.* 487, *seeing myself made game of, I leave them.*
quem posteā quam videt nōn adesse, ardēre atque furere coepit, *V.* 2,
92, *seeing that the man does not appear, he began to rage and fume.* ubī hoc
videt, init cōnsilium importūnī tyrannī, *V.* 5, 103, *seeing this, he adopted
the policy of a savage tyrant.* Plautus uses also quom extemplō. Such
protases often take on a causal sense (see also 1930).

1927. The present or perfect with **postquam** or **ut** is sometimes used in expressions equivalent to an emphasized accusative or ablative of time, the main verb
being **est** or **sunt** : as, septingentī sunt annī postquam inclita condita
Rōma est, E. in Varro, *RR.* 3, 1, 2, *'tis seven hundred years since inclyta Rome
was founded.* domō ut abiērunt hic tertius annus, Pl. *St.* 29, *this is the
third year since they left home.* annus est octāvus ut imperium obtinēs,
Ta. 14, 53, *it is the eighth year since you acquired empire.* For a similar use of
cum, see 1871.

1928. The pluperfect with **postquam**, denoting resulting state (1615),
occurs less frequently : as,

tum cum **P.** Āfricānus, posteā quam bis cōnsul fuerat, **L.** Cottam in
iūdicium vocābat, *Caecil.* 69, *at the time when Africanus, after he had twice
been consul, was bringing Cotta to judgement.* postquam omnium oculōs
occupāverat certāmen, tum āversam adoriuntur Rōmānam aciem, **L.**
22, 48, 4, *when every eye was fairly riveted on the engagement, that instant they
fell upon the Romans in the rear.* Not in Plautus, once in Terence, and
rare in classical writers.

1929. The pluperfect, less frequently the perfect, with **postquam** is used
attributively with nouns denoting time.

In this use **post** is often separated from **quam**, and two constructions
are possible : (*a.*) Ablative : annō post quam vōta erat aedēs Monētae
dēdicātur, L. 7, 28, 6, *the temple of Moneta is dedicated a year after it was
vowed.* Without post : quadringentēsimō annō quam urbs Rōmāna condita erat, patriciī cōnsulēs magistrātum iniēre, L. 7, 18, 1, *four hundred
years after Rome town was founded, patrician consuls entered into office.*
(*b.*) Accusative, with an ordinal, and post as a preposition, or, sometimes,
intrā : post diem tertium gesta rēs est quam dīxerat, *Mil.* 44, *the deed
was done the next day but one after he said it.* See 2419.

1930. The imperfect with **postquam** expresses action continuing
into the time of the main action. Such a protasis, especially when
negative, usually denotes the cause of the main action : as,

Appius, postquam nēmō adībat, domum sē recēpit, L. 3, 46, 9,
Appius, finding that nobody presented himself, went back home. posteā quam
ē scaenā explōdēbātur, cōnfūgit in huius domum, *RC.* 30, *after being
repeatedly hissed off the stage, he took refuge in my client's house.*

In old Latin this use is found only once, in Plautus; it is most common in Livy, but occurs frequently in Tacitus. So occasionally the present, generally when the main action is present (see also 1926): as, **postquam nec ab Rōmānīs vōbīs ūlla est spēs, nec vōs moenia dēfendunt, pācem adferō ad vōs**, L. 21, 13, 4, *now that it has become plain that you have no hope from the Romans, and that your walls are no protection to you, I bring peace unto you.* **postquam līberast, ubī habitet dīcere admodum incertē sciō**, Pl. *E.* 505, *now that she's free, I'm quite too ill informed to say where she lives.* **quae omnia intellegit nihil prōdesse, posteā quam testibus convincitur**, *V.* 5, 103, *he knows that all this is fruitless, now that he is being refuted by witnesses.* The perfect with **postquam** or **ut** occurs occasionally in this use with the present in the main clause: as, **animus in tūtō locōst, postquam iste hinc abiīt**, Pl. *Ps.* 1052, *my mind is easy, now that fellow's gone.* **nam ut in nāvī vecta's, crēdō timida's**, Pl. *B.* 106, *for after your voyage, of course you're nervous.*

1931. **postquam** and **ut** have sometimes the meaning of *ever since* or *as long as*: as,

postquam nātus sum, satur numquam fuī, Pl. *St.* 156, *since I was born I've never had enough to eat.* **tibī umquam quicquam, postquam tuos sum, verbōrum dedī?** Pl. *Most.* 925, *have I once ever cheated you as long as I have been your slave?* **neque meum pedem intulī in aedīs, ut cum exercitū hinc profectus sum**, Pl. *Am.* 733, *I have n't set foot in the house ever since I marched out with the army.* **ut illōs dē rē pūblicā librōs ēdidistī, nihil ā tē posteā accēpimus**, *Br.* 19, *we have had nothing from you since you published the work On the State.*

ubī, ut, simul atque.

1932. **ubī, ut,** or **simul atque (ac)** often introduces a clause denoting indefinite or repeated action: as,

adeō obcaecat animōs fortūna, ubī vim suam refringī nōn vult, L. 5, 37, 1, *so completely does fortune blind the mind when she will not have her power thwarted.* **ubī salūtātiō dēflūxit, litterīs mē involvō**, *Fam.* 9, 20, 3, *when my callers go, I always plunge into my book* (1613). **omnēs profectō mulierēs tē amant, ut quaeque aspexit**, Pl. *MG.* 1264, *all the ladies love you, every time one spies you.* **simul atque sē īnflēxit hīc rēx in dominātum iniūstiōrem, fit continuō tyrannus**, *RP.* 2, 48, *for the moment our king turns to a severer kind of mastery, he becomes a tyrant on the spot.* **Messānam ut quisque nostrūm vēnerat, haec vīsere solēbat**, *V.* 4, 5, *any Roman, who visited Messana, invariably went to see these statues* (1618). **hostēs, ubī aliquōs singulārēs cōnspexerant, adoriēbantur**, 4, 26, 2, *every time the enemy saw some detached parties, they would charge.* The imperfect in this use is not common in classical writers, and occurs but once, with **ubī**, in old Latin; the pluperfect is rare before the silver age. Clauses with **ut** generally contain some form of **quisque** (2396). Plautus uses **quom extemplō** with the present and perfect. The subjunctive is found with **ubī** and **ut quisque** in cases of repeated past action (1730).

1933. **ubī, ut,** or **simul atque** rarely introduces an imperfect or pluperfect of definite time: as, quid ubi reddēbās aurum, dīxistī patrī, Pl. *B.* 685, *what did you tell your father when you were returning the money?* ubĭ lūx adventābat, tubicinēs sĭgna canere, S. *I.* 99, 1, *when daylight was drawing on, the trumpeters sounded the call.* ubĭ nēmō obvius ībat, plēnō gradū ad hostium castra tendunt, L. 9, 45, 14, *finding nobody came to meet them, they advanced double quick upon the enemy's camp* (1930). The use of these tenses referring to definite time is very rare in old Latin, and found only with ut in Cicero.

1934. ubĭ or simul atque, referring to definite time, introduces the future or future perfect, when the apodosis is also future : as,

simul et quid erit certī, scrībam ad tē, *Att.* 2, 20, 2, *as soon as there is anything positive, I will write to you.* ego ad tē statim habēbō quod scrībam, simul ut vīderō Cūriōnem, *Att.* 10, 4, 12, *I shall have something to write you, as soon as ever I see Curio.* nam ubĭ mē aspiciet, ad carnuficem rapiet continuō senex, Pl. *B.* 688, *when the old man sees me, he'll hurry me off to Jack Ketch without any ado.* ubi prīmum poterit, sē illinc subdūcet, T. *Eu.* 628, *she'll steal away as soon as she can.* Plautus has also quom extemplō in this use, and Pliny the Younger ut primum.

◆

utĭ or ut.

1935. The relative adverb utĭ or ut (711) is found in the oldest Latin in the form utei, but ut was the prevalent form even in the time of Plautus. As a conjunctive particle, it accompanies both the indicative and the subjunctive. For ut in wishes, see 1540; in questions, 1568.

WITH THE INDICATIVE.

(A.) ut, *where.*

1936. utĭ or ut in the rare signification of *where*, accompanies the indicative: as, atque in eōpse adstās lapide, ut praecō praedicat, Pl. *B.* 815, *and there you stand right on the auction block, just where the crier always cries.* sīve in extrēmōs penetrābit Indōs, lītus ut longē resonante Ēōā tunditur undā, Cat. 11, 2, *or shall he pierce to farthest Ind, where by the long-resounding eastern wave the strand is lashed.* In classical Latin, ut in this sense is used only by the poets, as here and there in Lucilius, Catullus, Cicero's *Aratēa*, and Vergil. ubĭ is the word regularly used. For ut, *when*, see 1923.

(B.) ut, *as.*

1937. The indicative is used in the protasis of a comparative period introduced by utĭ or ut, *as.*

ut often has as a correlative ita, item, itidem, sīc, perinde, or similiter, and sometimes in old Latin and poetry aequē, adaequē, pariter, nōn aliter, nōn secus, īdem. sīc is sometimes drawn to the protasis, making sīcutĭ, sīcut; utĭ is sometimes strengthened by vel, making velutĭ, velut, *even as, just as.* quemadmodum often, and quōmodo sometimes, stands for ut. For the use of ut in old Latin in sentences in which classical Latin would employ the indirect question, see 1791. For coordinated comparative sentences without ut, see 1704.

333

perge ut īnstituistī, *RP.* 2, 22, *go on as you have begun.* ut volēs mēd esse, ita erō, Pl. *Ps.* 240, *as you will have me be, so will I be* (1625). ut sēmentem fēceris, ita metēs, *DO.* 2, 261, *as you sow, y'are like to reap* (1626). ut nōn omnem frūgem in omnī agrō reperīre possīs, sīc nōn omne facinus in omnī vītā nāscitur, *RA.* 75, *every crime does not start into being in every life, any more than you can find every fruit in every field* (1731). Also in asseverations : ita mē dī amābunt, ut ego hunc auscultō lubēns, Pl. *Aul.* 496, *so help me heaven, as I am glad to hear this man* (1622).

1938. ut . . . ita or sīc, *as* . . . *so*, often stand where concessive and adversative conjunctions might be used; *while* . . . *nevertheless, although* . . . *yet, certainly* . . . *but :* as,

ut nihil bonī est in morte, sīc certē nihil malī, *L.* 14, *while there is nothing good after death, yet certainly there is nothing bad.* quō factō sīcut glōriam auxit, ita grātiam minuit, Suet. *Oth.* 1, *by this action he increased his reputation, but lessened his popularity.* nec ut iniūstus in pāce rēx, ita dux bellī prāvus fuit, *L.* 1, 53, 1, *but while he was an unjust king in peace, he was not a bad leader in war.* This adversative correlation is found sometimes in Cicero, but is far more common in late writers.

1939. ut quisque, commonly with a superlative expression, is used in the protasis of a comparative period of equality, with ita or sīc and commonly another superlative expression in the apodosis : as,

ut quaeque rēs est turpissima, sīc maximē vindicanda est, *Caec.* 7, *the more disgraceful a thing is, the more emphatically does it call for punishment.* ut quisque optimē Graecē scīret, ita esse nēquissimum, *DO.* 2, 265, *that the better Greek scholar a man was, the greater rascal he always was* (1722). This construction is often abridged : as, sapientissimus quisque aequissimō animō moritur, *CM.* 83, *the sage always dies with perfect resignation.* optimus quisque praeceptor frequentiā gaudet, Quint. 1, 2, 9, *the best teachers always revel in large classes.* See 2397.

1940. ut often introduces a parenthetical idea, particularly a general truth or a habit which accounts for the special fact expressed in the main sentence : as,

nēmō, ut opīnor, in culpā est, *Clu.* 143, *nobody, as I fancy, is to blame.* excitābat flūctūs in simpulō, ut dīcitur, Grātidius, *Leg.* 3, 36, *Gratidius was raising a tempest in a teapot, as the saying is.* paulisper, dum sē uxor, ut fit, comparat, commorātus est, *Mil.* 28, *he had to wait a bit, as is always the case, while his wife was putting on her things.* hōrum auctōritāte adductī, ut sunt Gallōrum subita cōnsilia, Trebium retinent, 3, 8, 3, *influenced by these people they detain Trebius, as might have been expected, sudden resolutions being always characteristic of the Gauls.* sēditiōne nūntiātā, ut erat laenā amictus, ita vēnit in cōntiōnem, *Br.* 56, *an outbreak was reported, and he came to the meeting all accoutred as he was, with his sacrificial robe on.* Often elliptically : as, acūtī hominis, ut Siculī, *TD.* 1, 15, *a bright man, of course, being a Sicilian.* Aequōrum exercitus, ut quī permultōs annōs imbellēs ēgissent, trepidāre, *L.* 9, 45, 10, *the army of the Aequians alarmed and irresolute, and naturally, since they had passed a great many years without fighting* (1824, 1827).

1941. ut, *as for example,* is used in illustrations, particularly in abridged sentences (1057) : as, genus est quod plūrēs partēs amplectitur, ut 'animal.' pars est, quae subest generī, ut 'equos,' *Inv.* 1, 32, *a class is what embraces a number of parts, as 'living thing'; a part is what is included in a class, as 'horse.'* sunt bēstiae in quibus inest aliquid simile virtūtis, ut in leōnibus, ut in canibus, *Fin.* 5, 38, *there are brutes in which there is a something like the moral quality of man, as for instance the lion and the dog.*

1942. The parenthetical clause with ut or prout sometimes makes an allowance for the meaning of a word, usually an adjective, in the main sentence : as,

cīvitās ampla atque flōrēns, ut est captus Germānōrum, 4, 3, 3, *a grand and prosperous community, that is according to German conceptions.* ut captus est servōrum, nōn malus, T. *Ad.* 480, *not a bad fellow, as slaves go.* Sthenius ab adulēscentiā haec comparārat, supellēctilem ex aere ēlegantiōrem, tabulās pīctās, etiam argentī bene factī prout Thermī-tānī hominis facultātēs ferēbant, satis, *V.* 2, 83, *Sthenius had been a collector from early years of such things as artistic bronzes, pictures ; also of curiously wrought silver a goodly amount, that is as the means of a Thermae man went.* Often in abridged sentences : as, scrīptor fuit, ut temporibus illīs, lūculentus, *Br.* 102, *he was a brilliant historian for the times.* multae etiam, ut in homine Rōmānō, litterae, *CM.* 12. *furthermore, extensive reading, that is for a Roman.* ut illīs temporibus, praedīves, L. 4, 13, 1, *a millionaire, for those times.*

1943. ut, *as indeed, as in fact,* with the indicative, is used to represent that an action supposed, conceded, or commanded, really occurs : as,

sit Ennius sānē, ut est certē, perfectior, *Br.* 76, *grant, for aught I care, that Ennius is a more finished poet, as indeed he is.* utī erat rēs, Metellum esse ratī, S. *I.* 69, 1, *supposing that it was Metellus, as in fact it was.* This use begins in the classical period. It is found particularly with quamvīs, 1905 ; with sī, see 2017.

1944. ut, *as, like,* sometimes shows that a noun used predicatively is not literally applicable, but expresses an imputed quality or character : as,

Cicerō ea quae nunc ūsū veniunt cecinit ut vātēs, N. 25, 16, 4, *Cicero foretold what is now actually occurring, like a bard inspired.* canem et faelem ut deōs colunt, *Leg.* 1, 32, *they bow the knee to dog and cat as gods.* quod mē sīcut alterum parentem dīligit, *Fam.* 5, 8, 4, *because he loves me like a second father.* rēgiae virginēs, ut tōnstrīculae, tondēbant barbam patris, *TD.* 5, 58, *the princesses used to shave their father, just like common barber-girls.* In an untrue or a merely figurative comparison tamquam (1908) or quasi is used.

1945. In old Latin, prae is combined with ut: praeut, *compared with how :* as, parum etiam, praeut futūrumst, praedicās, Pl. *Am.* 374, *you say too little still compared with how 'twill be.* praeut is sometimes followed by a relative clause : as, lūdum iocumque dīcet fuisse illum alterum, praeut huius rabiēs quae dabit, T. *Eu.* 300, *he'll say the other was but sport and play, compared with what this youth will in his frenzy do.*

1946. In Plautus sīcut, with the indicative, has once or twice the meaning of *since:* as, quīn tū illam iubē abs tē abīre quō lubet : sīcut soror eius hūc gemina vēnit Ephesum, *MG.* 974, *why, bid her go away from you wherever she may choose, since her twin sister here to Ephesus is come.*

WITH THE SUBJUNCTIVE.

utī or ut.

NEGATIVE ut nē, nē, or ut nōn.

1947. The subjunctive with ut is: (A.) That of action desired (1540), in clauses of purpose; in these the negative is nē, or sometimes ut nē, and *and that not*, nēve or neu, rarely neque or nec. ut nē, though used at all periods (not by Caesar, Sallust, or Livy), is chiefly found in older Latin; afterwards nē alone took its place (1706). ut nōn is used when the negative belongs to a single word. (B.) That of action conceivable (1554), in clauses of result; in these the negative is ut nōn, ut nēmō, ut nūllus, &c.; or with emphasis on the negative, nēmō ut, nūllus ut, nihil ut; also vix ut, paene ut, prope ut.

1948. Final and consecutive clauses with ut are of two classes: I. Complementary clauses, that is, such as are an essential complement of certain specific verbs or expressions; such clauses have the value of a substantive, and may represent a subject, an object, or any oblique case. II. Pure final or consecutive clauses, in which the purpose or result of any action may be expressed, and which are not essential to complete the sense of a verb.

(A.) PURPOSE.

I. COMPLEMENTARY FINAL CLAUSES.

1949. (1.) The subjunctive with **ut** or **nē** is used in clauses which serve to complete the sense of verbs of will or aim.

1950. (*a*.) Verbs of will include those of desire, request, advice, resolution, stipulation, command, or permission.

Will may be suggested by a general verb or expression: as, dīcō, respondeō, nūntiō, &c.; or denoted by specific ones, of which some of the commonest are: desire: volō (mālō), concupīscō, optō. request: petō, postulō, flāgitō, ōrō, rogō, precor, obsecrō, implōrō, īnstō, *urge*, invītō. advice: suādeō, persuādeō, *persuade*, moneō, *bid*, admoneō, hortor, cēnseō, *propose, vote*. resolution, stipulation: dēcernō, statuō, *decree*, cōnstituō, placet, sanciō, pacīscor, pepigī. command: imperō, praecipiō, praescrībō, mandō, negōtium dō, ēdīcō, ferō, caveō, interdīcō. permission: concēdō, *allow*, permittō, committō, potestātem faciō, veniam dō, sinō, nōn patior.

1951. (*b*.) Verbs of aim include those of striving, accomplishing, or inducing; such are:

striving: agō or id agō, animum indūcō, temptō, operam dō, labōrō, nītor, ēnītor, mōlior, videō, prōspiciō, cūrō, nihil antīquius habeō quam, contendō, studeō, pūgnō. accomplishing: faciō (efficiō, perficiō), praestō; mereō; impetrō, adsequor, cōnsequor, adipīscor. inducing: moveō, excitō, incitō, impellō, perpellō, cōgō.

(*a.*) optāvit ut in currum patris tollerētur, *Off.* 3, 94, *he asked to be lifted into his father's chariot.* optō nē sē illa gēns moveat, *Fam.* 12, 19, 2, *I hope and pray that that nation may not stir.* Ubiī ōrābant, ut sibī auxilium ferret, 4, 16, 5, *the Ubians begged that he would help them.* Pausaniās ōrāre coepit nē ēnūntiāret, N. 4, 4, 6, *Pausanias began to beg that he would not tell.* hortātus est utī in officiō manēret, 5, 4, 2, *he urged him to remain steadfast in duty.* hortātur eōs nē animō dēficiant, Caes. *C.* 1, 19, 1, *he urges them not to get disheartened* (1752). suīs, ut idem faciant, imperat, 5, 37, 1, *he orders his men to do the same.* suīs imperāvit nē quod omnīnō tēlum rēicerent, 1, 46, 2, *he ordered his men not to throw any weapon at all back.* huic permīsit, utī in hīs locīs legiōnem conlocāret, 3, 1, 3, *he allowed this man to quarter his legion in these parts.* neque suam neque populī Rōmānī cōnsuētūdinem patī, utī sociōs dēsereret, 1, 45, 1, *that his practice and that of the Roman nation would not allow him to desert his allies.*

(*b.*) neque id agere ut exercitum teneat ipse, sed nē illī habeant quō contrā sē ūtī possint, Caes. *C.* 1, 85, 11, *and that his object was not to hold the army himself, but to prevent the other side from having an army which they could use against him.* XII nāvibus āmissīs, reliquīs ut nāvigārī commodē posset effēcit, 4, 31, 3, *a dozen vessels were lost, but he managed to sail comfortably with the rest.* eius bellī fāma effēcit nē sē pugnae committerent Sappīnātēs, L. 5, 32, 4, *the story of this war prevented the Sappinatians from hazarding an engagement.* sī ā Chrȳsogonō nōn impetrāmus ut pecūniā nostrā contentus sit, vītam nē petat, *RA.* 150, *if we do not succeed in making Chrysogonus satisfied with our money without his aiming at our life.* Aulum spē pactiōnis perpulit, utī in abditās regiōnēs sēsē īnsequerētur, S. *I.* 38, 2, *Aulus he induced by the hope of a pecuniary settlement to follow him to distant regions.* Antōnium pactiōne prōvinciae perpulerat, nē contrā rem pūblicam sentīret, S. *C.* 26, 4, *by agreeing to let Antony have a province, he had induced him not to be disaffected toward the government.*

1952. Many of these verbs often have a coordinated subjunctive (1705–1713), or, according to the meaning, admit other constructions, which must in general be learned by reading, or from the dictionary. The following points may be noticed :

1953. (*a.*) The verbs of resolving, **statuō, cōnstituō,** and **dēcernō,** and of striving, **nītor,** and **temptō,** have usually the complementary infinitive (2169), unless a new subject is introduced. For **volō** (**mālō**), and **cupiō,** see also 2189; for **iubeō, vetō, sinō,** and **patior,** 2198. **postulō,** *expect,* often has the same construction as **volō,** especially in old Latin (2194). For **imperō,** see 2202.

1954. (*b.*) Some of the above verbs, with the meaning *think* or *say,* have the accusative with the infinitive (2175, 2195): as, **volō, contendō,** *maintain,* **concēdō,** *admit,* **statuō,** *assume,* **dēcernō,** *judge,* **moneō,** *remind,* **persuādeō,** *convince.*

1955. (*c.*) Verbs of accomplishing sometimes express result rather than purpose, and when the result is negative, are completed by a clause with ut nōn (1965). For the infinitive with such verbs, see 2196.

1956. est with a predicate noun is sometimes equivalent to a verb of will or aim, and has the same construction.

So with words like **iūs, lēx, mūnus,** &c.: as, **iūs esse bellī ut** çuī **vīcissent hīs quōs vīcissent imperārent,** 1, 36, 1, *that rules of war entitled a conquerors to lord it over conquered.* **quis nescit prīmam esse historiae lēgem, nē quid falsī dīcere audeat?** *DO.* 2, 62, *who does not know that the first rule of history is that it shall not venture to say anything false?* **iūstitiae prīmum mūnus est ut nē cui quis noceat,** *Off.* 1, 20, *the first duty of justice is that a man harm nobody.* **nam id arbitror adprīmē in vītā esse ūtile, ' ut nē quid nimis,'** T. *Andr.* 60, *for this I hold to be a rule in life that's passing useful,* '*naught in overplus.*'

1957. (2.) The subjunctive with **ut** or **nē** is used in clauses which complete expressions of fear, anxiety, or danger.

ut, *that not, may not,* and **nē,** *lest, may,* were originally signs of a wish (1540): thus, **vereor, ut fīat,** *I am afraid; may it come to pass,* acquires the meaning of *I am afraid it may not come to pass* (1706); and **vereor, nē fīat,** *I am afraid; may it not come to pass,* of *I am afraid it may come to pass.* **metuō ut** is common in old Latin, and is used by Horace, but not by Caesar or Sallust, once by Cicero in the orations. **timeō ut** is rare, and first used by Cicero. **vereor ut** is not uncommon.

at vereor ut plācārī possit, T. *Ph.* 965, *but I'm afraid she can't be reconciled.* **nē uxor rescīscat metuit,** Pl. *As.* 743, *he is afraid his wife may find it out.* **ō puer, ut sīs vītālis metuō, et maiōrum nē quis amīcus frīgore tē feriat,** H. *S.* 2, 1, 60, *my boy, you'll not see length of days I fear, and that some grander friend may with his coldness cut you dead.* **nēquid sumn.ā dēperdat metuēns aut ampliet ut rem,** H. *S.* 1, 4, 31, *in dread lest from his store he something lose or may not add to his estate.* **metuō nē nōs nōsmet perdiderīmus uspiam,** Pl. *MG.* 428, *I'm afraid we've lost ourselves somewhere.* **sollicitus nē turba perēgerit orbem,** J. 5, 20, *apprehensive that the throng may have finished its round.* **nē nōn** is often, though rarely in old Latin, used for **ut,** and regularly when the expression of fear is negative: as, **nōn vereor nē hoc officium meum** P. Servīliō nōn probem, *V.* 4, 82, *I have no fear but I may make my services acceptable in the eyes of Servilius.* For **nōn metuō quīn,** see 1986.

1958. **vereor nē** is often equivalent to *I rather think,* and **vereor ut** to *hardly.* **vidē (videāmus, videndum est) nē,** and similar expressions, are sometimes used for **vereor nē,** to introduce something conjectured rather than proved: as,

vereor nē barbarōrum rēx fuerit, *RP.* 1, 58, *I rather think he was king over savages.* **vidē nē mea coniectūra multō sit vērior.** *Clu.* 97, *I rath. I think my conjecture is in better keeping with the facts.*

1959. Other constructions with expressions of fear are: (*a.*) Indirect question. (*b.*) Accusative with infinitive. (*c.*) Complementary infinitive as,

(*a.*) **erī semper lēnitās verēbar quorsum ēvāderet,** T. *Andr.* 175, *I was afraid how master's always gentleness would end.* **timeō quid sit,** T. *Hau.* 620, *I have my fears what it may be.* **timeō quid rērum gesserim,** Pl. *MG.* 397, *I am concerned to think what capers I have cut.* **metuō quid agam,** T. *Hau.* 720, *I'm scared and know not what to do* (1731). (*b.*) **ego mē cupiditātis rēgnī crīmen subitūrum timērem?** L. 2, 7, 9, *was I to fear being charged with aspiring to a throne?* (*c.*) **vereor cōram in ōs tē laudāre,** T. *Ad.* 269, *I am afraid to disgrace you with praise to the face* (2168).

1960. (3.) The subjunctive with **nē** is used in clauses which serve to complete the sense of verbs of avoiding, hindering, and resisting.

Such are: avoiding: **caveō, mē ēripiō, vītō.** hindering: **intercēdō, inter-dicō, recūsō, repugnō, temperō**; also the following which often have **quō-minus** (1977): **dēterreō, impediō, obsistō, obstō, officiō, prohibeō, teneō.** resisting: **resistō, repugnō, recūsō**; with these last often **quōminus.** Some of the above verbs when preceded by a negative also take **quīn** (1986); **prohibeō** and **impediō** have also the accusative with the infinitive (2203). For the subjunctive co-ordinated with **cavē**, see 1711.

nē quid eīs noceātur neu quis invītus sacrāmentum dīcere cōgātur ā Caesare cavētur, Caes. *C.* 1, 86, 4, *all precaution is taken by Caesar that no harm be done them, and that nobody be compelled to take the oath against his will.* **per eōs, nē causam dīceret, sē ēripuit,** 1, 4, 2, *thanks to this display of retainers he succeeded in avoiding trial.* **plūra nē scrībam, dolōre impedior,** *Att.* 11, 13, 5, *grief prevents me from writing more.* **nē qua sibī statua pōnerētur restitit,** N. 25, 3, 2, *he objected to having a statue erected in his honour.*

II. Pure Final Clauses.

1961. The subjunctive with **ut** or **nē** is used to de-note the purpose of the main action.

The purpose is often indicated in the main sentence by an expression like **ideō, idcircō, propereā, eā mente,** &c.

vigilās dē nocte, ut tuīs cōnsultōribus respondeās, *Mur.* 22, *you have to get up early in the morning to give advice to your clients.* **maiōrēs nostrī ab arātrō addūxērunt Cincinnātum, ut dictātor esset,** *Fin.* 2, 12, *our fathers brought Cincinnatus from his plough, to be dictator.* **dīcam auctiōnis causam, ut damnō gaudeant,** Pl. *St.* 207, *I'll tell the reason for the sale, that o'er my losses they may gloat.* **quīn etiam nē tōnsōrī collum commit-teret, tondēre fīliās suās docuit,** *TD.* 5, 58, *why, he actually taught his own daughters to shave, so as not to trust his throat to a barber.* **Caesar, nē gra-viōrī bellō occurreret, ad exercitum proficīscitur,** 4, 6, 1, *to avoid facing war on a more formidable scale, Caesar goes to the army.* **tē ulcīscar, ut nē inpūne in nōs inlūseris,** T. *Eu.* 941, *I'll be revenged on you, so that you shan't play tricks on me for nothing* (1947). **nē īgnōrārētis esse aliquās pācis vōbīs condiciōnēs, ad vōs vēnī,** L. 21, 13, 2, *I have come to you to let you know that you have some chances of peace* (1754). **ita mē gessī nē tibī pudōrī essem,** L. 40, 15, 6, *I comported myself in such a way that I might not be a mortification to you.* **Mariōnem ad tē eō mīsī, ut tēcum ad mē venī-ret,** *Fam.* 16, 1, 1, *I sent Mario to you with the intention of having him come with you to me.* **idcircō nēmō superiōrum attigit, ut hīc tolleret? ideō C. Claudius rettulit, ut C. Verrēs posset auferre?** *V.* 4, 7, *was that the reason why no former officials laid a finger on it, that this man might swoop it away? was that why Claudius returned it, that a Verres might carry it off?* **danda opera est, ut etiam singulīs cōnsulātur, sed ita, ut ea rēs aut prōsit aut certē nē obsit rēī pūblicae,** *Off.* 2, 72, *we must be particular in regarding the interests of individuals as well, but with this restriction, that our action may benefit, or at any rate may not damage the country.*

1962. The subjunctive with **ut** or **nē** is often used not to express the purpose of the main action, but in a parenthetical clause, as though dependant upon some verb unexpressed: as,

ut in pauca cōnferam, testāmentō factō mulier moritur, *Caec.* 17, *to cut a long story short, the woman makes her will and dies.* **sed ut hīc nē īgnōret, quae rēs agātur: dē nātūrā agēbāmus deōrum,** *DN.* 1,17, *but that our friend here may know what is up: we were just on the nature of the gods.* The tense is present, in late writers the perfect, as **ut sīc dīxerim,** Quint. 1, 6, 1. Here may also be mentioned the use of **nēdum** (rarely **nē** or, from Livy on, **nēdum ut**) with the present subjunctive (rarely the imperfect): as, **satrapa numquam sufferre eius sūmptūs queat: nēdum tū possīs,** T. *Hau.* 452, *a prince could n't stand her extravagance, much less could you.* This is found in Terence and Lucretius once each, in Cicero, and later; not in Caesar. The preceding clause is negative or involves a negative idea. From Livy on, the verb may be omitted: as, **vix clāmōrem eōrum, nēdum impetum tulēre,** L. 34, 20, 7, *they hardly stood their war cry, much less their charge.*

1963. The subjunctive is used in an assumption or concession with **ut** or **nē**, or if the negation belongs to a single word, with **ut nōn, nēmō,** &c.: as,

ut taceam, quoivīs facile scītū est quam fuerim miser, T. *Hec.* 296, *even supposing I say nothing, anybody can understand how unhappy I was.* **sed ut haec concēdantur, reliqua quī concēdī possunt?** *DN.* 3, 41, *but even supposing this be admitted, how can the rest be admitted?* **nē sit summum malum dolor, malum certē est,** *TD.* 2, 14, *grant that suffering is not the chiefest evil, an evil it assuredly is* (1553). **vērum ut hoc nōn sit, tamen praeclārum spectāculum mihī prōpōnō,** *Att.* 2, 15, 2, *but suppose this be not the case, still I anticipate a gorgeous show.* **ac iam ut omnia contrā opīniōnem acciderent, tamen sē plūrimum nāvibus posse perspiciēbant,** 3, 9, 6, *and even supposing everything turned out contrary to expectation, still they saw clearly that they had the advantage by sea.* **ut enim nēminem alium nisi T. Patinam rogāsset, scīre potuit prōdī flāminem necesse esse,** *Mil.* 46, *for even supposing he had asked nobody but Patina, he might have known that a priest must be appointed.* This use is common in Cicero, not found in Plautus or Sallust.

1964. The subjunctive with **ut** or **nē**, generally with ita as a correlative, sometimes has the force of a proviso: as,

ita probanda est clēmentia, ut adhibeātur sevēritās, *Off.* 1, 88, *mercy is to be commended, provided that strictness is employed.* **satis memoriae meae tribuent, ut maiōribus meīs dignum crēdant,** Ta. 4, 38, *they will pay respect enough to my memory, provided they consider me worthy of my ancestors.*

(B.) RESULT.

J. COMPLEMENTARY CONSECUTIVE CLAUSES.

1965. The subjunctive with **ut** or **ut nōn** is used in clauses which serve to complete the sense of certain verbs and expressions, chiefly of bringing to pass, happening, and following.

Such are: (*a.*) **faciō, efficiō** (unless they imply purpose, 1951); **fit, accidit, contingit, ēvenit, est,** *it is the case;* similarly **mōs est, cōnsuētūdō est,** &c. (*b.*) **proximum est, reliquum est, extrēmum est, relinquitur, restat, accēdit.** Or, of logical sequence, **sequitur, efficitur.**

(*a.*) **fēcērunt ut cōnsimilis fugae profectiō vidērētur,** 2, 11, 1, *they made their march look exactly like a stampede.* **splendor vester facit ut peccāre sine summō perīculō nōn possītis,** *V.* 1, 22, *your conspicuous position makes it impossible for you to do wrong without great peril.* **hīs rēbus fīēbat, ut minus lātē vagārentur,** 1, 2, 4, *so it came to pass that they did not rove round much.* **fit ut nātūrā ipsā ad ōrnātius dīcendī genus excitēmur,** *DO.* 2. 338, *it is sometimes the case that we are roused to a loftier style in oratory by sheer circumstance.* **potest fierī ut fallar,** *Fam.* 13, 73, 2, *it is possible that I am mistaken.* **fierī nōn potest ut eum tū nōn cōgnōverīs,** *V.* 2, 190, *it must be the case that you have made his acquaintance yourself.* **eādem nocte accidit, ut esset lūna plēna,** 4, 29, 1, *it came to pass on the same night that there was a full moon* (1758). **negāvit mōris esse Graecōrum ut in convīviō virōrum accumberent mulierēs,** *V.* 1, 66, *he said it was not etiquette among the Greeks for women to go to men's dinner parties.* **est hōc commūne vitium in līberīs cīvitātibus, ut invidia glōriae comes sit,** N. 12, 3, 3, *this is a common trouble in free communities, that envy is the attendant of a great name.*

(*b.*) **proximum est, ut doceam,** *DN.* 2, 73, *my next task is to prove.* **relinquēbātur ut neque longius ab āgmine legiōnum discēdī Caesar paterētur,** 5, 19, 3, *the consequence was that Caesar could not allow any very distant excursion from the main line of march.* **restat ut doceam omnia hominum causā facta esse,** *DN.* 2, 154, *lastly, I must prove that everything is made for man.* **accēdēbat ut tempestātem ferrent,** 3, 13, 9, *then, too, they could stand the gale.* **accēdit ut** is not found in old Latin; for **accēdit quod,** see 1845. **ita efficitur ut omne corpus mortāle sit,** *DN.* 3, 30, *thus it follows that every bodily substance is mortal.* **sequitur** and **efficitur,** *it follows,* often have the accusative with the infinitive (2207). For the subjunctive with **quam ut** after a comparative of disproportion, see 1896. For **fore** and **futūrum esse ut** as the periphrasis for the future infinitive, see 2233.

1966. Verbs of happening may often be rendered best by compacter expressions: thus, **hīs rēbus fīēbat ut,** *consequently ;* **fit ut,** *once in a while, sometimes, often ;* **fierī potest ut,** *possibly ;* **accidit ut,** *accidentally, unfortunately.*

1967. faciō ut, or with a negative, commonly **committō ut,** is used in circumlocutions for emphasis: as,

faciundum mihī putāvī, ut tuīs litterīs brevī respondērem, *Fam.* 3, 8, 1, *I thought I ought to take hold and write a few lines in answer to your letter.* **±go vērō nōn committam, ut tibī causam recūsandī dem,** *DO.* 2, 233, *no, no, sir, I will not be guilty, not I, of giving you an excuse to back out.* So particularly with **invītus, libenter, prope**: as, **invītus fēcī ut L. Flāminīnum ē senātū ēicerem,** *CM.* 42, *it was with great reluctance that I expelled Flamininus from the senate.*

1968. A subjunctive clause with **ut** is often used to define a preceding idea indicated in a general way by a neuter pronoun: as, post eius mortem nihilō minus Helvētiī id, quod cōnstituerant, **facere cōnantur, ut ē fīnibus suīs exeant,** I, 5, I, *after his death the Helvetians attempted just the same to carry out their resolution of moving out of their abodes* (1752). omnibus Gallīs idem esse faciendum, quod Helvētiī fēce-rint, ut domō ēmigrent, I, 31, 14, *that all the Gauls must do just as the Helvetians had done and move away from home.* Helvētiī, cum id, quod ipsī diēbus XX aegerrimē cōnfēcerant, ut flūmen trānsīrent, illum ūnō diē fēcisse intellegerent, lēgātōs mittunt, I, 13, 2, *when the Helvetians learned that the Roman commander had done in a single day what they had found it hard themselves to do in twenty, namely cross the river, they sent deputies* (1752). id aliquot dē causīs acciderat, ut subitō Gallī bellī renovandī cōnsilium caperent, **3,** 2, 2, *it was due to a variety of reasons that the Gauls suddenly conceived the idea of making war again* (1758). **hocine bonī esse officium servī exīstumas, ut erī suī corrumpat et rem et fīlium ?** Pl. *Most.* 27, *is this what you think the duty of a good slave, to waste his own master's property and corrupt his son ?*

1969. tantum abest, *so far from,* is sometimes followed by a double **ut,** the first introducing an unreal, and the second a real action : as,

tantum abest ut haec bēstiārum causā parāta sint, ut ipsās bēstiās hominum grātiā generātās esse videāmus, *DN.* 2, 158, *so far from these things being made for brutes, we see that brutes themselves were created for man.* This use, very rarely personal, begins with Cicero, and is common in his writings and in Livy. Not in Caesar, Sallust, or Tacitus. Sometimes instead of **ut** the second sentence is coordinated (1700) : **tantum abfuit ut īnflammārēs nostrōs animōs, somnum vix tenēbāmus,** *Br.* 278, *so far from your firing our heart, we could hardly keep awake.* Or, the idea is expressed by **ita nōn . . . ut :** as, **erat ita nōn timidus ad mortem, ut in aciē sit ob rem pūblicam interfectus,** *Fin.* 2, 63, *so far from being afraid of death, he fell in battle for his country.*

II. Pure Consecutive Clauses.

1970. The subjunctive is used with **ut** or **ut nōn** to denote result.

The result may be the result of an action or of a thing named in the main sentence. The main sentence often has a correlative to **ut,** expressing (*a.*) degree : as, **tantus,** *so great,* **tam,** *so* (with adjectives or adverbs). **adeō, tantopere.** (*b.*) quality : as, **is** (hīc, ille, iste), *such,* **tālis, ita, sīc.**

mōns altissimus impendēbat, ut facile perpaucī prohibēre possent, I, 6, I, *an exceeding high mountain hung over, so that a very few could block the way.* **dictitābant sē domō expulsōs, omnibus necessāriīs egēre rēbus, ut honestā praescrīptiōne rem turpissimam tegerent,** Caes. *C.* 3, 32. 4, *they stoutly declared that they were driven out of house and home, and lacked the necessaries of life, thus veiling dishonour under the name of respectability.*

(*a.*) **Ariovistus tantōs sibī spīritūs sūmpserat, ut ferendus nōn vidērētur,** I, 33, 5, *Ariovistus had put on such high and mighty airs as to seem intolerable.* **adeō angustō marī cōnflīxit, ut eius multitūdō nāvium explicārī nōn potuerit,** N. 2, 4, 5, *he went into action in such cramped sea-room, that his armada could not deploy,* of Xerxes (1757).

342

(*b*.) eōs dēdūxī testēs ut dē istīus factō dubium esse nēminī possit, *V.* 4, 91, *I have brought such witnesses that nobody can entertain a doubt of the defendant's guilt.* ita sē recipiēbat ut nihil nisi dē perniciē populī Rō-ṃānī cōgitāret, *Ph.* 4, 4, *he retreated, it is true, but retreated with his mind running on nothing but how to ruin the country.* illa, ex tūribulīs quae ēvellerat, ita scītē in aureīs pōculīs inligābat, ut ea ad illam rem nāta esse dicerēs, *V.* 4, 54, *what he had torn from the censers he attached to golden cups so cunningly that you would have said it was just made for that very purpose* (1731, 1559).

For the imperfect subjunctive connected with a main general present, see 1751; for the independent present or perfect subjunctive with a main secondary tense, see 1757.

---

ubī.

1971. ubī, in the sense of *where* (709), has the ordinary construction of a relative (1812–1831). For ubī, *when*, see 1923–1926 and 1932–1934; as a synonym of sī, *if*, see 2110.

---

quō or quī.

1972. quō, *whereby*, *wherewith*, or in old Latin sometimes quī (689), is the instrumental ablative from the relative and interrogative stem quī-. Combined with minus, *the less, not*, quō gives quōminus.

WITH THE INDICATIVE.

1973. The indicative is used with quō and a comparative in the protasis of a comparative period, with eō or hōc and a comparative as correlative (1393): as,

quō dēlictum maius est, eō poena est tardior, *Caec.* 7, *the greater the sin is, the slower is the punishment.* The eō or hōc is sometimes omitted: as, quō plūrēs sumus, plūribus rēbus egēbimus, *L.* 34, 34, 6, *the more numerous we are, the more things we shall need.* In late writers, the comparative is sometimes omitted in the main clause, very rarely in the subordinate clause. quantō . . . tantō are also used like quō . . . eō: as, quantō diūtius cōnsīderō, tantō mihī rēs vidētur obscūrior, *DN.* 1, 60, *the longer I puzzle over it, the more incomprehensible the question seems to me.* quantō magis extergeō, tenuius fit, Pl. *R.* 1301, *the more I polish, the slimmer it gets.* This form is sometimes used with quisque or quis of indefinite persons, instead of the commoner ut . . . ita or sīc (1939): as, quō quisque est sollertior, hōc docet labōriōsius, *RC.* 31, *the brighter a man is, the more wearisome he finds teaching.* quō quisque est maior, magis est plācābilis īrae, O. *Tr.* 3, 5, 31, *the greater be the man, the easier 'tis his anger to appease.*

WITH THE SUBJUNCTIVE.

1974. The subjunctive is used with quō to express purpose.

quō differs but little in meaning from ut of purpose. It is used (*a.*) particularly in clauses containing a comparative expression, or (*b*) in solemn law language.

(*a.*) **equitēs omnibus in locīs pugnant, quō sē legiōnāriīs mīlitibus praeferrent**, 2, 27, 2, *the troopers fought on every kind of ground, hoping to out-.hine the regular infantry thereby.* **medicō putō aliquid dandum esse, quō sit studiōsior**, *Fam.* 16, 4, 2, *I think it would be well to fee your medical man, to make him more attentive.* **id amābō adiūtā mē quō id fīat facilius**, T. *Eu.* 150, *help me in that, I pray, that it may be the easier done.* **sublāta erat celebritās virōrum ac mulierum, quō lāmentātiō minuerētur**, *Leg.* 2, 65, *the large attendance of both sexes was done away with, to make the weeping and wailing less harrowing.* (*b.*) **hominī mortuō nē ossa legitō, quō pos fūnus faciat**, Twelve Tables in *Leg.* 2, 60, *he shall not gather up the bones of a dead man, with intent to celebrate the funeral a second time* (1586). **quī eōrum coiit, coierit, quō quis iūdiciō pūblicō condemnārētur**, law in *Clu.* 148, *whosoever of that number conspired or shall have conspired to have anybody condemned in a criminal court.* Otherwise rarely used without a comparative expression, yet occasionally found thus in Plautus, Terence, Sallust, and Ovid: as, **hanc simulant parere quō Chremētem absterreant**, T. *Andr.* 472, *they're pretending that she's lying in, to frighten Chremes off.* So often in Tacitus.

1975. quō nē, in a negative clause of purpose, is found in a disputed passage in Horace, but not again until late Latin. For nōn quō, nōn eō quō, introducing an untenable reason, see 1855.

1976. In old Latin quī, *whereby, wherewith, withal*, is partly felt as a live relative pronoun in the ablative, and partly as a mere conjunction of purpose; as a pronoun it may even take a preposition; as a conjunction, it may refer to a plural antecedent (689): as, **quasi patriciīs puerīs aut monērulae aut anitēs aut cōturnīcēs dantur, quīcum lūsitent: itidem mī haec upupa, quī mē dēlectem datast**, Pl. *Cap.* 1002, *as to the sons of gentlemen or daws or ducks or quails are given, wherewith to play; just so to me this crow is given, to entertain myself withal.* **enim mihi quidem aequomst darī vehicla quī vehar**, Pl. *Aul.* 500, *in sooth 't were fair that carriages be given me, to ride withal.* The indicative occurs where the subjunctive would be used in classical Latin: as, **multa concurrunt simul, quī coniectūram hanc faciō**, T. *Andr.* 511, *a thousand things combine whereby I come to this conjecture.*

------◆------

quōminus.

1977. The subjunctive with quōminus (1972) is used to complete the sense of verbs of hindering or resisting.

˙ Such verbs are: **impediō, teneō,** *hinder,* **interclūdō, dēterreō, obstō, obsistō, resistō, repugnō, nōn recūsō** ; these verbs often have a subjunctive with nē (1960). Cicero rarely and Caesar never uses quōminus with impediō or prohibeō. For the accusative and infinitive with these verbs, see 2203. quōminus is also used with **moveor,** *am influenced,* **fit,** *it is owing to.* **stat per aliquem,** *somebody is responsible,* or indeed any expression implying hindrance. When the verb of hindering has a negative with it, quīn is often used ; see 1986.

nōn dēterret sapientem mors, quōminus rēī pūblicae suīsque cōn-
sulat, *TD.* 1, 91, *death does not hinder the wise man from working for country
and friends.* quid obstat, quōminus sit beātus? *DN.* 1, 95, *what is to hinder his being happy?* neque recūsāvit quōminus lēgis poenam subīret,
N. 15, 8, 2, *and he did not decline to submit to the penalty of the law.* Caesar,
ubi cōgnōvit per Afrānium stāre quōminus proeliō dīmicārētur, castra
facere cōnstituit, Caes. *C.* 1, 41, 3, *when Caesar learned that owing to Afranius there was no battle, he resolved to build a camp.* sī tē dolor corporis
tenuit, quōminus ad lūdōs venīrēs, fortūnae magis tribuō quam
sapientiae tuae, *Fam.* 7, 1, 1, *if it was bodily suffering that kept you from
coming to the performances, I think more highly of your luck than of your sense.*
Terence first uses quōminus thus, but only rarely. He also sometimes uses
the parts separately so that the true relative and negative forces appear: as,
sī sēnserō quicquam in hīs tē nūptiīs fallāciae cōnārī, quō fīant minus,
T. *Andr.* 196, *if I catch you trying on any trick in the matter of this marriage
through which it may not come off* (1451).

1978. In Tacitus, quōminus is sometimes found where quīn would be used in
classical Latin (1986): as, nec dubitātum quōminus pācem concēderent,
Ta. *H.* 2, 45, *there was no hesitation in granting peace.*

1979. It may be mentioned here that quō sētius with the subjunctive, instead
of quōminus, is found twice in Cicero's earliest extant prose, and twice in older
Latin.

------------◆------------

quīn.

1980. quīn is composed of quī, the ablative or locative of the interrogative and relative stem qui- (689), and -ne, *not.* It is used in
simple sentences and as a conjunctive particle.

1981. For the use of quīn, *why not*, in questions with the indicative, see
1526. Such questions have the sense of an affirmative command or exhortation (1531): as, quīn abīs, Pl. *MG.* 1087, *why won't you begone?* or *get you
gone.* quīn cōnscendimus equōs, L. 1, 57, 7, *why not mount*, or *to horse, to
horse.* For the use of quīn without interrogative force, see 1527.

1982. quīn is found occasionally with the subjunctive in a direct question in Plautus, Terence, Lucilius, Lucretius, Cicero, and Tacitus: thus,
quīn ego hōc rogem? Pl. *MG.* 426, *why should n't I ask this?* (1563).

1983. The subjunctive with the conjunctive particle quīn is used, particularly in old Latin, in connection with the common formula nūlla causa est
or its equivalents.

Such a subjunctive may be regarded as original (1786) or as due to the
indirect form of question (1773).

nūlla causast quīn mē condōnēs crucī, Pl. *R.* 1070, *there 's no reason
why you should n't deliver me up to execution.* quīn dēcēdam, nūlla causa
est, *Fam.* 2, 17, 1, *there is no reason why I should not retire.* quid causaest
quīn in pistrīnum rēctā proficīscar viā? T. *Andr.* 600, *what 's the reason
I don't march straight into the mill?* haud causificor quīn eam habeam,
Pl. *Aul.* 755, *I don't quibble against keeping her.*

1984. mīrum quīn with the subjunctive is used by Plautus in sarcastic expressions where mīrum is ironical: as, mīrum quīn tū illō tēcum dīvitiās ferās, Pl. *Tri.* 495, *strange enough, how you can't take your money there with you,* that is to Hades.

1985. The subjunctive with quīn (or ut nōn) is used after nōn possum, or nōn possum with an infinitive, usually facere, and with fierī nōn potest: as,

nōn enim possum quīn exclāmem, eugē, eugē, Lȳsitelēs, πάλιν, Pl. *Tri.* 705, *upon my word I must cry bravo, bravo, Lysiteles; encore!* facere nōn potuī quīn tibī sententiam dēclārārem, *Fam.* 6, 13, 1, *I could not help giving you my views.* fierī nūllō modō poterat, quīn Cleomenī parcerētur, *V.* 5, 104, *it was impossible not to spare Cleomenes.* ēheu, nequeō quīn fleam, quom abs tē abeam, Pl. *MG.* 1342, *O well-a-day, I needs must weep, for that from thee I part.* nōn potuistī ūllō modō facere, ut mihī illam epistulam nōn mitterēs, *Att.* 11, 21, 1, *you could not get along at all without writing me that letter* (1965).

1986. The subjunctive with quīn is used in clauses which complete the sense of verbs of restraining, abstaining, delaying, or doubting, when such verbs have a negative, expressed or implied.

Such verbs are (*a.*) restraining: temperō mihī, teneō, *restrain*, retineō, contineō, dēterreō, reprimō. abstaining: praetermittō, intermittō. delaying: cunctor, differō, exspectō, recūsō; nōn multum, nihil, paulum abest. (*b.*) doubting: dubitō, dubium est; a doubt may also be implied in other words, or forms of words: as, nōn metuō, nōn abest suspīciō, &c.

(*a.*) neque sibī hominēs barbarōs temperātūrōs exīstimābat, quīn in prōvinciam exīrent, 1, 33, 4, *and he thought, as they were savages, they would not restrain themselves, but would sally out into the province.* vix mē contineō quīn involem mōnstrō in capillum, T. *Eu.* 859, *I scarce can keep from flying at the caitiff's hair.* nihil praetermīsī, quīn Pompēium ā Caesaris coniūnctiōne āvocārem, *Ph.* 2, 23, *I left no stone unturned to prevent Pompey from joining Caesar.* abstinēre quīn attingās nōn queās, Pl. *B.* 915, *you can't keep from touching it.* (*b.*) nōn dubitat, quīn tē ductūrum negēs, T. *Andr.* 405, *he does n't doubt that you 'll refuse to marry.* quis dubitet, quīn in virtūte dīvitiae sint?* *Par.* 48, *who can doubt that there is money in virtue?* neque abest suspīciō quīn ipse sibī mortem cōnscīverit, 1, 4, 4, *and ground is not wanting for the belief that he made away with himself.*

1987. nōn dubitō has other constructions: (*a.*) Indirect question. (*b.*) Accusative with the infinitive (in some authors: chiefly Nepos and Livy and later writers). (*c.*) Meaning *not hesitate,* the infinitive alone (2169). quīn seldom follows this meaning.

(*a.*) nōn dubitō, quid nōbīs agendum putēs, *Att.* 10, 1, 2, *I have no doubt about what you think is our duty to do.* (*b.*) neque enim dubitābant hostem ventūrum, L. 22, 55, 2, *for they firmly believed the enemy would come.* (*c.*) quid dubitāmus pultāre? Pl. *B.* 1117, *why do we hesitate to knock?* nōlīte dubitāre quīn huic crēdātis omnia, *IP.* 68, *do not hesitate to trust all to him.*

1988. The subjunctive with quīn is often used after general negative assertions, or questions implying a negative: as, nēmō fuit omnīnō mīlitum quīn vulnerārētur, Caes. *C.* 3, 53, 3, *there was absolutely not a single soldier but was wounded.* nūllust Ephesī quīn sciat, Pl. *B.* 336, *there's not a soul at Ephesus but knows.* quis in circum vēnit, quīn is ūnōquōque gradū dē avāritiā tuā commonērētur? *V.* 1, 154, *who came to the circus without being reminded of your avarice at each and every step?* nūlla fuit cīvitās quīn partem senātūs Cordubam mitteret, nōn cīvis Rōmānus quīn convenīret, Caes. *C.* 2, 19, 2, *there was not a community but sent a part of its local senate to Corduba, not a Roman citizen, but went to the meeting.* For quī nōn after such expressions, see 1821. The main sentence often has tam, ita, sīc, or tantus: as, nēmō est tam fortis, quīn rēī novitāte perturbētur, 6, 39, 3, *there was nobody so brave but was demoralized by the strangeness of the situation.* nīl tam difficilest quīn quaerendō investīgārī possiet, T. *Hau.* 675, *there's naught so hard but may by searching be tracked out.* Instead of quīn, ut nōn or quī nōn is often used in such combinations (1821).

1989. The subjunctive in an untenable reason, negatively put, is sometimes introduced by nōn quīn instead of nōn quod nōn or nōn quō nōn (1855): as, nōn quīn parī virtūte aliī fuerint, *Ph.* 7, 6, *not that others may not have been his peers in virtue.*

1990. quīn is used very rarely instead of quōminus to introduce clauses completing the sense of verbs which have no negative expressed or implied: as, once each in the *Bellum Alexandrīnum,* in Tacitus, and in Seneca's prose.

---

dum, dōnec, quoad, quamdiū.

1991. With the temporal particles dum, *while, until,* and dōnec, *until* (in old Latin dōnicum and in Lucretius dōnique), may be conveniently treated the relative quaad or quoad (that is quā or quō combined with ad), *while, until,* and the comparative quamdiū, *as long as.*

1992. dum, *while,* means originally *a while* (1151): as, circumspice dum, Pl. *Tri.* 146, *look round you a while, a minute, just look round* (1573). dum servī meī perplacet mihi cōnsilium, dum haud placet, Pl. *Merc.* 348, *one while my slave's plan suits me completely, another while it doesn't suit.* dum . . . dum, Accius in *DN.* 2, 89, *one while . . . another.*

1993. As a pure conjunctive particle, dum, *while,* means either (A.) *in the time while,* or (B.) *all the time while;* in the latter sense quoad and quamdiū are also used. From *all the time while,* dum comes t mean (C.) *as long as, provided;* and (D.) *until;* in this sense quoad and dōnec are also used.

1994. The indicative is used in a protasis introduced by dum, quoad, or quamdiū, *while;* and the subjunctive in a protasis introduced by dum, *provided,* or *until.*

The subjunctive is also used for special reasons, as in indirect discourse (1725), by attraction (1728), of action conceivable (1731), or by late writers to express repeated past action (1730). See also 1997 and 2009, end.

347

(A.) dum, *in the time while.*

1995. The present indicative is regularly used with **dum,** *in the time while* (1739).

dum sometimes has as correlative subitō, repente ; iam, intereā, &c.

The main verb may be present, future, or past; as, dum haec dīcit, abiīt hōra, T. *Eu.* 341, *while he thus prated, sped an hour away.* īnficī dēbet iīs artibus quās sī, dum est tener, combiberit, ad maiōra veniet parātior, *Fin.* 3, 9, *he should be imbued with such arts as will, if absorbed while he is young, render him the better equipped to deal with weightier business.* nunc rem ipsam, ut gesta sit, dum breviter vōbīs dēmōnstrō, attendite, *Tul.* 13, *now give your attention to the case itself, while I set forth to you briefly how it occurred.* dum in hīs locīs Caesar morātur, ad eum lēgātī vēnērunt, 4, 22, 1, *while Caesar tarried in these regions, some envoys came to him.* dum haec aguntur, vōce clārā exclāmat, Pl. *Am.* 1120, *while this was going on, with clarion voice he cries aloud.* haec dum aguntur, intereā Cleomenēs iam ad Helōrī lītus pervēnerat, *V.* 5, 91, *while this was going on, Cleomenes meantime had already arrived at the shore of Helorum.* The phrase dum haec geruntur, *meanwhile,* is often used by the historians to shift the scene : as, dum haec in Venetīs geruntur, Q. Titūrius Sabīnus in fīnēs Venellōrum pervēnit, 3, 17, 1, *while this was going on among the Veneti, Sabinus arrived in the territory of the Venelli.* The present indicative is sometimes retained in indirect discourse, chiefly in poetry or late prose: as, dīc, hospes, Spartae nōs tē hīc vīdisse iacentīs, dum sānctīs patriae lēgibus obsequimur, *TD.* 1, 101, *tell it at Sparta, friend, that thou hast seen us lying here, obedient to our country's holy laws.* dīcit sēsē illī ānulum, dum lūctat, dētrāxisse, T. *Hec.* 829, *he says that, in the struggle, he pulled off her ring.*

1996. The future is rare and chiefly confined to old Latin: as,

animum advortite, dum huius argūmentum ēloquar cōmoediae, Pl. *prol. Am.* 95, *attention lend, while I set forth the subject of this comedy.* dum pauca dīcam, breviter attendite, *V.* 3, 163, *while I speak briefly, give me your attention a few moments.*

1997. The imperfect indicative is rare ; the imperfect subjunctive is sometimes used, chiefly by the poets and historians : as,

(*a.*) dum haec Vēīs agēbantur, interim capitōlium in ingentī perīculō fuit, L. 5, 47, 1, *while this was going on at Vei, the capitol meanwhile was in terrible peril.* The pluperfect of resulting state is rarer : as, dum in ūnam partem oculōs hostium certāmen āverterat, plūribus locīs capitur mūrus, L. 32, 24, 5, *while the eyes of the enemy were turned away in one direction toward the fight, the wall is carried in several places* (1615). (*b.*) dum sē rēx āverteret, alter ēlātam secūrim in caput dēiēcit, L. 1, 40, 7, *while the king was looking another way, the second man raised his axe and brought it down on his head.*

1998. The clause with **dum** often denotes the cause of the main action, particularly when the subjects of both verbs are the same and the action of the protasis is coincident with that of the apodosis (1733).

348

dum docent, discunt, Sen. *E.* 7, 8, *while they are teaching, they are learning,* or, *by teaching they learn.* **nīmīrum didicī etiam, dum in istum inquīrō, artificum nōmina,** *V.* 4, 4, *preposterous as it may seem, in hunting up evidence against the defendant, I have actually learned artists' names.* The main action is often one not anticipated or desired : as, **ita dum pauca mancipia retinēre volt, fortūnās omnīs lībertātemque suam perdidit,** *Caecil.* 56, *so in her attempt to keep a few human chattels, she sacrificed all her possessions and her own liberty.* **dum vītant stultī vitia, in contrāria currunt,** H. *S.* 1, 2, 24, *while fools essay a vice to shun, into its opposite they run.* Sometimes with the perfect : as, **dum Alexandrī similis esse voluit, L. Crassī inventus est dissimillimus,** *Br.* 282, *from his desire to be like Alexander, he came out just the opposite of Crassus.*

(B.) dum, quoad, quamdiū (dōnec), *all the time while.*

1999. **dum, quoad,** or **quamdiū,** *all the time while,* often has as correlative **tamdiū, tantum, tantummodo, tantisper, usque,** or **ita.** When **tamdiū** is used, **quam** often stands for **quamdiū.**

2000 (1.) When the main verb is present or future, the protasis with **dum, quoad,** or **quamdiū,** *all the time while,* is usually in the same tense as the main verb : as,

mane dum scrībit, Pl. *B.* 737, *wait while he writes.* **aegrōtō dum anima est, spēs esse dīcitur,** *Att.* 9, 10, 3, *as long as a sick man has breath he is said to have hope.* **vidua vīvitō vel usque dum rēgnum optinēbit Iuppiter,** Pl. *Men.* 727, *may'st widowed live e'en long as Jupiter shall reign.* **ego tē meum esse dīcī tantisper volō, dum quod tē dignumst faciēs,** T. *Hau.* 106, *I'll have thee called my son but just so long as thou shalt act as doth become thee.* **dum Latīnae loquentur litterae, quercus huic locō nōn deerit,** *Leg.* 1, 2, *as long as Latin literature has the gift of speech, this spot will not lack its oak* (1733). **quamdiū quisquam erit quī tē dēfendere audeat, vīvēs,** *C.* 1, 6, *as long as there shall be a soul who will venture to defend you, you shall live on.* **discēs quamdiū volēs, tamdiū autem velle dēbēbis quoad tē quantum prōficiās nōn paenitēbit,** *Off.* 1, 2, *you shall study as long as you want to, and it will be proper for you to want to, as long as you are satisfied with your progress.* **dandum hordeum et furfurēs usque quaad erunt lactantēs,** Varro *R.R.* 2, 7, 12, *give them barley and bran as long as they are sucklings.* **quoad,** *as long as,* is not found in Terence.

2001. (2.) With **quamdiū** the perfect is used when the main verb is perfect ; with **dum** or **quoad** the perfect or imperfect is used when the main verb is perfect or pluperfect, and the imperfect usually when the main verb is imperfect : as,

(*a.*) **quōrum quamdiū mānsit imitātiō, tamdiū genus illud dīcendī vīxit,** *DO.* 2, 94, *as long as the imitation of these men lasted, so long was that style in vogue.* **tenuit locum tamdiū quam ferre potuit labōrem,** *Br.* 236, *he held the position as long as he could stand the work.* In this use **quamdiū** is found first in Cicero.

(*b.*) **vīxit, dum vīxit, bene,** T. *Hec.* 461, *he lived well all the time he lived* (1733). **avus noster quoad vīxit, restitit M. Grātidiō,** *Leg.* 3, 36, *our grandfather as long as he lived, opposed Gratidius.*

(*c.*) **Massiliēnsēs quoad licēbat, circumvenīre nostrōs contendēbant,**
Caes. *C.* 1, 58, 1, *as long as the Massilia people had a chance, they kept trying
to surround our men.* **dum necesse erat, rēsque ipsa cōgēbat, ūnus
omnia poterat,** *RA.* 139, *as long as it had to be, and circumstances demanded,
one man controlled the world* (1733). From Sallust on, the present of vivid
narration (1590) is occasionally found with dum in this sense.

2002. In poetry and in late prose writers, beginning with Lucretius and Livy,
dōnec is used in the sense of *all the time while,* usually with the indicative, but sometimes with the subjunctive of repeated past action : as, **dōnec grātus eram tibī,
Persārum viguī rēge beātior,** H. 3, 9, 1, *as long as I was loved of thee, I flourished happier than the Persians' king.* **dōnec armātī cōnfertīque abībant,
peditum labor in persequendō fuit,** L. 6, 13, 4, *as long as they were moving off
under arms and in close array, the task of pursuit fell to the infantry.* **vulgus
trucīdātum est dōnec īra et diēs permānsit,** Ta. 1, 68, *the rank and file
were butchered as long as wrath and daylight held out.* **nihil trepidābant, dōnec
continentī velut ponte agerentur,** L. 21, 28, 10, *the elephants were not a bit
skittish as long as they were driven along what seemed a continuous bridge* (1730).
The future is rare : as, **nātus enim dēbet quīcumque est velle manēre in
vītā, dōnec retinēbit blanda voluptās,** Lucr. 5, 177, *whoe'er is born must wish
in life to abide, so long as him fond pleasure shall detain.* **dōnec eris fēlīx, multōs numerābis amīcōs,** O. *Tr.* 1, 9, 5, *as long as fortune smiles, thou troops
shalt count of friends.*

(C.) dum, *as long as, provided, so.*

2003. The present and imperfect subjunctive are used in provisos
introduced by **dum**, *as long as, provided, so.*

dum is sometimes accompanied by modo, *only,* or quidem, *that is ;* or
(from Terence on) modo is used without dum. The negative is nē (from
Ovid on, sometimes nōn) ; nē sometimes has as correlative ita.

ōderint dum metuant, Poet. in Suet. *Cal.* 30, *let them hate, so they fear.*
absit, dum modo laude partā domum recipiat sē, Pl. *Am.* 644, *let him go,
so only he come home with glory won.* **postulābant prō homine miserrimō,
quī vel ipse sēsē in cruciātum darī cuperet, dum dē patris morte quae-
rerētur,** *RA.* 119, *they made the request in behalf of a pitiable wretch, who would
be only too glad to be put to the rack himself, so his father's death might be inves-
tigated.* **itaque dum locus comminus pugnandī darētur, aequō animō
singulās bīnīs nāvibus obiciēbant,** Caes. *C.* 1, 58, 4, *therefore, so a chance
was given to fight hand to hand, they did not mind pitting one of their vessels
against two of the enemy's.* **sī ēī permissum esset, ita id sacrum faceret,
dum nē plūs quīnque sacrificiō interessent,** L. 39, 18, 9, *if he were allowed,
he might perform the sacrifice far better, provided that not more than five people
should have a part in the ceremonial.* **dum quidem nēquid percontēris
quod nōn lubeat prōloquī,** Pl. *Aul.* 211, *provided at least you ask nothing that
I may not like to disclose.* **volet, cīvis modo haec sit,** T. *Eu.* 889, *he'll consent, only let her be a free born maid.* **magnō mē metū līberābis, dum
modo inter mē atque tē mūrus intersit,** *C.* 1, 10, *you will relieve me of
great fear, provided only there be a wall interposed between you and myself.*

(D.) dum, quoad, dōnec, *until.*

2004. dum, quoad or dōnec, *until,* often has as correlative usque,
usque eō, usque ad eum fīnem or tamdiū.

dum, *until.*

2005. The subjunctive present is used in a protasis introduced by **dum,** *until,* when the main verb denotes either indefinite or present time, and the subjunctive imperfect when the
main verb is past.

The subjunctive is an extension of the subjunctive of desire (1540); the
clause denotes something expected or proposed.

is dum veniat sedens ibĭ opperībere, Pl. *B.* 48, *you shall sit there
waiting till he comes.* **ōrandī sunt, ut sī quam habent ulcīscendī vim,
differant in tempus aliud, dum dēfervēscat īra,** *TD.* 4, 78, *we must
always ask such people, if they have any chance to take vengeance, to put it off
to some other time, till their rage cool down.* **cēnseō latendum tantisper
ibīdem, dum effervēscit haec grātulātiō et simul dum audiāmus,
quemadmodum negōtium cōnfectum sit,** *Fam.* 9, 2, 4, *I advise lying low
where you are, while the present congratulation excitement is cooling off, and at
the same time till we may hear how the job was done.* **dum reliquae nāvēs eō
convenīrent, in ancorīs exspectāvit,** 4, 23, 4, *he waited at anchor till the rest
of the vessels should gather there* (1725). **Verginius dum collēgam cōnsu-
leret morātus, dictātōrem dīxit,** L. 4, 21, 10, *Verginius, after waiting till he
should consult his colleague, appointed a dictator.* **observāvit dum dormitā-
ret canēs,** Pl. *Tri.* 170, *he watched till the dog should be napping.*

2006. The present indicative with **dum,** *while,* is sometimes used where
the subjunctive might be expected with **dum,** *until* (1593). Other indicative
tenses are rarely thus used: as,

(*a.*) **expectābō, dum venit,** T. *Eu.* 206, *I will wait while he comes.* **ego
hīc tantisper, dum exīs, tē opperiar,** Pl. *Most.* 683, *I'll wait for you here a
while till you come out.* **ego in Arcānō opperior, dum ista cōgnōscō,** *Att.*
10, 3, *for myself I am waiting at the Arcae place, till I ascertain this.* (*b.*) **mihĭ
quidem usque cūrae erit, quid agās, dum quid ēgerīs, scierō,** *Fam.* 12, 19,
3, *for me I shall be anxious all the time to know what you are doing, till I know
what you have done.* **mānsit in condiciōne usque ad eum finem dum
iūdicēs rēiectī sunt,** *V. a. pr.* 16, *he stuck to his bargain till the jurors were
challenged.*

quoad, dōnec, *until.*

2007. quoad or **dōnec,** *until,* introduces a protasis in the present
subjunctive when the main verb is present or future; and in the
perfect indicative when the main verb is past or a general present.

quoad is found once in Plautus with the imperfect subjunctive (2008); in other
authors here and there with both moods; not in Tacitus. With **dōnec** the present subjunctive is found once in Plautus, rarely in late Latin and in poetry: the perfect indicative is found at all periods; the present indicative (1590), found once in
Plautus, is poetic and late. But **dōnec** is rarely used by Cicero, and never by Caesar
or Sallust. **dōnicum** is found in old Latin (not in Terence) with the indicative
(2009), and once in Nepos with the subjunctive of indirect discourse. **dōnique** is
found four times in Lucretius with the indicative, always before vowels (2009).
dōneque and **dōneque cum** seem to occur a few times in Vitruvius.

(*a.*) **ego hīc cōgitō commorārī, quoad mē reficiam,** *Fam.* 7, 26, 2, *I am thinking of staying here till I feel better.* **ea continēbis, quoad ipse tē videam,** *Att.* 13, 21, 4, *you will keep this back till I see you myself.* **expergē-factīque secuntur inānia saepe cervōrum simulācra, dōnec discussīs re-deant errōribus ad sē,** Lucr. 4, 995, *and when awakened, often they still keep hunting the shadowy forms of stags, until the delusion is shaken off and they come to themselves.* **magnus mīrandusque cliēns sedet ad praetōria rēgis, dōnec Bīthȳnō libeat vigilāre tyrannō,** J. 10, 160, *a vassal great and strange he sits in the king's gate, till it may suit his oriental majesty to wake.* **inter eadem pecora dēgunt, dōnec aetās sēparet ingenuōs,** Ta. *G.* 20, *they always live among the same flocks and herds, till maturity puts the free-born by themselves.*

(*b.*) **nostrī reppulērunt neque fīnem sequendī fēcērunt, quoad equi-tēs praecipitēs hostēs ēgērunt,** 5, 17, 3, *our people routed them and did not give up the pursuit till the cavalry drove the enemy headlong.* **Milō cum in senātū fuisset eō diē quoad senātus est dīmissus, domum vēnit,** *Mil.* 28, *after staying in the senate that day till the senate adjourned, Milo went home.* **numquam dēstitit ōrāre usque adeō dōnec perpulit,** T. *Andr.* 660, *he never ceased to tease until he gained his point.* **nec timuī, dōnec ad rēiciun-dōs iūdicēs vēnimus,** *V.* 1, 17, *I was afraid all the time till we came to challenging jurors.* The present indicative of vivid narration (1590) is found in Vergil and Livy : as, **sociī cōnsurgere tōnsīs, dōnec rōstra tenent sic-cum et sēdēre carīnae omnēs innocuae,** V. 10, 299, *with one accord the shipmates rose to oars, until the beaks dry land attain, and keels all sat unscathed.*

2008. An imperfect subjunctive is rarely found with **quoad,** *until* (1725): as, **haec diēs praestitūtast, quoad referret,** Pl. *Ps.* 623, *this day was set by which he was to pay.* **exercēbātur currendō et lūctandō ad eum fīnem, quoad stāns complectī posset,** N. 15, 2, 5, *he used to practise running and wrestling, till he could give a grip standing.* For **dōnec,** see 2009 at the end.

2009. Other constructions occur, chiefly in old Latin or poetry, with **dōnec,** or **dōnicum,** *until.* (*a.*) The future perfect : as, **haud dēsinam, dōnec perfēcerō hōc,** T. *Ph.* 419, *I shall not stop till I have finished this.* **dēlicta maiōrum luēs, dōnec templa refēceris,** H. 3, 6, 1, *for sins of sires thou shalt atone, till thou hast shrines repaired.* (*b.*) The future: **coquitō usque dōnec conmadēbit bene,** Cato, *RR.* 156, 5, *boil until it is very soft.* **ter centum rēgnābitur annōs, dōnec geminam partū dabit Īlia prōlem,** V. 1, 272, *for thrice a hundred years there will be kings, till Ilia gives birth to twins.* (*c.*) The perfect indicative, less frequently the present, introductory to a general present : **impedit piscīs usque adeō, dōnicum ēdūxit forās,** Pl. *Tru.* 38, *he always draws his net about the fish, until he's brought them out* (1613). **usque mantant neque id faciunt, dōnicum parietēs ruont,** Pl. *Most.* 116, *they keep waiting and don't do it until the walls are falling.* (*d.*) The pluperfect indicative : **horriferis'accībant vōcibus Orcum, dōnique eōs vītā prīvārant vermina saeva,** Lucr. 5, 996, *with horrid cries on Death they'd call till gripings sore had set them free from life.* The imperfect indicative is found once in Tacitus, who also has the infinitive of inti-mation (1539) once or twice. An imperfect or pluperfect subjunctive sometimes occurs where purpose is intimated, and in Livy and late Latin to express repeated past action: as, **dōnec ēgregius properāret exsul,** H. 3, 5, 45, *till he could hasten forth a peerless exile.* **trepidātiōnis aliquantum ēdēbant, dōnec quiētem ipse timor fēcisset,** L. 21, 28, 11, *the elephants always displayed some nervous-ness, till terror itself restored quiet* (1730). But the habit of using the imperfect subjunctive is very common in Tacitus where neither purpose nor repetition is inti-mated : as **neque proelium omīsit dōnec caderet,** Ta. 3, 20, *he ceased not fighting till he fell.*

352

quandō.

2010. quandō, originally a temporal particle, has the meaning *when*, which readily passes over to a causal meaning, *since, because*. In both meanings it introduces the indicative. For special reasons, however, the subjunctive is used, as in indirect discourse (1725) or of action conceivable (1731). quandō is also used to introduce a conditional protasis (2110).

In simple sentences, temporal quandō is used in pronoun questions (1526). As an indefinite adverb it has the meaning *ever*.

(A.) TEMPORAL quandō.

2011. quandō, *when*, introduces a temporal clause with the indicative.

The time is often indefinite or iterative; so usually in old Latin. quandō often has tum as correlative.

fīō Iuppiter quandō lubet, Pl. *Am.* 864, *I turn into Jupiter at my sweet will.* laudātō quandō illud quod cupis effēcerō, Pl. *Cu.* 364, *cry your bravo when I've done what you desire.* quandō occāsiō illaec periīt, post sērō cupit. Pl. *A:ul.* 249, *when that chance is lost, he wants it all too late* (1613). quandō omnēs creātī sunt, tum ad eōs deus fātur, *Tim.* 40, *when all were created, then to them spake the god.* quandō pars maior in eandem sententiam ībat, bellum erat cōnsēnsum, L. 1, 32, 12, *when the majority voted for the same motion, war was always agreed upon.* Temporal quandō is found sporadically at all periods; not in Terence or Caesar.

2012. quandōque, *whenever*, is found once in the Twelve Tables, a few times in Cicero (chiefly in legal formulae), three times in Horace, and here and there in later authors. Not in Caesar.

(B.) CAUSAL quandō.

2013. quandō, *since, seeing that*, introduces a causal clause with the indicative.

The reason is usually one known to the person addressed or one generally known (1884). quandō is often strengthened by quidem.

quandō hīc serviō, haec patriast mea, Pl. *Per.* 641, *now that I am a slave here, this is my country.* quīn ergō abeis, quandō respōnsumst? Pl. *MG.* 1085, *why don't you go then, since you've had your answer?* melius est, quandōquidem hoc numquam mī ipse voluit dīcere, T. *Ad.* 639, *better so, since he would n't ever tell me about it of his own accord.* quandō mē in hunc locum dēdūxit ōrātiō, docēbō. *DN* 3, 43, *seeing that my discourse has brought me to this point, I will show.* haec dētur cūra cēnsōribus, quandōquidem eōs in rē pūblicā semper volumus esse, *Leg.* 3, 47, *let this be the charge of the censors, seeing that we want such officers always in our state.* prō urbe ac penātibus dīmicandum esse, quandō Ītaliam tuērī nequīssent, L. 22, 8, 7, *that they must fight for home and country, now that they had failed to preserve Italy* (1724). Causal quandō is found at all periods, though not in Caesar, and in Cicero's orations only with quidem.

2014. quandōque, *inasmuch as,* is used a few times in a formal or legal sense in Cicero and Livy : as, quandōque hīsce hominēs iniussū populī Rōmānī Quirītium foedus ictum īrī spopondērunt, L. 9, 10, 9, *inasmuch as these persons have promised that a covenant should be made, without the order of the Roman nation of Quirites.*

SĪ.

2015. sī, in early Latin sei, is originally a locative, meaning *under those circumstances, so.* With the enclitic -ce, it forms sīce or sīc, *so.* The two are sometimes found as correlatives in colloquial style : as, sīc scrībēs aliquid, sī vacābis, *Att.* 12, 38, 2, *so you shall have time, so you will write something.* See 708.

CONDITIONAL PERIODS.

2016. A protasis introduced by sī, *so, if,* or nisi, *unless, if not,* states a condition ; the apodosis states action occurring under that condition. The conditional protasis and apodosis combined make a *Conditional Period.*

Thus, sī diēs est, *if it is day,* is a conditional protasis ; combined with an apodosis, lūcet, *it is light,* it makes a conditional period : sī diēs est, lūcet, *Inv.* 1, 86, *if it is day, it is light.*

2017. A parenthesis with ut (1943) is added when the speaker asserts that the action of the protasis is not only assumed, but actually occurs : as, sī virtūs digna est glōriātiōne, ut est, beātus esse poterit virtūte ūnā praeditus, *Fin.* 4, 51, *if virtue is entitled to glorification, as it really is, he will find it possible to be happy in the possession of virtue alone.* sī nox opportūna est ēruptiōnī, sīcut est, haec profectō noctis aptissima hōra est, L. 7, 35, 10, *if night is always favourable for a sortie, and it always is, this particular hour of the night is surely the very best time.*

2018. The apodosis is usually declarative. Often, however, it is interrogative, exclamatory, or imperative, or it may take any other form which the thought or the context may require. The apodosis has rarely a correlative to sī : as, igitur, *it follows that,* idcircō, *for all that,* tum, *then,* ita, sīc, *only,* eā condiciōne, *on condition ;* at, *but,* tamen, *nevertheless,* certē, saltem, *at any rate,* tum dēnique, tum dēmum, *then and not till then.*

2019. sī is sometimes followed by quidem or, from Cicero on, by modo : sī quidem, *that is if, since, even if,* sī modo, *if only.* sī tamen, *at least if,* is found in Lucretius, Sallust, the Augustan poets and in late writers. sīve . . . sīve (seu . . . seu) or, in old Latin, sī . . . sīve, *whether . . . or,* with the indicative or the subjunctive of the indefinite second person (1556), leaves a choice between two cases possible. By abbreviation of the protasis sīve becomes a coordinating particle : see 1672.

2020. The negative of **sī** is **sī nōn**, *if not* (**sī nēmō, sī nūllus,** &c.), or **nisi,** *unless, if not,* used especially of an exception or after a negative. **nisi sī,** chiefly in old, colloquial, or late Latin, or, particularly in solemn language or poetry, **nī** is sometimes used for **nisi.** A restriction, usually an ironical afterthought, may be introduced by **nisi forte** (rare before Cicero) or **nisi vērō** (in Cicero and Pliny the Younger) with the indicative.

nisi is sometimes found in an adversative sense in old and colloquial Latin, especially after **nesciō**; from Cicero on, it may be strengthened by **tamen.** For nisi quod, see 1848.

2021. When a second conditional period is opposed to a first, it is sometimes introduced by **sī** (or **sī autem**), but usually by **sīn** (or **sīn autem**). If the second period is negative, and its verb is not expressed, **minus or aliter** is preferred to **nōn.**

CLASSES OF CONDITIONAL PROTASES.

2022. Conditional protases may be divided into two classes:

2023. I. INDETERMINATE protases, that is such as merely suppose an action, without implying either its occurrence or its non-occurrence ; these may take :

(A.) Any tense of the indicative required by the sense ; or (B.) the present subjunctive, less frequently the perfect subjunctive, to express a condition in the future.

2024. II. Protases of ACTION NON–OCCURRENT, that is such as suppose action not taking place. These take the imperfect or pluperfect subjunctive.

Thus, in the period sī diēs est, lūcet, *Inv.* 1, 86, *if it is day, it is light,* the protasis *if it is day* is indeterminate, neither implying that *it is,* or *is not day.* But in sī vīveret, verba eius audīrētis, *if he were alive, you would hear his evidence, RC.* 42, the protasis denotes action non-occurrent, *if he were alive,* implying *but he is not.* The whole period, like the protasis, is either an *Indeterminate Period* or a *Period of Action non-occurrent.*

I. INDETERMINATE PROTASES.

(A.) INDICATIVE USE.

2025. The indicative in a conditional protasis may state present, past, or future time.

The mood and tense of the apodosis are determined by the sense. The following combinations occur :

(I.) PROTASIS IN THE PRESENT.

2026.   (*a.*) Apodosis in the Present.

sī sunt dī, beneficī in hominēs sunt, *Div.* 2, 104, *if there are gods, they are kind to men.* sī nescīs, tibī īgnōscō, *Fam.* 10, 26, 3, *if you do not know, I pardon you.* deus sum, sī hoc itast, T. *Hec.* 843, *I am a god, if this is so.* erus sī tuos domīst, quīn prōvocās ? Pl. *Ps.* 638, *in case your master is at home, why don't you call him out ?* hōc mortuō, aut sī quī ex relíquīs excellit dignitāte, succēdit, aut, sī sunt plūrēs parēs, dē prīncipātū contendunt, 6, 13, 9, *when this man dies, if there is any one of the rest superior in position, he always takes his place; or if there are several with equal claims, they have a contest about the supremacy.* sī vīs, potes, H. *S.* 2, 6, 39, *you can, if you will.* in corpore sī quid eius modī est quod reliquō corporī noceat, id ūrī secārique patimur, *Ph.* 8, 15, *in the human body if there is anything likely to damage the rest of the body, we always allow it to be cauterized and cut.* sī cui vēnae sīc moventur, is habet febrim, *Fat.* 15, *if a man's pulse beats thus and so, he always has fever.* The present is sometimes loosely used of future time (1593): as, sī illum relinquō, eius vītae timeō, T. *Andr.* 210, *if I desert him, I tremble for his life.* assequor omnia, sī properō; sī cunctor, āmittō, *Att.* 10, 8, 5, *I shall compass all my ends, if I hurry ; if I delay, I shall lose everything.* castra nunc vōbīs hostium praedae dō, sī mihī pollicēminī vōs fortiter operam nāvātūrōs, L. 7, 16, 4, *I give you the camp of the enemy as booty now, if you promise me you will quit you like men.*

2027.   (*b.*) Apodosis in the Perfect.

sī hominēs ratiōnem ā dīs datam in fraudem convertunt, nōn darī illam quam darī hūmānō generī melius fuit, *DN.* 3, 78, *if men apply reason, the gift of the gods, to purposes of mischief, it would have been better it should not be given to the human race than given* (1495). The perfect of the apodosis is ordinarily used of future time (1612) : as, occidī, sī tū vēra memorās, Pl. *Most.* 369, *I'm a dead man, if what you say is true.* nunc sī indicium faciō, interiī; sī taceō, interiī tamen, Pl. *MG.* 306, *now if I tell, I'm dead and gone : if I keep dark, I'm dead and gone the same.* nī illōs hominēs expellō, ego occidī plānissumē, Pl. *St.* 401, *if I don't drive those people off, all's up with me.* nam sī argentum prius adfert, continuō nōs ambō exclūsī sumus, Pl. *As.* 360, *for if he brings the money first, then we're at once left out in the cold.*

2028.   (*c.*) Apodosis in the Imperfect.

sed sī domīst, Dēmaenetum volēbam, Pl. *As.* 452, *but if he is at home, Demaenetus I wanted.* iam tum erat senex, senectūs sī verēcundōs facit, T. *Ph.* 1023, *he was already old, if age is what makes shamefastness.* sī singula vōs forte nōn movent, ūniversa certē tamen movēre dēbēbant, *DN* 2, 163, *if these points taken severally do not affect you, yet collectively they surely should have done so* (1495).

2029.   (*d.*) Apodosis in the Pluperfect.

cesseram, sī aliēnam ā mē plēbem fuisse voltis, quae nōn fuit, invidiae, *Sest.* 64, *I had yielded, if you will have it that the commons were opposed to me, though they were not, to hatred.* hoc mī ūnum relicuom fuerat malum, sī puerum ut tollam cōgit, T. *Hec.* 570, *this was the only evil left in store for me, if he compels me to adopt the child.*

2030.   (*e.*) Apodosis in the Future.

sī interpellās, ego tacēbō, Pl. *Men.* 1121, *if you persist in breaking in, I'll hold my tongue.* hīc tū sī laesum tē esse dīcis, patiar et concēdam; sī iniūriam tibī factam quereris, dēfendam et negābō, *Caecil.* 58, *if you assert that you are hurt in this matter, I am perfectly willing to admit it; but if you complain that it is a violation of your rights, I shall stoutly maintain the contrary.* Often in this combination the present is loosely used of future time (1593): as, nunc sī ille hūc salvos revenit, reddam suom sibī; sī quid eō fuerit, habeō dōtem unde dem, Pl. *Tri.* 156, *now if our absent friend comes safely back, I'll give him back his own again; if anything befalls him, I've wherewith a dower to give.* nisi id cōnfestim facis, ego tē trādam magistrātuī, N. 15, 4, 3, *if you do not do it at once, I will hand you over to a magistrate.* sī pāce fruī volumus, bellum gerendum est; sī bellum omittimus, pāce numquam fruēmur, *Ph.* 7, 19, *if we wish to enjoy peace, we shall have to make war; if we give up war, we never shall enjoy peace.* convincam, sī negās, *C.* 1, 8, *I will bring it home to you, if you deny it.* tibi dīvitiās dabō, sī impetrās, Pl. *MG.* 1213, *I'll make you rich, if you succeed.*

2031.   (*f.*) Apodosis in the Future Perfect.

sī nequeō facere ut abeās, egomet abierō, Pl. *Poen.* 442, *if I can't make you go, I'll instantly begone myself* (1629). sī id nōn facis, ego quod mē in tē sit facere dignum invēnerō, T. *Hau.* 107, *if you don't do it, I will have a proper course devised to use with you.*

2032.   (*g.*) Apodosis in the Imperative.

dā mihī hoc, mel meum, sī mē amās, Pl. *Tri.* 244, *give me this, honey mine, an thou lov'st me.* redargue mē, sī mentior, *Clu.* 62, *refute me, if I am not speaking the truth.* dēsilīte, mīlitēs, nisi vultis aquilam hostibus prōdere, 4, 25, 3, *jump overboard, men, unless you choose to abandon your eagle to the enemy.* nī iūdicātum facit, sēcum dūcitō, vincitō compedibus, Twelve Tables in Gell. 20, 1, 45, *unless he satisfies the judgement, the complainant shall take him with him, and put him in gyves* (1593, 1575). quā rē, sī haec ita sunt, sīc mē colitōte ut deum, *CM.* 81, *therefore, if this is so, you are to honour me as a god.*

2033. (*h.*) Apodosis in the Present Subjunctive.

sī quid habēs certius, velim scīre, *Att.* 4, 10, 1, *if you have any-thing more definite, I should like to know* (1554). sīn aliter animātus es, bene, quod agās, ēveniat tibī, Pl. *Tri.* 715, *but if you 're minded otherwise, may all you do betide you well* (1540). quod sī nōn possumus facere, mori-āmur, *Ph.* 7, 14, *if we cannot do it, let us die* (1547). sī mihī fīlius genitur, isque prius moritur, et cētera, tum mihī ille sit hērēs, *DO.* 2, 141, *if a son is born to me, and the boy dies before &c., &c., then so and so is to be my heir* (1593, 1548). sī est spēs nostrī reditūs, eam cōnfirmēs, *Fam.* 14, 4, 3, *if there is a hope of my coming back, strengthen that hope* (1550). eum sī reddis mihi, praetereā ūnum nummum nē duīs, Pl. *Cap.* 331, *if you restore my boy to me, you need n't give one penny more* (1551). sī hīc pernoctō, causae quid dīcam? T. *Ad.* 531, *if I sleep here, what reason can I give* (1563)?

(2.) PROTASIS IN THE PERFECT.

2034. (*a.*) Apodosis in the Present.

sī quid vēnāle habuit Heius, sī id quantī aestimābat, tantī vēndidit, dēsinō quaerere cūr ēmeris, *V.* 4, 10, *if Hejus had anything for sale, if he sold it at his own valuation, I stop enquiring why you bought.* sī vērē est ā nōbīs philosophia laudāta, eius tractātiō optimō quōque dignissima est, *Ac.* 2, 6, *if philosophy has been extolled by me with justice, its study is eminently worthy of the good.* sī honōris causā statuam dedērunt, inimīcī nōn sunt, *V.* 2, 150, *if they contributed a statue as a compliment, they are not enemies.* postēs quoiusmodī? . . . etiam nunc satis bonī sunt, sī sunt inductī pice, Pl. *Most.* 818, *what think you of the posts? . . . they're pretty good even now, if they are only smeared with pitch.* This combination is common in general con-ditional periods (1613): as, hominēs aegrī sī aquam gelidam bibērunt, prīmō relevārī videntur, *C.* 1, 31, *if sick people drink cold water, at first they always seem refreshed.* sī quod est admissum facinus, īdem dēcernunt, 6, 13, 5, *if a crime has been committed, they also act as judges.* abiūrant, sī quid crēditumst, Pl. *Cur.* 496, *they always swear they haven't it, if anything is trusted them.* sī puer parvus occidit, aequō animō ferendum putant, *TD.* 1, 93, *if a baby dies, they always think the affliction should be borne with resignation.*

2035. (*b.*) Apodosis in the Perfect.

sī peccāvī, īnsciēns fēcī, T. *Hau.* 631, *if I've done wrong, it was in igno-rance.* haec bona in tabulās pūblicās sī rediērunt, tabulae pūblicae conruptae sunt, *RA.* 128, *if this property has been entered on the state books, then the state books have been tampered with.* quō in bellō sī fuit error, commūnis ēī fuit cum senātū, *Ph.* 11, 34, *if there was a mistake in this war, it was common to him and the senate.* interiī, sī abiīt, Pl. *Ps.* 910, *I 'm lost, if he has gone* (1608). Also in general periods (1613): as, animī sī quandō vēra vīdērunt, ūsī sunt fortūnā atque cāsū, *Div.* 2, 108, *if the mind has ever seen the truth, it has used in every case luck and chance.* studiōsē equi-dem ūtor nostrīs poētīs, sed sīcubi illī dēfēcērunt, vertī multa dē Graecīs, *TD.* 2, 26, *I use our own poets carefully, it is true; but whenever they have failed me, I have always translated a great deal from Greek.*

358

2036. (*c.*) Apodosis in the Pluperfect.

sī illud iūre rogātum dīcere ausī sunt, oblītīne erant ? *PC.* 45, *if they ventured to say that that measure was brought forward in due form, had not they forgotten ?*

2037. (*d.*) Apodosis in the Future.

sī quis oriente canīculā nātus est, is in marī nōn moriētur, *if anybody is born when the dogstar is rising, he will never die at sea* (general) : sī Fabius oriente canīculā nātus est, Fabius in marī nōn moriētur, *Fat.* 12, *if Fabius was born when the dogstar was rising, Fabius will not die at sea* (particular). sī parum intellēxtī, dīcam dēnuō, Pl. *R.* 1103, *if you don't understand, I'll say again.* nōn ūtar eā cōnsuētūdine, sī quid est factum clēmenter, ut dissolūtē factum crīminer, *V.* 5, 19, *I will not avail myself of the common practice, and if a thing has been done in a spirit of mercy, charge that it was done in a lax way.* nisi iam factum aliquid est per Flaccum, fīet ā mē, *Fam.* 3, 11, 3, *unless something or other has been done already through Flaccus, it will be done by me.*

2038. (*e.*) Apodosis in the Imperative.

sī plūs minusve secuērunt, sē fraude estō, Twelve Tables in Gell. 20, 1, 49, *if they cut too much or too little, it shall be without penalty* (1613). sī vīdistis, dīcite, Pl. *R.* 323, *if ye have seen, declare.* sī quid est peccātum ā nōbīs, prōfer, T. *Hec.* 253, *declare it, if we've erred at all.* sī numquam avārē pretium statuī artī meae, exemplum statuite in mē, T. *Hau.* 48, *if never like a miser I have set a price upon my art, a pattern set in me.* sī quōs propīnquus sanguīs patrōnōs dedit, iuvāte perīclitantem, Ta. 3, 12, *if relationship has made any of you his advocates, help him in his straits.*

2039. (*f.*) Apodosis in the Present Subjunctive.

sī nūlla colōris prīncipiīs est reddita nātūra, extemplō ratiōnem reddere possīs, Lucr. 2, 757, *if atoms have no colour, you might explain at once* (1556). meritō maledīcās mī, sī nōn id ita factumst, Pl. *Am.* 572, *you might with perfect right abuse me, if it is not so* (1556).

2040. (*g.*) Apodosis in the Imperfect Subjunctive.

sī nēmō hāc praeteriit, postquam intrō abiī, cistella hīc iacēret, Pl. *Cist.* 683, *if nobody has passed along this way, since I went in, a casket must have been lying here* (1560). nam cūr tam variae rēs possent esse requīrō, ex ūnō sī sunt ignī pūrōque creātae ? Lucr. 1, 645, *for how could things so motley be, I ask, if they are made of pure and simple fire* (1565) ?

2041. (*h.*) Apodosis in the Pluperfect Subjunctive.

sī Antōniō Crassus ēloquēns vīsus nōn est, tibī numquam Cotta vīsus esset, *O.* 106, *if Antony did not hold Crassus eloquent, you would never have held Cotta so* (1561).

(3.) PROTASIS IN THE IMPERFECT.

2042. (*a.*) Apodosis in the Present.

sī tum nōn pertimēscēbās, nē nunc quidem perhorrēscis? *V.* 4, 78, *if you were not getting afraid then, are you not getting scared even now?* sī quī senēs āc dēfōrmēs erant, eōs in hostium numerō dūcit, *V.* 5, 64, *if any were old and homely, he considers them in the light of enemies* (1590). sī ad illum hērēditās veniēbat, vērī simile est ab illō necātum, *Inv.* 1, 89, *if the inheritance was coming to so and so, it is likely that the murder was committed by that man.* adulēscentī nihil est quod suscēnseam, sī illum minus nōrat, T. *Ph.* 361, *I have no cause for anger with the youth, if he was not acquainted with the man.*

2043. (*b.*) Apodosis in the Perfect.

sed sī properābās magis, prīdiē nōs tē hūc dūxisse oportuit, Pl. *Poen.* 525, *but if you were in greater haste, you should have brought us here the day before.*

2044. (*c.*) Apodosis in the Imperfect.

This combination is used chiefly of contemporaneous action (1732), in general conditional periods: as, sī quod erat grande vās, laetī adferēbant, *V.* 4, 47, *if any good-sized vase was ever found, they would always bring it to him in high glee.* atque ea sī erant, magnam habēbās dīs grātiam, Pl. *As.* 143, *and if them you ever had, you were monstrous grateful to the gods.* sī quae rēs erat maior, populus commovēbātur, *Sest.* 105, *if a thing of more than ordinary importance occurred, the populace was always aroused.* hī, sī quid erat dūrius, concurrēbant, 1, 48, 6, *whenever there was any pretty sharp work, these men would always fall to.* For the subjunctive in such protases, see 2071.

2045. (*d.*) Apodosis in the Future.

flēbunt Germānicum etiam īgnōtī: vindicābitis vōs, sī mē potius quam fortūnam meam fovēbātis, Ta. 2, 71, *as for weeping for Germanicus, that will be done by strangers too; vengeance will be yours, if you honoured in me more the man than the position.* See *Att.* 14, 1, 1.

2046. (*e.*) Apodosis in the Present Subjunctive.

fac animō magnō sīs, et sī turbidissima sapienter ferēbās, tranquilliōra laetē ferās, *Fam.* 6, 14, 3, *be of great heart, and if you bore anarchy like a stoic, bear a more orderly condition of things with good cheer* (1550).

2047. (*f.*) Apodosis in the Imperfect Subjunctive.

sī amābās, invenīrēs mūtuom, Pl. *Ps.* 286, *you should have borrowed, if you were in love* (1559). quod sī meīs incommodīs laetābantur, urbis tamen perīculō commovērentur, *Sest.* 54, *if they did exult over my mishaps, still they ought to have been touched by the danger to Rome* (1559).

(4.) Protasis in the Pluperfect.

2048. (*a.*) Apodosis in the Present.

sī hoc ita fātō datum erat, ut ad pācem petendam venīrem, laetor tē mihī sorte potissimum datum, ā quō peterem, L. 30, 30, 3, *if it was so ordained by fate that I should come to sue for peace, I am glad that you are allotted me, of all men in the world, to sue from.*

2049. (*b.*) Apodosis in the Perfect.

tum id, sī falsum fuerat, fīlius quōr nōn refellit? T. *Ph.* 400, *if that had been untrue, why did not at the time your son disprove it?* vel officiō, sī quid dēbuerat, vel errōrī, sī quid nescierat, satis factum esse dūxit, *D.* 13, *he thought he had done enough for duty, if he had been under any obligation, enough for delusion, if he had been acting under mistaken ignorance.*

2050. (*c.*) Apodosis in the Imperfect.

sed in aedibus quid tibi meīs nam erat negōtī mē absente, nisi ego iusseram? Pl. *Aul.* 427, *but what business had you in my house in my absence, unless I had ordered?* sī nihil in istā pugnā Rōsciī fēcerant, quam ob causam tantīs praemiīs dōnābantur? *RA.* 108, *if the Rosciuses had not done service in that fight, why were they presented with such rewards?* Often of antecedent action, in general conditional periods: as, sī quicquam caelātī adspexerat, manūs abstinēre, iūdicēs, nōn poterat, *V.* 4, 48, *if he ever caught sight of a bit of chased work, why, gentlemen, he never could keep his hands off.* stomachābātur senex, sī quid asperius dīxeram, *DN.* 1, 93, *the old gentleman was always nettled, if I said anything harsh.* ac seu longum post tempus vēnerat hospes, sīve convīva per imbrem vīcīnus, bene erat nōn piscibus urbe petītīs, H. *S.* 2, 2, 118, *and if a friend dropped in, after an absence long, or neighbour, come to take pot-luck upon a rainy day, we feasted not on fish brought out from town.* For the subjunctive in such protases, see 2071.

2051. (*d.*) Apodosis in the Imperfect Subjunctive.

ante sōlem exorientem nisi in palaestram vēnerās, haud mediocrīs poenās penderēs, Pl. *B.* 426, *ere sunrise so you came not to the wrestling school, amercement strong you had to pay* (1552).

(5.) Protasis in the Future.

2052. (*a.*) Apodosis in the Present.

eam sei cūrābeis, perbonast, Pl. *Merc.* 526, *if you'll take care of her, she is first-rate.* quod sī perferre nōn poterō, opprimī mē mālō, *RA.* 10, *if I cannot succeed in bearing it, I would rather be crushed.*

2053. (*b.*) **Apodosis in the Perfect.**

quam nisi dēfendēs, Rōmulus nōn bene vīdit avēs, Prop. 4 (5), 6, 43, *unless thou savest her, 'twas ill that Romulus espied his birds.* āctumst, sī quidem tū mē hīc lūdificābere, T. *Eu.* 717, *all's up, that is in case you fool me here* (1612). cui sī esse in urbe licēbit, vīcimus, *Att.* 14, 20, 3, *if he shall be allowed to stay in town, the day is ours* (1612).

2054. (*c.*) **Apodosis in the Future.**

sī erum īnsimulābis malitiae, male audiēs, T. *Ph.* 359, *you'll hear what you won't like, if you insinuate anything wrong against master.* vīcīnīs bonus estō : sī tē libenter vīcīnitās vidēbit, facilius tua vēndēs ; sī aedificābis, operīs, iūmentīs, māteriē adiuvābunt, Cato, *RR.* 4, *be obliging to your neighbours : if the neighbourhood looks on you with favour, you will find a readier sale for your produce ; if you fall to building, they will help you with labour, draught animals, and building material.* sī id audēbis dīcere, causam in-imīcī tuī sublevābis, *Caecil.* 12, *if you venture to say that, you will promote the cause of your enemy.* sī fortūna volet, fīēs dē rhētore cōnsul ; sī volet haec eadem, fīēs dē cōnsule rhētor, J. 7, 197, *if fortune shall ordain, a mag-nate from a teacher thou shalt be ; again shall she ordain, a teacher from a magnate shalt thou be.* nōn modo nōn laedētur causa nōbilitātis, sī istīs hominibus resistētis, vērum etiam ōrnābitur, *RA.* 138, *the interests of the nobility will not be damaged, if you resist those creatures ; oh no, on the contrary, they will be promoted.* The clause with sī is apt to take the future perfect (2061). The future in the apodosis often denotes action holding good at all times : as, dēfēnsor prīmum, ∷ poterit, dēbēbit vītam eius, quī īnsimu-lābitur, quam honestissimam dēmōnstrāre, *Inv.* 2, 35, *the advocate ought in the first place, if he can, to prove that the life of the accused is eminently re-spectable.* quod adsequemur, sī cavēbimus nē in perturbātiōnēs incidā-mus, *Off.* 1, 131, *we shall attain this end if we take care not to be subject to fits of passion.* Sometimes in exemplifications : sī patriam prōdere cōnābitur pater, silēbitne fīlius ? *Off.* 3, 90, *if a father shall try to betray his country, will the son keep silent ?* But see 2090.

2055. (*d.*) **Apodosis in the Future Perfect.**

oculum ego ecfodiam tibī : : dīcam tamen ; nam sī sīc nōn licēbit, luscus dīxerō, Pl. *Tri.* 463, *I'll dig your eye out : : but I'll speak, nathless ; for if I may not as I am, I'll say my say as one-eyed man.* sed sī tē aequō ani-mō ferre accipiet, neclegentem fēceris, T. *Andr.* 397, *but if he sees you take it placidly, you'll have him off his guard.* The more usual combination is as in 2062.

2056. (*e.*) **Apodosis in the Imperative.**

vir tuos sī veniet, iube domī opperīrier, Pl. *Cist.* 592, *in case your hus-band comes, tell him to wait at home.* Almost always the second imperative is used (1577) : as, sī volet, suō vīvitō, Twelve Tables in Gell. 20, 1, 45, *if the prisoner wish, he may subsist on his own food.* sī veniet nūntius, facitō ut sciam, Pl. *St.* 148, *if a messenger shall come, be sure you let me know.* sī dē mē ipsō plūra dīcere vidēbor, īgnōscitōte, *Sest.* 31, *if I seem to harp too much on myself, you must excuse me.*

2057. (*f.*) Apodosis in the Present Subjunctive.

sī quid erit, quod scrībendum putēs, velim faciās, *Att.* 11, 13, 5, *if there shall be anything which you think worth writing, I wish you would write* (1555). nam sī altera illaec magis īnstābit, forsitan nōs reiciat, T. *Ph.* 717, *for if the other lady presses more, perhaps he'll throw us out* (1554). peream, sī tē ferre poterunt, Brut. in *Fam.* 11, 23, 2, *may I die, if they shall find it possible to endure you* (1541). sī quandō illa dīcet ' Phaedriam intrō mittāmus,' Pamphilam cantātum prōvocēmus, T. *Eu.* 441, *if ever she shall say ' let us have Phaedria in,' then let us call out Pamphila to sing* (1548). habeat, sī argentum dabit, Pl. *R.* 727, *she's welcome to them, if she pays the cash* (1548).

2058. (*g.*) Apodosis in the Perfect Subjunctive.

sī mē audiētis, adulēscentēs, sōlem alterum nē metuerītis, *RP.* 1, 32, *if you will hearken to me, my young friends, never fear a double sun* (1551). sīn erit ille gemitus ēlāmentābilis, vix eum virum dīxerim, *TD.* 2, 57, *but if his groan be a long-drawn wail, I could scarcely call him a man* (1558).

(6.) Protasis in the Future Perfect.

2059. (*a.*) Apodosis in the Present.

salvae sunt, sī istōs flūctūs dēvītāverint, Pl. *R.* 168, *they are saved, if they escape those waves* (1593). rēx sum, sī ego illum hominem adlexerō, Pl. *Poen.* 671, *I'm a millionaire, if I allure the man* (1593). crīmen probāre tē cēnsēs posse, sī nē causam quidem maleficī prōtuleris ? *RA.* 72, *do you think you can prove your charge, if you do not even bring forward a motive for the crime ?* quod sī meam spem vīs improbōrum fefellerit, commendō vōbīs meum parvum fīlium, *C.* 4, 23, *but if the might of the wicked disappoints my hope, unto your keeping do I commend the little son of mine.*

2060. (*b.*) Apodosis in the Perfect.

victus sum, sī dīxeris, Pl. *Am.* 428, *I am beaten if you tell* (1612). sī sēnserit, periī, T. *Andr.* 213, *if he scents it, I'm done for* (1612). sī cōnservātus erit, vīcimus, *Fam.* 12, 6, 2, *if he is saved, our success is assured* (1612). tum, hercule, illō diē quō ego cōnsul sum creātus, male gesta rēs pūblica est, sī tuleritis, L. 3, 19, 11, *in that case it was indeed a bad day for the country when I was made consul, if you make the proposition* (1608).

2061. (*c.*) Apodosis in the Future.

perībō, sī nōn fēcerō, sī faxō vāpulābō, Pl. in Gell. 3, 3, 8, *I shall be done for if I don't do it, if I do, I shall be done up too* (1626). oculum ego ecfodiam tibī, sī verbum addideris, Pl. *Tri.* 463, *I'll gouge your eye out for you, if you say another word.* sī tē interficī iusserō, residēbit in rē pūblicā reliqua coniūrātōrum manus, *C.* 1, 12, *if I order you to be dispatched, the rest of the gang of conspirators will be left in the state.*

363

2062.   (*d.*) **Apodosis in the Future Perfect.**

sī dīxerō mendācium, solēns meō mōre fēcerō, Pl. *Am.* 198, *if fiction I relate, I shall have done but in my usual way.* sī tū argentum attuleris, cum illō perdiderō fidem, Pl. *Ps.* 376, *if you, sir, bring the cash, I'll break my word to him.* respīrārō, sī tē vīderō, *Att.* 2, 24, 5, *I shall be myself again, if I see you.* pergrātum mihī fēceris, sī dē amīcitiā disputāris, *L.* 16, *you will do me a very great favour, if you will discourse on friendship.*

2063.   (*e.*) **Apodosis in the Imperative.**

Generally the longer forms of the imperative are used (1577) : patrōnus sī clientī fraudem fēcerit, sacer estō, Twelve Tables in Serv. to V. 6, 609, *if a patron shall cheat his client, let him be doomed.* servītum tibi mē abdū- citō, nī fēcerō, Pl. *Ps.* 520, *if I don't do it, take me off to be your slave.* hoc sī effēceris, quodvīs dōnum ā mē optātō, T. *Eu.* 1056, *if you do this, ask any gift you please of me.* sī mē adsequī potueris, ut tibī vidēbitur, sepelītō, *TD.* 1, 103, *if you can ever find me, then bury me as you think best.* Rarely the shorter forms : inpinge pugnum, sī muttīverit, Pl. *B.* 800, *drive your fist into him if he says booh.* sī tumidōs accēdere fastūs sēnseris, inceptō parce referque pedem, O. *AA.* 1, 715, *if thou shalt see disdain come swelling high, give o'er and beat retreat.*

2064.   (*f.*) **Apodosis in the Present Subjunctive.**

sibī habeat, sī nōn extemplō ab eō abdūxerō, Pl. *Per.* 164, *he may keep her, if I don't carry her off that minute* (1548). sī tē potuisse superārī dīxerō, *Planc.* 6, *if I say that you can be sur- passed, I should own myself swept along like a blind man* (1556). tum magis adsentiāre, sī ad maiōra pervēnerō, *RP.* 1, 62, *you would agree all the more if I come at once to weightier points* (1556).

Some Special Uses.

2065. An indicative protasis with sī is often used to assume a general truth as a proof either for another general truth, or for a particular fact.

(*a.*) sī voluptātis sēnsum capit, dolōrēs etiam capit, *DN.* 3, 32, *if it is susceptible of pleasure, it is also susceptible of pain.* sī omnēs, quī rēī pūb- licae cōnsulunt, cārī nōbīs esse dēbent, certē in prīmīs imperātōrēs. sī ferae partūs suōs dīligunt, quā nōs in līberōs nostrōs indulgentiā esse dēbēmus, *DO.* 2, 168, *if all people who are devoted to the public service are dear to us, then assuredly our military men ought always to be particularly dear. If wild beasts always love their young, how kind ought we always to be to our own children.* (*b.*) sī pietātī summa tribuenda laus est, dēbētis movērī, cum Q. Metellum tam piē lūgēre videātis, *DO.* 2, 167, *if filial affection is always to be held in high honour, you ought to be touched in this instance, seeing such affectionate grief in Metellus.* sī nox opportūna est ēruptiōnī, sīcut est, haec profectō noctis aptissima hōra est, *L.* 7, 35, 10, *if night is always favourable for a sortie, and it always is, this particular hour of the night is the very best time.*

2066. An indicative protasis with sī often assumes a fact, past or present, as an argument for another fact, or for a general truth.

In this case the apodosis, which is usually a question, often takes the subjunctive (1565).

sī Sūlla potuit efficere, ut dictātor dīcerētur, cūr hīc nōn possit? *Att.* 9, 15, 2, *if Sulla could succeed in being appointed dictator, why cannot this man?* sī Zēnōnī licuit inaudītum rēī nōmen impōnere, cūr nōn liceat Catōnī? *Fin.* 3, 15, *if Zeno was allowed to give a new name to a thing, why should not Cato be allowed?* quod sī Graecī leguntur ā Graecīs, quid est cūr nostrī ā nostrīs nōn legantur? *Fin.* 1, 6, *but if Greeks are read by Greeks, why should not Romans be read by Romans?*

2067. An indicative protasis with sī often assumes a fact which is declared in the apodosis to be no reason for another fact.

In this case the negative usually begins the period. sī, for which quia or etsī is sometimes substituted, sometimes has idcircō, īlicō, or continuō, rarely proptereā or ideō, as correlative in the apodosis.

nōn, sī tibī anteā prōfuit, semper prōderit, *Ph.* 8, 12, *even if it has done you good in the past, that is no reason why it always will in the future.* nōn sī Opīmium dēfendistī, idcircō tē istī bonum cīvem putābunt, *DO.* 2, 170, *suppose you did defend Opimius, that is no reason why your friends will think you a patriot.* nec sī omne ēnūntiātum aut vērum aut falsum est, sequitur īlicō, esse causās immūtābilīs, quae prohibeant secus cadere atque cāsūrum sit, *Fat.* 28, *and even if every aeclaration is either true or false, it does not follow without any further ado that there are unchangeable causes to prevent a thing falling out different from the way it promises to fall out.* nōn continuō, sī mē in gregem sīcāriōrum contulī, sum sīcārius, *RA.* 94, *it does not forthwith follow that if I have joined a band of bravoes, I am a bravo.*

mīror, mīrum sī.

2068. mīror or mīrum est (mīra sunt) may introduce a conditional protasis, instead of a clause with quod (1851) or the accusative with the infinitive (2188).

Generally the main clause is actually or virtually negatived: as, minus mīrandumst, illaec aetās sī quid illōrum facit, Pl. *B.* 409, *'tis not to be wondered at, if youth does things like that.* idne tū mīrāre, sī patrissat fīlius? Pl. *Ps.* 442, *can you, sir, wonder at it if the son plays the father?* nec mīrum sī ūtēbātur cōnsiliō, *Quinct.* 18, *and it is no wonder if he followed the advice.* mīrer, sī vāna vestra auctōritās est? L. 3, 21, 4, *can I think it strange if your influence is of no account* (1565)? Rarely the main clause is positive: as, mīrābar hoc sī sīc abīret, T. *Andr.* 175, *I wondered if it was going to end so* (1773). mīror sī quemquam amīcum habēre potuit, L. 54, *I wonder if he could have had a friend in the world.* In old colloquial style mīrum nī is found: as, mīrum nī hīc mē exossāre cōgitat, Pl. *Am.* 319, *strange that he does n't think of boning me.* ubi nunc ipsus? : : mīrum nī domīst, T. *Andr.* 598, *where is he now? : : at home of course.* So once in Livy: mīrum esse nī castra hostium oppugnentur, L. 3, 28, 5, *that he should n't be surprised if the enemy's camp were being stormed* (1724). gaudeō sī is found once in Cicero, and terreō, metus est sī, or the like occurs a few times in Tacitus. For sī in expressions of trial, hope, expectation, &c., see 1777.

365

THE SUBJUNCTIVE FOR THE INDICATIVE.

2069. The indicative in the protasis is occasionally replaced by the subjunctive, as follows :

2070. (1.) The present or perfect subjunctive is sometimes used in general present suppositions, regularly in the indefinite second person singular, rarely with other persons (1730) : as,

(*a.*) nam dolī nōn dolī sunt nisi astū colās, sed malum maxumum, sī id palam prōvenit, Pl. *Cap.* 221, *for tricks are never tricks, unless you handle them with craft, but damage dire, in case the thing gets out ;* here the indicative prōvenit shows that colās is due to the person. nec calidae citius dēcēdunt corpore febrēs, textilibus sī in pictūrīs ostrōque rubentī iactēris, quam sī in plēbēiā veste cubandum est, Lucr. 2, 34, *nor sooner will hot fevers leave the limbs, if on gay tapestries and blushing purple you should toss, than if perforce your bed you make on pallet rude.* quod est difficile, nisi speciem prae tē bonī virī ferās, *Off.* 2, 39, *and this is a hard thing, unless you have the exterior of a good man.* nec habēre virtūtem satis est nisi ūtāre, *RP.* 1, 2, *and to have virtue is not enough, unless one use it.* sīquoi mūtuom quid dederīs, fit prō propriō perditum, Pl. *Tri.* 1051, *if aught you've lent to anyone, 't is not your own, but lost.* nam nūllae magis rēs duae plūs negōtī habent, sī occēperīs exōrnāre, Pl. *Poen.* 212, *for no two things give more trouble if you once begin to fit them out.* nūlla est excūsātiō peccātī, sī amīcī causā peccāverīs, *L.* 37, *it is no excuse for a sin if you have sinned from friendship.*

(*b.*) suōs quisque opprimī nōn patitur, neque, aliter sī faciat, ūllam inter suōs habet auctōritātem, 6, 11, 4, *nobody suffers his vassals to be put down, and if he ever act otherwise, he has no influence among his people.* laeduntur artēriae, sī ācrī clāmōre compleantur, Cornif. 3, 21, *it always hurts the windpipe, if it be filled out with a sharp scream.* turpis excūsātiō est, sī quis contrā rem pūblicam sē amīcī causā fēcisse fateātur, *L.* 40, *it is always a discreditable apology, if a man confess that he has been unpatriotic from motives of friendship.* Britannī iniūncta imperiī mūnera impigrē obeunt, sī iniūriae absint, Ta. *Agr.* 13, *the Britons are always perfectly ready to perform the duties enjoined on them by the Roman government, if they be not maltreated.*

2071. (2.) The imperfect or pluperfect subjunctive is sometimes used in general past suppositions (1730).

This use begins with Catullus and Caesar, the indicative being the regular classical construction (2044, 2050).

chommoda dīcēbat, sī quandō commoda vellet dīcere Arrius, Cat. 84, 1, *hadvantages said Arrius, if advantages he ever meant to say.* sī quis prehenderētur, cōnsēnsū mīlitum ēripiēbātur, Caes. *C.* 3, 110, 4, *every time a man was taken up, he was rescued by the joint action of the rank and file.* sīn autem locum tenēre vellent, nec virtūtī locus relinquēbātur, neque coniecta tēla vītāre poterant, 5, 35, 4, *but if on the other hand they undertook to hold their position, there was never any opening for bravery, nor could they ever dodge the shower of missiles.* sīn Numidae propius accessissent, ibī virtūtem ostendere, S. *I.* 58, 3, *they showed forth their valour every time the Numidians drew near* (1535).

(B.) SUBJUNCTIVE USE.

2072. The present or perfect subjunctive may be used in a conditional protasis of future time.

2073. The apodosis is usually in the present subjunctive, less frequently in the perfect subjunctive. The imperfect and pluperfect subjunctive are rare (2089).

2074. The indicative is sometimes used in the apodosis, especially in expressions of ability, duty, &c. (1495); **nōn possum** is regularly in the indicative when the protasis is also negative. For the future indicative the periphrastic form is sometimes used.

2075. In the early period, before the imperfect subjunctive had been shifted to denote present time in conditional sentences (2091), the present subjunctive was used to express action non-occurrent in present time. Examples of this use are found in Plautus: as, **sī honestē cēnseam tē facere posse, suādeam; vērum nōn potest; cave faxīs**, Pl. *MG.* 1371, *if I thought that you could do the thing with credit to yourself, I should advise you to; but 'tis impossible; so don't you do it.* **vocem tē ad cēnam, nisi egomet cēnem forīs**, Pl. *St.* 190, *I should ask you home to dine, if I were not dining out myself.* Such sentences must not be confused with those in which an action from the nature of things impossible is represented as of possible occurrence.

(I.) Protasis in the Present Subjunctive.

2076. (*a.*) Apodosis in the Present Subjunctive.

at pigeat posteā nostrum erum, sī vōs eximat vinculīs, Pl. *Cap.* 203, *but it may rue our master by and by, if he should take you out of bonds.* **quid sī ēveniat dēsubitō prandium, ubī ego tum accumbam?** Pl. *B.* 79, *suppose a lunch should suddenly come off, where is your humble servant then to lie* (1563)? **hanc viam sī asperam esse negem, mentiar**, *Sest.* 100, *if I say that this path is not rough, I should not tell the truth.* **sī deus tē interroget, quid respondeās?** *Ac.* 2, 80, *if a god ask you, what would you answer?* **haec sī tēcum patria loquātur, nōnne impetrāre dēbeat?** *C.* 1, 19, *if thy country plead with thee thus, ought she not to carry her point?* **sī existat hodiē ab īnferīs Lycūrgus, sē Spartam antīquam āgnōscere dīcat**, L. 39, 37, 3, *if Lycurgus rise this day from the dead, he would say that he recognized the Sparta of yore.* **eōs nōn cūrāre opīnor, quid agat hūmānum genus; nam sī cūrent, bene bonīs sit, male malīs, quod nunc abest**, E. in *Div.* 2, 104, *DN.* 3, 79, *but little care the gods, I trow, how fares the race of man; for should they care, the good were blest, the wicked curst; a thing that really cometh not to pass.*

2077.   (*b.*) Apodosis in the Perfect Subjunctive.

sī aequom siet mē plūs sapere quam vōs, dederim vōbīs cōnsilium catum, Pl. *E.* 257, *if it becoming be for me to have more wit than ye, sage counsel might I give* (1558).   aufūgerim potius quam redeam, sī eō mihi redeundum sciam, T. *Hec.* 424, *I'd run away sooner than go back, if I should hear I had to* (1558).   nec satis sciō, nec sī sciam, dīcere ausim, L. *praef.* 1, *in the first place I do not know very well, and secondly if I should know, I should not venture to say* (1555).   iniussū tuō extrā ōrdinem numquam pugnāverim, nōn sī certam victōriam videam, L. 7, 10, 2, *without orders from you I never should fight out of ranks, no, not if I saw victory was certain* (1558).   tum vērō nēquīquam hāc dextrā capitōlium servāverim, si cīvem commīlitōnemque meum in vincula dūcī videam, L. 6, 14, 4, *upon my word, in that case I should prove to have saved the capitol in vain, if I saw a townsman and brother-in-arms of mine haled to jail.*   multōs circā ūnam rem ambitūs fēcerim, sī quae variant auctōrēs omnia exequī velim, L. 27, 27, 12, *I should make a long story about one subject, if I should undertake to go through all the different versions of the authorities.*

2078.   (*c.*) Apodosis in the Present Indicative.

quī sī decem habeās linguās, mūtum esse addecet, Pl. *B.* 128, *if you should have a dozen tongues, 'tis fit you should be dumb* (2074).   sī prō peccātīs centum dūcat uxōrēs, parumst, Pl. *Tri.* 1186, *if he should wed a hundred wives in payment for his sins, 'tis not enough.*   intrāre, sī possim, castra hostium volō, L. 2, 12, 5, *I propose to enter the camp of the enemy, if I be able.*   tē neque dēbent adiuvāre, sī possint, neque possunt, sī velint, *V.* 4, 20, *they ought not to help you, if they could, and cannot, if they would.*   sī vōcem rērum nātūra repente mittat, quid respondēmus? Lucr. 3, 931, *if Nature of a sudden lift her voice, what answer shall we make?*   sī quaerātur, idemne sit pertinācia et persevērantia, dēfīnītiōnibus iūdicandum est, *T.* 87, *if it be asked whether obstinacy and perseverance are the same, it must be settled by definitions* (2074).

2079.   (*d.*) Apodosis in the Future.

quadrīgās sī īnscendās Iovis atque hinc fugiās, ita vix poteris effugere īnfortūnium, Pl. *Am.* 450, *Jove's four-in-hand if you should mount, and try to flee from here, even so you'll scarce escape a dreadful doom.*   sīquidem summum Iovem tē dīcās dētinuisse, malam rem effugiēs numquam, Pl. *As.* 414, *e'en shouldst thou say imperial Jove detained thee, chastisement thou'lt ne'er avoid.*   sī frāctus inlābātur orbis, inpavidum ferient ruīnae, H. 3, 3, 7, *should heaven's vault crumbling fall, him all undaunted will its ruin strike.*   neque tū hoc dīcere audēbis, nec sī cupiās, licēbit, *V.* 2, 167, *you will not dare to say this, sir, nor if you wish, will you be allowed.*

2080.   (*e.*) Apodosis in the Future Perfect.

nōn tantum, sī proeliō vincās, glōriae adiēceris, quantum adēmeris, sī quid adversī ēveniat, L. 30, 30, 21, *you will not acquire as much glory, if you succeed in battle, as you will lose, if any reverse occur.*

2081. (*f.*) Apodosis in the Periphrastic Future.

nōn latūrus sum, sī iubeās maxumē, Pl. *B.* 1004, *I don't intend to be the bearer, should you urge me e'er so much.* quid, sī hostēs ad urbem veniant, factūrī estis? L. 3, 52, 7, *suppose the enemy march on the town, what do you intend to do?*

2082. (*g.*) Apodosis in the Imperfect Subjunctive.

cantus et Lūnam dēdūcere temptat et faceret, sī nōn **aera repulsa sonent,** Tib. 1, 8, 21, *magic essays to draw Luna down and would succeed if clashing brass should not resound* (1560). nē sī nāvigāre quidem velim, ita gubernārem, ut somniāverim; praesēns enim poena sit, *Div.* 2, 122, *again, suppose I undertake to go sailing, I should not lay my course as I may have dreamed; for the penalty would be swift* (1560). sī hodiē bella sint, quāle Etrūscum fuit, quāle Gallicum; possētisne ferre Sextium cōnsulem esse? L. 6, 40, 17, *suppose there be wars to-day like the Etruscan and the Gallic wars: could you bear to see Sextius consul* (1565)?

2083. (*h.*) Apodosis in the Pluperfect Subjunctive.

carmina nī sint, ex umerō Pelopis nōn nituisset ebur, Tib. 1, 4, 63, *suppose there be no verse, from Pelops' shoulder ne'er had ivory gleamed* (1561).

(2.) PROTASIS IN THE PERFECT SUBJUNCTIVE.

2084. (*a.*) Apodosis in the Present Subjunctive.

dēbeam, crēdō, istī quicquam furciferō, sī id fēcerim, T. *Eu.* 861, *I should be, forsooth, responsible to the rogue, if I should do it* (1556). sī dē caelō vīlla tācta siet, dē eā rē verba utī fiant, Cato, *RR.* 14, 3, *if the villa be struck by lightning, let there be utterances about the case* (1547). sī ā corōnā relictus sim, nōn queam dīcere, *Br.* 192, *if I should ever be abandoned by my audience, I should not be able to speak.* id sī acciderit, sīmus armātī, *TD.* 1, 78, *if this have happened, let us be on our guard* (1548). cūr ego simulem mē, sī quid in hīs studiīs operae posuerim, perdidisse? *Par.* 33, *why should I have the affectation to say that if I have spent any time in these pursuits, I have thrown it away* (1563)? See also 2090.

2085. (*b.*) Apodosis in the Perfect Subjunctive.

sī paululum modo quid tē fūgerit, ego perierim, T. *Hau.* 316, *should you have missed the smallest point, a dead man I should be.* See also 2090.

2086. (*c.*) Apodosis in the Future Indicative.

sī forte līber fierī occēperim, mittam nūntium ad tē, Pl. *MG.* 1362, *if haply I should be by way of getting free, I'll send you word.* sī forte morbus amplior factus siet, servom intrō iisse dicent Sōstratae, T. *Hec.* 330, *if her illness should get worse, they'll say a slave of Sostrata's went in there.*

2087. (*d.*) Apodosis in the Periphrastic **Future.**

sī Vēis incendium ortum sit, Fīdēnās inde quaesītūrī sumus ? L.
5, 54, 1, *if a fire break out at Vei, are we going to move from there to Fidenae ?*

2088. (*e.*) Apodosis in the Imperfect Subjunctive.

sīquis hoc gnātō tuō tuos servos faxit, quālem habērēs grātiam ?
Pl. *Cap.* 711, *suppose a slave of yours has done this for a son of yours, how grateful should you have been ?*

CONVERSION TO PAST TIME.

2089. An indeterminate subjunctive protasis is rarely thrown into the
past, the present and perfect becoming respectively imperfect and pluperfect. In this case the form is the same as that of a protasis of action non-
occurrent (2091), and the conversion occurs only when it is evident from the
context that past action is supposed, which may or may not have occurred :
as,

cūr igitur et Camillus dolēret, sī haec post trecentōs et quīnquāgintā ferē annōs ēventūra putāret, et ego doleam, sī ad decem mīlia
annōrum gentem aliquam urbe nostrā potītūram putem ? *TD.* 1, 90,
*why then would Camillus have fretted, if he thought this would occur after a
lapse of some three hundred and fifty years, and why should I fret, if I think
that some nation may seize Rome some ten thousand years hence ?* erat sōla illa
nāvis cōnstrāta ; quae sī in praedōnum pugnā versārētur, urbis īnstar
habēre inter illōs pīrāticōs myoparōnēs vidērētur, *V.* 5, 89, *this was the
only vessel with a deck ; and supposing she figured in the engagement with the
corsairs, she would have loomed up like a town, surrounded by those pirate cock-
boats.* Sardus habēbat ille Tigellius hoc ; Caesar sī peteret nōn quicquam prōficeret, H. *S.* 1, 3, 4, *Tigellius the Sardian had this way ; supposing Caesar asked him, naught had he availed.*

PERIODS OF EXEMPLIFICATION.

2090. The present subjunctive is particularly common in exemplifica-
tion. The perfect is sometimes used in the protasis, rarely in the apodosis : as,

sī pater fāna expīlet, indīcetne id magistrātibus fīlius ? *Off.* 3, 90, *if
a father should plunder temples, would the son report it to the magistrates ?* sī
quis pater familiās supplicium nōn sūmpserit, utrum is clēmēns an
crūdēlissimus esse videātur ? *C.* 4, 12, *assume for the sake of argument that
a householder have not inflicted punishment, would he seem merciful, or a monster of cruelty ?* sī scierīs aspidem occultē latēre uspiam, et velle aliquem imprūdentem super eam adsīdere, improbē fēcerīs, nisi
monuerīs nē adsīdat, *Fin.* 2, 59, *suppose a man should know, e. g. that there
was a snake hiding somewhere, and that somebody was going to sit down on the
snake unawares ; he would do wrong, if he did not tell him he must not sit down
there.* In such periods the future is also used, but less frequently : see 2054

II. PROTASES OF ACTION NON-OCCURRENT.

2091. A conditional period in which the non-occurrence of the action is implied takes the imperfect or pluperfect subjunctive both in the protasis and in the apodosis. The imperfect usually denotes present or indefinite time, and the pluperfect denotes past time.

For the present subjunctive in such conditions, see 2075.

2092. The imperfect sometimes denotes past time (1559). When future time is referred to, the protasis is usually in the imperfect of the periphrastic future, commonly the subjunctive, but sometimes the indicative (2108).

2093. The apodosis is very rarely in the present subjunctive (2098). The periphrastic future is sometimes used, commonly in the indicative (2097, 2100).

(1.) PROTASIS IN THE IMPERFECT SUBJUNCTIVE.

2094. (*a.*) **Apodosis in the Imperfect Subjunctive.**

(a.) Protasis and apodosis both denoting present action ; this is the usual application : sī intus esset, ēvocārem, Pl. *Ps.* 640, *I should call him out, if he were in.* is iam prīdem est mortuus. sī vīveret, verba eius audīrētis, *RC.* 42, *that person has long been dead ; if he were alive, you would hear his evidence.* adnuere tē videō ; prōferrem librōs, sī negārēs, *DN.* I, 113, *I see you nod assent ; I should bring out the books, if you maintained the opposite.* sī **L.** Mummius aliquem istōrum vidēret Corinthium cupidissimē trāctantem, utrum illum cīvem excellentem, an ātriēnsem dīligentem putāret ? *Par.* 38, *if Mummius should see one of your connoisseurs nursing a piece of Corinthian, and going into perfect ecstasies over it, what would he think ? that the man was a model citizen or a thoroughly competent indoor-man ?* quod sī semper optima tenēre possēmus, haud sānē cōnsiliō multum egērēmus, *OP.* 89, *now if we could always be in possession of what is best, we should not ever stand in any special need of reasoning.*

(b.) Protasis and apodosis both denoting past action : haec sī neque ego neque tū fēcimus, nōn siit egestās facere nōs ; nam sī esset unde id fieret, facerēmus ; et tū illum tuom, sī essēs homō, sinerēs nunc facere, T. *Ad.* 103, *if neither you nor I have acted thus, 'twas poverty that stinted us ; for if we 'd had the means, we should have done so too ; and you would let that boy of yours, if you were human, do it now.* Here esset refers to past time, essēs to present. num igitur eum, sī tum essēs, temerārium cīvem putārēs ? *Ph.* 8, 14, *would you therefore have thought him, if you had lived then, a hotheaded citizen ?* sī ūniversa prōvincia loquī posset, hāc vōce ūterētur ; quoniam id nōn poterat, hārum rērum āctōrem ipsa dēlēgit, *Caecil.* 19, *if the collective province could have spoken, she would have used these words ; but since she could not, she chose a manager for the case herself.*

2095. (*b.*) **Apodosis in the Pluperfect Subjunctive.**

invēnissēmus iam diū, sei vīveret, Pl. *Men.* 241, *were he alive, we should have found him long ago.* sī mihi secundae rēs dē amōre meō essent, iam dūdum sciō vēnissent, T. *Hau.* 230, *if everything were well about my love, I know they would have been here long ago.* quae nisi essent in senibus, nōn summum cōnsilium maiōrēs nostrī appellāssent senātum, *CM.* 19, *unless the elderly were in general characterized by these qualities, our ancestors would not have called the highest deliberative body the body of elders.*

2096. (*c.*) **Periphrastic Apodosis.**

quibus, sī Rōmae esset, facile contentus futūrus erat, *Att.* 12, 32, 2, *with which, if he were in Rome, he would readily be satisfied* (2093). quōs ego, sī tribūnī mē triumphāre prohibērent, testēs citātūrus fuī rērum ā mē gestārum, L. 38, 47, 4, *the very men whom I was to call to bear witness to my deeds, if the tribunes should refuse me a triumph.*

(2.) PROTASIS IN THE PLUPERFECT SUBJUNCTIVE.

2097. (*a.*) **Apodosis in the Imperfect Subjunctive.**

(a.) Protasis denoting past, apodosis present action: sī ante voluissēs, essēs ; nunc sērō cupis, Pl. *Tri.* 568, *if you had wished it before, you might be ; as it is, you long too late.* sī nōn mēcum aetātem ēgisset, hodiē stulta vīveret, Pl. *MG.* 1320, *if she had n't spent her life with me, she'd be a fool to-day.* sī tum illī respondēre voluissem, nunc rēī pūblicae cōnsulere nōn possem, *Ph.* 3, 33, *if I had chosen to answer the man then, I should not be able to promote the public interest now.* quō quidem tempore sī meum cōnsilium valuisset, tū hodiē egērēs, nōs līberī essēmus, *Ph.* 2, 37, *if by the way at that time my counsel had been regarded, you, sir, would be a beggar to-day and we should be free.*

(b.) Protasis and apodosis both referring to past: ōlim sī advēnissem, magis tū tum istūc dīcerēs, Pl. *Cap.* 871, *if I had come before, you'd have said so then all the more.* num igitur, sī ad centēsimum annum vīxisset, senectūtis eum suae paenitēret? *CM.* 19, *suppose therefore he had lived to be a hundred, would he have regretted his years?* Indōs aliāsque sī adiūnxisset gentēs, impedimentum maius quam auxilium traheret, L. 9, 19, 5, *if he had added the Indians and other nations, he would have found them a hindrance rather than a help in his train.*

2098. (*b.*) **Apodosis in the Pluperfect Subjunctive.**

sī appellāssēs, respondisset nōminī, Pl. *Tri.* 927, *if you had called him, he'd have answered to his name.* nisi fūgissem, medium praemorsisset, Pl. in Gell. 6, 9, 7, *if I had n't run away, he'd have bitten me in two.* sī vēnissēs ad exercitum, ā tribūnīs vīsus essēs ; nōn es autem ab hīs vīsus ;

nōn es igitur ad exercitum profectus, *Inv.* 1, 87, *if you had come to the army, you would have been seen by the tribunes ; but you have not been seen by them ; therefore you have not been to the army.* sī beātus umquam fuisset, beātam vītam usque ad rogum pertulisset, *Fin.* 3, 76, *if he had ever been a child of fortune, he would have continued the life of bliss to the funeral pyre.* nisi mīlitēs essent dēfessī, omnēs hostium cōpiae dēlērī potuissent, 7, 88, 6, *unless the soldiers had been utterly exhausted, the entire force of the enemy might have been exterminated* (2101). quod sī Catilīna in urbe remānsisset, dīmicandum nōbīs cum illō fuisset, *C.* 3, 17, *but if Catiline had staid in town, we should have had to fight with the villain* (2101).

2099. (*c.*) Apodosis in the Present Subjunctive.

vocem ego tē ad mē ad cēnam, frāter tuos nisi dīxisset mihī tē apud sē cēnātūrum esse hodiē, Pl. *St.* 510, *I should like to invite you home to dinner, if my brother had n't told me that you were to dine with him to-day.*

2100. (*c.*) Periphrastic Apodosis.

(a.) sī tacuisset, ego eram dictūrus, Pl. *Cist.* 152, *if she had held her peace, I was going to tell* (2093). sī P. Sēstius occīsus esset, fuistisne ad arma itūrī? *Sest.* 81, *if Sestius had been slain, were you disposed to rush to arms?* conclāve illud, ubī erat mānsūrus, sī īre perrēxisset. conruit, *Div.* 1, 26, *the suite of rooms where he was going to spend the night, if he had pushed on, tumbled down.* Teucrās fuerat mersūra carīnās, nī prius in scopulum trānsfōrmāta foret, O. 14, 72, *she had gone on to sink the Trojan barks unless she had been changed into a rock.* (b.) quem sī vīcisset, habitūrus esset impūnitātem sempiternam, *Mil.* 84, *and if he overcame him, he would be likely to have exemption from punishment forever and ever* (2093). aut nōn fātō interiit exercitus, aut sī fātō, etiam sī obtemperāsset auspiciīs, idem ēventūrum fuisset, *Div.* 2, 21, *the destruction of his army was either not due to fate, or if to fate, it would have happened all the same, even if he had conformed to the auspices.*

INDICATIVE APODOSIS.

2101. (I.) The apodosis of verbs of ability, duty, &c. (1495–1497), including the gerundive with **sum**, is often in the indicative, the imperfect taking the place of the imperfect or pluperfect subjunctive, and the perfect that of the pluperfect subjunctive. But the subjunctive is also found, especially **possem** rather than **poteram**.

2102. (*a.*) Apodosis in the Imperfect Indicative.

(a.) Of present action : quod sī Rōmae Cn. Pompēius prīvātus esset, tamen ad tantum bellum is erat mittendus, *IP.* 50, *now if Pompey were at Rome, in private station, still he would be the man to send to this important war.* quem patris locō, sī ūlla in tē pietās esset, colere dēbēbās, *Ph.* 2, 99, *whom you ought to honour as a father, if you had any such thing as affection in you.*

373

(b.) Of past action : quid enim poterat Heius respondēre, sī esset improbus ? *V.* 4, 16, *for what answer could Hejus have given, if he were an unprincipled man ?* sī sordidam vestem habuissent, lūgentium Perseī cāsum praebēre speciem poterant, L. 45, 20, 5, *if they had worn dark clothing, they might have presented the mien of mourners for the fall of Perseus.*

2103.   (*b.*) Apodosis in the Perfect Indicative.

nōn potuit reperīre, sī ipsī sōlī quaerendās darēs, lepidiōrēs duās, Pl. *MG.* 803, *if you assigned the search to Sol himself, he couldn't have found two jollier girls.* quō modo pultāre potuī sī nōn tangerem ? Pl. *Most.* 462, *how could I have knocked, if I hadn't touched the door ?* licitumst, sī vellēs, Pl. *Tri.* 566, *you might have been, if you'd wished.* sī meum imperium exsequī voluissēs, interemptam oportuit, T. *Hau.* 634, *if you had been willing to follow my commands, she should have been dispatched.* cōnsul esse quī potuī, nisi eum vītae cursum tenuissem ā pueritiā? *RP.* 1, 10, *how could I have been consul unless from boyhood I had taken that line in life ?* sī eum captīvitās in urbem pertrāxisset, Caesarem ipsum audīre potuit, Ta. *D.* 17, *if captivity had carried him to the city, he could have heard Caesar himself.* Antōnī gladiōs potuit contemnere, sī sīc omnia dīxisset, J. 10, 123, *Antonius' swords he might have scorned, if all things he had worded so.* sī ūnum diem morātī essētis, moriendum omnibus fuit, L. 2, 38, 5, *if you had staid one day, you must all have died.*

2104. (2.) Other verbs also sometimes have a past indicative apodosis, usually an imperfect or pluperfect, to denote an action very near to actual performance, which is interrupted by the action of the protasis.

Naturally such a protasis generally contains an actual or a virtual negative ; but positive protases are found here and there, chiefly in late writers.

2105.   (*a.*) Apodosis in the Perfect Indicative.

paene in foveam dēcidī, nī hīc adessēs, Pl. *Per.* 594, *I had almost fallen into a snare, unless you were here.* nec vēnī, nisi fāta locum sēdemque dedissent, V. 11, 112, *nor had I come, unless the fates a place and seat had given.* pōns sublicius iter paene hostibus dedit, nī ūnus vir fuisset Horātius Cocles, L. 2, 10, 2, *the pile-bridge all but gave a path to the enemy, had it not been for one heroic soul, Horatius Cocles.*

2106.   (*b.*) Apodosis in the Imperfect Indicative.

quīn lābēbar longius, nisi mē retinuissem, *Leg.* 1, 52, *why, I was going to drift on still further, if I had not checked myself.* sī per L. Metellum licitum esset, mātrēs illōrum veniēbant, *V.* 5, 129, *if Metellus had not prevented, the mothers of those people were just coming ;* here the protasis may be held to contain a virtual negative ; so in the last example on this page. castra excindere parābant, nī Mūciānus sextam legiōnem opposuisset, Ta. *H.* 3, 46, *they were preparing to destroy the camp, had not Mucianus checked them with the sixth legion.* sī dēstināta prōvēnissent, rēgnō imminēbat, Ta. *H.* 4, 18, *had his schemes succeeded, he was close upon the throne.*

2107.   (*c.*) Apodosis in the Pluperfect Indicative.

quīngentōs simul, nī hebes machaera foret, ūnō ictū occīderās, Pl. *MG.* 52, *five hundred, had your glaive not blunted been, at one fell swoop you'd slain.*   praeclārē vīcerāmus, nisi Lepidus recēpisset Antōnium, *Fam.* 12, 10, 3, *we had gained a splendid victory, if Lepidus had not taken Antony under his protection.*   quod ipsum fortūna ēripuerat, nisi ūnīus amīcī opēs subvēnissent, *RabP.* 48, *even this boon fortune had wrenched from him, unless he had been assisted by a single friend.*   sī gladium nōn strīnxissem, tamen triumphum merueram, L. 38, 49, 12, *if I had not drawn my sword, I had still earned my triumph.*   perierat imperium, sī Fabius tantum ausus esset quantum īra suādēbat, Sen. *de Ira,* 1, 11, 5, *the empire had been lost, if Fabius had ventured as far as passion urged.*

2108.   (3.) Periphrastic Protasis.

(*a.*) ac sī tibī nēmō respōnsūrus esset, tamen causam dēmōnstrāre nōn possēs, *Caecil.* 43, *and even supposing that nobody were going to answer you, still you would not be able to make the case good* (2092).   plūribus vōs, mīlitēs, hortārer, sī cum armātīs dīmicātiō futūra esset, L. 24, 38, 9, *I should exhort you at greater length, my men, if there was to be a tug with armed men* (2092).   (*b.*) sī domum tuam expugnātūrus eram, nōn temperāssem vīnō in ūnum diem? L. 40, 14, 4, *if I intended to capture your house, should I not have abstained from wine for a day* (2092)?

Variation of the Protasis.

2109. Instead of a conditional protasis with **sī** or **nisi**, equivalents are often used.

2110. Thus, the protasis may be coordinated (1701), or be introduced by a relative pronoun (1812), by quod (1843), cum (1859, 1860), ubī (1932), ut or nē (1963), dum, dum modo, modo (2003), or quandō (2011). Or the protasis may be intimated by sine, *without*, cum, *with*, by a participle or ablative absolute, by a wish, or otherwise : as,

(*a.*) nēmō umquam sine magnā spē immortālitātis sē prō patriā offerret ad mortem, *TD.* 1, 32, *nobody would ever expose himself to death for his country without a well-grounded conviction of immortality.*   cum hāc dōte poteris vel mendīcō nūbere, Pl. *Per.* 396, *with such a dowry you can e'en a beggar wed.*   Sūlla, crēdō, hunc petentem repudiāsset, *Arch.* 25, *Sulla, I suppose, would have turned my client away, if he petitioned him.*   quae legentem fefellissent, trānsferentem fugere nōn possunt, Plin. *Ep.* 7, 9, 2, *what would have escaped a reader can't escape a translator.*   vīvere ego Britannicō potiente rērum poteram? Ta. 13, 21, *as for me, could I live, if Britannicus were on the throne* (2102)?   nisi tē salvō salvī esse nōn possumus, *Marc.* 32, *without you safe, safe we cannot be.*   aspicerēs utinam, Sāturnia: mītior essēs, O. 2, 435, *would thou couldst see, Saturnia: thou wouldst gentler be.*

(*b.*) habet ōrātiōnem tālem cōnsul, quālem numquam Catilīna vīctor habuisset, *Sest.* 28, *he makes a speech — yes, and he a consul — such as a Catiline would never have made, if flushed with success.* revereāris occursum, nōn reformīdēs, Plin. *Ep.* I, 10, 7, *you might well be abashed in his presence, but you would not be afraid.* di immortālēs mentem illī perditō ac furiōsō dedērunt ut huic faceret īnsidiās ; aliter perīre pestis illa nōn potuit, *Mil.* 88, *the immortal gods inspired that mad miscreant to waylay my client ; otherwise, that monster could not have been destroyed.* For the use of absque in a coordinate protasis in Plautus and Terence, see 1701, 1421.

2111. The verb of the protasis is sometimes omitted : as in abridged sentences (1057), or when it may be easily supplied (1036).

aut enim nēmō, aut sī quisquam, ille sapiēns fuit, *L.* 9, *for either nobody or, if anybody, that was a wise man.* sī ēveniet, gaudēbimus : sīn secus, patiēmur, Pl. *Cas.* 377, *if it shall come to pass, glad shall we be ; if else, we shall endure.* mē voluisse, sī haec cīvitās est, cīvem esse mē ; sī nōn, exsulem esse, *Fam.* 7, 3, 5, *that I wished, if this is a commonwealth, to be a citizen of it ; if it is not, to be an exile.* sūmeret alicunde . . . sī nūllō aliō pactō, faenore, T. *Ph.* 299, *he could have got it from somebody or other . . . if in no other way, on usury* (2113).

VARIATION OF THE APODOSIS.

2112. The apodosis is sometimes represented by the accusative of exclamation (1149), or the vocative : as,

mortālem graphicum, sī servat fidem, Pl. *Ps.* 519, *O what a pattern creature, if he keeps his word.* ō miserum tē, sī intellegis, miseriōrem, sī nōn intellegis, hoc litterīs mandārī, *Ph.* 2, 54, *wretched man if you are aware, more wretched if you are not aware, that all this is put down in black and white.* inimīce lāmnae, Crīspe Sallustī, nisi temperātō splendeat ūsū, H. 2, 2, 2, *thou foe to bullion, Crispus Sallustius, so it shine not with tempered use.* Also the future participle in poetry and in prose from Livy on.

2113. The verb of the apodosis, or the entire apodosis, is often omitted. In the latter case an appended verb might easily be mistaken for the apodosis.

quid sī caelum ruat ? T. *Hau.* 719, *what if the sky should fall ?* quō mihi fortūnam, sī nōn concēditur ūtī ? H. *E.* I, 5, 12, *why wealth for me, if wealth I may not use ?* nisi restituissent statuās, vehementer minātur, *V.* 2, 162, *he threatens vengeance dire, if they did not put the statues back in their place.* quae supplicātiō sī cum cēterīs cōnferātur, hoc interest, *C.* 3, 15, *if this thanksgiving be compared with all others, there would be found the following difference.* nōn edepol ubi terrārum sim sciō, sī quis roget, Pl. *Am.* 336, *upon my word I don't know where on earth I am, if anyone should ask.* sī Valeriō quī crēdat, quadrāgintā mīlia hostium sunt caesa, L. 33, 10, 8, *if anybody believe such a man as Valerius, there were forty thousand of the enemy slain.* A clause with sī or nisi is often used parenthetically : as, sī placet, sī vidētur, sīs, sultis, *if you please,* sī quaeris, *if you must know, in fact,* sī dīs placet, *please heaven,* nisi mē fallit, *if I am not mistaken, &c.,* &c. For wishes introduced by ō sī, without an apodosis, see 1546.

2114. The apodosis is sometimes expanded by inserted expressions. So particularly by vereor nē, equivalent to fortasse (1958), nōn dubitō quīn, to profectō (1986), or a form of sum with a relative pronoun: as,

quae cōnētur sī velim commemorāre, vereor nē quis exīstimet mē causam nōbilitātis voluisse laedere, *RA.* 135, *if I should undertake to set forth his high and mighty schemes, possibly it might be thought that I wished to damage the cause of the conservatives.* sī tum P. Sēstius animam ēdidisset, nōn dubitō quīn aliquandō statua huic statuerētur, *Sest.* 83, *if Sestius had given up the ghost then, a statue would doubtless at some day have been set up in his honour.* quod ille sī repudiāsset, dubitātis quīn ēī vīs esset adlāta? *Sest.* 62, *if he had rejected this, have you any doubt that violent hands would have been laid on him?* sescenta sunt quae memorem, sī sit ōtium, Pl. *Aul.* 320, *there are a thousand things that I could tell, if I had time.*

2115. For expressions of trial, hope, or expectation, followed by a conditional protasis with sī, see 1777.

CONCESSIVE PROTASES.

etsī, tametsī (tamenetsī), etiamsī.

2116. etsī, tametsī, *though*, etiamsī, *even if*, or sometimes simple sī, *if*, is used to introduce a concessive protasis. The verb of the protasis is either indicative or subjunctive; but the indicative is the prevailing construction, especially with etsī. The apodosis often has tamen as an adversative correlative, even with tametsī.

etsī is rare in poetry; not in Sallust. Sometimes it is used like quamquam to append a fresh main sentence (2153). tametsī belongs chiefly to colloquial style, though Sallust often uses it; not in the Augustan poets or Tacitus. etiamsī is not found in Plautus or Caesar.

(*a*.) nōn vīdī eam, etsī vīdī, Pl. *MG.* 407, *I saw her not, although I saw her.* quō mē habeam pactō, tametsī nōn quaeris, docēbō, Lucilius in Gell. 18, 8, 2, *I'll tell you how I am, though you do not inquire.* etiamsī multī mēcum contendent. tamen omnīs superābō, *Fam.* 5, 8, 4, *though I shall have many rivals, yet I will outdo them all.* tametsī causa postulat, tamen praeterībō, *Quinct.* 13, *though the case calls for it, still I will let it pass.* Caesar, etsī in hīs locīs mātūrae sunt hiemēs, tamen in Britanniam proficīscī contendit, 4, 20, 1, *though the winter always sets in early in these parts, nevertheless Caesar made haste to proceed to Britain.* Caesar, etsī intellegēbat, quā dē causā ea dīcerentur, Indutiomarum ad sē venīre iussit, 5, 4, 1, *though Caesar was aware of his motives in saying so, he directed Indutiomarus to come to him.*

(*b*.) etsī taceās, palam id quidem est, Pl. *Aul.* 418, *though you should hold your tongue, still that at least is plain.* etsī nihil aliud Sūllae nisi cōnsulātum abstulissētis, tamen eō contentōs vōs esse oportēbat, *Suil.* 90, *even though you had robbed Sulla of nothing but the consulship, still you ought to be satisfied with that.* equidem, etiamsī oppetenda mors esset, in patriā māllem quam in externīs locīs, *Fam.* 4, 7, 4, *for my part, even though death were to be faced, I should prefer it in my native land rather than abroad.*

377

CONDITIONAL COMPARISONS.

quasi (quam sī), tamquam sī, ut or velut sī.

2117. **sī** following a word meaning *than* or *as* is used with the subjunctive in conditional comparisons.

In this use, **quasi** (quam˙sī twice in Tacitus) and **tamquam sī** are found at all periods. **ut sī** is found in Terence once, in Cicero (not in the orations), once in Livy, sometimes in later writers. **velut sī** begins with Caesar; not in Cicero. **ac sī** is found once in the *Bell. Hisp.* and in late Latin.

2118. **sī** is often omitted after **tamquam**, and (from Livy on) sometimes after **velut**. After **quasi** it is sometimes inserted in Plautus, Lucretius, and late Latin. **ceu** is sometimes used, chiefly in poetry, for **tamquam sī**. The main clause often has as correlative **ita, sīc, perinde, proinde, similiter,** or **nōn secus.**

2119. The tense of the subjunctive is usually regulated by the sequence of tenses, in Cicero nearly always with **quasi** and **tamquam sī**.

quid mē sīc salūtās quasi dūdum nōn vīderīs? Pl. *Am.* 682, *why dost thou greet me thus as if but now thou hadst not looked on me?* quid ego hīs testibus ūtor, quasi rēs dubia sit? *Caecil.* 14, *why do I employ these witnesses, as if it were a case involving doubt?* tamquam sī claudus sim, cum fūstīst ambulandum, Pl. *As.* 427, *I have to take my walks with a stick, as if I were a lame man.* tamquam extrūderētur, ita cucurrit, *Ph.* 10, 10, *he rushed away as if he had been kicked out.* quod absentis Ariovistī crūdēlitātem, velut sī cōram adesset, horrērent, I, 32, 4, *because they trembled at Ariovistus's barbarity, absent as he was, just as if he stood before their eyes.* mē quoque iuvat, velut ipse in parte labōris ac perīculī fuerim, ad fīnem bellī Pūnicī pervēnisse, L. 31, 1, 1, *I feel glad myself at having finally reached the end of the Punic war, as if I had had a direct hand in the work and the danger.*

2120. The imperfect or pluperfect subjunctive is sometimes used, even when the leading verb is in a primary tense, to mark action more distinctly as non-occurrent (2091) : as,

eius negōtium sīc velim suscipiās, ut sī esset rēs mea, *Fam.* 2, 14, *I wish you would undertake his business, just as if it were my own affair.* mē audiās, precor, tamquam sī mihī quirītantī intervēnissēs, L. 40, 9, 7, *listen to me, I pray you, as if you had come at a cry from me for help.* iūs iūrandum perinde aestimandum quam sī Iovem fefellisset, Ta. I, 73, *as for the oath, it must be counted exactly as if he had broken one sworn on the name of Jupiter.* This is the more usual way in Cicero with ut sī.

2121. quasi, ut, or, from Livy on, tamquam or velut, *as if,* is sometimes used with participle constructions, nouns, and abridged expressions: as,

quasi temere dē rē pūblicā locūtus in carcerem coniectus est, *DN.* 2, 6, *on the ground that he had been speaking without good authority about a state matter, he was clapped in jail.* restitēre Rōmānī tamquam caelestī vōce iussī, I, 12, *the Romans halted as if bidden by a voice from heaven.* laetī, ut explōrātā victōriā, ad castra pergunt, 3, 18, 8, *in high spirits, as if victory were assured, they proceeded to the camp.*

2122. In old Latin, quasi is found a few times for the original **quam sī** after a comparative: as, **mē nēmō magis respiciet, quasi abhinc ducentōs annōs fuerim mortuos**, Pl. *Tru.* 340, *nobody will pay any more attention to me than if I had been dead two centuries.* It is also used (once in classical Latin, *CM.* 71) in periods of actual comparison, like **tamquam** (1908), with the indicative: as, **senex ille illī dīxit, quasi ego nunc tibi dīcō**, Pl. *St.* 545, *that old man said to him, as I now say to you.* For its use in figurative comparisons, see 1908, 1944. For **tamquam** introducing a reason &c., see 1909, a late usage found rarely with **quasi** and **ut**.

CONNECTION OF SEPARATE SENTENCES OR PERIODS.

2123. Separate sentences or periods have a connective more commonly in Latin than in English. Sometimes, however, like the members of single periods, they are for special reasons put *asyndetically* (1637).

(A.) WITHOUT A CONNECTIVE.

2124. Asyndeton is common with two or more separate sentences or periods:

2125. (*a.*) To represent a series of actions as occurring at the same moment: as,

hīc diffīsus suae salūtī ex tabernāculō prōdit; videt imminēre hostēs; capit arma atque in portā cōnsistit; cōnsequuntur hunc centuriōnēs; relinquit animus Sextium gravibus acceptīs vulneribus, 6, 38, 2, *despairing of his life, he comes out of the tent; sees the enemy close at hand; seizes arms and takes his stand at the gate; the centurions rally round him; Sextius becomes unconscious, receiving severe wounds.*

2126. (*b.*) When an occurrence is represented as consisting of many successive actions: the *Enumerative Asyndeton*: as,

perōrāvit aliquandō, adsēdit. surrēxī ego. respīrāre vīsus est, quod nōn alius potius dīceret. coepī dīcere. usque eō animadvertī, iūdicēs, eum aliās rēs agere, antequam Chrȳsogonum nōmināvī; quem simul atque attigī, statim homō sē ērēxit, mīrārī vīsus est. intellēxī quid eum pupugisset, *RA.* 60, *after a while he wound up, took his seat; up rose your humble servant. He seemed to take courage from the fact it was nobody else. I began to speak. I noticed, gentlemen, that he was inattentive all along till I named Chrysogonus; but the moment I touched on him, the creature perked up at once, seemed to be surprised. I knew what the rub was.*

2127. (*c.*) When the last sentence sums up the result of the preceding with emphasis: the *Asyndeton of Summary*: as, hī dē suā salūte dēspērantēs, aut suam mortem miserābantur, aut parentēs suōs commendābant. plēna erant omnia timōris et lūctūs, Caes. *C.* 2, 41, 8, *despairing of their lives, they either bewailed their own death, or strove to interest people in their parents. In short, it was one scene of terror and lamentation.*

(B.) WITH A CONNECTIVE.

2128. Separate sentences or periods may be connected: (1.) by pronominal words: (*a.*) demonstrative or determina- tive; (*b.*) relative; (2.) by conjunctions and adverbs.

(1.) PRONOMINAL WORDS.

(*a.*) DEMONSTRATIVE AND DETERMINATIVE WORDS AS CONNECTIVES.

2129. hīc and is serve as connectives at the beginning of a new period. In English the equivalent word is usually placed not at the beginning as a connective, but after some words.

Gallia est dīvīsa in partēs trēs, quārum ūnam incolunt Belgae, aliam Aquītānī, tertiam Celtae. hī omnēs linguā, īnstitūtīs, lēgibus inter sē differunt, 1, 1, 1, *Gaul is divided into three parts, one of which is occu- pied by Belgians, another by Aquitanians, and the third by Kelts. In language, customs, and laws these are all different from each other.* apud Helvētiōs nōbilissimus fuit Orgetorīx. is M. Messālā et M. Pīsōne cōnsulibus coniūrātiōnem nōbilitātis fēcit, 1, 2, 1, *among the Helvetians the man of highest rank was Orgetorix. In the consulship of Messala and Piso he got up a conspiracy among the nobles.* angustōs sē fīnīs habēre arbitrābantur. hīs rēbus adductī cōnstituērunt ea quae ad proficīscendum pertinērent comparāre. ad eās rēs cōnficiendās biennium sibī satis esse dūxērunt. ad eās rēs cōnficiendās Orgetorīx dēligitur. is sibī lēgātiōnem sus- cēpit, 1, 2, 5, *they thought they had a narrow territory; so they resolved in consequence to make such preparations as were necessary for a move. They considered two years ample to do this. Orgetorix is chosen to do this. He took upon himself the office of envoy.*

2130. Particularly common are demonstrative words at the beginning of a new period, to show that the first action necessarily took place or was natural.

Dionȳsius tyrannus Syrācūsīs expulsus Corinthī puerōs docēbat; usque eō imperiō carēre nōn poterat, *TD.* 3, 27, *after his expulsion from Syracuse, the tyrant Dionysius kept school at Corinth; so incapable was he of getting along without governing.*

(*b*.) Relatives as Connectives.

2131. qui serves to connect a new period when it may be translated by a demonstrative, or when it is equivalent to **et is, is autem,
is enim, is igitur**: as,

perpetrāret Anicētus prōmissa. quī nihil cunctātus poscit sum-
mam sceleris, Ta. 14, 7, *Anicetus must carry out his agreement. Without any
ado he asks to have the entire management of the crime.* For other examples,
see 1835.

2132. The neuter accusative **quod**, *as to that, as to which,
whereas, now, so,* is used to connect a new period, especially before
sī, nisi, etsī, utinam (1837): as,

quod sī tū valērēs, iam mihī quaedam explōrāta essent, *Att.* 7, 2, 6,
*whereas if you were well yourself, some points would have been clear to me before
this.* quod sī diūtius alātur contrōversia, fore utī pars cum parte
cīvitātis cōnflīgat, 7, 32, 5, *now if the dispute ħe kept up any longer, one half
of the community would quarrel with the other.* quod nisi mīlitēs essent
dēfessī, omnēs hostium cōpiae dēlērī potuissent, 7, 88, 6, *so if the
soldiers had not been utterly spent, all the forces of the enemy might have been
exterminated.*

(2.) CONJUNCTIONS AND ADVERBS.

2133. The conjunctions and adverbs used to coordinate sentences
are : (*a*.) copulative and disjunctive ; (*b*.) concessive and adversative ;
(*c*.) causal and illative.

(*a*.) Copulative and Disjunctive.

et, neque or **nec, -que, atque** or **ac, aut.**

et.

2134. **et,** *and,* simply adds, as in English (1645). But it is
often used in such a connection that a modification of the translation is required to bring out the sense.

2135. **et** may continue the discourse with a concessive sentence,
which is to be followed by an adversative. In such cases **quidem**
often stands in the concessive sentence: as,

prīmōrēs cīvitātis eadem ōrant. et cēterī quidem movēbant minus ;
postquam Sp. Lucrētius agere coepit, cōnsul abdicāvit sē cōnsulātū,
L. 2, 2, 8, *the head men of the state make the same request. Now the others did
not influence him much. But when Lucretius began to take steps the consul re-
signed his consulship.*

2136. et, *and strange to say, and if you'd believe it,* introduces something unexpected : as,

iamque trēs laureātae in urbe statuae, et adhūc raptābat Āfricam Tacfarinās, Ta. 4, 23, *there were already three triumphal statues in Rome, and, strange to say, Tacfarinas was still harrying Africa.*

2137. et, *and really, and in fact, and to be sure;* in this sense it is usually followed immediately by the verb : as,

multa quae nōn volt videt. et multa fortasse quae volt! *CM.* 25, *one sees much that one would not. Aye, and much perhaps that one would!*

2138. et introducing a sentence explaining in detail a general idea before given may be translated *namely :* as,

cōnsulēs religiō tenēbat, quod prōdigiīs aliquot nūntiātīs, nōn facile litābant. et ex Campāniā nūntiāta erant Capuae sepulchra aliquot dē caelō tācta, L. 27, 23, 1, *the consuls were detained by scruple, because several prodigies were reported, and they could not readily obtain good omens ; namely from Campania it was reported that at Capua several tombs were struck by lightning.*

2139. et, *and also, and besides :* as,

Pūnicae quoque victōriae sīgnum octō ductī elephantī. et nōn minimum fuēre spectāculum praecēdentēs Sōsis et Moericus, L. 26, 21, 9, *as an emblem of the Punic victory also, elephants to the number of eight marched in parade. And furthermore not the least attractive part of the pageant were Sosis and Moericus, moving at the head of the line.*

2140. et, *and yet,* introduces a contrast or opposition : as,

canōrum illud in vōce splendēscit etiam in senectūte, quod equidem adhūc nōn āmīsī; et vidētis annōs, *CM.* 28, *the musical element in the voice actually improves in old age, and this I have not yet lost. And yet you see my years.*

neque or nec.

2141. nec, *and really . . . not, and in fact . . . not:* as,

magnō cum perīculō suō, quī forte patrum in forō erant, in eam turbam incidērunt. nec temperātum manibus foret, nī properē cōnsulēs intervēnissent, L. 2, 23, 9, *it was with great personal risk to such of the fathers as happened to be in the market place, that they got into the crowd. And in fact acts of violence would have occurred, unless the consuls had made haste to interfere.*

2142. nec, *and to be sure . . . not :* as,

centum vīgintī līctōrēs cum fascibus secūrēs inligātās praeferēbant. nec attinuisse dēmī secūrem, cum sine prōvocātiōne creātī essent, interpretābantur, L. 3, 36, 4, *a hundred and twenty lictors with rods displayed axes bound in them. And to be sure they explained the matter thus, that there would have been no propriety in having the axe taken out, since the officers were appointed without any appeal.*

2143. nec, *not . . . either, nor either, neither :* as,

eō annō vīs morbī levāta. neque ā pēnūriā frūmentī perīculum fuit, L. 4, 25, 6, *that year the violence of the plague grew less. Nor was there any danger from lack of grain either.*

2144. nec, *but . . . not :* as,

missī tamen fētiālēs. nec eōrum verba sunt audīta, L. 4, 30, 14, *however the fetials were sent. But they were not listened to.*

-que.

2145. -que, *and likewise :* as,

huic duōs flāminēs adiēcit. virginēsque Vestae lēgit, L. 1, 20, 2, *to this god he assigned two special priests. And he likewise chose maids for Vesta.*

2146. -que, *and in fact, and so, and in general :* as,

tum quoque male pugnātum est. obsessaque urbs foret, nī Horātius esset revocātus, L. 2, 51, 2, *then also there was an unsuccessful engagement. And in fact Rome would have been besieged, unless Horatius had been recalled.*

atque or ac.

2147. atque, *and besides, and more than that, and actually :* as,

ex quō efficitur animantem esse mundum. atque ex hōc quoque intellegī poterit in eō inesse intellegentiam, quod certē est mundus melior quam ūlla nātūra, *DN.* 2, 32, *from which it follows that the universe is alive. And more than that, we can see that it has sense from the following circumstance, that the universe is certainly superior to any element of the universe.*

2148. atque, *and so, and consequently :* as,

impedior religiōne quōminus expōnam quam multa P. Sēstius sēnserit. atque nihil dīcō praeter ūnum, *Sest.* 8, *I am prevented by scruples from setting forth how much Sestius was aware of. And so I will only say one thing.*

aut.

2149. aut is used to add a new sentence in the sense of aliōquī, *or else, otherwise,* or as if nisi, *unless,* preceded : as,

omnia bene sunt ĕī dīcenda, aut ēloquentiae nōmen relinquendum est, *DO.* 2, 5, *he must be able to speak well on all subjects, or else he must waive the name of an eloquent man.*

(*b*.) CONCESSIVE AND ADVERSATIVE.

2150. A new concessive period is introduced by sānē, quidem, omnīnŏ, *to be sure,* or fortasse, *perhaps :* as,

Plīnius et Cluvius nihil dubitātum dē fidē praefectī referunt. sānē Fabius inclīnat ad laudēs Senecae, Ta. 13, 20, *Pliny and Cluvius say that there was no doubt about the loyalty of the prefect. Fabius, it must be admitted, is always inclined to eulogize Seneca.* id fortasse nōn perfēcimus; cōnātī quidem saepissimē sumus, *O.* 210, *perhaps we have not attained to it ; still we have very often made the attempt.*

2151. A new adversative sentence is introduced by **autem**, *again*, **sed**, **vērum**, *but*, **vērō**, *but, indeed*, **at**, *but*, or **tamen, nihilō minus**, *nevertheless*.

These words when used to connect sentences have the same meaning as when used to connect the parts of a sentence (1676).

2152. atquī, rarely atquin, *and yet, but*, is used chiefly in dialogue. It introduces a strong objection, sometimes in the form of a conditional protasis. From Cicero on, it is sometimes found after a question, to introduce an earnest denial.

nōn sum apud mē : : atquī opus est nunc quom maxumē ut sīs, T. *Ph.* 204, *I 'm all abroad : : but that 's just exactly where you must n't be now.* nōn vereor condiscipulōrum nē quis exaudiat : : atquī cavendum est, *Leg.* 1, 21, *I 'm not afraid of being overheard by any of my fellow-students : : and yet you must be on your guard.* sine veniat. atquī sī illam digitō attigerit ūnō, oculī īlicō ecfodientur, T. *Eu.* 739. *let him come on. But if he lays a finger on the maid, we 'll scratch his eyes out on the spot.* quid vērō ? modum statuārum habērī nūllum placet ? atquī habeātur necesse est, *V.* 2, 144, *what ? is there, think you, to be no end to your statues ? Yet there must be.*

2153. quamquam, etsī, tametsī, *though*, and nisi, *but*, are sometimes used to coordinate a new period, correcting the preceding : as,

carēre sentientis est, nec sēnsus in mortuō, nē carēre quidem igitur in mortuō est. quamquam quid opus est in hōc philosophārī ? *TD.* 1, 88, *foregoing requires a sentient being, and there is no sensation in a dead man ; therefore there is no foregoing either in a dead man. And yet what is the use of philosophizing over this ?* utram mālīs vidē ; etsī cōnsilium quod cēpī rēctum esse sciō, T. *Hau.* 326, *of these two states choose which you will ; though I am sure my plan's the right one.* cūr ego nōn adsum ? tametsī hoc minimē tibī deest, *Fam.* 2, 7, 2, *why am I not with you ? though this is the very last thing you need.* spērābam dēfervisse adulēscentiam : ecce autem dē integrō ! nisi quidquid est, volō hominem convenīre, T. *Ad.* 152, *I hoped his youthful passion had cooled down ; yet here it is afresh ! But be it what it may, I want to see the fellow.*

(*c.*) CAUSAL AND ILLATIVE.

2154. nam, enim, *for*, or namque, etenim, *for you see*, introduces a new period which gives the reason of the foregoing : as,

quā quidem ex rē hominum multitūdō cōgnōscī potuit : nam minus hōrīs tribus mūnītiōnem perfēcērunt, 5, 42, 4, *and from this by the way their numbers could be gauged ; for they made a breastwork in less than three hours.* quem meminisse potestis : annō enim ūndēvīcēsimō post eius mortem hī cōnsulēs factī sunt, *CM.* 14, *you can remember him : for the present consuls were created only nineteen years after his death.*

2155. The originally asseverative meaning of **nam** appears, even in the classical period, in colloquial language: as, **tibī ā mē nūlla ortast iniūria : : nam hercle etiam hoc restat**, T. *Ad.* 189, *I've ne'er done you a wanton wrong: : aye verily that's still to come.* In old Latin, it sometimes introduces a question: as, **nam quae haec anus est?** T. *Ph.* 732, *why, who's this old woman?* Frequently it introduces an explanation or illustration, and, from Cicero on, a remark or question made in passing: as, **sīc enim sēsē rēs habet: nam Odyssīa Latina est sīc tamquam opus Daedalī**, *Br.* 71, *the case stands thus: the Odyssey in Latin is, you may say, a regular work of Daedalus* (1908). **vīvō Catōne multī ōrātōrēs flōruērunt: nam A. Albīnus**, *Br.* 81, *many orators flourished in Cato's lifetime: for example, Albinus.* **nam quid dē aedīle loquar?** *Sest.* 95, *for why speak of the aedile?* **enim** does not differ essentially in use from **nam**; for its meaning in old Latin, see 1688. **namque** is rare until Livy, and usually (always in old Latin) stands before a vowel. **etenim** is common only in classical Latin.

2156. For **quippe**, *why*, often used as a coordinating word, see 1690.

2157. **proinde** or **proin**, *therefore, so*, introduces a command or direction based upon the foregoing: as,

ōrātiōnem spērat invēnisse sē, quī differat tē : proin tū fac apud tē ut siēs, T. *Andr.* 407, *he trusts he's found some phrase wherewith he may confound you: so see you have your wits about you.* **frūstrā meae vītae subvenīre cōnāminī.** **proinde abīte, dum est facultās**, 7, 50, 6, *in vain ye try to save my life. So away, while ye have the power.* **iam undique silvae et sōlitūdō magna cōgitātiōnis incitāmenta sunt.** **proinde cum vēnābere, licēbit pugillārēs ferās**, Plin. *Ep.* 1, 6, 2, *then again the surrounding woods and the loneliness are powerful stimulants to meditation. So when you go hunting, you can take a note book with you.*

2158. A conclusion is denoted by **ergō**, **itaque** or **igitur**, *therefore, so*, introducing a new period: as,

nihil est praestantius deō ; ab eō igitur mundum necesse est regī. **nūllī igitur est nātūrae subiectus deus.** **omnem ergō regit ipse nātūram**, *DN.* 2, 77, *nothing is more excellent than god. Therefore the universe must be governed by him. Therefore god is in no respect subject to nature. Consequently he rules all nature himself.* For the position of these words in their clauses, see 1688 ; for **ergō igitur** and **itaque ergō**, 1689. For **hinc**, **inde**, **eō**, **ideō**, **idcircō**, **proptereā**, as coordinating words, see 1691.

AFFIRMATIVE COORDINATION.

2159. A new sentence affirmative of a foregoing is often introduced by an emphatic **sīc** or **ita**.

These words often introduce a general truth which is deduced from the first statement.

vīsne igitur tē īnspiciāmus ā puerō ? sīc opīnor ; ā prīncipiō ōrdiāmur, *Ph.* 2, 44, *would you like to have us look into your record from boyhood? Yes, I think it would be well ; let us begin at the beginning.* **quī dīligēbant hunc, illī favēbant. sīc est volgus : ex vēritāte pauca, ex opīniōne multa aestimat**, *RC.* 29, *everybody who loved him, smiled on the other man. Yes, that is always the way of the world : it seldom judges by truth, often by hearsay.*

NOUNS OF THE VERB.

THE INFINITIVE.

2160. The infinitive is in its origin a verbal substantive.

2161. The present infinitive active is an ancient dative, closely resembling in meaning and use the English infinitive with *to*. It originally marked action merely in a general way, without indication of voice or tense. In virtue of this original timeless character, the present often represents action which is really past or future ; in such cases the time must be inferred from the context.

2162. The present infinitive active gradually approached the character of a verb, and the original substantive nature being forgotten, it was supplemented by a passive, and by forms for completed and for future action, active and passive.

2163. The infinitive has furthermore two other properties of the verb : (*a.*) it is modified by an adverb, not by an adjective ; and (*b.*) it is followed by the construction of its verb.

OLD AND POETICAL USE OF THE INFINITIVE.

THE INFINITIVE OF PURPOSE.

2164. The infinitive denotes purpose : (*a.*) when loosely added to a substantive and to old Latin, (*b.*) with verbs of motion, **eō, veniō, currō, mittō,** in old or poetical Latin, and (*c.*) in the combination **dō bibere,** *give to drink,* in old, colloquial, or poetical Latin : as,

(*a.*) **occāsiō benefacta cumulāre,** Pl. *Cap.* 423, *a chance to pile up kindnesses.* Parallel with a gerund : **summa ēlūdendī occāsiōst mihi nunc senēs et Phaedriae cūram adimere argentāriam,** T. *Ph.* 885, *I've now a splendid chance the greybeards of eluding and Phaedria to rescue from his money cares.* (*b.*) **recurre petere rē recentī,** Pl. *Tri.* 1015, *run back to get it ere it is too late.* **voltisne eāmus vīsere ?** T. *Ph.* 102, *do you think we'd better go to call ?* **parasītum mīsī nudiusquārtus Cāriam petere argentum,** Pl. *Cur.* 206, *my parasite I sent four days ago to Caria, to fetch the cash.* **nec dulcēs occurrent ōscula nātī praeripere,** Lucr. 3, 895, *nor shall thy children dear come running kiss on kiss to snatch.* **nōn nōs ferrō Libycōs populāre penātīs vēnimus,** V. 1, 527, *we are not come with steel to harry Libya's hearths.* (*c.*) **bibere dā usque plēnīs cantharīs,** Pl. *Per.* 821, *keep giving on to drink with brimming bowls.* **bibere** is thus used by Plautus, Terence, Cato, and Livy, and by Cicero once with **ministrō.** In classical prose, purpose is expressed by the subjunctive with **ut** or a relative pronoun, or by a gerund or gerundive with ad or **causā.**

2165. In poetry, the infinitive of purpose is used with **synonymes of dō** also, and with verbs of leaving, taking away, taking up, &c.

huic lōrīcam dōnat habēre, V. 5, 259, *on him a corselet he bestows to wear.* trīstitiam et metūs trādam protervīs in mare Crēticum portāre ventīs, H. 1, 26, 1, *sadness and fears I 'll to the wanton winds consign, to sweep into the Cretic sea.* quis sibi rēs gestās Augustī scrībere sūmit? H. *E.* 1, 3, 7, *who takes it on himself Augustus' deeds to pen?* quem virum aut hērōa lyrā vel ācrī tībiā sūmis celebrāre? H. 1, 12, 1, *what hero or what demigod dost thou take up, to ring his praises on the rebec or the piercing pipe?*

THE INFINITIVE WITH ADJECTIVES.

2166. The infinitive is sometimes used with adjectives, chiefly by poets of the Augustan age, and late prose writers, often in imitation of a Greek idiom: as,

indoctum iuga ferre nostra, H. 2, 6, 2, *not taught our yoke to bear.* avidī committere pugnam, O. 5, 75, *hot to engage in fight.* sōlī cantāre perītī Arcades, V. *E.* 10, 32, *Arcadians alone in minstrelsy are skilled.* vitulus niveus vidērī, H. 4, 2, 59, *a bullock snow-white to behold,* i. e. vīsū (2274). These infinitives are of different kinds, some of them resembling a complementary infinitive, others a gerund or gerundive construction, the supine in -tū (-sū), &c., &c.

THE ORDINARY USE OF THE INFINITIVE.

2167. The infinitive is ordinarily used either as object or as subject of a verb.

(A.) THE INFINITIVE AS OBJECT.
THE COMPLEMENTARY INFINITIVE.

2168. The present infinitive is often used to complete the meaning of certain kinds of verbs which imply another action of the same subject: as,

prō Pompēiō ēmorī possum, *Fam.* 2, 15, 3, *I could die the death for Pompey* (1495). quid habēs dīcere? *Balb.* 33, *what have you to say?* scīre volēbat, *V.* 1, 131, *he wanted to know.* hoc facere dēbēs, *RabP.* 7, *you ought to do this.* Caesar Rhēnum trānsīre dēcrēverat, 4, 17, 1, *Caesar had resolved to cross the Rhine.* fugā salūtem petere contendērunt, 3, 15, 2, *they tried to save themselves by flight.* num negāre audēs? *C.* 1, 8, *do you dare deny it?* vereor dīcere, T. *Andr.* 323, *I am afraid to tell.* num dubitās id facere? *C.* 1, 13, *do you hesitate to do that?* mātūrat ab urbe proficīscī, 1, 7, 1, *he makes haste to leave Rome.* Dīviciācus Caesarem obsecrāre coepit, 1, 20, 1, *Diviciacus began to entreat Caesar.* Dolābella iniūriam facere persevērat, *Quint.* 31, *Dolabella persists in doing wrong.* illī pecūniam pollicērī nōn dēsistunt, 6, 2, 1, *these people did not stop offering money.* diem ēdictī obīre neglēxit, *Ph.* 3, 20, *he failed to keep the day named in the edict.* īrāscī amīcīs nōn temere soleō, *Ph.* 8, 16, *I am not apt to get provoked with friends without just cause.* illī rēgibus pārēre didicerant, *Ph.* 3, 9, *the men of old were trained to bow the knee to kings* (1615). dextram cohibēre mementō, J. 5, 71, *remember that you keep hands off.*

2169. The verbs or verbal expressions which are supplemented by an infinitive are chiefly such as mean *can, will* or *wish, ought, resolve, endeavour, dare, fear, hesitate, hasten, begin, continue, cease, neglect, am wont, learn, know how, remember, forget, seem.* The infinitive in this combination contains the leading idea. For the occasional use of the perfect infinitive with some of these verbs, see 2223.

Some of the commonest of these verbs are possum, queō, nequeō; volō, nōlō, mālō, cupiō, studeō; dēbeō; cōgitō, meditor, statuō, cōnstituō, dēcernō, parō; cōnor, nītor, contendō; audeō; vereor; cunctor, dubitō, festīnō, mātūrō, īnstituō, coepī, incipiō, pergō, persevērō, dēsinō, dēsistō, omittō, supersedeō, neglegō, nōn cūrō; soleō, adsuēscō, cōnsuēscō; discō, sciō, nesciō, recordor, meminī, oblīvīscor; videor.

2170. The infinitive is also used with many verbal expressions equivalent to the above verbs, such as habeō in animō, cōnsilium est, certum est, parātus sum, &c., &c., or with parātus alone, adsuēfactus, &c., &c. Furthermore, in poetry and late prose, the place of many of the above verbs is often taken by livelier or fresher synonymes, such as valeō for possum, from Lucretius on, ardeō, *burn,* for volō, cupiō, or absiste, fuge, parce, &c., for nōlī (1584), &c., &c.

2171. A predicate noun used in the construction of the complementary infinitive, is put in the nominative : as,

Aelius Stōicus esse voluit, *Br.* 206, *Aelius wanted to be a Stoic.* esse quam vidērī bonus mālēbat, S. *C.* 54, 6, *he chose to be good rather than seem good.*

THE ACCUSATIVE WITH THE INFINITIVE.

2172. A very common form of a dependent sentence is that known as the *Accusative with the Infinitive.*

Thus, of the two coordinate sentences sciō: iocāris tū nunc, Pl. *Most.* 1081, *I know : you are jesting now,* the second may be put in a dependent form, the two sentences blending into one : sciō iocārī tē nunc, *I know you to be jesting now.*

2173. The subject of an infinitive is put in the accusative.

Thus, in eum vident, *they see him,* eum is the object of vident (1134). If sedēre is added, eum vident sedēre, *V.* 5, 107, *they see him sit,* or *they see that he is sitting,* eum is at the same time the object of vident and the subject of sedēre. But the accusative by degrees becoming detached from the main verb, and closely interlocked with the infinitive, the combination is extended to cases where the main verb is intransitive or passive.

2174. A predicate noun referring to a subject accusative is itself put in the accusative : as,

tē esse arbitror puerum probum, Pl. *Most.* 949, *I think you are a good boy.* nēminem vīvum capī patiuntur, 8, 35, 5, *they do not allow anybody to be made prisoner alive* (2198).

VERBS OF PERCEIVING, KNOWING, THINKING, AND SAYING.

2175. The accusative with the infinitive is used with active verbs or verbal expressions of perceiving, knowing, thinking, and saying: as,

patēre tua cōnsilia nōn sentīs? *C.* 1, 1, *you don't feel that your plots are all out?* huic fīlium scīs esse? T. *Hau.* 181, *you are aware that this man has a son?* Pompēiōs cōnsēdisse terrae mōtū audīvimus, Sen. *NQ.* 6, 1, 1, *we have heard that Pompei has been swallowed up by an earthquake*, 63 A. D., 17 years before its utter destruction. saepe audīvī inter ōs atque offam multa intervenīre posse, Cato in Gell. 13, 18 (17), 1, *I have often heard ''twixt cup and lip there's many a slip.'* dīcit montem ab hostibus tenērī, 1, 22, 2, *he says the hill is held by the enemy.* dīxtin dūdum illam dīxisse, sē expectāre fīlium? T. *Hec.* 451, *did n't you say a while ago the woman said that she was looking for her son?*

Some of the commonest of these verbs are: (*a.*) audiō, animadvertō, sentiō, videō. (*b.*) accipiō, intellegō, sciō, nesciō. (*c.*) arbitror, cēnseō, cōgitō, crēdō, exīstimō, meminī, opīnor, putō, recordor, suspicor. (*d.*) adfīrmō, āiō, dēmōnstrō, dīcō, disputō, doceō, fateor, nārrō, negō, nūntiō, ostendō, prōmittō, scrībō, sīgnificō, spērō, trādō. (*e.*) rūmor est, nōn mē fugit, certus sum, nōn nescius sum, &c., &c. Also occasionally verbs used in the sense of *think* or *say*, as mittō, *send word*, and substantives or pronouns expressing a thought or judgement.

2176. The accusative with the infinitive is sometimes introduced by a neuter pronoun, or by sīc or ita: as, illud negābis, tē dē rē iūdicātā iūdicāvisse? *V.* 2, 81, *will you deny this, that you sate in judgement on a matter that was already decided?* sīc accēpimus, nūllum bellum fuisse, *V.* 5, 5, *we have been told this, that there was not any war.* Sometimes by an ablative with dē: as, dē hōc Verrī dīcitur, habēre eum perbona toreumata, *V.* 4, 38, *about this man report is made to Verres that he had some choice bits of embossed work.*

2177. (1.) Passive verbs of this class are commonly used personally in the third person of the present system, with the subject, and the predicate noun, if used, in the nominative: as,

hī centum pāgōs habēre dīcuntur, 4, 1, 4, *these people are said to have a hundred cantons.* nūlla iam exīstimantur esse iūdicia, *V. a. pr.* 43, *there are thought to be no courts of law any longer.* pōns prope effectus nūntiābātur, Caes. *C.* 1, 62, 3, *the bridge was reported to be well-nigh done.*

2178. Such personal passives are much more common in the writers of Cicero's day than in old Latin. Particularly so arguō, audiō, cōgnōscō, comperiō, concēdō, dēfendō, dēmōnstrō, dīcō, doceō, excūsō, exīstimō, inveniō, iūdicō, līberō, memorō, negō, nūntiō, ostendō, postulō, putō, reperiō, trādō.

2179. (2.) With the first or second person the personal construction is rare: as, quod nōs bene ēmisse iūdicātī sumus, *Att.* 1, 13, 6, *that we are thought to have made a good bargain.* cum inveniāre improbissimā ratiōne esse praedātus, *V.* 4, 3, *when you prove to have been robbing most abominably.* But with videor, *seem*, the personal construction is the rule in all three persons, and in the perfect system as well as the present.

2180. (3.) In the perfect system, and also usually in the gerundive construction (2246), verbs of this class are commonly impersonal: as,

trāditum est Homērum caecum fuisse, *TD.* 5, 114, *the tradition is that Homer was blind.* **ubī tyrannus est, ibī dīcendum est nūllam esse rem pūblicam,** *RP.* 3, 43, *wherever there is an absolute ruler, there we must maintain there is no commonwealth.*

2181. (4.) With some verbs of this class, the impersonal construction is preferred even in the present system. Thus, commonly **intellegitur,** *it is understood,* as impersonal; regularly in classical Latin **crēditur;** with a dative in Cicero and Caesar **dīcitur, nūntiātur.** The impersonals **cernitur, fertur, memorātur, prōditur, vidētur,** are rare.

2182. The personal construction is sometimes extended to other verbs or verbal expressions, especially in poetry: as, **colligor,** *O. A.* 2, 6, 61, *I am inferred,* for **colligitur. nōnnūllīs magistrātūs veniēbant in suspīciōnem nōs dēmorātī esse,** Lentulus in *Fam.* 12, 15, 5, *the magistrates were suspected by some of having delayed us* (1491).

2183. With verbs of thinking and saying the subject accusative is sometimes omitted.

(*a.*) Oftenest thus **mē nōs, tē vōs,** or **sē**: as, **stultē fēcisse fateor,** i. e. **mē,** Pl. *B.* 1013, *I own I've acted like a fool.* **cōnfitēre vēnisse,** i. e. **tē,** *RA.* 61, *confess you came.* **quae imperārentur facere dīxērunt,** i. e. **sē,** 2, 32, 3, *they said they would do as ordered* (2221). Often the future without **esse**: as, **refrāctūrōs carcerem minābantur,** i. e. **sē,** L. 6, 17, 6, *they threatened to break the jail open.* (*b.*) Less frequently an accusative of **is**: as, **oblītum crēdidī,** i. e. **eum,** *Fam.* 9, 2, 1, *I imagined he had forgotten.* Such omissions are common in old Latin, Cicero, Caesar, Livy, and in poetry.

2184. When the accusative is not expressed, a predicate noun is sometimes put in the nominative, chiefly in poetry, in imitation of a Greek idiom: as,

phasēlus ille quem vidētis, hospitēs, ait fuisse nāvium celerrimus, Cat. 4, 1, *the clipper you see yonder, friends, says she was once the fleetest of the fleet.* **uxor invictī Iovis esse nescīs,** H. 3, 27, 73. *thou knowest not thou art the bride of the unconquerable Jove.* Similarly with verbs of emotion (2187): as, **gaudent esse rogātae,** *O. AA.* 1, 345, *they are glad to have been asked.* **gaudent perfūsī sanguine frātrum,** V. *G.* 2, 510, *they're glad to have been imbued with brothers' blood.*

VERBS OF ACCUSING.

2185. The verbs of accusing, **arguō** and **īnsimulō,** take the accusative with the infinitive like verbs of saying: as,

cīvīs Rōmānōs necātōs esse arguō, *V.* 5, 149, *my accusation is that Romans have been slain.* **occīdisse patrem Sex. Rōscius arguitur,** *RA.* 37. *Roscius is charged with the murder of his father.* **īnsimulāre coepērunt Epicratem litterās pūblicās corrūpisse,** *V.* 2, 60, *they began to accuse Epicrates of having falsified records of state.*

VERBS OF HOPING, PROMISING, AND THREATENING.

2186. The accusative with the future infinitive is used with verbs of hoping, promising, and threatening: as,

id sēsē effectūrōs spērābant, 7, 26, 2, *they hoped to carry it out.* pollicentur sēsē ēi dēditūrōs, 5, 20, 2, *they volunteer to surrender to him.* But
sometimes the present infinitive alone : see 2236.

VERBS OF EMOTION.

2187. The accusative with the infinitive is sometimes used with
verbs of joy, grief, surprise, or wonder : as,

venīre tū mē gaudēs, Pl. *B.* 184, *thou art glad I'm come.* doluī pācem
repudiārī, *Marc.* 14, *I felt sorry peace was rejected.* These verbs often have
the construction with quod, or in old Latin with quia (1851).

2188. Some of the commonest of these verbs are doleō, gaudeō, laetor,
mīror, &c., &c.; and from Cicero on, angor, indignor, lūgeō, sollicitō.

VERBS OF DESIRE.

2189. (1.) The accusative with the infinitive is commonly used
with volō (mālō, nōlō), and cupiō, when the subject of the infinitive
is not the same as that of the verb : as,

Catilīnam perīre voluī, *Ph.* 8, 15, *I wished Catiline to die.* māluit hominēs peccāre quam deōs, *V.* 2, 22, *he wanted men to sin rather than gods.*
tē tuā fruī virtūte cupimus, *Br.* 331, *we wish you to reap the benefit of your
high character.*

2190. (2.) Even when the subjects denote the same person, the accusative is sometimes used with the infinitive : as,

ēmorī mē mālim, Pl. *As.* 810, morī mē mālim, T. *Eu.* 66, *I'd rather
die.* magnuficē volō mē virōs summōs accipere, Pl. *Ps.* 167, *I'm going
to entertain some highborn gentlemen in style.* Oftenest when the infinitive
is esse, vidērī, putārī, or dīcī : as, cupiō mē esse clēmentem, cupiō mē
nōn dissolūtum vidērī, *C.* 1, 4, *I wish to play the man of mercy, and yet I
do not wish to seem over lax.* Rarely thus with dēsīderō, nōlō, optō, and
studeō, and in Sallust with properō.

2191. For the perfect active with these verbs, see 2228 ; for the perfect passive,
2229.

2192. volō, mālō, and cupiō are often coordinated with the subjunctive of
desire (1707). volō and mālō often have the subjunctive with ut, particularly in
old Latin (1950).

2193. Verbs of resolving sometimes take the accusative with the infinitive : as,
certum offirmāre est viam mē, T. *Hec.* 454, *I am resolved to hold the way.*
So, from Cicero on, sometimes cēnseō, dēcernō, and sentiō, in the exceptional
sense of volō or iubeō, *think it best:* as, velle et cēnsēre eōs ab armīs discēdere, *S. I.* 21, 4, *that they wished and thought it best for those people to give up
fighting.*

2194. The accusative with the infinitive is sometimes used with verbs of demanding : as, hau postulō equidem mēd in lectō accumbere, Pl. *St.* 488, *I
can't expect, not I, to sprawl upon a couch.* hīc postulat sē absolvī? *V.* 3, 138,
does this man ask to be acquitted? Similarly with ōrō and praecipiō in late
writers.

2195. The accusative with the infinitive is sometimes found with **suādeō** and **persuādeō** in Terence, Lucretius, and Vergil, and with **precor** in Ovid and late prose.

Verbs of Accomplishing.

2196. Verbs of accomplishing rarely have the accusative with the infinitive: as, **tālis ōrātōrēs vidērī facit, quālis ipsī sē vidērī volunt,** *Br.* 142, of delivery, *it makes orators appear just as they wish to appear themselves.* Oftenest in poetry. In prose usually the subjunctive with **ut** (1951).

Verbs of Teaching and Training.

2197. The verbs of teaching and training, **doceō** and **adsuēfaciō**, may take an accusative of a substantive and an infinitive expressing the thing taught: as,

quīn etiam tondēre fīliās suās docuit, *TD.* 5, 58, *why more than that, he actually taught his own daughters to shave,* of Dionysius, tyrant of Syracuse. **equōs eōdem remanēre vestīgiō adsuēfēcērunt,** 4, 2, 3, *they have their horses trained to stand stock-still* (1608). Compare 1169.

Verbs of Bidding and Forbidding and of Allowing.

2198. The accusative with the infinitive is used with **iubeō** and **vetō, sinō** and **patior**: as,

mīlitēs ex oppidō exīre iussit, 2, 33, 1, *he ordered the soldiers to go out of the town.* **pontem iubet rescindī,** 1, 7, 2, *he orders the bridge torn up.* **lēx peregrīnum vetat in mūrum ascendere,** *DO.* 2, 100, *it is against the law for a foreigner to get up on the wall.* **castra vāllō mūnīrī vetuit,** Caes. *C.* 1, 41, 4, *he gave orders that the camp should not be fortified with a palisade.* **vīnum ad sē inportārī nōn sinunt,** 4, 2, 6, *wine they will not allow to be brought into their country.* Cicero is the first to use **vetō** thus. Other constructions also occur with these words: see 1708, 1950, 1953, &c.

2199. The person ordered or forbidden is often omitted, when stress is laid on the action merely, or when the person is obvious from the context: as, **castra mūnīre iubet,** i.e. **mīlitēs,** 2, 5, 6, *he gives orders to construct a camp.* **iussērunt prōnūntiāre,** i.e. **tribūnōs et centuriōnēs,** 5, 33, 3, *they gave orders to proclaim.* **īdemque iussērunt simulācrum Iovis facere maius,** i.e. **cōnsulēs,** *C.* 3, 20, *and they furthermore gave directions to make a statue of Jupiter, a bigger one.*

2200. **iubeō** is sometimes coordinated with the subjunctive, especially in old Latin (1708). Sometimes it has the subjunctive with **ut**, especially in resolves of the people.

2201. In the passive, **iubeō, vetō,** and **sinō** are used personally, the accusative of the person ordered or forbidden becoming nominative: as, **iubentur scrībere exercitum,** L. 3, 30, 3, *they are ordered to raise an army.* **Nōlānī mūrōs adīre vetitī,** L. 23, 16, 9, *the men of Nola were not allowed to go to the walls.* **hīc accūsāre eum nōn est situs,** *Sest.* 95, *this man was not allowed to accuse him.*

2202. imperō often has the accusative with a passive or deponent infinitive, or with fierī : as, **praesentem pecūniam solvī imperāvī,** *Att.* 2, 4, 1, *I have given orders for ready money to be paid.* Rarely with an active infinitive parallel with a passive: as, **eō partem nāvium convenīre commeātumque com-portārī imperat,** Caes. *C.* 3, 42, 2, *he orders part of the vessels to rendezvous there, and grain to be brought.* In the passive, a personal **imperor** occurs, like iubeor (2201): as, **in lautumiās dēdūcī imperantur,** *V.* 5, 68, *orders are given for them to be taken to the quarries.* See also 1950. permittō has sometimes the accusative with the infinitive from Tacitus on, usually the subjunctive with ut (1950).

2203. The verbs of hindering, prohibeō and impediō, sometimes have the accusative with the infinitive: as, **barbarī nostrōs nāvibus ēgredī prohibē-bant,** 4, 24, 1, *the savages undertook to prevent our people from disembarking.* The infinitive used with prohibeō is usually passive or deponent. **quid est igitur quod mē impediat ea quae probābilia mihī videantur sequī?** *Off.* 2, 8, *what is there then to hinder me from following what seems to me to be probable?* See also 1960 and 1977.

The Infinitive as a Substantive Accusative.

2204. The accusative with the infinitive, or the infinitive alone, regarded as a neuter substantive, may be used as the object of a verb, or in apposition with the object: as,

(*a.*) leporem gustāre fās nōn putant, 5, 12, 6, *tasting hare they count a sin.* errāre malum dūcimus, *Off.* 1, 18, *going astray we hold a bad thing.* (*b.*) ad id quod īnstituistī, ōrātōrum genera distinguere aetātibus, istam dīligentiam esse accommodātam putō, *Br.* 74, *I think your accurate schol-arship is just the thing for your projected task — classifying public speakers chronologically.*

2205. The infinitive as a substantive is rarely preceded by the preposition inter in late prose: as, multum interest inter dare et accipere, Sen. *Ben.* 5, 10, 2, *there is a vast difference between ' give ' and ' take.'* Cicero has it thus once in a translation (*Fin.* 2, 43). In poetry praeter is thus used rarely.

2206. In poetry, the infinitive is used as a substantive object with such verbs as dō, reddō, adimō, perdō: as, hīc verērī perdidit, Pl. *B.* 158, *this youth has lost his sense of shame.*

(B.) The Infinitive as Subject.

2207. The accusative with the infinitive, or the in-finitive alone, present or perfect, may be used as the subject of a verb, in apposition with the subject, or as a predicate nominative: as,

(*a.*) mendācem memorem esse oportēre, Quintil. 4, 2, 91, *that a liar should have a good memory.* (*b.*) sequitur illud, caedem senātum iūdicāsse contrā rem pūblicam esse factam, *Mil.* 12, *next comes this point, that the senate adjudged the homicide an offence against the state.* (*c.*) exitus fuit ōrā-tiōnis, sibī nūllam cum hīs amīcitiam esse posse, 4, 8, 1, *the end of the speech was that he could not have any friendship with these people.*

2208. The infinitive is used as the subject (*a*.) with impersonal verbs, (*b*.) with **est, putātur, habētur,** &c., and an abstract substantive, a genitive, or a neuter adjective in the predicate.

2209. (*a*.) Some of the commonest impersonal verbs are **appāret, decet, expedit, licet, lubet, oportet, praestat, pudet, rēfert.** Also in classical Latin, **attinet, condūcit, cōnstat, dēdecet, exsistit, fallit, interest, iuvat, liquet, obest, paenitet, patet, pertinet, placet, displicet, prōdest,** which are used as live verbs by Lucretius and Sallust also. Similarly in Plautus and Terence **fortasse.**

2210. The infinitive is occasionally used as a subject with verbs other than the above (2209): as, **nōn cadit invidēre in sapientem,** *TD.* 3, 21, *envy does not square with our ideas of a sage.* **carēre hoc sīgnificat, egēre eō quod habēre velīs,** *TD.* 1, 88, *careō means not having what you would like to have.*

2211. (*b*.) Some of the commonest abstracts used thus with **est** are **fāma, fās · and nefās, fidēs, iūs, laus, opus, mōs, tempus.** From Cicero on, **opīniō** and **prōverbium.** In Plautus, **audācia, cōnfīdentia, miseria, negōtium, scelus,** &c. For genitives, see 1237. Neuter adjectives are such as **aequum, inīquum, cōnsentāneum, crēdibile, incrēdibile, manifestum, necesse, pār, rēctum,** &c., &c.

2212. The accusative is not expressed when it is indefinite, *you, a man, a person, anybody,* frequently also when it is implied in some other case in the sentence: as,

nōn tam praeclārum est scīre Latīnē quam turpe nescīre, *Br.* 140, *it is not so creditable to be a Latin scholar as it is disreputable not to be.* **mihī inter virtūtēs grammaticī habēbitur aliqua nescīre,** Quintil. 1, 8, 21, *in my eyes it will be one merit in a classical scholar not to be omniscient.* **temporī cēdere semper sapientis est habitum,** *Fam.* 4, 9, 2, *bowing to the inevitable has always passed as a mark of wisdom.* **peccāre licet nēminī,** *Par.* 20, *no man is at liberty to sin.* An indefinite **hominem, aliquem,** or **tē,** is rare: as, **illa laus est, līberōs hominem ēducāre,** Pl. *MG.* 703, *it is a crown of glory for a man a family to rear.*

2213. (1.) A predicate noun referring to the unexpressed indefinite subject of the infinitive is put in the accusative: as,

nōn esse cupidum pecūnia est, nōn esse emācem vectīgal est, contentum vērō suīs rēbus esse maximae sunt dīvitiae, *Par.* 51, *for a man not to have desires, is money down, not to be eager to buy is an income; but to be satisfied with what you have is the greatest possible wealth.* A plural predicate is rare: as, **esset ēgregium domesticīs esse contentōs,** *O.* 22, *it would be a grand thing for people to be satisfied with home examples.*

2214. (2.) When the subject of the infinitive is implied in a dative, a predicate noun may also be in the dative . as,

mihī neglegentī esse nōn licet, *Att.* 1, 17, 6, *it will not do for me to be careless.* With a dative and licet, however, the predicate is sometimes in the accusative: as, **quod sī cīvī Rōmānō licet esse Gādītānum,** *Balb.* 29, *now if a Roman is allowed to be a Gaditanian.* Regularly so, when the subject is indefinite and not expressed (2212): as, **haec praescrīpta servantem licet magnificē vīvere,** *Off.* 1, 92, *a man who holds to these rules may live a noble life.*

2215. The infinitive, used as a substantive in the nominative or accusative sometimes has a neuter attribute.

Chiefly thus ipsum, hoc ipsum, tōtum hoc : as, **ipsum Latīnē loquī est in magnā laude pōnendum,** *Br.* 140, *just the mere ability of talking good Latin is to be accounted highly creditable.* Rarely a possessive, **meum, tuum** : as, **ita tuom cōnfertō amāre nē tibi sit probrō,** Pl. *Cur.* 28, *so shape thy wooing that it be to thee no shame.*

THE INFINITIVE OF EXCLAMATION.

2216. The infinitive alone, or the accusative with the infinitive, is sometimes used in exclamations of surprise, incredulity, disapproval, or lamentation : as,

nōn pudēre, T. *Ph.* 233, *not be ashamed.* **sedēre tōtōs diēs in vīllā,** *Att.* 12, 44, 2, *sitting round whole days and days at the country place.* **at tē Rōmae nōn fore,** *Att.* 5, 20, 7, *only to think you won't be in Rome.* **hoc posterīs memoriae trāditum īrī,** L. 3, 67, 1, *to think this will be passed down to generations yet unborn.* Often with a -ne, transferred from the unexpressed verb on which the infinitive depends (1503) : as, **tēne hoc, Accī, dīcere, tālī prūdentiā praeditum,** *Clu.* 84, *what ? you to say this, Accius, with your sound sense.* The exclamatory infinitive is chiefly confined to Plautus, Terence, and Cicero.

THE INFINITIVE OF INTIMATION.

2217. This infinitive has already been spoken of ; see **1535–1539.**

THE TENSES OF THE INFINITIVE.

2218. The present infinitive represents action as going on, the perfect as completed, and the future as not yet begun, at the time of the action of the verb to which the infinitive is attached.

The forms of the infinitive are commonly and conveniently called tenses, though this designation is not strictly applicable.

THE PRESENT TENSE.

2219. In itself, the present infinitive denotes action merely as going on, without any reference to time. With some verbs, however, which look to the future, the present relates to action in the immediate future. With verbs of perceiving, knowing, thinking, and saying, it denotes action as going on at the time of the verb : as, (*a.*) facinus est vincīre cīvem Rōmānum, *V.* 5, 170, *it is a crime to put a Roman in irons.* (*b.*) audīre cupiō, *Caec.* 33, *I am eager to hear.* Antium mē recipere cōgitō a. d. v Nōn. Māi., *Att.* 2, 9, 4, *I am meditating going back to Antium the third of May.* (*c.*) errāre eōs dīcunt, 5, 41, 5, *they say those people are mistaken.* tempus dīxī esse, T. *Hec.* 687, *I said it was time.* dīcēs tibī Siculōs esse amīcōs? *V.* 2, 155, *will you say the Sicilians are friends of yours ?*

2220. The present infinitive is sometimes used with meminī, recordor, memoriā teneō, and with some analogous expressions, such as accēpimus, fertur, &c., to represent merely the occurrence of action really completed, without indicating its completion : as,

meminī ad mē tē scrībere, *D.* 38, *I remember your writing to me.* meministis fierī senātūs cōnsultum, *Mur.* 51, *you remember a decree of the senate being passed.* sed ego īdem recordor longē omnibus anteferre Dēmosthenem, *O.* 23, *and yet I remember putting Demosthenes far above everybody else.* hanc accēpimus agrōs et nemora peragrāre, *HR.* 24, *we have heard of this goddess's scouring fields and groves.* Q. Maximum accēpimus facile cēlāre, tacēre, *Off.* 1, 108, *we have heard of Fabius's ready cleverness in keeping dark and holding his tongue.* But the perfect is used when the action is to be distinctly marked as completed : as, meministis mē ita distribuisse causam, *RA.* 122, *you remember that I arranged the case thus.* Sometimes present and perfect are united : as, Helenē capere arma fertur, nec frātrēs ērubuisse deōs, Prop. 3, 14, 19 (4, 13, 19), *Helen is said to fly to arms, and not to have blushed in presence of her brother gods.* Here capere relates to the same completed action as the more exact ērubuisse.

2221. With verbs of saying, used in the narrower sense of promising, the present infinitive sometimes stands for the future (2236) : as,

crās māne argentum mihī mīles dare sē dīxit, T. *Ph.* 531, *the soldier spoke of paying me the money early in the morning.* mē āibat accersere, Pl. *Ps.* 1118, *he said he'd fetch me* (2186). quae imperārentur facere dīxērunt, 2, 32, 3, *they agreed to do what was commanded.*

2222. The present infinitive dependent on a past tense of dēbeō, oportet, possum, often requires the English perfect infinitive in translation : as, quid enim facere poterāmus? *Pis.* 13, *for what else could we have done?* See, however, 1495. For the infinitive perfect, see 2230.

THE PERFECT TENSE.

2223. (1.) The perfect active infinitive sometimes serves as a complement of dēbeō, volō, possum, &c. (2168) : as,

tametsī statim vīcisse dēbeō, tamen dē meō iūre dēcēdam, *RA.* 73, *though I am entitled to come off victorious at once, yet I will waive my right ;* compare vīcī, *I am victorious,* 1608. nīl vetitum fēcisse volet, J. 14, 185, *nothing forbidden will he wish to have done ;* compare fēcī, *I am guilty.* unde illa potuit didicisse ? *Div.* 2, 51, *from what source could he have all that information acquired ?* bellum quod possumus ante hiemem perfēcisse, L. 37, 19, 5, *the war which we can have ended up before winter.*

2224. (2.) In prohibitions, the perfect active infinitive often serves as a complement of nōlō or volō (2168).

Thus, in old Latin, nōlītō dēvellisse, Pl. *Poen.* 872, *do not have had it plucked.* Particularly so when dependent on nē velit or nē vellet, in legal style : as, nē quis convēnisse sacrōrum causā velit, L. 39, 14, 8, *that nobody may presume to have banded with others for the observance of the mysteries.* BACAS · VIR · NEQVIS · ADIESE · VELET, CIL. I, 196, 7, inscription of 186 B. C., *that no male should presume to have had resort to the Bacchants* (765; 48). nē quid ēmisse velit īnsciente dominō, Cato, *RR.* 5, 4, *he must not venture to have bought anything without his master's knowledge,* of a head farm-steward.

2225. In poetry of the Augustan age, the complementary perfect infinitive active is sometimes dependent on a verb of will or effort, such as cūrō, labōrō, tendō : as, tendentēs opācō Pēlion inposuisse Olympō, H. 3, 4, 51, *on shadowy Olympus striving Pelion to have piled.*

2226. Any past tense of the indicative, when made dependent on a verb of perceiving, knowing, thinking, or saying, is represented by the perfect infinitive.

Thus, in **Theophrastus scrībit Cīmōnem hospitālem fuisse : ita enim vīlicīs imperāvisse, ut omnia praebērentur,** *Off.* 2, 64, *Theophrastus says in his book that Cimon was the soul of hospitality : he had directed his stewards to furnish everything required ;* the **fuisse** represents **erat** or **fuit,** and the **imperāvisse** may represent **imperābat, imperāvit,** or perhaps **imperāverat,** of direct discourse. **praecō dīxisse prōnūntiat,** *V.* 2, 75, *the crier proclaims ' speaking finished '* (1605).

2227. The perfect infinitive passive with fuisse denotes a past resulting state : as,

dīcō Mithridātī cōpiās omnibus rēbus ōrnātās atque īnstrūctās fuisse, urbemque obsessam esse, *IP.* 20, *I must tell you that Mithridates's troops were completely armed and equipped, and that the town was under siege.* Here ōrnātās fuisse represents ōrnātae erant (1615), and obsessam esse represents obsidēbātur (1595).

2228. (1.) The perfect active infinitive is sometimes used with nōlō or volō, especially in poetry, when the subject of the infinitive is not the same as that of the verb (2189) : as,

hanc tē ad cēterās virtūtēs adiēcisse velim, L. 30, 14, 6, *I only wish you had this good quality added to the rest.*

2229. (2.) volō often has an emphatic perfect passive infinitive, usually without esse (2230) ; less frequently cupiō and rarely nōlō : as,

factum volō, Pl. *B.* 495, *As.* 685, *I want it done,* i. e. I will. illōs monitōs etiam atque etiam volō, *C.* 2, 27, *I want those people cautioned over and over.* Particularly common in Cicero, not in Caesar or Sallust. Also with impersonal infinitives (1479) : as, oblīvīscere illum adversāriō tuō voluisse cōnsultum, *Att.* 16, 16ᶜ, 10, *you must forget that the man wanted your enemy provided for.*

2230. The perfect infinitive passive or deponent, commonly without **esse**, is often used in Plautus, Terence, and Cicero, by assimilation with past tenses of verbs of propriety, such as **aequum est, convenit, decet,** and **oportet** : as, **nōn oportuit relīctās,** T. *Hau.* 247, *they should n't have been left.* **tē Iovī comprecātam oportuit,** Pl. *Am.* 739, *you should have said your prayers to Jove.* The perfect active is less common : as, **cāvisse oportuit,** Pl. *Am.* 944, *you should have been upon your guard.* For **volō, cupiō, nōlō,** see 2229.

2231. The perfect infinitive of completed action is very common with such expressions as **satis est, satis habeō, iuvat, melius est, paenitet,** &c., also with verbs of emotion, such as **gaudeō,** &c. : as, **mē quoque iuvat ad finem bellī Pūnicī pervēnisse,** L. 31, 1, 1, *I am delighted myself to have reached the end of the Punic war.* Oftentimes, however, in verse, the use of the perfect is partly due to the metre.

THE FUTURE TENSE.

2232. The future infinitive is only used as a representative of the indicative, and not as a substantive.

2233. For the future infinitive active or passive, a circumlocution with **fore** or **futūrum esse** with **ut** and the subjunctive present or imperfect is often used. This construction is necessary when the verb has no future participle or supine : as,

spērō fore ut contingat id nōbīs, *TD.* 1, 82, *I hope we may be so fortunate.* **clāmābant fore ut ipsī sē dī ulcīscerentur,** *V.* 4, 87, *they cried out that the gods would avenge themselves.*

2234. fore with the perfect participle of a passive or deponent, represents the future perfect of direct discourse : as, **dēbellātum mox fore rēbantur,** L. 23, 13, 6, *they thought the war would soon be over.*

2235. (1.) The future infinitive is commonly used with **iūrō, minor, polliceor, prōmittō,** and **spērō,** especially when the leading verb and the infinitive have the same subject : as,

iūrāvit sē nisi victōrem in castra nōn reversūrum, Caes. *C.* 3, 87, 5. *he swore he would not come back to camp except as a victor.* **quod sē factūrōs minābantur,** Caes. *C.* 2, 13, 4, *which they threatened they would do.* **obsidēs datūrōs pollicitī sunt,** 4, 27, 1, *they volunteered to give hostages.*

2236. (2.) A looser present infinitive is sometimes used with the above verbs, especially in old Latin, generally without a subject accusative. Thus with **iūrō** by Cato and Plautus, and with **minor,** *proclaim with threats,* by Lucretius. Similarly **dare pollicentur,** 6, 9, 7, *they offer to give.* **reliquōs dēterrērī spērāns,** Caes. *C.* 3, 8, 3, *hoping that the rest were scared.* **spērō nostram amīcitiam nōn egēre testibus,** *Fam.* 2, 2, *I trust our friendship needs no witnesses.* As **possum** has no future infinitive, the present of this verb is necessarily used : as, **tōtīus Galliae sēsē potīrī posse spērant,** 1, 3, 8, *they hope to be able to get the control of the whole of Gaul.*

———◆———

THE GERUNDIVE AND GERUND.

2237. The gerundive is a verbal adjective (899). The gerund is a neuter verbal substantive, used only in the oblique cases of the singular. Both gerundives and gerunds express, in a noun form, the uncompleted action of the verb.

2238. Gerundives and gerunds, like the English verbal in *-ing*, were originally neither active nor passive (288), but might stand for either an active or a passive. In time a prevailing passive meaning grew up in the gerundive, and a prevailing active meaning in the gerund.

A gerund may be followed by the same case as its verb; but for the gerund of verbs of transitive use, see 2242, 2255, 2259, 2265.

2239. Both gerundives and gerunds are modified like verbs, by adverbs, not by adjectives.

(1.) THE GERUNDIVE CONSTRUCTION.

2240. The gerundive expresses, in an adjective form, the uncompleted action of a verb of transitive use exerted on a substantive object, the substantive standing in the case required by the context, and the gerundive agreeing with it.

In this construction, which is called the *gerundive construction*, the substantive and gerundive blend together in sense like the parts of a compound.

male gerendō negōtiō in aere aliēnō vacillant, *C.* 2, 21, *owing to bad business-managing they are staggering under debts.* studium agrī colendī, *CM.* 59, *the occupation of land-tilling.* vir regendae rēī pūblicae scientissimus, *DO.* 1, 214, *a man of great experience in state-managing.*

(2.) THE GERUND.

2241. The gerund expresses, in a substantive form, the uncompleted action of a verb which has no direct object.

ars vīvendī, *Fin.* 1, 42, *the art of living.* nōn est locus ad tergiversandum, *Att.* 7, 1, 4, *'tis no time for shill-I-shall-I-ing.* sum dēfessus quaeritandō, Pl. *Am.* 1014, *I'm all worn out with hunting.* sē experiendō didicisse, Ta. 1, 11, *he had learned by experience.*

2242. Gerunds of verbs of transitive use are exceptionally found with a substantive object (2255, 2259, 2265), and regularly with neuter pronouns and neuter plural adjectives to avoid ambiguity (1106). See also 2247.

agendī aliquid discendīque causā, *Fin.* 5, 54, *for the sake of doing or learning something.* faciendī aliquid vel nōn faciendī vēra ratiō, Plin. *Ep.* 6, 27, 4, *the true ground for doing or not doing a thing.* artem sē trādere vēra ac falsa diiūdicandī, *DO.* 2, 157, *that he passed along the art of distinguishing between the true and the false.* regendī cūncta onus, Ta. 1, 11, *the burden of governing the world.*

CASES OF GERUNDS AND GERUNDIVES.

NOMINATIVE.

2243. The nominative of the gerundive construction, as the subject of **sum**, denotes action which is to be done.

The combination acquires the meaning of obligation or propriety, and this meaning also passes over to the accusative with **esse**. The person who has the action to do is put in the dative of the possessor (1215). Instead of the dative, the ablative with **ab** is sometimes used, particularly where the dative would be ambiguous.

tibī haec cūra suscipienda est, *V.* 4, 69, *the undertaking of this care exists for you,* i.e. *you must undertake this charge.* Caesarī omnia ūnō tempore erant agenda: vēxillum prōpōnendum, sīgnum tubā dandum, ab opere revocandī mīlitēs, aciēs īnstruenda, mīlitēs cohortandī, sīgnum dandum, 2, 20, 1, *for Caesar there was everything to be done at the same moment: the standard to be raised, bugle call given, soldiers summoned in from their work, line of battle to be formed, soldiers harangued, signal given for engagement.* quaerenda pecūnia prīmum est; virtūs post nummōs, H. *E.* 1, 1, 53, *there is money-making to be the first aim: character second to dollars.* adeundus mihī illic est homō, Pl. *R.* 1298, *I must draw near this fellow.* Caesar statuit sibī Rhēnum esse trānseundum, 4, 16, 1, *Caesar made up his mind that he must cross the Rhine.* ego istum tenendum cēnseō, L. 21, 3, 6, *for my part, I think that young man ought to be kept at home.* ēī ego ā mē referendam grātiam nōn putem? *Planc.* 78, *should I not think that I ought to show my gratitude to him?* quid ā mē amplius dīcendum putātis? *V.* 3, 60, *what more do you think that I need say?*

2244. fruendus, fungendus, potiundus, ūtendus, vēscendus, are also used in this construction, chiefly in the oblique cases; in the nominative the impersonal construction (2246) is usual. These verbs sometimes have a transitive use in old Latin (1380).

nōn paranda nōbīs sōlum ea, sed fruenda etiam est, *Fin.* 1, 3, *that is a thing which we must not only obtain, but enjoy as well,* of wisdom. nec tamen est potiunda tibī, O. 9, 754, *she is not to be won by thee.* Examples of the oblique cases in this use are cited below.

2245. habeō with the gerundive, as an equivalent of est mihĭ, est tibĭ, &c. (2243), is sometimes found, chiefly in late writers and particularly in Tacitus: as,

multĭ habent in praediīs, quibus frūmentum aut vīnum aliudve quid dēsit, inportandum, Varro, *RR.* 1, 16, 2, *many on whose estates corn or wine or something else is lacking, have to bring it in.* multum interest utrumne dē fūrtō dīcendum habeās an dē cīvibus trucīdātīs, Ta. *D.* 37, *it makes a great difference whether you have to speak about a theft or about the murder of Romans.* sī nunc prīmum statuendum habērēmus, Ta. 14, 44, *if we had to decide the point to-day for the first time.*

2246. The neuter of verbs of intransitive use takes the impersonal construction with est. Verbs ordinarily transitive also take the impersonal construction when used without an object.

nunc est bibendum, H. 1, 37, 1, *now drinking exists,* i.e. *now we must drink.* inambulandumst, Pl. *As.* 682, *I must be moving on.* ego amplius dēlīberandum cēnseō, T. *Ph.* 457, *I opine there must be more pondering.* linguae moderandumst mihĭ, Pl. *Cu.* 486, *I must check my tongue.* omne animal cōnfitendum est esse mortāle, *DN.* 3, 32, *it must be admitted that every living thing is destined to die.* nēmō umquam sapiēns prōditōrī crēdendum putāvit, *V.* 1, 38, *no wise man ever held that a traitor was to be trusted.*

2247. The impersonal construction with an object in the accusative, is old-fashioned and rare.

canēs paucōs habendum, Varro, *RR.* 1, 21, *one should keep but few dogs.* aeternās quoniam poenās in morte timendumst, Lucr. 1, 111, *since punishment eterne they have in death to fear.* This construction occurs oftenest in Lucretius and Varro; once in Plautus, a few times in Cicero for special reasons, and here and there in later writers. Not in Caesar or Horace.

2248. The gerundive sometimes acquires, in itself, the meaning of obligation or propriety, which it properly has only when combined with sum, and becomes a mere adjective, used in any case.

fōrmā expetendā līberālem virginem, Pl. *Per.* 521, *a freeborn maid of shape delectable.* L. Brūtō, principe huius maximē cōnservandī generis et nōminis, *Ph.* 3, 11, *Brutus, the first of this most highly cherished house and name.* huic timendō hostī obvius fuī, L. 21, 41, 4, *I met this dreadful foe.* Athēnās, multa vīsenda habentīs, L. 45, 27, 11, *Athens, which contains many sights worth a visit.* For volvendus &c., see 288.

2249. The attributive gerundive (2248), particularly with a negative, in- privative, or vix, may denote possibility, like the verbal in -bilis: as,

labōrēs nōn fugiendōs, *Fin.* 2, 118, *inevitable labours.* Polybius, haud-quāquam spernendus auctor, L. 30, 45, 5, *Polybius, an authority by no means despicable.* īnfandum, rēgīna, iubēs renovāre dolōrem, *V.* 2, 3, *thou bidst me, queen, rehearse that woe unspeakable.* vix erat crēdendum, 5, 28, 1, *it was hardly credible.* praedicābile aliquid et glōriandum ac prae sē ferendum, *TD.* 5, 49, *something laudable and vauntable and displayable as well.*

ACCUSATIVE.

2250. (1.) The accusative of the gerundive construction is used with **locō** and **condūcō**, with **suscipiō, habeō,** and **cūrō,** and with verbs of giving or assigning.

With the verbs of giving or assigning (such as **dō, trādō, committō, attribuō, dīvidō, relinquō, permittō, dēnotō**), the emphasis often gravitates towards the substantive, and the gerundive, as an explanatory appendage, acquires the meaning of purpose. So in Plautus with the verbs of asking (**rogō** and **petō**); in Cicero with **posco.**

(*a.*) **caedundum condūxī ego illum :: tum optumumst locēs efferendum,** Pl. *Aul.* 567, *I engaged him for killing : : then you'd better contract for his funeral* (1709). **sīgnum conlocandum cōnsulēs locāvērunt,** *Cat.* 3, 20, *the consuls let out the erecting of the statue.* **redemptor quī columnam illam condūxerat faciendam,** *Div.* 2, 47, *the contractor who had undertaken the making of that pillar.* **vellem suscēpissēs iuvenem regendum,** *Att.* 10, 6, 2, *I wish you had undertaken training the young man.* **aedem habuit tuendam,** *V.* 1, 130, *he had the looking after the temple.* **agrum dē nostrō patre colendum habēbat,** T. *Ph.* 364, *he had the tilling of a farm from my father.*

(*b.*) COIRAVIT · BASILICAM · CALECANDAM, CIL. I, 1166, *he superintended the town hall plastering.* **pontem faciendum cūrat,** 1, 13, 1, *he attends to a bridge's being made,* i. e. *has it made.* **cōnsulibus senātus rem pūblicam dēfendendam dedit,** *Ph.* 8, 15, *the senate entrusted the defence of the state to the consuls.* **agrōs plēbī colendōs dedit,** *RP.* 3, 16, *he gave lands to the common people to till.* **Antigonus Eumenem propīnquīs sepeliendum trādidit,** N. 18, 13, 4, *Antigonus delivered Eumenes to his kinsfolk to be buried.* **attribuit ncs trucīdandōs,** *C.* 4, 13, *us he handed over to be slaughtered.* **sauciōs mīlitēs cūrandōs dīvidit patribus,** L. 2, 47, 12, *he apportioned the wounded soldiers among the senators to cure.* **haec porcīs comedenda relinquēs,** H. *E.* 1, 7, 19, *you'll leave them to the pigs to eat.* **cīvīs Rōmānōs trucīdandōs dēnotāvit,** *IP.* 7, *he specified Romans for slaughter.*

(*c.*) **quae ūtenda vāsa semper vīcīnī rogant,** Pl. *Aul.* 96, *traps that the neighbours are always asking the use of.* **artoptam ex proxumō ūtendam petō,** Pl. *Aul.* 400, *I'm going for the use of a breadpan from next door.*

2251. When such a verb is passive, the accusative becomes nominative.

simulācrum Dīānae tollendum locātur, *V.* 4, 76, *the moving of the statue of Diana is let out.* **dīlaceranda ferīs dabor ālitibusque praeda,** *Cat.* 64, 152, *I shall be given a prey for beasts and birds to tear.* **trādĭtīque fētiālibus Caudium dūcendī,** L. 9, 10, 2, *and they were delivered to the fetials to be taken to Caudium.*

2252. (2.) The accusative of the gerundive construction or gerund is used with a preposition, usually **ad.** If the verb is of transitive use, the gerundive is proper, not the gerund (2240).

This construction is used with verbs (including verbs of hindering), with substantives generally to denote purpose, and with adjectives which have the meaning of *capable, fit, easy, useful,* &c., &c.

(*a.*) hic in noxiāst, ille ad dīcendam causam adest, T. *Ph.* 266, *when A's in trouble, B turns up to make excuses for him.* ad pācem petendam ad Hannibalem vēnit, L. 21, 13, 1, *he is come to Hannibal to sue for peace.* ad eās rēs cōnficiendās 'Orgetorīx dēligitur, 1, 3, 3, *Orgetorix is chosen to do this.* dant sē ad lūdendum, *Fin.* 5, 42, *they devote themselves to playing.* palūs Rōmānōs ad īnsequendum tardābat, 7, 26, 2, *a morass hindered the Romans from pursuit.* ut peditēs ad trānseundum impedīrentur, Caes. *C.* 1, 62, 2, *so that the infantry were hampered in crossing.* (*b.*) causa ad obiūr- gandum, T. *Andr.* 150, *a reason for finding fault.* spatium sūmāmus ad cōgitandum, *Fin.* 4, 1, *let us take time for thought.* alter occāsiōnem sibī ad occupandam Asiam oblātam esse arbitrātur, *IP.* 4, *the other thinks a chance is given him for seizing all Asia.* (*c.*) homo nōn aptissimus ad iocandum, *DN.* 2, 46, *a man not very well fitted to be a joker.* nimis doctus illest ad male faciendum, Pl. *E.* 378, *too well the fellow's trained at playing tricks.* ūtēbātur eō cibō quī esset facillimus ad concoquendum, *Fin.* 2, 64, *he made use of the sort of food which was easiest to digest.*

2253. Other prepositions are sometimes used: as, **inter**, in old Latin, Vergil, Livy, and later writers; **ob**, once in Ennius, rarely in Cicero and Sallust; **in** very rarely, but even in Cicero; **ante** (Vergil, Livy), **circā** (post-Augustan), **propter** (Varro, Val. Max.), all rare.

mōrēs sē inter lūdendum dētegunt, Quintil. 1, 3, 12, *character discovers itself during play.* ob rem iūdicandam pecūniam accipere, *V.* 2, 78, *to take money for passing judgement on a case.*

DATIVE.

2254. The dative of the gerundive construction is used with adjectives, verbs, and phrases of ability, attention, and adaptation, with titles of office, and with **comitia**, *election.*

This construction is not very common in classical Latin, where few verbs and substantives take it instead of the usual ad and the accusative (2252). In old Latin, it is also joined to adjectives and participles; in Cicero it is thus used only with **accommodātus.** From Livy on, the construction becomes a very favourite one. Caesar has it only as below and 3, 4, 1.

tālīs iactandīs tuae sunt cōnsuētae manūs, Pl. *Vid.* 33, *your hands are used to throwing dice.* optumum operī faciundō, Pl. *R.* 757, *most suitable for carrying on his trade.* praeesse agrō colendō, *RA.* 50, *to superintend farm managing.* cum diēs vēnisset rogātiōnī ferendae, *Att.* 1, 14, 5, *when the day came for proposing the bill.* hībernīs oppugnandīs hunc esse dictum diem, 5, 27, 5, *that this was the day set for attacking the winter quarters.* cōnsul plācandīs dīs habendōque dīlēctū dat operam, L. 22, 2, 1, *the con- sul devotes himself to proᵗitiating the gods and raising troops.* Dēmosthenēs cūrātor mūrīs reficiendīs fuit, *OG.* 19, *Demosthenes was commissioner for repairing the walls.* IIIvirī rēī pūblicae cōnstituendae, L. *Epit.* 120, *a commission of three for reorganizing the state.* comitia collēgae subrogandō habuit, L. 2, 8, 3, *he held an election for appointing a colleague.*

2255. In the dative, a transitive gerund with an object in the accusative is found four times in Plautus; in Ovid, Livy, and Vitruvius once each.

2256. Late writers sometimes use the dative of the gerundive construction instead of a final clause (1961) : as,

subdūcit ex aciē legiōnem faciendīs castrīs, Ta. 2, 21, *he withdraws a legion from the field to build a camp.* nīdum mollibus plūmīs cōnsternunt tepēfaciendīs ōvīs, simul nē dūrus sit īnfantibus pullīs, Plin. *NH.* 10, 92, *they line the nest with soft feathers to warm the eggs, and also to prevent it from being uncomfortable to their young brood.*

2257. The dative of the gerund is used chiefly by old and late writers, and is confined in the best prose to a few special phrases.

ōsculandō meliust pausam fierī, Pl. *R.* 1205, *'tis better that a stop be put to kissing.* tū nec solvendō erās, *Ph.* 2, 4, *you were neither solvent.* SC · ARF, i. e. scrībendō arfuērunt, CIL. I, 196, 2, *there were present when the document was put in writing.* quod scrībendō adfuistī, *Fam.* 15, 6, 2, *because you were present at the writing.*

GENITIVE.

2258. (1.) The genitive of the gerundive construction or gerund is used with substantives or adjectives.

(*a.*) tacendī tempus est, Pl. *Poen.* 741, *it 's time to be still.* spēs potiundī oppidī, 2, 7, 2, *the hope of overpowering the town* (2244). summa difficultās nāvigandī, 3, 12, 5. *the greatest difficulty in sailing.* proeliī committendī sīgnum dedit, 2, 21, 3, *he gave the signal for beginning the battle.* exemplō eōrum clādēs fuit ut Mārsī mitterent ōrātōrēs pācis petendae, L. 9, 45, 18, *their downfall was a warning to the Marsians to send envoys to sue for peace.* sīve nāvēs dēiciendī operis essent missae, 4, 17, 10, *or if vessels for breaking down the works had been sent.* Particularly with causā, grātiā, or rarely ergō (1257), to denote purpose : as, frūmentandī causā, 4, 12, 1, *for foraging.* vītandae suspīciōnis causā, *C.* 1, 19, *to avoid suspicion.* mūneris fungendī grātiā, *RP.* 1, 27, *for the sake of doing one's duty.* illiusce sacrī coercendī ergō, Cato, *RR.* 139, *because of thinning out yon hallowed grove.*

(*b.*) quam cupida eram hūc redeundī, T. *Hec.* 91, *how eager I was to return here.* homine perītō dēfīniendī, *Off.* 3, 60, *a man accomplished in drawing distinctions.* perpessus est omnia potius quam cōnsciōs dēlendae tyrannidis indicāret, *TD.* 2, 52, *he stood out against the worst sooner than betray his confederates in the overthrow of the tyranny.* īnsuētus nāvigandī, 5, 6, 3, *unused to sailing.* studiōsus audiendī, N. 15, 3, 2, *an eager listener.* nescia tolerandī, Ta. 3, 1, *ignorant what patience was.* nandī pavidus, Ta. *H.* 5, 14, *afraid to swim.* With adjectives, the gerundive construction is not found in Plautus and Terence, and the gerund not in Plautus. Terence has the gerund with cupidus, Cato with studiōsus. The construction is of slow growth before Tacitus, who greatly developed it.

2259. In the genitive, a transitive gerund with an object in the accusative is rare except in Plautus ; ordinarily the gerundive is used (2240).

tē dēfrūdandī causā, Pl. *Men.* 687, *for the purpose of cheating you.* **cupidus tē audiendī,** *DO.* 2, 16, *eager to hear you.* **summa ēlūdendī occāsiōst mihi nunc senēs,** T. *Ph.* 885, *I 've now a splendid chance the graybeards of eluding.* **nē suī līberandī** (2260) **atque ulcīscendī Rōmānōs occāsiōnem dīmittant,** 5, 38, 2, *that they should not let slip the chance of freeing themselves and taking vengeance on the Romans.* **sīgnum colligendī vāsa dedit,** L. 24, 16, 14, *he gave the signal to pack their things.*

2260. nostrī, vostrī (or vestrī), and suī, being singular in form (649) have often a singular gerundive.

nōn tam suī cōnservandī quam tuōrum cōnsiliōrum reprimendōrum causā profūgērunt, *C.* 1, 7, *they fled, not so much to protect themselves as to crush your plans.* **vēnisse tempus ulcīscendī suī,** *Sest.* 28, *that the time was come for them to revenge themselves.* **vestrī adhortandī causā,** L. 21, 41, 1, *for the purpose of encouraging you.*

2261. Sometimes another genitive appears beside the genitive of the gerund, each perhaps dependent on the main word. This use is found in old Latin, Lucretius, Varro, and here and there in Cicero, as well as in late Latin.

nōminandī istōrum tibī erit cōpia, Pl. *Cap.* 852, *you will have a chance to name them.* **poenārum solvendī tempus,** Lucr. 5, 1225, *the time of paying penalties.* **exemplōrum ēligendī potestās,** *Inv.* 2, 5, *a chance of picking out examples.* **lūcis tuendī cōpiam,** Pl. *Cap.* 1008, *a chance to look upon the light.*

2262. (2.) The genitive of the gerundive construction is used predicatively with **sum.**

rēgium imperium, quod initiō cōnservandae lībertātis fuerat, S. *C.* 6, 7, *the authority of the king, which had originally served to uphold freedom.* **cētera in** XII **minuendī sūmptūs sunt lāmentātiōnisque fūnebris,** *Leg.* 2, 59, *the rest of the contents of the Twelve Tables are conducive to the abating of extravagance and keening at funerals.* **concordiam ōrdinum, quam dissolvendae tribūnīciae potestātis rentur esse,** L. 5, 3, 5, *the union of the classes, which they believe serves to break down the power of the tribunes.* This use is not common. It is found rarely in Sallust and Cicero; chiefly in Livy.

2263. The genitive of the gerundive construction, without a substantive or adjective (2258) or the verb **sum** (2262), is occasionally used to denote purpose : as,

quae ille cēpit lēgum ac lībertātis subvortundae, S. *Fr. Phil.* 10, *which he began in order to overthrow freedom and the laws,* of civil war. **ūnum vincīrī iubet, magis ūsurpandī iūris quam quia ūnīus culpa foret,** Ta. *H.* 4, 25, *he ordered one into irons, more to vindicate his authority than because an individual was to blame.* This use occurs very rarely in Sallust, chiefly in Tacitus and late Latin. Once in Terence with the gerund.

2264. Tacitus has the genitive of the gerundive construction two or three times with a judicial verb (1280) to denote the charge: as, **occupandae rēī pūblicae arguī nōn poterant,** Ta. 6, 10, *they could not be charged with an attempt on the throne.*

ABLATIVE.

2265. In the ablative a transitive gerund with a substantive object is not uncommon.

frātrem laudandō, *Leg.* 1, 1, *in quoting your brother.* **largē partiendō praedam,** L. 21, 5, 5, *by a lavish distribution of the spoil.* This use is particularly common in Livy. Not in Caesar.

2266. (1.) The ablative of the gerundive construction or gerund denotes means, less often cause, rarely manner and circumstances, or time, or respect.

Means : **Caesar dandō sublevandō īgnōscundō, Catō nihil largiundō glōriam adeptus est,** S. *C.* 54, 3, *Caesar gained reputation by giving, helping, and pardoning, Cato by lavishing no gifts.* **opprimī sustentandō ac prōlātandō nūllō pactō potest,** *C.* 4, 6, *it cannot be crushed by patience and procrastination.* Livy has this ablative with the adjective **contentus** (1377): **nec iam possidendīs pūblicīs agrīs contentōs esse,** 6, 14, 11, *that they were no longer satisfied with the occupation of the public lands.* Cause : **aggerundā curvom aquā,** Pl. *Cas.* 124, *bowed with water carrying.* **flendō turgidulī rubent ocellī,** Cat. 3, 18, *with weeping red and swollen are her eyne.* Manner and circumstances : rare in old Latin and Cicero : not in Caesar : **bellum ambulandō cōnfēcērunt,** Caelius in *Fam.* 8, 15, 1, *they strolled through the war.* **senex vincendō factus,** L. 30, 28, 5, *maturing in victories.* Time : **cum plausum meō nōmine recitandō dedissent,** *Att.* 4, 1, 6, *when they had applauded on the reading of my name.* **partibus dīvidendīs ipsī regiō ēvēnit,** L. 25, 30, 6, *at the distribution, the district fell to him.* Respect : **Latīnē loquendō cuivīs erat pār,** *Br.* 128, *in his use of Latin he was a match for anybody.*

2267. (2.) The ablative of the gerundive construction or gerund is also accompanied by a preposition, **ab, dē, in,** or **ex ;** rarely by **prō.**

nūllum tempus illī umquam vacābat aut ā scrībendō aut ā cōgitandō, *Br.* 272, *he never had any time free from writing or from thinking.* **quod verbum ductum est ā nimis intuendō fortūnam alterīus,** *TD.* 3, 20, *a word which is derived from 'looking too closely at' another's prosperity,* of the word invidia. **cōnsilium illud dē occlūdendīs aedibus,** T. *Eu.* 784, *that idea about barring up the house.* **nihil dē causā discendā praecipiunt,** *DO.* 2, 100, *they give no instruction about studying up a case.* **vostra ōrātiō in rē incipiundā,** T. *Ph.* 224, *your remarks when we started in with this affair.* **Āfricānī in rē gerundā celeritātem,** *V.* 5, 25, *Africanus's swiftness in execution.* **vix ex grātulandō ēminēbam,** Pl. *Cap.* 504, *I barely got my head above their congratulations.* **quae virtūs ex prōvidendō est appellāta prūdentia,** *Leg.* 1, 60, *a virtue which from 'foreseeing' is called foresight.* **prō līberandā amīcā,** Pl. *Per.* 426, *for setting free a leman.* **prō ope ferendā,** L. 23, 28, 11, *instead of going to the rescue.* In this use ab is not found in Plautus or Terence, nor prō in Terence. cum is found in Quintilian, **super** once in Horace, then in Tacitus, sine once in Varro.

2268. With a comparative expression, the ablative of the gerundive is found once: **nūllum officium referendā grātiā magis necessārium est,** *Off.* 1, 47, *no obligation is more binding than the returning of a favour.* The gerundive construction in the ablative of separation (1302) is found rarely in Livy and Pliny the younger; Livy has also the gerund: as, **Verminam absistere sequendō coēgit,** L. 29, 33, 8, *he forced Vermina to abandon his pursuit.*

THE SUPINE.

2269. The supine is a verbal substantive. The form in **-um** is an accusative. The form in **-ū** is used sometimes as a dative, sometimes as an ablative.

THE SUPINE IN -um.

2270. The supine in **-um** denotes purpose with verbs of motion (1166): as,

abiīt piscātum, Pl. *R.* 898, *he's gone a fishing.* **neu noctū īrem obambulātum,** Pl. *Tri.* 315, *not to go a prowling by night.* **legiōne ūnā frūmentātum missā,** 4, 32, 1, *one legion being sent a foraging.* **sessum it praetor,** *DN.* 3, 74, *the praetor is going to take his seat.* **spectātum veniunt, veniunt spectentur ut ipsae,** O. *AA.* 1, 99, *they come to see and eke for to be seen.* This use is very common in Plautus and Terence, less common in Cicero and Caesar. It is found not infrequently in Sallust and particularly in Livy; sporadically in the Augustan poets. In late prose it is almost confined to archaistic writing. In classical Latin, purpose is more commonly expressed by the subjunctive with **ut** or a relative pronoun, or by a gerundive or gerund with **ad** or **causā.** See also 2164.

2271. The most common supines in **-um** are **cubitum, dormītum, ēreptum, frūmentātum, grātulātum, nūntiātum, oppugnātum, ōrātum, pāstum, perditum, petītum, salūtātum, sessum, supplicātum.** They are found chiefly with **eō** and **veniō. nūptum** is also common with **dō, collocō,** &c., and supines are occasionally found with other verbs implying motion.

2272. The supine in **-um** may be followed by the same construction as its verb: as,

(*a.*) Accusative: **deōs salūtātum atque uxōrem modo intrō dēvortor domum,** Pl. *St.* 534, *I'll just turn in home to greet my gods and my wife.* **lēgātōs ad Caesarem mittunt rogātum auxilium,** 1, 11, 2, *they send envoys to Caesar to beg aid.* **oppugnātum patriam nostram veniunt,** L. 21, 41, 13, *they come to assail our country.* Classical writers generally avoid this use of the accusative. (*b.*) Dative: **servītum tibi mē abdūcitō,** Pl. *Ps.* 520, *take me away to slave for you.* **nōn ego Grāis servītum mātribus ībō,** V. 2, 786, *not I shall go to be the serf of Grecian dames.* (*c.*) Subordinate clause: **lēgātī veniēbant: Aeduī questum quod Harūdēs fīnēs eōrum populārentur,** 1, 37, 1, *envoys came: the Aeduans to complain 'because the Harudians were laying their country waste'* (1853). **lēgātōs ad Caesarem mīsērunt ōrātum nē sē in hostium numerō dūceret,** 6, 32, 1, *they sent envoys to Caesar to beg that he would not regard them in the light of enemies.*

407

2273. The supine in -um followed by īrī forms the future passive infinitive: as,

eum exceptum īrī putō, *Att.* 7, 22, 1, *I think that there is a going to capture him*, i. e. *that he is going to be captured.* Here īrī is used impersonally and eum is the object of exceptum. This infinitive is found half a dozen times in old Latin, often in Cicero, rarely in other writers; not in the Augustan poets. For the common periphrasis, see 2233.

THE SUPINE IN -Ū.

2274. The supine in -ū is used with fās, nefās, and adjectives, chiefly of such meaning as *easy, good, pleasant, strange*, or their opposites.

Only a few supines in -ū are found; the commonest are audītū, cōgnitū, dictū, factū, inventū, memorātū, nātū, vīsū.

sī hoc fās est dictū, *TD.* 5, 38, *if heaven allows us to say so.* difficile dictū est dē singulīs, *Fam.* 1, 7, 2, *it is hard to say in the case of individuals.* quaerunt quod optimum factū sit, *V.* 1, 68, *they ask what the best thing is to do.* quid est tam iocundum cōgnitū atque audītū? *DO.* 1, 31, *what pleasure is greater to mind and ear?* palpebrae mollissimae tāctū, *DN.* 2, 142, *the eyelids are very soft to the touch.* With such adjectives the dative is commonly used (1200); or, particularly with facilis or difficilis, the gerundive construction with ad (2252); for the infinitive, see 2166. The supine in -ū is found chiefly in Cicero and Livy. Very rare in old Latin, Sallust, Caesar (who has only factū and nātū), and the poets. From the elder Pliny and Tacitus on, it gets commoner.

2275. The supine in -ū sometimes introduces a subordinate sentence, but it is never used with an object in the accusative.

quoivīs facile scītū est quam fuerim miser, T. *Hec.* 296, *anybody can easily understand how unhappy I was.* incrēdibile memorātū est quam facile coaluerint, S. *C.* 6, 2, *it is an incredible tale how readily they grew into one.* vidētis nefās esse dictū miseram fuisse tālem senectūtem, *CM.* 13, *you see that it were a sin to say that an old age like his was unhappy.*

2276. The supine in -ū is found rarely with opus est (1379), dīgnus and indīgnus (1392): as,

ita dictū opus est, T. *Hau.* 941, *thus thou must needs say.* nihil dignum dictū āctum hīs cōnsulibus, L. 4, 30, 4, *nothing worth mentioning was done this year.* For dignus with quī and the subjunctive, see 1819; for opus est with the infinitive, 2211.

2277. In Plautus and Cato, the supine in -ū is very rarely used like an ablative of separation (1302): as, nunc opsonātū redeō, Pl. *Men.* 288, *I'm only just back from catering.* prīmus cubitū surgat, postrēmus cubiʼum eat, Cato, *RR.* 5, 5, *let him be first to get up from bed and last to go to bed.* Statius imitates this use in *Ach.* 1, 119.

408

THE PARTICIPLE.

2278. The participle is a verbal adjective. Like the adjective, it is inflected to agree with its substantive. Like the verb, it may be modified by an adverb, it is active or passive, and it expresses action as continuing, completed, or future. It may also be followed by the same case as its verb.

TIME OF THE PARTICIPLE.

2279. (1.) The time to which the participle refers is indicated by the verb of the sentence.

āēr effluēns hūc et illūc ventōs efficit, *DN.* 2, 101, *the air by streaming to and fro produces winds.* convēnī hodiē adveniēns quendam, T. *Eu.* 234, *I met a man as I was coming to-day.* manūs tendentēs vītam ōrābant, L. 44, 42, 4, *with hands outstretched they begged their lives.* Croesus Halyn penetrāns magnam pervertet opum vim, oracle in *Div.* 2, 115, *Croesus, when Halys he shall cross, will overthrow a mighty realm.* benignitātem tūam mihī expertō praedicās, Pl. *Merc.* 289, *thou vauntest to me who 've proved thy courtesy.* cōnsecūtus id quod animō prōposuerat, receptuī canī iussit, 7, 47, 1, *having accomplished what he had designed, he gave orders to sound the retreat.* Dionӯsius Syrācūsīs expulsus Corinthī puerōs docēbat, *TD.* 3, 27, *after his expulsion from Syracuse, Dionysius kept school at Corinth.* lēgātī dīxērunt sē rē dēlīberātā ad Caesarem reversūrōs, 4, 9, 1, *the envoys said that they would come back to Caesar after they had thought the matter over.*

2280. (2.) The perfect participle of deponents is sometimes used with past tenses or their equivalents to denote incomplete contemporaneous action. So occasionally a perfect passive.

(*a.*) Metellum esse ratī portās clausēre, S. *I.* 69, 1, *supposing that it was Metellus, they closed their gates.* gāvīsus illōs retinērī iussit, 4, 13, 6, *with pleasure he gave orders for their detention.* persuādent Rauracīs utī eōdem ūsī cōnsiliō proficīscantur, 1, 5, 4, *they coaxed the Rauraci to adopt the same plan and go.* sōlātus iussit sapientem pāscere barbam, H. *S.* 2, 3, 35, *consoling me he bade me grow a philosophic beard.* This use is found in old Latin and in Cicero very rarely. Sallust and Caesar use a few verbs thus. It is not uncommon in the Augustan poets and Livy. In late writers, especially Tacitus, it is frequent. (*b.*) servum sub furcā caesum mediō ēgerat circō, L. 2, 36, 1, *he had driven a slave round, flogged under the fork, right in the circus.* With this compare servus per circum, cum virgīs caederētur, furcam ferēns ductus est, *Div.* 1, 55, *a slave with the fork on his neck was driven through the circus, flogged with rods the while* (1872). But the perfect passive has its ordinary force (2279) in verberibus caesum tē in pistrīnum dēdam, T. *Andr.* 199, *I 'll give you a flogging and then put you in the mill.*

2281. For the perfect participle with forms of sum and fuī, see 1608, 1609; for the conative present participle, 2301; reflexive, 1482.

THE ATTRIBUTIVE PARTICIPLE.

2282. The present or perfect participle is often used as an adjective to express a permanent condition : as,

ācrem ōrātōrem, incēnsum et agentem et canōrum forī strepitus dēsīderat, *Br.* 317, *the noisy forum requires an impetuous speaker, inspired and dramatic and sonorous.* L. Abuccius, homo adprīmē doctus, Varro, *RR.* 3, 2, 17, *Abuccius, an eminently learned man.* aliī facētī, flōrentēs etiam et ōrnātī, *O.* 20, *others are brilliant, even bright and elegant.* id tibī renūntiō futūrum ut sīs sciēns, T. *Andr.* 508, *I give you notice this will happen, that you may be prepared.*

2283. The future participle is found as an adjective in the Augustan poets and in late writers. Cicero, however, has futūrus in this use with rēs and a few other words, and has ventūrus once.

dā mānsūram urbem, V. 3, 85, *grant a city that shall abide.* firmus pariēs et dūrātūrus, Ta. *D.* 22, *a strong and durable wall.* sīgna ostenduntur ā dīs rērum futūrārum, *DN.* 2, 12, *signs of future events are disclosed by the gods.* For the future participle with forms of sum, see 1633.

2284. Many participles have become complete adjectives, and as such are capable of composition or comparison, or take the case required by an adjective.

(*a.*) nōmen invictī imperātōris, *V.* 4, 82, *the invincible general's name.* pūrus et īnsōns sī vīvō, H. *S.* 1, 6, 69, *pure and guiltless if I live* (749). (*b.*) solūtus venēficae scientiōris carmine, H. *Epod.* 5, 71, *freed by some craftier witch's charm.* homo ērudītissimus, Verrēs, *V.* 4, 126, *Verres, most accomplished of men.* (*c.*) tibi sum oboediēns, Pl. *MG.* 806, *I 'm your obedient* (1200). tē cōnfīdō ea factūrum quae mihī intellegēs maximē esse accommodāta, *Fam.* 3, 3, 2, *I feel confident that you will do what you shall feel most appropriate to my interests* (1201). For the genitive with such participles, see 1266.

2285. A perfect participle in agreement with a substantive often contains the leading idea, and may be translated like an abstract substantive with a genitive dependent. The nominative is rarely thus used. The present participle in this use is rare, the future late.

This construction expresses the completed action of the verb in precisely the same way that the gerundive construction (2240) expresses uncompleted action.

(*a.*) Joined with substantives: iniūriae retentōrum equitum Rōmānōrum, 3, 10, 2, *the outrages of Roman knights detained,* i. e. *in the detention of Roman knights.* servātī cōnsulis decus, L. 21, 46, 10, *the credit of saving the consul.* male administrātae prōvinciae urgēbātur, Ta. 6, 29, *he was charged with maladministration of his province.* ō quid solūtīs est beātius cūris ? Cat. 31, 7, *oh what is sweeter than the putting off of care ?*

(*b.*) Joined with prepositions: ab conditā urbe ad līberātam, L. 1, 60, 3, *from the foundation of the city to the liberation thereof.* post nātōs hominēs improbissimus, *Br.* 224, *the greatest reprobate since the creation of man.* ante cīvitātem datam, *Arch.* 9, *before the gift of the citizenship.*

(*c.*) In the nominative: very rare before Livy: **dēpressa hostium classis,** *Arch.* 21, *the sinking of the enemy's fleet.* **angēbant ingentis spīritūs virum Sicilia Sardiniaque āmissae,** L. 21, 1, 5, *what tortured the high-souled hero was the loss of Sicily and Sardinia.* **cuius turbāvit nitidōs exstīnctus passer ocellōs,** J. 6, 7, *whose sparkling eyne the sparrow's death bedimmed.*

2286. This use of the participle, though old, is not common before Livy, who, like Tacitus, has it frequently, both with substantives and with prepositions. Very rare in Caesar, rare in Cicero, who, however, uses it both with substantives and with a few prepositions. In old Latin (not in Terence), it is found with the substantives **opus** and **ūsus,** in Cato with **post,** in Varro with **propter :** as, **mī homine conventōst opus,** Pl. *Cur.* 302, *I needs must see the man.* **propter mare congelātum,** Varro, *RR.* 1, 2, 4, *by reason of the freezing of the sea water.* For the participle alone with **ūsus est** and **opus est,** see 1382.

THE SUBSTANTIVE PARTICIPLE.

2287. Participles sometimes become substantives, especially ₜthe perfect participle: as,

vīvit gnāta, T. *Ph.* 749, *your daughter's alive.* **dē dēmēnsō suō,** T. *Ph.* 43, *out of his allowance.* **īnstitūtum tenēbimus,** *TD.* 4, 7, *we will hold to our fundamental idea.* Adverbs, not adjectives, are commonly used to qualify perfect participles used as substantives; for examples, see 1440. The masculine singular is rarely used as a substantive; the neuter, both singular and plural, is common, particularly with prepositions.

2288. The masculine plural of the perfect participle, when used as a substantive, generally denotes a definite class of persons : as,

ut damnātī in integrum restituantur, vīnctī solvantur, *V.* 5, 12, *that the condemned go scot-free, the imprisoned are set at liberty.* **Catilīna cum expedītīs in prīmā aciē vorsārī,** S. *C.* 60, 4, *Catiline bustling round in the van with the light infantry.* **ēvocātīs equōs sūmit,** 7, 65, 5, *he took away the veterans' horses.* Rarely not denoting a definite class : as, **missī intercipiuntur,** 5, 40, 1, *the men who had been sent* (i.e. on a particular occasion) *are cut off.*

2289. The perfect participle alone sometimes serves as the subject of a sentence instead of an abstract substantive (2285) : as,

nōtum furēns quid fēmina possit, V. 5, 6, *the knowledge of what a woman in her wrath can do.* **prōnūntiātum repente nē quis violārētur, multitūdinem exuit armīs,** L. 4, 59, 7, *the sudden proclamation that nobody was to be harmed, deprived the people of their weapons.* This use is found chiefly in Livy, once or twice in Cicero; not in Caesar or Sallust. See 1382.

2290. The present participle is rarely a substantive in the nominative and ablative singular, but often in the other cases.

in cōnstituentibus rem pūblicam, *Br.* 45, *among the founders of a state.* **multae īnsectantēs dēpellunt,** *DN.* 2, 127, *many drive off their pursuers.* **nec praeterita nec praesentia abs tē, sed futūra exspectō,** *Fam.* 2, 8, 1, *I do not expect from you the past or the present, but the future.*

2291. The genitive plural of the present participle is often best translated by an English abstract : as,

cachinnōs inrīdentium commovēbat, *Br.* 216, *he provoked guffaws of derision.* mixtōs terrentium paventiumque clāmōrēs, L. 22, 5, 4, *mingled cries of exultation and terror.* prīmō gaudentium impetū, Ta. *H.* 1, 4, *in the first outburst of joy.*

2292. The future participle is very rarely used as a substantive.

audītūrum dictūrī cūra dēlectat, Quintil. 11, 3, 157, *deliberation on the part of one who is on the point of speaking attracts his prospective hearer.* havē, imperātor, moritūrī tē salūtant, Suet. *Claud.* 21, *emperor, all hail! the doomed give thee greeting.* This use is found in late writers, as in Tacitus and Curtius once each, and half a dozen times in Pliny the younger. Cicero and Sallust have futūrus thus (2283) : as, abs tē futūra exspectō, *Fam.* 2, 8, 1, *from you I expect the future.* supplicia in post futūrōs composuit, S. *Fr. Lep.* 6, *he invented penalties for men unborn.*

THE APPOSITIVE PARTICIPLE.

2293. The appositive participle is a loose substitute for a subordinate sentence introduced by a relative or by a conjunctive particle.

2294. (1.) The appositive participle may represent a relative sentence : as,

nōvī ego Epicūrēōs omnia sigilla venerantēs, *DN.* 1, 85, *why, I know Epicureans who bow the knee to all sorts of graven images.* Conōn mūrōs dīrutōs ā Lȳsandrō reficiendōs cūrat, N. 9, 4, 5, *Conon superintended the rebuilding of the walls which had been destroyed by Lysander.* The future participle is poetic and late (2283) : as, servēs itūrum Caesarem in Britannōs, H. 1, 35, 29, *guard Caesar who against the Britons is to march.*

2295. (2.) The appositive participle, representing other sentences, may express various relations : as, (*a.*) time, (*b.*) cause or means, (*c.*) purpose, (*d.*) concession, (*e.*) hypothesis, (*f.*) description or the manner of an action, like an adverb.

For the ablative absolute in such relations, see 1362–1374, particularly 1367.

(*a.*) Time : vehemēns sum exoriēns, quom occidō vehementior, Pl. *R.* 71, *furious am I at my rising, when I set more furious still.* occīsus est ā cēnā rediēns, *RA.* 97, *he was murdered on his way home from a dinner-party.* ūnam noctem sōlam praedōnēs commorātī, accēdere incipiunt Syrācūsās, *V.* 5, 95, *the freebooters, after tarrying but one night, began to draw near Syracuse.* The future is late (2283) : as, prīmum omnium virōrum fortium itūrī in proelia canunt, Ta. *G.* 3, *as the chief of all brave heroes, they sing of him when they are on the point of going to battle,* of Hercules.

412

(*b.*) Cause or means: **mōtum exspectāns dīlectum habēre īnstituit,** 6, 1, 1, *since he anticipated a rising, he determined on recruiting troops.* **moveor tālī amīcō orbātus,** *L.* 10, *I am certainly affected at being bereaved of such a friend.* **dextrā datā fidem futūrae amīcitiae sanxisse,** L. 1, 1, 8, *by giving his right hand he gave a pledge of future friendship.* **quae contuēns animus accēdit ad cōgnitiōnem deōrum,** *DN.* 2, 153, *through the contemplation of these, the mind arrives at a knowledge of the gods.* The future participle is late: as, **neque illīs iūdicium aut vēritās, quippe eōdem diē dīversa parī certāmine postulātūrīs,** Ta. *H.* 1, 3c, *they had neither sound judgement nor sincerity, since on the same day they were to make conflicting demands with equal vehemence.*

(*c.*) Purpose: the future participle, commonly with a verb of motion: **ad Clūsium vēnērunt, legiōnem Rōmānam castraque oppugnātūrī,** L. 10, 26, 7, *they came to the neighbourhood of Clusium, to assail the Roman legion and camp.* **ascendit ipse, lātūrus auxilium,** Plin. *Ep.* 6, 16, 9, *he went aboard in person to go to the rescue.* **laetō complērant litora coetū vīsūrī Aeneadas,** V. 5, 107, *in happy company they'd filled the strand to see Aeneas' men.* **rediēre omnēs Bonōniam, rursus cōnsiliātūrī,** Ta. *H.* 2, 53, *they all went back to Bologna for a second consultation.* This use appears first in C. Gracchus as cited by Gellius, then once in Cicero and Sallust each, and a few times in the poets. From Livy on, it grows commoner. In the poets, Livy, and Tacitus, it is sometimes joined with a conditional idea or protasis: as, **ēgreditur castrīs Rōmānus, vāllum invāsūrus nī cōpia pugnae fieret,** L. 3, 60, 8, *the Roman marches out of camp, proposing to assault the stockade unless battle were offered.*

(*d.*) Concession: **quī mortālis nātus condiciōnem postulēs immortālium,** *TD.* 3, 36, *thou who, though born to die, layest claim to the state of the deathless.* **bēstiīs, quibus ipsa terra fundit pāstūs abundantīs nihil labōrantibus,** *Fin.* 2, 111, *the beasts, on which, though they toil not, earth lavishes sustenance in profusion.* Often with **tamen** or the like accompanying the verb: as, **ibī vehementissimē perturbātus Lentulus tamen et sīgnum et manum suam cōgnōvit,** *C.* 3, 12, *thereupon Lentulus, though thrown into the most extreme confusion, did yet recognize his own hand and seal.* For **quamquam** and **quamvīs,** see 1900, 1907. Ovid and Propertius sometimes have **licet** (1710): as, **isque, licet caelī regiōne remōtōs, mente deōs adiīt,** O. 15, 62, *he in the spirit to the gods drew nigh, though they are far away in heaven's domain.* The future participle is rare and late.

(*e.*) Hypothesis: **quid igitur mihī ferārum laniātus oberit nihil sentientī?** *TD.* 1, 104, *what hurt will the clawing of wild beasts do me if I have no feeling?* **appārēbat nōn admissōs prōtinus Carthāginem itūrōs,** *L.* 21, 9, 4, *it grew obvious that, if not given audience, they would go to Carthage forthwith.* For other examples, see 2110. For the participle with **quasi** or **ut,** and in late writers with **tamquam** or **velut,** see 2121. The future participle is rare and late.

(*f.*) Description or manner: **haec properantēs scrīpsimus,** *Att.* 4, 4ª, *I have written this hastily,* i. e. *in haste yours truly.* **dictātor et magister equitum triumphantēs in urbem rediēre,** L. 2, 20, 13, *the dictator and his master of the horse returned to the city in triumph.* **incendēbat haec flētū et pectus verberāns,** Ta. 1, 23, *he lent passion to his words with tears and beating of his breast.* **vinctōs aspiciunt catēnīs līberōs suōs,** *V.* 5, 108, *they behold their own children held in bondage.*

2296. The participle with a negative may be translated by *without*: as,

id illa ūnivorsum abripiet haud existumāns quantō labōre partum, T. *Ph.* 45, *my lady'll grab it all without a thought of all the toil it cost to get.* nōn rogātōs ultrō offerre auxilium, L. 34, 23, 3, *that without being asked, they offer assistance of their own accord.*

THE PREDICATIVE PARTICIPLE.

2297. habeō is sometimes used with certain perfect participles to express an action continuing in its consequences. faciō, dō, and in old Latin reddō and cūrō, with a perfect participle, are emphatic substitutes for the verb to which the participle belongs.

(*a.*) quae nōs nostramque adulēscentiam habent dēspicātam et quae nōs semper omnibus cruciant modīs, T. *Eu.* 383, *who hold us and our youth in scorn and torment us in every way.* in eā prōvinciā pecūniās magnās collocātās habent, *IP.* 18, *they have invested large funds in that province.* Clōdiī animum perspectum habeō, cōgnitum, iūdicātum, *ad Br.* I, I, I, *Clodius's mind I have looked into thoroughly, probed, formed a judgement on.* clausum lacū ac montibus et circumfūsum suīs cōpiīs habuit hostem, L. 22, 4, 5, *his enemy he had shut in by lake and mountains and surrounded by his troops.* See also 1606.

(*b.*) missa haec face, T. *Ad.* 906, *let this pass.* vērum haec missa faciō, *RA.* 76, *but I let this pass.* Mānlium missum fēcit, *Off.* 3, 112, *he let Manlius go.* factum et cūrātum dabō, Pl. *Cas.* 439, *I'll have it done and seen to.* strātās legiōnēs Latīnōrum dabō, L. 8, 6, 6, *I will lay the Latin legions low.* ego iam tē commōtum reddam, T. *Andr.* 864, *I'll soon have you worked up.* inventum tibi cūrābō tuom Pamphilum, T. *Andr.* 684, *I'll have your Pamphilus looked up for you.* In classical writers, faciō only is found in this use and only with the participle of mittō; dō occurs in late writers; reddō and cūrō only in old Latin. All these verbs are usually in the future tense or its equivalent. For volō, cupiō, and nōlō with the infinitive passive without esse, see 2229.

2298. The present participle is used predicatively with verbs signifying *represent*, and with verbs denoting the exercise of the senses or mind: as,

facit Sōcratem disputantem, *DN.* I, 31, *he represents Socrates discussing.* quasi ipsōs indūxī loquentēs, *L.* 3, *I have brought on the men themselves as speaking.* nōn illum miserum, ignārum cāsūs suī, redeuntem ā cēnā vidētis? *RA.* 98, *do you not see the poor man, little dreaming of his fate, returning from the dinner?* nōn audīvit dracōnem loquentem, *Div.* 2, 141, *he did not hear the serpent speaking.* This use is found in Plautus, Terence, Cicero, Sallust, Horace, Nepos, Vitruvius, and Livy. Once in Piso (consul 133 B.C.), as cited by Gellius, 7, 9, 6. Verbs denoting the exercise of the senses or mind take the accusative with the infinitive to denote the fact or action; see 2175. For audiō with cum, see 1870. For the infinitive without esse with verbs of emotion, see 2184.

2299. A passive with a verb meaning *represent* is expressed, for lack of a present passive participle, by the infinitive (2175). The infinitive active is rare.

(*a.*) cōnstruī ā deō atque aedificārī mundum facit, *DN.* 1, 19, *he rep-resents the world being put together and built by the gods.* (*b.*) poētae impen-dēre saxum Tantalō faciunt, *TD.* 4, 35, *the poets represent a rock hanging over Tantalus.* Rarely the participle (2298) and the infinitive are united : as, Polyphēmum Homērus⁰ cum ariete conloquentem facit eiusque lau-dāre fortūnās, *TD.* 5, 115, *Homer represents Polyphemus chatting with the ram and his envy of the ram's estate.* But the perfect infinitive active must be used when the action is to be distinctly marked as completed, for lack of a perfect active participle : as, fēcit Dolābella Verrem accēpisse, *V.* 1, 100, *Dolabella represented Verres as having received.*

———◆———

APPENDIX.

(A.) SOME OCCASIONAL PECULIARITIES OF VERBS.

2300. In many cases where in English a verb like *wish* or *try to have* a thing done, *can*, *must*, or *am allowed to*, is used, the equivalent Latin verb is omitted. As this use generally extends through the entire system of the verb, examples of the nouns of the verb and of subordinate sentences thus used, are conveniently included here.

THE CONATIVE USE.

2301. A verb is sometimes used to denote action proposed, attempted, or begun, but not necessarily carried out. This is called the *Conative Use* of the verb : as,

ancillās dēdō, T. *Hec.* 773, *I try to give,* or *I offer up the servant girls.* sine ūllā dubitātiōne condemnant, *Clu.* 75, *without a moment's hesitation they vote to condemn.* dum id inpetrant, Pl. *Cap.* 233, *as long as they're trying to get it.* sī plācēs inlacrimābilem Plūtōna, H. 2, 14, 5, *shouldst thou the stonyhearted Pluto strive to melt.* sī discēdās, J. 7, 50, *should you attempt to leave.* in cūriam abiēcit, quam vīvus ēverterat, *Mil.* 90, *he shoved the corpse into the senate house, which the man in his lifetime had done his best to overthrow.* adsurgentem rēgem umbōne resupīnat, L. 4, 19, 5, *with the boss of his shield he put the king flat on his back, when he tried to get up.*

2302. This use is particularly common in the imperfect indicative : as,

nostrōs ingredī prohibēbant, 5, 9, 6, *they tried to stop our people from getting in.* Apellēs faciēbat, Plin. *NH. praef.* 26, *Apelles undertook to do this,* or *an attempt of Apelles's.* sēdābant tumultūs, sēdandō interdum movēbant, L. 3, 15, 7, *they tried to quell the riotings, but by trying they started them once in a while afresh.* num dubitās id mē imperante facere, quod iam tuā sponte faciēbās? *C.* 1, 13, *do you possibly hesitate to do at my command what you wanted to do, as it was, yourself?* The conative use is not very common in old Latin, but more frequent from Cicero and Caesar on.

2303. When the conative use is to be expressed more distinctly, a form of **volō** or **cōnor** is used, or a frequentative, like **vēnditō**, *try to sell,* **adventō**, *strive to come.*

THE CAUSATIVE USE.

2304. A verb is sometimes used to denote not what the subject actually does himself, but what he has another do. This is called the *Causative Use* of the verb: as,

animī causā mihi nāvem faciam, Pl. *R.* 932, *just for diversion I'll build me a yacht.* cum vellet sibī ānulum facere, aurificem iussit vocārī, *V.* 4, 56, *wanting to make him a ring, he ordered a goldsmith to be called.* complūrēs pauperēs mortuōs suō sūmptū extulit, N. 5, 4, 3, *he buried a good many poor dead people at his own expense,* i. e. had them buried. Also in the passive: as, tondēmur, Quintil. 1, 6, 44, *we get shaved.* When greater exactness is required, having a thing done may be expressed more distinctly by **faciō (1965),** by **cūrō (2250),** or by iubeō.

THE POTENTIAL USE.

2305. A verb is sometimes used to indicate action that can be done, and especially action that can be done at any time. This is called the *Potential Use* of the verb: as,

clārē oculīs videō, Pl. *MG.* 630, *I can see distinctly.* proptereā quod inter fīnēs Helvētiōrum et Allobrogum Rhodanus fluit isque nōnnūllīs locīs vadō trānsītur, 1, 6, 2, *because the Rhone runs between the district of the Helvetians and Allobrogans, and the river in some places can be forded,* or *is fordable.* Particularly with a negative: as, apertē adūlantem nēmō nōn videt, *L.* 99, *an open flatterer anybody can see through.* nōn facile dīiūdicātur amor vērus et fictus, *Fam.* 9, 16, 2, *real love and pretended love cannot easily be told apart.* ubī Crassus animadvertit, suās cōpiās nōn facile dīdūcī, nōn cunctandum exīstimāvit, 3, 23, 7, *when Crassus saw that his forces could not easily be divided, he thought he ought to lose no time.* quoniam prōpositum nōn tenuerat. Caes. *C.* 3, 65, 4, *seeing that he had not succeeded in carrying out his plan.* Sometimes this idea is expressed by the subjunctive **(1554).**

THE OBLIGATORY USE.

2306. A verb is sometimes used to denote obligatory action. This is called the *Obligatory Use* of the verb: as,

paulisper commorātus est, *Mil.* 28, *he had to wait.* aegra trahēbant corpora, *V.* 3, 140, *they had to drag their sickly frames along.* caruī patriā. *Sest* 145, *I had to keep away from the country of my birth.* senātor populī Rōmānī pernoctāvit in pūblicō, *V.* 4, 25, *a senator of Rome was fain to sleep in the streets.* serēmus aliquid in dērelictō solō, *Br.* 16, *we shall have to sow something in an abandoned field.* erat summa inopia pābulī, adeō ut foliīs equōs alerent. Caes. *C.* 3, 58, 3, *there was an utter lack of fodder, so that they were fain to feed their horses on leaves.*

THE PERMISSIVE USE.

2307. A verb is sometimes used to denote permitted action. **This is** called the *Permissive Use* of the verb: as,

Verrēsne habēbit domī suae candēlābrum Iovis ? *V.* 4, 71, *shall Verres be allowed to have at his house a candelabra of Jupiter?* petit ut ipse dē eō statuat, 1, 19, 5, *he asks to be allowed to sit in judgement himself on the man.* Pīsō ōrāvit ut manēret, Ta. 2, 81, *Piso asked to be allowed to stay.*

(B.) INDIRECT DISCOURSE.

(Ōrātiō Oblīqua.)

2308. The speech or thought of another, quoted in his own words, is called *Direct Discourse* (1723).

2309. The speech or thought of another, dependent on a verb of saying or thinking, is called *Indirect Discourse* (1723).

One may, of course, quote his own words or thoughts indirectly, as well as those of another (1726).

2310. The verb of thinking or saying is often not distinctly expressed, but only implied in the context (1725).

2311. The principles which govern the change of direct discourse into indirect discourse have been already set forth in the foregoing pages; but, for the convenience of the learner, they are here put together.

MOOD.

(A.) MAIN SENTENCES.

2312. Declarative sentences of direct discourse are put in the accusative with the infinitive, and interrogative and imperative sentences of direct discourse are put in the subjunctive, in indirect discourse.

(a.) For examples of declarative sentences, see 2175–2184.

(*b.*) Interrogative (1773): quid vellet? cūr in suās possessiōnēs venīret? 1, 44, 7, *what did he mean? why this movement into his property?* from Ariovistus's reply to Caesar.   dictātor litterās ad senātum mīsit: deum benignitāte Vēiōs iam fore in potestāte populī Rōmānī; quid dē praedā faciendum cēnsērent? L. 5, 20, 1, *the dictator sent this letter to the senate: through the bounty of the gods Vei would soon belong to the Roman nation; what did they think should be done about the booty?*

(*c.*) Imperative (1547): Cicerō respondit: sī ab armīs discēdere velint, sē adiūtōre ūtantur lēgātōsque ad Caesarem mittant, 5, 41, 7, *Cicero replied: if they wished to lay down their arms, let them take his advice and send envoys to Caesar.*   nūntius ēi domō vēnit: bellum Athēniēnsēs et Boeōtōs indīxisse Lacedaemoniīs; quārē venīre nē dubitāret, N. 17, 4, 1, *a message reached him from home: the Athenians and Boeotians had declared war on the Lacedaemonians; so he was to come without delay.*   See also 1707, 1708.

2313. Rhetorical questions (that is, declarations made for effect in the form of questions) in the first or third person in the direct discourse are put in the accusative with the infinitive in indirect discourse: as,

sī veteris contumēliae oblīvīscī vellet, num etiam recentium iniūriārum memoriam dēpōnere posse? 1, 14, 3, *if he were inclined to disregard the old affront, could he also forget their fresh insults?* from Caesar's reply to the Helvetians.   haud mīrum esse Superbō ēi inditum Rōmae cōgnōmen: an quicquam superbius esse quam lūdificārī sīc omne nōmen Latīnum? cui nōn appārēre adfectāre eum imperium in Latīnōs? L. 1, 50, 3, *no wonder Rome dubbed him 'the Proud': could there be a greater sign of pride than this mockery of the whole Latin nation? who did not see that he aspired to dominion over the Latins?*   This use is not found in old Latin. It occurs once or twice in Cicero's letters and a few times in Caesar.   In Livy and late writers, it is not uncommon.   Such questions in the second person require the subjunctive (2312).

2314. Questions which are in the subjunctive in direct discourse retain the subjunctive in indirect discourse: as,

quod vērō ad amīcitiam populī Rōmānī attulissent, id iīs ēripī quis patī posset? 1, 43, 8, *who could allow them to be stripped of what they had possessed when they became the friends of the Roman nation?* (1565).

(B.) Subordinate Sentences.

2315. The verb of a subordinate sentence, introduced by a relative word or a conjunctive particle, stands in the subjunctive in indirect discourse (1722).

For the indicative with **dum**, *in the time while*, retained in indirect discourse, see 1995

sapientissimum esse dīcunt eum, cui quod opus sit ipsī veniat in mentem; proximē accēdere illum quī alterīus bene inventīs obtemperet, *Clu.* 84, *they say he is the wisest man who thinks out of himself what is expedient; and that the man who avails himself of the wise devices of another comes next.* ad haec Ariovistus respondit: iūs esse bellī, ut quī vīcissent iīs quōs vīcissent, quemadmodum vellent imperārent, 1, 36, 1, *to this Ariovistus answered: that it was the right of war for the conquerors to dictate to the conquered such terms as they pleased.*

2316. Relative sentences equivalent to main sentences (1835) may be put in the accusative with the infinitive : as,

ūnum medium diem fuisse, quem tōtum Galbam in cōnsīderandā causā compōnendāque posuisse, *Br.* 87, *that a single day intervened and that this whole day Galba employed in studying up and arranging the case.* This use is found in Cicero, rarely in Caesar, in Livy, and a few times in other authors. Not in old Latin.

2317. So also sentences introduced by certain conjunctive particles are occasionally put in the accusative with the infinitive : as,

id quod saepe dictum est: ut mare ventōrum vī agitārī atque turbārī, sīc populum Rōmānum hominum sēditiōsōrum vōcibus concitārī, *Clu.* 138, *the oft-repeated saying: as the sea is ruffled and tossed by the mighty winds, so the people of Rome are stirred up by the talk of agitators.* honōrificum id mīlitibus fore, quōrum favōrem ut largitiōne et ambitū male adquīrī, ita per bonās artēs haud spernendum, *Ta. H.* 1, 17, *that would be a mark of respect to the troops, and their good will, though usually won by bribery and corruption, was certainly no small gain if honourably come by.* fugere senātum testēs tabulās pūblicās cēnsūs cuiusque, cum interim obaerātam plēbem obiectārī aliīs atque aliīs hostibus, *L.* 6, 27, 6, *that the senate sought to avoid evidence of each man's property through making public returns, while at the same time the commons lay bankrupt and at the mercy of one enemy after another.* ut and quemadmodum are found with this infinitive in Cicero, Livy, and Tacitus; cum interim and sī nōn in Livy; quia in Livy and Seneca; quamquam in Livy and Tacitus; nisi forte in Tacitus. For quam with the infinitive, see 1898.

2318. Relative sentences which are not a part of the quotation, but an addition of the writer's, or which are a circumlocution equivalent to a substantive, are marked by the indicative (1729) : as,

Condrūsōs, Eburōnēs, Caeroesōs, Paemānōs, quī ūnō nōmine Germānī appellantur, arbitrārī ad XL mīlia, 2, 4, 10, *that they reckoned the Condrusians, Eburonians, Caeroesians and Paemanians (who are all called by one name Germans) at forty thousand.* For other examples of such sentences, see 1729.

2319. Sentences containing the thought of another, introduced by a relative pronoun or by causal, temporal, or other conjunctive particles, take the subjunctive, though not appended to the accusative with the infinitive (1725) : as,

421

numquis, quod bonus vir esset, grātiās dīs ēgit umquam ? *DN.* 3, 87, *did anybody ever thank the gods 'because he was a good man' ?* (1853). mihī loquitur nec rēctē quia tibī aurum reddidī et quia nōn tē dēfraudāverim, Pl. *B.* 735, *he's always pitching into me because I returned you the money and 'because I did n't do you out of it'* (1856, 1853). aedem Dīiovī vōvit, sī eō diē hostēs fūdisset, L. 31, 21, 12, *he vowed a temple to infernal Jove, 'if he should rout the enemy on that day.'* For other examples, see 1725, 1852, 1853, 1884, &c.

2320. Sometimes a verb of saying or thinking is added, and is itself irrationally put in the subjunctive. For examples, see 1727.

(2.) TENSE.

(A.) OF THE INFINITIVE.

2321. The tenses of the infinitive follow their usual law (2218), representing the action as present, past, or future, from the speaker's point of view.

nūntiātum est Ariovistum ad occupandum Vesontiōnem contendere trīduīque viam ā suīs fīnibus prōfēcisse, 1, 38, 1, *it was reported that Ariovistus was pressing on* (2219) *to seize Vesontio, and that he had done a three days' journey from his own borders* (2226). fāma est āram esse in vestibulō templī, L. 24, 3, 7, *rumour has it that there is an altar in the vestibule of the temple* (2219). lēgātī haec sē ad suōs relātūrōs dīxērunt, 4, 9, 1, *the envoys said they would report this to their countrymen* (2232). For other examples, see 2175–2203; for the infinitive equivalent of the indicative imperfect and pluperfect, see 2226, 2227.

(B.) OF THE SUBJUNCTIVE.

2322. The tenses of the subjunctive follow the law of the sequence of tenses ; see 1745.

The tenses are usually imperfect or pluperfect, as the verb introducing a quotation is usually past.

Sōcratēs dīcere solēbat, omnēs in eō quod scīrent, satis esse ēloquentēs, *DO.* 1, 63, *Socrates used to maintain that all men were eloquent enough in a matter which they understood* (1766). dīcēbam quoad metuerēs, omnia tē prōmissūrum, *Ph.* 2, 89, *I said that as long as you were afraid, you would promise everything* (1771). cōgnōvit Suēbōs posteā quam pontem fierī comperissent, nūntiōs in omnēs partēs dīmīsisse, 4, 19, 2, *he ascertained that after the Suebans had learned of the building of the bridge, they had sent out messengers in every direction* (1772). For other examples, see 1746–1772.

2323. But the present and perfect subjunctive are often used, especially when the main verb is present, or for vividness after a secondary tense.

Alexandrum Philippus accūsat quod largitiōne benevolentiam Macedonum cōnsectētur, *Off.* 2, 53, *Philip accuses Alexander of courting the favour of the Macedonians by the use of money* (1746, 1853). initium quod huic cum mātre fuerit simultātis audīstis, *Clu.* 17, *you have heard the origin of the enmity which was between the defendant and his mother* (1746). Ariovistus respondit: stīpendium capere iūre bellī quod victōrēs victīs imponere cōnsuerint, 1, 44, 1, *Ariovistus answered that it was by the laws of war that he took the tribute which victors were wont to lay upon the vanquished* (1755). For other examples, see 1746–1772.

2324. The future of direct discourse is represented in indirect discourse by the imperfect, and the future perfect by the pluperfect subjunctive.

sē quod ē rē pūblicā esset factūrum, L. 28, 45, 3, *that he would do what should be for the interests of the state* (1766). sē nōn ante coeptūrum quam ignem in rēgiīs castrīs cōnspexisset, L. 30, 5, 5, *that he would not begin before he saw fire in the royal camp* (1766, 1921). The present or perfect subjunctive also is found when the main verb requires. For other examples, see 1746–1772.

(3.) PRONOUN.

2325. ego and nōs, of direct discourse, are represented by sē in indirect discourse, and meus and noster by suus. tū and vōs, of direct discourse, are represented in indirect discourse by ille, or, when less emphatic, by is.

For the use of the reflexive pronoun, see 2338–2342.

sē prius in Galliam vēnisse quam populum Rōmānum, 1, 44, 7, *that he came into Gaul before the Roman nation*, said Ariovistus of himself. sē ā patribus maiōribusque suīs didicisse, 1, 13, 6, *that they had learned from their fathers and ancestors*, said the Helvetians of themselves. trānsīsse Rhēnum sēsē nōn suā sponte, 1, 44, 1, *that he had crossed the Rhine not of his own accord*, was the assertion of Ariovistus. quī nisi dēcēdat, sēsē illum nōn prō amīcō sed hoste habitūrum. quod sī eum interfēcerit, multīs sēsē prīncipibus populī Rōmānī grātum esse factūrum, 1, 44, 11, *that unless he withdrew, he should consider him not a friend but a foe. Why, if he killed him, he should do a favour to numerous leading men in the Roman nation.* Here Ariovistus is reported as speaking to Caesar.

CONDITIONAL PERIODS IN INDIRECT DISCOURSE.

(A.) PROTASIS.

2326. The protasis of every kind (2023, 2024) has the verb in the subjunctive in indirect discourse (2315).

2327. The tense of the protasis is generally imperfect or pluperfect (2322): as,

Ariovistus respondit: sī ipse populō Rōmānō nōn praescrīberet, nōn oportēre sēsē ā populō Rōmānō impedīrī, 1, 36, 1, *Ariovistus answered: if he did not dictate to the Roman nation, no more ought the Roman nation to interfere with him* (2026). quae sī fēcisset, Pompēium in Hispāniās itūrum, Caes. *C.* 1, 10,3, *if he did that, Pompey would go to the Spains* (2061).

2328. But indeterminate protases (2023) are sometimes put in the present or perfect subjunctive in indirect discourse, even with a main secondary tense: as,

Ariovistus respondit: sī iterum experīrī velint, sē parātum esse dēcertāre, 1, 44, 1, *Ariovistus answered that if the Romans wanted to try again, he was ready to fight it out* (2026). quī nisi dēcēdat, sēsē illum prō hoste habitūrum, 1, 44, 11, *that unless he withdrew, he should consider him an enemy* (2054).

2329. Protases of action non-occurrent (2024) remain in the imperfect or pluperfect, even with a main primary tense.

licet Varrō Mūsās, Aelī Stilōnis sententiā, Plautīnō dīcat sermōne locutūrās fuisse sī Latīnē loquī vellent, Quintil. 10, 1, 99, *though Varro, following Stilo's dictum, may say that the Muses would have spoken in the style of Plautus, if they had wanted to speak Latin* (2095). quaeret ab accūsātōribus quid factūrī essent, sī in eō locō fuissent, Cornif. 2, 22, *he will ask the accusers what they would have done if they had been in that predicament* (2099).

(B.) APODOSIS.

2330. In indeterminate conditional periods (2023), the apodosis simply follows the general rule (2312): as,

Iovem sīc aiunt philosophī, sī Graecē loquātur, loquī, *Br.* 121, *the philosophers say that this is Jove's style of speaking, if Jove speaks Greek* (2026). sīn bellō persequī persevērāret, reminīscerētur prīstinae virtūtis Helvētiōrum, 1, 13, 4, *if he persisted in following them up with war, let him call to mind the old time valour of the Helvetians* (2056). in prōvinciīs intellegēbant sī is quī esset cum imperiō emere vellet, fore utī quod quisque vellet quantī vellet auferret, *V.* 4, 10, *in the provinces they saw that if a man clothed in authority should wish to be a buyer, he would carry off every time whatever he wished at what he wished* (2233; 2054 or 2076). futūrum esse, nisi prōvīsum esset, ut Rōma caperētur, *Div.* 1, 101, *that unless precaution was taken, Rome would be captured* (2233, 2061). For other examples, see 2327, 2328.

2331. In conditional periods of action non-occurrent (2024), the future participle with **fuisse**, is used in apodoses of the active voice: as,

an Cn. Pompēium cēnsēs maximārum rērum glōriā laetātūrum fuisse, sī scīret sē in sōlitūdine Aēgyptiōrum trucīdātum īrī, *Div.* 2, 22, *do you suppose that Pompey would have taken any pleasure in the fame which his peerless exploits brought him if he had known that he was going to be butchered in the wilds of Egypt?*

In one instance, found in Caesar, the future participle with **esse** occurs, representing the imperfect subjunctive of present time (2091):

Caesarem arbitrārī profectum in Ītaliam; neque aliter Carnūtēs interficiundī Tasgetiī cōnsilium fuisse captūrōs, neque Eburōnēs, sī ille adesset, ad castra ventūrōs esse, 5, 29, 2, *that he thought Caesar was gone into Italy; otherwise, the Carnutes would not have formed their design of killing Tasgetius, and the Eburones, if he were at hand, would not be assaulting the camp.* Here the context shows that **ventūrōs esse** represents the imperfect subjunctive. But ordinarily it might seem to represent the future indicative. Hence, to avoid ambiguity, the Romans generally did not try to express present time in apodoses of this class in indirect discourse.

2332. The perfect infinitive is exceptionally used; this is based upon the indicative in apodosis (2104).

memoriā teneō solitum ipsum nārrāre sē studium philosophiae ācrius hausisse, nī prūdentia mātris incēnsum animum coërcuisset, Ta. *Agr.* 4, *I remember that he used to say that he had drunk in the study of philosophy with too great eagerness, had not his discreet mother checked his ardent soul* (2105 or 2107).

2333. possum, in the apodosis of a conditional period of action non-occurrent (2101), is regularly put in the perfect infinitive in indirect discourse: as,

Platōnem exīstimō, sī genus forēnse dīcendī trāctāre voluisset, gravissimē potuisse dīcere, *Off.* 1, 4, *I think that if Plato had only chosen to cultivqte forensic eloquence, he might have been a most impressive speaker* (2103). **cum dīcerent sē potuisse in amplissimum locum pervenīre, sī sua studia ad honōrēs petendōs cōnferre voluissent,** *Clu.* 153, *saying they might have risen to the proudest position, if they had only chosen to apply their energies to a political career* (2103).

2334. **futūrum fuisse ut** with the imperfect subjunctive is rarely used in apodoses of the passive voice (2331): as,

Theophrastus accūsāsse nātūram dīcitur quod hominibus tam exiguam vītam dedisset: quōrum sī aetās potuisset esse longinquior, futūrum fuisse ut omnī doctrīnā hominum vīta ērudīrētur, *TD.* 3, 69, *it is said that Theophrastus took nature to task 'for giving man such a short life; if the period could have been longer man's life would have been informed with knowledge of every sort'* (2099). See also Caes. *C.* 3, 101, 2.

——————◆——————

(C.) PRONOUNS.

THE PERSONAL PRONOUN.

2335. For the use of the nominatives **ego tū, nōs vōs,** see 1029. The genitive plurals **nostrŭm** and **vestrŭm** are used as partitive, **nostrī** and **vestrī** as objective genitives: as,

nēmō nostrŭm, *RA.* 55, *not one cf us* (1242).   ab utrīsque **vestrŭm**, *Fam.* 11, 21, 5, *by each of you* (1243).   grāta mihī vehementer est memoria nostrī tua, *Fam.* 12, 17, 1, *your remembrance of me is exceedingly agreeable to me* (1260).   nostrī nōsmet paenitet, T. *Ph.* 172, *we're discontented with our lot* (1283).   For the adjective instead of the possessive or objective genitive, see 1234, 1262.

The Reflexive sē and suus.

2336. The reflexive regularly refers to the subject of the verb : as,

fugae sēsē mandābant, 2, 24, 2, *they betook themselves to flight.*   animō servit, nōn sibī, Pl. *Tri.* 308, *he serves his passions, not his better self.*   est amāns suī virtūs, *L.* 98, *virtue is fond of itself.*   dūcit sēcum ūnā virginem, T. *Eu.* 229, *he is leading a girl along with him.*   Caesar cōpiās suās dīvīsit, Caes. *C.* 3, 97, 3, *Caesar divided his forces.*   For sē ipse, see 2376; for sē or suus quisque, see 2397.

2337. The reflexive sometimes refers to a word not the subject, when that word is specially emphasized or easily made out from the context.   This holds chiefly of **suus**, which is used with great freedom : as,

Alexandrum uxor sua occīdit, *Inv.* 2, 144, *Alexander was murdered by his own wife.*   dēsinant īnsidiārī domī suae cōnsulī, *C.* 1, 32, *let them cease to waylay the consul in his own house and home.*   suās rēs Syrācūsānīs restituit, *L.* 29, 1, 17, *he restored their property to the Syracuse people.*

2338. In the construction of the accusative with the infinitive (2175), the reflexive is regularly used when the subject of the infinitive refers to the subject of the verb : as,

Vārus imperium sē habēre dīxit, *Lig.* 22, *Varus said that he had authority.*   id sēsē effectūrōs spērābant, 7, 26, 2, *they hoped to accomplish it* (2235).

2339. The reflexive, in this construction, sometimes refers to an emphasized word not the formal subject of the verb : as,

canum custōdia quid sīgnificat aliud nisi sē ad hominum commoditātēs esse generātōs? *DN.* 2, 158, *the watchfulness of the dog— does not it show that he was created for the convenience of man ?*

2340. When the subject of the infinitive is different from that of the verb, the reflexive sometimes refers to the subject of the verb, sometimes to that of the infinitive : as,

Ariovistus respondit omnēs Galliae cīvitātēs ad sē oppugnandum vēnisse, 1, 44, 1, *Ariovistus answered that all the states of Gaul had come to attack him,* i.e. Ariovistus.   nēminem sēcum sine suā perniciē contendisse, 1, 36, 6, *that no man had contended with him without his own undoing;* sēcum refers to Ariovistus, the subject of the main verb respondit, suā to nēminem.

2341. In subordinate subjunctive clauses of purpose, indirect discourse, or indirect question, the reflexive refers to the subject of the main sentence : as,

huic mandat, ut ad sē quam prīmum revertātur, 4, 21, 2, *he instructs him to come back to himself as soon as possible.* excruciābit mē erus, quia sibī nōn dīxerim, Pl. *MG.* 859, *my master'll torture me 'because I have not told him.'* Paetus omnīs librōs, quōs frāter suus relīquisset, mihī dō-nāvit, *Att.* 2, 1, 12, *Paetus made me a present of all the books 'that his brother left.'* For the use of is for sē, see 2370.

2342. The reflexive, in such subordinate clauses, sometimes refers to an emphatic word not the main subject : as,

identịdem fēlīcem Priamum vocābat, quod superstes omnium suōrum exstitisset, Suet. *Tib.* 62, *he was for ever calling Priam 'Fortune's darling, because he outlived all his kith and kin.'*

2343. The reflexive referring to the main subject is sometimes irregularly used in subordinate indicative clauses.

Epamīnōndās ēī, quī sibī successerat, exercitum nōn trādidit, *Inv.* 1, 55, *Epaminondas did not deliver the army to his successor.* centum bovēs mīlitibus dōnō dedit, quī sēcum fuerant, L. 7, 37, 3, *he gave a hundred oxen to the soldiers who had been with him.*

EQUIVALENTS FOR A RECIPROCAL PRONOUN.

2344. The place of a reciprocal pronoun, *each other,* is supplied by inter nōs, inter vōs, inter sē, or by alter or alius followed by another case of the same word : as,

inter nōs nātūrā cōniūnctī sumus, *Fin.* 3, 66, *we are united with each other by nature.* Cicerōnēs puerī amant inter sē, *Att.* 6, 1, 12, *the Cicero boys are fond of each other.* cum alius aliī subsidium ferret, 2, 26, 2, *when they were helping each other.* For uterque, see 2400. The reciprocal idea is sometimes expressed by the form of the verb: as, fulvā lūctantur harēnā, V. 6, 643, *they wrestle with each other on the yellow sand* (1487).

2345. From Livy on, invicem inter sē, invicem sē, or invicem alone, is often used in the expression of reciprocal relations : as,

invicem inter sē grātantēs, L. 9, 43, 17, *mutually congratulating each other.* invicem sē antepōnendō, Ta. *Agr.* 6, *mutually preferring one another.* ut invicem ardentius dīligāmus, Plin. *Ep.* 7, 20, 7, *that we may love each other more ardently.*

THE POSSESSIVE PRONOUN.

2346. The possessive of the personal and reflexive pronoun is regularly omitted, unless it is required for emphasis or contrast : as,

ōra manūsque tuā lavimus, Fērōnia, lymphā, H. *S.* 1, 5, 24, *our hands and faces in thy rill, Feronia, we bathe.* The possessive sometimes has the meaning of *proper, appropriate, favourable ;* as, suō locō dīcam, Quintil. 1, 1, 36, *I shall tell in the proper place.* For the possessive pronoun used instead of the possessive or objective genitive, see 1234, 1262.

THE DEMONSTRATIVE PRONOUN.

hīc.

2347. **hīc** points out what is near the speaker in place, time, or thought: as,

hī domum mē ad sē auferent, Pl. *Men.* 847, *these fellows will hale me off to their house.* nōn mē exīstimāvī in hōc sermōne usque ad hanc aetātem esse ventūrum, *Br.* 232, *I did not think that in this discourse I should get down to the present generation.* reliquum omne tempus huius annī, *V.* 1, 30, *all the rest of this year.*

2348. **hīc** sometimes points out the speaker with pathos, or with emphasis, particularly in comedy.

haec arma et hunc mīlitem propitiō flūmine accipiās, L. 2, 10, 11, *receive these arms and this soldier in thy gracious stream*, the prayer of Horatius Cocles to Father Tiber. tibī erunt parāta verba, huic hominī verbera, T. *Hau.* 356, *you'll get a chiding, this child a hiding.* fēcisset nī haec praesēnsisset canēs, Pl. *Tri.* 172, *and he'd have done it, unless this dog had got scent of it in time*, where the speaker means himself.

2349. The neuter plural **haec** sometimes means *the realm, our country, our state, the* [Roman] *world*: as,

haec, quae iam prīdem vastāre studēs, *C.* 1, 21, *the realm which you have long sought to lay in ruins.* quī haec dēlēre cōnātī sunt, *C.* 4, 7, *who have tried to destroy the state.* servus est nēmō quī nōn haec stāre cupiat, *C.* 4, 16, *there lives no slave that wills not our country should abide.*

2350. **hīc**, as expressing a familiar, every-day thing, occasionally has a shade of contempt, either alone, or with **volgāris, cottīdiānus** or the like: as,

mittit hominī mūnera satis largē, haec ad ūsum domesticum, *V.* 4, 62, *he sent him some presents — pretty liberal ones, commonish things for household use.* mittō hāsce artīs volgārīs, coquōs, pistōrēs, *RA.* 134, *I'll skip your everyday common occupations — such as cooks, bakers, &c., &c.* taedet cottīdiānārum hārum fōrmārum, T. *Eu.* 297, *I'm sick of your everyday beauties.*

2351. When **hīc** relates to the words of a sentence, it points out what has preceded or is to follow, or emphasizes a word referred to by a preceding relative.

For **hīc** used to introduce a new sentence, see 2129.

haec habuī dē senectūte quae dīcerem, *CM.* 85, *this was what I had to say on Old Age.* sed haec hāctenus; nunc ad ostenta veniāmus, *Div.* 2, 53, *so much for this; let us now go on to portents.* fēcit pācem hīs condiciōnibus, *N.* 8, 3, 1, *he made peace on the following terms.* dīcitur locūtus in hanc ferē sententiam esse, *L.* 6, 40, 2, *it is said that he spoke to somewhat the following effect.* quaesierat ex mē Scīpiō quidnam sentīrem dē hōc quod duo sōlēs vīsōs esse cōnstāret, *RP.* 1, 19, *Scipio had asked me what I thought about this, that it was generally agreed that two suns had been seen.*

2352. hīc and ille are often opposed, particularly in contrasts of classes : as,

laudātur ab hīs, culpātur ab illīs, H. *S.* 1, 2, 11, *one side praises him, the other condemns.* illud est album, hoc dulce, canōrum illud, hoc bene olēns, hoc asperum, *Ac.* 2, 21, *that is white, this is sweet, that sonorous, this fragrant, this rough.* ōrātor, nōn ille volgāris sed hīc excellēns, *O.* 45, *an orator, not of the common sort, but the superior one of whom we are speaking.*

2353. In transitions, ille introduces a new thing, hīc denotes *the aforementioned :* as,

sed haec vetera ; illud vērō recēns, Caesarem meō cōnsiliō interfectum, *Ph.* 2, 25, *but this is all ancient history ; here, however, is something new, that Caesar was killed at my suggestion.*

2354. When hīc and ille refer to two different persons or things named in the sentence, hīc commonly refers to the nearer word, ille to the remoter word; or hīc sometimes refers to what is nearer the mind of the speaker, even though it be remoter in the sentence.

(*a.*) Caesar beneficiīs ac mūnificentiā magnus habēbātur, integritāte vītae Catō. Ille mānsuētūdine et misericordiā clārus factus, huic sevēritās dignitātem addiderat, *S. C.* 54, 2, *Caesar was esteemed great for his liberality and generosity, Cato for his unsullied life. The former became famous through his humanity and mercy, the latter's dignity was heightened by his austerity.* (*b.*) cavē Catōnī antepōnās nē istum quidem ipsum quem Apollō, ut ais, sapientissimum iūdicāvit : huius enim facta, illīus dicta laudantur, *L.* 10, *suffer not Cato to find a rival even in your man himself, whom, as you say, Apollo declared wisest of mankind; for our Cato is renowned for deeds, the other for doctrines.*

2355. hīc and ille are used together, chiefly in poetry, to explain something past by a present thing : as,

hunc illum poscere fāta reor, *V.* 7, 272, *this I think is he whom the fates require.* hunc illum fātīs externā ab sēde profectum portendī generum, *V.* 7, 255, *this was the man whom destiny foretold should fare from foreign home to be his son-in-law.*

iste.

2356. iste points out something near to, belonging to, or imputed to the person addressed : as,

cum istā sīs auctōritāte, nōn dēbēs adripere maledictum ex triviō, *Mur.* 13, *carrying the influence that you do, you ought not to take to street-corner abuse.* multae istārum arborum meā manū sunt satae, *CM.* 59, *many of the trees you see there were planted by my own hand.* salem istum quō caret vestra nātiō, inrīdendīs nōbīs nōlītōte cōnsūmere, *ND.* 2, 74, *do not waste in ridiculing us that wit which your fraternity sadly needs.* Often with tuus or vester : as, īsdem hīc sapiēns dē quō loquor oculīs quibus iste vester intuēbitur, *Ac.* 2, 105, *the sage of whom I speak will look with the same eyes as the sage you boast of.*

2357. From its use in addressing opponents or in talking at them, **iste** is common in contemptuous phrases : as,

tū istīs faucibus, istīs lateribus, istā gladiātōriā tōtīus corporis firmitāte, *Ph.* 2, 63, *you with that gullet of yours, those swollen flanks, that prizefighter's bulky make-up.* nōn erit ista amīcitia, sed mercātūra quaedam, *ND.* 1, 122, *such a thing will not be a friendship, but a sort of traffic.*

ille.

2358. ille points to what is remote in place, time, or thought : as,

ergō illī intellegunt quid Epicūrus dīcat, ego nōn intellegō ? *Fin.* 2, 13, *do those gentlemen then understand what Epicurus means and I not ?* populus Rōmānus nihil aequē atque illam veterem iūdiciōrum vim gravitātemque requīrit, *Caecil.* 8, *the Roman people miss nothing so much as the ancient vigour and firmness attaching to public trials.* hīs autem dē rēbus sōl mē ille admonuit ut brevior essem, *DO.* 3, 209, *but on these topics yonder sun has warned me to be pretty brief.* For other examples, see 2352–2355.

2359. ille is used to point out a celebrity, often one of the past. So, particularly without a proper name, in allusive style, referring to what is famed in story.

(*a.*) hīc est ille Dēmosthenēs, *TD.* 5, 103, *this is the famous Demosthenes.* Athēniēnsis ille Themistoclēs, *DO.* 2, 299, *Themistocles the great, of Athens.* illud Solōnis, *CM.* 50, *Solon's memorable words.* Mēdēa illa, *IP.* 22, *Medea famed in story.* (*b.*) vīribus ille cōnfīsus periit, J. 10, 10, *the man in the story lost his life through confidence in his strength.* illae rēgiae lacrimae, *Plin. Ep.* 3, 7, 13, *the monarch's historic tears,* of Xerxes.

2360. Indicating change of subject, ille is *this other man.* In such cases it is often best expressed in English by a proper name or a descriptive word.

ad sē adulēscentem iussit venīre. at ille, ut ingressus est, cōnfestim gladium dēstrinxit, *Off.* 3, 112, *he gave orders to admit the young man. But this other, the moment he entered, drew his sword.* rūsticus expectat dum dēfluat amnis : at ille lābitur et lābētur, *H. E.* 1, 2, 42, *he is a peasant waiting for the river to go down : but the river flows and will flow on.*

2361. In concessions, ille often precedes quidem ; in translation no pronoun is required.

librī scrīptī incōnsīderātē ab optimīs illīs quidem virīs, sed nōn satis ērudītīs, *TD.* 1, 6, *books rashly written by men respectable enough but of insufficient education.* est tarda illa medicīna, sed tamen magna, *TD.* 3, 35, *it is a powerful remedy, though slow in its working.* hīc, is, and iste are used rarely in this way.

2362. In poetry ille may serve : (1.) To repeat a thing with emphasis : as,

arma virumque canō Trōiae quī prīmus ab ōrīs Ītaliam vēnit, multum ille et terrīs iactātus et altō, *V.* 1, 1, *arms and the man I sing, from Troja's shore the first to come to Italy, much tossed that man by land and sea.*

2363. (2.) To emphasize the second of two ideas : as,

nunc dextrā ingemināns ictūs, nunc ille sinistrā, V. 5, 457, *now with his right redoubling blows, now mighty with his left.* nōn tamen Euryalī, non ille oblītus amōrum, V. 5, 334, *still not Euryalus forgetting, no, not he his love !*

2364. (3.) As a provisional subject, to anticipate the real subject, and keep the attention in suspense till the real subject comes with emphasis : as,

ac velut ille canum morsū dē montibus altīs āctus aper substitit, V. 10, 707, *and e'en as he, goaded by bite of hounds from mountains high, the boar hath paused.*

THE DETERMINATIVE PRONOUN.

is.

2365. is refers to something named in the context. When some feeling is to be expressed, such as admiration, or oftener contempt, homō is often put for is.

(*a.*) petit ā rēge et eum plūribus verbīs rogat ut id ad sē mittat, *V.* 4, 64. *he solicits the king and begs him at considerable length to send it to him.* nōndum mātūrus imperiō Ascanius erat, tamen id imperium ēī ad pūberem aetātem incolume mānsit, L. 1, 3, 1, *Ascanius was not yet old enough for the throne, but that throne was kept safe for him till he came of age.* (*b.*) ego hominem callidiōrem vīdī nēminem quam Phormiōnem. veniō ad hominem, ut dīcerem argentum opus esse, T. *Ph.* 591, *a shrewder man than Phormio I never saw, not I ! I went to him to tell him that I needed money.* nēquam esse hominem et levem sciēbam, *Sest.* 22, *I knew the fellow was worthless and frivolous.*

2366. (1.) is refers to something named before or after : as,

eius omnis ōrātiō versāta est in eō, ut scrīptum plūrimum valēre oportēre dēfenderet, *DO.* 1, 244, *his whole speech turned on the contention that the written word should be paramount.* Melitēnsis Diodōrus est ; is Lilybaeī multōs iam annōs habitat, *V.* 4, 38, *Diodorus is from Melita ; he has lived many years at Lilybaeum.* For other examples of is used to connect sentences, see 2129.

2367. With a connective, is denotes an important addition : as,

vincula et ea sempiterna, *C.* 4, 7, *imprisonment and that too perpetual.* annum iam audientem Cratippum idque Athēnīs, *Off.* 1, 1, *after a year's study under Cratippus, and that too in Athens.* erant in eō plūrimae litterae nec eae volgārēs, *Br.* 265, *he was a man of very deep reading and that of no common sort either.*

2368. (2.) is indicates something explained or restricted by a relative or indefinite, quī, quīcumque, sī quis : as, haec omnia is fēcī, quī sodālis Dolābellae eram, *Fam.* 12, 14, 7, *all this I did, I that was Dolabella's bosom friend* (1807).   ūnus ex eō numerō quī ad caedem parātī erant, S. *I.* 35, 6, *one of the number that were ready to do murder* (1804).   neque is sum quī mortis perīculō terrear, 5, 30, 2, *but I am not the man to be scared by danger of death, no, not I* (1818).   quīcumque is est, ēī mē profiteor inimīcum, *Fam.* 10, 31, 3, *whoever he may be, I proclaim myself his enemy* (1814).   cum ipse Aliēnus ex eā facultāte, sī quam habet, aliquantum dētrāctūrus sit, *Caecil.* 49, *seeing that even Alienus is to suppress some part of that eloquence, if any he may have.*   See also 1795, 1798.   For id quod, see 1811.

2369. For the use of is instead of a relative repeated in a different case, see 1833.

2370. is sometimes is loosely used for the reflexive **sē** (2341); here the point of view of the writer shows itself.

Mīlēsiōs nāvem poposcit, quae eum Myndum prōsequerētur, *V.* 1, 86, *he asked the Milesians for a ship to escort him to Myndus.*   suōs omnēs castrīs continuit ignēsque fierī prohibuit, quō occultior esset eius adventus, Caes. *C.* 3, 30, 5, *he confined his troops to camp and forbade the kindling of fires, in order to keep his coming a greater secret.*

The Pronoun of Identity.

īdem.

2371. **īdem**, *the same,* often connects two different predicates to the same person or thing.   In this case, it may be variously rendered by *likewise, also, all the same, on the other hand, at once, very, nevertheless.*

ūtēbātur eō cibō quī et suāvissimus esset et īdem facillimus ad concoquendum, *Fin.* 2, 64, *he made use of such food as was both very dainty and likewise very easy to digest.*   ita fiet ut nōn omnēs quī Atticē, eīdem bene dīcant, *Br.* 291, *so it will be found that not all who speak Attic are also good speakers.*   multī quī ut iūs suum et lībertātem tenērent volnera excēpērunt fortiter et tulērunt, īdem omissā contentiōne dolōrem morbī ferre nōn possunt, *TD.* 2, 65, *many who have met heroically and endured wounds, to preserve their rights and their freedom, are nevertheless, when no contest is involved, unable to bear the pain of a disease.*

2372. īdem is often used with other pronouns, hīc, iste, istūc, ille: as,

haec eadem centuriōnibus mandābant, 7, 17, 8, *they confided these same sentiments to their centurions.*   multae aliae idem istuc cupiunt, Pl. *MG.* 1040, *many other ladies want just what you want.*

2373. *The same as* is expressed by īdem followed by **quī, atque or ac, ut, quasi, cum,** sometimes in poetry by the dative.

īdem sum quī semper fuī, Pl. *Am.* 447, *I 'm the same man I 've always been.* pōmārium sēminārium ad eundem modum atque oleāgineum facitō, Cato, *RR.* 48, *make your fruit-tree nursery in the same way as your nursery for olive-trees* (1653). eīsdem ferē verbīs ut disputātum est, *TD* 2, 9 *in pretty much the same words as were used in the actual argument* (1937). ut eōdem locō rēs sit quasi ea pecūnia lēgāta nōn esset, *Leg.* 2, 53, *so that the position is the same as if the money had not been bequeathed* (2120). tibī mēcum in eōdem est pistrīnō vīvendum, *DO.* 2, 144, *you must live in the same mill as I.* Homērus eādem aliīs sōpītu' quiētest, Lucr. 3, 1037, *Homer sleeps the same sleep as others.*

THE INTENSIVE PRONOUN.

ipse.

2374. ipse, *self,* is used in contrasts.

2375. ipse may contrast the chief person with subordinates, or a person with any thing belonging to him.

Catilīna ipse pertimuit, profūgit; hī quid exspectant? *C.* 2, 6, *Catiline, their head, has fled in abject terror ; his minions here, what wait they for?* eī mūnītiōnī, quam fēcerat. T. Labiēnum lēgātum praefēcit; ipse in Italiam magnīs itineribus contendit, 1, 10, 3, *he put Labienus, his lieutenant, in charge of the fortification he had made ; he hurried, himself, to Italy with forced marches.* tēmētī nihil adlātum intellegō : : at iam adferētur, sī ā forō ipsus redierit, Pl. *Aul.* 355. *I see there 's no wine brought : : but it soon will be, if the governor comes back from down town.* 'ipse dīxit ;' "ipse" autem erat Pȳthagorās, *DN.* 1, 10, *' the old man said so ;' now "the old man" was Pythagoras.* nāvis tantum iactūrā factā, incolumēs ipsī ēvāsērunt, *L.* 30, 25, 8, *the vessel only was lost, and the sailors escaped in safety.*

2376. ipse is often used with personals and reflexives agreeing with the emphatic word. But the nominative is usually preferred, especially when ipse stands before the other pronoun, or when it stands after per mē, per sē. After mēmet, nōbīsmet, nōsmet, &c. it agrees with these words.

(*a.*) neque enim potest exercitum is continēre imperātor, quī sē ipsum nōn continet, *IP.* 38, *for no commander can keep his army under control who does not keep his own self under control.* miles frātrem suum, dein sē ipsum interfēcit, Ta. *H.* 3, 51, *a soldier slew his own brother, then himself.* (*b.*) ipse sē quisque dīligit, *L.* 80, *every man loves himself.* bellum per sē ipse, iniussū populī ac senātūs, fēcit, *L.* 1, 49, 7, *he made war on his own responsibility, without orders from the people and senate.* Iūnius necem sibī ipse cōnscīvit, *DN.* 2, 7, *Junius killed himself.* nōn egeō medicīnā, mē ipse cōnsōlor, *L.* 10, *I need no medicine, I am my own comforter.* (*c.*) ut nōbīsmet ipsīs imperēmus, *TD.* 2, 47, *that we should govern ourselves.*

2377. ipse alone sometimes stands for an emphatic sē or suus : as, pertimuērunt nē ab ipsīs dēscīsceret et cum suīs in grātiam redīret, N. 7, 5, 1, *they were much afraid that he would abandon them and come into favour with his compatriots again.* ea molestissimē ferre hominēs dēbent, quae ipsōrum culpā contrācta sunt, *QFr.* 1, 1, 2, *people should be most vexed at things which are brought about through fault of their own.*

2378. ipse is used in many combinations where *self* is an inadequate translation. It may sometimes be translated by:

2379. (1.) *Actual, positive, even.*

habet certōs suī studiōsōs, quōs valētūdō modo bona sit, tenuitās ipsa dēlectat, *Br.* 64, *he has a clique of admirers, who are charmed by positive scragginess, provided the health be good.* hōc ipsum ēlegantius pōnī meliusque potuit, *Fin.* 2, 100, *even this might have been put more logically and better.*

2380. (2.) *Regular, proper, real.*

flagrantem invidiā propter interitum C. Gracchī ipse populus Rōmānus perīculō līberāvit, *Sest.* 140, *though greatly detested in consequence of the death of Gracchus, he was acquitted by the Roman people proper.* cīvēs Rōmānī permultī in illō oppidō cōniūnctissimō animō cum ipsīs Agrigentīnīs vīvunt, *V.* 4, 93, *a great many Romans live in that town in most friendly relations with the natives of Agrigentum.*

2381. (3.) *As well, likewise, too,* for which, from Livy on, et ipse is used.

hoc Rīpheus, hoc ipse Dymās, omnisque iuventūs laeta facit, *V.* 2, 394, *this Ripheus doth, this Dymas too, and all the youth alert.* cōgitātiō Locrōs urbem recipiendī, quae sub dēfectiōnem Ītaliae dēscīverat et ipsa ad Poenōs, *L.* 29, 6, 1, *a project for recovering the city of Locri, which, on the revolt of Italy, had likewise gone over to the Carthaginians.*

2382. (4.) *Alone, mere.*

nōn sōlum adventus malī, sed etiam metus ipse adfert calamitātem, *IP.* 15, *not only the coming of misfortune, but even the mere dread of it brings disaster.*

2383. (5.) *Exactly, just,* with numerals and dates, or *right,* of place.

annīs LXXXVI ipsīs ante mē cōnsulem, *Br.* 61, *exactly 86 years before my consulship.* Kalendīs ipsīs Novembribus, *C.* 1, 8, *on the 1st of November precisely.* in ipsō vadō dēprehēnsus Indutiomarus interficitur, 5, 58, 6, *right at the ford Indutiomarus is caught and killed.* suprā ipsum balneum habitō, Sen. *Ep.* 56, 1, *I live right over a bath.*

2384. (6.) *Of oneself, voluntarily, of one's own motion.*

valvae subitō sē ipsae aperuērunt, *Div.* 1, 74, *the temple-door suddenly opened of itself.* Catilīnam vel ēiēcimus vel ēmīsimus vel ipsum ēgredientem verbīs prōsecūtī sumus, *C.* 2, 1, *we have driven Catiline out, or let him out, or, when he was going out of his own motion, wished him god-speed.*

THE INTERROGATIVE PRONOUN.

uter and quis.

2385. **uter,** *whether? which?* is used in questions about two things; **quis** and **quī**, *who? what?* in questions about more than two, though sometimes loosely of two things.

uter est īnsānior hōrum? H. *S.* 2, 3, 102, *which of these is the greater crank?* praeclārē apud eundem est Platōnem, similiter facere eōs quī inter sē contenderent uter potius rem pūblicam administrāret, ut sī nautae certārent quis eōrum potissimum gubernāret, *Off.* 1, 87, *in the same Plato is the excellent saying that for people to fall out with one another about which of two men should manage a state, were just as if the crew of a ship should quarrel about which of them should be pilot.* ut quem velīs, nesciās, *Att.* 16, 14, 1, *so that you don't know which to choose,* as between Octavian and Antony.

2386. **quis** and **quid** ask to have a thing named; **quī** and **quod** to have it described. But see 685.

quis Diōnem Syrācosium doctrīnīs omnibus expolīvit? nōn Platō? *DO.* 3, 139, *who refined Syracusan Dio with learning of every sort? was it not Plato?* quid rīdēs, H. *S.* 2, 5, 3, *why dost thou laugh?* (1144). quis fuit igitur? : : iste Chaerea. : : quī Chaerea? T. *Eu.* 823, *who was he then? : : your precious Chaerea. : : what Chaerea?* quem frūctum petentēs scīre cupimus illa quō modō moveantur? *Fin.* 3, 37, *with what practical end in view do we seek to know how yon bodies in the sky keep in motion?*

THE RELATIVE PRONOUN.

2387. The relative pronoun has already been treated; see 1792–1837.

THE INDEFINITE PRONOUN.

quis or quī; quispiam.

2388. **quis** or **quī**, *a, some, somebody,* always stands after one or more words of the sentence. **quis** or **quī** is used after **sī** (nisi, sīve). **nē, num, utrum, an, quō,** or **quandō,** in preference to **aliquis,** unless emphasis is intended.

dīxerit quis, *Off.* 3, 76, *somebody may say.* malum quod tibī dī dabunt, Pl. *Am.* 563, *some curse the gods will bring upon thee.* hī, sī quid erat dūrius, concurrēbant; sī quī equō dēciderat, circumsistēbant, 1, 48, 6, *if there was ever any sharpish work, these men would rally; if a man fell from his horse, they would close round him.* praecipit atque interdīcit ūnum omnēs peterent Indutiomarum, neu quis quem vulneret, 5, 58, 4, *he charges them and forbids them; they were all to assail Indutiomarus alone; and nobody was to wound anybody* (2402).

435

2389. quispiam, *a, some, one or another.*

forsitan quispiam dīxerit, *Off.* 3, 29, *peradventure somebody may say.* quispiam dīcet, *V.* 3, 111, *somebody will say.* cum quaepiam cohors impetum fēcerat, hostēs vēlōcissimē refugiēbant, 5, 35, 1, *every time one or another cohort charged, the enemy fled back quick speed* (2394).

aliquis.

2390. aliquis or **aliquī** *some one, some one or other*, has always some affirmative emphasis, and is opposed to the idea of *all, much, none :* as,

nōn enim dēclāmātōrem aliquem dē lūdō, sed perfectissimum quaerimus, *O.* 47, *for it is not some spouter from school that we aim to find, but the ideal orator.* omnēs ut aliquam perniciōsam bēstiam fugiēbant, *Clu.* 41, *everybody avoided him, like some dangerous wild animal or other.* audē aliquid Gyarīs dīgnum sī vīs esse aliquid, J. 1, 73, *venture some deed that deserves transportation, if you care to be something grand.* nōn sine aliquā spē, *D.* 7, *not without some hope.* quaerō sitne aliqua āctiō an nūlla, *Caec.* 33, *I ask whether there is some ground for an action or none.* num igitur aliquis dolor post mortem est ? *TD.* 1, 82, *is there, then, some sense of pain after death ?* With emphasis after sī (2388) : sī aliquid dē summā gravitāte Pompēius, multum de cupiditāte Caesar remīsisset, aliquam rem pūblicam nōbīs habēre licuisset, *Ph.* 13, 2, *if Pompey had sacrificed really something of his importance, and Caesar a good deal of his ambition, we might have had what would have been to some degree a commonwealth.*

2391. aliquis is sometimes equivalent to aliquis alius : as,

cum M. Pīsone et cum Q. Pompēiō aut cum aliquō, *Br.* 310, *with Piso or Pompey or some other man.* ea mihī cottīdiē aut tūre aut vīnō aut aliquī semper supplicat, Pl. *Aul. prol.* 23, *she always offers me incense or wine or something else every day.*

quīdam.

2392. quīdam, *a, a certain,* denotes a thing which we cannot describe or do not care to.

nōn inrīdiculē quīdam ex mīlitibus decimae legiōnis dīxit : plūs quam pollicitus esset, Caesarem facere, 1, 42, 6, *one of the privates of the Tenth said a very dry thing : that ' Caesar was doing more than he engaged to.'* accurrit quīdam nōtus mihi nōmine tantum, H. *S.* 1, 9, 3, *up trots a man I knew by name alone.* assimilis quīdam mūgituī sonus, Suet. *Galb.* 18, *a mysterious sound like the lowing of a cow.* vidēmus nātūram suō quōdam itinere ad ultimum pervenīre, *DN.* 2, 35, *nature reaches perfection by a kind of road of her own.* Often in translations from Greek : as, aliīs librīs ratiōnem quandam per omnem nātūram rērum pertinentem vī dīvīnā esse adfectam putat, *DN.* 1, 36, *in other works he supposes ' a kind of Reason pervading all nature and endowed with divine power,* of Zeno's doctrine.

2393. quīdam is often used to soften an exaggeration or a metaphor, sometimes to denote contempt.

ēloquentissimōs hominēs innumerābilīs quōsdam nōminābat, *DO.* 1, 91, *great speakers he named, absolutely without number.* ad omnīs enim meōs impetūs quasi mūrus quīdam bonī nōmen imperātōris oppōnitur, *V.* 5, 2, *for against all assaults of mine the name of a good commander is set up, like a regular wall.* sed aliud quoddam fīlum ōrātiōnis tuae, *L.* 25, *but there is quite a different fibre to your speech.* nōn est eōrum urbānitāte quādam quasi colōrāta ōrātiō, *Br.* 170, *their language lacks the tinge of an indefinable metropolitan element.* Theomnāstus quīdam, homo rīdiculē īnsānus, *V.* 4, 148, *a person of the name of Theomnastus, an absurd, crack-brained creature.*

quisque.

2394. quisque, *each, each in particular, each by himself,* applies what is stated of all to each several case, out of a number more than two.

laudātī prō cōntiōne omnēs sunt, dōnātīque prō meritō quisque, *L.* 38, 23, 11, *they were collectively commended in assembly convened, and received presents, each in proportion to his deserts.* quotiēns quaeque cohors prōcurrerat, magnus numerus hostium cadēbat, 5, 34, 2, *as the cohorts successively charged, a great number of the enemy fell every time* (2389). mēns cuiusque, is est quisque, nōn ea figūra quae digitō dēmōnstrārī potest, *RP.* 6, 26, *the mind of a man is always the man, and not that shape which can be pointed out by the finger.*

2395. quisque is sometimes used in a relative and demonstrative sentence both.

quod cuique obtigit, id quisque teneat, *Off.* 1, 21, *let every man keep what he has got.* id enim est cuiusque proprium, quō quisque fruitur atque ūtitur, *Fam.* 7, 30, 2, *for that is always a man's property which he has the enjoyment and use of.*

2396. In a complex sentence, consisting of a main and a relative sentence, quisque is usually expressed but once, and then in the unemphatic relative sentence. In English, the equivalent of quisque goes with the main sentence.

nēmō fuit quī nōn surrēxerit, tēlumque quod cuique fors offerēbat, adripuerit, *V.* 4, 95, *not a man but sprang from his bed, and seized in every instance such a weapon as chance threw in his way.* theātrum cum commūne sit, rēctē tamen dīcī potest, eius esse eum locum, quem quisque occupārit, *Fin.* 3, 67, *though the theatre is open to all, still it may be said with perfect propriety, that each spectator is entitled to the seat he has taken.* Messānam ut quisque nostrūm vēnerat, haec vīsere solēbat, *V.* 4, 5, *any Roman, who went to Messana, invariably went to see these statues* (1939). eōrum ut quisque prīmus vēnerat, sub mūrō cōnsistēbat, 7, 48, 2, *as they successively arrived, each man of them took his stand under the wall.*

2397. quisque is often used with sē or suus, superlatives, and ordinals, holding an unemphatic place *after* these words: as, ipse sē quisque dīligit, *L*. 80, *a man always loves his own self.* suos quoique mōs, T. *Ph.* 454, *every man his own way.* huic prō sē quisque nostrūm medērī velle dēbēmus, *L. Agr.* 1, 26, *this evil we ought to wish to remedy, according to our several abilities.* optimum quidque rārissimum est, *Fin.* 2, 81, *ever the fairest is the rarest.* nam in forō vix decumus quisquest, quī ipsus sēsē nōverit, Pl. *Ps.* 973, *for in the marketplace there's scarce one man in every ten that knows himself.* quīntō quōque annō Sicilia tōta cēnsētur, *V.* 2, 139, *at the end of every four years all Sicily is assessed.* quamquam prīmum quidque explicēmus, *Fam.* 12, 1, 1, *but stay — let me explain things successively;* or, *one thing after another.* litterās mīsit, ut is ānulus ad sē prīmō quōque tempore adferrētur, *V.* 4, 58, *he sent a letter directing said ring to be sent to him without delay.*

2398. In old Latin quisque is sometimes equivalent to quīcumque or quisquis, *whoever:* as, quisque obviam huic occesserit īrātō, vāpulābit, Pl. *As.* 404, *whoever meets him in his wrath will catch it.* In cuiusque generis and cuiusque modī, it means *any and every:* as, tot hominēs cuiusque modī, *V.* 4, 7, *so many people of every sort,* i. e. cuicuimodī. The neuter quidquid for quidque is not uncommon: as, cum prōcessit paulum et quātenus quicquid sē attingat perspicere coepit, *Fin.* 5, 24, *when it has progressed a little and has begun to discover how far each thing affects it.* Masculine quisquis for quisque is doubtful (see *Fam.* 6, 1, 1).

uterque.

2399. uterque, *each,* is used of two individuals, and utrīque of two sets or parties. But sometimes utrīque is used of two individuals.

(*a*.) ut illa nātūra caelestis et terrā vacat et ūmōre, sīc utriusque hārum rērum hūmānus animus est expers, *TD.* 1, 65, *even as the heavenly nature is free from the earthy and the humid, so the soul of man has no part in either of these qualities* (1243). nūtū tremefactus uterque est polus, O. *F.* 2, 489, *at his nod trembled each pole* (1243). Aetōliōrum utraeque manūs Hēraclēam sēsē inclūsērunt, *L.* 36, 16, 5, *both bands of the Aetolians shut themselves up in Heraclea.* (*b*.) sex filiī nōbīs, duae filiae sunt, utraeque iam nūptae, *L.* 42, 34, 4, *we have six sons and two daughters, both already married.*

2400. Reciprocal relations (2344) are sometimes expressed by uterque followed by a different case of alter; rarely by uterque and a different case of the same word.

(*a*.) quōrum uterque contempsit alterum, *Off.* 1, 4, *each of whom lightly esteemed the other.* (*b*.) abdūcī nōn potest : : quī nōn potest ? : : quia uterque utrīquest cordī, T. *Ph.* 799, *she's not to be taken from him : : why is n't she ? : : because they're heart to heart.* This doubling of uterque is found only half a dozen times ; not in Cicero.

quivis and quilibet ; utervis and uterlibet.

2401. quīvīs and quīlibet, *any you please,* are used either in affirmative or negative sentences. When two are spoken of, utervīs or uterlibet is used.

(*a.*) **ut quīvīs intellegere posset,** *V.* 5, 17, *so that any fool might know.* **faciat quidlubet,** T. *Hau.* 464, *let him do anything he likes.* (*b.*) **quī utramvīs rēctē nōvit, ambās nōverit,** T. *Andr. prol.* 10, *who knows either well, knows both.* **utrumlibet ēlige,** *Quinct.* 81, *choose either you like.*

quisquam and ūllus.

2402. quisquam (692), *a single one, any one at all,* and **ūllus,** *any,* are used chiefly in negative sentences or in interrogative, conditional, and comparative sentences implying negation, or with **sine.**

vēnī Athēnās, neque mē quisquam ibī adgnōvit, *TD.* 5, 104, *I came to Athens and not a person there knew me* (1659). **interdīcit omnibus, nē quemquam interficiant,** 7, 40, 4, *he warns them collectively against killing any man at all* (2388). **hunc suā quisquam sententiā ex hāc urbe expellet ?** *Mil.* 104, *will anybody at all, by his vote, banish this man from Rome ?* **quis hoc fēcit ūllā in Scythiā tyrannus ?** *Pis.* 18, *what tyrant ever did this in any Scythia ?* **sī quisquam est timidus, is ego sum,** *Fam.* 6, 14, 1, *if anybody is timid, I am the man.* **quī saepius cum hoste cōnflīxit quam quisquam cum inimīcō concertāvit,** *IP.* 28, *who has measured swords oftener with the enemy than anybody ever wrangled with an opponent in private life.* **sine ūllō metū in ipsum portum penetrāre coepērunt,** *V.* 5, 96, *without a bit of fear they began to make their way right into the harbour.* **nēmō quisquam** and **nihil quicquam** are old and late : as, **lepidiōrem uxōrem nēmō quisquam habet,** Pl. *Cas.* 1008, *nobody has a jollier wife.* **noster malī nīl quicquam prīmō,** T. *Ph.* 80, *our young master did n't make any trouble at first.*

2403. nēmō is generally used for **nōn quisquam, nēmō umquam** for **numquam quisquam, nihil** for **nōn quicquam,** and **nūllus** for **nōn ūllus.** If only two are spoken of, **neuter** is used. The plural **neutrī** is used of two parties.

nēmōst miserior mē, T. *Hau.* 263, *no man's unhappier than I.* **nēmō igitur vir magnus sine aliquō adflātū dīvīnō umquam fuit,** *DN.* 2, 167, *nobody who is a great man was ever without some divine inspiration.* **ab nūllō ille līberālius quam ā Cluentiō trāctātus est,** *Clu.* 161, *by no man has he been treated more generously than by Cluentius.* **neutrum eōrum contrā alterum iuvāre,** Caes. *C.* 1, 35, 5, *to help neither of them against the other.* **neutrī alterōs prīmō cernēbant,** L. 21, 46, 4, *neither party saw the others at first.*

(D.) NUMERALS.

2404. Numerals are divided into Adjectives : *Cardinal,* **ūnus,** *one,* **duo,** *two,* &c. ; *Ordinal,* **prīmus,** *first,* **secundus,** *second,* &c. ; *Distributive,* **singulī,** *one each,* **bīnī,** *two each,* &c. ; and Numeral Adverbs : **semel,** *once,* **bis,** *twice,* &c.

For the inflection of numerals, see 637–643.

ARABIC.	CARDINALS.	ORDINALS.
1	ūnus, *one* (638)	prīmus, *first* (643)
2	duo, *two* (639)	secundus, *second*
3	trēs, *three* (639)	tertius, *third*
4	quattuor, *four*	quārtus, *fourth*
5	quīnque, *five*	quīntus, *fifth*
6	sex, *six*	sextus, *sixth*
7	septem, *seven*	septimus, *seventh*
8	octō, *eight*	octāvus, *eighth*
9	novem, *nine*	nōnus, *ninth*
10	decem, *ten*	decimus, *tenth*
11	ūndecim, *eleven*	ūndecimus, *eleventh*
12	duodecim	duodecimus
13	tredecim	tertius decimus
14	quattuordecim	quārtus decimus
15	quīndecim	quīntus decimus
16	sēdecim	sextus decimus
17	septendecim	septimus decimus
18	duodēvīgintī	duodēvīcēsimus
19	ūndēvīgintī	ūndēvīcēsimus
20	vīgintī, *twenty*	vīcēsimus, *twentieth*
21	vīgintī ūnus or ūnus et vīgintī	vīcēsimus prīmus or ūnus et vīcēsimus
22	vīgintī duo or duo et vīgintī	vīcēsimus alter or alter et vīcēsimus
28	duodētrīgintā	duodētrīcēsimus
29	ūndētrīgintā	ūndētrīcēsimus
30	trīgintā	trīcēsimus
40	quadrāgintā	quadrāgēsimus
50	quīnquāgintā	quīnquāgēsimus
60	sexāgintā	sexāgēsimus
70	septuāgintā	septuāgēsimus
80	octōgintā	octōgēsimus
90	nōnāgintā	nōnāgēsimus
99	ūndēcentum	ūndēcentēsimus
100	centum, *one hundred*	centēsimus, *one hundredth*
101	centum ūnus or centum et ūnus	centēsimus prīmus or centēsimus et prīmus
200	ducentī (641)	ducentēsimus
300	trecentī	trecentēsimus
400	quadringentī	quādringentēsimus
500	quīngentī	quīngentēsimus
600	sescentī	sescentēsimus
700	septingentī	septingentēsimus
800	octingentī	octingentēsimus
900	nōngentī	nōngentēsimus
1,000	mīlle, *thousand* (642)	mīllēsimus, *thousandth*
2,000	duo mīllia	bis mīllēsimus
5,000	quīnque mīllia	quīnquiēns mīllēsimus
10,000	decem mīllia	deciēns mīllēsimus
50,000	quīnquāgintā mīllia	quīnquāgiēns mīllēsimus
100,000	centum mīllia	centiēns mīllēsimus
1,000,000	deciēns centēna mīllia	deciēns centiēns mīllēsimus

DISTRIBUTIVES.	NUMERAL ADVERBS.	ROMAN.
singulī, *one each* (643)	semel, *once*	I
bīnī, *two each*	bis, *twice*	II
ternī, trīnī, *three each*	ter, *thrice*	III
quaternī, *four each*	quater, *four times*	IIII or IV
quīnī, *five each*	quīnquiēns, *five times*	V
sēnī, *six each*	sexiēns, *six times*	VI
septēnī, *seven each*	septiēns, *seven times*	VII
octōnī, *eight each*	octiēns, *eight times*	VIII
novēnī, *nine each*	noviēns, *nine times*	VIIII or IX
dēnī, *ten each*	deciēns, *ten times*	X
ūndēnī, *eleven each*	ūndeciēns, *eleven times*	XI
duodēnī	duodeciēns	XII
ternī dēnī	terdeciēns	XIII
quaternī dēnī	quater deciēns	XIIII or XIV
quīnī dēnī	quīndeciēns	XV
sēnī dēnī	sēdeciēns	XVI
septēnī dēnī	septiēns deciēns	XVII
duodēvīcēnī	octiēns deciēns	XVIII
ūndēvīcēnī	noviēns deciēns	XVIII or XIX
vīcēnī, *twenty each*	vīciēns, *twenty times*	XX
vīcēnī singulī or singulī et vīcēnī	vīciēns semel or semel et vīciēns	XXI
vīcēnī bīnī or bīnī et vīcēnī	vīciēns bis or bis et vīciēns	XXII
duodētrīcēnī	duodētrīciēns	XXVIII
ūndētrīcēnī	*ūndētrīciēns	XXVIIII or XXIX
trīcēnī	trīciēns	XXX
quadrāgēnī	quadrāgiēns	XXXX or XL
quīnquāgēnī	quīnquāgiēns	L
sexāgēnī	sexāgiēns	LX
septuāgēnī	septuāgiēns	LXX
octōgēnī	octōgiēns	LXXX
nōnāgēnī	nōnāgiēns	LXXXX or XC
ūndēcentēnī	*ūndēcentiēns	LXXXXVIIII or XCIX
centēnī, *a hundred each*	centiēns, *a hundred times*	C
centēnī singulī	centiēns semel or centiēns et semel	CI
ducēnī	ducentiēns	CC
trecēnī	trecentiēns	CCC
quadringēnī	quadringentiēns	CCCC
quīngēnī	quīngentiēns	D
sescēnī	sescentiēns	DC
septingēnī	septingentiēns	DCC
octingēnī	octingentiēns	DCCC
nōngēnī	nōngentiēns	DCCCC
singula mīllia, *a thousand*	mīlliēns, *a thousand times*	∞
bīna mīllia [*each*	bis mīlliēns	∞∞
quīna mīllia	quīnquiēns mīlliēns	
dēna mīllia	deciēns mīlliēns	
quīnquāgēna mīllia	quīnquāgiēns mīlliēns	
centēna mīllia	centiēns mīlliēns	
deciēns centēna mīllia	deciēns centiēns mīlliēns	X

NOTATION.

2406. Numbers are noted by combinations of the characters I = 1; V = 5; X = 10; ⌄, later ⌄, ⊥, or L = 50; C = 100; D = 500; Ⅽ or CↃ, post-Augustan M = 1000.

2407. Of these signs, V seems to be the half of X, which may be Etruscan in origin. The original signs for 50 and 1000 were taken from the Chalcidian Greek alphabet (18 ·9), in which they represented sounds unknown to early Latin. Thus, ⌄, in the Chalcidian alphabet representing **ch** (49), was used by the early Romans for 50, and became successively ⌄, ⊥, and L. The form ⌄, is found very rarely, ⌄ oftener, in the Augustan period; ⊥ is common during the last century of the republic and in the early empire; L, due to assimilation with the Roman letter, appears in the last century of the republic. The sign for 1000 was originally Ⅽ (Chalcidian **ph**); it became CↃ (the common classical form), ∞, or ⋈; the form M as a numeral appears in the second century A. D., although M is found much earlier as an abbreviation for **mīllia** in M · P, that is **mīllia passuum**. For 100, the sign Ⲑ (Chalcidian **th**) may have been used originally; but C (the abbreviation for **centum**) came into use at an early period. The sign D, = 500, is the half of Ⅽ.

2408. To denote 10,000 the sign for 1000 was doubled: thus, Ⓟ, written also Ⓠ, ⌄, ⋔. Another circle was added to denote 100,000: thus, ⓪, written also Ⓠ, ⌄, ⋔. The halves of these signs were used for 5000 and 50,000: thus, Ⅾ) and Ⅾ); variations of these last two signs are found, corresponding to the variations of the signs of which they are the halves.

2409. From the last century of the republic on, thousands are sometimes indicated by a line drawn above a numeral, and hundreds of thousands by three lines enclosing a numeral: as, V̄ = 5000; ⌈x⌉ = 1,000,000.

2410. To distinguish numerals from ordinary letters, a line is often drawn above them: as, V̄Ⅰ = 6. This practice is common in the Augustan period; earlier, a line is sometimes drawn across the numeral, as, Ħ = 2; Ᵽ = 500.

2411. Of the two methods of writing the symbols for 4, 9, 14, 19, &c., the method by subtraction (IV, IX, XIV, XIX, &c.) is rarer, and is characteristic of private, not public inscriptions.

SOME FORMS OF NUMERALS.

2412. **quīnctus**, the older form of **quīntus** (170, 4) is sometimes found in old and even in classical writers. Instead of **septimus** and **decimus**, the older **septumus** and **decumus** are not uncommon (28).

2413. In the ordinals from *twentieth* upwards, the older forms **vīcēnsumus** or **vīcēnsimus**, **trīcēnsumus** or **trīcēnsimus**, &c., &c., are not infrequently found instead of **vīcēsimus**, **trīcēsimus**, &c., &c. (63; 28).

2414. In the numeral adverbs from **quīnquiēns** upwards, later forms in **-iēs** (63) are often found: as, **quīnquiēs**, **deciēs**, &c., &c.

2415. In cardinals and ordinals from *thirteen* to *seventeen* inclusive, the larger number sometimes comes first, and in cardinals et is sometimes used, though rarely in Cicero.

decem trēs, L. 37, 30, 7, *thirteen.* fundōs decem et trēs relīquit, *RA.* 20, *he left thirteen farms.* Rarely the smaller number comes first with et : as, dē tribus et decem fundīs, *RA.* 99, *of the thirteen farms.*

2416. Numbers from 18 to 99 inclusive which end in 8 or 9 are usually expressed by subtraction, as in the list (2405); less frequently (not in Cicero, rarely in classical writers) by addition : as, decem et octō, 4, 19, 4 ; decem novem, Ta. *H.* 2, 58.

2417. In compound numbers from *twenty-one* to *ninety-seven* inclusive, except those which end in *eight* or *nine* (2416), the smaller number with et usually comes first or the larger number without et, as in the list. But rarely the larger number comes first with et: as, vīgintī et septem, *V.* 4, 123, *twenty and seven.*

2418. In numbers from a *hundred and one* upwards, the larger number comes first, either with or without et ; but with distributives et is not used. With cardinals and ordinals the smaller number sometimes comes first with et; as, iīs rēgiīs quadrāgintā annīs et ducentīs praeteritīs, *RP.* 2, 52, *after these two hundred and forty years of monarchy were ended.*

SOME USES OF NUMERALS.

CARDINALS AND ORDINALS.

2419. Dates are expressed either by cardinals with a plural substantive or by ordinals with a singular substantive : as,

dictātor factus est annīs post Rōmam conditam CCCCXV, *Fam.* 9, 21, 2, *he was made dictator* 415 U. C. (1393). annō trecentēsimō quīnquāgēsimō post Rōmam conditam, Nōnīs Iūnīs, *RP.* 1, 25, *on the 5th of June,* 350 U. C. (1350). The ordinal is also used with a substantive not used in the singular : as, mancipia vēnībant Sāturnālibus tertiīs, *Att.* 5, 20, 5, *the slaves were sold on the third day of the Saturnalia.* As the Romans, however, had no fixed official era, they had no dates in the modern sense, and marked the year by the names of the consuls.

DISTRIBUTIVES.

2420. Distributives are used to denote an equal division among several persons or things, and in expressions of multiplication : as,

bīnī senātōrēs singulīs cohortibus praepositī, L. 3, 69, 8, *two senators were put over every cohort:* sometimes when singulī is added, the cardinal is used, thus: singulīs cēnsōribus dēnāriī trecentī imperātī sunt, *V.* 2, 137, *every censor was assessed* 300 *denars.* bis bīna, *DN.* 2, 49, *twice two.* Poets use multiplication freely, partly for variety, but mainly from metrical necessity.

2421. Distributives are also used with substantives which have no singular, or which have a different meaning in the singular; but in this use *one* is always ūnī, not singulī, and *three* is often trīnī, not ternī: as.

ut ūna castra iam facta ex bīnīs vidērentur, Caes. *C.* 1, 74, 4, *so that one camp seemed now to have been formed out of two.* trīnīs catēnīs vinctus, 1, 53, 5, *in triple irons.* Similarly with things in pairs, as: bovēs bīnī, Pl. *Pers.* 317, *a yoke of oxen.*

2422. Poets sometimes use the singular of distributives: as, centēnāque arbore flūctum verberat, V. 10, 207, *and with a hundred beams at every stroke the wave he smites.* duplicī nātūrā et corpore bīnō, Lucr. 5, 879, *twynatured and of body twain.* The plural is sometimes used in verse for the cardinal: centum bracchia . . . centēnāsque manūs, V. 10, 565, *a hundred arms . . . and hundred hands.*

Other Numerals.

2423. Other numerical adjectives are *multiplicatives*, ending in -plex; they are: simplex, *onefold*, *simple*, sēscuplex, *one and a half fold*, duplex, triplex, quadruplex, quīncuplex, septemplex, decemplex, centuplex; and *proportionals*, used mostly in the neuter as substantives: duplus, *twice as great*, triplus, *three times as great*, quadruplus, septuplus, octuplus. Besides these there are other adjectives derived from numerals: as, prīmānus, *soldier of the first:* prīmārius, *first rate:* bīmus, *twinter, two-year-old ;* &c., &c.

Expression of Fractions.

2424. *One half* may be expressed by dīmidium or dīmidia pars; other fractions with 1 as a numerator by ordinals, with or without pars : as, tertia pars or tertia, $\frac{1}{3}$.

2425. If the numerator is greater than 1 it is usually expressed by the cardinal feminine, with the ordinal feminine for the denominator: as, duae septimae, $\frac{2}{7}$. But besides these forms there are others, namely :

2426. (1.) Fractions with a numerator less by 1 than the denominator, except $\frac{1}{2}$, may be expressed by cardinals with partēs, as, duae partēs, $\frac{2}{3}$; trēs partēs, $\frac{3}{4}$; quattuor partēs, $\frac{4}{5}$.

2427. (2.) Fractions with 12 or its multiples as a denominator are expressed in business language by the parts of an ās: thus,

$\frac{1}{12}$, uncia	$\frac{1}{3}$, triēns	$\frac{7}{12}$, septunx	$\frac{5}{8}$, dēxtāns
$\frac{1}{6}$, sextāns	$\frac{5}{12}$, quīncunx	$\frac{2}{3}$, bēs	$\frac{11}{12}$, deūnx
$\frac{1}{4}$, quadrāns	$\frac{1}{2}$, sēmis	$\frac{3}{4}$, dōdrāns	$\frac{12}{12}$, ās

ex āsse hērēs, Quintil. 7, 1, 20, *heir to the whole ;* relīquit hērēdēs ex bēsse nepōtem, ex tertiā parte neptem, Plin. *Ep.* 7, 24, 2, *she left her grand son heir to* $\frac{2}{3}$*, her granddaughter to* $\frac{1}{3}$. hērēdem ex dōdrante, N. 25, 5, 2, *heir to* $\frac{3}{4}$.

2428. Sometimes fractions are expressed by addition: as, dīmidia et quarta, $\frac{3}{4}$; pars tertia et septima, $\frac{10}{21}$; sometimes by division of the denominator: as, dīmidia quīnta, $\frac{1}{10}$.

(E.) PROSODY.

I. RULES OF QUANTITY.

(A.) In Classical Latin.

2429. The length of the vowel in some classes of syllables, as used in the classical period, may be conveniently fixed in the memory by the following rules. For the usage of older writers, see 126, 129, 132 and 2464–2472. For the general principles of length of vowels and syllables, see 33–41 ; 121–134 ; 177–178.

MONOSYLLABLES.

2430. Monosyllables ending in a vowel or a single consonant have the vowel long : as,

dōs, sōl; ā for ab; ē for ex or ec-, pēs for *peds; ablative quā, quī; quīn for *quīne ; locative sei, commonly sī ; sīc (708) ; dative and ablative plural quīs (688).

Exceptions.

2431. The vowel is short in:

2432. (*a*.) Monosyllables ending in b, d, m, and t : as, ab, ad, dum, dat.

2433. (*b*.) The indefinite qua, N. and Ac.; the enclitics -que (rarely -quē), -ne, -ve, -ce ; and in the words cor, fel, mel ; os, *bone ;* ac, vir, is, pol, quis (N.) ; fac, fer, per, ter ; an, bis, in, cis ; nec, vel. N. hĭc is rarely short (664). For the quantity of es, see 747.

POLYSYLLABLES.

PENULTS.

2434. Disyllabic perfects and perfect participles have the vowel of the penult long when it stands before a single consonant : as,

vēnī, vīdī, vīcī (862) ; fōvī (864), fōtus (917).

445

Exceptions.

2435. (*a.*) Nine perfects have the penult short (859–861):
bibī, -fidī   dedī, scidī   stetī, stitī   tulī, -tudī, per-culī.

2436. (*b.*) Ten perfect participles have the penult short (918; see also 919):
citus, datus itum, ratus -rutus, satus situs, status litus, quitus.

Final Syllables.

(I.) Ending in a Vowel.

2437. In words of more than one syllable, final **a** and **e** are short; final **o, u,** and **i,** are long: as,

(*a.*) N. aquila; Pl. N. and Ac. oppida, cētera, omnĭa.

(*b.*) N. ille; N. and Ac. rēte; impūne (701); V. bone; Ab. tempore; Inf. prōmere; Imperat. rege (826); Pres. Ind. and Imperat. querere; Perf. rēxēre.

(*c.*) N. sermō; D. and Ab. verbō; vērō (704). iō. regō, erō, amābō, rēxerō (826); estō.

(*d.*) N. and Ac. cornū (587); D. and Ab. metū (590, 425, 593); diū.

(*e.*) G. frūmentī; V. Vergilī (459); G. domī (594); D. nūllī, orbī; Ab. sitī (554). Imperat. vestī (845). Inf. querī, locārī; Ind. Perf. rēxī (856), rēxistī.

Exceptions in a.

2438. (*a.*) Final **a** is long in the ablative, in indeclinable words, and in the imperative: as,

(*a.*) Ab. mēnsā (426).

(*b.*) quadrāgintā; many indeclinable words are ablatives: as, contrā, iūxtā, (707). The indeclinable heia, ita, and quia (701), have short a.

(*c.*) Imperat. locā (845). But puta, *for instance,* has short a. (130, 4).

2439. (*b.*) Final **a** is long in some Greek nominatives and vocatives: as, N. Electrā; V. Aenēā, Pallā.

Exceptions in e.

2440. (*a.*) Final **e** is long in cases of nouns with stems in -ē- (596), in adverbs from stems in -o-, and in the imperative singular active of verbs in -ēre: as,

(*a.*) diē (G., D., or Ab.), hodiē, prīdiē; see also 603.

(*b.*) altē (705); also ferē, fermē and ohē or ōhē; but **e** is always short in bene and male; īnferne and superne.

(*c.*) docē (845); for cave, see 130, 4.

2441. (*b.*) Final **e** is long in the endings of some Greek nouns : as, N. **crambē**, **Circē** ; V. **Alcīdē** ; Ne. Pl. N. and Ac. **cētē, melē, pelagē, tempē.**

Exceptions in o.

2442. (*a.*) Final **o** is short in the nominatives **ego, duo.** It is sometimes shortened in **homo** (130, 3) and in the nominative of other stems in **-n-** (484, 485) : as, **mentio, Nāso, virgo. o** is regularly short in **endo**, in the ablatives **cito** and **modo**, used as adverbs, and in many other words in late poetry : as, **īlico, immo, ergo, quando, octo**, &c. ; very rarely in the ablative of the gerund.

2443. (*b.*) Before Ovid, **o** of the present indicative is regularly long. It is shortened only in the following words (130, 3) : in

volo, six times (Cat., 4 times ; Hor., Prop.).

scio, twice (Verg.).

nescio, six times (Verg., twice ; Hor., twice ; Tib., Prop.) ;

and once each in **eo** and **veto** (Hor.), **dēsino** (Tib.), and **findo** (Prop.). From Ovid on, short **o** is not uncommon.

Short **o** in other forms of the verb is rare : as, **dīxero** (Hor.) ; **esto, ero, dabo** (Ov.) ; but **o** is always short in the imperative **cedo**, *give, tell.*

Exceptions in u.

2444. Final **u** is short in **indu** and **noenu.**

Exceptions in i.

2445. (*a.*) Final **i** is short in **nisi, quasi,** and **sīcuti**; also in the endings of some Greek nouns : as N. and Ac. **sināpi** ; V. **Pari, Amarylli** ; D. **Paridi, Minōidi** ; Pl. D. **Trōasi.**

2446. (*b.*) Final **i** is common in **mihĭ, tibĭ, sibĭ** ; **ibĭ, ubĭ** (129, 2).

(2.) Ending in a Single Consonant not s.

2447. A final syllable ending in a single consonant not **s** has its vowel short : as,

dōnec. illud. animal (536) ; **semel. agmen. calcar** (537) ; **soror, stultior** (132). **moror, loquar, fatēbor** (132) ; **regitur, regimur, reguntur. regit** (826) ; **amat, sciat, pōnēbat** ; **tinnit, possit** ; **iacet, neget, esset** (132).

Exceptions.

2448. (*a.*) The last vowel is long in **allēc**, and in compounds of **pār** ; in the contracted genitive plural of stems in **-u-** : as **currūm** ; in all cases of **illic** and **istic** except the nominative masculine, in the adverbs **illūc** and **istūc**, and sometimes in **nihīl.** Also in the endings of some Greek nouns : as, N. **āēr, aethēr, sīrēn** ; Ac. **Aenēān.**

2449. (*b.*) In the short form of the genitive plural of stems in **-o-** and **-ā-**, the vowel was originally long, but afterwards short : as, **dīvŏm** (462), **caelicolŭm** (439).

2450. (*c.*) The last vowel is long in **iīt** and **petiīt** and their compounds.

(3.) ENDING IN s.

2451. Final syllables in is and us have the vowel short; those in as, es, and os, have the vowel long: as,

(*a.*) N. lapis, fīnis; G. lapidis, fīnis; magis. Indic. Pres. regis (826); Fut. eris (851, 826), eritis, locābis (853, 826), locābitis.

(*b.*) N. dominus; currus; N. and Ac. tempus; prius; rēgibus; īmus; regimus.

(*c.*) aetās; Pl. Ac. mēnsās (424). Indic. Pres. locās (840); Imp. erās (848); regēbās (847); Plup. rēxerās (880); Subj. Pres. regās, vestiās, doceās (842).

(*d.*) N. hērēs; sēdēs; nūbēs; Cerēs; fidēs; Pl. N. and Ac. rēgēs (424); Indic. Pres. docēs (840); Fut. regēs (852); Subj. Pres. siēs (841); locēs (843); Imp. essēs (850); regerēs (849); Plup. rēxissēs (881).

(*e.*) N. custōs; arbōs; Pl. Ac. ventōs (424).

Exceptions in is.

2452. (*a.*) Final is has ī in all plural cases: as,

N. and Ac. omnīs; D. and Ab. viīs, locīs (108, *a*), vōbīs. Also in the nominatives singular Quirīs and Samnīs, usually in sanguīs (486), and twice in pulvīs.

2453. (*b.*) Final is has ī in the second person singular of verbs in -īre, in māvīs, in compounds of sīs, and in all present subjunctives singular: as, duīs, edīs, velīs, mālīs, nōlīs. For -rīs of the perfect subjunctive and the future perfect, see 877, 878, 883, 884.

Exceptions in us.

2454. u is long in the nominative singular of consonant stems with ū before the final stem consonant: as, tellūs, stem tellūr-; palūs, once palus (Hor.), stem palūd-; in the genitive singular and nominative and accusative plural of nouns with stems in -u-: as, frūctūs; and in the ending of some Greek names: as, N. Panthūs; G. Sapphūs.

Exceptions in as.

2455. Final as has short a in anas and in the ending of some Greek nouns: as, N. Īlias; Pl. Ac. cratēras.

Exceptions in es.

2456. Final es has short e in the nominative singular of stems in -d- and -t- which have the genitive in -idis, -itis, and -etis (475, 476): as, praeses, teges, comes (but ē in abiēs, ariēs, and pariēs), also, in penes, in compounds of es, *thou art*, and in the endings of some Greek nouns: as, N. Cynosarges; Pl. N. Arcades, cratēres.

Exceptions in os.

2457. Final os has short o in the nominative of stems in -o-: as, servos, suos, Dēlos; also in compos. impos, and exos; and in the endings of some Greek nouns: as, N. and Ac. epos; G. chlamydos, Erīnyos.

POSITION.

2458. For the general rule of position, see 177, 178; but, except in the thesis of a foot, a final syllable ending with a short vowel generally remains short before a word beginning with two consonants or a double consonant: as, **molliă strāta, nemorōsă Zacўnthos, lūcĕ smaragdī.**

In Horace such a final syllable is never lengthened before a word beginning with two consonants.

HIDDEN QUANTITY.

2459. A vowel which stands before two consonants, or a double consonant, belonging to the same word, so that its natural quantity cannot be determined from the scansion of the word, is said to possess *Hidden Quantity.*

2460. The natural quantity of such a vowel may sometimes be ascertained: (*a.*) from the statements of ancient writers; (*b.*) from the way in which the vowel is written in Latin inscriptions (see 24, 29); (*c.*) from the transliteration of the word into other languages, especially Greek; (*d.*) from the etymology of the word, or from a comparison of it with kindred words in other Indo-European languages; (*e.*) from comparison with derived words in the Romance languages. But all these kinds of evidence must be used with great caution.

2461. For the length of a vowel before **ns, nf,** and certain other groups of consonants, see 122.

2462. In inceptive verbs (834) the ending **-scō** is thought to be always preceded by a long vowel: as, **crēscō, nāscor, proficīscor.**

2463. In the perfect indicative active, perfect participle passive and kindred formations of verbs in **-gō** preceded by a short vowel, as **agō, regō,** the theme syllable shows a long vowel: as, **lēxī, rēxī, tēxī; āctus, lēctus; rēctor; āctitō.**

(B.) Some Peculiarities of Quantity in Old Latin.

2464. For the preservation of a long vowel in certain specific endings in old Latin, see 132.

2465. Final **-āl** is sometimes preserved long in the nominative singular: as, **bacchānāl** (Plaut.); also the syllable **-es** in the nominative singular of stems in **-t-** which have the genitive in **-itis** (477): as **mīlēs** (Plaut.) 171, 1.

2466. Hic, illic and istic, when adverbs, have a long final syllable; but when nominative singular masculine, have the final syllable regularly short.

2467. In Plautus **frūstrā** always where determinable (seven times) has the final syllable short. **contrā** sometimes has a short final syllable in old Latin.

2468. In Latin poetry down to the time of Cicero, final s often does not " make position " before a following consonant (66) ; as, **tempŭs fert** (Plaut.) ; **magĭs stetisse** (Ter.).

2469. The first syllable of ille, illic (the pronoun), **quippe, immō, inde, unde, nempe, omnis**, and perhaps **iste**, is sometimes shortened.

In **ille, illic, quippe**, and **immō** the shortening is, some hold, due to the fact that in common speech one of the double consonants was often pronounced faintly or not at all ; while in **inde, unde, nempe**, and **omnis** the nasal was very faintly sounded before the following consonant. But some authorities hold that always in **nempe**, and sometimes in **ille, quippe, inde, unde**, and perhaps **iste**, before an initial consonant final **e** disappears, and the word becomes a monosyllable.

LAW OF IAMBIC SHORTENING.

2470. A long syllable, preceded by a short monosyllable or by a short initial syllable, and immediately preceded or followed by the verse-ictus, may be shortened : as, **ét hŭnc, dómŏ mē, ad ŭxŏrem, volŭntăte**.

The short monosyllable may be a word which has become monosyllabic by elision : as, **ég(o) hănc**.

2471. If the syllable to be shortened is the first of a word of more than one syllable, or the second of a polysyllable, it must be one which is long by position, not by nature. There are some possible exceptions to this rule, such as **verĕbămini** (T. *Ph.* 902) ; but these are few and doubtful.

2472. Iambic shortening took place not only in verse, but also to a considerable extent in common speech, particularly in iambic words (see 130), in which the accent coöperated with the verse-ictus to produce the shortening.

II. FIGURES OF PROSODY.

HIATUS.

2473. For hiatus within a word, and the means by which it is avoided, see 114–120.

2474. Hiatus between two words is much more common in old Latin than in writers of the classical period. The precise extent to which it is allowed by the early dramatists is matter of dispute. The following cases may be mentioned in which the Latin poets admit hiatus :

2475. (1.) After interjections : as, **hahahae homo**, T. *Ph.* 411 ; **ō et praesidium**, H. 1, 1, 2.

2476. (2.) After proper names, and words of Greek origin : as, **ancillam ferre Venerī aut Cupīdinī**, Pl. *As.* 804 ; **Thrēiciō Aquilōne**, H. *Epod.* 13, 3.

2477. (3.) In the principal caesura of a verse. So especially in Plautus and Terence after the fourth foot of the iambic septenarius, and in Plautus in the principal break in the iambic octonarius, trochaic septenarius and trochaic octonarius.

2478. (4.) Often in the dramatists where there is a change of speakers: as, quī potuit vidēre ? : : oculīs : : quō pactō ? : : hiantibus, Pl. *Merc.* 182.

2479. (5.) Probably sometimes in cases of repetition, enumeration, or sharp antithesis, and where there is an important pause in the sense: as, eam volt meretrīcem facere : ea mē dēperit, Pl. *Cur.* 46; sī pĕreŏ, hominum manibus periisse iuvābit, V. 3, 606.

2480. Vergil sometimes admits hiatus when the final syllable ending in a vowel is preceded or followed (or both) by two short syllables: as, lāmentīs gemitūque et fēmĭnĕō ŭlŭlātū, V. 4, 667.

ELISION.

2481. For elision within a word, see 119.

2482. In verse a final vowel is generally elided before a vowel or h : as,

quidve moror, s(ī) omnīs ūn(ō) ōrdin(e) habētis Achīvōs, V. 2, 102.
Such a vowel was probably faintly sounded, not dropped altogether.

2483. Elision is frequent in most of the early poets; but writers of the Augustan and succeeding ages regarded it with increasing disfavour. The elision of a long vowel before a short was in general avoided; but there are numerous exceptions.

2484. Monosyllabic interjections do not suffer elision.

2485. Monosyllables ending in a diphthong seldom suffer elision before a short vowel.

2486. Diphthongs arising from Synizesis (2499) are sometimes elided in early Latin verse, but not in verse of the classical period.

2487. The monosyllables quī (plural), dŏ, stŏ, rē, spē, are thought never to suffer elision before a short vowel.

2488. The dactylic poets very rarely elide the final syllable of an iambic (‿ —) or Cretic (— ‿ —) word before a short vowel.

2489. Elision seldom occurs if the syllable to be elided is immediately prece- by a vowel : as in de(am) et.

2490. The final syllable of a Greek word is rarely elided.

2491. Elision is more common toward the beginning of a verse than toward the end.

2492. Elision rarely occurs in the first syllable or last syllable of a verse ; but see under Synapheia (2510), and for the elision of the enclitic -que or -ve at the end of a dactylic hexameter, see 2568.

2493. ECTHLIPSIS (Gr. ἔκθλιψις, *a squeezing out*). Final m and a preceding short vowel are usually elided before a vowel or h : as,

mōnstr(um) horrend(um) īnform(e) ingēns, cui lūmen ademptum,
V. 3, 658.

In such cases the ending was probably not cut off altogether, but was given a faint nasal sound.

2494. Sometimes a monosyllable ending in a short vowel and m is not elided before a vowel: as quăm ego (Ter.) ; súnt cŭm odōre (Lucr.).

Such unelided monosyllables are most frequent in the early dramatists, and in them usually fall under the verse-ictus. See 61.

2495. The monosyllables dem, stem, rem, spem, sim, are thought never to be elided before a short vowel.

2496. After a word ending with a vowel, -m, or -us, the verb est often loses its e : as, bonast, bonumst, bonust, vīsust. So, too, es sometimes loses its vowel: as homo's, adeptus'. This usage reflects the actual pronunciation of common speech.

2497. SEMI–HIATUS OR SEMI–ELISION. A long final vowel is sometimes shortened before a vowel. This may occur either in the arsis (2520), or in a resolved thęsis : as, án quĭ amant (Verg.) ; léc-tulŏ ērudītulĭ (Cat.) ; nam quĭ aget (Ter.).

This kind of shortening is not frequent except in the early dramatists, who often shorten under the verse-ictus a monosyllable ending in a long vowel and followed by an initial vowel (as in the third example above).

2498. SYNALOEPHA (Greek συναλοιφή, *a smearing together*) is a general term used to denote the means of avoiding hiatus. It includes elision and synizesis, though some grammarians use it in the same sense as synizesis.

2499. Synizesis (Greek συνίζησις, *a settling together*). Two vowels (or a vowel and a diphthong) which belong to different syllables sometimes coalesce so as to form one syllable. This is called *Synizesis*, and is especially common in the early dramatists. Examples are : meō, eadem, cuius, aurei. See 117.

Some grammarians would include under Synizesis only cases in which a short vowel is subordinated to a following long ; as tŭo.

2500. The term *Synaeresis* (Greek συναίρεσις, *a taking together*) is sometimes used as a synonym for Synizesis. The ancient grammarians, however, used it in the sense of Contraction (118).

2501. DIALYSIS (Greek διάλυσις, *a breaking up*). Conversely, two vowels which usually form a diphthong are sometimes separated so as to form two syllables : as coëpī (Lucr.) for coepī.

This, however, is really the survival of the original forms (120).

2502. The name DIAERESIS (Greek διαίρεσις, *a separating*) is sometimes used as a synonym for Dialysis; but it is better to restrict it to the meaning defined in 2542.

2503. HARDENING. A vocalic i or u is sometimes made consonantal before another vowel : as, abíete, aríete (Verg.) ; cōnsilium (Hor.) ; omnia (Lucr.). See 117 and 83.

This usage is sometimes included under Synizesis (2499), while some grammarians term it Synaeresis (2500).

2504. SOFTENING. Conversely, a consonantal i or u sometimes becomes vocalized before a vowel, thus giving an additional syllable : as, silüae for silvae (Hor.) ; ēvolüisse for ēvolvisse (Ov.). See 52.

This usage is sometimes included under the name Dialysis (2501).

2505. DIASTOLÉ (Greek διαστολή, *a drawing asunder*). A syllable which in verse of the classical period is generally short is sometimes used as long for metrical convenience. The syllable so employed generally falls under the verse-ictus, and in most cases is immediately followed by the principal caesura, or by a pause in the sense. Examples are :

terga fatīgāmūs hastā, nec tarda senectus, V. 9, 610.
tum sīc Mercurium adloquitūr ac tālia mandat, V. 4, 222.
caeca timēt aliunde fāta, H. 2, 13, 16.

In many such cases this lengthening is not arbitrary, but the " lengthened " syllable is one that was originally long (see 132).

2506. The enclitic -que is sometimes lengthened under the ictus when another -que precedes or follows in the arsis : as, cālōnēs famulīque metallīquĕ caculaeque (Accius).

2507. SYSTOLÉ (Greek συστολή, *a drawing together*). Conversely a syllable which in verse is regularly long is sometimes shortened for metrical convenience : as, dedĕrunt (Hor.), nūllĭus (Hor.), imperat. commodă (Cat.).

In most cases this shortening is not arbitrary, but represents a pronunciation which was in actual use, especially among the common people.

2508. SYNCOPÉ (Greek συγκοπή, *a cutting short*). A short vowel is often dropped between two consonants : as, surpitę for surripite (Hor.), repostum for repositum (Verg.).
This usage doubtless reflects the common pronunciation ; see 110, 111.

2509. TMESIS (Greek τμῆσις, *a cutting*) is the separation of the parts of a word : as, septem subiecta triōnī = septemtriōnī subiecta (Verg.).

This usually occurs only in compounds ; but early poets sometimes divided other words : as, saxō cere comminuit brum for saxō cerebrum comminuit (Ennius).

453

2510. SYNAPHEIA (Greek συνάφεια, *a joining together*) is the linking together of two verses belonging to the same system. Here elision or word division may occur at the end of the first verse: as,

> Iōve nōn probante u-
> xōrius amnis, H. 1, 2, 19.

> Iam licet veniās marīt(e),
> uxor in thalamō tibī est, Cat. 61, 191.

III. VERSIFICATION.

BY HERMAN W. HAYLEY, PH.D.

2511. RHYTHM (Gr. ῥυθμός, from ῥεῖν, *to flow*) is the effect of regularity produced by the discrimination of a movement or sound into uniform intervals of time. It is often marked by a stress or *ictus* recurring at fixed intervals.

Rhythm is by no means confined to verse. Music, dancing, and even the regular beat of a trip-hammer, have rhythm. Particular kinds of movement are often called rhythms, as anapaestic rhythms, dactylic rhythms, &c.

2512. METRE (Gr. μέτρον, *a measure*) is the definite measurement of verse by feet, lines, strophes, systems, &c.

2513. Latin verse is quantitative, the rhythm depending upon the quantity of the syllables (but see 2548). The ictus naturally falls upon a long syllable (or its equivalent). English verse, on the other hand, is accentual, its rhythm depending upon the accent of words.

QUANTITY.

2514. SIGNS OF QUANTITY. A long syllable is indicated by —, a short one by ⌣. A syllable which varies in quantity, being sometimes long, sometimes short, is indicated by ⌣̄ or ⌣̆.

In the following metrical schemes, ⌣̄ indicates that the long is more usual or more strictly in accordance with the rhythm than the short. The reverse is indicated by ⌣̆.

2515. The UNIT OF MEASURE is the duration of a short syllable and is called a *Time*, *Tempus*, or *Mora*. The *mora* did not have an absolute length, but varied with the nature of the rhythm. For greater convenience, however, it is assumed that its length was uniform, and equalled that of an eighth note ♪ A long syllable, being equal to two shorts, has a length of two *morae*, which is assumed to be the same as that of our quarter-note ♩ Hence in notation ⌣ = ♪ and — = ♩

2516. PROTRACTION. A long syllable may be prolonged (*Protraction*) so as to have a length of three *morae*, in which case it is called a *triseme* (marked ⌊⌋), or of four *morae*, when it is termed a *tetraseme* (marked ⌊⌋). See 2537 and 2541.

2517. CORREPTION. A long or short syllable may be shortened so as to occupy less than its normal time. This is called *Correption* (Lat. *correptiō, a shortening*). See 2523 and 2524.

2518. RESOLUTION AND CONTRACTION. In some kinds of verse a long syllable may be, as it were, broken up (*Resolution*) into the equivalent two shorts; and conversely two short syllables may in some cases be united (*Contraction*) into the equivalent long.

FEET.

2519. FEET. Latin verse (like English) is measured by groups of syllables called *Feet*. Each of these groups has a definite length of so many *morae* (2515).

It is theoretically more accurate to make the foot purely a time-division, as some authorities do; but the definition given above is sanctioned by established usage.

2520. ARSIS and THESIS. Every complete foot consists of two parts, an accented and an unaccented. The part on which the rhythmical accent or *ictus* falls is called the *Thesis* (Gr. θέσις, *a setting down*). The unaccented part of the foot is termed the *Arsis* (Gr. ἄρσις, *a raising*).

The name *Thesis* originally referred to the setting down of the foot in beating time or marching, or to the movement of the leader's hand in making the downward beat; and *Arsis* in like manner meant the raising of the foot or hand. But the Roman grammarians misunderstood the Greek terms, supposing them to refer to the lowering and raising of the voice, and so interchanged them. Hence many modern writers prefer to use *Arsis* to denote the accented, and *Thesis* the unaccented, part of the foot.

KINDS OF FEET.

2521. The feet in common use are the following: —

FEET OF THREE MORAE.			
Name.	Sign.	Musically.	Example.
Trochee	– ‿	♩ ♪	dūcit
Iambus	‿ –		legunt
Tribrach	‿ ‿ ‿		hominis

FEET OF FOUR MORAE.			
Dactyl	– ‿ ‿		dūcimus
Anapaest	‿ ‿ –		regerent
Spondee	– –		fēcī
Proceleusmatic	‿ ‿ ‿ ‿		hominibus

FEET OF FIVE MORAE.			
Cretic	– ‿ –		fēcerint
First Paeon	– ‿ ‿ ‿		lēgeritis
Fourth Paeon	‿ ‿ ‿ –		celeritās
Bacchīus	‿ – –		regēbant

FEET OF SIX MORAE.			
Choriambus	– ‿ ‿ –		horribilēs
Ionic *ā māiōre*	– – ‿ ‿		dēdūcimus
Ionic *ā minōre*	‿ ‿ – –		relegēbant

2522. Other feet mentioned by the ancient grammarians are : —

Name.	Sign.	Name.	Sign.
Pyrrhic	‿ ‿	Antispast . .	‿ – – ‿
Amphibrach . .	‿ – ‿	Second Paeon .	‿ – ‿ ‿
Antibacchīus or ⎱ .	– – ‿	Third Paeon .	‿ ‿ – ‿
Palimbacchīus ⎰ .		First Epitrite .	‿ – – –
Molossus	– – –	Second Epitrite .	– ‿ – –
Dispondee . . .	– – – –	Third Epitrite .	– – ‿ –
Ditrochee . . .	– ‿ – ‿	Fourth Epitrite	– – – ‿
Diiambus . . .	‿ – ‿ –		

But these are of little practical importance, as most of them never are employed in Latin poetry, and the few which do occur are used only as substitutes for other feet.

CYCLIC FEET.

2523. A dactyl occurring in $\frac{3}{8}$ time did not have the value of 2 *morae* + 1 + 1, but was given instead that of $1\frac{1}{3} + \frac{2}{4} + \frac{2}{4}$; in other words both arsis and thesis suffered correption (2517), but the ratio between them remained unchanged. Such a dactyl is called *cyclic*, and is marked — ‿‿, or musically ♪ ♪ ♪ There is also a *cyclic anapaest*, marked ‿‿ — or ♪ ♪ ♪.

Some scholars, however, hold that the cyclic dactyl had approximately the value $1\frac{1}{2} + \frac{1}{2} + 1$, or ♩. ♪, and mark it —‿ ‿. In like manner they mark the cyclic anapaest ‿ ‿—. The true nature of these cyclic feet is very uncertain.

IRRATIONAL SYLLABLES AND FEET.

2524. A long syllable sometimes stands in place of a short. A syllable thus used is called *irrational* (marked >) because it destroys the normal ratio between arsis and thesis. The foot which contains such a syllable is itself called irrational. The most common irrational foot is the *irrational spondee* (— > when it stands for a trochee; > — when it replaces an iambus), which is found in iambic, trochaic, and logaoedic rhythms.

Probably the irrational long suffered a slight correption (2517), so that its duration was between that of the ordinary long and that of a short syllable.

RHYTHMS.

2525. The different rhythms or metres are named trochaic, iambic, &c., according to their fundamental feet.

2526. Much of the Latin poetry (though not by any means all) was written to be sung. The Greeks and Romans employed in their music not only common (or $\frac{2}{4}$) time and triple ($\frac{3}{8}$, $\frac{3}{4}$) time, but also $\frac{5}{8}$ time, which last is very rarely used in modern music.

2527. The Greek and Roman metricians divided the rhythms into three classes, according to the ratio between arsis and thesis in their fundamental feet. These classes were: — (*a*.) the *Equal Class* (γένος ἴσον, *genus pār*) in which thesis and arsis are equal in duration, as in dactylics, anapaestics, &c.; (*b*.) the *Double Class* (γένος διπλάσιον, *genus duplex*) in which the thesis has twice the duration of the arsis, as in trochaics, iambics, &c.; (*c*.) the *Hemiolic Class* (γένος ἡμιόλιον, *genus sēscuplex*) in which the thesis has one and a half times the duration of the arsis, as in bacchiacs, cretics, etc.

2528. ASCENDING AND DESCENDING RHYTHMS. Rhythms in which the thesis follows the arsis (as in iambics) are called *ascending;* those in which it precedes the arsis (as in trochaics) are termed *descending.*

ANACRUSIS.

2529. The ancients recognized both ascending **and** descending rhythms (2528), and regarded the former class as at least equal in importance to the latter; but many modern scholars since the time of Bentley have preferred to treat all rhythms as descending, regarding the first arsis of an ascending rhythm as merely answering to a preliminary upward beat in music. Such an initial arsis was named by Gottfried Hermann *Anacrŭsis* (Gr. ἀνάκρουσις, *a striking up*).

Scholars have been influenced to adopt the anacrustic theory in its widest extent largely by the fact that in most modern music a measure must commence with a downward beat, a rule which did not hold in ancient music. By this theory an iambic verse becomes trochaic with anacrusis, an anapaestic verse dactylic with anacrusis, &c. But in many cases those kinds of verse which begin with an arsis were subject to different rules of construction from those which begin with a thesis. Hence it seems best to restrict anacrusis to logaoedic verse, in which it undoubtedly occurs.

2530. The anacrusis may be a long syllable, a short syllable, or two shorts (but not two longs). It is often irrational (2524). In metrical schemes it is often set off from the rest of the verse by a vertical row of dots: thus, :

GROUPS OF FEET.

2531. A group of two feet is called a *dipody*, one of three a *tripody*, one of four a *tetrapody*, one of five a *pentapody*, and one of six a *hexapody*. The dipody is the measure of trochaic, iambic, and anapaestic verse. Other kinds of verse are measured by the single foot.

A single foot is sometimes called a *monopody*. A group of three half feet, i. e. a foot and a half, is sometimes called a *trithemimeris*, one of two and a half feet a *penthemimeris*, one of three and a half a *hephthemimeris*, &c.

2532. A *Rhythmical Series, Rhythmical Sentence*, or *Colon* is a group of two or more feet (but not more than six) which are united into a rhythmic whole by strengthening one of the ictuses, so that it becomes the principal or dominant ictus of the whole group.

2533. THE VERSE. A rhythmical series, or group of two (or even three) series, which forms a distinct and separate whole is called a *Verse*. The final syllable of a verse must terminate a word (except in cases of synapheia, see 2510), and may be either long or short (whence it is termed *syllaba anceps*) without regard to the rhythm. Hiatus (2474) is freely allowed at the end of a verse (though in rare cases elision occurs before a vowel at the beginning of the following verse; see 2492 and 2568).

A verse is generally (but not always) written as one line. Hence, the words "verse" and "line" are often used as synonyms.

SYLLABA ANCEPS.

2534. In the present work, the final syllable of each verse is marked long or short as the rhythm may require, without reference to its quantity in a given example; and in the general schemes it is to be understood that the final syllable is *syllaba anceps* (2533) unless the contrary is expressly stated.

2535. DICOLIC AND ASYNARTETIC VERSES. A verse which consists of two rhythmical series (or cola) is called *dicolic*. If the series of which the verse is made up are quasi-independent of each other, so that hiatus or syllaba anceps occurs in the caesura, the verse is styled *asynartetic* (Gr. ἀσυνάρτητος, *not joined together*).

2536. NAMES OF VERSES. Verses are called *trochaic, iambic, dactylic*, &c., according to their fundamental (or characteristic) feet. A verse which contains one foot (or one dipody if iambic, trochaic, or anapaestic; see 2531) is called a *monometer*, one of two a *dimeter*, one of three a *trimeter*, one of four a *tetrameter*, one of five a *pentameter*, and one of six a *hexameter*.

Trochaic, iambic, and anapaestic verses are often named by Latin adjectives in *-ārius* (used as nouns) denoting the number of feet. Thus, such a verse of eight feet is called an *octōnārius*, one of seven a *septēnārius*, one of six a *sēnārius*, &c. A short verse which is employed to close a system (2547), or to mark a metrical or musical transition between longer verses, is called a *clausula*.

CATALEXIS, PAUSE, SYNCOPE.

2537. CATALEXIS. A verse, the last foot of which is incomplete, is said to suffer *Catalexis* (Gr. κατάληξις, *a stopping short*) or to be *catalectic;* one of which the last foot is complete is called *acatalectic*.

It is usually the last part of the foot that is omitted; but (according to the theory now generally accepted) in catalectic iambic verses it is the last arsis that is omitted, the preceding thesis being protracted (2516) to compensate for the loss, thus : ∪ ⌣́ ⌣́

2538. A verse in which both the last arsis and the next to the last are suppressed, so that a whole foot appears to be wanting, is called *brachycatalectic*.

2539. A verse is said to be catalectic *in syllabam, in disyllabum*, or *in trisyllabum*, according to the number of syllables remaining in the last foot. Thus, the dactylic tetrameter _ ∪ ∪ | _ ∪ ∪ | _ ∪ ∪ | _ is catalectic *in syllabam*, but _ ∪ ∪ | _ ∪ ∪ | _ ∪ ∪ | _ ∪ is catalectic *in disyllabum*.

2540. PAUSES. Theoretically all the feet (or dipodies; see 2531) into which a verse is divided must be equal in duration. Hence, when a final syllable (or two final syllables) is lost by catalexis, compensation is made for the loss by a pause at the end of the verse. Such a pause, which serves to fill out the last measure, answers to a *rest* in music.

A pause of one *mora* is often indicated by the sign ∧, and one of two *morae* by ⌅.

2541. SYNCOPE is the omission of one or more arses in the body of a verse. Compensation is made for the suppression of an arsis by protracting (2516) the preceding thesis.

CAESURA.

2542. CAESURA AND DIAERESIS. A *Caesūra* (literally *a cutting*, from *caedo, I cut*) is the break in a verse produced by the ending of a word within a foot. When the end of a word coincides with the end of a foot, the break is called a *Diaeresis* (Gr. διαίρεσις, *a separating*). A caesura is marked ‖, a diaeresis ‡.

The word *caesura* is often loosely used to include both caesura proper and diaeresis.

2543. Strictly speaking, there is a caesura (or diaeresis, as the case may be) wherever a word ends within a verse ; but the main incision in the verse is so much more important than the rest that it is often called the *principal caesura*, or simply *the caesura*.

2544. Caesuras are named according to their position in the verse ; thus a caesura after the third half-foot (i. e. in the second foot) is called *trithemimeral* (from Gr. τριθημιμερής, *containing three halves*), one after the fifth half-foot (i. e. in the third foot) *penthemimeral* (Gr. πενθημιμερής, *consisting of five halves*), one after the seventh half-foot (i. e. in the fourth foot) *hephthemimeral* (Gr. ἐφθημιμερής), &c.

The Latin names *caesūra sēmiternāria* (= the trithemimeral caesura), *sēmiquīnāria* (= the penthemimeral), *sēmiseptēnāria* (= the hepthemimeral), &c., are sometimes used. For the *masculine* and *feminine* caesuras, see **2557.**

STROPHE. SYSTEM.

2545. THE STROPHE. A fixed number of verses recurring in a regular order is called a *Strophe*. A strophe commonly contains verses of different kinds, but some strophes are composed of verses which are all alike. The most common strophes in Latin poetry are either *distichs* (i. e. groups of two lines each), *tristichs* (of three lines each), or *tetrastichs* (of four).

Strophes and verses are frequently named after some poet who made use of them. So the Alcaic strophe (named after Alcaeus), the Sapphic strophe (named after Sappho), the Glyconic verse (named after Glycon), the Asclepiadean (after Asclepiades), the Phalaecean (after Phalaecus), the Pherecratean (after Pherecrates), &c.

2546. A *Stichic Series* is a series of verses of the same kind not combined into strophes.

2547. THE SYSTEM. A group of rhythmical series (see 2532) which is of greater extent than a verse is called a *System*. Long systems, such as are common in Greek poetry, are comparatively rare in Latin verse.

Few verses have more than two rhythmical series ; none more than three.

2548. Although in all probability the Latin accent was mainly one of stress rather than of pitch, it seems to have been comparatively weak. Hence, when it conflicted with the metrical ictus, it could be the more easily disregarded. But accentual or semi-accentual poetry seems to have existed among the common people even in the Augustan age, and even in classical Latin verse in certain cases (as in the last part of the dactylic hexameter) conflict between ictus and accent was carefully avoided. After the third century A. D. the accent exerted a stronger and stronger influence upon versification, until in the Middle Ages the quantitative Latin verse was quite supplanted by the accentual.

NUMERI ITALICI.

2549. Some of the earliest remains of Latin literature are believed to show a rhythmical structure. These are chiefly prayers, imprecations, sacred songs and the like, couched in a set form of words. Of the rules according to which these **carmina** were composed, almost nothing is known. According to one theory, they are wholly accentual, and are composed of rhythmical series, each series containing four theses. Frequently an arsis is suppressed, and compensation for the omission is made by dwelling longer upon the thesis. As an example is given the prayer in Cato, *Dē Rē Rūsticā*, 141 :

> Mǎrs páter tē précor | quaésóque útī síēs | vólēns própítiús
> míhí dómó | fámiliaéque nóstraé, &c.

THE SATURNIAN.

2550. THE SATURNIAN is the best known and most important of the old Italian rhythms; but its nature long has been, and still is, matter of high dispute. There are two principal theories as to its character, the quantitative and the accentual, each of which is advocated by many distinguished scholars.

2551. (1.) THE QUANTITATIVE THEORY. According to this theory, the Saturnian is a verse of six feet, with an anacrusis (2529). There is a break after the fourth arsis, or more rarely after the third thesis. Each thesis may be either a long syllable or two shorts; each arsis may be a short syllable, a long, or two shorts, but an arsis is not resolved before the principal break or at the end of the verse. Hiatus is common, especially at the principal break in the verse. A short final syllable may be lengthened by the influence of the verse-ictus. An arsis is frequently suppressed, especially the penultimate arsis. Two arses are never suppressed in the same half-verse, and rarely two in the same verse. Examples of the Saturnian, measured quantitatively, are :

> Dabúnt malúm Metéllī ‡ Naévió poétae.

> Novém Iovís concórdēs ‡ fíliaé sorórēs.
> (Naevius.)

Virúm mihí, Caména, ‡ ínsecé versútum.
(Livius Andronicus.)

Eōrúm sectám sequóntur ‡ múltī mórtālēs.
(Naevius.)

Compare in English: "The queén was ín the párlour, éating bréad and hóney."

2552. Most of the Roman grammarians who discussed the nature of the Saturnian seem to have regarded it as quantitative. In modern times the quantitative theory has been advocated by Ritschl, Buecheler, Havet, Christ, Lucian Mueller, W. Meyer, Reichardt and many others.

2553. (2.) THE ACCENTUAL THEORY. According to this theory, the Saturnian is an accentual verse, constructed without regard to quantity. It is divided by the principal break into two halves, the first of which has three theses. The second half usually has three, but may have only two, in which case it is usually preceded by an anacrusis (2529). Two accented syllables are regularly separated by an unaccented syllable, but in strictly constructed Saturnians the second and third unaccented syllables are regularly separated by two unaccented ones. Hiatus was at first freely admitted, but in the Saturnians of the second century B. C. occurs only at the principal break. Examples of the Saturnian, measured according to this theory, are:

Dábunt málum Metéllī ‡ Naéviō poétae.

Nóvem Ióvis concórdēs ‡ fíliaé sorórēs.
(Naevius.)

Vírum míhi, Caména, ‡ ínsecé versútum.
(Livius Andronicus.)

Eōrum séctam sequóntur ‡ múltī mórtālēs.
(Naevius.)

2554. The accentual theory was held by the scholiast on V. *G.* 2, 385, and in modern times has been upheld (in one form or another) by O. Keller, Thurneysen, Westphal, Gleditsch, Lindsay and others. The brief statement given above agrees essentially with that of O. Keller. Gleditsch holds that each half-verse has four accents, as: Dábunt málum Metéllī ‖ Naéviō poétaé; Lindsay that the first hemistich has three accents and the second two, as: Dábunt málum Metéllī ‖ Naéviō poétae. The whole question is still far from its final settlement.

DACTYLIC RHYTHMS.

2555. These are descending rhythms belonging to the *Equal Class* (see 2527). In them the fundamental foot is the dactyl ($\angle \cup \cup$), for which its metrical equivalent, the spondee ($\angle$ —), is frequently substituted.

THE DACTYLIC HEXAMETER.

2556. The DACTYLIC HEXAMETER is the verse regularly employed in epic, didactic, and bucolic poetry, and is used by the Latin writers oftener than any other measure. It consists of six feet, the last of which is a spondee (but with the privilege of *syllaba anceps;* see 2534). The fifth foot is usually a dactyl; but sometimes a spondee is employed, in which case the verse is called *spondaic.* In each of the other four feet either a dactyl or a spondee may be used. The scheme is therefore:

$$\acute{}\smile\smile \mid \acute{}\smile\smile \mid \acute{}\smile\smile \mid \acute{}\smile\smile \mid \acute{}\smileebar \mid \acute{}\,\underline{}$$

2557. A caesura which comes immediately after the thesis of a foot is called *masculine;* one which falls in the middle of the arsis (i. e. after the first short of a dactyl) is termed *feminine.* The Roman writers show a strong preference for masculine principal caesuras, and in general their treatment of the caesura is more strict than that of the Greek poets.

2558. The principal caesura in the Latin hexameter is most frequently the penthemimeral (2544): as in:

Arma virumque canō ‖ Troiae quī prīmus ab ōrīs
(V.1, 1).

Next in order of frequency stands the hephthemimeral, which is usually accompanied by a secondary trithemimeral, and in many cases also by a feminine caesura in the third foot: as in the verse,

Īnsīgnem ‖ pietāte ‖ virum ‖ tot adīre labōrēs
(V. 1, 10).

If the secondary trithemimeral caesura is lacking, the penthemimeral is usually accompanied by a feminine caesura in the second foot. Sometimes, though more rarely, the principal break in the line is the feminine caesura in the third foot (often called the "caesura after the third trochee"), as in the verse

Spargēns ūmida mella ‖ sopōriferumque papāver
(V. 4, 486).

2559. The diaeresis (see 2542) after the fourth foot (often called "bucolic diaeresis" from its use by pastoral writers) sometimes occurs, but is much less common in Latin hexameters than in Greek. An example is

Dīc mihi, Dāmoetā, ‖ cuium pecus ? ‡‡ An Meliboeī ?
(V. *E.* 3, 1).

This diaeresis, though common in Juvenal, is rare in most of the Latin poets (even the bucolic), and when it does occur, it is usually accompanied by a penthemimeral caesura. Lucian Mueller and others deny that the bucolic diaeresis ever forms the principal break in a line.

2560. When a line has several caesuras, it is often hard to determine which is the principal one. In general, masculine caesuras out-rank feminine; the penthemimeral takes precedence over the hephthemimeral, and the latter over all other caesuras. But if the hephthemimeral, or even one of the minor caesuras, coincides with an important pause in the sentence, it may out-rank the penthemimeral. Thus in the verse

> **Paulāt(im) adnābam ‖ terrae; ‖ iam tūta tenēbam**
> (V. 6, 358),

the principal caesura is after **terrae**, not adnābam.

Lines without a principal caesura are rare. An instance is

> **Nōn quīvīs videt inmodulāta poēmata iūdex**
> (H. *AP.* 263).

2561. The great flexibility of the hexameter makes it an admirable vehicle of poetic expression. Accumulated spondees give the verse a slow and ponderous movement: as in the line

> **Ill(ī) in|ter sē|sē ‖ ma|gnā vī | bracchia | tollunt**
> (V. *G.* 4, 174).

The multiplication of dactyls imparts to the verse a comparatively rapid and impetuous motion, as in the famous verse

> **Quadrupe|dante pu|trem ‖ soni|tū quatit | ungula | campum**
> (V. 8, 596).

But even when dactyls are numerous, the Latin hexameter, "the stateliest measure ever moulded by the lips of man," should not be read with the jerky ⅜ movement which is characteristic of the English hexameter.

2562. The following passage may serve to illustrate the movement of the hexameter, and to show how the use of the different caesuras imparts variety to the measure:

> **Ō soci|ī ‖ —nequ(e) e|n(im) īgnā|rī ‖ sumus | ante ma|lōrum—**
> **ō pas|sī gravi|ōra, ‖ da|bit deus | hīs quoque | finem.**
> **Vōs et | Scyllae|am ‖ rabi|em ‖ peni|tusque so|nantēs**
> **accē|stis scopu|lōs, ‖ vōs | et Cȳ|clōpea | saxa**
> **exper|tī; ‖ revo|cāt(e) ani|mōs, ‖ mae|stumque ti|mōrem**
> **mittite: | forsan et | haec ‖ ō|lim ‖ memi|nisse iu|vābit.**
> (V. 1, 198).

Compare in English:

> Rolls and rages amain the restless, billowy ocean,
> While with a roar that soundeth afar the white-maned breakers
> Leap up against the cliffs, like foemen madly rejoicing.

NOTES ON THE HEXAMETER.

2563. (1.) In all probability, the hexameter was originally a composite verse, made up of two tripodies, or of a tetrapody and a dipody. Hence hiatus in the principal caesura is not very rare, even in the Augustan poets. The stress upon the first and fourth theses was probably stronger than that upon the other four.

2564. (2.) In the second half of the hexameter, particularly in the fifth and sixth feet, verse-ictus and word-accent show a strong tendency to coincide.

2565. (3.) A monosyllable rarely stands before the principal caesura or at the end of the verse. When the verse ends in a monosyllable, the thesis of the last foot is generally a monosyllable also, as in the line

Crīspīnus minimō mē prōvocat ; accipe, sī vīs
(H. *S.* 1, 4, 14).

Exceptions to this rule sometimes occur when the poet wishes to produce a particular effect, as in

Parturient montēs, nāscētur rīdiculus mūs
(H. *AP.* 139).

2566. (4.) A hexameter generally ends in a word of two or three syllables, almost never in one of four, rarely in one of five. But *spondaic* verses (2556) generally end with a word of four syllables, more rarely with one of three, almost never with one of two.

2567. (5.) Spondaic verses are comparatively rare in Ennius and Lucretius, but become more frequent in Catullus. They are not common in Vergil, Horace, Propertius and Ovid, and do not occur at all in Tibullus. Persius has one spondaic verse, Valerius Flaccus one, Claudian five, Silius Italicus six, Statius seven. Ennius has lines composed entirely of spondees, and so in one instance (116, 3) Catullus. Ennius also resolves the thesis of a dactyl in a few cases.

2568. (6.) A verse which is connected with the following one by elision (2492) is called hypermetrical. Such verses are rare, and usually end with the enclitics -que or -ve.

2569. (7.) The dactylic hexameter was introduced into Latin literature by Ennius, and was further perfected by Lucilius, Lucretius, and Cicero, who took him as their model. Catullus and the group to which he belonged followed Alexandrian models more closely, while the great poets of the Augustan age carried the technique of the hexameter to its highest perfection. Horace in his lyric poetry treats the hexameter with great strictness; but in the Satires and Epistles he handles it with much freedom, imparting to the measure a more colloquial character by the frequent use of spondees and by less rigorous treatment of the caesura.

The Dactylic Pentameter.

2570. The Dactylic Pentameter is a verse consisting of two catalectic dactylic tripodies, separated by a fixed diaeresis. Spondees are admitted in the first tripody, but not in the second. The final thesis of the first tripody is protracted to a tetraseme (2516) to compensate for the omission of the arsis. The scheme is therefore

$$\underline{\ } \underset{\smile\smile}{\ } \mid \underline{\ } \underset{\smile\smile}{\ } \mid \underline{\llcorner} \# \underline{\ } \smile \smile \mid \underline{\ } \smile \smile \mid \underline{\ } \overline{\wedge}$$

2571. (1.) The verse is not asynartetic (2535), neither *syllaba anceps* nor hiatus being allowed at the end of the first tripody.

2572. (2.) This verse is known as the pentameter because the ancient grammarians measured it

$$\underline{\ }\smile\smile\mid\underline{\ }\smile\smile\mid\underline{\ }\underline{\ }\mid\smile\smile\underline{\ }\mid\smile\smile\underline{\ }$$

2573. The pentameter is rarely used except in combination with the hexameter, with which it forms the so-called *Elegiac Distich:*

$$\stackrel{\prime}{\smile}\!\smile\mid\!-\!\smile\!\smile\mid\!-\!\smile\!\smile\mid\stackrel{\prime}{\smile}\!\smile\mid\stackrel{\prime}{\smile}\!\overline{\smile}\!\mid\stackrel{\prime}{\smile}\!-$$
$$\stackrel{\prime}{\smile}\!\smile\mid\stackrel{\prime}{\smile}\!\smile\mid\stackrel{\prime}{\smile}\!\#\stackrel{\prime}{\smile}\cup\cup\mid\stackrel{\prime}{\smile}\cup\cup\mid\stackrel{\prime}{\smile}\!\overline{\wedge}$$

2574. The Elegiac Distich is used chiefly in elegiac poetry (whence the name), in amatory verse and in epigrams. The end of the pentameter generally coincides with a pause in the sense. As examples of the Elegiac Distich, the following may serve :

> Quam legis | ex il|lā ‖ tibi | vēnit e|pistola | terrā
> lātus u|b(ī) aequore|īs ‡ additur | Hister a|quīs.
> Sī tibi | contige|rit ‖ cum | dulcī | vīta sa|lūte,
> candida | fortū|nae ‡ pars manet | ūna me|ae.
>
> <div align="right">O. <i>Tr.</i> 5, 7, 1.</div>

Compare in English (but see 2561 *ad fin.*) :

> " These lame hexameters the strong-winged music of Homer !
> No — but a most burlesque, barbarous experiment . . .
> Hexameters no worse than daring Germany gave us,
> Barbarous experiment, barbarous hexameters."
>
> (TENNYSON).

2575. The Elegiac Distich was introduced into Roman poetry by Ennius, who used it in epigrams. Varro employed it in his *Saturae*, and Catullus seems to have been the first of the Latins who used it in Elegiac poetry. The elegiac and amatory poets of the Augustan age, especially Ovid, perfected it, and wielded it with unequalled grace and ease.

2576. Ovid nearly always closes the pentameter with a disyllabic word ; but earlier poets, especially Catullus, are less careful in this regard. Elision is less frequent in the pentameter than in the hexameter. It sometimes occurs in the main diaeresis of the pentameter, though rarely.

THE DACTYLIC TETRAMETER ACATALECTIC (or *Alcmanian*).

2577. This verse is chiefly used in composition with a trochaic tripody to form the Greater Archilochian verse (2677) ; but it occurs alone once in Terence (*Andria* 625), and is employed in stichic series (2546) by Seneca The scheme is :

$$\stackrel{\prime}{\smile}\!\smile\mid\stackrel{\prime}{\smile}\!\smile\mid\stackrel{\prime}{\smile}\!\smile\mid\stackrel{\prime}{\smile}\cup\cup$$

An example is :

> hocine | crēdibi|l(e) aut memo|rābile
>
> <div align="right">(T. <i>Andr.</i> 625).</div>

This verse is often called *Alcmanian* because it was used by the Greek poet Alcman.

THE DACTYLIC TETRAMETER CATALECTIC (or *Archilochian.*)

2578. This verse consists of four dactylic feet, the last one being incomplete. The scheme is:

$$\perp \smallsmile\smallsmile \mid \perp \smallsmile\smallsmile \mid - \smallsmile\smallsmile \mid \perp \smallsmile \wedge$$

An example is:

Cármine | pérpetu|ṓ cele|brā́r(e) et

(H. 1, 7, 6).

This verse differs from the preceding in that the last foot is always a trochee or spondee, never a dactyl. It is used only in the Alcmanian strophe (2724).

THE DACTYLIC TRIMETER CATALECTIC (or *Lesser Archilochian*).

2579. This verse has the scheme:

$$\perp \smallsmile \smallsmile \mid \perp \smallsmile \smallsmile \mid \perp \bar{\wedge}$$

An example is:

Árbori|búsque co | maé

(H. 4, 7, 2).

It is used chiefly in the First Archilochian Strophe (see 2725). In form it is the same as the second half of the pentameter (2570).

2580. These verses (2578, 2579) are often called *Archilochian* because they were first used by the Greek poet Archilochus.

IAMBIC RHYTHMS.

2581. These are ascending rhythms (2528)in ⅜ time. The fundamental foot is the Iambus ($\smallsmile \perp$), for which its metrical equivalent the tribrach $\smallsmile \smallsmile \smallsmile$, the irrational spondee $> \perp$, the irrational dactyl $> \smallsmile \smallsmile$, the cyclic anapaest $\smallsmile\smallsmile \perp$, or the proceleusmatic $\smallsmile\smallsmile \smallsmile \smallsmile$ is sometimes substituted.

2582. The Greek poets excluded all feet except the iambus and tribrach, and in comedy the anapaest, from the even places in iambic verse. The Latin poets were not so strict: but when one of the even feet was formed by a word or a word-ending, they did not usually allow the foot to be a spondee or an anapaest, but required it to be an iambus.

467

THE IAMBIC TRIMETER OR SENARIUS.

2583. The IAMBIC TRIMETER is the verse most frequently used by the Roman dramatists. It consists of six iambic feet, or three iambic dipodies. The ictus on the second thesis of each dipody was probably weaker than that upon the first thesis. Some ancient authorities, however, held that the ictus on the second thesis was the stronger. The last foot is always an iambus. The normal scheme is therefore:

$$\cup \; \underline{\angle} \; | \; \cup \; \underline{\angle} \; | \; \cup \; \underline{\angle} \; | \; \cup \; \underline{\angle} \; | \; \cup \; \underline{\angle} \; | \; \cup \; \underline{\angle}$$

Some prefer (see 2529) to regard this verse as a trochaic trimeter catalectic with anacrusis. The normal scheme will then be:

$$\cup \; \vdots \; \underline{\angle} \; \cup \; | \; \underline{\angle} \; \cup \; | \; \underline{\angle} \; \cup \; | \; \underline{\angle} \; \cup \; | \; \underline{\angle} \; \cup \; | \; \underline{\angle} \; \wedge$$

2584. The Latin poets differ widely in their treatment of the Senarius, some (especially Plautus, Terence, and the other early dramatists) handling it with great freedom, while others (especially Phaedrus and Publilius Syrus) conform more closely to Greek models. We may therefore distinguish two periods:

(A.) Early Period.

2585. Any one of the substitutions enumerated in 2581 is admitted in any foot except the last. The scheme is therefore:

$$
\begin{array}{ccccccc}
\gtrless\,\underline{\angle} & | & \gtrless\,\underline{\ldots} & | & \gtrless\,\underline{\angle} & | & \gtrless\,\underline{\ldots} & | & \gtrless\,\underline{\angle} & | & \cup\,\underline{\ldots} \\
\cup\,\cup\,\cup | & \cup\,\cup\,\cup | & \cup\,\cup\,\cup | & \cup\,\cup\,\cup | & \cup\,\cup\,\cup | \\
\gtrdot\,\cup\,\cup | & \gtrdot\,\cup\,\cup | & \gtrdot\,\cup\,\cup | & \gtrdot\,\cup\,\cup | & \gtrdot\,\cup\,\cup | \\
\rotatebox{0}{w}\,\underline{\angle} | & \rotatebox{0}{w}\,\underline{\ldots} | & \rotatebox{0}{w}\,\underline{\angle} | & \rotatebox{0}{w}\,\underline{\ldots} | & \rotatebox{0}{w}\,\underline{\angle} | \\
\rotatebox{0}{w}\,\cup\,\cup | & \rotatebox{0}{w}\,\cup\,\cup | & \rotatebox{0}{w}\,\cup\,\cup | & \rotatebox{0}{w}\,\cup\,\cup | & \rotatebox{0}{w}\,\cup\,\cup |
\end{array}
$$

The main caesura is usually penthemimeral (2544); but it is sometimes hephthemimeral, in which case there is generally a secondary caesura in, or diaeresis after, the second foot.

The following passage may serve to show the rhythm:

> Ubi vén|t(um) ad ae|dīs ‖ ést | Dromō | pultát | pultát | forēs ;
> anŭs quaé|dam prō|dit ; ‖ haéc | ub(i) ape|rit ŏs|tium,
> contínu(ō) | hic sē | conié|cit ‖ in|tr(ō), ego cón|sequor ;
> anŭs fóri|bus ob|dit ‖ pés|sul(um), ad | lānám | redit.
> Hīc scí|rī potu|it ‖ aut_| nusqu(am) ali|bī, Clí niạ,
> quō stúdi|ō vī|tam ‖ suám | t(ē) absen|t(e) exē|gerit,
> ubi d(ē) ín |prōvī|sōst ‖ ín|terven|tum múli|erī, &c.
>
> T. *Hau.* 275.

⏑ _́ | ⏑ _ | >‖ _́ | ⏑ _ | >_́ | ⏑ _
⏑ _́ | >_ | ⏑ ‖ _́ | ⏑⏑⏑ | ⏑ _́ | ⏑ _
> ⏑̆ ⏑ | >_ | >_́ | ⏑ ‖ _ | ⏑⏑ _́ | ⏑ _
⏑⏑ ⏑̆ ⏑ | ⏑ _ | >‖ _́ | ⏑ _ | >_́ | ⏑ _
>_́ | >⏑⏑ | ⏑ ‖ _́ | >⏑⏑ | >_́ | ⏑ _
> ⏑̆ ⏑ | >_ | >‖ _́ | >_ | >_́ | ⏑ _
⏑⏑ _́ | >_ | >‖ _́ | >_ | >⏑̆ ⏑ | ⏑ _

2586. (1.) In the early dramatists, substitutions are very numerous, and lines which follow the normal scheme are rare. Substitutions are most frequent in the first foot.

2587. (2.) Four shorts rarely stand in succession unless they belong to the same foot. Hence a dactyl or tribrach is seldom followed by an anapaest.

2588. (3.) The dactyl and proceleusmatic are rare in the fifth foot. The proceleusmatic occurs chiefly in the first foot.

2589. (4.) The fifth foot is very often a spondee. It must not be a pure iambus except (*a*.) when the line ends with a polysyllable of four or more syllables; (*b*.) when it ends with a word which forms a Cretic (2521); (*c*.) when it ends with an iambic word preceded by one which forms a Fourth Paeon (2521), or by an anapaestic word which is itself preceded by a final short syllable; (*d*.) when there is a change of speakers before the last foot; (*e*.) when elision occurs in the fifth or sixth foot.

2590. (5.) The main caesura is rarely preceded by a monosyllable.

2591. (6.) In the Senarius, and in the other iambic and trochaic verses of the early dramatists, a resolved arsis or thesis is usually placed so that its first syllable *begins a word*, or so that the two shorts of the resolved arsis or thesis are *enclosed* by other syllables belonging to the same word. Hence a dactylic word with the ictus on the penult or ultima (e. g. **tempóre**) rarely occurs. But there are occasional exceptions to the rule, especially in the case of words that are closely connected (e. g. a preposition with its case).

(B.) Later Period.

2592. Later writers conform more closely to Greek usage, but differ from one another in the degree of strictness with which they follow it. The general scheme is:

ᐅ _́ | ⏑ _ | ᐅ ‖ _́ | ⏑ _ | ᐅ _́ | ⏑ _
⏑ ⏑̆ ⏑ | ⏑⏑⏑ | ⏑ ‖ ⏑̆ ⏑ | ⏑⏑⏑ | ⏑ ⏑̆ ⏑
> ⏑̆ ⏑ | | > ‖ ⏑̆ ⏑ |
[⏑⏑ _́] | [⏑⏑ _] |
[⏑⏑ ⏑̆ ⏑] |.

The main caesura is usually the penthemimeral (2544). The hephthemimeral sometimes occurs, but usually in connection with the penthemimeral, or with a diaeresis after the second foot. If the hephthemimeral is used without either of these, the second and third trochees of the line must form one word, as in

ut gaú|det īn|sití|va ‖ dē|cerpḗns | pira.

(H. *Epod.* 2, 19.)

2593. (1.) The anapaest is rare in nearly all classical writers; Catullus does not admit it at all, and Horace only five times in all. The proceleusmatic is admitted in the first foot by Seneca, the author of the *Octāvia*, Phaedrus, Publilius Syrus and Terentianus Maurus; other writers exclude it altogether. Catullus keeps the fifth foot pure, and Horace does not admit the tribrach in the fifth foot.

2594. (2.) Catullus (4 and 29), Horace (*Epod.* 16), Vergil (*Cat.* 3, 4, 8), and the authors of the *Priāpēa* sometimes use the *pure* iambic trimeter, without resolutions or substitutions.

2595. (3.) Phaedrus follows in part the earlier usage, admitting the spondee, dactyl, and anapaest, in every foot except the last. The dactyl he employs chiefly in the first, third, and fifth feet, the anapaest in the first and fifth. The proceleusmatic he admits only in the first.

2596 The rhythm of the Senarius may be illustrated by the following lines :

> But one amid the throng of eager listeners,
> A sable form with scornful eye and look averse,
> Out-stretched a lean fore-finger and bespake Haroun.

THE CHOLIAMBUS (or *Scazon*).

2597. The CHOLIAMBUS is an iambic trimeter in which a trochee has been substituted for the final iambus. The penultimate syllable is therefore long instead of short. The caesura is generally the penthemimeral (2544). If it is hephthemimeral, there is regularly a diaeresis after the second foot. The scheme is :

$$\breve{\bar{\;}} \perp \mid \cup \perp \mid \breve{\bar{\;}} \perp \mid \cup \perp \mid \cup \perp \mid \perp \cup$$
$$[\cup \, \dot{\cup} \, \cup] \mid \cup \cup \cup \mid \cup \dot{\cup} \cup \mid \cup \cup \cup \mid$$
$$> \dot{\cup} \, \cup \mid \quad \mid > \dot{\cup} \, \cup \mid \quad \mid$$
$$\sim \perp \mid$$

An example is :

> Fulsḗ|re quon|dam ‖ cán|didī| tibī | sṓlēs.

> (Cat. 8, 3.)

2598. (1). The anacrustic scheme (see 2529) of the choliambus is :

$$\overset{\sim}{\breve{\;}} : \perp \cup \mid \perp \breve{\;} \mid \perp \cup \mid \perp \cup \mid \dot{\perp} \mid \perp \cup$$
$$: \dot{\cup} \cup \cup \mid \cup \cup \cup \mid \dot{\cup} \cup \cup \mid \cup \cup \cup \mid$$

i. e. trochaic trimeter with anacrusis (2529), syncope (2541), and protraction (2516).

2599. (2.) Resolutions and substitutions are less common in the choliambus than in the ordinary trimeter. No monosyllable except **est** is admitted at the end of the line. The tribrach in the first foot is rare, and the fifth foot is regularly an iambus.

2600. (3.) The verse is named *Choliambus* (i. e. "lame" or "limping iambus") or *Scazon* ("hobbler") from its odd, limping movement. It is sometimes called Hipponactean from its inventor Hipponax, and is chiefly used to produce a satiric or ludicrous effect. It was introduced into Roman poetry by Cn. Mattius, and was employed by Varro, Catullus, Persius, Petronius, Martial, and others.

THE IAMBIC TRIMETER CATALECTIC.

2601. The IAMBIC TRIMETER CATALECTIC occurs in Horace (1, 4 and 2, 18). The caesura is regularly penthemimeral (2544). Resolutions are not admitted, except in one doubtful case, rēgumque puerīs (2, 18, 34), where pŭĕrīs may be read (with synizesis; see 2499). The scheme is:

$$\breve{\sigma} \perp | \cup \perp | \breve{\sigma} \| \perp | \cup \perp | \cup \angle \perp$$
$$[\cup \cup \cup] |$$

Examples are:

Meá | renī|det ‖ ín | domō | lacŭ|nar.

(H. 2, 18, 2.)

$$\cup \perp | \cup \perp | \cup \| \perp | \cup \perp | \cup \angle \perp$$

Seu pó|scit a|gnā sí|ve mā|lit haé|dō.

$$> \perp | \cup \perp | > \| \perp | \cup \perp | \cup \angle \perp$$

(H. 1, 4, 12.)

2602. (1.) The anacrustic scheme is:

$$\breve{\sigma} \vdots \perp \cup | \perp \breve{\sigma} \# \perp \cup | \perp \cup | \angle \perp \Lambda,$$

i. e. trochaic trimeter catalectic with anacrusis (2529), syncope (2541), and protraction (2516).

2603. (2.) Horace seems to have changed his practice with reference to the first foot. In 1, 4 the first foot is a spondee in nine lines out of ten; in 2, 18, it is a spondee in only two lines out of twenty.

THE IAMBIC TETRAMETER ACATALECTIC (or *Octonarius*).

2604. This verse consists of four iambic dipodies, or eight complete iambic feet. The substitutions enumerated in 2581 are admitted in the first seven feet; but the last foot is always an iambus. The principal break in the line is usually a diaeresis after the fourth foot (which in that case must be a pure iambus), or a caesura after the arsis of the fifth. The full scheme is:

$$\breve{\sigma} \perp | \breve{\sigma} \perp | \breve{\sigma} \perp | \breve{\sigma} \perp | \breve{\sigma} \perp | \breve{\sigma} \perp | \breve{\sigma} \perp | \cup \perp$$
$$\cup \stackrel{\shortmid}{\cup} \cup | \cup \cup \cup | \cup \stackrel{\shortmid}{\cup} \cup | \cup \cup \cup | \cup \stackrel{\shortmid}{\cup} \cup | \cup \cup \cup | \cup \stackrel{\shortmid}{\cup} \cup |$$
$$> \stackrel{\shortmid}{\cup} \cup | > \cup \cup | > \stackrel{\shortmid}{\cup} \cup | > \cup \cup | > \stackrel{\shortmid}{\cup} \cup | > \cup \cup | > \stackrel{\shortmid}{\cup} \cup |$$
$$\cup\cup \perp | \cup\cup \perp | \cup\cup \perp | \cup\cup \perp | \cup\cup \perp | \cup\cup \perp | \cup\cup \perp |$$
$$\cup\cup \stackrel{\shortmid}{\cup} \cup | \cup\cup \cup \cup | \cup\cup \stackrel{\shortmid}{\cup} \cup | \cup\cup \cup \cup | \cup\cup \stackrel{\shortmid}{\cup} \cup | \cup\cup \cup \cup | \cup\cup \stackrel{\shortmid}{\cup} \cup |$$

2605. The following lines are examples of this metre:

Enĭm vé|rō, Dā|ve. níl|locīst ‡ sēgníti|ae neque | sōcór|diae,
quant(um) ín|tellē|xī módo | senis ‡ sentén|tiam | dē nŭ|ptiīs:
quae sĭ|nōn a|stū pró|viden|tur ‖ m(ē)aút|erum | pessúm | dabunt.

(T. *Andr.* 206.)

$$\cup\cup \perp | > \perp | \cup \perp | \cup \perp \# > \stackrel{\shortmid}{\cup} \cup | > \cup \cup | > \perp | \cup \perp$$
$$> \perp | > \perp | > \stackrel{\shortmid}{\cup} \cup | \cup \perp \# > \perp | \cup \perp | > \perp | \cup \perp$$
$$> \perp | > \perp | > \perp | \cup \perp | > \| \perp | \cup \perp | > \perp | \cup \perp$$

2606. Compare in English :

He smote the rock, and forth a tide of crystal waters streamed amain ;
Up sprang the flowrets from the ground, and Nature smiled o'er all the
plain.

2607. (1.) The iambic octonarius is chiefly a comic verse. Terence has about
eight hundred lines in this measure, Plautus only about three hundred, Varro a few.

2608. (2.) Substitutions are much less common than in the senarius, especially in
the even feet.

2609. (3.) When there is a diaeresis after the fourth foot, so that the line is divided
into two equal halves, the verse is *asynartetic* (2535). There seems, however, to be no
certain instance of hiatus in the diaeresis in the Terentian plays.

IAMBIC SEPTENARIUS.

(A.) Early Usage.

2610. The IAMBIC SEPTENARIUS consists of seven and a half
iambic feet. In any of the complete feet the substitutes mentioned in
2581 are admitted. There is usually a diaeresis after the fourth foot,
which in that case must be a pure iambus. If there is not such a
diaeresis, there is generally a caesura after the arsis of the fifth foot.
The scheme of substitution is : —

$$\partial\perp \mid \partial\,\underline{\ }\mid \partial\,\underline{\ }\mid \partial\,\underline{\ }\mid \partial\,\perp\mid \partial\,\underline{\ }\mid \partial\,\perp\mid \partial\,\overline{\wedge}$$
$$\smile\,\smile\,\smile\mid\smile\smile\smile\mid\smile\,\smile\,\smile\mid\smile\smile\smile\mid\smile\,\smile\,\smile\mid\smile\smile\smile\mid\smile\,\smile\,\smile\mid$$
$$>\,\smile\,\smile\mid>\smile\smile\mid>\,\smile\,\smile\mid>\smile\smile\mid>\,\smile\,\smile\mid>\smile\smile\mid>\,\smile\,\smile\mid$$
$$\backsim\,\perp\mid\backsim\,\underline{\ }\mid\backsim\,\perp\mid\backsim\,\underline{\ }\mid\backsim\,\perp\mid\backsim\,\underline{\ }\mid\backsim\,\perp\mid$$
$$\backsim\,\smile\,\smile\mid\backsim\smile\smile\mid\backsim\,\smile\,\smile\mid\backsim\smile\smile\mid\backsim\,\smile\,\smile\mid\backsim\smile\smile\mid$$

2611. Examples of the Septenarius are the lines :

Spērā|bit sūm|ptum síbi | senex ‖ levā|t(um) ess(e) hā|runc ábi|tū :
n(ē) ill(e) haúd | scit hoc | paulúm | lucrī ‖ quant(um) é|ī da|mn(ī)
    adpór|tet.
Tū nés|ciēs | quod scís, | Dromō, ‖ sī sápi|ēs. Mū|tum dí|cēs.
                   (T. *Hau.* 746.)

$$>\,\underline{\perp}\mid>\,\underline{\ }\mid>\,\smile\,\smile\mid\smile\underline{\ }\,\|\,\smile\,\perp\mid>\,\underline{\ }\mid>\,\smile\,\smile\mid>\,\overline{\wedge}$$
$$>\,\underline{\perp}\mid\smile\,\underline{\ }\mid>\,\underline{\perp}\mid\smile\underline{\ }\,\|\,>\,\perp\mid>\,\underline{\ }\mid>\,\perp\mid\smile\,\overline{\wedge}$$
$$>\,\underline{\perp}\mid\smile\,\underline{\ }\mid>\,\perp\mid\smile\underline{\ }\,\|\,>\,\smile\,\smile\mid>\,\underline{\ }\mid>\,\underline{\ }\mid>\,\overline{\wedge}$$

Compare in English :

"**Now** who be ye would cross Lochgyle, this dark and stormy water?"
                                (Campbell.)

2612. (1.) The Iambic Septenarius of the early comedy is not properly a "tetrameter catalectic" like the Greek, for the penultimate syllable is sometimes resolved, which is never the case in the Greek catalectic tetrameter. For the same reason the ordinary anacrustic (2529) scheme of the early Septenarius is erroneous; for a triseme cannot be resolved.

2613. (2.) When there is a diaeresis after the fourth foot, the verse is asynartetic (see 2535).

2614. (3.) The Septenarius seems not to have been used in tragedy.

(B.) Later Usage.

2615. Varro and Catullus (25) employ a form of the Septenarius which conforms more closely to Greek models, keeping the arses of the even feet pure and rarely admitting resolutions. There is regularly a diaeresis after the fourth foot. The scheme is : —

ˇ ⏌ | ∪ ⏌ | ˇ ⏌ | ∪ ⏌ ‖ ˇ ⏌ | ∪ ⏌ | ˇ ⏌ ⏌

or anacrustically (2529)

ˇ ⋮ ⏌ ∪ | ⏌ ˇ | ⏌ ∪ | ⏌ ‖ ˇ | ⏌ ∪ | ⏌ ˇ | ⏌ | ⏌ ∧

2616. Catullus does not admit resolutions at all, save in one very doubtful case (25, 5). Varro seems to admit them in the first foot only.

IAMBIC DIMETER ACATALECTIC (or *Quaternarius*).

2617. The IAMBIC DIMETER ACATALECTIC consists of two complete iambic dipodies or four iambic feet. In the first three feet the tribrach, irrational spondee, irrational dactyl and cyclic anapaest are admitted; but the proceleusmatic is very rare, except in the first foot of the *Versus Reizianus* (2625), (of which a Quaternarius forms the first colon). The scheme for substitution is :

ˇ ⏌ | ˇ ⏌ | ˇ ⏌ | ∪ ⏌
∪ ⏑ ∪ | ∪ ∪ ∪ | ∪ ⏑ ∪ |
> ⏑ ∪ | > ∪ ∪ | > ⏑ ∪ |
⏜ ⏌ | ⏜ ⏌ | ⏜ ⏌ |
[⏜ ⏑ ∪] | [⏜ ∪ ∪] | ⏜ ⏑ ∪ |

Examples are:

Rogitá|re quasi | diffíci|le sit
⏜ ⏌ | ∪ ∪ ∪ | > ⏑ ∪ | ∪ ⏌   (T. *Eu.* 209).

Ast égo | vicis|sim rí|serō
> ⏑ ∪ | ∪ ⏌ | > ⏌ | ∪ ⏌   (H. *Epod.* 15, 24).

Perŭn|xit hōc | Iá|sonem
∪ ⏌ | ∪ ⏌ | ∪ ⏌ | ∪ ⏌   (H. *Epod.* 3, 12).

2618. (1.) The verse may also be regarded as a trochaic dimeter catalectic with anacrusis (2529), with the normal scheme:

$$\cup \vdots \; \perp \cup \; | \; \perp \cup \; | \; \perp \cup \; | \; \perp \wedge$$

2619. (2.) Horace admits resolutions only four times, the tribrach once in the second foot and the dactyl thrice in the first.

2620. (3.) Plautus (except in a few instances), Terence, and Horace employ the dimeter only as a *clausula* (2536) to longer verses. Petronius, Seneca, and Prudentius use it to form *systems* (2547); but it is rarely so employed by earlier writers.

THE IAMBIC DIMETER CATALECTIC (or *Ternarius*).

2621. This is like the preceding verse, except that the last foot is incomplete. Examples are: —

Nequ(e) íd | perspice|re quí|ví

$$\cup \perp | > \cup \cup | \cup \; {\scriptstyle \perp} \; \perp \qquad \text{(Pl. } Cap. \; 784).$$

Date; móx | eg(o) hūc | revór|tor

$$\cup\!\cup \; \perp \; | \cup \perp | \cup \; {\scriptstyle \perp} \; \perp \qquad \text{(T. } Andr. \; 485).$$

2622. (1.) The verse may also be regarded as a syncopated catalectic trochaic dimeter with anacrusis (2529). The normal scheme will then be : —

$$\cup \vdots \; \perp \cup \; | \; \perp \cup \; | \; {\scriptstyle \perp} \; | \; \perp \wedge$$

2623. (2.) Plautus and Terence use this verse as a *clausula* (2536). Petronius is the first who employs it to form *systems* (2547).

OTHER IAMBIC VERSES.

2624. Other short iambic verses, the acatalectic dipody (e. g. eg(o) íllúm | famē, | eg(o) íllúm | sití, Pl. *Cas.* 153), and the catalectic tripody (e. g. inóps | amā|tor, Pl. *Tri.* 256) sometimes occur, but are rare.

THE VERSUS REIZIANUS.

2625. This is a composite verse, consisting of two cola, an iambic dimeter acatalectic and an iambic tripody catalectic. The scheme is therefore,

$$\eth \perp \; | \; \eth \; {\scriptstyle \perp} \; | \; \eth \perp \; | \cup {\scriptstyle \perp} \# \; \eth \perp \; | \; \eth \perp \; | \cup \bar\wedge$$
$$\cup \check\cup \cup \; | \; \cup \cup \cup \; | \; \cup \check\cup \cup \; | \; [\cup \check\cup \cup] | \cup \check\cup \cup \; |$$
$$> \check\cup \cup \; | \; > \cup \cup \; | \; > \check\cup \cup \; | \qquad > \check\cup \cup \; | > \check\cup \cup \; |$$
$$\cup\!\cup \perp | \cup\!\cup \; {\scriptstyle \perp} \; | \; \cup\!\cup \perp | \qquad \cup\!\cup {\scriptstyle \perp} \; | \; \cup\!\cup \perp |$$
$$\cup\!\cup \check\cup \cup | [\cup\!\cup \cup \cup] | [\cup\!\cup \check\cup \cup] | \qquad \cup\!\cup \check\cup \cup \; | \; \cup\!\cup \check\cup \cup$$

Examples are: —

Sed in aé|dibus | quid tíbi | meīs ╫ n(am) erát | negó|tí
m(ē) absén|te, nis(i) e|go iús|seram ? ╫ volo scí|re.   Tac(ē) ér|gō
Quia vē|nimŭs coc|t(um) ad nú|ptiās. ╫ Quid tū, | malŭm, cú|rās.

(Pl. *Aul.* 427.)

2626. The nature of the second colon of this verse has long been disputed. Reiz and Christ treat it substantially as above; Studemund regards it as a syncopated iambic dimeter catalectic ($\cup \_\_ \cup \sqsubset \_\_ \cup$), Spengel and Gleditsch as anapaestic, Leo as logaoedic, Klotz as sometimes logaoedic and sometimes anapaestic! The view of Christ (*Metrik*[2], p. 348) seems, on the whole, the most reasonable, though the question cannot be said to be fully decided. The tribrach is rare in the second colon, but there seems to be a case in Plautus, *R.* 675 b.

2627. For other iambic verses and combinations of verses, see special editions of the dramatists.

TROCHAIC RHYTHMS.

2628. These are descending rhythms in $\frac{3}{8}$ time. The fundamental foot is the trochee $\_\!' \cup$, for which its metrical equivalent the tribrach $\cup\!\!\!\! \diagup \cup \cup$, the irrational spondee $\_\!' >$, the cyclic dactyl $\_\!' \curvearrowright$, the irrational anapaest $\cup\!\!\!\! \diagup \cup >$, and (rarely) the proceleusmatic $\cup\!\!\!\! \diagup \cup \curvearrowright$, are sometimes substituted.

THE TROCHAIC TETRAMETER CATALECTIC (or *Septenarius*).

2629. The TROCHAIC TETRAMETER CATALECTIC is, next to the iambic trimeter, the verse most frequently used by the early Roman dramatists. It consists of seven and a half trochaic feet, or four trochaic dipodies (the last one being incomplete). The ictus on the second thesis of each dipody was probably weaker than that on the first thesis. The normal scheme is: —

$$\_\!' \cup \mid \_\!' \cup \mid \_\!' \cup \mid \_\!' \cup \mid \_\!' \cup \mid \_\!' \cup \mid \_\!' \cup \mid \_\!' \wedge$$

As in the case of the senarius, we may distinguish two periods in the usage: —

(A.) Early Period.

2630. The tribrach is admitted in any of the complete feet, and the irrational spondee, cyclic dactyl, and irrational anapaest in any of the first six feet. Terence does not admit the proceleusmatic in the Septenarius (nor in any other kind of trochaic verse), but Plautus admits it in the first foot. The seventh foot of the Septenarius is usually a trochee, but the tribrach sometimes occurs there. The principal break in the line is usually a diaeresis after the fourth foot (which in that case must not be a dactyl), often accompanied by a secondary diaeresis after the second foot. Sometimes, however, the principal break is a diaeresis after the fifth foot, in which case there is generally a secondary diaeresis after the third foot or a caesura in the fourth. The full scheme of substitutions is: —

$$\_\!' \diagdown \mid \_\!' \diagdown \mid \_\!' \diagdown \mid \_\!' \diagdown \mid \_\!' \diagdown \mid \_\!' \diagdown \mid \_\!' \cup \mid \_\!' \wedge$$
$$\cup\!\!\!\! \diagup \cup \cup \mid \cup \cup \cup \mid \cup\!\!\!\! \diagup \cup \cup \mid \cup \cup \cup \mid \cup\!\!\!\! \diagup \cup \cup \mid \cup \cup \cup \mid \cup\!\!\!\! \diagup \cup \cup \mid$$
$$\_\!' \curvearrowright \mid \_\!' \curvearrowright \mid \_\!' \curvearrowright \mid \_\!' \curvearrowright \mid \_\!' \curvearrowright \mid \_\!' \curvearrowright \mid [\_\!' \curvearrowright]$$
$$\cup\!\!\!\! \diagup \cup > \mid \cup \cup > \mid \cup\!\!\!\! \diagup \cup > \mid \cup \cup > \mid \cup\!\!\!\! \diagup \cup > \mid \cup \cup > \mid$$
$$[\cup\!\!\!\! \diagup \cup \curvearrowright]$$

The following lines are examples of the Septenarius:—

Séquere | sīs, erŭm | quí lū|dificās ‡ díctīs | dēlī|ránti|bus
quī quoni(am) | erŭs quod | ímpe|rāvit ‡ néglē|xistī | pérse|quī,
núnc ve|nīs eti(am) | últr(ō) in|rīsum ‡ dóminum|: quae neque | fíe|rī
póssunt | neaue fan|d(ō) úmqu(am) ac|cēpit ‡ quísquam | prōfers, |
   cárnu|fex.   (Pl. *Am.* 585.)

$$\smile \smile \smile | \underline{}\,\underline{} | \underline{} > | \smile \smile > \ddagger \underline{} > \ | \ \underline{} > | \underline{} \smile | \underline{} \wedge$$
$$\underline{}\,\underline{} | \smile\smile\smile | \underline{} \smile | \ \underline{} > \ddagger \underline{} > \ | \ \underline{} > | \underline{} \smile | \underline{} \wedge$$
$$\underline{} \smile \ | \underline{}\,\underline{} | \underline{} > | \ \underline{} > \ddagger \smile\smile > | \underline{}\,\underline{} | \underline{} \smile | \underline{} \wedge$$
$$\underline{} > \ | \smile\smile > | \underline{} > | \ \underline{} > \ddagger \underline{} > \ | \ \underline{} > | \underline{} \smile | \underline{} \wedge$$

2631. (1.) When there is a diaeresis after the fourth foot, the verse is *asynartetic* (2535). In Plautus hiatus in the diaeresis is not rare; but there seems to be no *certain* instance of it in Terence (see *Ph.* 528, *Ad.* 697).

2632. (2.) An anapaest is not allowed to follow a dactyl.

2633. (3.) The seventh foot is usually a trochee; rarely a tribrach or dactyl. The tribrach and dactyl are seldom found in the fourth foot.

(B.) Later Usage.

2634. The later and stricter form of the Septenarius keeps the arses of the odd feet pure, and regularly shows a diaeresis after the fourth foot.

$$\underline{} \smile | \underline{}\,\breve{} | \underline{} \smile | \underline{}\,\breve{} \ddagger \underline{} \smile | \underline{}\,\breve{} | \underline{} \smile | \underline{} \wedge$$

Resolutions occur, but are far less common than in the earlier form of the verse. The strict form of the Septenarius is found in Varro, Seneca, and often in late poets (as Ausonius, Prudentius, &c.).

2635. The rhythm of the Septenarius may be illustrated by this line:—

"Comrades, leave me here a little, while as yet 'tis early morn."
                                                (Tennyson.)

THE TROCHAIC TETRAMETER ACATALECTIC (or *Octonarius*).

2636. The TROCHAIC TETRAMETER ACATALECTIC is chiefly confined to the lyrical portions of the early comedy. It consists of four complete trochaic dipodies or eight trochaic feet. The tribrach, irrational spondee, irrational anapaest and cyclic dactyl may stand in any foot save the last. The last foot is regularly a trochee or a tribrach, though (the last syllable being *syllaba anceps*, 2533) an apparent spondee or anapaest, but not a dactyl, may arise. The principal break in the line is regularly a diaeresis after the fourth foot (which in that case must not be a dactyl). Occasionally, however, there is instead a caesura in the fourth or fifth foot. The scheme is:—

$$\underline{}\,\breve{} | \underline{}\,\breve{} | \underline{}\,\breve{} | \underline{}\,\breve{} | \underline{}\,\breve{} | \underline{}\,\breve{} | \underline{}\,\breve{} | \underline{}\,\breve{}$$
$$\smile\smile\smile | \smile\smile\smile | \smile\smile\smile | \smile\smile\smile | \smile\smile\smile | \smile\smile\smile | \smile\smile\smile | [\smile\smile\smile]$$
$$\underline{}\,\smile | \underline{}\,\smile | \underline{}\,\smile | \underline{}\,\smile\smile | \underline{}\,\smile | \underline{}\,\smile | \underline{}\,\smile |$$
$$\smile\smile > | \smile\smile > | \smile\smile > | \smile\smile > | \smile\smile > | \smile\smile > | \smile\smile > | [\smile\smile >]$$

Example:—

Cénse|ō. Sed|heús tū.| Quid vīs? ‡ Cénsēn | posse | m(e) óffir|māre?
(T. *Eu.* 217).

‿‿|‿‿|‿>|‿>‡‿>|‿‿|‿>|‿‿

Compare in English:—

Over stream and mount and valley sweeps the merry, careless rover,
Toying with the fragrant blossoms, beating down the heads of clover.

2637. (1.) When there is a diaeresis after the fourth foot, the verse is *asynartetic* (2535).
2638. (2.) The Octonarius is essentially a lyric metre, and is much less common than the Septenarius.

THE TROCHAIC TETRAMETER CLAUDUS (or *Scazon*).

2639. This verse is a trochaic tetrameter acatalectic, with syncope **and** protraction in the seventh foot. The normal scheme is:

‿‿|‿‿|‿‿|‿‿|‿‿|‿‿|‿ |‿‿

An example is:—

Néc co|ruscus | ímber | altō ‖ nūbi|lō ca|déns | múltus

‿‿|‿‿| ‿‿|‿>‡‿‿|‿‿|‿ |‿‿
(Varro, *Sat. fr.* 557 Buech.).

2640. (1.) Substitutions are much rarer in this verse than in the ordinary trochaic octonarius.

2641. (2.) The Scazon was introduced among the Greeks by Hipponax, whence it is sometimes called the Hipponactean. Varro seems to be the only Roman poet who uses it.

THE NINE-SYLLABLED ALCAIC.

2642. This verse consists of two complete trochaic dipodies, with anacrusis. The second foot is always an irrational spondee. The scheme is:—

⌣ ¦ ‿‿|‿>|‿‿|‿‿

An example is:—

Sil|vaé la|bōran|tés ge|lūque.
(H. 1, 9, 3.)

This verse occurs only in Horace, where it forms the third line of the Alcaic Strophe (see 2736).

THE TROCHAIC DIMETER ACATALECTIC (or *Quaternarius*).

2643. This verse consists of two complete trochaic dipodies. It is **very rare,** but there are probably a few instances of it in Plautus, e. g. *Per.* 31:—

Básili|c(ō) accipi|ére | víctū

⌣⌣⌣|‿⌣⌣|‿‿|‿‿

THE TROCHAIC DIMETER CATALECTIC (or *Ternarius*).

2644. This consists of two trochaic dipodies, the second being incomplete. It occurs in the early dramatists and in Horace. The scheme for Plautus and Terence is : —

$$\text{— ⏓ | — ⏓ | — ⏑ | — ⋏}$$
$$\text{⏑ ⏑ ⏑ | ⏑ ⏑ ⏑ | [⏑ ⏑ ⏑]}$$
$$\text{— ⏡ | — ⏡ |}$$
$$\text{⏑ ⏑ > | ⏑ ⏑ > |}$$

The Horatian scheme is : —

$$\text{— ⏑ | — ⏑ | — ⏑ | — ⋏}$$

Examples are : —

Aút un|d(e) auxili|úm pe|tam

(T. *Ph.* 729).

Nón e|bur ne|qu(e) aúre|um

(H. 2, 18, 1).

2645. (1.) This is sometimes called the Euripidean verse, from its use by Euripides. The tribrach in the third foot is rare, and is not found in Terence. Horace keeps all the feet pure.

2646. (2.) Plautus and Terence often use this verse between trochaic tetrameters, but sometimes employ several *Ternarii* in succession, as in Plaut. *E.* 3-6, *Cas.* 953-6, *Ps.* 211-13.

THE TROCHAIC TRIPODY ACATALECTIC.

2647. This verse is confined to the early drama, where it is employed as a *clausula* (2536), especially with Cretics. It consists of three complete trochaic feet. The same substitutions are admitted in every foot that are allowed in the first two feet of the Ternarius (2644). An example is : —

Haú bonŭm | teneō | sérvom

$$\text{— ⏡ | ⏑ ⏑ > | — ⏑}$$

(Pl. *Most.* 721).

This verse is sometimes called the *Ithyphallic*.

THE TROCHAIC TRIPODY CATALECTIC.

2648. This verse is employed by the early dramatists, usually either as a *clausula* (2536) or in groups of two lines each. Terence generally uses it in the former way, Plautus in the latter. The scheme of substitutions is : --

$$\text{— ⏓ | — ⏓ | — ⋏}$$
$$\text{⏑ ⏑ ⏑ | ⏑ ⏑ ⏑ |}$$
$$\text{— ⏡ | — ⏡ |}$$
$$\text{⏑ ⏑ > | ⏑ ⏑ > |}$$

Example : —

Qu(ī) ímpi|ger fu|í

$\underline{\mathit{l}} \cup | \underline{\mathit{l}} \cup | \underline{\mathit{l}} \wedge$

(Pl. *R.* 925).

In one instance (*R.* 924 ff.) Plautus has six catalectic tripodies in succession.

OTHER TROCHAIC VERSES.

2649. The Trochaic Monometer Acatalectic is sometimes used by Plautus as a *clausula* (2536) to Cretic tetrameters. It consists of one complete trochaic dipody, e. g. **nímis in|epta' s**, *R.* 681. **iúre in|iūstās**, *Am.* 247. Terence uses the *catalectic* monometer twice (*Eu.* 292, *Ph.* 485) at the beginning of a scene, e. g. **Dŏri|ō**, *Ph.* 485. Plautus has a few other trochaic verses and combinations of verses, for which see special editions of his plays.

LOGAOEDIC RHYTHMS.

2650. Logaoedic verse consists of dactyls and trochees combined in the same metrical series. The dactyls are "cyclic" (see 2523), occupying approximately the time of trochees, and hence the verse moves in ⅜ time. Except in the "Lesser Alcaic" verse (2663), only one dactyl may stand in a single series; and a dactyl must not occupy the last place in a line.

2651. (1.) The name "logaoedic" (Gr. λογαοιδικός, from λόγος, *speech*, *prose*, and ἀοιδή, *song*) may refer to the apparent change of rhythm (due to the mixture of dactyls and trochees), in which logaoedic verse resembles prose; but this is a disputed point.

2652. (2.) In the logaoedic verses of Horace, an irrational spondee almost always takes the place of a trochee before the first dactyl; and if an apparent choriambus ($\underline{\mathit{l}} \cup \cup | \underline{\mathit{l}}$; see 2521) is followed by another apparent choriambus in the same verse, the two are regularly separated by a caesura. These rules are not observed by Catullus.

2653. (3.) Anacrusis (2529) and syncope (2541) are very common in logaoedic verse.

2654. The following are the principal logaoedic rhythms : —

DIPODY.

THE ADONIC.

2655. This is a logaoedic dipody, with the scheme : —

$$\underline{\mathit{l}} \cup \cup | \underline{\mathit{l}} \cup$$

Examples are : —

Térruit | úrbem	(H. 1, 2, 4).
Rắra iu|véntus	(H. 1, 2, 24).

2656. (1.) Some regard the Adonic as a syncopated catalectic tripody:

$$\_ \smile\smile \mid \sqcup \mid \_ \wedge$$

2657. (2.) A Latin Adonic should consist of a disyllable + a trisyllable, or the reverse. This rule did not hold in Greek, where such lines occur as ὦ τὸν Ἄδωνιν. Elision is not allowed in the Latin Adonic. Late Latin poets (like Terentianus) sometimes employ the Adonic in stichic series (2546).

TRIPODIES.

THE ARISTOPHANIC.

2658. This is a logaoedic tripody acatalectic, with a dactyl in the first place. The scheme is therefore:—

$$\_ \smile\smile \mid \_ \smile \mid \_ \smile$$

There is no fixed caesura. Examples are:—

Quíd latet | út ma|rínae

Fúnera | né vi|rílis

(H. 1, 8, 13).

(H. 1, 8, 15).

Some authorities write the scheme as:

$$\_ \smile\smile \mid \_ \smile \mid \sqcup \mid \_ \wedge$$

i. e. a syncopated logaoedic tetrapody catalectic.

THE PHERECRATEAN (or *Pherecratic*).

2659. This verse is used by Catullus (34, 61), and by Horace (as the third line of the Third Asclepiadean Strophe: see 2733). It is a logaoedic tripody, with the dactyl in the second place. The scheme is:—

$$\begin{array}{c} [\_ \smile] \mid \\ \_ > \mid \_ \smile\smile \mid \_ \smile \\ [\smile \_] \mid \end{array}$$

The trochee and iambus are admitted in the first foot by Catullus, but not by Horace. The iambus is very rare. There is no fixed caesura. Examples are:—

Grắtō, | Pýrrha, sub | ántrō

(H. 1, 5, 3).

With initial trochee: Lűte|úmve pa|pắver

(Cat. 61, 195).

With initial iambus: Púel|laéque ca|nắmus

(Cat. 34, 4).

Some authorities prefer to regard the Pherecratean as a syncopated logaoedic etrapody catalectic, with the scheme: —

$$[\overline{}\ \cup]\ |$$
$$\overline{} > |\ \underline{} \cup | \ \underline{} |\ \underline{} \wedge$$
$$[\cup\ \overline{}]\ |$$

TETRAPODIES.

THE GLYCONIC.

2660. This verse is used by Catullus (34, 61), by Horace (in the First, Second, and Third Asclepiadean Strophes: see 2731, 2732, 2733), and by Seneca and other later writers. It is a logaoedic tetrapody catalectic, with a dactyl in the second place. The scheme is: —

$$[\overline{}\ \cup]\ |$$
$$\overline{} > |\ \underline{} \cup | \ \underline{} \cup |\ \underline{} \wedge$$
$$[\cup\ \overline{}]\ |$$

The trochee and iambus in the first foot occur in Catullus, but not in Horace (except in the doubtful case, 1, 15, 36). There is generally a trithemimeral caesura; more rarely one in the arsis of the second foot. Examples are: —

Quém mor|tís ‖ timu|ít gra|dúm

(H. 1, 3, 17).

With initial trochee: Mónti|úm ‖ domi|n(a) út fo|rés

(Cat. 34, 9).

With initial iambus: Púel|l(ae) ét ‖ pue|r(ī) ínte|grí

(Cat. 34, 2).

2661. (1.) This verse in composition with the Pherecratean forms the *Priapean* (2674).

2662. (2.) In admitting the trochee and iambus in the first foot, Catullus follows Greek models, while Horace adheres to the stricter Roman usage, as laid down by the grammarians of his own day. Seneca observes the same rule as Horace, but some of the later writers (e. g. Terentianus) revert to the earlier and freer usage.

THE LESSER (or DECASYLLABIC) ALCAIC.

2663. This verse is a logaoedic tetrapody acatalectic, with dactyls in the first and second places. The scheme is: —

$$\underline{} \cup | \ \underline{} \cup | \ \underline{} \cup | \ \underline{} \cup$$

There is no fixed caesura, though there is frequently a break after the thesis, or in the arsis, of the second foot. Examples are: —

Flúmina | cónstite|rínt a|cútŏ

(H. 1, 9, 4).

Móntibus | ét Tibe|rím re|vértī

(H. 1, 29, 12).

PENTAPODIES.

THE PHALAECEAN (or *Hendecasyllable*).

2664. This verse is a logaoedic pentapody with the dactyl in the second place. The Greek poets admitted the trochee and iambus, as well as the spondee, in the first foot, and Catullus followed their example; but in Petronius, Martial, and the *Priāpēa* the first foot is always a spondee, and in later writers nearly always. Horace does not use the Phalaecean. There is no fixed caesura, though the penthemimeral is often found. **The scheme is:—**

$$[\bar{}\, \cup]\,|$$
$$\bar{} > \,|\, \bar{} \cup\cup\,|\, \bar{} \cup\,|\, \bar{} \cup\,|\, \_\,\cup$$
$$[\cup\, \_]\,|$$

Examples are:—

Cúius | vís fie|rí li|bélle | múnus
(Mart. 3, 2, 1).

With initial trochee: **Dĕ di|ĕ faci|tís me|í so|dálēs**
(Cat. 47, 6).

With initial iambus: **Ágit | péssimus | ómni|úm po|éta**
(Cat. 49, 5).

Compare in English:—
" Look, I come to the test, a tiny poem
All composed in a metre of Catullus."

(Tennyson.)

2665. The Phalaecean is a favourite metre in epigrams. It was used by Sappno, Phalaecus (from whom it took its name), and other Greek poets, and was introduced into Roman poetry by Laevius and Varro. It is a favourite metre with Catullus, and is found in the fragments of Cinna, Cornificius and Bibaculus, in the *Priāpēa*, in Petronius, Statius, Martial, &c. In Catullus 55, a spondee is often employed instead of the dactyl, the two kinds of feet alternating in the latter verses of the poem; but this innovation seems not to have found favour.

THE LESSER SAPPHIC.

2666. This verse is a logaoedic pentapody acatalectic, with the dactyl in the third place. The scheme is:—

$$\bar{} \cup \,\Big|\, \Big[\genfrac{}{}{0pt}{}{\bar{}}{\bar{}} \genfrac{}{}{0pt}{}{>}{\cup}\Big] \,\Big|\, \bar{} \,\|\, \cup\cup\,|\, \bar{} \cup \,|\, \bar{} \cup$$

The trochee in the second foot was admitted by Alcaeus and Sappho, and occurs in Catullus, but not in Horace. In Horace the caesura regularly falls after the thesis, or (less frequently) in the arsis, of the dactyl; but in Catullus, as in Sappho and Alcaeus, it has no fixed position. Examples of this verse are:—

With masculine caesura: **Iám sa|tís ter|rís ‖ nivis | átque | dírae**
(H. 1, 2, 1).

With feminine caesura: **Phoébe | sílvā|rúmque ‖ po|téns Di|ána**
(H. *C. S.* 1).
With trochee in second foot: **Seú Sa|cás sa|gíttife|rósve | Párthōs**
(Cat. 11, 6).

THE GREATER (or HENDECASYLLABIC) ALCAIC.

2667. This verse is a logaoedic pentapody catalectic, with **anacrusis and**
with the dactyl in the third foot. The scheme is:—

$$\smile \colon \mid \_ \smile \mid \_ > \sharp \_ \smile\smile \mid \_ \smile \mid \_ \wedge$$

There is nearly always a diaeresis after the second foot. **Examples are:—**
Ō|mātre | púlchrā ‡ fília | púlchri|ór
(H. **1, 16, 1**).
Vi|dés ut | áltā ‡ stét nive | cándi | dúm
(H. **1, 9, 1**).

2668. Alcaeus admitted a trochee in the second foot, and allowed the anacrusis to
be either long or short; but Horace admitted only the spondee in the second foot, and
usually (in Bk. 4 always) employed a long anacrusis. Horace also differed from his
predecessor in assigning a fixed place to the caesura, which in Alcaeus has no regular
position.

COMPOSITE LOGAOEDIC VERSES.

THE LESSER ASCLEPIADEAN.

2669. This is a composite verse, consisting of two series, a **syncopated**
logaoedic tripody + a logaoedic tripody catalectic. There is **regularly a**
diaeresis between the two series. The scheme is:—

$$\_ > \mid \_ \smile \mid \_ \quad \sharp \_ \smile \mid \_ \smile \mid \_ \wedge$$

Examples are :—
Maécē|nās ata|vís ‡ édite| régi|bús
(H. **1, 1, 1**).
Quís dē|síderi|ŏ ‡ sít pudor | aút mo|dús
(H. **1, 24, 1**).

THE GREATER ASCLEPIADEAN.

2670. This is a composite verse, consisting of three series. It differs from
the preceding (2669) in having a syncopated logaoedic dipody ($\_ \smile\smile \mid \_$)
inserted between the two tripodies. The three series are regularly separated
by diaeresis. The scheme is therefore:—

$$\_ > \mid \_ \smile \mid \_ \quad \sharp \_ \smile \mid \_ \quad \sharp \_ \smile \mid \_ \smile \mid \_ \wedge$$

Examples are :—
Núllam¹, Váre, sa|crá ‡ víte pri|ús ‡ séveris | árbo|rém
Círcā | míte so|lúm ‡ Tíburis | ét ‡ moénia | Cáti|lí.)
(H. **1, 18, 1–2**).

THE GREATER SAPPHIC.

2671. This is a composite verse, consisting of a syncopated logaoedic tetrapody + a syncopated logaoedic tetrapody catalectic. There is regularly a diaeresis between the two series, and a caesura after the thesis of the first dactyl. The scheme is : —

$$\_ \cup \cdot \mid \_ > \mid \_ \parallel \backsim \mid \_ \quad \sharp \_ \backsim \mid \_ \cup \mid \_ \mid \_ \wedge$$

An example is : —

Tḗ de|ōs ō|rō ‖ Syba|rín ♯ cŭr prope|rēs a|mán|dṓ

(H. 1, 8, 2).

2672. (1.) The second series has the same form as the Aristophanic, if the latter be written as a tetrapody (see 2658 *ad fin.*).

2673. (2.) Horace (1, 8) is the only Latin poet who makes use of the Greater Sapphic. It seems to be an imitation of the Greek Sapphic : —

$$\_ \backsim \mid \_ \quad \mid \_ \backsim \mid \quad \_ \mid \_ \backsim \mid \_ \cup \mid \_ \quad \mid \_ \wedge, \text{ e. g.}$$

δεῦτέ νιν ἅβραι Χάριτες καλλίκομοί τε Μοῖσαι

but if so, the imitation is not exact.

THE PRIAPEAN.

2674. This verse is employed by Catullus (17) and in the *Priāpēa* (86). It consists of a syncopated logaoedic tetrapody + a syncopated logaoedic tetrapody catalectic. There is regularly a diaeresis between the two parts, but hiatus and *syllaba anceps* are not allowed at the end of the first series. The scheme is : —

$$\_ \eth \mid \_ \backsim \mid \_ \cup \mid \_ \sharp \_ \eth \mid \_ \backsim \mid \_ \mid \_ \wedge$$

Examples are : —

Ṓ Co|lṓnia | quaé cu|pís ♯ pónte | lŭdere | lón|gṓ

(Cat. 17, 1).

Húnc lū|cúm tibi | dḗdi|cṓ ♯ cṓnse|crōque Pri|ā́|pé.

(Cat. *Fr.*).

The first series has the same form as the Glyconic (2660), and the second series has the same form as the Pherecratean, if the latter be written as a tetrapody (see 2659 *ad fin.*).

DACTYLO-TROCHAIC RHYTHMS.

2675. DACTYLO-TROCHAIC verse, like logaoedic, is composed of dactyls and trochees ; but whereas in logaoedic verse the dactyls and trochees occur within the same metrical series, in dactylo-trochaic they always form separate series. Hence dactylo-trochaic verses are always composite, consisting of two or more series in combination.

2676. It is uncertain whether the dactyls in dactylo-trochaic verse were cyclic (2523) or whether there was a change of time in the middle of the verse.

THE GREATER ARCHILOCHIAN.

2677. This verse is composed of a dactylic tetrameter acatalectic + a trochaic tripody. There is regularly a diaeresis after the first colon, and a caesura after the third thesis. The fourth foot is always a pure dactyl. The third foot is very often a spondee. The scheme is : —

$$\underline{\text{—}} \, \smile\smile \mid \underline{\text{—}} \, \smile\smile \mid \underline{\text{—}} \parallel \smile\smile \mid \underline{\text{—}} \smile\smile \sharp \underline{\text{—}} \, \smile \mid \underline{\text{—}} \, \smile \mid \underline{\text{—}} \, \smile$$

An example is : —

Sólvitur | ácris hi|éms ‖ grā|tā vice ‖ véris | ét Fa|vŏnī
(H. 1, 4).

In Archilochus the verse is said to have been asynartetic (2535); but Horace and Prudentius do not allow hiatus or *syllaba anceps* in the diaeresis, and Prudentius sometimes neglects the diaeresis altogether.

THE IAMBELEGUS.

2678. This verse consists of a trochaic dimeter catalectic with anacrusis + a Lesser Archilochian (2579). No resolutions are allowed in the first colon, and the dactyls in the second colon are never replaced by spondees. There is regularly a diaeresis between the two cola. The scheme is : —

$$\breve{\text{—}} \vdots \underline{\text{—}} \, \smile \mid \underline{\text{—}} \, \breve{\text{—}} \mid \underline{\text{—}} \, \smile \mid \underline{\text{—}} \, \wedge \sharp \underline{\text{—}} \, \smile\smile \mid \underline{\text{—}} \, \smile\smile \mid \underline{\text{—}} \, \overline{\wedge}$$

An example is : —

Rū|pĕre | nec mā|tér do|mum ‡ caérula | tĕ reve|hét
(H. *Epod.* 13, 16).

2679. This verse occurs only in the Second Archilochian Strophe (2726) of Horace. Some authorities treat the first colon as an iambic dimeter. The name Iambelegus was given to the verse because the ancient grammarians regarded it as a dactylic pentameter for the first half of which an iambic colon had been substituted.

THE ELEGIAMBUS.

2680. This verse consists of the same cola as the Iambelegus (2678), but in reverse order. Spondees are not admitted in the first colon, and no resolutions occur in the second colon. There is regularly a diaeresis between the cola. The scheme is : —

$$\underline{\text{—}} \, \smile\smile \mid \underline{\text{—}} \, \smile\smile \mid \underline{\text{—}} \, \overline{\wedge} \sharp \breve{\text{—}} \vdots \underline{\text{—}} \, \smile \mid \underline{\text{—}} \, \breve{\text{—}} \mid \underline{\text{—}} \, \smile \mid \underline{\text{—}} \, \wedge$$

An example is : —

Scríbere | vérsicu|lŏs ‖ a|mŏre | percus|súm gra|vī
(H. *Epod.* 11, 2).

2681. This verse occurs only in the Third Archilochian Strophe (2727) of Horace. The name Elegiambus is given to it as being the reverse of the Iambelegus (see 2679).

ANAPAESTIC RHYTHMS.

2682. In these the fundamental foot is the anapaest $\smile\smile\underline{\text{—}}$, for which its metrical equivalents the spondee $\text{—} \, \underline{\text{—}}$, dactyl $\text{—} \, \smile\smile$ and proceleusmatic $\smile\smile\smile\smile$ are sometimes substituted.

2683. The anapaestic verse of the early Latin comedy is extremely irregular, and its limits are often hard to define. Spondees and apparent bacchii (reduced to anapaests by the law of iambic shortening; see 2470) are extremely common, and metrical irregularities of various kinds abound. The Latin language has so few anapaestic words that it does not lend itself readily to this rhythm. Terence wisely abstained altogether from anapaestic verse. Varro, Seneca, and Prudentius and other late writers wrote anapaests conforming more closely to Greek models.

THE ANAPAESTIC TETRAMETER ACATALECTIC (or *Octonarius*).

2684. This consists of four anapaestic dipodies or eight complete anapaestic feet. There is regularly a diaeresis after the fourth foot, and the last thesis of the line is never resolved. Hiatus and *syllaba anceps* sometimes occur in the diaeresis, the verse being asynartetic (2535). The scheme is: —

⏑⏑⌣́⏐⏑⏑⌣̇⏐⏑⏑⌣́⏐⏑⏑⌣ ‡ ⏑⏑⌣́⏐⏑⏑⌣̇⏐⏑⏑⌣́⏐⏑⏑⌣̇
‒⌣́⏐‒⌣̇⏐‒⌣́⏐‒⌣ ‡ ‒⌣́⏐‒⌣̇⏐‒⌣́⏐‒⌣̇
‒⏑⏑⏐‒⏑⏑⏐‒⏑⏑⏐‒⏑⏑ ‡‒⏑⏑⏐‒⏑⏑⏐‒⏑⏑⏐‒⏑⏑
⏑⏑⏑⏑⏐⏑⏑⏑⏑⏐⏑⏑⏑⏑⏐⏑⏑[⏑⏑⏑⏑]‡⏑⏑⏑⏑⏐⏑⏑⏑⏑⏐⏑⏑⏑⏑⏐⏑⏑⏑⏑

Examples are: —

Neque quód | dubitem | neque quód | timeam ‡ me(ō) ĭn péc |
    tore con | ditŭmst cón | silium

                     (Pl. *Ps.* 575).

Quid míhi | meliust | quid mágis | in remst ‡ qu(am) ā
    cór|pore vī|tam sē|clūdam

                     (Pl. *R.* 220).

2685. The proceleusmatic is very rare in the fourth foot, but the spondee is very common there. Some editors divide the anapaestic octonarii into dimeters (or *quaternarii*) and write them as such.

THE ANAPAESTIC TETRAMETER CATALECTIC (or *Septenarius*).

2686. This is like the preceding, except that the last foot is incomplete. The seventh thesis may be resolved. There is regularly a diaeresis after the fourth foot, and hiatus and *syllaba anceps* sometimes occur in the diaeresis. The scheme is: —

⏑⏑⌣́⏐⏑⏑⌣̇⏐⏑⏑⌣́⏐⏑⏑⌣̇ ‡ ⏑⏑⌣́⏐⏑⏑⌣̇⏐⏑⏑⌣́⏐⏑⌣̄
‒⌣́⏐‒⌣̇⏐‒⌣́⏐‒⌣̇ ‡ ‒⌣́⏐‒⌣̇⏐‒⌣́⏐
‒⏑⏑⏐‒⏑⏑⏐‒⏑⏑⏐‒⏑⏑ ‡‒⏑⏑⏐‒⏑⏑⏐‒⏑⏑⏐
⏑⏑⏑⏑⏐⏑⏑⏑⏑⏐⏑⏑⏑⏑⏐⏑⏑[⏑⏑⏑⏑]‡⏑⏑⏑⏑⏐⏑⏑⏑⏑⏐⏑⏑⏑⏑⏐

Examples are: —

Em né|m(ō) habet hō|r(um)? occí|distī. ‡ dīc ígi|tur quis ha|bet
  né;scīs   (Pl. *Aul.* 720).

Hunc hómi|nem decet | aur(ō) éx|pend(ī) : huic ‖ decĕt státu|am
statu(ī) | ex aú|rō
(Pl. *B.* 640).

THE ANAPAESTIC DIMETER ACATALECTIC
(or *Quaternarius*).

2687. This verse consists of two anapaestic dipodies, or four complete
anapaestic feet. There is generally a diaeresis after the second foot, and the
fourth thesis is not resolved. The scheme is : —

ᵕ ᵕ ⏌ | ᵕᵕ ⏌ ‖ ᵕᵕ ⏌ | ᵕᵕ ⏌
⎯ ⏌ | ⎯ ⏌ ‖ ⎯ ⏌ | ⎯ ⏌
⎯ ᵕ ᵕ | ⎯ ᵕ ᵕ ‖ ⎯ ᵕ ᵕ |
ᵕ ᵕ ᵕ ᵕ | ᵕ ᵕ ᵕ ᵕ ‖ ᵕ ᵕ ᵕ ᵕ |

Examples are : —

Quod lúbet | nōn lubet ‖ iam cón|tinuō.
Ita m(ē) Ámor| lass(um) ani|mī lú|dificat,
fugat, ágit | appetĭt ‖ raptát | retinet
(Pl. *Cist.* 214).

This verse is often used to form systems, which frequently end in a paroemiac
(see 2688).

THE ANAPAESTIC DIMETER CATALECTIC (or *Paroemiac*).

2688. This verse consists of two anapaestic dipodies or four anapaestic
feet, the last foot being incomplete. The third thesis is sometimes resolved.
There is no fixed caesura. The scheme is : —

ᵕ ᵕ ⏌ | ᵕ ᵕ ⏌ | ᵕ ᵕ ⏌ | ᵕ ⋀
⎯ ⏌ | ⎯ ⏌ | ⎯ ⏌ |
⎯ ᵕ ᵕ | ⎯ ᵕ ᵕ | ⎯ ᵕ ᵕ |
ᵕ ᵕ ᵕ ᵕ | ᵕ ᵕ ᵕ ᵕ | ᵕ ᵕ ᵕ ᵕ |

Examples are : —

Volucér| pede cor| pore púl| cher
(Ausonius).

Nimĭs tán| d(em) eg(o) ăbs tē | conté|mnor.
Quipp(e) égo | tē nĭ| conté|mnam,
stratió|ticus homo| quī clúe|ar ?
(Pl. *Ps.* 916).

2689. (1.) The Paroemiac is generally used to close a system of acatalectic anapaestic dimeters; but sometimes several paroemiacs in succession form a system (as in
the second example above), especially in Ausonius, Prudentius, and other late poets.

2690. (2.) Other anapaestic verses sometimes occur, especially in the early comedy, but they are rare.

CRETIC RHYTHMS.

2691. These are rhythms of the Hemiolic class (2527), in ⅜ time. The fundamental foot is the Cretic ($\underline{\prime} \cup \underline{\cdot}$).

Either (but not *both*) of the two longs of a Cretic is sometimes resolved (giving the First Paeon $\underline{\prime} \cup \cup \cup$ or the Fourth Paeon $\cup \cup \cup \underline{\cdot}$); but there is rarely more than one resolution in a single verse. The middle short is sometimes replaced by an irrational long (giving $\underline{\prime} > \underline{\cdot}$, or if there is resolution, $\cup \cup > \underline{\cdot}$ or $\underline{\prime} > \cup \cup$); but this never occurs in the last foot of a verse, and but rarely when the middle syllable is the penult of a spondaic word (e. g. nōs nostrās).

2692. (1.) The ictus on the first long of the Cretic was probably (at least in most cases) stronger than that on the second. The first long and the short form the thesis, the second long the arsis, $\underline{\prime} \cup \mid \underline{\cdot}$

2693. (2.) The impetuous, swinging movement of the Cretic rhythm fits it for the expression of passionate emotion.

The Cretic Tetrameter Acatalectic.

2694. This verse consists of four complete Cretic feet. There is usually a diaeresis after the second foot, but sometimes there is instead a caesura after the first long of the third foot. Resolution is not admitted before the diaeresis or the end of the line. The irrational long middle syllable is admitted in the first and third feet. The scheme is : —

$$\underset{\smile\smile}{\prime} \gtrless \overset{\cdot}{\smile\smile} \mid \underset{\smile\smile}{\prime} \cup \underline{\cdot} \# \underset{\smile\smile}{\prime} \gtrless \overset{\cdot}{\smile\smile} \mid \underset{\smile\smile}{\prime} \cup \underline{\cdot}$$

Examples are : —

  Út malīs | gaúdeant ‖ átqu(e) ex in|cómmodīs
                        (T. *Andr.* 627).

  Déind(e) uter|qu(e) ímperā|tŏr ‖ in medi|(um) éxeunt
                        (Pl. *Am.* 223).

2695. This verse is common in the *cantica* of the early drama, and is often repeated to form systems. Hiatus and *syllaba anceps* sometimes occur in the diaeresis.

The Cretic Tetrameter Catalectic.

2696. This is similar to the preceding, except that the last foot is incomplete. The scheme is : —

$$\underset{\smile\smile}{\prime} \gtrless \overset{\cdot}{\smile\smile} \mid \underset{\smile\smile}{\prime} \cup \underline{\cdot} \# \underset{\smile\smile}{\prime} \gtrless \overset{\cdot}{\smile\smile} \mid \underset{\smile\smile}{\prime} \cup \overline{\wedge}$$

Examples are : —

  Sí cadēs,| nón cadēs ‖ quín cadam| técum
                        (Pl. *Most.* 329).

  Nŏv(ī) eg(o) hoc| saéculum ‖ mŏribus| quíbŭs sit
                        (Pl. *Tri.* 283).

OTHER CRETIC VERSES.

2697. The Cretic trimeter acatalectic sometimes occurs, though rarely: **e. g.**

Iám revor|tár. diūst| i(am) íd mihī
(Pl. *Most.* 338).

More frequent is the dimeter acatalectic, which has the scheme: —

$$\text{—}\cup\cup \ \smile \ \text{—}\cup\cup \ | \ \text{—}\cup\cup \ \cup \ \text{—}$$

This is often compounded with a trochaic tripody catalectic: e. g.

Hóc ub(ĭ) Am|phítru(ō) erus ‡ cónspi|cátus|ést
(Pl. *Am.* 242),

and sometimes with a trochaic tripody acatalectic (e. g. Pl. *Ps.* 1248), a trochaic dipody acatalectic (e. g. Pl. *Cap.* 214), or a *Thymelicus* — ∪ ∪ ∪ — (e. g. Pl. *Am.* 245). For other kinds of Cretic verses, see special editions of the early dramatists.

BACCHĪAC RHYTHMS.

2698. These are rhythms of the Hemiolic class (2527), in 3/8 time. The fundamental foot is the Bacchīus (∪ _́_ _́_). Either (or both) of the two longs of a bacchius is sometimes resolved. For the initial short syllable an irrational long is sometimes substituted. Occasionally two shorts are so substituted, especially in the first foot of a verse.

2699. (1.) The ictus on the first long of the bacchīus was probably stronger **than** that on the second long.

2700. (2.) The bacchiac rhythm, like the Cretic, has an impetuous and passionate character.

THE BACCHIAC TETRAMETER ACATALECTIC.

2701. This verse consists of four complete bacchiac feet. There is generally a caesura after the first long of the second or third foot, or (more rarely) a diaeresis after the second foot. An irrational long (or two shorts) may be substituted for the initial short only in the first and third feet. Resolution is not allowed before the caesura or the end of the verse. The scheme is: —

$$[\overset{\smile}{\cup\cup}] \ \cup \text{—} \ \cup \text{—} \ | \ \cup \ \text{—}\| \cup \text{—} \ | \ [\overset{\smile}{\cup\cup}] \ \cup \text{—} \ \cup \text{—} \ | \ \cup \ \cup \text{—} \ \text{—}$$

Examples are: —

Habénd(um) et | ferúnd(um) hoc ‡ onúst cum | labóre
(Pl. *Am.* 175).

At támen ubi | fidḗs? ‖ sī | rogḗs nīl | pudént hīc
(T. *Andr.* 637).

Vetulaé sunt | min(ae) ámb(ae). At ‡ bonás fuís|se crḗdō
(Pl. *B.* 1129).

2702. (1.) There are seldom more than two resolutions in the same verse, and never more than three. Bacchiac tetrameters are often repeated to form systems.

2703. (2.) According to some authorities, bacchiac tetrameters catalectic sometimes occur, e. g. Pl. *Cas.* 656, 867, *Men.* 969, 971, *Most.* 313, *Poen.* 244.

OTHER BACCHIAC VERSES.

2704. (1.) Bacchiac dimeters are occasionally found, especially as *clausulae* to bacchiac systems. An example is : —

$$\text{Ad aétā | t(em) agúndam}$$

(Pl. *Tri.* 232).

An acatalectic dimeter is not seldom compounded with a catalectic iambic tripody: e. g.

$$\text{Rerín tēr | in ánnō } \tfrac{++}{++} \text{ t(ū) hās tón|sitá|rí ?}$$

(Pl. *B.* 1127).

2705. (2.) Bacchiac hexameters occur in a few instances, as : —

$$\text{Satín par|va rés est | volúptā|t(um) in vít(ā) at|qu(e) in aétā | t(e) agúndā}$$

(Pl. *Am.* 633).

2706. (3.) Hypermetrical combination of bacchii into a system appears to occur in Varro, *Sat. Men.* fr. 405 Buech.

CHORIAMBIC RHYTHMS.

2707. In these, the fundamental foot is the choriambus ($\underline{\prime} \cup \cup \underline{\cdot}$). True choriambic verse is very rare in Latin poetry, though apparent choriambi of the form $\underline{\prime} \cup\cup | \_$ or $\underline{\prime} \cup\cup | \underline{\prime}$ are common in logaoedic verse (2652).

Apparently, however, in Terence, *Ad.* 611–13,

$$\text{Út neque quid | mḗ faciam | néc quid agam } \tfrac{++}{++} \text{ certúm | sit.}$$
$$\text{mémbra metū | débilia | súnt, animus } \tfrac{++}{++} \text{ timó|re}$$
$$\text{óbstipuit, | péctore cōn|sístere nīl } \tfrac{++}{++} \text{ cōnsi|lí quit,}$$

there are three choriambic trimeters, the first two with iambic close, the third with trochaic. In the second line there is *syllaba anceps* at the end of the second choriambus. In Plautus, *Casina* 629, *Menaechmi* 110, and perhaps *Asinaria* 133, we have a choriambic dimeter + an acatalectic trochaic dipody.

Owing to the frequent occurrence of the apparent choriambus in certain kinds of logaoedic verse, the metricians of Horace's day regarded them as really choriambic. Hence the rule mentioned in 2652, a rule unknown to Greek writers of logaoedic verse.

IONIC RHYTHMS.

2708. In these, the fundamental foot is the Ionic, of which there are two forms, the Ionic *ā māiōre* $\underline{\prime} \underline{\cdot} \cup\cup$, so called because it begins with the greater part (i. e. the thesis) of the foot, and the Ionic *ā minōre* $\cup\cup \underline{\prime} \underline{\cdot}$, which receives its name from the fact that it begins with the less important part of the foot (i. e. the arsis).

2709. (1.) Ionics *ā minōre* are often treated as Ionics *ā māiōre* with anacrusis, $\cup\cup | \underline{\prime} \underline{\cdot} \cup\cup$, &c. See 2529 *ad fin.*

2710. (2.) Ionic verse shows numerous resolutions and irrational longs, especially in early Latin. The accumulation of short syllables imparts to the verse a wild and passionate character.

2711. (3.) *Anaclăsis* (Gr. ἀνάκλασις, "a bending back") is an exchange of place between a short syllable and the preceding long (e. g. $\underline{\prime}\ \cup\ \underline{\cdot}\ \cup$ for $\underline{\prime}\ \underline{\cdot}\ \cup\cup$ or $\cup\cup\ \underline{\prime}\ \cup\ |\ \underline{\cdot}\ \cup\ \underline{\prime}\ \underline{\cdot}$ for $\cup\cup\ \underline{\prime}\ \underline{\cdot}\ |\ \cup\cup\ \underline{\prime}\ \underline{\cdot}$), and is very frequent in Ionic verse.

The Ionic ā māiōre Tetrameter Catalectic (or *Sotadean*).

2712. This verse consists of four Ionic *ā māiōre* feet, the last foot being incomplete. In the early Latin poets, beginning with Ennius, the Sotadean is treated with much freedom: resolution, contraction (2518), anaclasis (2711), and irrational longs are freely admitted. Examples are: —

Nám quam varia | sínt genera po|ḗmatōrum, | Baébī,
quámque longē | dístinct(a) ali|(a) áb aliīs sīs, | nósce
(Accius, *Didasc.* p. 305 **M.**).

$\underline{\prime}\_\cup\curvearrowright|\ \underline{\prime}\cup\cup\cup\cup|\ \underline{\prime}\cup\_>|\ \underline{\prime}\_\barwedge$
$\underline{\prime}\cup\_>|\ \underline{\prime}\_\cup\cup\ |\ \underline{\jmath}\cup\cup\_>|\ \underline{\prime}\_\barwedge$

Compare in Greek: —

σείων μελί|ην Πηλίαδα | δεξιὸν κατ᾽ | ὦμον (Sotades).

2713. Later poets (Petronius, Martial, Terentianus Maurus) are more strict in their usage, admitting (with very few exceptions) only the forms $\underline{\jmath}\cup\_\cup\cup,\underline{\prime}\cup\cup\cup\cup,\underline{\prime}\cup\_\cup$ besides the normal $\underline{\prime}\_\cup\cup$. Hence their scheme is: —

$\underline{\prime}\_\cup\cup\ |\ \underline{\prime}\_\cup\cup\ |\ \underline{\prime}\_\cup\cup\ |\ \underline{\prime}\_\barwedge$
$\underline{\jmath}\cup\_\cup\cup|\ \underline{\jmath}\cup\_\cup\cup|\ \underline{\jmath}\cup\_\cup\cup|$
$\underline{\prime}\cup\cup\cup\cup|\ \underline{\prime}\cup\cup\cup\cup|\ \underline{\prime}\cup\cup\cup\cup|$
$\underline{\prime}\cup\_\cup|\ \underline{\prime}\cup\_\cup|\ \underline{\prime}\cup\_\cup|$

Examples are: —

Móllēs, vete | rḗs Dēlia|cí manū re|císī
péde tendite, | cúrs(um) addite, | cónvolāte | plántā
(Petron. 23).

Laevius and Varro employ Ionic *ā māiōre* systems of considerable length.

The Ionic ā minōre Tetrameter Catalectic (or *Galliambic.*)

2714. This consists of four Ionic *ā minōre* feet, the last one incomplete. *Anaclasis*, resolution, and contraction are extremely common, and the multiplication of short syllables gives the verse a peculiarly wild and frenzied movement. Catullus very rarely admits Ionics that are not anaclastic (*never* in the first half of the verse, except the doubtful cases 63, 18; 54; 75); but Varro is less strict in this regard. The penultimate long is nearly always resolved. There is rarely more than one resolution in the same half-verse. A diaeresis regularly occurs after the second foot. The scheme is ·━-·

‿‿ ‿́‿⌣̣ | ⏑̣̆ ⏑ ⌣́‿ – ⫮ ‿‿ ‿́‿ ⌣̣ | ⏑̣̆ ⏑ ‿́ ⊼

Examples are: —

   Ades, ínquit, | Ō Cybébē, ‖ fera mónti|um deá
                                (Maecenas).

   ⏑⏑‿́⏑ | ‿⏑‿́ ‿ ⫮ ⏑⏑ ‿ ⏑ |‿‿⏑ ‿́ ⊼

   Super álta | vectus Áttis ‖ celerí ra|te mariá
                               (Catullus 63, 1).

   ⏑⏑‿́⏑ | ‿⏑‿́ ‿ ⫮ ⏑⏑ ‿́ ⏑ | ⏑⏑⏑ ‿́ ⊼

   Quō nós de|cet citātīs ‡ celeráre | tripudiís
                                (*Id.* 63, 26).

   ‿ ‿́ ⏑ | ‿ ⏑ ‿́ ‿ ⫮ ⏑⏑ ‿́ ⏑ | ⏑⏑⏑ ‿́ ⊼

   Ego iúvenis, | eg(o) adulḗscēns ‡ eg(o) ephḗbus,| ego puér
                                (*Id.* 63, 63).

   ⏑ ⏑ ⏑̆ ⏑ ⏑ | ⏑⏑⏑ ‿́ ‿ ⫮ ⏑⏑ ‿́ ⏑ | ⏑ ⏑ ⏑ ‿́ ⊼

   Tibi týpana | nōn inánī ‖ sonitū́ mā|tri' deúm
                         (Varro, *Sat. Men.* 132 Buech.).

   ⏑ ⏑ ⏑̆ ⏑ ⏑ | ‿ ⏑ ‿́ ‿ ⫮ ⏑⏑ ‿́ ‿ | ⏑ ⏑ ‿́ ⊼

2715. It has been suggested that Catullus probably *felt* the rhythm not as Ionic, but as trochaic or logaoedic: —

⏑⏑̆ | ‿́ ⏑ | ⏓̇ ⏑ | ‿̣ | ⏓̇ ⫮ ⏑⏑̆ | ⏑́ ⏑ ⏑ | ⏑ ⏑ ⏑ | ‿́ ∧,

or the like.

   This view has much in its favour; but the true nature of the rhythm is still matter of dispute.

   2716. Compare the Greek: —

       Γαλλαὶ μη|τρὸς ὀρείης| φιλόθυρσοι| δρομάδες,
and in English: —

   " Perished many a maid and matron, many a valorous legionary,
    Fell the colony, city and citadel, London, Verulam, Camuloduné."
                            (Tennyson).

   2717. Horace (3, 12) employs a system of ten pure Ionics *ā minŏre*, e. g.: —

Miserā́rum (e)st | nequ(e) amṓrī ,| dare lū́dum | neque dúlcī
mala vīnō | laver(e) aút ex|animārī
metuéntīs | patruaé ver|bera línguae.

There is generally a diaeresis after each foot.

Lyric Metres of Horace.

2718. The following is a list of the Horatian lyric metres: —

2719. (I.) The Iambic Trimeter (see 2592 ff.). *Epode* 17.

2720. (II.) The Iambic Strophe, an iambic trimeter (2592) followed by an iambic dimeter acatalectic (2617):—

⏒ ´– | ⏑ – | ⏒ ‖ ´– | ⏑ – | ⏒ ´– | ⏑ –
⏒ ´– | ⏑ – | ⏒ ´– | ⏑ – *Epodes* 1–10.

So in Archilochus, e.g.:—

Ὦ Ζεῦ πάτερ, Ζεῦ, σὸν μὲν οὐρανοῦ κράτος,
σὺ δ' ἔργ' ἐπ' ἀνθρώπων ὁρᾷς. (Fr. 88, Bergk).

2721. (III.) The Hipponactean or Trochaic Strophe, a trochaic dimeter catalectic (2644) followed by an iambic trimeter catalectic (2601):—

´– ⏑ | – ⏑ | ´– ⏑ | – ∧
⏒ ´– | ⏑ – | ⏒ ‖ ´– | ⏑ – | ⏑ ´– – *C.* 2, 18.

2722. (IV.) The First Pythiambic Strophe, a dactylic hexameter (2556) followed by an iambic dimeter acatalectic (2617):—

´– ⏖ | ´– ⏖ | ´– ‖ ⏖ | ´– ⏖ | ´– ⏑ ⏑ | ´– –
⏒ ´– | ⏑ – | ⏒ ´– | ⏑ – *Epodes* 14 *and* 15.

So in Archilochus, e.g.:—

ἄψυχος, χαλεπῇσι θεῶν ὀδύνῃσιν ἕκητι
πεπαρμένος δι' ὀστέων. (Fr. 84, Bergk).

2723. (V.) The Second Pythiambic Strophe, a dactylic hexameter (2556) followed by a pure iambic trimeter (2594):—

´– ⏖ | ´– ⏖ | ´– ‖ ⏖ | ´– ⏖ | ´– ⏖ | ´– –
⏑ ´– | ⏑ – | ⏑ ‖ ´– | ⏑ – | ⏑ ´– | ⏑ – *Epode* 16.

So the Greek epigrammatists, e.g.:—

Οἶνός τοι χαρίεντι πέλει ταχὺς ἵππος ἀοιδῷ·
ὕδωρ δὲ πίνων οὐδὲν ἂν τέκοι σοφόν. (Nicaenetus).

2724. (VI.) The Alcmanian Strophe, a dactylic hexameter (2556) followed by a dactylic tetrameter catalectic (2578):—

´– ⏖ | ´– ⏖ | ´– ‖ ⏖ | ´– ⏖ | ´– ⏖ | ´– –
´– ⏖ | ´– ⏖ | ´– ⏖ | ´– ⏑ ∧ *C.* 1, 7, 28; *Epode* 12.

2725. (VII.) The First Archilochian Strophe, a dactylic hexameter (2556) followed by a Lesser Archilochian (2579):—

´– ⏖ | ´– ⏖ | ´– ‖ ⏖ | ´– ⏖ | ´– ⏑ ⏑ | ´– –
´– ⏑ ⏑ | ´– ⏑ ⏑ | ´– ⊼ *C.* 4, 7.

2726. (VIII.) The Second Archilochian Strophe, a dactylic hexameter (2556) followed by an iambelegus (2678):—

´– ⏖ | ´– ⏖ | – ‖ ⏖ | ´– ⏖ | ´– ⏑ ⏑ | ´– –
⏒ ⋮ ´– ⏑ | ´– ⏒ | ´– ⏑ | – ∧ ‡ ´– ⏑ ⏑ | ´– ⏑ ⏑ | ´– ⊼
Epode 13.

2727. (IX.) The THIRD ARCHILOCHIAN STROPHE, an iambic trimeter (2592) followed by an elegiambus (2680) : —

$$\breve{\circ} \stackrel{\angle}{} | \cup \stackrel{\angle}{} | \breve{\circ} \stackrel{\angle}{} | \cup \stackrel{\angle}{} | \breve{\circ} \stackrel{\angle}{} | \cup \stackrel{\angle}{}$$
$$\stackrel{\angle}{} \cup \cup | \stackrel{\angle}{} \cup \cup | \stackrel{\angle}{} \overline{\wedge} \# \breve{\circ} \vdots \stackrel{\angle}{} \cup | \stackrel{\angle}{} \breve{\circ} | \stackrel{\angle}{} \cup | \stackrel{\angle}{} \wedge$$

Epode 11.

Compare Archilochus fr. 85, Bergk (elegiambus; the trimeter is lost) : —

ἀλλά μ' ὁ λυσιμελής, ὦ 'ταῖρε, δάμναται πόθος.

2728. (X.) The FOURTH ARCHILOCHIAN STROPHE, a Greater Archilochian (2677) followed by an iambic trimeter catalectic (2601) : —

$$\stackrel{\angle}{} \overline{\cup\cup} | \stackrel{\angle}{} \overline{\cup\cup} | \stackrel{\angle}{} \| \overline{\cup\cup} | \stackrel{\angle}{} \cup \cup \# \stackrel{\angle}{} \cup | \stackrel{\angle}{} \cup | \stackrel{\angle}{} \cup$$
$$\breve{\circ} \stackrel{\angle}{} | \cup \stackrel{\angle}{} | \breve{\circ} \| \stackrel{\angle}{} | \cup \stackrel{\angle}{} | \cup \stackrel{\angle}{} \quad \stackrel{\angle}{} \qquad \textit{C.} \text{ 1, 4.}$$

So Archilochus, e. g. : —

τοῖος γὰρ φιλότητος ἔρως ὑπὸ καρδίην ἐλυσθεὶς
πολλὴν κατ' ἀχλὺν ὀμμάτων ἔχευεν (Fr. 103, Bergk).

See, however, 2677 *ad fin.*

2729. (XI.) The LESSER ASCLEPIADEAN METRE, a series of Lesser Asclepiadeans (2669) employed stichically (2546) : —

$$\stackrel{\angle}{} > | \stackrel{\angle}{} \cup | \stackrel{\angle}{} \# \stackrel{\angle}{} \cup | \stackrel{\angle}{} \cup | \stackrel{\angle}{} \wedge \qquad \textit{C.} \text{ 1, 1; 3, 30; 4, 8.}$$

So Alcaeus, e. g. : —

ἦλθες ἐκ περάτων γᾶς ἐλεφαντίναν
λάβαν τῶ ξίφεος χρυσοδέταν ἔχων (Fr. 33, Bergk).

2730. (XII.) The GREATER ASCLEPIADEAN METRE, a series of Greater Asclepiadeans (2670) employed stichically (2546) : —

$$\stackrel{\angle}{} > | \stackrel{\angle}{} \cup | \stackrel{\angle}{} \# \stackrel{\angle}{} \cup | \stackrel{\angle}{} \# \stackrel{\angle}{} \cup | \stackrel{\angle}{} \cup | \_ \wedge$$

C. 1, 11, 18; 4, 10.

So Alcaeus, e. g. : —

μηδὲν ἄλλο φυτεύσῃς πρότερον δένδριον ἀμπέλω
(Fr. 44, Bergk).

Many editors hold (with Meineke) that the Horatian odes were written in tetrastichs (2545), and hence that this metre and the preceding were employed by Horace in strophes of four lines each. Catullus (30) seems to use the Greater Asclepiadean by distichs, and so apparently Sappho (fr. 69, Bergk). But as to these points there is still much dispute.

2731. (XIII.) The FIRST ASCLEPIADEAN STROPHE, a Glyconic (2660) followed by a Lesser Asclepiadean (2669) : —

$$\stackrel{\angle}{} > | \stackrel{\angle}{} \cup | \stackrel{\angle}{} \cup | \stackrel{\angle}{} \wedge$$
$$\stackrel{\angle}{} > | \stackrel{\angle}{} \cup | \stackrel{\angle}{} \# \stackrel{\angle}{} \cup | \stackrel{\angle}{} \cup | \stackrel{\angle}{} \wedge$$

C. 1, 3, 13, 19, 36; 3, 9, 15, 19, 24, 25, 28; 4, 1, 3.

Cf. Alcaeus : —

> νῦν δ' [αὖτ'] οὗτος ἐπικρέτει
> κινήσαις τὸν ἀπ' ἴρας πύματον λίθον.　　(Fr. 82, Bergk).

In one instance, *C.* 4, 1, 35, elision occurs at the end of the Glyconic.

2732. (XIV.) The SECOND ASCLEPIADEAN STROPHE, three Lesser Asclepiadeans (2669) followed by a Glyconic (2660) : —

$$\underline{\perp} > \mid \underline{\perp} \smile\smile \mid \underline{\llcorner} \; \# \; \underline{\perp} \smile\smile \mid \underline{\perp} \smile \mid \underline{\perp} \; \wedge$$
$$\underline{\perp} > \mid \underline{\perp} \smile\smile \mid \underline{\llcorner} \; \# \; \underline{\perp} \smile\smile \mid \underline{\perp} \smile \mid \underline{\perp} \; \wedge$$
$$\underline{\perp} > \mid \underline{\perp} \smile\smile \mid \underline{\llcorner} \; \# \; \underline{\perp} \smile\smile \mid \underline{\perp} \smile \mid \underline{\perp} \; \wedge$$
$$\underline{\perp} > \mid \underline{\perp} \smile\smile \mid \underline{\perp} \smile \mid \underline{\perp} \; \wedge$$

C. 1, 6, 15, 24, 33; 2, 12; 3, 10, **16; 4, 5, 12.**

2733. (XV.) The THIRD ASCLEPIADEAN STROPHE, two Lesser Asclepiadeans (2669), a Pherecratean (2659) and a Glyconic (2660) : —

$$\underline{\perp} > \mid \underline{\perp} \smile\smile \mid \underline{\llcorner} \; \# \; \underline{\perp} \smile\smile \mid \underline{\perp} \smile \mid \underline{\perp} \; \wedge$$
$$\underline{\perp} > \mid \underline{\perp} \smile\smile \mid \underline{\llcorner} \; \# \; \underline{\perp} \smile\smile \mid \underline{\perp} \smile \mid \underline{\perp} \; \wedge$$
$$\underline{\perp} > \mid \underline{\perp} \smile\smile \mid \underline{\perp} \smile$$
$$\underline{\perp} > \mid \underline{\perp} \smile\smile \mid \underline{\perp} \smile \mid \underline{\perp} \; \wedge$$

C. 1, 5, 14, 21, 23; 3, 7, **13;** 4, 13.

Compare Alcaeus (Pherecratean followed by Glyconic ; apparently two Lesser Asclepiadeans preceded, but they are lost) : —

> λάταγες ποτέονται
> κυλιχνᾶν ἄπο Τηΐαν.　　(Fr. 43, Bergk).

2734. (XVI.) The GREATER SAPPHIC STROPHE, an Aristophanic (2658) followed by a Greater Sapphic (2671) : —

$$\underline{\perp} \smile\smile \mid \underline{\perp} \smile \mid \underline{\perp} \smile$$
$$\underline{\perp} \smile \mid \underline{\perp} > \mid \underline{\perp} \parallel \smile\smile \mid \underline{\llcorner} \; \# \; \underline{\perp} \smile\smile \mid \underline{\perp} \smile \mid \underline{\llcorner} \mid \underline{\perp} \; \wedge$$

C. 1, 8.

2735. (XVII). The SAPPHIC STROPHE, three Lesser Sapphics (2666) and an Adonic (2655) : —

$$\underline{\perp} \smile \mid \underline{\perp} > \mid \underline{\perp} \parallel \smile\smile \mid \underline{\perp} \smile \mid \underline{\perp} \smile$$
$$\underline{\perp} \smile \mid \underline{\perp} > \mid \underline{\perp} \parallel \smile\smile \mid \underline{\perp} \smile \mid \underline{\perp} \smile$$
$$\underline{\perp} \smile \mid \underline{\perp} > \mid \underline{\perp} \parallel \smile\smile \mid \underline{\perp} \smile \mid \underline{\perp} \smile$$
$$\underline{\perp} \smile\smile \mid \underline{\perp} \smile$$

C. 1, 2, 10, 12, 20, 22, 25, 30, 32, 38; 2, 2, 4, 6, 8, 10, 16; 3, 8, **11, 14, 18,** 20, 22, 27; 4, 2, 6, 11; *Carmen Saeculare.* Also in Catullus 11 and **51.**

So Sappho : —

> φαίνεταί μοι κῆνος ἴσος θέοισιν
> ἔμμεν ὤνερ ὅστις ἐναντίος τοι
> ἰζάνει καὶ πλασίον ἆδυ φωνεύ-
> σας ὑπακούει.　　(Fr. 2, Bergk).

Sappho apparently treated the third Sapphic and the Adonic as continuous; but Horace and Catullus allow *syllaba anceps* (and Horace in four cases, 1, 2, 47; 1, 12, 7, and 31; 1, 22, 15, hiatus) at the end of the third line. On the other hand, both Catullus and Horace sometimes join the third line to the fourth (by dividing a word, Hor. 1, 2, 19; 25, 11; 2, 16, 7; Cat. 11, 11; by elision Hor. 4, 2, 23; *Car. Saec.* 47; Cat. 11, 19), and in a few instances the second to the third (Hor. 2, 2, 18; 16, 34; 4, 2, 22; Cat. 11, 22, all by elision) by *synapheia* (see 2510). In Horace, the last foot of the third line is nearly always an irrational spondee.

2736. (XVIII.) The ALCAIC STROPHE, two Greater Alcaics (2667), a nine-syllabled Alcaic (2642) and a Lesser Alcaic (2663):—

$$\breve{\supset} \; \vdots \; \underline{\cancel{}} \cup \mid \underline{\cancel{}} > \# \underline{\cancel{}} \cup\cup \mid \underline{\cancel{}} \cup \mid \underline{\cancel{}} \wedge$$
$$\breve{\supset} \; \vdots \; \underline{\cancel{}} \cup \mid \underline{\cancel{}} > \# \underline{\cancel{}} \cup\cup \mid \underline{\cancel{}} \cup \mid \underline{\cancel{}} \wedge$$
$$\breve{\supset} \; \vdots \; \underline{\cancel{}} \cup \mid \underline{\cancel{}} > \mid \underline{\cancel{}} \cup \mid \underline{\cancel{}} \cup$$
$$\underline{\cancel{}} \cup\cup \mid \underline{\cancel{}} \cup\cup \mid \underline{\cancel{}} \cup \mid \underline{\cancel{}} \cup$$

C. 1, 9, 16, 17, 26, 27, 29, 31, 34, 35, 37; 2, 1, 3, 5, 7, 9, 11, 13, 14, 15, 17, 19, 20; 3, 1, 2, 3, 4, 5, 6, 17, 21, 23, 26, 29; 4, 4, 9, 14, 15.

So Alcaeus:—

> Ἀσυνέτημι τῶν ἀνέμων στάσιν·
> τὸ μὲν γὰρ ἔνθεν κῦμα κυλίνδεται,
> τὸ δ' ἔνθεν· ἄμμες δ' ἀν τὸ μέσσον
> νᾶϊ φορήμεθα σὺν μελαίνᾳ.   (Fr. 18, Bergk).

In the Greek poets the last two lines are sometimes joined by *synapheia* (2510), and Horace has elision at the end of the third verse in 2, 3, 27; 3, 29, 35. But he frequently admits hiatus in that place.

2737. (XIX.) The IONIC SYSTEM, a system of ten pure Ionics *à minōre* (see 2717):—

$$\cup\cup \underline{\cancel{}} - \mid \cup\cup \underline{\cancel{}} - \mid \cup\cup \underline{\cancel{}} - \mid \cup\cup \underline{\cancel{}} -$$
$$\cup\cup \underline{\cancel{}} - \mid \cup\cup - - \mid \cup\cup \underline{\cancel{}} - \mid \cup\cup \underline{\cancel{}} -$$
$$\cup\cup \underline{\cancel{}} - \mid \cup\cup \underline{\cancel{}} -$$ *C.* 3, 12.

Lyric Strophes of Catullus.

2738. Catullus in 34 uses a strophe consisting of three Glyconics (2660) followed by a Pherecratean (2659):—

$$\begin{bmatrix} \underline{\cancel{}} \cup \\ - > \\ \cup - \end{bmatrix} \mid \underline{\cancel{}} \cup\cup \mid \underline{\cancel{}} \cup \mid \underline{\cancel{}} \wedge$$
$$\begin{bmatrix} \underline{\cancel{}} \cup \\ \underline{\cancel{}} > \\ \cup - \end{bmatrix} \mid \underline{\cancel{}} \cup\cup \mid \underline{\cancel{}} \cup \mid \underline{\cancel{}} \wedge$$
$$\begin{bmatrix} \underline{\cancel{}} \cup \\ \underline{\cancel{}} > \\ \cup - \end{bmatrix} \mid \underline{\cancel{}} \cup\cup \mid \underline{\cancel{}} \cup \mid \underline{\cancel{}} \wedge$$
$$\begin{bmatrix} \underline{\cancel{}} \cup \\ \underline{\cancel{}} > \\ \cup - \end{bmatrix} \mid \underline{\cancel{}} \cup\cup \mid \underline{\cancel{}} \cup$$

In 61 he employs a strophe consisting of *four* Glyconics followed by a Pherecratean.

2739. Index of Horatian Odes and their Metres.

The Roman numerals in the table refer to the numbers assigned to the various strophes in 2719–2737.

BOOK.	ODE.	METRE.	BOOK.	ODE.	METRE.	BOOK.	ODE.	METRE.
I	1	XI.	2	1	XVIII.	3	23	XVIII.
	2	XVII.		2	XVII.		24	XIII.
	3	XIII.		3	XVIII.		25	XIII.
	4	X.		4	XVII.		26	XVIII.
	5	XV.		5	XVIII.		27	XVII.
	6	XIV.		6	XVII.		28	XIII.
	7	VI.		7	XVIII.		29	XVIII.
	8	XVI.		8	XVII.		30	XI.
	9	XVIII.		9	XVIII.			
	10	XVII.		10	XVII.	4	1	XIII.
	11	XII.		11	XVIII.		2	XVII.
	12	XVII.		12	XIV.		3	XIII.
	13	XIII.		13	XVIII.		4	XVIII.
	14	XV.		14	XVIII.		5	XIV.
	15	XIV.		15	XVIII.		6	XVII.
	16	XVIII.		16	XVII.		7	VII.
	17	XVIII.		17	XVIII.		8	XI.
	18	XII.		18	III.		9	XVIII.
	19	XIII.		19	XVIII.		10	XII.
	20	XVII.		20	XVIII.		11	XVII.
	21	XV.					12	XIV.
	22	XVII.	3	1–6	XVIII.		13	XV.
	23	XV.		7	XV.		14	XVIII.
	24	XIV.		8	XVII.		15	XVIII.
	25	XVII.		9	XIII.			
	26	XVIII.		10	XIV.			
	27	XVIII.		11	XVII.	*Carmen*		
	28	VI.		12	XIX.	*Saecu-*		XVII.
	29	XVIII.		13	XV.	*lare..*		
	30	XVII.		14	XVII.			
	31	XVIII.		15	XIII.	Epodes	1–10	II.
	32	XVII.		16	XIV.		11	IX.
	33	XIV.		17	XVIII.		12	VI.
	34	XVIII.		18	XVII.		13	VIII.
	35	XVIII.		19	XIII.		14	IV.
	36	XIII.		20	XVII.		15	IV.
	37	XVIII.		21	XVIII.		16	V.
	38	XVII.		22	XVII.		17	I.

ABBREVIATIONS USED IN CITING THE AUTHORS.

2740. In Part First, in which authors are occasionally cited, but without direct reference to their works, the usual abbreviations are employed: as Plaut., Ter., Cic., Verg., Hor., &c., &c.

2741. In Part Second, the principles adopted are as follows:

2742. (1.) A reference consisting of figures alone (as, 2, 2, 3), denotes book, chapter, and section of Caesar *de Bello Gallico.*

2743. (2.) A reference to a work (in italics), without a preceding abbreviation for the author's name (as, *TD.* 1, 2; *Mil.* 3), denotes the book and section, or the section only, of a work by Cicero. The abbreviations used to denote his works are given in the list below (2745).

2744. (3.) A reference made to Vergil (V.), followed by figures alone, is a reference to the *Aeneid:* as, V. 1, 20. Similarly, H. stands alone for the *Odes* of Horace; O. alone for the *Metamorphoses* of Ovid; and Ta. alone for the *Annals* of Tacitus.

2745. (4.) Roman letters are used in the abbreviations of the names of authors, *italics* in the abbreviations of the names of their works, as in the following List: —

LIST OF ABBREVIATIONS.

Abbreviations.	Authors and Works.	Abbreviations.	Authors and Works.
Caes.	Caesar.	*Fin.*	*de Finibus.*
C.	*de Bello Civili.*	*Fl.* or *Flacc.*	*prō Flaccō.* [*sis.*
See 2742.	*de Bello Gallicō.*	*HR.*	*de Haruspicum Respōn-*
Cat.	Catullus.	*IP.*	*dē Imperiō Pompēī.*
See 2743.	Cicero.	*Inv.*	*de Inventiōne.*
Ac.	*Acadēmica.*	*L.*	*Laelius.*
ad *Br.*	ad *Brūtum Epistulae.*	*LAgr.*	*dē lēge Agrāriā.*
Agr.	*dē lēge Agrāriā.*	*Leg.*	*dē Lēgibus.*
Arch.	*prō Archiā.*	*Lig.*	*prō Ligāriō.*
Att.	ad *Atticum Epistulae.*	*Marc.*	*prō Marcellō.*
Balb.	*prō Balbō.*	*Mil.*	*prō Milōne.*
Br.	*Brūtus.*	*Mur.*	*prō Mūrēnā.*
C.	*in Catilīnam.*	*O.*	*Ōrātor.*
Caec.	*prō Caecinā.*	*Off.*	*dē Officiīs.* [*tōrum.*
Caecil.	*Dīvinātiō in Caecilium.*	*OG.*	*de Optimō Genere Ōrā-*
Cael.	*prō Caeliō.*	*OP.*	*de Ōrātōriā Partītiōne.*
CM.	*Catō Maior.*	*Par.*	*Paradoxa.* [*bus.*
Clu.	*prō Cluentiō.*	*PC.*	*de Prōvinciīs Cōnsulāri-*
D.	*prō Dēiotarō.*	*Ph.*	*Philippicae.*
Div.	*dē Dīvinātiōne.*	*Pis.*	*in Pisōnem.*
DN.	*dē Deōrum Nātūrā.*	*Pl.*or *Planc.*	*prō Planciō.*
DC.	*dē Ōrātōre.*	*Q.* or *Quint*	*prō Quintiō.* [*Epistulae.*
Fam.	ad *Familiārēs Epistulae.*	*QFr.*	ad *Quīntum Frātrem*
Fat.	*dē Fātō.*	*RA.*	*prō Rōsciō Amerinō.*

RC.	prō Rōsciō Cōmoedō.	Most.	Mostellāria.
RP.	dē Rē Pūblicā. [nis reō.	Per.	Persa.
Rab.	prō Rabīriō perduelliō-	Poen.	Poenulus.
RabP.	prō Rabīriō Posthumō.	Ps.	Pseudolus.
Scaur.	prō Scaurō.	R.	Rudēns.
Sest.	prō Sēstiō.	St.	Stichus.
Sull.	prō Sūllā.	Tri.	Trinummus.
T. or Top.	Topica. [nēs.	Tru.	Truculentus.
TD.	Tusculānae Disputātiō-	Vid.	Vīdulāria.
Tim.	Timaeus.	Plin. Ep.	Pliny's Epistulae.
Tul.	prō Tulliō.	Plin. NH.	Pliny's Nātūrālis His-
V. a. pr.	in Verrem āctiō I.	Prop.	Propertius. [toriae.
V.	in Verrem āctiō II.	Publil. Syr.	Publilius Syrus.
Corn., Cornif.	Cornificius.	Quint. or Quintil.	Quintilian.
E.	Ennius.		
Fest.	Festus.	S.	Sallust.
Gell.	Gellius.	C.	Catilīna. [Lepidī.
H.	Horace.	Fr. Lep.	Fragmenta Ōrātiōnis
AP.	Ars Poetica.	Fr. Phil.	Fragmenta Ōrātiōnis
See 2744.	Carmina.	I.	Iugurtha. [Philippī.
E.	Epistulae.	Sen.	Seneca.
Epod.	Epōdoi.	Ben.	dē Beneficiīs.
S.	Sermōnēs.	Ep.	Epistulae.
J.	Juvenal.	St.	Statius.
L.	Livy.	Th.	Thēbais.
Lucil.	Lucilius.	Suet.	Suetonius.
Lucr.	Lucretius.	Aug.	Augustus.
Macrob.	Macrobius.	Cal.	Caligula.
Sat.	Sāturnālia.	Cl.	Claudius.
Mart.	Martial.	Galb.	Galba.
N.	Nepos.	Iul.	Iūlius.
O.	Ovid.	Tib.	Tiberius.
A.	Amōrēs.	T.	Terence.
AA.	Ars Amātōria.	Ad.	Adelphoe.
F.	Fāstī.	Andr.	Andria.
See 2744.	Metamorphōsēs.	Eu.	Eunūchus.
Tr.	Trīstia.	Hec.	Hecyra.
Pl.	Plautus.	Hau.	Hauton Timōrūmenos.
Am.	Amphitruō.	Ph.	Phormiō.
As.	Asināria.	Ta.	Tacitus.
Aul.	Aululāria.	See 2744.	Annālēs.
B.	Bacchidēs.	A. or Agr.	Agricola.
Cap.	Captīvī.	D.	Dialogus.
Cas.	Casina.	G.	Germānia.
Cist.	Cistellāria.	H.	Historiae.
Cu. or Cur.	Curculiō.	Tib.	Tibullus.
E.	Epidicus.	V.	Vergil.
Men.	Menaechmī.	See 2744.	Aenēis.
Mer.	Mercātor.	E.	Eclogae.
MG.	Miles Glōriōsus.	G.	Geōrgica.

INDEX OF SUBJECTS.

Index of Subjects.

Index of Subjects.

Conditional — *continued.*
2103-2105 ; apod. in plup. indic., 2104, 2107.

Variation of prot., 2109-2111 ; variation of apod., 2112-2115 ; forms which apod. may take, 2018 ; coordinated member equivalent to prot., 1574, 1701 ; imper. as prot., 1574 ; prot. expressed by abl. abs., 2295 ; prot. expressed by partic., 2295 ; conditional comparisons, 2117-2122 ; protases in ind. disc., 2326-2329 ; apodoses in ind. disc., 2330-2334 ; sentence, quisquam and ūllus in, 2402.

Conjugation,
defined, 397 ; of sum, 744-750 ; of possum, 744, 751-753 ; of dō, 744, 754-757 ; of bibō, serō, sistō, 744, 758 ; of inquam, 759-761 ; of eō, 759, 762-767 ; of quʒō, nequeō, 759, 768 ; of edō, 769-771 ; of volō, 772-774 ; of nōlō, 772, 775-777 ; of mālō, 772, 778, 779 ; of ferō, 772, 780, 781 ; of verbs in -ere (third conjug.), 782-784 ; of aiō, 785-787 ; of fīō, 785, 788-790 ; of verbs in -iō, -ere, 784-791 ; of verbs in -āre (first conjug.), 792, 793 ; of verbs in -ēre (sec. conjug.), 794, 795 ; of verbs in -īre (fourth conjug.), 796, 797 ; of deponent verbs, 798-801 ; of periphrastic forms, 802-804 ; see Stems, Person, Formation.

Conjunctional,
see Conjunctive.

Conjunctions,
defined, 13 ; origin of, 696 ; copulative, use of, 1644-1661, 1687-1692, 1881, 2133-2149 ; combination of different, 1662-1666 ; disjunctive, use of, 1667-1675, 2133-2149 ; adversative, use of, 1676-1686, 2133, 2150-2153 ; postpositive, 1676 ; quamquam as, 1899, 1900 ; quamvīs as, 1904, 1905 ; quī, 1976 ; concessive, use of, 2133, 2150-2153 ; causal and illative, use of, 2133, 2154-2158 ; affirmative coordination, 2159 ; see Connectives.

Conjunctive,
particle sentences, 1838-2122 ; introduced by quod, quia, 1838 1858 ; by nōn quod, nōn quō, &c., 1855 ; by cum, 1859-1881 ; by quoniam, 1882-1884 ; by quotiēns, quotiēnscumque, 1885-1887 ; by quam, 1888-1898 ; by quantus, ut, 1892 ; by quamquam, 1899-1902 ; by quam-

Conjunctive — *continued.*
vīs, 1903-1906 ; by quamlibet, 1907 ; by tamquam, 1908-1910 ; by quemadmodum, 1908 ; by antequam, priusquam, 1911-1921 ; by prīdiē quam, postrīdiē quam, 1922 ; by postquam, ubī, ut, cum prīmum, 1923-1934 ; by utī, ut, nē, 1935-1970 ; by ubī, 1971 ; by quō, quī, 1972-1976 ; by quantō, 1973 ; by quōminus, 1977, 1978 ; by quō sētius, 1979 ; by quīn, 1980-1990 ; by dum, dōnec, quoad, quamdiū, 1901-2009 ; by modo, 2003 ; by quandō, quandōque, 2010-2014 ; by sī, nisi, &c., 2015-2115 ; by etsī, tametsī, tamenetsī, etiamsī, sī, 2116 ; by quasi, quam sī, tamquam sī, &c., 2117-2122 ; particle sentences, in ind. disc., 2315, 2317, 2319.

Connection,
of the parts of sentence, 1636-1692 ; of sentences or periods, 2123-2159 ; relationship, &c., words of, with gen., 1203.

Connectives,
compound sentence without, 1636-1642 ; separate sentences or periods without, 2124-2127 ; relatives as, 2131 ; demonstrative and determinative words as, 2129, 2130 ; concessive words as, 2150-2153 ; disjunctive words as, 1667-1675, 2134-2149 ; copulative words as, 1644-1661, 2134-2149 ; adversative words as, 1676-1686, 2150-2153 ; other words than conjunctions as, 1687-1692 ; causal words as, 2154-2158 ; illative words as, 2154-2158 ; affirmative coordination, 2159.

Consecutive,
sentences, defined, 1716 ; tense of, after secondary, 1757-1759 ; complementary, 1948, 1965-1969 ; pure, 1948, 1970.

Consonants,
cons. and vowel i and u, 22-28 ; x double cons., how sounded, 70 ; x makes long syllable, 177 ; doubled cons., how written and how pronounced, 80 ; doubled, never ends a word, 177 ; doubled, makes long syllable, 177 ; pronunciation of, 53-72 ; classification of the consonants, 73-79 ; consonant changes, 146-174, see Substitution, Development, Disappearance, Assimilation, Dissimilation, Interchange ; mute or f followed by l or r,

510

Index of Subjects.

Genitive case — *continued.*
objective, 1260–1262; objective, **nostrī, vestrī**, 2335.

With adjectives, 1263–1270, 1203, 1204; with **cōnscius** and dat., 1265; with partic., 1266; with **similis**, 1204; with **dignus, indignus**, 1269.

With verbs, 1271–1294; with verbs of valuing, &c., 1271–1275, 1279; with **rēfert** and **interest**, 1276–1279; with judicial verbs, 1280–1282; with **miseret, paenitet, piget, pudet, taedet,** 1283, 1284; with **misereor, misereō, miserēscō,** 1285; with personal verbs of desiring, loathing, admiring, dreading, 1286; with verbs of memory, 1287–1291; with verbs of participation and mastery, 1292; with verbs of fulness and want, 1293; with verbs of separating and abstaining, 1294.

Of exclamation, 1295; with **mihĭ est nōmen, nōmen dō,** &c., 1213, 1214; with **opus,** 1383; with **post** and **intrā** in expressions of time, 1396; with preps., 1406, 1413, 1419, 1420, 1232; possess., with infin., 1237, 2208, 2211, 1232; of gerundive construction and gerund, 2258–2264, 2164.

Genus,
par, duplex, sesculex, 2527.

Gerund.
no plur. of, 416; a verbal noun, 732, 2237; formation of, 899; dat. of doer of action with, 1215, 1478, 2243; abl. with **ab** with, 2243; in reflexive sense, 1482; treated, 2237–2268; character of, 2237–2239; with and without obj., 2241, 2242; of verbs of trans. use, 2242, 2255, 2259, 2265; use of acc. of, with **ad,** 2252, 2164; with other preps., 2253; use of dat. of, 2255, 2257; in gen., 2259; denoting purpose, 2263; with **causā** expressing purpose, 2164; use of abl. of, 2265–2268; denoting means, cause, &c., 2266; with preps., 2267; in abl. of separation, 2268.

Gerundive,
a verbal noun, 732, 2237: formation of, 899, 288; originally neither act. nor pass., 288, 2238; dat. of possessor with, 1215, 1478, 2243; abl. with **ab** with, 2243; treated, 2237–2268; character of, 2237–2239; the construction, 2240: use of nom. of, 2243–2249, 2251; with **sum,** 2243; inflection of, with **sum,**

Gerundive — *continued.*
804; with **sum** in conditional periods, 2101; **fruendus, fungendus,** &c., 2244; **habeō** with, 2245; impersonally, 2246, 2180, 2244; impersonally with obj., 2247; adjectively, 288, 2248; denoting possibility, 2249; with pass., 2251; use of acc. of, 2250–2253, 2243; with verbs, 2250; with **ad,** 2252, 2164; with other preps., 2253; use of dat. of, 2254, 2256, 1208; use of gen. of, 2258–2264; with subst. or adj., 2258, 2259; with **nostrī,** &c., 2260, 2261; predicately with **sum,** 2262; with **causā** expressing purpose, 2164; alone, denoting purpose, 2263; with judicial verbs, 2264; use of abl. of, 2265–2268; denoting means, cause, &c., 2266; with preps., 2267; in abl. of separation, 2268; with compar. expression, 2268.

Giving,
verbs of, subjv. coordinated with, 1712; with gerundive construction, 2250.

Glides, consonantal, 167.
Glyconic, 2660–2662.
Gnomic, see **Often.**
Gradation,
quantitative vowel, 135; qualitative, 145.

Grave accent, 90.
Greek,
characters of the alphabet, 17, 18; words, **eu** in, 101; changed in Latin, 172, 2; quantity in, 125; 127, 8, 9; patronymics, 279; nouns, gender of, 406, 408, 570; nouns of **-ā-** decl., forms of, 443–445; of **-o-** decl., 466; of cons. decl., 508–512; of **-i-** decl., 565; idiom, imitated in Latin with dat. of **volēns,** &c., 1218; acc., see **Part concerned.**

Grief,
verbs of, with **quod, quia,** 1851; with **cum,** 1851, 1875; with acc. and infin., 2187, 2188, 2184.

Gutturals,
44; 77; guttural mute stems, decl. of, 471–473.

Haplology, 179.
Happening,
verbs of, case with, 1181–1185; **quī** with, 1826, 1850; **quod** with, introducing coincident action, 1850; **cum** with, 1874, 1850: with result clause, 1965; with result clause, how translated, 1966.

Index of Subjects.

Hardening, 2503.

Harming,
verbs of, case with, 1205–1210.

Having,
verbs of, with two accusatives, 1167.

Hearing,
verbs of, in pres. of past action, 1592; with indirect question, 1774.

Helping,
expressions of, case with, 1181–1185.

Hemiolic class,
of rhythms, 2527.

Hendecasyllabic Alcaic, 2667, 2668.

Hendecasyllable, 2664, 2665.

Hephthemimeral caesura, 2544.

Hephthemimeris, 2531.

Hesitate,
verbs meaning, with **quīn,** 1987; with infin., 2169.

Hexameter,
defined, 2536; dactylic, 2556–2569; bacchiac, 2705.

Hexapody, 2531.

Hiatus,
within a word, 114–116; between words, 2473–2480; at end of verse, 2533.

Hidden quantity, 2459–2463.

Hiding,
verbs of, with two accusatives, 1169–1171; with acc. and prepositional phrase, 1170.

Hindering,
verbs of, with **nē,** 1960, 1977; with **quōminus,** 1960, 1977; with **quīn,** 1986; with acc. and infin., 2203; with acc. of gerundive construction or gerund, 2252.

Hipponactean verse,
2597–2600, 2639–2641; strophe, in Horace, 2721.

Hiring,
verbs of, with gen., 1274; with abl., 1388–1392.

Historical,
perf., 1602–1604, see **Perfect;** infin., see **Intimation;** pres., see **Vivid narration.**

Hope,
expressions of, with **sī, sī forte,** 1777; with acc. and infin., 2186; with pres. infin., 2186.

Horace,
lyric metres of, 2718–2737, 2739.

Hortatory,
see **Desire.**

Hostility,
words of, with gen., 1203.

Hypothesis,
expressed by abl. abs., 1367; expressed by partic., 2295; variation of prot., 2109–2111.

Hypermetrical verse, 2568.

Iambelegus, 2678, 2679.

Iambic,
words, last syllable of, shortened in verse, 129; shortening, law of, 120, 2470; rhythms, 2581–2627; trimeter (senarius), 2583–2596; choliambus, 2597–2600; trimeter catalectic, 2601–2603; tetrameter acatalectic, 2604–2609; septenarius, 2610–2616; dimeter acatalectic, 2617–2620; dimeter catalectic, 2621–2623; acatalectic dipody and catalectic tripody, 2624; versus Reizianus, 2625, 2626; trimeter, in Horace, 2719; strophe, in Horace, 2720.

Iambus, 2521.

Ictus,
2511; in combination with word accent, 2548.

Identity,
pron. of. decl. of, 676–678; use of, 2371–2373; see **idem.**

Illative,
words, use of, 2133, 2154–2158.

Illustrations,
ut in, 1941; introduced by **nam,** 2155.

Imparisyllables,
defined, 469; decl. of, cons. stems, 471–512; -i- stems, 529–569; gender of, 571–584.

Imperative,
with short final vowel, 130, 4; tense of, 716, 1575; of **dīcō, dūcō, faciō,** 113, 846; of compounds of **dūcō,** 846; accent of compounds of **dīc, dūc,** 88; endings of, 297, 731; in -d, 748; formation of, 844–846; perf., 879, 813; sing., of more than one, 1075; with **quīn,** 1527; in commands, 1571–1580; accompanied by **amābō, age, sānē,** &c., 1572, 1573, 1992; in protasis of conditional sentence, 1574, 2032, 2038, 2056, 2063; use of third person and longer forms, 1575–1578; the fut., 1575; **fac, fac ut, cūrā ut, vidē,** &c., 1579; periphrastic perf. pass., 1580; in prohibitions, 1581–1586; **nōn**

Inscriptions — *continued.*
ĭdem in, 678; of quī, quis in, 690;
person endings in, 729; form of sum
in, 748; form of possum in, 753;
forms of eō in, 764, 765; form of tulī
in, 781; fut. perf. in, 884, 888; perf.
subjv. in, 877, 887; pass. infin. in, 897,
965; use of nom. in, 1114.

Instrument,
suffixes denoting, 238–245, 213, 224;
abl. of, 1377–1384, 1476, 1477.

Instrumental case,
meaning of, 1300; uses of, 1356–1399,
see **Ablative.**

Intensive,
verbs, definition and formation of,
371–374; pron., decl. of, 656, 657, 679,
680; use of, 2374–2384; see **ipse.**

Intention,
dat. of, 1223–1225.

Interest,
dat. of, 1205–1210; expressed by
emotional dat., 1211.

Interjections,
defined, 14; used with nom., 1117,
1123; used with voc., 1123; used with
dat., 1206; used with acc., 1149, 1150;
used with gen., 1295; hiatus after, 2475;
monosyllabic, not elided, 2484.

Intermediate,
coordinate sentence, treated, 1693–
1713.

Interrogations,
neg. adv. in, 1443; as apod. in tam
. . . quam sentences, 1889.

Interrogative adverbs, 711, 1526.

Interrogative implication,
infin. of intimation with, 1538.

Interrogative pronouns,
decl. of, 658, 659, 681–694; adj. and
subst. forms of, 683–685; use of, in
simple sentences, 1526–1533, 1787–
1791; in subjv. questions, 1563–1570;
in indirect question, 1785, 1786; quid
tibī hanc cūrātiōst rem, 1136:
of kindred meaning with verb, 1144,
1840, 1851; with verbs of intrans. use,
1183–1186; with emotional dat., 1211;
with rēfert, interest, 1276–1279;
rel. developed from, 1795, 1808; difference between uter and quis, quī,
2385; difference between quis, quid,
and quī, quod, 2386.

Interrogative sentences,
defined, 1025; quisquam and ūllus
in, 2402; see **Questions.**

Interrogative subjunctive,
1563–1569; in subordinate sentence,
1731; in indirect question, 1786.

Intimation,
infin. of, 1534–1539, 1717, 1868, 1869,
1924, 2009.

Intransitive use,
verbs of, used impersonally in pass.,
724, 1479; verbs of trans. use used as,
1133; used transitively, 1137, 1139,
1191; with dat., 1181–1191, 1205; use
of gerundive of, 2246.

Ionic,
rhythms, 2708–2717; ā māiōre, 2708–
2713; ā minōre, 2708, 2709, 2714–2717;
system, in Horace, 2737.

Ionic ā māiōre,
defined, 2521; see **Ionic.**

Ionic ā minōre,
defined, 2521; see **Ionic.**

Irrational syllables and feet,
2524.

Irregular,
verbs, defined, 743; conjugated, 744–
781, see **Conjugation.**

Islands,
names of, in acc., with expressions of
motion, 1157, 1158; constructions with,
to denote place from which, 1307–1310;
constructions with, to denote place in
or at which, 1331–1336, 1342, 1343;
rel. advs., ubī, quō, unde, referring
to, 1793.

Iterative,
see **Frequentative.**

Ithyphallic verse, 2647.

Joy,
verbs of, with quod, quia, 1851;
with cum, 1851, 1875; with acc. and
infin., 2187, 2188, 2184.

Judicial,
verbs, with gen., 1280–1282; with abl
1280–1282; with gen. of gerundive con
struction, 2264.

Keeping,
verbs of, with two accusatives, 1167;
with pred. abl., 1363.

Kindred,
derivation, acc. of, 1140, 1173; mean
ing, acc. of, 1141.

Know how,
verbs meaning, with infin., 2169.

Index of Subjects.

Index of Subjects.

Pluperfect tense — *continued.*
following perf. infin., or perf. partic.,
1767; with **cum**, 1872, 1873; with
quotiēns, quotiēnscumque, 1887;
with **antequam, priusquam**, 1914,
1920, 1921; with **posteā quam,
postquam**, &c., 1924; with **dōnec**,
2009; with indef. rel. pron. or adv., 1814;
in conditional prot., 2024, 2071, 2089,
2091, 2096, 2098-2107; in conditional
apod., 2024, 2041, 2071, 2073, 2083,
2089, 2091, 2095, 2099; with **quasi,
tamquam sī**, &c., 2120; in ind. disc.
representing a fut. perf., 2324; in
conditional apod. of direct discourse,
how represented in ind. disc., 2331-
2334.

Plural number,
in nouns, defined, 414; lacking, see
Defective; with different meaning
from sing., 418, 480; of material
substs., 416, 1108; of abstracts, 416,
1109; of proper names, 416, 1105; of
names of countries, 1107; in generalizations and in poetry, 1110; adjs. in,
used as substs., 1103, 1104, 1106; in
substs., in agreement, 1077-1081; in
adjs., prons., and partic., in agreement,
1082-1098; in verbs, defined, 722; with
sing. and plur. subjects, 1062-1076;
of modesty, 1074; of gerundive with
nostrī, &c., 2261.

Polysyllables,
quantity of penult in, 2434-2436;
quantity of final syllable in, 2437-2457.

Position,
syllables long by, 177; syllable containing vowel before mute or **f** followed
by **l** or **r**, 178; final short vowel before
word beginning with two consonants or
double cons., 2458; final **s** does not always make, 2468; of preps., 1433-1437.

Positive,
expressing disproportion, 1454; used
in comparison of adjs. and advs., 1457,
1458; combined with a compar., 1458;
expressed by compar. with abl., 1464;
see **Comparison, Affirmative.**

Possession,
adj. suffixes implying, 298, 302-330;
expressed by dat., 1207, 1212-1216; expressed by gen., 1232-1238.

Possessive compounds, 385.

Possessive pronouns,
decl. of, 652-655; agreement of, 1082-
1098; used instead of gen. of personal
or reflexive pron., 1234, 1262; with

Possessive pronouns — *continued.*
word in apposition in gen., 1235; with
rēfert and **interest**, 1277; gen. of,
with infin., 1237, 2208, 2211; implying
antecedent to rel., 1807; of reflexive,
referring to subj. of verb, 2336; of reflexive, referring to word not subj. of
verb, 2337; of reflexive, in construction
of acc. with infin., 2338-2340; of reflexive, in subordinate clauses, 2341-2343;
omitted, 2346; meaning *proper, appropriate, favourable,* 2346; see **meus**, &c.

Possessor,
dat. of, 1212-1216, 1478, 2181, 2243.

Possibility,
expressed by subjv., 1554-1562; denoted by gerundive, 2249; verbal expressions of, see **Ability.**

Postpositive,
words, 1676, 1688; preps., 1433-1436.

Posttonic syllable,
102.

Potential,
use of verb, 2305; see **Action conceivable.**

Prayer,
duim, &c. in, 756; forms of perf.
subjv. and fut. perf. in, 887; expressed
by imper., 1571; in verse, 2549.

Predicate,
defined, 1023, 1035; omitted, 1036;
enlarged, 1048-1054; pred. subst., verb
agreeing with, 1072; agreement of pred.
subst., 1077-1081; in oblique case,
1052, 1363; pred. adj., agreement of,
1082-1098; pred. nom., with verb of indeterminate meaning, 1035; with other
verbs, 1051; infin. as pred. nom., 2207;
noun, in nom. with complementary
infin., 2171; in acc., referring to subj.
acc. 2174; in nom., with verbs of perceiving, knowing, &c., used in pass.,
2177; in nom., with verbs of perceiving,
knowing, &c., used in act., 2184; in
acc., referring to unexpressed indef. subj.
of infin., 2213; in dat., with implied
subj. of infin., 2214; in acc., with verbs
of making, choosing, naming, &c., 1167,
1168; pred. uses of gen., 1236, 1237,
1239, 1251; pred. use of abl. of quality,
1375; with **ūtor**, 1381; pred. partic.
with **ūsus est, opus est**, 1382; pred.
use of prepositional expressions, 1428;
pron. agreeing with pred. subst., 1097,
1806; pred. use of gen. of gerundive
construction, 2262-2264; see **Predicative.**

532

Index of Subjects.

Predicative,
dat., 1219–1225; partic., 2297–2299.

Prefixes,
advs. as verbal, 1402–1409.

Prepositions,
defined, 11, 696, 1402; as proclitics, 92; accent of, when following case, 92; how written in inscriptions and mss., 92; as positive, 357; compounded with nouns or noun stems, 381–383, 385, 390; compounded with verbs, 391, 392; inseparable, 392, 1409; origin of, 696, 1402–1404; function of, 1405; inflected forms of substs. used as, 1406, 1413, 1419, 1420; trace of adverbial use in tmesis, 1407; use as advs. and as preps. discussed, 1412–1416, 1421; used with acc., 1410–1416; used with abl., 1415–1421; used with abl. proper, 1415, 1419–1421; used with loc. abl., 1299, 1416; used with instrumental abl., 1300; with acc. or abl., 1422–1425, 1415; substs. combined by, 1426–1428; repetition of, with two or more substs., 1429; omission of, with a second subst., 1430; two, with one subst., 1431, 1432; position of, 1433–1437; in oaths, 1437; verbs compounded with, cases after, 1137, 1138, 1188–1191, 1194–1199, 1209; with infin. as obj., 2205; with gerundive construction or gerund in acc., 2252, 2253; in abl., 2267; with subst. and partic., 2285, 2286; for special uses of different preps., see Index of Latin Words.

Present stems,
used as roots, 190–194, 855; roots used as, 738–743, 828, 844.

Present system,
of verbs, formation of, 828–853.

Present tense,
indicative formation of, 828–840; -īt, -āt, -ēt, 132; -ōr, 132; dat. of possessor with, 1216, 1478, 2181; uses of, in simple sentence, 1587–1593, 1601; of pres. action, 1587; of customary or repeated action, or general truth, 1588; of past action, still continued, 1589; of vivid narration, 1590, 1639; the annalistic, 1591; of verbs of hearing, seeing, saying, 1592; in quotations, 1592; of fut. action, 1593, 2026; in letters, 1601; sequence of, 1717, 1740–1746, 1749–1753, 2322–2324, 2326–2329; in subordinate sentence, rel. time, 1733–1735; independent, 1738; with cum, 1860–1862, 1866, 1867, 1869, 1871; with

Present tense — *continued.*
quoniam, 1883; with **antequam, priusquam,** 1915, 1918; with **postquam, ubī, ut,** &c., 1926, 1927, 1930, 1932; with **dum, dōnec, quoad, quamdiū,** 1995, 2000, 2001, 2006, 2007, 2009; in conditional prot., 2023, 2026–2033, 2065–2068, 2074; in conditional apod., 2023, 2026, 2034, 2042, 2048, 2052, 2059, 2078.
Subjunctive, formation of, 841–843; -īt, -āt, -ēt, 132; -ār, 132; in wishes, 1541, 1542; in exhortations, prohibitions, &c., 1548, 1550, 1551; of action conceivable, 1556; of repeated action, 1730; primary, 1762; referring to fut. time, 1743, 1749; following perf. definite, 1754; following secondary in rel., causal, and concessive sentences, 1756; following secondary in consecutive sentences, 1757; following secondary in indirect question, 1760; following secondary in ind. disc., 2328; in sequence with adjacent verb, 1761; of action non-occurrent, in pres. sequence, 1763; in sequence with perf. infin., 1768; with **antequam, priusquam,** 1912, 1915, 1919; with **ut** purpose, 1961; with **dum, dōnec, quoad,** 2003, 2005, 2007; with **modo,** 2003; in conditional prot., 2023, 2070, 2072, 2076–2083, 2090, 2093, 2096; in conditional apod., 2023, 2033, 2039, 2046, 2057, 2064, 2070, 2076, 2084, 2090; with **quasi, tamquam sī,** &c., 2119; in ind. disc. representing a fut., 2324.
Infinitive, see **Infinitive.**
Participle, see **Participles.**

Preventing,
see Hindering.

Priapean, 2674.

Price,
gen. of, 1271; abl. of, 1388–1392.

Primary tenses, 1717, 1762.

Primitive,
defined, 198; substs., 204–245, see **Substantives**; adjs., 280–297, 305, see **Adjectives**; verbs, theme in, 738–741; inflection of, 743–791; formation of pres. stem of, 828–838; list of, 922–986, see **Verbs.**

Principal cases, 1111, 1112.

Principal parts,
of the verb, 733–735; classification of verbs according to, **920–1022, see Verbs.**

Privation,
see **Separation.**

533

Separating,
verbs of, with dat., 1195, 1209; with gen., 1294; with abl., 1302–1306, 1294; with gerundive construction or gerund, 2268; adjs. of, with gen., 1263; with abl., 1306.

Separation,
expressed by supine in **-ū,** 2277; see **Separating.**

Septēnārius,
defined, 2536; iambic, 2610–2616; trochaic, 2629–2635; anapaestic, 2686.

Sequence of tenses,
1745–1772; subjv. subordinate to indic., 1746–1761; subjv. subordinate to subjv., 1762–1765; subjv. subordinate to noun of verb, 1766–1769; subjv. in ind. disc. or by attraction, 1770–1772, 2322–2324, 2326–2329.

Series,
rhythmical, 2532, 2533; stichic, 2546.

Service,
adjs. of, with dat., 1200.

Serving,
verbs of, with dat., 1181, 1182.

Sharing,
verbs meaning, with gen., 1263.

Shortening,
of vowels, 124–132; of vowel before another vowel, 124; in final syllable, 129–132; in nom. of **-ā-** stems, 130, 1; 436; in neut. plur., 130, 2; 461; in abl. ending **e** of cons. stems, 502; in verb endings, 130, 132; in nom. ending **-or,** 132; in **mihī, tibī, sibī, ibī, ubī, alicubī, nēcubi, sīcubi, ubinam, ubivīs, ubicumque, ibīdem,** 129, 2; in iambic words in verse, 129, 1; before **-n** for **-sn,** 129, 1; in perf. ending **-ērunt,** 857; in perf. subjv., 876; variations of quantity, 134; in first syllable of **ille, illic, quippe, immō,** &c., 2469; iambic, rule of, 2470–2472; vowel before another vowel retained long, 127; long vowel in specific endings in Old Latin, 132.

Showing.
verbs of, with two accusatives, 1167.

Sibilants,
79.

Simple,
words, defined, 181; formative suffixes, defined, 200; sentence, defined, 1024, see **Sentence.**

Singular number,
in nouns, defined, 414; lacking, see **Defective;** with different meaning from plur., 418, 480; in substs., in agreement, 1077–1081, see **Agreement;** in adjs., prons., partic., in agreement, 1082–1098, see **Agreement;** in collective sense. 1099; of a class, 1100; neut., of adjs. used as substs., 1093, 1101, 1250; of other adjs. used as substs., 1102, 1103; in verbs, defined, 722; in verbs, in agreement, 1062–1076, 1080, see **Agreement;** of gerundive, with **nostrī,** &c., 2260.

Smell,
verbs of, with acc., 1143.

Softening, 2504.

Sonants, 75.

Sotadean, 2712, 2713.

Sound,
one of the divisions of Latin Grammar, treated, 1, 16–179; change of, in vowels, 55–113; change of, in diphthongs, 80–88; change of, in consonants, 114–154; see **Substitution, Development, Disappearance, Assimilation, Dissimilation. Interchange. Lengthening, Shortening, Weakening, Hiatus, Contraction, Elision, Affinities, Pronunciation, Accent, Quantity.**

Sounds,
continuous, defined, 51; momentary, defined, 51; classified, 54.

Source,
abl. of, 1312–1315, 1426; expressed by gen., 1232; expressed by adj., 1427.

Space,
extent of, denoted by acc., 1151–1156, 1398, 1475; denoted by abl., 1153, 1399.

Sparing,
expressions of, case with, 1181–1185.

Specification,
abl. of, 1385; acc. of, see **Part concerned;** gen. of, see **Genitive.**

Spirants, 78.

Spondaic verse,
defined, 2556; use, 2566, 2567.

Spondee,
defined, 2521; irrational, 2524.

Statements,
general, with **antequam. priusquam,** 1912–1914; particular, with **antequam. priusquam, 1915–1921.**

INDEX OF LATIN WORDS.

THE REFERENCES ARE TO SECTIONS.

547

clangō, defective, 808.
clārēscō, prin. parts of, 976.
classis, decl. of, 521, 555.
claudō, claudeō, defective, 808.
claudō, clūdō, prin. parts of, 958; compounds of, 958; form clūdō, 109.
clāvis, decl. of, 519, 551, 555.
Clōdius, form of, 97.
clueō, defective, 809.
Cn., abbreviation for **Gnaeus**, 18.
cōdex, form of, **97.**
coemō, prin. parts of, 937.
coëō, with dat., 1186.
coepī, defective, 812; synopsis of, 812; forms of pres. system, 99, 813, 940; form coēpī, 120, 813, 863; form coeptūrus, 814; prin. parts of, 940; use of act. and pass. of, 1483.
coerceō, prin. parts of, 1006.
cōgnōscō, form of, 169, 2; perf. partic. of, 919; prin. parts of, 965; used personally in pass., 2178.
cōgō, prin. parts of, 937.
collis, decl. of, 556; gender of, 579.
colō, prin. parts of, 972.
colus, gender of, 447.
com-, compounds of, with dat., 1188, 1189, 1194; other constructions with, 1190, 1196, 1197.
combūrō, prin. parts of, 953.
comedō, conjug. of, 771.
comitia, with gerundive construction, 2254.
commīnīscor, prin. parts of, 980.
commiserēscit, construction with, 1283.
commodum, acc. as adv., 701, 1196.
commonĕfaciō, with double acc., 1291; with acc. and gen. or dē and abl., 1291.
commoneō, with double acc., 1291; with acc. and gen. or dē and abl., 1291.
commūnis, constructions with, 1202, 1238.
commūtō, with abl., 1389; with cum, 1389.
cōmō, prin. parts of, 953.
comparō, construction with, 1197.
compectus, 980.
compede, compedium, 532; stems of, 569; gender of, 532, 572.
compercō, forms of, 930; comperce with infin. for nōlī, 1584.
comperiō, comperior, forms of, 1012; used personally in pass., 2178.
compescō, prin. parts of, 976; compesce with infin. for nōlī, 1584.
compingō, prin. parts of, 938; perf. of, 863.

complector, pres. stem of, 835; prin. parts of, 985.
compleō, with gen., 1293; with abl., 1386.
complicō, prin. parts of, 993.
complūrēs, decl. of, 623.
compos, defective, 624; with gen., 1263; quantity of second **o** in, 2457.
comprimō, prin. parts of, 958.
compungō, prin. parts of, 954.
concēdō, coordinated, 1710; with purpose clause, 1950; with acc. and infin., 1954; used personally in pass., 2178.
concidō, perf. of, 860.
concinō, prin. parts of, 972.
concitus (concītus), 919.
concolor, decl. of, 537, 559.
concors, decl. of, 532, 559.
concrēduō, 756.
concupīscō, prin. parts of, **968.**
concurrō, with dat., 1186.
condignē, with abl., 1392.
condōnō, with double acc., 1172.
cōnficior, cōnfīō, 790.
cōnfīdō, forms of, 801, 1488; with dat., 1181; with abl., 1349.
cōnfiteor, prin. parts of, 1010.
cōnfricō, prin. parts of, 993.
cōnfringō, prin. parts of, 938.
congruō, prin. parts of, 947; **congru-ēre** for congruere, 819.
cōnīveō, prin. parts of, 1000.
conlocō, with in and abl., 1424; with gerundive construction, 2250; with supine, 2271.
conquīrō, prin. parts of, 967.
conrigō, prin. parts of, 953.
conrumptus, 938.
cōnscius, with gen., 1263; with gen. and dat. or dat. alone, 1265; with gen. of gerundive construction or gerund, 2258.
cōnserō, prin. parts of, 922.
cōnspergō, prin. parts of, 958.
cōnstituō, prin. parts of, 947; with in and abl., 1424; with purpose clause 1950; with infin., 1953, 2169.
cōnsulō, prin. parts of, 972.
cōnsultus, adj., with gen., 1263; with iūre, 1268.
contāgēs, decl. of, 603.
contendō, with dat., 1186; with purpose clause, 1951; with acc. and infin., 1954; with infin., 2169.
conticēscō, conticīscō, prin. parts of, 976.
contineō, with quīn, 1986.

Index of Latin Words.

Index of Latin Words.

Index of Latin Words.

gemō, prin. parts of, 972; with acc., 1139.
generātus, with abl., 1312.
genius, voc. sing. of, 459.
genū, gender of, 586; decl. of, 592.
gerō, form of, 154; prin. parts of, 953.
gignō, forms of, 973; genitus with abl., 1312.
glīs, decl. of, 538, 544; stems of, 569; gender of, 579.
glīscō, defective, 808.
glŏmus, 62, 491.
glōrior, with abl., 1349.
glūbō, defective, 808.
Gnaeus, abbreviated, 20; diphthong before vowel in, 125.
gracilis, comparison of, 345.
gradior, conjug. of, 799; compounds of, 791, 799, 986; pres. stem of, 836; prin. parts of, 986.
grātia, sing. and plur. of, meaning, 418; grātiā, gen. of definition with, 1257; grātiā, expressing cause, &c., 1317; grātiā,resembling prep.,1406; grātiās agō with quod and cum, 1852, 1875; eā grātiā . . . quod, 1854; grātiā with gen. of gerundive construction or gerund, 2258.
grātulor, with quod, 1852; with cum, 1852, 1875.
grave est, implying non-occurrent action, 1496.
grex, decl. of, 472; gender of, 581.
grūs, gender and decl. of, 494.

h, from guttural aspirate, 152; not a cons., 177; medial, disappearance of, 151; elision before, 2482, 2493.
habeō, prin. parts of, 1004; compounds of, 1004; with prō and abl., 1168; with dat., 1222; with gen. of value, 1271; habētō, 1576; with perf. partic., 1606, 2297; with gerundive, 2245, 2250.
Hadria, gender of, 433.
haereō, defective, 905; prin. parts of, 1000; with dat., 1186.
hau, use of, 1450.
haud, see haut.
hauddum, following cum, 1868.
hauriō, fut. partic. of, 905; forms of, 1014.
hausciō, formation of, 396, 1450.
haut, haud, with adjs., advs., verbs, 1449; haud sciō an, &c., 1449, 1554, 1782.

havĕ, avĕ, 805.
hebeō, defective, 809.
hebes, decl. of, 533, 635.
hēia, with voc. nom. and voc., 1123; with short final vowel, 2438.
hem, with voc. nom. and voc., 1123.
hercle, in answers, 1513.
herī, here, 1341.
heu, with nom. of exclamation, 1117; with acc., 1149; with gen., 1295.
heus, with voc. nom. and voc., 1123.
hīc, decl. of, 658-665; nom. plur., hīsce, 461, 664, 665; dat. and abl. plur., hībus, 664, 665; formation of, 659, 662; with short vowel, 664, 2466; inscriptional forms of, 665; full form with -ce, 663; hoice, 658; hīcine, 663; with correlatives, 695; huius, quantity, 153, 2. Adj. equivalent to gen., 1098; rules for agreement of, 1094-1098; neut. acc. used adverbially, 1156; neut. with partitive gen., 1248; huius as gen. of value, 1272; with rel., 1797; correlative of quī, 1831; used instead of repeated rel., 1833; correlative of ut, ut nōn, 1970; hōc . . . quō, 1973; as connective, 2129, 2130; hoc ipsum, tōtum hoc, as attribute of infin., 2215; pointing out what is near in place, time, or thought, 2347; referring to the speaker, 2348; haec meaning the realm, our country, &c., 2349; expressing something familiar, with shade of contempt, 2350; referring to words of a sentence, 2351; hīc and ille contrasted, 2352-2355; in concessions, 2361; idem used with, 2372.
hīc, adv., 708, 1340; defined by loc., 1340; quantity of vowel in, 2466.
hiemps (hiems), form of, 167, 495; decl. of, 430.
hinc, adv., 710; as coordinating word, 1691.
hīscō, defective, 808.
Hispalis, decl. of, 518, 549, 554; in abl. with in, 1335.
homō, hominēs sunt quī, 1822: hominem as indef., 2212; expressing feeling, as admiration or contempt, 2365; with short final vowel, 2442, form, 144.
honōrificus, comparison of, 353.
horreō, prin. parts of, 1006; with acc., 1139.
horrēscō, prin. parts of, 976.
hosticapās, nom., 436.
hostis, decl. of, 517, 552.
hūc, with gen., 1254.

559

Index of Latin Words.

Index of Latin Words.

nēquam, comparison of, 353; indeclinable, 431; as adj., 431.

neque, with imper., 1581; introducing parenthesis, 1642; as copulative conj., 1644, 1657, 2141–2144; **neque . . . neque**, 1657; preferred to **et nōn**, 1659; **nec . . . nōn**, 1660; **neque . . . haud**, 1660; after a neg., 1661; **neque . . . et, et . . . neque**, 1665; **neque . . . -que**, 1665; **neque . . . ac**, 1665; in purpose clauses, 1947; see **nec.**

nequeō, conjug. of, 768; form of **nequit**, 828; pass. forms of, 768, 1484; prin. parts of, 922; translation of, 1445.

nesciō, formation of, 396; translation of, 1445; with **nisi**, 2020; with infin., 2169; with acc. and infin., 2175; with **o** shortened, 2443; **nesciō an**, 1782; **nesciō quis**, &c., 1788, 1789; **nesciō quōmodo**, as adv., 712, 1788, 1789; **nesciō quō pactō**, as adv., 712, 1788, 1789.

neu, 1674; see **nēve.**

neuter, form of, 120; gen. sing. of, 127, 6; 618–620, 657, 694; decl. of, 618–620, 694; translation of, 1445; use of sing. and plur., 2403.

nēve, form of, 1674; with imper., 1581, 1586; in purpose clauses, 1947.

nex, gender of, 581.

nī, 2020; with **mīrum**, 2068.

nigrēscō, inceptive verb, prin. parts of, 976.

nihil, form of, 144, 150, 455; used adverbially, 1144; with partitive gen., 1248; translation of, 1445; with **nōn**, 1452; for **nēmō**, 1462; **nihil minus** in answers, 1513; with subjv. in exhortations, 1547; after **et, atque, -que**, 1659; **nihil est quod**, 1822, 1841; **nihil habeō quod**, 1822; **ut nihil**, **nihil ut**, 1947, **nihil quicquam**, 2402; used for **nōn quicquam**, 2403; **nihil abest**, with **quin**, 1086; **nihil aliud quam**, 1895; **nihilī**, as gen. of value, 1272; **nihilō**, as abl. of value, 1391; **nihilō minus**, 1676, 1686; **cum nihilōminus**, 1868; **nihilō minus** introducing adversative sentence, 2151; **nihilum**, form of, 150, 455; **nīl**, form of, 151, 455; with **ī** in second syllable, 2448.

nimiō, with compar., 1459.

nimis, with partitive gen., 1248.

nimium, with partitive gen., 1248.

nisi, introducing subst. with which verb agrees, 1073; with abl. abs., 1374; **nisi quod**, 1848; **nisi quia**, 1848; **nisi sī**, 2020; in adversative sense, after **nesciō**, with **tamen**, 2020; as neg. of **sī**, 2016, 2020; **nisi forte**, **vērō**, 2020; coordinating, 2153; **nisi fōrte** with infin. in. ind. disc., 2317; followed by **quis**, **quī**, indef., 2388; with short final vowel, 2445.

niteō, prin. parts of, 1006.

nitor, prin. parts of, 983; with abl., 1349; with **haud**, 1449; with purpose clause, 1951; with infin., 1953, 2169.

nix, gender and decl. of, 494, 500; use of plur. of, 1108.

nō, prin. parts of, 991.

nōbilis, comparison of, 359.

noceō, prin. parts of, 1006.

noctū, 533, 703.

noenu, form of, 99, 699, 1444, 2444; use of, 1444.

noenum, form of, 99, 455, 699, 1444; use of, 1444.

nōlō, form of, 775, 396; conjug. of, 772, 775–777; form of **nōlim**, &c., 841; imper. of, 844; prin. parts of, 922; translation of, 1445; use of **nōlim**, **nōlō**, 1555; use of **nōllem**, 1560; use of **nōlī**, **nōlīte**, 1583, 1584; **nōlim** with subjv., 1585; coordination of forms of, 1707; with infin., 2169; with acc. and infin., 2189, 2190, 2228; with perf. act. infin., in prohibitions, 2224; with perf. pass. infin., 2229.

nōmen, decl. of, 481; **mihī, est nōmen**, case with, 1213; **nōmen dō, indō**, &c., case with, 1214; gen. of definition with, 1256; gen. of definition with **nōmine**, 1257; abl. of, with judicial verbs, 1280; **nōmine** resembling prep., 1406.

nōmus, 892.

nōn, formation, 99, 455, 699, 1444; common use of, 1443, 1494; **nōn, nēmō**, &c., 1452; **nēmō nōn**, &c., 1452; **nōn . . . nōn**, 1452; in questions, 1502; **nōnne . . . nōn**, 1506; **an nōn**, 1508, 1519; with and without particles in answers, 1513; with wishes, 1540; with subjv. in exhortations, 1547; with subjv. of action conceivable, 1554; with subjv. questions, 1563, 1566; with imper., 1582; with fut. expressing prohibition, 1624; after **et, atque (ac)**, **-que**, 1659; **ut nōn**, 1947; **nē nōn**, 1957; with **dum** and subjv., 2003; **sī**

Index of Latin Words.

570

Index of Latin Words.

plangō, prin. parts of, 954.
plaudō, prin. parts of, 958 ; compounds of, 958.
plēbs (plēps, plēbēs), pronunciation of, 54 ; decl. of, 524, 534, 603.
plēnus, with gen., 1263; with abl., 1268, 1387.
-pleō, prin. parts of, 1001.
plērique, use of, 1244 ; with abl. abs., 1366.
plērumque, with partitive gen., 1248.
-plicō, prin. parts of, 993; compounds of, 993.
pluit, defective, 815 ; form plūvit, 823 ; prin. parts of, 947 ; impersonal, 1034.
plūrimum, comparison of, 363.
plūrimus, formation of, 352; comparison of, 355 ; plūrimum with partitive gen., 1248; plūrimī as gen. of value, 1271; quam plūrimō as abl. of value, 1391.
plūs, adj. and adv., comparison of, 355, 363; defective, 355; decl. of, 623 ; with partitive gen., 1248 ; plūris as gen. of value, 1271, 1274, 1279; without quam, 1328; with quam, 1328; with abl., 1328; plūrēs with subjv. of action conceivable, 1556.
pol, quantity, 2433.
polleō, defective, 809.
polliceor, with acc. and infin., 2186; with fut. infin., 2235 ; with pres. infin., 2236.
pōne, not compounded, 1406; prep., 1410.
pōnō, form of, 111; forms of, 972; nōmen pōnō, case with, 1214; with in and abl., 1424.
populō, populor, 800, 1488.
por-, inseparable prep., 392, 1409.
porrigō, porgō, prin. parts of, 953.
porticus, gender of, 588.
pos, prep. 1410.
poscō, form of. 170, 10; pres. stem of, 834; perf. of compounds of, 860; prin. parts of, 927; with double acc., 1169; with ab and abl., 1170; constructions with pass. qf, 1171.
possum, conjug. of, 744. 751; form of, 752, 753 ; potis sum, &c., for, 752 ; defective, 753 ; old and rare forms of, 753; pass. forms of, 753, 1484 ; prin. parts of, 922 ; potēns, 922 ; with haud, 1449 ; with superl., 1466, 1892 ; implying non-occurrent action, 1496 ; ir subjv., 1498 ; sī potuerō, 1632 ; quod (quantum) . . . possum,

1830 ; nōn possum quīn (ut nōn), &c., 1985; nōn possum in conditions, 2074 ; in past tense with pres. infin., translation of, 2222 ; with perf. infin., 2223 ; use of pres. infin. of, loi fut., 2236 ; in perf. infin. in conditional apodoses in ind. disc., 2333.
post, forms of, 1410; compounds of, with dat., 1195 ; in expressions of time, 1394–1397 ; followed by quam or cum in expressions of time, 1397 ; with fut. perf., 1630; with subst. and partic., 2285, 2286.
poste, prep., 1410.
posteā, with partitive gen., 1253.
postera, defective, 356.
posterī, use of, 347.
posterior, formation of, 348 ; comparison of, 356.
posthabeō, prin. parts of, 1004.
postid, with partitive gen., 1253 ; prep., 1410.
postideā, with partitive gen., 1253.
postquam, posteā quam, posquam, with infin., 1539, 1924 ; with indic. and subjv., 1923–1931.
pōstrēmus, formation of, 352 ; comparison of, 356; with partitive meaning, 1249.
postrīdiē, as adv., 1341; with gen., 1413, 1232; with acc., 1406, 1413 ; postrīdiē quam, 1922.
postulō. with subjv. coordinated, 1708 ; with ut, 1950; used personally in pass., 2178; with acc. and infin., 1953, 2194.
postumus, formation of, 351 ; comparison of, 356.
pote, forms of, used with or without sum, 752 ; ut pote quī, 1827 ; ut pote cum, 1879.
potior, forms of, 791, 799 ; prin. parts of, 981; with gen., 1292 ; with abl., 1379; with acc., 1380; use of gerundive of, 2244.
potis, with or without sum, 752.
potius, after vel, 1670; with sīv., 1672: potius quam, 1897.
pōtus, with act. meaning, 907.
prae, prep., 1417 ; comparison of, 357 ; compounds of, with acc., 1137; compounds of, with dat., 1188, 1189, 1194 ; compounds of, other constructions with, 1190, 1191, 1196 ; with abl. proper, 1297 ; expressing cause, &c., 1317; prae quam, 1895 ; prae quam quod, 1895.

571

pudet, forms of, 815, 817; impersonal, 1034; construction with, 1283; used personally, 1284; with subj. infin., 2209.

pugnō, with dat., 1186.

pungō, perf. of, 823, 858; prin. parts of, 925.

puppis, decl. of, 519, 550, 555.

pūtēscō, prin. parts of, 976.

putō, with **prō** and abl., 1168; with gen. of value, 1271; coordinated, 1696; used personally in pass., 2178; **putārī,** subj. of, omitted with verbs of desire, 2190; **puta,** *for instance,* with short final vowel, 2438.

putus, 919.

q, written for **c,** 20, 690; followed by **u,** 27, 64, 177, see **qu.**

qu, before consonants or when final, changed to **c,** 158; other changes, 156; 170, 3 and 4.

quā . . . quā, 1687.

quaad, 1991.

quadrāns, decl. of, 533; gender of, 580; meaning of, 2427.

quaerō, prin. parts of, 967; prin. parts of compounds of, 967; **sī quaeris,** 2113.

quaesō, with imper., 1572.

quālis, in questions, 1526; agreement of, 1802; **tālis . . . quālis,** 1831.

quam, form of, 702; introducing subst. with which verb agrees, 1073; after a compar., 1324-1327, 1329; after **alius** and **alter,** 1323; after **amplius, longius, plūs, minus,** 1328; in expressions of time, 1397; in comparisons, 1457, 1458; **quam prō,** after compar., 1461; with superl., 1466, 1892; in questions, 1526; moods with, 1888; in compar. period of equality, 1889; **tam . . . quam,** 1831, 1889; **nōn minus, nōn magis . . . quam.** 1889; **aequē, . . . quam,** 1890; **perinde . . . quam,** 1890; **iūxtā . . . quam,** 1890; **tam . . . quam** coordinating words, 1891; **tam . . . quam quī,** 1892; **quam . . . tam** with double compar. or superl., 1893; ιn compar. period of inequality, 1894; **suprā quam,** 1894; **īnfrā quam,** 1894; **ūltrā quam,** 1894; **extrā quam,** 1894; **nihil aliud, nōn aliud quam,** 1895; **secus quam,** 1895; **bis tantō quam,** 1895; **prae quam,** 1895; **contrā quam,** 1895; **praeter quam quod,** 1895; **super quam quod,** 1895; **insuper quam,** 1895; **prō quam,** 1895; **advorsum quam,**

1895; **magis quod,** &c., . . . **quam quō,** &c., 1855; **quam, quam ut, quam quī,** wιth subjv. after compar. denoting disproportion, 1896; **potius, citius (ante, prius) quam, potius quam ut,** 1897; with infin., 1898; **priusquam, antequam,** 1593, 1626, 1911-1921; **prīdiē quam, postrīdiē quam,** 1922; **postquam, posteā quam, posquam,** 1923-1931; **intrā . . . quam,** 1929; **tamdiū . . . quam,** 1999; **quam sī,** 2117.

quamdiū, accent of, 92; use of, 1991, 1994, 1999-2001.

quamlibet, use of, 1907.

quamquam, with abl. abs., 1374, 1900; as adv., 1899; as conj. with indic., subjv., adj., partic., 1899-1902; coordinating, 2153; with infin. in ind. disc., 2317.

quamvīs, with abl. abs., 1374; use of, 1903-1907.

quandō, used with accusative of exclamation, 1150; in questions, 1526; **nesciō quandō,** 1788; as indef. adv., 2010; temporal, 2010, 2011; causal, 2013; with **quidem,** 2013; as prot. of conditional period, 2110; followed by **quis, quī,** indef., 2388; with shortened **o,** 2442.

quandōque, 2012, 2014.

quantō . . . tantō, 1831, 1973.

quantum, introducing subst. with which verb agrees, 1073; **quantum . . . tantum,** 1831.

quantus, neut. with partitive gen., 1248; **quantum est** with gen., 1259; **quantī** as gen. of value, 1271, 1274, 1279; in questions, 1526; with **-ne,** 1529; agreement of, 1802; **quantum . . . possum,** &c., 1830, 1892.

quasi, with abl. abs., 1374: in figurative expressions, 1944; in conditional comparisons, 2117-2120; with partic., nouns, and abridged expressions, 2121: after a compar., 2122; in actual comparisons, 2122: followed by **sī,** 2118; **idem quasi,** 2373; with short final vowel, 2445.

quatiō, pres. stem of, 836; prin. parts of, 961; compounds of, 961.

-que, enclitic, 93; connecting substs. with sing. or plur. verb, 1064-1066; use of, as copulative conj, 1644, 1646, 1647, 1649-1651, 1655, 1656, 2145, 2146, **-que . . . -que,** 1650; meaning *but,* 1655; **-que nōn,** &c., 1659; **et . . .**

Index of Latin Words.

relicuus (reliquus), with partitive meaning, 1249.
rēnēs, gender of, 583.
renideō, defective 809.
reor, perf. partic. of, 918, 2436; prin. parts of, 1008.
reparcō, forms of, 930.
repellō, prin. parts of, 932.
reperiō, prin. parts of, 1011.
replicō, prin. parts of, 993.
rēpō, prin. parts of, 953.
reprimō, with quīn, 1986.
repugnō, with nē, 1960, 1977; with quōminus, 1960, 1977.
requiēs, decl. of, 477, 603; gender of, 572.
rēs, gen. and dat. sing. of, 127, 4; decl. of, 601, 602; malam rem and in malam rem, 1165; repeated in rel. sentence, 1796; quae rēs, 1811; form rē not elided before short vowel, 2487; form rem not elided before short vowel, 2495.
resideō, prin. parts of, 997.
resipīscō, prin. parts of, 968.
resistō, with nē, 1960, 1977; with quōminus, 1960, 1977.
resonō, forms of, 993.
respondeō, prin. parts of, 995.
restis, decl. of, 520, 550.
rēte, decl. of, 528, 557.
retendō, forms of, 924.
reticeō, prin. parts of, 1004.
retineō, with quīn, 1986.
rettulī, rētulī, 781, 861.
retundō, prin. parts of, 931.
reus, with gen., 1263.
revīvēscō (-vīvīscō), 959.
revortor, forms of, 801.
Rhodus, in loc., 1334.
rideō, prin. parts of, 1000.
rigeō, prin. parts of, 1006.
rigēscō, prin. parts of, 976.
rōbur, gender of, 408; decl. of, 489.
rōdō, prin. parts of, 958.
rogō, with double acc., 1159; with dē and abl , 1170; constructions with pass. of, 1171; with gerundive construction, 2250.
rubēscō, prin. parts of, 976.
rubus, gender of. 408.
rudēns, gender of, 580.
rudis, with gen., 1263.
rumex, gender of, 408.
rumpō, prin. parts of, 938; compounds of, 938.
ruō, perf. partic. of, 918, 2436; prin. parts of, 947.

rursum, russum, rūsum, accusatives as adverbs, 701.
rūs, decl. of, 430, 491; loc. rūrī, 504; use of rūrī, 1337; acc. as adv., 699; acc. without prep., 1162; use of abl. rūre, 1311; use of loc. abl. rūre, 1344, 1345; rūre as adv., 703.

s, sound of, 65; followed by u, 27, 65; (and ss) used for z, 21, 67; intervocalic, 155; ss from tt, 159; changed to r, 154, 488; (and st), initial, disappearance of, 169, 4; medial, disappearance of, 170, 2; final, disappearance of, 66, 171; ns, quantity of vowel preceding, 122, a; final syllables in, quantity of vowel of, 2451-2457; does not always make position, 2468.
sacer, comparison of, 358; constructions with, 1202, 1238.
saepe, comparison of, 364.
saepiō, prin. parts of, 1014.
Sagra, gender of, 406.
sāl, decl. of, 430, 482; gender of, 583.
saliō, prin. parts of, 1019; compounds of, 1019.
sam, pron., 675.
Samnis, accent of, 88; decl. of, 533; quantity of i in, 2452.
sanciō, forms of, 1014.
sānē, introducing concessive period, 2150; sānē quam, 1790; sānē, sānē quidem, in answers, 1512; with imper., 1572.
sānēscō, prin. parts of, 976.
sanguis, form of, 171, 4; decl. of, 486; gender of, 579; quantity of i in, 2452.
sapiō, pres. stem of, 836; prin. parts of, 969; compounds of, 969.
sarciō, prin parts of, 1014.
sās (for suās), 653.
satin, in questions, 1510.
satis, verbs combined with, followed by dat., 1187; with partitive gen., 1248; satis est implying non-occurrent action, 1496; satis est, &c., with perf. infin., 2231.
satisdō, conjug. of, 757.
satius est, implying non-occurrent action, 1496.
scalpō, prin. parts of, 953.
scandō, prin. parts of, 950; compounds of, 950.
scīlicet, form of, 712; in answers, 1512.
scindō, perf. of, 859, 860, 2435; prin. parts of, 934.

576

Index of Latin Words.

scio, pres. stem of, 837; imper. of, 846; fut. scibo, 852; prin. parts of, 1016; with haud, 1449, 1554, 1782; scito, scitote, 1576; scin, coordinated, 1787; scio quid, &c., as indef., 1788; with infin., 2169; with acc. and infin., 2175; with o shortened, 2443.
scirpus, gender of, 408.
scisco, prin. parts of, 565.
scribo, prin. parts of, 953.
sculpo, prin. parts of, 953.
seco, prin. parts of, 993; compound of, 993.
securis, decl. of, 520, 550, 554.
securus, with gen., 1264.
secus, comparison of, 364; defective, 430; secus quam, 1895; non secus, correlative of ut, 1937; of quasi, tamquam si, &c., 2118.
sed, set, use of, 1676, 1679; after non modo, &c., 1680-1682; coordinating rel. sentence, 1820; non quod, &c., . . . sed, &c., 1855; introducing adversative sentence, 2151.
sed- (se-), as inseparable prep., 392, 1409; as prep., 1417.
sedeo, perf. of, 862; prin. parts of, 997; compounds of, 997.
sedes, decl. of, 476, 566.
seges, gender of, 572.
Seleucia, abl. of, with in, 1334.
sementis, decl. of, 519, 551, 555.
semis, decl. of, 539; meaning of, 2427.
senatus, gen. sing. senati, senatuos, 590, 593.
senesco, prin. parts of, 976.
senex, comparison of, 353; decl. of, 500.
sentes, gender of, 579.
sentio, prin. parts of, 1015.
sepelio, prin. parts of, 1017.
septemplex, decl. of, 531.
septunx, 2427.
sequor, prin. parts of. 978.
series, decl. of, 607.
sero, *string*, prin. parts of, 972.
sero, *sow*, conjug. of, 744, 758; root verb, reduplicated, 744, 758; form of serit, 828; perf. partic. of, 918, 2436; prin. parts of, 922; prin. parts of compounds of, 922; satus with abl., 1312.
sestertius, gen. plur. of, 462.
setius, comparison of, 364; with quo, 1979.
seu, see sive.
sextans, gender of, 580; meaning of, 2427.

si, sei, adv., 708; with wishes, 1546; with pres. indic. of fut. action, 1593; with fut. perf., 1626; si or si forte in questions, 1777; form of, 2015; correlatives of, 2015, 2018; with quidem, 2019; with modo, 2019; with tamen, 2019; si (sive) . . . sive, 2019; neg. of, si non, nisi, nisi si, ni, 2020; si autem, minus, aliter, 2021; in conditions, 2025-2115; with miror, mirum est, mira sunt, gaudeo, terreo, metus est, 2068; si placet, &c., 2113; etsi, si, &c., concessive, 2116; quasi, quam si, tamquam si, &c., 2117-2122; si non with infin. in ind. disc., 2317; siquis referring to is, 2368; followed by quis, qui, indef., 2388.
sic, form of, 113, 2015; adv., 708; correlative of tamquam, 1908; correlative of ut, 1831, 1937, 1970; preceding quin, 1988; correlative of si, 2015, 2018; correlative of quasi, tamquam si, &c., 2118; expressing affirmative coordination, 2159; introducing acc. and infin., 2176.
sicubi, quantity, 129,2; form of, 129, 709.
sicunde, form of, 146, 710.
sicut, after quamvis, 1905; form of, 1937; meaning *since*, 1946.
sicuti, with short final vowel, 2445.
Sicyoni, Sicyone, 1331.
sido, prin. parts of, 943.
sileo, prin. parts of, 1006.
silex, gender of, 581.
similis, comparison of, 345; constructions with, 1204; agreeing with abl. of quality, 1240.
similiter, correlative of ut, 1937; correlative of quasi, tamquam si, &c., 2118.
simplex, decl. of, 531.
simul, as adv. and prep., 701, 1421, with et, 1648; simul . . . simul, 1687.
simul atque, ac, et, ut, and simul, use of, 1923-1934, 1613.
sin, 2021.
sine, prep., 1417; with abl. proper, 1297; position of, 1434; intimating prot. of conditional period, 2110; with gerundive construction or gerund, 2267.
sino, pres. stem of, 833; forms of, 893, 964; perf. partic. of, 918, 2436; with subjv. coordinated, 1710; with purpose clause, 1950; with acc. and infin., 2198; used personally in pass., 2201.

577

Index of Latin Words.

sis (for sī vīs), 774; with imper., 1572;
parenthetical, 2113.
sīs, determinative pron., 675.
sistō, conjug. of, 744, 758; root verb,
reduplicated, 744, 758; form of sistit,
828; perf. of, 133, 859, 2435; perf. of
compounds of, 860; perf. partic. of,
918, 2436; prin. parts of, 922.
sitis, decl. of 518, 548, 554.
sīve, conjunction, use of, 1667, 1672,
1673; followed by quis, quī, indef.,
2388; see sī.
societās, formation, 103, a.
sōcors, decl. of, 559.
sōdēs, with imper., 1572.
soleō, forms of, 801, 1488.
sōlum, with nōn, 1680, 1682.
sōlus, gen. sing. of, 126, 6; 618-620; decl.
of, 618-620; gen. in apposition with possess. pron., 1235; sōlus est quī, 1822.
solvō, prin. parts of, 947; constructions
with, 1303, 1304.
sonō, forms of, 820 ; defective, 905;
prin. parts of, 993; compound of, 993.
sorbeō, forms of, 1006; compounds of,
1006.
sors, decl. of, 533, 543, 556.
sortior, prin. parts of, 1021.
sōs, determinative pron., 675.
sōspes, decl. of, 477, 624. 625.
spargō, prin. parts of, 958; compounds
of, 958.
Sparta, abl. of, with in, 1334
spatium, use of abl. of, 1399.
speciēs, decl. of, 606, 607.
speciō, spiciō, pres. stem of, 836;
forms of, 956.
specus, gender of, 588; decl. of, 592.
spernō, pres. stem of, 833; prin. parts
of, 964.
spērō, with acc. and infin., 2175, 2186;
with fut. infin., 2235 ; with pres. infin.,
2236.
spēs, defective, 600, 602; spē with
compar., 1330; form spē not elided
before short vowel, 2487; form spem
not elided before short vowel, 2495.
spoliō, constructions with, 1303, 1304.
spondeō, perf. of, 173, 2; 859; prin. parts
of, 995 ; compounds of, 995.
spuō, prin. parts of, 947.
squāleō, defective, 809.
sta, stūc (for ista, istūc), 667.
statuō, 367; prin. parts of, 947; compounds of, 947; with in and abl., 1424;
with purpose clause, 1950; with infin.,
1953, 2169; with acc. and infin., 1954.

sternō, prin. parts of, 964.
sternuō, pres. stem of, 833; prin. parts
of, 948.
stertō, prin. parts of, 972.
stinguō, prin. parts of, 954.
stirps, gender of, 580.
stō, pres. stem of, 837; perf. of, 173, 2;
859, 2435; perf. of compounds of, 860;
defective, 905; prin. parts of, 989; with
abl., 1349; stat per aliquem with
quōminus, 1977; form stō not elided
before short vowel, 2487; form stem
not elided before short vowel, 2495.
strepō, prin. parts of, 972.
strīdeō, perf. of, 862; prin. parts of, 997.
strigilis, decl. of, 519, 551, 555.
stringō, prin. parts of, 954.
struō, perf. of, 164, 1; 865, 867; prin. parts
of, 953.
studeō, prin. parts of, 1006; with purpose clause, 1951; with infin., 2169;
with acc. and infin., 2190.
studiōsus, with gen. of gerundive construction or gerund, 2258.
stupeō, prin. parts of, 1006.
stupēscō, prin. parts of, 976.
Styx, gender of, 406.
suādeō, prin. parts of, 1000; with subjv.
coordinated, 1712; with purpose clause,
1950; with acc. and infin., 2195.
sub, form of, 164, 2; compounds of,
with dat., 1188, 1189, 1194; compounds
of, other constructions with, 1190, 1191,
1196; with loc. abl., 1299; with acc.
and abl., 1422, 1423.
subcumbō, prin. parts of, 974.
subinde, pronunciation of, 93.
subitō, with cum, 1869.
subrepsit, 975.
subrupiō, forms of, 975.
subter, with acc., 1410; with abl., 1416.
subtundō, forms of, 931.
suēscō, perf. of, 871; prin. parts of, 968.
sūgō, prin. parts of, 953.
suī, decl. of, 644-651; use of gen. of, 1234;
sē, subj. of infin., omitted, 2183; suī
with gerundive, 2260, 2261; in ind. disc.
representing ego and nōs of direct discourse, 2325; referring to subj. of verb,
2336; referring to word not subj. of verb,
2337; use in construction of acc. with
infin., 2338-2340; use in subordinate
clauses, 2341-2343; inter sē, invicem
inter sē, invicem sē, expressing
reciprocal relations, 2344, 2345; is used
for, 2370; ipse with, 2376; ipse standing for, 2377; sē quisque, 2397.

578

Index of Latin Words.

Index of Latin Words.

ut, utei, utī, form of, 1935; with gen.,
1254; with satin in questions, 1510;
in wishes, 1540; with subjv. in exhortations, 1547; with questions, 1568, 1569;
coordinated member equivalent to result
clause with, 1700; sciō ut as indef.,
1788; with dignus, indignus, 1819;
quam ut, 1896; general statement of
use in subordinate clause, 1947, 1948;
ut nē, 1947; ut nōn, 1947; nēmō
ut, vix ut, &c., 1947; in complementary final clauses, 1949-1960; after expressions of fear, &c., 1957, 1958; in
pure final clauses, 1961-1964; in parenthetical clauses, 1962; expressing assumption or concession, 1963, 2110; in
provisos, 1964; in complementary consecutive clauses, 1965-1969; tantum
abest ut . . . ut, 1969; in pure consecutive clauses, 1970; after nōn possum, &c., 1985.
How, in questions and exclamations,
1528.
As, with infin., 1539; with fut. perf.,
1626; coordinated member equivalent
to comparative sentence with, 1704; ut
quī, 1827, 1828; ut pote quī, 1827;
ut . . . ita, sīc, item, 1831; ut pote
cum, 1879; with superl., 1892; ut or
sīcut after quamvīs, 1905; correlatives of, 1937; sīcuti, sīcut, velutī,
velut, 1937; with adversative correlation, 1938; with quisque, 1939;
introducing parenthesis, 1940; in illustrations, 1941: ut, prout, making
allowance, 1942; meaning *as indeed*,
as in fact, 1943; meaning *like*, 1944;
praeut, 1945; sīcut, *since*, 1946;
with infin. in ind. disc., 2317; īdem
ut, 2373.
  ut, ut prīmum, simul ut, *when*,
use of, 1923-1934; with quisque,
1932.
  ut, *where*, 1936.
  ut, ut sī, in conditional comparisons,
2117, 2121.
uter, form of, 146; formation of, 347:
gen. sing. of, 162, 618-620, 657, 693;
decl. of, 618-620, 693; as rel. or indef.,
693; in questions, 1526; with -ne,
1529; distinguished from quis, quī,
2385.
ūter, decl. of, 525.
utercumque, decl. of, 694.
uterlibet, decl. of, 694; use of, 2401.
uterque. gen. sing. of, 127, 6; 657. 694;
decl. of, 691: utriusque with gen. of

pron., 1254; as subst. and as adj., 1243;
of two individuals, 2399; utrīque, of
two sets, 2399; utrīque, of two individuals, 2399; combined with different
case of alter or different case of same
word to express reciprocal relations,
2400.
utervīs, decl. of, 694; use of, 2401.
ūtilis, comparison of, 359; constructions
with, 1201.
utinam, in wishes, 1540.
ūtor, prin. parts of, 983; with abl., 1379,
1381; use of gerundive of, 2244.
utrum . . . an, anne, an nōn, 1517,
1519; utrum . . . an . . . an, 1521;
utrum . . . -ne . . . an, 1522;
utrumne . . . an, 1522; utrum,
alone, 1523; as pron., 1522; utrum
. . . -ne . . . an, utrumne . . .
an, 1779; followed by quis, quī, indef., 2388.

v, the character, as vowel and as cons.,
22; as cons., 25, 26; sound of, 69:
after q, g, s, 27, 177; interchange of
vowel and cons., 52; changed to b, 161:
medial, disappearance of, 153, 1.
vacō, constructions with, 1303, 1304.
vacuus, with gen., 1264; with abl.,
1306; with prep., 1306.
vādō, defective, 808; prin. parts of,
958.
vae, with dat., 1206.
vafer, comparison of, 358.
vāh, with nom. of exclamation, 1117.
valeō, defective, 905; prin. parts of,
1006.
valēscō, prin. parts of, 976.
vallēs (vallis), 541.
vānēscō. prin. parts of, 976.
vannus, gender of, 447.
vas, gender and decl. of, 475.
vās, decl. of, 492; gender of, 578.
vātēs, decl. of, 478, 566.
-ve, enclitic, 93; appended to nē, 1581,
1586, 1674; use of, 1667, 1674; quantity, 2433; at end of verse, 2568.
vēcors, decl. of, 532.
vectis, gender of, 579.
vehō, prin. parts of, 953.
vel, with superl., 1466, 1671; meaning *if
you will, even, perhaps, for instance*,
1671; use of, 1667, 1669, 1670; followed by etiam, potius, dīcam,
1670; in sense of aut, 1670; quantity,
2433.
vellō, see vollō.

582

Index of Latin Words.